The Seasons
of Women

The
Seasons
of
Women

An Anthology

Edited by

GLORIA NORRIS

W·W· Norton & Company

New York   London

For my mother

Mary Ella Turnipseed Norris

Truly a woman for all seasons

Copyright © 1996 by Gloria Norris
All Rights Reserved
Printed in the United States of America
First Edition

The text of this book is composed in 11/13 Electra
with the display set in Lucian
Composition and Manufacturing by the Haddon Craftsmen, Inc.
Book design and illustration by Margaret McCutcheon Wagner

Library of Congress Cataloging-in-Publication Data
The seasons of women: an anthology / edited by Gloria Norris.
p.cm.
ISBN 0-393-03860-2
1.Women—United States—Literary collections. 2. American
literature—Women authors. I. Norris, Gloria.
PS508.W7S4 1995
810.8´09287—dc20   95-34475

W. W. Norton & Company, Inc.
500 Fifth Avenue, New York, N.Y. 10110
W. W. Norton & Company Ltd.
10 Coptic Street, London WC1A 1PU

1 2 3 4 5 6 7 8 9 0

Contents

 # Introduction

GLORIA NORRIS

THIS collection of stories, memoirs, and personal essays by contemporary American women celebrates the passions, joys, losses, courage, sorrows, quests, and wisdom of women through all the seasons of their lives. The title does not suggest that women like trees, are fated to only four seasons in their existence: a burgeoning, green spring; luxuriant, sensuous summer; the bittersweet last glory of autumn, followed by a cold, frozen winter.

No, women's lives are rich in new experiences and relationships in each decade of life. Each year that we live brings new pleasures, new obstacles, new rewards, some green and bright summery moments, along with the ebbing of some options. Most of us, however, busy living and doing, do not think of ourselves as passing through a season or cycle. Looking over our pasts, like old scrapbooks or photo albums, we are jolted by random memories and nostalgia. We say such things as:

"She was the first little girlfriend I had. I loved to stay over at her house. . . ."

"Ah, he was my first date. . . . I'll never forget that night."

"That was the worst job I ever had . . . but it pushed me to find a new career."

"When I moved out of my parents' to my own apartment, I finally knew I was grown up and on my own."

"Sometime in my thirties, I decided to stop pleasing everybody else and discover who I really was. . . ."

"When the kids went to college, I started a whole new life."

"The year my mother died, I changed so much myself. . . ."

Our seasons also overlap. Our love for our parents continues long after childhood, and even as we pass into middle age, we are still renegotiating our relations with them; some part of us remains a daughter. We are mothers while also working away at jobs and careers. As for romantic love, a woman may search for a partner at sixteen, twenty-six, or sixty-six.

Women also flower at different times in their lives. A young woman, miserable through all her teen years, may hit her stride in her twenties. Many women discover later life is a deeply satisfying season, after their families have been raised, or when their careers reach a new peak, or simply as age helps us narrow down who we are and what our lives mean. As May Sarton writes in her journal of her seventieth year, "I felt that my face is better now, and I like it better . . . because I am a far more complete and richer person that I was at twenty-five, when ambition and personal conflicts were paramount. . . ."

Thus this collection presents the universal, though infinitely varied, experiences of women, in seven seasons that follow a generally chronological track—but with a bit of license here and there. We begin with "When I Was a Girl," dealing with childhood and adolescence and move along to "Looking for Love," "Finding Direction," "Love, Marriage and in Between," "Motherhood," "Family and Friends," and "The Fullness of Life."

ONE of my deepest pleasures in editing *The Seasons of Women* was that it helped me discover a sense of the evolution of my own life as a woman. When I was a teenager, for example, I suffered from the common fallacy that there was a kind of cliff that women fell off when they reached, say, forty. I pitied my mother and her friends who had disappeared into this chasm where nothing new could ever happen; any hope for surprise had disappeared from their existence. I couldn't imagine that they had complex relationships, sexual lives, rewarding friendships, or daily pleasures that had become richer because they had lived and experienced the slowly unfolding process of discovering themselves for several decades.

Reading the stories of "When I Was a Girl" takes us back to that wonderful innocent state of girlhood arrogance, when we are intent on discovering *everything*—all the mysteries the adults hide from us—while we are sure life will be *different* for us. The girls in these stories burn to know what their mothers are hiding from them. At the same time they are reluctant to accept motherly wisdom as the final word. Isabel Huggan's Elizabeth, for example, treads a thin line: her mother has ordered her to "be nice" to an unpopular girl who tags along with Elizabeth's friends on pain of being publicly spanked before her girl friends. Elizabeth will die from humiliation if she is caught disobeying. But when she's safely out of sight of her mother and faced with a hard choice about how to treat the annoying Celia, she follows her own instinct.

Here, too, is the never-to-be forgotten first of having a best girl friend.

"My Lucy Friend Who Smells like Corn" celebrates a little girl's excitement in having a best friend and imagining how she would feel being part of Lucy's family. These first loves chisel our characters and shape how well we will reach out and connect with others in the future.

Our next season, "Looking for Love," is also filled with discoveries that seem ours alone—too fresh to have been experienced by anyone before us in the human race. Sharon Olds's poem "First Boyfriend" captures the thrill of a young woman's first love, from the feel of the boy's arms around her to the odor of his leather car seat.

Going farther along the road, Mary McCarthy's Dottie, a proper Bostonian and new Vassar graduate, steps out of character when she recklessly goes home with a man she's met at a classmate's wedding. In his rooming house Dottie not only has her first sexual experience but, despite his perfunctory lovemaking, enjoys not one but two orgasms. McCarthy's wittily poignant tale has become a classic—perhaps because it captures so neatly both the ecstasy and the incongruousness of most young women's first sexual experience. Dottie's healthy pleasure in her body is followed by her comic postcoital dialogue—not with her lover but a cozy imaginary talk with her mother about the evening.

More experience in love brings more seasoning of our emotions, as dramatized in the stories of Lee Smith, Terry McMillan, and Jean Stafford. For as we fall in love once, twice, and many more times, gradually we discover that being in love is about more than the beloved who we think holds the single key to our happiness. Three quite different women—Smith's married woman having an affair, McMillan's black professional woman searching among the no-commit "New Men of the Nineties," and Stafford's rapturously engaged young woman—learn that by loving someone, each discovers something valuable and unknown in herself. It is by loving someone else that we learn about ourselves—and grow.

"Finding Direction" is a season not limited to any one age. A woman can change her path at any time in many areas of life. Many of us find much of our direction from the work we do. But it's one thing to work at a job and another to decide this is *you*. Perri Klass's story of her grueling year of medical internship shows how hard she found it to move from *acting* like a doctor, making life-and-death decisions, to *feeling* she'd become one. Nor does "finding direction" for a young woman mean any longer that she will be herded toward neatly "female" interests. Annie Dillard's autobiography of her childhood recollects the 1950s Christmas in Pittsburgh when she was ten and unexpectedly received a microscope set. Annie secludes herself in the family basement with her new microscope, and her excited solitary discoveries change her life.

Divorce upends many women's lives. In J. California Cooper's exuberant story, however, shy, retiring Molly is suddenly left by her domineering husband and is amazed to discover the things he told her she could never do suddenly open to her.

Finding new direction can be a matter of changing oneself internally—altering old destructive patterns, and moving toward greater health and self-love. Lauren Slater's "Striptease" describes how she, a teenage anorexic, stopped her "obsessive desire to be thin thin thin" started to enjoy eating, and began to flourish and live again.

By now it will have become obvious that *The Seasons of Women* has a decidedly contemporary focus. I have deliberately made my choices from writing published in the last thirty years. This is not to scant the profound insight into female experience given us by writers like Virginia Woolf, Ellen Glasgow, and Willa Cather. Rather it is because in only the past three decades have women gained the freedom to write about all the areas of women's emotions and psyches—no zones forbidden. What was unsayable (and almost unthinkable) for earlier women writers are open terrain today.

In these pages, for example, Lynn Sharon Schwartz can depict the passionate sex that takes place between a happily married couple—a side of the marital relationship that was once daintily tucked between chapter breaks. Terry McMillan's Robin expresses her white-hot rage at the marriage-shy men of the nineties with a needling accuracy that makes us whoop aloud. Abby Frucht brings to life, detail by detail, the agonizing and ignominious moments of childbirth, as well as the more slowly felt joy of her new motherhood. Carolyn Heilbrun lays out the ways that women are redefining those once-feared years when they are "neither young nor old"; by letting go of old expectations of living through male admiration, we can forge a rich new season with its own remarkable power and fullness.

Recent writing also offers a new bounty from women writers of color who are showing us strong women characters previously invisible to us. Though the speech, situations, and customs shaping their heroines' lives are beguilingly fresh, the conflicts these women face are instantly recognizable, such as Amy Tan's young heroine wilting under fire from her domineering Chinese mother, Ntozake Shange's black single mother trying not to hobble her three lively, gifted daughters, and Judith Ortiz Cofer's dual tugs of love and separateness, as she watches an old home movie of her Puerto Rican family's party, her mother wearing a red dress and stiletto heels that bespeak the fact that the mother lives forever in a culture separate from her Americanized daughter.

This anthology also is enriched by the current outpouring of women's memoirs, essays, and autobiographies. Women, it seems, are discarding the masks and invented characters of fiction to write directly of the actual details and emotions of their lives. We feel sufficiently empowered now to see our own daily struggles as moral and dramatic theater worthy of sharing as a part of human revelation. Since the momentous day I first learned to read, fiction has been the wonderful imaginative roadway for me to learn how other people live, breathe, and cope. Yet I find that these autobiographical forms help me see my own life with a fresh immediacy and sense of drama. Indeed, as you read one of these "non-fiction" selections, you will find it hard to guess whether it is fiction or memoir, for the colorful, evocative prose and dramatic tension of fiction are nowadays put to excellent use in nonfiction.

For most of us, relationships form the warp and woof of our lives. We can move simultaneously from a sense of sharing love with one person in our lives to loneliness in other areas to suffocation at being too tightly bound by others who love us. A great number of these writers illuminate this great human seesaw between the deep need for love and connection and the need to be true to oneself. They show both comedy and drama in the myriad pleasures and pains of relationships—between parent and child, lovers, married couples, female friends.

But while each kind of relationship, such as mother and daughter, has universal tensions, each particular relationship is unique; the pair is happy or unhappy in its own way. So in the wise hands of these writers, we do enjoy reading about a situation that intrigues us, but the deeper pleasure arises from the characters brought to life, such as the pain and bewilderment of Barbara Kingsolver's sensitive, loving young woman and man, who have been living together for seven years and think themselves as bonded as any marriage—until they move to an isolated cabin without their old friends and they must discover if they can love each other in a new way.

Anne Tyler's long-married Maggie and Ira quarrel when they get lost on a journey to a wedding. But the way warmhearted Maggie and laconic, but loyal Ira fight—and make up—delights us as much for the idiosyncrasies of their characters as for what they tell us about the truths and compromises of a good, long marriage.

The relationship between mother and child not only shifts with that particular mother and one particular child but, as any mother knows, changes day by day and undergoes even more sea changes as the child grows up. These infinite shadings of maternal love are shown in situations that run from the amazed discovery of Mary Gordon's mother, on an ordinary day, of the depth of her love for her children to Adrienne Rich's journal recording the crowded mix of tenderness, rage, heartbreak, and guilt a mother feels in a single day to Kelly Cherry's mature mother who must love her daughter enough to let her live her own life.

The extraordinary courage that women summon to confront loss and go on living is a theme that emerges again and again. Gloria Naylor's young mother faces the death of her daughter and must pass through the grieving that will lead her back to life. Joan Gould's memoir of her early widowhood demonstrates the bravery a widow needs to avoid turning her deceased husband into a false saint who will rule her life beyond the grave. Helen Norris's Mrs. Moonlight is a remarkable, lovable character, an aging woman whose memory is failing yet who drums up the courage to call an old lover she hasn't seen for sixty years and run off with him to live in a treehouse. She makes one cheer for the indomitable human spirit.

Female friendships are an enduring bond of strength in our lives, and the friendships in these pages range from Pam Houston's hauntingly brief companionship between two western young women to Grace Paley's lifelong friends who start with a spat on a New York stoop and are still holding each other up (and sometimes sniping at each other) four decades later.

Finally as these writers richly illustrate, it is through our relationships—by loving others—that we discover our own vulnerability, passion, and common humanity. In "Skin, Where She Touches Me," Dorothy Allison writes of her love for "the two most important women in my life—my mother and my first lover—who taught me I was just like everyone else, capable of emotional and erotic obsessions, deeply needy and hungry for affection. . . . That knowledge, the human insight I gained from discovering myself passionate, capable of great joy, vulnerability, and love, had been astonishing. . . . My skin was as thin as anyone's."

I sometime ago passed forty and learned that I did not fall off into the ghostly existence I once imagined the fate of middle-aged women. Once the crisis of turning forty had passed, in fact, I slowly realized that my life was richer and more interesting than in any previous decade. I had become much more "I"—a person with values, memories, relationships that enriched my feelings and capacity to appreciate life—than when I was ten, twenty, or thirty and had much less chance to know how circumstances and my inner qualities would shape me. Yet I learned much more about my own evolution as a person from sharing the experiences of other women's seasons in these pages, crystallized through the special lens of their artistry and truth-telling. As one of Grace Paley's characters observes, our memories of the past "thicken the present and give all kind of advice for the future." I hope that other readers, too, will remember much that they have forgotten about key events in their own lives. That they will see connections never noticed—such as how one's first love led, in a convoluted line, to one's present love. And these will thicken the present sense of themselves and point to the future that may be.

The final season of this book, "The Fullness of Life," is more of an exciting prophecy, a foretelling of how later life is opening up for us. This section about women over fifty offers perhaps the most revolutionary thoughts about women's possibilities being published today.

I could point to many cultural and economic reasons for this new vision of later life. The baby boomers are turning fifty. Thus books on menopause, spiritual enrichment, and even dying are suddenly being brought out of dark corners of bookstores and thrust onto the best-seller racks. On a crasser note, the beauty industry is discovering a rich market in older women, and cosmetic advertisements that formerly emphasized "moisturizing" and "hot color" are changing to "age-defying" and offering glamorous mature models. However, I think that women themselves are spontaneously doing the redefining from their own life experiences.

Whatever the cause, the last five or ten years have brought a new vein of writing in fiction and essays by women who tell us the last third of life holds unsuspected riches. These range from Gloria Steinem's "Fifty is What Forty Used to Be"—a report on this extended longevity of women and the newly acknowledged sexual appeal of older women—to Carolyn Heilbrun's brilliantly argued exegesis of the "Coming of Age" that women can enjoy when they no longer depend on the "gaze of men" and discover new rewards in a new season of their lives. The hope, spiritual fullness, humor, and adventure offered by the women in this section ring deep.

Loss is feared, mourned, and survived by these women. They celebrate the rewards of wisdom and the increasing sense of simply being oneself, no longer bound by so many obligations to others or careers. May Sarton's extraordinary journal of her seventieth year sums up *The Seasons of Women*. She chronicles both the loneliness of no longer having "a central person" in her life as well as the pleasure of her gardening, friends, dog, and an audience of readers. This is a woman still living at full tilt. As she puts it, "it is these days a very good life for an old raccoon of seventy."

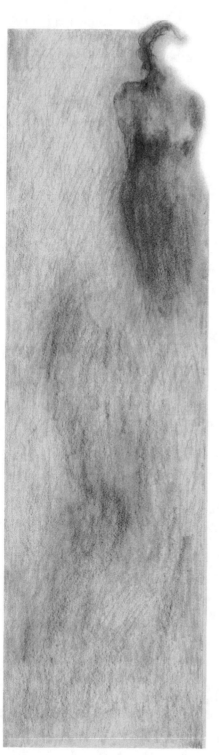

When I Was a Girl

OUR girlhoods are haunted by *not knowing*—about the adult world and about who we are ourselves. These girlhood experiences reveal how our frustration at *not knowing* drives us to adventure and the *finding out* that follows. Gail Godwin's "Over the Mountain" combines both these childhood passions. A ten-year-old girl lives with her grandmother and mother in The Piping Hot rooming house and enjoys the privilege of being her mother's confidante, learning Kitty's grown-up secrets. But do mothers ever tell us all their truths? Susan Minot's two teenage sisters, on the other hand, are the oldest of a large Irish Catholic family and assume they already know it all. They look upon their mother with weary cynicism—until Mum surprises them with a sudden view of womanly joy they can never forget.

Two stories show how friendships help us learn who *we* are. In "My Lucy Friend Who Smells like Corn," Sandra Cisneros celebrates the joy of having a best girl friend, to share hair flip-flops and Popsicles. In "Celia Behind Me," Elizabeth is fearful herself of being ridiculed by other little girls, and when an unpopular girl tags after her, she is faced with the painful choice of being friendly or cruel.

Finding out how babies are made is one of the burning questions of girlhood, and in "Summer Fruits," from her autobiography, Kate Simon brings to life a lush Bronx summer in which she spies on her pregnant mother and her friends who talk about "women's things." By summer's end Kate has begun to fathom some of the mystery; "The tall door to their secret gardens was beginning, maybe just a crack, to open to me."

AS WE grow older, we awkwardly try to define ourselves by where we stand with others. Two stories of adolescence bring to life the powerful and often painful drive to be liked and belong. Louise Erdrich's Indian girl, Mary, has been abandoned by her mother and taken in by her aunt Fritzie in Fargo, South Dakota. Mary's older cousin Sita is annoyed by her presence and deserts her the first day at school. But with the help of a freak accident Mary makes an unusual name for herself in her new Catholic school.

In Carson McCullers's "That Green and Crazy Summer," tomboy-ish Frankie's mother is long dead, and she lives with her father. Shunned by girls her own age who are already budding into womanhood, she belongs to "no club and was a member of nothing." Frankie struggles to make do with the company of her little cousin John Henry. Frankie discovers that belonging even to a group of two, which she and John Henry make up, is sometimes a sudden gift to the spirit. But even the best of our affiliations usually are bound by time. We move on in a search for connection that continues through every age.

Over the Mountain

GAIL GODWIN

IF YOU have grown to love your life, it seems ungrateful to belabor old injustices, especially those that happened in childhood, that place of sheltered perspectives where you were likely to wake up and go to bed without anyone ever disabusing you of your certainty that all days were planned around you. After all, isn't it possible that the very betrayal that flags your memory and constricts your heart led to a development in character that enabled you to forge your present life?

This is not a belaboring. I know by now that behind every story that begins "When I was a child" there exists another story in which adults are fighting for their lives. It is because I accept this that I am ready to go back and fill in some of the blank spaces in the world of a ten-year-old girl whose mother takes her on an overnight train journey. The train carries them out of their sheltered mountains to a town some thousand feet below. The mother and daughter walk around this town, whose main attraction is that the mother spent her happy girlhood years there. The mother and her little girl stay the night in a respectable boardinghouse. The next day, they get on the northbound version of yesterday's train and go back to the mountains.

Why do I remember nothing particular about that journey? I, with my usually prodigious memory for details? Except for a quality of light and atmosphere—the lowland town throbbed with a sociable, golden-yellow heat that made people seem closer, whereas our mountain town had a cool, separating blue air that magnified distances—I have no personal images of this important twenty-four hours. I say important because it was a landmark in my life: it was the first time I had gone away alone with my mother.

Despite the fact that I believe I now know why that excursion lies blank among my memory cells, there is something worth exploring here.

The feeling attached to that event, even today, signals the kind of buried affect that shapes a life.

WE WERE NOT, our little unit of three, your ordinary "nuclear" family, but, as I had known nothing else, we seemed normal enough to me. Our living arrangements were somewhat strange for a trio of females with high conceptions of their privileges in society, but, as my grandmother hastened to tell people, it was because of the war. And when the war ended, and all the military personnel who had preempted the desirable dwellings had departed from town, and we continued to stay where we were, I accepted my mother's and grandmother's continual reminders that "it was only a matter of time now until the right place could be found."

The three of us slept in one gigantic room, vast enough to swallow the two full-sized Persian carpets that had once covered my grand-mother's former living room and dining room and still reproach us with its lonely space, even when we filled it with all the furniture from the two bedrooms of her previous home. The rest of her furniture crowded our tiny living room and dark, windowless kitchen and then spilled out into the shabby public entrance hall of our building, euphemistically called "the lobby" by our landlord and my grandmother. My grand-mother spent a lot of time trying to pounce on a tenant in the act of sit-ting on "our" sofa in the lobby, or winding up "our" old Victrola. She would rush out of our apartment like a fury and explain haughtily that this furniture did not belong to the lobby, it was our furniture, only bid-ing its time in this limbo until it could be resettled into the sort of room to which it was accustomed. She actually told one woman, whom she caught smoking while sitting on "our" sofa, to please "consider this fur-niture invisible in the future." The woman ground out her cigarette on the floor, told my grandmother she was crazy, and went upstairs.

Our building was still known in town by its old name: The Piping Hot. During the twenties, when Asheville overflowed with land-boom speculators and relatives visiting TB patients, this brown-shingled mon-strosity had been thrown up on a lot much too small for it. It had come into existence as a commercial establishment whose purpose was to make money on not-too-elegant people willing to settle for a so-so room and a hot "home-cooked" meal. Therefore, it had none of those quaint redeeming features of former private residences fallen on hard times. The reason our bedroom was so huge was simple: it had been the dining room.

It was a pure and simple eyesore, our building: coarse, square, and

mud-colored, it hulked miserably on its half acre with the truculent insecurity of a social interloper. It was a building you might feel sorry for if
you were not so busy feeling sorrier for yourself for living in it. Probably
the reason its construction had been tolerated at all on that leafy, genteel
block was because its lot faced the unsightly physical plant of the proud
and stately Manor Hotel, which rambled atop its generous acreage on
the hill across the street; moreover, the guests at the Manor were prevented by their elevation from seeing even the roof of the lowlier establishment. Our landlord had bought Piping Hot when it went out of business just before the war, chopped it up into as many "apartments" as he
could get away with legally, and now collected the rents. Whenever he
was forced to drop by, breathless and red-faced, a wet cigar clamped in
one corner of his mouth, he would assure my grandmother he had every
intention of sowing grass in the bare front yard, of having someone come
and wash the filthy windows of the lobby, of cutting down the thorny
bushes with their suspicious red berries that grew on either side of the
squatty, brown-shingled "shelter" at the sidewalk's edge, where Negro
maids often sat down to rest on their way to the bus stop from the big
houses at the upper end of the street.

The most "respectable" tenants lived on the ground floor which must
have been some consolation to my grandmother. The Catholic widow,
Mrs. Gannon, and her two marriageable daughters lived behind us in a
rear apartment which had been made over from pantries and half of the
old kitchen. (Our kitchen had been carved out of the other half.) When
my grandmother or Mrs. Gannon felt like chatting, either had only to
tap lightly on the painted-over window above her sink; they would gossip
about the upstairs tenants while snapping beans or peeling potatoes at
their facing sinks. The apartment across the lobby was inhabited by
another widow, the cheerful Mrs. Rhinehart, who went limping off to
work in a china shop every day; her numerous windowsills (her apartment was the Piping Hot's ex-sunporch) were crowded with delicate
painted figurines. She suffered from a disease that made one leg twice
the width of the other. Among the three widows existed a forbearing
camaraderie. Mrs. Rhinehart did not like to gossip, but she always
stopped and listened pleasantly if my grandmother waylaid her in the
lobby; and, though both my grandmother and Mrs. Gannon thought
Mrs. Rhinehart had too many little objects in her windows for good taste,
they always amended that, at any rate, she was a brave lady for standing
in a shop all day on that leg; and when sailors trekked regularly past our
side windows on the way to call on the Gannon girls, my grandmother
did not allow her imagination to run as wild as she would have if those
same sailors had been on their way to one of the apartments upstairs.

Except for the policeman and his wife, whose stormy marital life thudded and crashed directly above our bedroom, the other upstairs apartments were filled with people my grandmother referred to simply as "the transients." They didn't stay long. You would have to be pretty desperate to stay long in those rear upstairs apartments, which were weird amalgams of former guest rooms, opening into hallways or one another in inconvenient, embarrassing ways, their afterthought bathrooms and kitchens rammed into ex-closets and storage rooms. We didn't even bother to learn their names, those constantly changing combinations of women, of women and children and the occasional rare man, who occupied those awkward upper quarters. They were identified merely by their affronts: the two working girls who clopped around most of the night in their high heels; the woman with the little boy who had written the dirty word in chalk on the sidewalk shelter; the woman who sat down on "our" sofa and stomped out her cigarette on the floor.

THOSE were the politics of our building. There were also, within our family unit, the politics of my mother's job, the politics of my school, and the subtler triangular dynamics that underpinned life in our apartment.

"Today has been too much for my nerves," my grandmother would say as we huddled over her supper at one end of our giant mahogany dining table which, even with its center leaf removed, took up most of the kitchen. "I was out in the lobby trying to wipe some of the layers of dust off those windows when I happened to look out and there was that little boy about to eat some of the berries on those poison bushes. I rushed out to warn him, only to have his mother tell me she didn't want him frightened. Would she rather have him frightened or dead? Then, not five minutes later, the LaFarges' Negro maid came along and sat down in our shelter and I happened to see her hike her dress up and her stockings were crammed with eggs. I had to debate with myself whether I shouldn't let the LaFarges know. . . ."

"I hope you didn't," said my mother, rolling her eyes at me in that special way which my grandmother was not meant to see.

"No. You have to let them get away with murder if you're going to keep them. I remembered that. Do you remember Willy Mae, when we lived in Greenville?"

My mother laughed. Her voice was suddenly younger and she looked less tired. Greenville was the town on the other side of the mountain where, in a former incarnation, she had lived as a happy, protected young girl. But then a thought pinched her forehead, crimping the smoothness between her deep blue eyes. "I do wish that ass Dr. Busey could see through that snake Lu Ann Leach," she said.

"Kathleen. Lower your voice."

My mother gave an exasperated sigh and sent me a signal: *We've got to get out of here. After supper we'll go to the drugstore.*

"He hasn't said anything about her staying on at the college, has he?" asked my grandmother *sotto voce*, casting her eyes balefully towards the painted-over window above our sink behind which even a good friend like Mrs. Gannon might be straining to hear how other people's daughters were faring in this uncertain world without a man.

"No, but he hasn't said anything about her leaving, and now she's taken over the literary magazine. She was only supposed to fill in for Miss Pennell's operation and Miss Pennell has been back three weeks. The college can't afford to keep all three of us. There aren't that many students taking English. All the GIs want their math and science so they can go out and make *money*."

"Well, they have to keep you," declared my grandmother, drawing herself up regally.

"They don't have to do anything, Mother." My mother was losing her temper.

"What I mean is," murmured my grandmother in a conciliatory manner to ward off a "scene" which might be overheard, "they will naturally want to keep you, because you're the only one with your M.A. I'm so thankful that Poppy lived long enough so we could see you through your good education."

"You should see the way she plays up to him," my mother went on, as if she hadn't heard. "She has that plummy, little-girl way of talking, and she asks his *advice* before she'll even go to the bathroom. If she weren't a Leach, people couldn't possibly take her seriously; she couldn't get a job in a kindergarten."

"If only Poppy had lived," moaned my grandmother, "you would never have had to work."

"My work is all I've *got*," blurted my mother passionately. "I mean, besides you two, of course."

"Of course," agreed my grandmother. "I only meant if he had lived. Then we could have had a nice house, and you could have worked if you wanted."

My mother's eyes got round, the way they did when someone had overlooked an important fact. She was on the verge of saying more, but then with an effort of her shoulders harnessed her outburst. She sat with her eyes still rounded, but cast down, breathing rapidly through her nostrils. I thought she looked lovely at such times.

"Can we walk to the drugstore and look at the magazines?" I asked.

"If you like," she said neutrally. But, as soon as my grandmother rose to clear the dishes, she sneaked me a smile.

"The thing is, no matter how much I wipe at those lobby windows from the inside," my grandmother said, as much to herself as to us, "they can never be clean. They need to be washed from the outside by a man. Until they are, we will be forced to look through dirt."

"IT WAS on the tip of my tongue to say, 'If you stay *out* of the lobby you won't have to worry about the dirt,' " my mother told me as we walked to the drugstore a block away.

"That would have been perfect!" I cried, swinging her hand. "Oh, why *didn't* you?" I was a little overexcited, as I always was when the two of us finally made it off by ourselves. Here we were, escaped together at last, like two sisters from an overprotective mother. Yet even as the spring dusk purpled about our retreating figures, we both knew she was watching us from the window: she would be kneeling in the armchair, her left hand balancing her on the windowsill, her right hand discreetly parting the white curtains; she could watch us all the way to our destination. She had left the lights off in the apartment, to follow us better.

"It would have been cruel," my mother said. "That lobby is her outside world."

Though complaining about my grandmother often drew us closer, I could see my mother's point. It was not that we didn't love her; it was that the heaviness of her love confined us. She worried constantly that something would happen to us. She thought up things, described them aloud in detail, which sometimes ended up scaring us all. (The mother of the little boy about to eat the berry had been right.)

We had reached the corner of our block. As we waited for a turning car to go by, we looked up and saw the dining-room lights of the Manor Hotel twinkling at us. The handful of early spring guests would just be sitting down to eat.

I looked up at one of the timbered gables. "There's nobody in Naomi Benjamin's room yet," I said.

"The season will be starting soon. All the rooms will be filled. But never again will I ever write *anybody's* autobiography. Unless I write my own someday."

My mother and grandmother had been so excited last summer when Naomi Benjamin, an older woman from New York who had come to our mountains for her health, offered my mother five hundred dollars to "work with her on her autobiography." Someone at the Manor had told Naomi that my mother was a published writer, and she had come down from the hill to call on us at The Piping Hot and make her offer. We were impressed by her stylish clothes and her slow, gloomy way of expressing herself, as if the weight of the world lay behind her carefully chosen words. But, before the end of the summer, my mother was in a rage. Sometimes, after having "worked with" Naomi Benjamin all afternoon, and after typing up the results at night, my mother would lie back and rant while my grandmother applied a cold washcloth to her head and told her she was not too young to get a stroke. "A stroke would be something *happening*," snarled my mother, "whereas not a damn thing has happened to that woman; how dare she aspire to autobiography!" "Well, she is Jewish," reflected my grandmother. "They never have an easy time." "Ha!" spat my mother. "That's what I thought. I thought I'd learn something interesting about other ways of suffering, but there's not even that. I'd like to tell her to take her five hundred dollars and buy herself some excitement. That's what she really needs." "Kathleen, tension can burst a blood vessel. . . ." "I wish to God I could make it up," my mother ranted on, growing more excited, "at least I wouldn't be dying of boredom!" "I'm going to phone her right now," announced my grandmother, taking a new tack; "I'm going to tell her you're too sick to go on." "No, no, no!" My mother sprang up, waving the cold cloth aside. "It's all right. I'm almost finished. Just let me go walk up and down the street for a while and clear my head."

WE HAD REACHED the drugstore in the middle of the next block, our oasis of freedom. We passed into its brightly lit interior, safe for a time behind brick walls that even my grandmother's ardent vision could not penetrate. Barbara, the pharmacist, was doing double duty behind the soda fountain, but when she looked up and saw it was us she went on wiping the counter; she knew that, despite her sign (THESE MAGAZINES ARE FOR BUYING, not for browsing), we would first go and look through the pulp magazines to see if there was any new story by Charlotte Ashe. But we always conducted our business as quickly and unobtrusively as possible, so as not to set a bad example for other customers; we knew it pained Barbara to see her merchandise sinking in value with each browser's fingerprints, even though she admired my mother and was in on the secret that Charlotte Ashe's name had been created from the name of this street and the first half of the name of our town.

There was no new story by Charlotte Ashe. It was quite possible all of them had appeared by now, but my mother did not want to spoil our game. It had been a while since Charlotte Ashe had mailed off a story.

During the war, when my mother worked on the newspaper, it had been easier to slip a paragraph or two of fiction into the typewriter on a slow-breaking news day. But now the men had come home, to reclaim their jobs at the newspaper, and fill up the seats in the classroom where my mother taught; there was less time and opportunity to find an hour alone with a typewriter and let one's romantic imagination soar—within the bounds of propriety, of course.

We sat down at the counter. It would not do to make Barbara wait on us in a booth. She was, for all her gruff tones, the way she pounced on children who tried to read the comic books, the pharmacist. As if to emphasize this to customers who might confuse her with a mere female employee, Barbara wore trousers and neckties and took deep, swinging strides around her store; she even wore men's shoes.

"Kathleen, what'll you have?"

"A Coke, please, Barbara, for each of us. Oh, and would you put a tiny squirt of ammonia in mine? I've got a headache coming on."

"How tiny?" Barbara's large hand with its close-clipped nails hovered over the counter pump that discharged ammonia.

"Well, not too tiny."

Both women laughed. Barbara made our Cokes, giving my mother an indulgent look as she squirted the pump twice over one of the paper cups. All the other customers got glasses if they drank their beverages in the store, but my grandmother had made us promise never to drink from a drugstore glass after she saw an ex-patient of the TB sanatorium drink from one. "Your cups, ladies," said Barbara ironically, setting them ceremoniously before us. She and my mother rolled their eyes at each other. Barbara knew all about the promise; my mother had been forced to tell her after Barbara had once demanded gruffly, "Why can't you all drink out of glasses like everybody else?" But Barbara did not charge us the extra penny for the cups.

We excused ourselves and took our Cokes and adjourned to a booth, where we could have privacy. As there were no other customers, Barbara loped happily back into her rear sanctum of bottles and pills.

At last I had my mother all to myself.

"How was school today?"

"We had field-day practice," I said. "Mother Donovan was showing us how to run the three-legged race and she pulled up her habit and she has really nice legs."

"That doesn't surprise me, somehow. She must have had a real vocation, because she's certainly pretty enough to have gotten married. How are you and Lisa getting along?"

"We're friends, but I hate her. I hate her and she fascinates me at the same time. What has she *got* that makes everybody do what she wants?"

"I've told you what she's got, but you always forget."

"Tell me again. I won't forget."

My mother swung her smooth pageboy forward until it half curtained her face. She peered into the syrupy depths of her spiked Coke and rattled its crushed ice, as if summoning the noisy fragments to speak the secret of Lisa Gudger's popularity. Then, slowly, she raised her face and her beautiful dark blue eyes met mine. I waited, transfixed by our powerful intimacy.

"You are smarter than Lisa Gudger," she began, saying her words slowly. "You have more imagination than Lisa Gudger. And, feature by feature, you are prettier than Lisa Gudger. . . ."

I drank in this litany, which I did remember from before.

"But Lisa likes herself better than you like yourself. Whatever Lisa has, she thinks it's best. And this communicates itself to others, and they follow her."

This was the part I always forgot. I was forgetting it again already. I stared hard at my mother's face. I could see myself reflected in the small pupils, contracted from the bright drugstore lights; I watched the movement of her lips, the way one front tooth crossed slightly over the other. The syllables trying to contain the truth about a girl named Lisa Gudger broke into smaller and smaller particles and escaped into the air as I focused on my mother, trying to show her how well I was listening.

I partially covered up by asking, after it was over, "Do you hate Lu Ann Leach the way I hate Lisa?"

"Now that's an interesting question. Now, Lisa Gudger would not have had the imagination to ask that question. I do hate Lu Ann, because she's a real threat; she can steal my job. I hate her because she's safe and smug and has a rich father to take care of her if everything else falls through. But Lu Ann Leach does not fascinate me. If I could afford it, I would feel pity for her. See, I've figured her out. When you've figured someone out, they don't fascinate you anymore. Or at least they don't when you've figured out the kind of thing I figured out about her."

"Oh, what? What have you figured out?"

"Shh." My mother looked around towards Barbara's whereabouts. She leaned forward across our table. "Lu Ann hates men, but she knows how to use them. Her hatred gives her a power over them, because she just doesn't care. But I'd rather be myself, without that power, if it means the only way I can have it is to become like Lu Ann Leach. She's thirty, for God's sake, and she still lives with her parents."

"But you live with your mother."

"That's different."

"How is it different?"

My mother got her evasive look. This dialogue had strayed into channels where she hadn't meant it to. "It's a matter of choice versus necessity," she said, going abstract on me.

"You don't hate men, then?" I could swear I'd heard her say she had: the day she got fired from the newspaper, for instance.

"Of course I don't. They're the other half of the world. You don't hate men, do you?" She gave me a concerned look.

I thought of Men. There was the priest at school, Father Lilley, whose black skirts whispered upon the gravel; there was Jovan, our black bus driver; there was Hal the handyman who lived in a basement apartment under the fifth-grade classroom with his old father, who drove the bus on Jovan's day off. There was Don Olson, the sailor I had selected as my favorite out of all those who passed our window on their way to see the Gannon girls; I would lie in wait for him at our middle-bedroom window, by the sewing machine, and he would look in and say, "Hi there, beautiful. I might as well just stop here." Which always made me laugh. One day my grandmother caught me in the act of giving him a long list of things I wanted him to buy me in town. "She's just playing, she doesn't mean it," she cried, rushing forward to the window. But he brought me back every item on the list. And there was my father, who had paid us one surprise visit from Florida. His body shook the floor as he strode through our bedroom to wash his hands in the bathroom. He closed the bathroom door behind him and locked it. My mother made me tell everybody he was my uncle, because she had already told people he had been killed in the war: a lie she justified because, long ago, he had stopped sending money, and because people would hire a war widow before they would a divorced woman. Still, I was rather sorry not to be able to claim him; with his good-looking face and sunburnt ankles (he wore no socks, even with his suit), he was much more glamorous than my friends' dull business fathers.

"Sure. I like men," I told my mother in the booth. I was thinking particularly of Don Olson. The Gannon girls were fools to let him get away.

"Well, good," said my mother wryly, shaking her ice in the paper cup. "I wouldn't want that on my conscience. That I'd brought you up to hate men."

As if we had conjured him up by our tolerant allowance of his species, a Man materialized in front of our booth.

"Well looky here what I found," he said, his dark brown eyes dancing familiarly at us.

My mother's face went through an interesting series of changes. "Why, what are you doing home?" she asked him.

It was Frank, one of her GI students from the year before, who was always coming by our apartment to get extra help on a term paper, or asking her to read a poem aloud so he could understand it better. Once last year, out of politeness, I had asked him to sign my autograph book; but whereas her other GIs had signed things like "Best of luck from your friend Charles," or "To a sweet girl," Frank had written in a feisty slant: "To the best daughter of my best teacher." His page troubled me, with its insinuating inclusion of himself between my mother and me; also, his handwriting made "daughter" look like "daughtlet." It was like glimpsing myself from a sudden unflattering angle: a "daughtlet." And what did he mean *best* daughter? I was my mother's only daughter. At the end of last spring, when I knew he would be transferring to Georgia Tech, I took a razor and carefully excised his page.

"I can't stay out of these mountains," said Frank, reaching for a chair from a nearby table and fitting it backwards between his legs. Barbara looked out from the window of her pharmacy, but when she saw who it was did not bother to come out.

"I should think it would be nice to get out of them for a change," said my mother.

"Well, what's stopping you?" asked Frank, teetering forward dangerously on two legs of his chair. He rested his chin on the dainty wrought-iron back of the chair and assessed us, like a playful animal looking over a fence.

My mother rolled her eyes, gave her crushed ice a fierce shake, and emptied the last shards into her mouth. They talked on for a few more minutes, my mother asking him neutral questions about his engineering courses, and then she stood up. "We've got to be getting back or Mother will start worrying that we've been kidnapped."

He stood up, too, and walked us to the door with his hands in his pockets. "Want a ride?"

"One block? Don't be silly," said my mother.

He got into a little gray coupe and raced the motor unnecessarily, I thought, and then spoiled half of our walk home by driving slowly along beside us with his lights on.

"I wish we could go off sometime, just by ourselves," I said in the few remaining steps of cool darkness. My grandmother had pulled down the shades and turned on the lamp, and we could see the shadow of the top of her head as she sat listening to the radio in her wing chair.

"Well, maybe we can," said my mother. "Let me think about it some."

We went inside and the three of us scrubbed for bed and the women creamed their faces. I got in bed with my mother, and, across the room, my grandmother put on her chin strap and got into her bed. We heard the policeman coming home; his heavy shoes shook the whole house as he took the stairs two at a time. "He has no consideration," came my grandmother's reproachful voice from the dark. There soon followed their colorful exchange of abuses, the wife's shrieks and the policeman's blows. "It's going too far this time," said my grandmother, "he's going to kill her, I'm going to call the police." "You can't call the police on the police, Mother. Just wait, it'll soon be over." And my mother was right: about this time the sound effects subsided into the steady, accelerated knocking against our ceiling which would soon lead to silence. "If Poppy had lived, we would not be subjected to this," moaned my grandmother. "Even he couldn't keep life out," sighed my mother, and turned her back to me for sleep.

OUR TRIP alone together came to pass. I don't know how my mother talked my grandmother out of going with us. She was a respectful daughter, if often impatient, and would not have hurt my grandmother's feelings for the world. And it would have been so natural for my grandmother to come: she was the only one of us who could ride free. The widow of a railroad man, she could go anywhere she wanted on Southern Railways until the end of her life.

But, at any rate, after what I am sure were exhaustive preparations sprinkled with my grandmother's imaginative warnings of all the mishaps that might befall us, we embarked—my mother and I—from Biltmore Train Station south of Asheville. My grandmother surely drove us there in our ten-year-old Oldsmobile, our last relic of prosperity from the days when Poppy lived. I am sure we arrived at the station much too early, and that my grandmother probably cried. Poppy had been working at Biltmore Station when my grandmother met him. His promotions had taken them out of her girlhood mountains to a series of dusty piedmont towns which she had never liked; and now here she was back in the home mountains, in the altitude she loved—but old and without him. My mother and I were going to the first of the towns to which he had been transferred when my mother had been about the age I was now.

I DO NOT remember our leaving from Biltmore Station or our returning to it the next afternoon. That is the strange thing about those twenty-four hours. I have no mental pictures that I can truly claim I inhabited during that time span. Except for that palpable recollection of the golden heat which I have already described, there are no details. No vivid scenes. No dialogues. I know we stayed in a boardinghouse, which my grandmother, I am sure, checked out in advance. It is possible that the owner might have been an old acquaintance, some lady fallen on harder times, like ourselves. Was this boardinghouse in the same neighborhood as the house where my mother had lived? I'm sure we must have walked by that house. After all, wasn't the purpose of our trip—other than going somewhere by ourselves—to pay a pilgrimage to the scene of my mother's happy youth? Did we, then, also walk past her school? It seems likely, but I don't remember. I do have a vague remembrance of "downtown," where, I am sure, we must have walked up and down streets, in and out of stores, perhaps buying something, some small thing that I wanted; I am sure we must have stopped in some drugstore and bought two Cokes in paper cups.

Did the town still have streetcars running on tracks, jangling their bells: or was it that my mother described them so well, the streetcars that she used to ride when she lived there as a girl?

I do not know.

We must have eaten at least three meals, perhaps four, but I don't remember eating them.

We must have slept in the same bed. Even if there had been two beds in the room, I would, sooner or later, have crawled in with my mother. I always slept with her.

M Y AMNES IA comes to a stunning halt the moment the trip is over. My grandmother has picked us up from Biltmore Station and there I am, on Charlotte Street again, in the bedroom *née* dining room of the old Piping Hot.

It is late afternoon. The sun is still shining, but the blue atmosphere of our mountains has begun to gather. The predominant color of this memory is blue. I am alone in the bedroom, lying catty-cornered across the bed with my head at the foot; I am looking out the window next to the one where I always used to lie in wait for the sailor, Don Olson, on his way to call on the Gannon girls. The bedspread on which I am lying is blue, a light blue, with a raised circular pattern in white; it smells clean. Everything in this room, in this apartment, smells clean and womanly. There is the smell of linen which has lain in lavender-scented drawers; the smell of my mother's Tweed perfume, which she dabs on lightly before going to teach at the college; the acerbic, medicinal smell of my grandmother's spirits of ammonia, which she keeps in a small green cutglass bottle and sniffs whenever she feels faint; the smell of a furniture polish, oil-based, which my grandmother rubs, twice a week, into our numerous pieces of furniture.

Where are they? Perhaps my grandmother is already in the kitchen, starting our early supper, hardly able to contain her relief that our trip without her is over. Perhaps my mother is out by herself in the late sunshine, taking one of her walks to clear her head; or maybe she is only in the next room, reading the Sunday paper, grading student themes for the following day, or simply gazing out at the same view I was gazing at, thinking her own thoughts.

I looked out at the end of that afternoon. The cars were turning from Charlotte Street into Kimberly, making a whishing sound. I could see the corner wall of the drugstore. But there was no chance of going there after supper, because we had already been away for more time than ever before.

An irremediable sadness gathered about me. *This time yesterday, we were there*, I thought; *and now we are here and it's all over.* How could that be? For the first time, I hovered, outside my own body, in that ghostly synapse between the anticipated event and its aftermath. I knew what all adults know: that "this time yesterday" and "this time tomorrow" are often more real than the protracted now.

It's over, I thought; and perhaps, at the blue hour, I abandoned childhood for the vaguely perceived kingdom of my future. But the knot in my chest that I felt then—its exact location and shape—I feel now, whenever I dredge up that memory.

A LOT of things were over, a lot of things did come to an end that spring. My mother announced that she would not be going back to teach at the college. (Lu Ann Leach took her place, staying on into old age—until the college was incorporated into the state university.) And then, on an evening in which my grandmother rivaled the policeman's wife in her abandoned cries of protest, my mother went out for a walk and reappeared with Frank, and they announced to us that they were married. The three of us left that night, but now we are talking about a different three: my mother, Frank, and me. All that summer we lived high on a mountain—a mountain that, ironically, overlooked the red-tiled roofs of the Manor Hotel. Our mountain was called Beaucatcher, and our address was the most romantic I've ever had: 1000 Sunset Drive. Again we were in a house with others, but these others were a far cry from the panicked widows and lonely mothers of Charlotte Street. Downstairs lived a nightclub owner and his wife and her son (my age) from an earlier marriage; upstairs lived a gregarious woman of questionable virtue. One night, a man on the way upstairs blundered by accident into my room—I now had a room, almost as large as the one we three had shared in the life below—and Frank was so incensed that he rigged up a complicated buzzer system: if my door opened during the night, the buzzer-alarm would go off, even if it was I who opened it. That summer I made friends with the nightclub owner's stepson, learned to shoot out streetlights with my own homemade slingshot, and, after seeing a stray dog dripping blood, was told about the realities of sex. First by the boy, the stepson, in his own words; then, in a cleaned-up version, by my mother. I invited Lisa Gudger up to play with me; we got into Frank's bottle of Kentucky Tavern and became roaring drunk; and I beat her up. My mother called Mrs. Gudger to come and get Lisa, and then hurriedly sewed onto Lisa's ripped blouse all the buttons I had torn off.

MY GRANDMOTHER, who had screamed she would die if we left her, lived on through the long summer. And through another summer, during which we were reconciled. Frank had quit Georgia Tech to marry my mother, and worked as a trainee in Kress's. Within a year, my mother and Frank had moved back to the old Piping Hot. They now had the former apartment of the policeman and his wife. My grandmother slept on in her bed downstairs, and I divided my time between them.

A few years later, we left my grandmother again. Frank was being transferred to a town on the other side of the mountain. One of those hot little towns a thousand feet below. After we had been away for some months, my grandmother shocked us all by getting her first job at the age most people were thinking about retiring. At the time most people were coming home from work, my grandmother pinned on her hat and put on her gloves and hid all of Poppy's gold pieces and his ring and his watch in a secret fold of her purse, and took the empty bus downtown to her job. She worked as night housemother at the YWCA residence for working girls. It was a job made in heaven for her: she sat up waiting for the girls. If they came in after midnight, they had to ring and she let them in with an admonition. After three admonitions she reported them to the directress, a woman she despised. We heard all about the posturings and deceptions of this directress, a Mrs. Malt, whenever we visited. My grandmother's politics had gone beyond the lobby into the working world; she was able to draw Social Security because of it.

WHEN our brand-new "nuclear family" arrived in the little lowland town where Frank was to be the assistant manager of Kress's, we moved into a housing development. Our yard had no grass, only an ugly red clay slope that bled into the walkway every time it rained. "I guess I'll never know what it's like to have grass in the front yard," I said, in the sorrowful, affronted, doom-laden voice of my grandmother. "Hell, honey," replied Frank with his mountain twang, "if you want grass in this world, you've got to plant it." I forgive him for his treachery now, as I recall the thrill of those first tiny green spikes, poking up out of that raw, red soil.

Years and years passed. I was home on a visit to my mother and Frank and their little daughter and their two baby sons. "You know, it's awful," I told Mother, "but I can't remember a single thing about that trip you and I took that time on the train. You know, to Greenville. Do you remember it?"

"Of course I do," she said, her eyes going that distant blue. "Mother took us to the station and we had a lovely lunch in the dining car, and then we went to all my old haunts, and we stayed the night at Mrs. — — 's, and then we got back on the train and came home. It was a lovely time."

"Well, I wish I could remember more about it."

"What else would you like to know?" asked Frank, who had been listening, his eyes as warm and eager to communicate as my mother's were cool and elegiac.

But she suddenly got an odd look on her face. "Frank," she said warningly.

"Well hell, Kathleen." He hunched his shoulders like a rebuked child.

"Frank, please," my mother said.

"Well, I was there, too," he flared up.

"You were not! That was another time we met in Greenville." But her eyes were sending desperate signals and her mouth had twisted into a guilty smirk.

"The hell it was. The second time we went, it was to get married."

Then he looked at me, those brown eyes swimming with their eager truths. She had turned away, and I didn't want to hear. Fat chance. "I drove down," he said. "I followed your train. You were sick on the train and you had to have a nap when you got there. I waited till your mother met me on the corner after you fell asleep. And then after you fell asleep that night. Well, dammit, Kathleen," he said to the cool profile turned away from him, "it's the truth. Did the truth ever hurt anybody?"

He went on to me, almost pleading for me to see his side. "I don't know what we would have done without you," he said. "You were our little chaperon, in a way. Don't you *know* how impossible it was, in those days, ever to get her alone?"

My Lucy Friend Who Smells like Corn

SANDRA CISNEROS

LUCY ANGUIANO, Texas girl who smells like corn, like Frito Bandito chips, like tortillas, something like that warm smell of *nixtamal* or bread the way her head smells when she's leaning close to you over a paper cut-out doll or on the porch when we are squatting over marbles trading this pretty crystal that leaves a blue star on your hand for that giant cat-eye with a grasshopper green spiral in the center like the juice of bugs on the windshield when you drive to the border, like the yellow blood of butterflies.

Have you ever eaten dog food? I have. After crunching like ice, she opens her big mouth to prove it, only a pink tongue rolling around in there like a blind worm, and Janey looking in because she said Show me. But me I like that Lucy, corn smell hair and aqua flip-flops just like mine that we bought at the K mart for only 79 cents same time.

I'm going to sit in the sun, don't care if it's a million trillion degrees outside, so my skin can get so dark it's blue where it bends like Lucy's. Her whole family like that. Eyes like knife slits. Lucy and her sisters. Norma, Margarita, Ofelia, Herminia, Nancy, Olivia, Cheli, *y la* Amber Sue.

Screen door with no screen. *Bang!* Little black dog biting his fur. Fat couch on the porch. Some of the windows painted blue, some pink, because her daddy got tired that day or forgot. Mama in the kitchen feeding clothes into the wringer washer and clothes rolling out all stiff and twisted and flat like paper. Lucy got her arm stuck once and had to yell Maaa! and her mama had to put the machine in reverse and then her hand rolled back, the finger black and later, her nail fell off. *But did your arm get flat like the clothes? What happened to your arm? Did they have to pump it with air?* No, only the finger, and she didn't cry neither.

Lean across the porch rail and pin the pink sock of the baby Amber Sue on top of Cheli's flowered T-shirt, and the blue jeans of *la* Ofelia over the inside seam of Olivia's blouse, over the flannel nightgown of Margarita so it don't stretch out, and then you take the work shirts of their daddy and hang them upside down like this, and this way all the clothes don't get so wrinkled and take up less space and you don't waste pins. The girls all wear each other's clothes, except Olivia, who is stingy. There ain't no boys here. Only girls and one father who is never home hardly and one mother who says *Ay! I'm real tired* and so many sisters there's no time to count them.

I'm sitting in the sun even though it's the hottest part of the day, the part that makes the streets dizzy, when the heat makes a little hat on the top of your head and bakes the dust and weed grass and sweat up good, all steamy and smelling like sweet corn.

I want to rub heads and sleep in a bed with little sisters, some at the top and some at the feets. I think it would be fun to sleep with sisters you could yell at one at a time or all together, instead of alone on the fold-out chair in the living room.

When I get home Abuelita will say *Didn't I tell you?* and I'll get it because I was supposed to wear this dress again tomorrow. But first I'm going to jump off an old pissy mattress in the Anguiano yard. I'm going to scratch your mosquito bites, Lucy, so they'll itch you, then put Mercurochrome smiley faces on them. We're going to trade shoes and wear them on our hands. We're going to walk over to Janey Ortiz's house and say *We're never ever going to be your friend again forever!* We're going to run home backwards and we're going to run home frontwards, look twice under the house where the rats hide and I'll stick one foot in there because you dared me, sky so blue and heaven inside those white clouds. I'm going to peel a scab from my knee and eat it, sneeze on the cat, give you three M & M's I've been saving for you since yesterday, comb your hair with my fingers and braid it into teeny-tiny braids real pretty. We're going to wave to a lady we don't know on the bus. Hello! I'm going to somersault on the rail of the front porch even though my *chones* show. And cut paper dolls we draw ourselves, and color in their clothes with crayons, my arm around your neck.

And when we look at each other, our arms gummy from an orange Popsicle we split, we could be sisters, right? We could be, you and me waiting for our teeth to fall and money. You laughing something into my ear that tickles, and me going Ha Ha Ha Ha. Her and me, my Lucy friend who smells like corn.

Wildflowers

SUSAN MINOT

"MAYBE we should help her," said Sophie, sitting on the window seat of the front room. The open windows let in the luffing of sails and the clanging of halyards, but louder than that were dishes, making a clatter in the kitchen.

"She hasn't asked," said Caitlin with a smile. Their feet, barely touching, did not move. Out in the harbor sailboats were circling one another, tacking this way and that, positioning themselves before the starting gun. Kids in rowboats shot jackknife sprays with their oars while other kids watched from railings above. Mum passed by the living room and out the door. Sophie and Caitlin heard her squeal in the wind and rolled their eyes. She reappeared on the dock carrying a plate of brownies in one hand and a vase of flowers in the other. Her dress fluttered about her, the vase bent back like a torch. It was part of it for the ladies giving the Saturday race teas to bring flowers, usually from their own gardens—careful arrangements of dahlias and zinnias and sweet william. Mum had brought wildflowers—loosestrife and buttercups and queen anne's lace. There was no space for a garden at the Vincents', with the dock in front and Main Street just up the steps—the vegetable garden was in another place entirely—so Mum gathered flowers up island. She found fields everywhere shimmering down to the sea, flowers scattered and random, not boxed inside walls. On her bedside table she kept a small vase, always fresh.

"She's feeling her oats," Sophie said, watching Mum head for the clubhouse at the end of the dock. Inside the mahogany darkness, other bright dresses were crossing back and forth.

"She thinks she needs to say hello to everyone in sight," said Caitlin.

Upstairs along the hall a series of doors slammed in the draft, one after another.

"Guess-Who must be racing today," said Sophie.

Caitlin, studying the scene, nodded.

THE CROWD that showed up two hours later at the clubhouse was not large but it was dense. Everyone clustered together; they'd known each other a long time. Beneath the pyramid of yachting flags were familiar tennis hats and faded salmon shorts, warped topsiders and yellowing socks. Short, lime-green skirts, fashionable anywhere else in 1970, were here on North Eden nothing new. They were what the ladies wore and always had worn playing golf.

Apart from the crowd, slumped against the tackle shed, were the way-ward teenagers in torn blue jeans and Indian prints. Caitlin and Sophie, among them, snuck drags from a furtive cigarette. Mum was sitting near the clubhouse doorway in front of a silver samovar, handing cups of tea upward with napkins pressed beneath. Chicky, the youngest Vincent, was waiting near her elbow for a cookie. According to their grandmother, Chicky looked exactly like Dad. She had said the same thing about each baby, as Mum had had them, seven of them one right after another. Caitlin and Sophie, the first babies, had been dressed in blue for the first years of their lives, in honor of the Blessed Virgin. Mum had been taught by nuns. After her seventh baby, she stopped listening to the pope. She was thirty-nine years old now, her last baby, Chicky, was six, and for the first time since marrying Dad, she had no little fists clutching at her hem, the way they would in department stores. "Hold on," she'd say before weaving off through crowded aisles.

"Just one," she whispered to Chicky. He snuck a cookie from a china plate. Around the corner kids were lined up for ice cream being scooped out of a cardboard tub by freckled Amy Haffenreffer, who preferred the company of children. Out on the thorofare by the spindle, the last of the sailboats were tacking in to the finish line, each at a different angle, all at a heel.

Caitlin nudged Sophie. Mum was pouring a cup of tea. The man next to her had a grayish-white spot on the back of his dark head, and Mum's eyes were lit with a brightness. When her sister Grace visited, sitting on the porch in her smart wool dresses and silk kerchiefs and black sunglasses, telling New York stories, Mum would get that look, giggling now and then in an odd, excited way. The first time the girls had seen it had been years ago in the lamplight, when they'd all spent the night in the cabin on Boxed Island. Mum came flying out of the cricket darkness, her nightgown luminous, a fiery look in her eye. She was pant-ing. On her way to the outhouse, she'd seen a fox, a silver fox. "It streaked across my path," she said. Her hands trembled and toyed with the ruffle at her neck; her pupils were lit in bright points from the oil lamp.

"No such thing," said Dad, thumping at a flimsy mattress.

Mum stood there transfixed. She turned to her babies, all six of them in diminishing sizes, rolled up in flannel sleeping bags. "As silver as the Silver Orient," she said. It was from a story they all knew, one Mum had read to them, about the train that took off from its tracks and flew over the Alps.

Later when the cabin was dark, Caitlin and Sophie heard Mum and Dad mumbling across the room. "Oh they'll forget about it by tomorrow," Mum said. But they didn't. It was one of those things they remembered and mentioned now and then, about that time the silver fox streaked across Mum's path and how her eyes were lit, not with fright, and how Dad said there was no such thing.

When Mum handed the man a cup of tea, the look was there: thrilled. Wilbur Kittredge had his collar turned up against his tanned skin. He was the head of a large international company. He made bombs.

The Kittredge estate was set high on a bluff of North Eden. The main house had a long porch that overlooked the bay where humped islands scattered off into tiny dots. The estate had stables and an electric fence and guest cottages and a walled-in garden where stone satyrs huddled, ears pointed, fingers secretly at their lips. They had exotic animals, antelopes and a snow leopard and crocodiles, and special guests. A Balinese fire dancer had performed under the moon; an American Indian had constructed an authentic teepee. The topiary garden was designed by an Italian monk to depict a tennis match. A man sculpted in privet served a green ball to a sculpted woman in a flared privet skirt crouched at a slender privet hedge. Each year the Kittredges had a clambake and invited the whole island—all the summer people, that is, and certain islanders who knew who they were. But the main attraction was the carriages. Wilbur Kittredge had over forty antique carriages lined up in a special barn. There were scenes painted on the shiny doors, polished brass railings, leather seats and velvet seats and fringed surreys with wicker sides. When Dad was home in Marshport during the week, Mum went on rides.

Wilbur Kittredge was a special friend of Mum's. Over the years, he'd sent her presents, strange items from strange lands. One package held an odd wreath of shellacked flowers, which Mum hung over the mitten basket. Caitlin and Sophie knew that if Dad had given her something like that it would have gone straight to the cellar. Some things just weren't Mum's taste. When his first son, Gus, was born, after three girls, Dad brought Mum gladiolas. To make it worse, they were yellow. His presents made Mum bite her lip; there was a whole world of things "not me" or "a little off." Dad learned to leave the sales slip in the box.

THE TEENAGERS were discussing various figures in the crowd. "Ol' Will Kittredge is looking pretty dapper," said Westy Granger sullenly.

"Is your father up?" asked Trisha Holt, who had painted a rose on her cheek.

Everyone on the island minded each other's business. You always knew who was up or not. Everyone knew that Wilbur Kittredge's wife was at a spa in California.

"He got up yesterday," Sophie said. "He's probably at the garden." The vegetable garden was in the middle of the island on a bit of land their grandfather had bought long ago. The garden was one of Dad's projects. He'd grown the plants from seed in soil cubes that sat on a green plastic tray in the laundry room. He studied each seed as if it were a jewel, releasing it and brushing the dirt over with his baby finger. Each night he brought back something for supper: small clubs of zucchini, ripe tomatoes, string beans with their raw fiber-glass skin, and carrots luminous under creases of dirt.

Dad had other projects. For after-dinner, he liked to carve small birds. He was rebuilding the back walkway. There were mooring lines to be spliced onto buoys. When they were little, Dad built a lot of things, a bicycle hutch, a playhouse down in the woods, a treehouse with three separate platforms. Whenever a new baby came home, he'd built something for it. He constructed a bassinet with a step around it so the girls could stand and watch while Mum gave the baby a bath. They watched her fold the diapers fiercely, her eyes with an intent glare, clenching pins in her teeth, pins with plastic tulips on them.

To Caitlin and Sophie it seemed there always was a new baby. When it came home from the hospital, Caitlin and Sophie dressed up as Indians and made cards for Mum. The bundle got picked up and put down, and when it was left in its carriage, it lifted its head to stare at the back. Caitlin and Sophie looked into the black carriage at the baby's head bobbing around like a buoy, staring at nothing. It could stare at nothing for hours.

It was in the baby carriage that Frances died. She was the fifth baby. Only Caitlin and Sophie could remember it, being six and five. It was in the afternoon. Mum came home with shopping bags crinkling, wearing her Boston suit and with her hair in a puff from the hairdresser's. Delilah and Gus were there—everyone always came running into the hall when Mum came home. She picked Baby Frances out of the carriage where it was parked on the porch. Mum went tucking at the baby's throat. Suddenly she was in a hurry, pulling the baby tight to her, touching the baby's face. The kids all looked. Mum spat out, "Get down in the playroom," more mean than she'd ever yelled before. They weren't important anymore at all. Mum ran into the TV room and Caitlin saw her put her mouth on top of Baby Frances's mouth, trying to dial the phone at the same time. Then she slammed it down and went tearing out the hall and down the steps and onto the driveway toward the Birches'.

The next day and for a while after the driveway was filled with cars and the house with people. Caitlin and Sophie found ashtrays next to their toothbrushes in the bathroom and teacups on the piano bench. Baby Frances, they were told, was now in heaven and the grown-ups looked down at them as if they didn't understand. There were flowers everywhere, baskets on tables, pots on the floor, carefully shaped pyramids or clipped round globes.

One day, Sophie saw Mum sitting alone in the living room, where no one ever was, on the arm of a chair in a slouch. Her thumb moved slowly up and down her elbow, smoothing it over.

Downstairs in the playroom Caitlin said it was because Mum still missed Baby Frances. Sophie said she did too.

"Well," Delilah said, "I'm not going to die."

"You have to," Caitlin said. "Everyone in the world has to."

"Not me," Delilah said, pressing her eyelashes down. "I'm going to be the first one in the world not to."

"But that's impossible, Delilah."

"Just wait."

They were all drawing pictures of the family, cards to give Mum and Dad. You lined everyone up according to age. In the sky they put an angel with a halo and wings and black hair for Baby Frances.

The next baby, Sherman, came less than a year after. He was a bad crier. He had a long high screech that would suddenly stop as if a switch had been thrown. After a long silence he'd launch again into even higher wails, gasps to make up for the time spent not breathing.

AMONG the tea drinkers on the wharf was a trio of strangers to North Eden, two swarthy men and a statuesque blond woman near the sail closet. They looked European.

"Kittredge houseguests," said Westy Granger.

"I bet they're folksingers," said Trisha Holt. "They look like Peter, Paul, and Mary."

"More like a Swedish movie star," said Westy's friend with the long hair. "Quite a T-shirt on her."

"The mystery woman perhaps," said Westy.

The other night they were careening home from a moonless party at Blind Man's Beach when they came upon a dark carriage clip-clopping along the Middle Road. Red lamps were swinging from points up front and there were two silhouettes under the fringed awning. The car slowed down and pulled to the side and everyone looked. Next to Mr. Kittredge was a woman with a hat on. Caitlin dug her elbow into Sophie's rib. A thin fly whip passed across the rosy lights, waving them on. Westy screeched forward and began to sing the chorus of an antiwar song and everyone joined in.

The fact that Mr. Kittredge made bombs did not, according to Mum, mean that he was bad. She recognized the bad guys. She threw her shoe at Nixon when he was on TV. She distributed leaflets after the bombing of Cambodia and gave cocktail parties with Patricia Meyer, the only other Democrat in Marshport, to raise money for their candidates. Years before, on a tour of the Capitol, they visited their senator and afterward Mum brought Caitlin and Sophie to visit Mr. Kittredge. Mum liked to look at other people's houses. While she was touring the greenhouse and the collection rooms and the new addition, Caitlin and Sophie swam in the Kittredges' slate pool without anyone watching, something they'd never done before. None of the other Kittredges were there but they never were. The afternoon air was hushed, with only heat bugs going, and when it started to rain, the girls slipped into the pool house. It had an automatic ice maker and ceramic elephants under glass tabletops, cushions trimmed in green bamboo patterns, and a pair of tusks taller than the girls, guarding the doorway. Silver frames showed the blond Kittredge daughters in bathing suits, waist-deep in turquoise water, glinting gold jewelry. When Mum and Mr. Kittredge got back, he lifted a trapdoor and led them down cement steps into a cement room, the bomb shelter. In the corner were boxes of dried food stacked up like bricks. Of all the things she saw, Mum said, the glass orchids were her favorite. Mum always told the girls her favorite things.

WILBUR KITTREDGE poked his head out of the clubhouse door and waved to the two men and the blond woman. They appeared amused with their surroundings, observing the scene with an air of irony. Wilbur Kittredge seemed to share their private joke and greeted them warmly when they joined him. Mum turned in her seat to be introduced, her shoulders stiff, her smile polite, and her eyes lightning-quick, taking it all in.

BEFORE dinner each evening, Caitlin practiced her driving. She and Mum took the loop by the vegetable garden with the windows rolled down. Lumbering down the rutted road, the station wagon would scrape its fender on the deep holes, making Mum wince. This evening after the race tea when Caitlin looked over, Mum's face was pensive. A few strands of hair were caught in the side of her mouth but she didn't brush them away. They drove by the pond choked with lily pads and high-blown weeds, and passed the fence Dad had made. He'd also built a hitching post at the parking place and when they rounded the corner they found it occupied. Tied up to it was a horse and carriage.

"Oh," said Mum, sitting forward. The glint in her eye showed that she knew the carriage, and well. It was one of the smaller carriages, with a black hood curving over a double seat, no windows. The horse's long face was close to the car, its blinders out like absurd shutters, staring at them. Further back, in the gray shade of the bonnet, they could see the back of Wilbur Kittredge's head and the silvery spot on it. Behind him, with a different glow, was a white T-shirt arching upward.

"Turn around," Mum said.

Caitlin shifted into neutral and the engine roared.

"Back up." Mum was looking everywhere but forward. The car went stuttering backward in jerks. Once around the corner, they stopped and switched places and Mum drove home.

The wind dies down at that time of day and the bay past Clam Cove, its mud flat shiny, was pearly and still, a silk tablecloth with sailboats sitting on top, motionless.

"I didn't think we should get any nearer," said Mum after a while. "Those are especially spirited horses. They spook." The crease in her forehead hinted at deeper knowledge. Whatever it was, she kept it to herself.

NOT LONG after, the island fell under the spell of a heat wave that wouldn't let up. It lasted for the rest of the summer. A limpid air hung over the glassy thorofare, which remained undulating and languid and pale blue. Screams and splashes could be heard day and night as kids ran drumming off the floats. Over the Labor Day weekend was the Kittredges' annual clambake, but the Vincents didn't go. Dad had played too long on the golf course that day and was out with heat stroke. He shut himself in his room, pulled the shades down, and lay in the dark. Mum, who sometimes went to parties without him, this year did not feel up to it and went to bed early too. At the end of the summer, the Vincents returned to Marshport and once again Wilbur Kittredge's postcards appeared on the hall table—greetings from distant lands like Peru or Zanzibar or the Seychelle Islands—cheerful notes dashed off in a loose, large hand, unsigned.

The following spring, after her fortieth birthday, Rosie Vincent gave birth for the eighth time. It was a girl, Miranda Rose. Everyone was excited; there hadn't been a baby in the house for years.

Mum sat up in bed in her pretty nightgown, the pillows behind her bordered in *fleurs-de-lis*, holding her new treasure. Everyone hovered around, knocking against the dust ruffle, lying diagonally at her feet. Mum gazed into the infant eyes, seeing their strange clarity. She touched the tiny nose. She uncurled the fiddlehead fists and showed them to everyone lolling around. "You see?" she said. "Her father's hands exactly."

Then came the feeding. They watched her unbutton the nightgown and feel inside for the bosom. After fixing it to the baby mouth, and satisfied with it, she looked up. Caitlin and Sophie saw it—that wild look—only this time there was something added. It was aimed at them and it said: There is nothing in the world compares with this.

The eye was fierce. The baby stayed fast. There is nothing so thrilling as this. Nothing.

Celia behind Me

ISABEL HUGGAN

THERE was a little girl with large smooth cheeks and very thick glasses who lived up the street when I was in public school. Her name was Celia. It was far too rare and grown-up a name, so we always laughed at it. And we laughed at her because she was a chubby, diabetic child, made peevish by our teasing.

My mother always said, "You must be nice to Celia, she won't live forever," and even as early as seven I could see the unfairness of that position. Everybody died sooner or later, I'd die too, but that didn't mean everybody was nice to me or to each other. I already knew about mortality and was prepared to go to heaven with my two aunts who had died together in a car crash with their heads smashed like overripe melons. I overheard the bit about the melons when my mother was on the telephone, repeating that phrase and sobbing. I used to think about it often, repeating the words to myself as I did other things so that I got a nice rhythm: "Their heads smashed like melons, like melons, like melons." I imagined the pulpy insides of muskmelons and watermelons all over the road.

I often thought about the melons when I saw Celia because her head was so round and she seemed so bland and stupid and fruitlike. All rosy and vulnerable at the same time as being the most *awful* pain. She'd follow us home from school, whining if we walked faster than she did. Everybody always walked faster than Celia because her short little legs wouldn't keep up. And she was bundled in long stockings and heavy underwear, summer and winter, so that even her clothes held her back from our sturdy, leaping pace over and under hedges and across backyards and, when it was dry, or when it was frozen, down the stream bed and through the drainage pipe beneath the bridge on Church Street.

Celia, by the year I turned nine in December, had failed once and was behind us in school, which was a relief because at least in class there wasn't someone telling you to be nice to Celia. But she'd always be in the playground at recess, her pleading eyes magnified behind those ugly lenses so that you couldn't look at her when you told her she couldn't play skipping unless she was an ender. "Because you can't skip worth a fart," we'd whisper in her ear. "Fart, fart, fart," and watch her round pink face crumple as she stood there, turning, turning, turning the rope over and over.

As the fall turned to winter, the five of us who lived on Brubacher Street and went back and forth to school together got meaner and meaner to Celia. And, after the brief diversions of Christmas, we returned with a vengeance to our running and hiding and scaring games that kept Celia in a state of terror all the way home.

My mother said, one day when I'd come into the kitchen and she'd just turned away from the window so I could see she'd been watching us coming down the street, "You'll be sorry, Elizabeth. I see how you're treating that poor child, and it makes me sick. You wait, young lady. Some day you'll see how it feels yourself. Now you be nice to her, d'you hear?"

"But it's not just me," I protested. "I'm nicer to her than anybody else, and I don't see why I have to be. She's nobody special, she's just a pain. She's really dumb and she can't do anything. Why can't I just play with the other kids like everybody else?"

"You just remember I'm watching," she said, ignoring every word I'd said. "And if I see one more snowball thrown in her direction, by you or by anybody else, I'm coming right out there and spanking you in front of them all. Now you remember that!"

I knew my mother, and knew this was no idle threat. The awesome responsibility of now making sure the other kids stopped snowballing Celia made me weep with rage and despair, and I was locked in my room after supper to "think things over."

I thought things over. I hated Celia with a dreadful and absolute passion. Her round guileless face floated in the air above me as I finally fell asleep, taunting me: "You have to be nice to me because I'm going to die."

I did as my mother bid me, out of fear and the thought of the shame that a public spanking would bring. I imagined my mother could see much farther up the street than she really could, and it prevented me from throwing snowballs or teasing Celia for the last four blocks of our homeward journey. And then came the stomach-wrenching task of making the others quit.

"You'd better stop," I'd say. "If my mother sees you she's going to thrash us all."

Terror of terrors that they wouldn't be sufficiently scared of her strap-wielding hand; gut-knotting fear that they'd find out or guess what she'd really said and throw millions of snowballs just for the joy of seeing me whipped, pants down in the snowbank, screaming. I visualized that scene all winter, and felt a shock of relief when March brought such a cold spell that the snow was too crisp for packing. It meant a temporary safety for Celia, and respite for me. For I knew, deep in my wretched heart, that were it not for Celia I was next in line for humiliation. I was kind of chunky and wore glasses too, and had sucked my thumb so openly in kindergarten that "Sucky" had stuck with me all the way to Grade 3 where I now balanced at a hazardous point, nearly accepted by the amorphous Other Kids and always at the brink of being laughed at, ignored or teased. I cried very easily, and prayed during those years—not to become pretty or smart or popular, all aims too far out of my or God's reach, but simply to be strong enough not to cry when I got called Sucky.

During that cold snap, we were all bundled up by our mothers as much as poor Celia ever was. Our comings and goings were hampered by layers of flannel bloomers and undershirts and ribbed stockings and itchy wool against us no matter which way we turned; mitts, sweaters, scarves and hats, heavy and wet-smelling when the snot from our dripping noses mixed with the melting snow on our collars and we wiped, in frigid resignation, our sore red faces with rough sleeves knobbed over with icy pellets.

Trudging, turgid little beasts we were, making our way along slippery streets, breaking the crusts on those few front yards we'd not yet stepped all over in glee to hear the glorious snapping sound of boot through hard snow. Celia, her glasses steamed up even worse than mine, would scuffle and trip a few yards behind us, and I walked along wishing that some time I'd look back and she wouldn't be there. But she always was, and I was always conscious of the abiding hatred that had built up during the winter, in conflict with other emotions that gave me no peace at all. I felt pity, and a rising urge within me to cry as hard as I could so that Celia would cry too, and somehow realize how bad she made me feel, and ask my forgiveness.

It was the last day before the thaw when the tension broke, like northern lights exploding in the frozen air. We were all a little wingy after days of switching between the extremes of bitter cold outdoors and the heat of our homes and school. Thermostats had been turned up in a desperate attempt to combat the arctic air, so that we children suffered scratchy, tingly torment in our faces, hands and feet as the blood in our bodies roared in confusion, first freezing, then boiling. At school we had to go outside at recess—only an act of God would have ever prevented recess, the teachers had to have their cigarettes and tea—and in bad weather we huddled in a shed where the bicycles and the janitor's outdoor equipment were stored.

During the afternoon recess of the day I'm remembering, at the end of the shed where the girls stood, a sudden commotion broke out when Sandra, a rich big girl from Grade 4, brought forth a huge milk-chocolate bar from her pocket. It was brittle in the icy air, and snapped into little bits in its foil wrapper, to be divided among the chosen. I made my way cautiously to the fringe of her group, where many of my classmates were receiving their smidgens of sweet chocolate, letting it melt on their tongues like dark communion wafers. Behind me hung Celia, who had mistaken my earlier cries of "Stop throwing snowballs at Celia!" for kindness. She'd been mooning behind me for days, it seemed to me, as I stepped a little farther forward to see that there were only a few pieces left. Happily, though, most mouths were full and the air hummed with the murmuring sound of chocolate being pressed between tongue and palate.

Made bold by cold and desire, I spoke up. "Could I have a bit, Sandra?" She turned to where Celia and I stood, holding the precious foil in her mittened hand. Wrapping it in a ball, she pushed it over at Celia. Act of kindness, act of spite, vicious bitch or richness seeking expiation? She gave the chocolate to Celia and smiled at her. "This last bit is for Celia," she said to me.

"But I can't eat it," whispered Celia, her round red face aflame with the sensation of being singled out for a gift. "I've got di-a-beet-is." The word. Said so carefully. As if it were a talisman, a charm to protect her against our rough healthiness.

I knew it was a trick. I knew she was watching me out of the corner of her eye, that Sandra, but I was driven. "Then could I have it, eh?" The duress under which I acted prompted my chin to quiver and a tear to start down my cheek before I could wipe it away.

"No, no, no!" jeered Sandra then. "Suckybabies can't have sweets either. Di-a-beet-ics and Suck-y-ba-bies can't eat chocolate. Give it back, you little fart, Celia! That's the last time I ever give you anything!"

Wild, appreciative laughter from the chocolate-tongued mob, and they turned their backs on us, Celia and me, and waited while Sandra crushed the remaining bits into minuscule slivers. They had to take off their mitts and lick their fingers to pick up the last fragments from the foil. I stood there and prayed: "Dear God and Jesus, I would please like very much not to cry. Please help me. Amen." And with that the clanging recess bell clanked through the playground noise, and we all lined up, girls and boys in straight, straight rows, to go inside.

After school there was the usual bunch of us walking home and, of course, Celia trailing behind us. The cold of the past few days had been making us hurry, taking the shortest routes on our way to steaming cups of Ovaltine and cocoa. But this day we were all full of that peculiar energy that swells up before a turn in the weather and, as one body, we turned down the street that meant the long way home. Past the feed store where the Menonites tied their horses, out the back of the town hall parking-lot and then down a ridge to the ice-covered stream and through the Church Street culvert to come out in the unused field behind the Front Street stores; the forbidden adventure we indulged in as a gesture of defiance against the parental "come right home."

We slid down the snowy slope at the mouth of the pipe that seemed immense then but was really only five feet in diameter. Part of its attraction was the tremendous racket you could make by scraping a stick along the corrugated sides as you went through. It was also long enough to echo very nicely if you made good booming noises, and we occasionally titillated each other by saying bad words at one end that grew as they bounced along the pipe and became wonderfully shocking in their magnitude . . . poopy, Poopy, POOpy, POOOOPy, POOOOPPYYY!

I was last because I had dropped my schoolbag in the snow and stopped to brush it off. And when I looked up, down at the far end, where the white plate of daylight lay stark in the darkness, the figures of my four friends were silhouetted as they emerged into the brightness. As I started making great sliding steps to catch up, I heard Celia behind me, and her plaintive, high voice: "Elizabeth! Wait for me, okay? I'm scared to go through alone. Elizabeth?"

And of course I slid faster and faster, unable to stand the thought of being the only one in the culvert with Celia. Then we would come out together and we'd really be paired up. What if they always ran on ahead and left us to walk together? What would I ever do? And behind me I heard the rising call of Celia, who had ventured as far as a few yards into the pipe, calling my name to come back and walk with her. I got right to the end, when I heard another noise and looked up. There they all were, on the bridge looking down, and as soon as they saw my face began to chant, "Better wait for Celia, Sucky. Better get Celia, Sucky."

The sky was very pale and lifeless, and I looked up in the air at my breath curling in spirals and felt, I remember this very well, an exhilarating, clear-headed instant of understanding. And with that, raced back into the tunnel where Celia stood whimpering half-way along.

"You little fart!" I screamed at her, my voice breaking and tearing at the words. "You little diabetic fart! I hate you! I hate you! Stop it, stop crying, I hate you! I could bash your head in I hate you so much, you fart, you fart! I'll smash your head like a melon! And it'll go in pieces all over and you'll die. You'll die, you diabetic. You're going to die!" Shaking her, shaking her and banging her against the cold, ribbed metal, crying and sobbing for grief and gasping with the exertion of pure hatred. And then there were the others, pulling at me, yanking me away, and in the moral tones of those who don't actually take part, warning me that they were going to tell, that Celia probably was going to die now, that I was really evil, they would tell what I said.

And there, slumped in a little heap, was Celia, her round head in its furry bonnet all dirty at the back where it had hit against the pipe, and she was hiccupping with fear. And for a wild, terrible moment I thought I had killed her, that the movements and noises her body made were part of dying.

I ran.

I ran as fast as I could back out the way we had come, and all the way back to the schoolyard. I didn't think about where I was going, it simply seemed the only bulwark to turn to when I knew I couldn't go home. There were a few kids still in the yard but they were older and ignored me as I tried the handle of the side door and found it open. I'd never been in the school after hours, and was stricken with another kind of terror that it might be a strappable offense. But no-one saw me, even the janitor was blessedly in another part of the building, so I was able to creep down to the girls' washroom and quickly hide in one of the cubicles. Furtive, criminal, condemned.

I was so filled with horror I couldn't even cry. I just sat on the toilet seat, reading all the things that were written in pencil on the green, wooden walls. *G.R. loves M.H.* and *Y.F. hates W.S. for double double sure. Mr. Becker wears ladies pants.* Thinking that I might die myself, die right here, and then it wouldn't matter if they told on me that I had killed Celia.

But the inevitable footsteps of retribution came down the stone steps before I had been there very long. I heard the janitor's voice explaining he hadn't seen any children come in and then my father's voice saying that the others were sure this is where Elizabeth would be. And they called my name, and then came in, and I guess saw my boots beneath the door because I suddenly thought it was too late to scrunch them up on the seat and my father was looking down at me and grabbed my arm, hurting it, pulling me, saying "Get in the car, Elizabeth."

Both my mother and my father spanked me that night. At first I tried not to cry, and tried to defend myself against their diatribe, tried to tell them when they asked, "But whatever possessed you to do such a terrible thing?" But whatever I said seemed to make them more angry and they became so soured by their own shame that they slapped my stinging buttocks for personal revenge as much as for any rehabilitative purposes.

"I'll never be able to lift my head on this street again!" my mother cried, and it struck me then, as it still does now, as a marvellous turn of phrase. I thought about her head on the street as she hit me, and wondered what Celia's head looked like, and if I had dented it at all.

Celia hadn't died, of course. She'd been half-carried, half-dragged home by the heroic others, and given pills and attention and love, and the doctor had come to look at her head but she didn't have so much as a bruise. She had a dirty hat, and a bad case of hiccups all night, but she survived.

Celia forgave me, all too soon. Within weeks her mother allowed her to walk back and forth to school with me again. But, in all the years before she finally died at seventeen, I was never able to forgive her. She made me discover a darkness far more frightening than the echoing culvert, far more enduring than her smooth, pink face.

Summer Fruits

KATE SIMON

THE SHAPES of things changed in the summertime. The smoke from the hat factory next door became fat and slow, oozing like a chorus of fat ladies in pink, blue, yellow, purple dresses. The edges of buildings shook and melted. Cold, dry faces opened and glistened with sweat. The spikey park flowers bent and hung. The sidewalks sweated, the walls sweated, and out of the heat and wetness came heavily ornate, lazy bunches of grapes, the opulent shine and swell of plums, the rubies of pomegranate seeds set in their yellow embroidery. (When I came to know Keats' "Ode to Autumn" and the Ingres women in his "Turkish Bath," they became again the languid airs and shapes of my childhood summers.)

Summertime was life, wide and generous, fat King Cole lolling on his throne listening to his fiddlers three, a smiling dolphin turning, playing in big, shining waters. Summer was another country whose fathers had, suddenly, bare, shy arms, whose mothers padded like cats on bare feet. Time was still summer air, as slow and round as pregnant women. In the mornings, time sat quietly, waiting for me as I commanded it to, watching me think, shape, arrange the world. The breakfast farina and milk should be mountains and rivers and I heaped mounds and scraped tunnels with my spoon to make it so. The sun that lit up the rung of a chair, if it hid behind the cloud, would the chair become something else? And if I decided to call the chair a table and said it many times, would the back disappear and the seat broaden to become a table? My brother's pinches (he was still asleep; I hated sleeping, it stole things from me) hurt me. Why didn't I feel anything when I pinched him, just as hard? (I still find myself searching for that answer.)

Cloaked in the royal robes of omnipotent childhood, I went down — it was very early — to check the condition of my domain and my subjects. I was the queen of my block. No one but I knew it and I knew it well, each morning making a royal progress on my empty street, among my big garbage cans, my limp window curtains, my sheet of newspaper slowly turning and sliding in the gutter, my morning glory on Mrs. Roberti's porch vine, my waiting stoops fronting my sleeping houses; my hat factory on the corner of 179th Street, resting from its hours of blowing pink and blue and purple dye smoke; my Kleins, my Rizzos, my Petrides, my Clancys safely in bed, guarded by my strength and will. Even after I had been heavily assaulted with school proofs that very little of the world was mine, that history existed of itself and not as a huge crowded stage hurriedly arranged the day I was born, I maintained a deep interest in my subjects, moving out of absolute control to the more subtle control of observer and critic. (My father, no fool, sensing the menace inherent in the long stares half hidden by my thatch of flaxen hair, accused my mother of having brought forth a silent white snake.)

Early one July morning, the sidewalk already soft and steamy like the bed I had left, I made my usual surveillance, this morning the good fairy tiptoeing through the sleeping castle in the sleeping forest. All was well: the De Santis garage door was locked; the factory door was locked. The Morettis' gray cat was stalking a sparrow, and I hoped she would get it since she wasn't a good mouser and must have a disappointing life. As I watched the cat—a dummy, not good at sparrows either—the clanking of bars and the rumble of turning bolts told me that the factory doors were opening. The oldest De Santis boy, still chewing on a breakfast roll, came out of his stucco house to set a chair on the porch for his grandmother. Annie's father in his working cap, carrying a brown paper lunch bag, ran down the stairs of their house and turned briskly in the direction of the El station. Windows and doors shot open, the trickle of voices thickened, and the legs of the fathers on their way to work became a jumble of zigzags on the sidewalk. I watched my show, contented with its expectedness, hoping a little for the unexpected. Maybe Mr. Kaplan would be wearing his new hat to work, like the gentleman and hero he was. Two Sundays ago he had shouted up at a towering *goy* who wouldn't let him sit on a nearby park bench, "Because I'm a Jew and you're a Christian, I should kiss your ass? You can kiss *my* ass." If not Mr. Kaplan's hat, maybe Mrs. Santini would come out on her porch, chewing yesterday's spaghetti and pushing it into the mouth of her new baby, like what birds did, and then nurse it from a pale flood of breast. Maybe, with luck, I might see one of the sleek men who looked like knives, nobody's fathers or immigrant uncles, run quickly out of the houses of "*nafkas*," a word whispered by the mothers as they rocked their baby carriages in the street, a word, like many, I didn't quite understand yet sensed fairly accurately.

The stage was filling nicely. The milkman was coming around the corner, little boys—not my dopey brother, thank God—were tumbling into the streets. Suddenly, from around the corner, at the back of the factory, the sounds of yelping, wailing, shrieking. I ran, to see something Lon Chaney might have invented as a mad doctor. Dogs, back to back stuck together, trying to pull away from each other, screaming as they pulled. They snapped their teeth at the air, their eyes rolled in anguish, their legs arched and pawed in a crazy dance, their rumps rubbed and twisted, but they couldn't separate. Two factory workers stopped for a moment, watched, exchanged a phrase and a smile, and walked on. I couldn't understand why two grown men couldn't, wouldn't separate the dogs who must have sat in some glue that was tearing their skins and fur as they pulled.

I ran back to my house and leaped up the tenement stairs, past the open doors that drew relief from the cool stone landings. Past Mrs. Petrides' floor, past Mrs. Schwartz's, past Mrs. Szekely's and up to our own, where Mrs. Haskell, with no children to feed or dress, sat reading love advice, fanning herself with the rest of the *Graphic*. I gasped "Hello" and dashed into our apartment. "Mama! Mama! Come down quick. There are two dogs stuck together, maybe some mean person glued them. They can't separate and it hurts them. They're screaming. Please, Mama, it's terrible, get them apart."

The expected move to the door didn't happen. Even with her new big belly, my mother would run down the four flights when Marie Moretti shouted up from the stairwell that her mother's new baby was twisting funny, or when Mrs. Bernstein called across the yard that her stinking old father was sick and needed cupping. Now she stood at the stove and continued stirring the soup as she poured in barley. "Please, Ma, please hurry."

"No. I'm staying here and so are you. Mind your own business. Play in the house." The round face and the mouth like summer fruit had become dry and flat, she looked like the assistant principal, an iron lady. Another "Please" would have been useless, I knew. I must have done something wrong and I went away from the strange woman as far as I could, to the back fire escape to watch the colored smoke from the factory fade into the sky. I counted the mattresses flopping out of the open windows on Monterey Avenue, across from the empty lot below. I took out my box of cloth scraps to try the pink with the blue; no, the yellow with the blue, the shiny with the dull; two shinys. I was going to stay on the fire escape forever, burn in the sun, freeze in the snow, never go back into the kitchen with the woman with the stone face and the ugly hump-back on her belly. She called me in for a glass of milk. I went and drank it in the kitchen, both of us very quiet, a nervous quiet like the first day in a new class. I shouldn't have told her about the dogs. I didn't ask her why. She didn't tell me.

The day of the glued dogs led off many watchful days, days of going out only with Mama. I was her helper, her monitor, much, much older now than my brother, in gray shade while he darted and dazzled in the full sun of the street. They were slow troublesome walks. I didn't want to be with her when her belly burst open and spilled a hundred tiny babies like watermelon seeds. Or it might crack open and a skinny little blind chick would fall to the sidewalk, or out of the crack would slide the long, shining blue of a skinless rabbit like those on the hooks of the Italian butcher shop. I couldn't say I wouldn't go with her, but I hated this swollen person who used to be as lively as jumping rope and never scared. Now she was scared when she stepped off the sidewalk, scared of the boxes flung around in the market, scared of crippled people and Mary Sugar Bum, who staggered around singing like a penny whistle. Once her skirt caught in a band of metal on the stair rail. She tripped, lost her footing, but didn't fall, nothing to make a fuss about. But she sat down on one of the steps and burst into tears. I couldn't understand why, nothing had happened, she hadn't even torn her skirt or scraped her knee and I hadn't ever seen her cry except when she laughed very hard. She was becoming a big ugly crybaby, and lazy. She had to rest a lot and I didn't really know what "resting" meant. She told me to go down and play but I wouldn't. I sat in the kitchen reading about and envying the Dutch Twins who clomped around in noisy wooden shoes—and people let them—or ice-skated and ice-skated all day through the winter. Sometimes I would take, very careful with the latch, a few cherries from the icebox. I ate them slowly, stroking the silk skin, looking at the way the stems jumped up like dancers, crunching into the juicy blood red and sucking the pit until it, too, felt like silk. While I examined and bit and sucked, I heard from across the courtyard Ruthie rumbling her way through scales on her new piano and the sighs of steam from the factory.

Our walks grew shorter, the descent down the stairs slow and careful, I gripping her hand, bracing myself against the pull of the belly, maybe ready to fall and bounce like an enormous ball, thudding down, down, along the four flights of stairs and into the street. As the descent became more difficult—and frightening, I suppose—my mother stopped for a few minutes of what the men referred to as "women's talk" with the neighbors before we went on toward the park or around the block. While they talked, I bounced my ball, staying as close as I discreetly could to the low words. "They had to pull the baby from her with instruments. She screamed for two days." "She always lost them in the fourth month." "The cord got twisted around the neck, so it died." Bounce, bounce, bounce, foot over the ball on the fourth bounce, waiting for the key words, how a baby got into a belly and just how it got out, but they never came. There was repeated mention of nine months. Did that mean that it took nine months for a baby to ripen like a banana to be peeled, a peach to be sliced when it was ready? It must hurt, otherwise the women wouldn't be whispering about screaming. As I bounced the ball, a heat of terror and guilt burned through me and turned to icy nausea in my stomach. I had done this to my mother, made her shout with pain for hours and hours, while doctors dug and ripped at her with "instruments," big pliers and saws that tore her flesh and skin. No wonder my mother could get so mad at me sometimes for reasons I didn't understand. Bouncing, still bouncing the ball, I wondered why she didn't fight this baby off? Or maybe she didn't know it was coming in, like nits in hairs, like worms in puppies and babies? I kept waiting for words that would unlock the door the women guarded, for the light that would make everything clear and nice, like the neat gardens and the clear people with clear smiles in books.

Instead, the women moved into the commonness of headaches and sore throats, a winding, boring exchange of symptoms and cures I'd heard before. . . .

At the end of August that year, the temperature rose to near 100 and stayed, motionless, thick. It was too hot to walk, too hot to go to the library, too hot to play in the street. My brother took his train of spools down to Jimmy Petrides' house; Bianca's grandmother was sick so I couldn't swing in her yard, and I was mad at Becky, who stole my best pencil and denied it. I had finished reading the Belgian Twins and French Twins. I couldn't play with the big doll in the closet that had been there for two years. It was mine, bought for me by old Uncle David, but my father said I couldn't play with it, it was too good. . . . My mother suggested that if I was very careful, I might play with the bowls in the china closet and the basket of tiny flowers, but I must put them back very carefully. I didn't feel like being careful, so when she went to her room to lie down, I just sat and waited. I looked at the light behind the drawn window shade, listened to the crickets on the green lot, traced with my pinkie the red roses and green leaves stitched into the tablecloth in the dining room. When I heard my mother's light snoring, I slipped into the hall, through the open door and up the stairs to the roof.

This was my second kingdom, a continuous black, romantic terrain of tar and low brick dividers that marked off the houses, which stretched from one end of the block to the other. Here I could walk high above the street, in the sky and unshadowed sun. It was here that my subjects spent the hottest nights, when it became a place of dark figures dragging white sheets that billowed like sails and waves as they sank on spreads of newspaper. The sleepy children were put down to curl on each other, fitting like sections of orange. At one side of the pale patches of sheet, the fathers talked quietly while the mothers sat whispering on the other side. From the factory at the end of the row, dye vat vapors stained the thin, smoky dark of the summer night. On this slow-breathing afternoon there was no one around. The hot tar squeaked under my feet as I practiced stepping like Mae Murray with dainty, pointed toes over the brick dividers. I picked some of the hot shining tar from between the bricks and chewed it, a forbidden thing. It tasted of sun and dust, stiffer and better than bubble gum, better than rubber bands. As I chewed and pointed my toes, wondering how close I could get to the edge of the roof before I became too frightened, I heard funny little sounds. They seemed to come from behind a skylight of the middle houses. Like an Indian scout I moved carefully, watching out for the pebbles that might slide under my feet and, rattling, give me away. Following the little gasps and moans and giggles, I reached a side of the skylight from which I could peer around to the front. A man and woman were squirming together like big, tangled worms. Their clothing was all mixed up, open, closed; some off, some on. Clasping, turning, legs and arms grasping and lashing like an octopus, a behind thumping like an angry gorilla, they were stuck as the dogs were but not hurting. I watched for a while as their gasps and moans became shuddery little "Oohs" like being splashed with cold water. More crazies, getting dirty and sweaty, messing up their clothing, hugging, digging, twisting on the hot sticky tar.

I ran back to my skylight, forgetting the twinkle-toe steps, laughing and laughing. Down the stairs and into the apartment to tell my mother about this funny thing I saw. She was still on her bed, awake now and smiling. "What's so funny? What are you laughing at? What happened?" I was about to tell her when I looked at her face, the face that had turned to stone when I asked her to help the dogs. I looked at her belly; maybe the people on the roof were making a belly. Quite easily, smoothly, I began to play the secrets game, as comfortable in my evasions as grown-ups were. "Nothing much, Mama. Sarah was trying to imitate Nita Naldi. She was trying to slink vampy with her fat behind and pigeon toes." "Did she say anything? Tell me." "Nothing, Ma, honest." "She probably said dirty words, that Sarah, didn't she?" "Yes, Mama." "Don't tell me then, don't repeat them." "All right, Mama, I won't."

All that day I could feel the laughter bubbling in me, I could see the whipping bodies of the dogs and the people mixed up with the swell of my mother's body. I washed my face and combed my hair without being told to; I cut the cucumbers neatly, in even slices, almost as well as my mother did, when I helped with supper. The tall door to their secret gardens was beginning, maybe just a crack, to open to me. I didn't know just what I knew, but I knew I was closer to knowing.

A Cold Frozen Day

LOUISE ERDRICH

ON THE first day of school that next fall, we walked out of the door together, both carrying fat creamy tablets and new pencils in identical wooden pencil boxes, both wearing blue. Sita's dress was new with sizing, mine was soft from many washings. It didn't bother me to wear Sita's hand-me-downs because I knew it bothered her so much to see those outgrown dresses, faded and unevenly hemmed by Fritzie, diminished by me and worn to tatters, not enshrined as Sita probably wished.

We walked down the dirt road together and then, hidden from Fritzie's view by the short pines, we separated. Or rather, Sita ran long legged, brightly calling, toward a group of girls also dressed in stiff new material, white stockings, unscuffed shoes. Colored ribbons, plumped in bows, hung down their backs. I lagged far behind. It didn't bother me to walk alone.

And yet, once we stood in the gravel school yard, milling about in clumps, and once we were herded into rows, and once Celestine began to talk to me and once Sita meanly said I'd come in on the freight train, I suddenly became an object of fascination. Popular. I was new in Argus. Everybody wanted to be my friend. But I had eyes only for Celestine. I found her and took her hand. Her flat black eyes were shaded by thick lashes, soft as paintbrushes. Her hair had grown out into a tail. She was strong. Her arms were thick from wrestling with her brother Russell, and she seemed to have grown even taller than a month ago. She was bigger than the eighth-grade boys, almost as tall as Sister Leopolda, the tallest of all the nuns.

We walked up the pressed-rock stairs following our teacher, a round-faced young Dominican named Sister Hugo. And then, assigned our seats in alphabetical order, I was satisfied to find myself in the first desk, ahead of Sita.

Sita's position soon changed, of course. Sita always got moved up front because she volunteered to smack erasers together, wash blackboards, and copy out poems in colored chalk with her perfect handwriting. Much to her relief, I soon became old hat. The girls no longer clustered around me at recess but sat by her on the merry-go-round and listened while she gossiped, stroked her long braid and rolled her blue eyes to attract the attention of the boys in the upper grade.

Halfway through the school year, however, I recaptured my classmates' awe. I didn't plan it or even try to cause the miracle, it simply happened, on a cold frozen day late in winter.

Overnight that March, the rain had gone solid as it fell. Frozen runnels paved the ground and thick cakes of ice formed beneath the eaves where the dripping water solidified midair. We slid down the glossy streets on the way to school, but later that morning, before we got our boots and coats from the closet for the recess hour, Sister Hugo cautioned us that sliding was forbidden. It was dangerous. But once we stood beneath the tall steel slide outdoors, this seemed unfair, for the slide was more a slide than ever, frozen black in one clear sheet. The railings and steps were coated with invisible glare. At the bottom of the slide a pure glass fan opened, inviting the slider to hit it feet first and swoop down the center of the school yard, which was iced to the curbs.

I was the first and only slider.

I climbed the stairs with Celestine behind me, several boys behind her, and Sita hanging toward the rear with her girl friends, who all wore dainty black gum boots and gloves, which were supposed to be more adult, instead of mittens. The railings made a graceful loop on top, and the boys and bolder girls used it to gain extra momentum or even somersault before they slid down. But that day it was treacherous, so slick that I did not dare hoist myself up. Instead, I grabbed the edges of the slide. And then I realized that if I went down at all, it would have to be head first.

From where I crouched the ride looked steeper, slicker, more dangerous than I'd imagined. But I did have on the product of my mother's stolen spoons, the winter coat of such heavy material I imagined I would slide across the school yard on it as if it were a piece of cardboard.

I let go. I went down with terrifying speed. But instead of landing on my padded stomach I hit the ice full force, with my face.

I blacked out for a moment, then sat up, stunned. I saw forms run toward me through a haze of red and glittering spots. Sister Hugo got to me first, grabbed my shoulders, removed my wool scarf, probed the bones of my face with her strong, short fingers. She lifted my eyelids, whacked my knee to see if I was paralyzed, waggled my wrists.

"Can you hear me?" she cried, mopping at my face with her big manly handkerchief, which turned bright red. "If you hear me, blink your eyes!"

I only stared. My own blood was on the cloth. The whole playground was frighteningly silent. Then I understood my head was whole and that no one was even looking at me. They were all crowded at the end of the slide. Even Sister Hugo was standing there now, her back turned. When several of the more pious students sank to their knees, I could not contain myself. I lurched to my feet and tottered over. Somehow I managed to squeeze through their cluster, and then I saw.

The pure gray fan of ice below the slide had splintered, on impact with my face, into a shadowy white likeness of my brother Karl.

He stared straight at me. His cheeks were hollowed out, his eyes dark pits. His mouth was held in a firm line of pain and the hair on his forehead had formed wet spikes, the way it always did when he slept or had a fever.

Gradually, the bodies around me parted and then, very gently, Sister Hugo led me away. She took me up the stairs and helped me onto a cot in the school infirmary.

She looked down at me. Her cheeks were red from the cold, like polished apples, and her brown eyes were sharp with passion.

"Father is coming," she said, then popped quickly out.

As soon as she was gone, I jumped off the cot and went straight to the window. An even larger crowd had collected at the base of the slide, and now Sister Leopolda was setting up a tripod and other photographic equipment. It seemed incredible that Karl's picture should warrant such a stir. But he was always like that. People noticed him. Strangers gave him money while I was ignored, just like now, abandoned with my wounds. I heard the priest's measured creak on the stairs, then Sister Hugo's quick skip, and I jumped back.

Father opened the back door and allowed his magnificence to be framed in it for a moment while he fixed me with his most penetrating stare. Priests were only called in on special cases of discipline or death, and I didn't know which one this was.

He motioned to Sister Hugo, and she ducked from the room.

He drew a chair up beneath his bulk and sat down. I lay flat, as if for his inspection, and there was a long and uncomfortable silence.

"Do you pray to see God?" he asked finally.

"Yes!" I said.

"Your prayers were answered," Father stated. He folded his fingers into the shape of a church and bit harshly on the steeple, increasing the power of his stare.

"Christ's Dying Passion," he said. "Christ's face formed in the ice as surely as on Veronica's veil."

I knew what he meant at last, and so kept silent about Karl. The others at Saint Catherine's did not know about my brother, of course. To them the image on the ice was that of the Son of God.

As long as the ice on the playground lasted, I was special in the class again, sought out by Sita's friends, teachers, even boys who were drawn to the glory of my black eyes and bruises. But I stuck with Celestine. After the sliding, we were even better friends than before. One day the newspaper photographer came to school and I made a great commotion about not having my picture taken unless it was with her. We stood together in the cold wind, at the foot of the slide.

GIRL'S MISHAP SHAPES MIRACLE was the headline in the *Argus Sentinel*.

For two weeks the face was cordoned off and farmers drove for miles to kneel by the cyclone fence outside of Saint Catherine's school. Rosaries were draped on the red slats, paper flowers, little ribbons and even a dollar or two.

And then one day, the sun came out and suddenly warmed the earth. The face of Karl, or Christ, dispersed into little rivulets that ran all through the town. Echoing in gutters, disappearing, swelling through culverts and collecting in basements, he made himself impossibly everywhere and nowhere all at once so that all spring before the town baked hard, before the drought began, I felt his presence in the whispering and sighing of the streams.

That Green and Crazy Summer

CARSON McCULLERS

IT HAPPENED that green and crazy summer when Frankie was twelve years old. This was the summer when for a long time she had not been a member. She belonged to no club and was a member of nothing in the world. Frankie had become an unjoined person who hung around in doorways, and she was afraid. In June the trees were bright dizzy green, but later the leaves darkened, and the town turned black and shrunken under the glare of the sun. At first Frankie walked around doing one thing and another. The sidewalks of the town were gray in the early morning and at night, but the noon sun put a glaze on them, so that the cement burned and glittered like glass. The sidewalks finally became too hot for Frankie's feet, and also she got herself in trouble. She was in so much secret trouble that she thought it was better to stay at home—and at home there was only Berenice Sadie Brown and John Henry West. The three of them sat at the kitchen table, saying the same things over and over, so that by August the words began to rhyme with each other and sound strange. The world seemed to die each afternoon and nothing moved any longer. At last the summer was like a green sick dream, or like a silent crazy jungle under glass. And then, on the last Friday of August, all this was changed: it was so sudden that Frankie puzzled the whole blank afternoon, and still she did not understand.

"It is so very queer," she said. "The way it all just happened."

"Happened? Happened?" said Berenice.

John Henry listened and watched them quietly.

"I have never been so puzzled."

"But puzzled about what?"

"The whole thing," Frankie said.

And Berenice remarked: "I believe the sun has fried your brains."

"Me too," John Henry whispered.

Frankie herself almost admitted maybe so. It was four o'clock in the afternoon and the kitchen was square and gray and quiet. Frankie sat at the table with her eyes half closed, and she thought about a wedding. She saw a silent church, a strange snow slanting down against the colored windows. The groom in this wedding was her brother, and there was a brightness where his face should be. The bride was there in a long white train, and the bride also was faceless. There was something about this wedding that gave Frankie a feeling she could not name.

"Look here at me," said Berenice. "You jealous?"

"Jealous?"

"Jealous because your brother going to be married?"

"No," said Frankie. "I just never saw any two people like them. When they walked in the house today it was so queer."

"You jealous," said Berenice. "Go and behold yourself in the mirror. I can see from the color in your eye."

There was a watery kitchen mirror hanging above the sink. Frankie looked, but her eyes were gray as they always were. This summer she was grown so tall that she was almost a big freak, and her shoulders were narrow, her legs too long. She wore a pair of blue black shorts, a B.V.D. undervest, and she was barefooted. Her hair had been cut like a boy's, but it had not been cut for a long time and was now not even parted. The reflection in the glass was warped and crooked, but Frankie knew well what she looked like; she drew up her left shoulder and turned her head aside.

"Oh," she said. "They were the two prettiest people I ever saw. I just can't understand how it happened."

"But what, Foolish?" said Berenice. "Your brother come home with the girl he means to marry and took dinner today with you and your Daddy. They intend to marry at her home in Winter Hill this coming Sunday. You and your Daddy are going to the wedding. And that is the A and the Z of the matter. So whatever ails you?"

"I don't know," said Frankie. "I bet they have a good time every minute of the day."

"Less us have a good time," John Henry said.

"Us have a good time?" Frankie asked. "Us?"

The three of them sat at the table again and Berenice dealt the cards for three-handed bridge. Berenice had been the cook since Frankie could remember. She was very black and broad-shouldered and short. She always said that she was thirty-five years old, but she had been saying that at least three years. Her hair was parted, plaited, and greased close to the skull, and she had a flat and quiet face. There was only one thing wrong about Berenice—her left eye was bright blue glass. It stared out fixed and wild from her quiet, colored face, and why she had wanted a blue eye nobody human would ever know. Her right eye was dark and sad. Berenice dealt slowly, licking her thumb when the sweaty cards stuck together. John Henry watched each card as it was being dealt. His chest was white and wet and naked, and he wore around his neck a tiny lead donkey tied by a string. He was blood kin to Frankie, first cousin, and all summer he would eat dinner and spend the day with her, or eat supper and spend the night; and she could not make him go home. He was small to be six years old, but he had the largest knees that Frankie had ever seen, and on one of them there was always a scab or a bandage where he had fallen down and skinned himself. John Henry had a little screwed white face and he wore tiny gold-rimmed glasses. He watched all of the cards very carefully, because he was in debt; he owed Berenice more than five million dollars.

"I bid one heart," said Berenice.

"A spade," said Frankie.

"I want to bid spades," said John Henry. "That's what I was going to bid."

"Well, that's your tough luck. I bid them first."

"Oh, you fool jackass!" he said. "It's not fair!"

"Hush quarreling," said Berenice. "To tell the truth, I don't think either one of you got such a grand hand to fight over the bid about. I bid two hearts."

"I don't give a durn about it," Frankie said. "It is immaterial with me."

As a matter of fact this was so: she played bridge that afternoon like John Henry, just putting down any card that suddenly occurred to her. They sat together in the kitchen, and the kitchen was a sad and ugly room. John Henry had covered the walls with queer, child drawings, as far up as his arm would reach. This gave the kitchen a crazy look, like that of a room in the crazy-house. And now the old kitchen made Frankie sick. The name for what had happened to her Frankie did not know, but she could feel her squeezed heart beating against the table edge.

"The world is certainly a small place," she said.

"What makes you say that?"

"I mean sudden," said Frankie. "The world is certainy a sudden place."

"Well, I don't know," said Berenice. "Sometimes sudden and sometimes slow."

Frankie's eyes were half closed, and to her own ears her voice sounded ragged, far away:

"To me it is sudden."

For only yesterday Frankie had never thought seriously about a wedding. She knew that her only brother, Jarvis, was to be married. He had become engaged to a girl in Winter Hill just before he went to Alaska. Jarvis was a corporal in the army and he had spent almost two years in Alaska. Frankie had not seen her brother for a long, long time, and his face had become masked and changing, like a face seen under water. But Alaska! Frankie had dreamed of it constantly, and especially this summer it was very real. She saw the snow and frozen sea and ice glaciers. Esquimau igloos and polar bears and the beautiful Northern lights. When Jarvis had first gone to Alaska, she had sent him a box of homemade fudge, packing it carefully and wrapping each piece separately in waxed paper. It had thrilled her to think that her fudge would be eaten in Alaska, and she had a vision of her brother passing it around to furry Esquimaux. Three months later, a thank-you letter had come from Jarvis with a five-dollar bill enclosed. For a while she mailed candy almost every week, sometimes divinity instead of fudge, but Jarvis did not send her another bill, except at Christmas time. Sometimes his short letters to her father disturbed her a little. For instance, this summer he mentioned once that he had been in swimming and that the mosquitoes were something fierce. This letter jarred upon her dream, but after a few days of bewilderment, she returned to her frozen seas and snow. When Jarvis had come back from Alaska, he had gone straight to Winter Hill. The bride was named Janice Evans and the plans for the wedding were like this: her brother had wired that he and the bride were coming this Friday to spend the day, then on the following Sunday there was to be the wedding at Winter Hill. Frankie and her father were going to the wedding, traveling nearly a hundred miles to Winter Hill, and Frankie had already packed a suitcase. She looked forward to the time her brother and the bride should come, but she did not picture them to herself, and did not think about the wedding. So on the day before the visit she only commented to Berenice:

"I think it's a curious coincidence that Jarvis would get to go to Alaska and that the very bride he picked to marry would come from a place called Winter Hill. Winter Hill," she repeated slowly, her eyes closed, and the name blended with dreams of Alaska and cold snow. "I wish tomorrow was Sunday instead of Friday. I wish I had already left town."

"Sunday will come," said Berenice.

"I doubt it," said Frankie. "I've been ready to leave this town so long. I wish I didn't have to come back here after the wedding. I wish I was going somewhere for good. I wish I had a hundred dollars and could just light out and never see this town again."

"It seems to me you wish for a lot of things," said Berenice.

"I wish I was somebody else except me."

So the afternoon before it happened was like the other August afternoons. Frankie had hung around the kitchen, then toward dark she had gone out into the yard. The scuppernong arbor behind the house was purple and dark in the twilight. She walked slowly. John Henry West was sitting beneath the August arbor in a wicker chair, his legs crossed and his hands in his pockets.

"What are you doing?" she asked.

"I'm thinking."

"About what?"

He did not answer.

Frankie was too tall this summer to walk beneath the arbor as she had always done before. Other twelve-year-old people could still walk around inside, give shows, and have a good time. Even small grown ladies could walk underneath the arbor. And already Frankie was too big; this year she had to hang around and pick from the edges like the grown people. She stared into the tangle of dark vines, and there was the smell of crushed scuppernongs and dust. Standing beside the arbor, with dark coming on, Frankie was afraid. She did not know what caused this fear, but she was afraid.

"I tell you what," she said. "Suppose you eat supper and spend the night with me."

John Henry took his dollar watch from his pocket and looked at it as though the time would decide whether or not he would come, but it was too dark under the arbor for him to read the numbers.

"Go on home and tell Aunt Pet. I'll meet you in the kitchen."

"All right."

She was afraid. The evening sky was pale and empty and the light from the kitchen window made a yellow square reflection in the darkening yard. She remembered that when she was a little girl she believed that three ghosts were living in the coal house, and one of the ghosts wore a silver ring.

She ran up the back steps and said: "I just now invited John Henry to eat supper and spend the night with me."

Berenice was kneading a lump of biscuit dough, and she dropped it on the flour-dusted table. "I thought you were sick and tired of him."

"I am sick and tired of him," said Frankie. "But it seemed to me he looked scared."

"Scared of what?"

Frankie shook her head. "Maybe I mean lonesome," she said finally.

"Well, I'll save him a scrap of dough."

After the darkening yard the kitchen was hot and bright and queer.

The walls of the kitchen bothered Frankie—the queer drawings of Christmas trees, airplanes, freak soldiers, flowers. John Henry had started the first pictures one long afternoon in June, and having already ruined the wall, he went on and drew whenever he wished. Sometimes Frankie had drawn also. At first her father had been furious about the walls, but later he said for them to draw all the pictures out of their systems, and he would have the kitchen painted in the fall. But as the summer lasted, and would not end, the walls had begun to bother Frankie. That evening the kitchen looked strange to her, and she was afraid.

She stood in the doorway and said: "I just thought I might as well invite him."

So at dark John Henry came to the back door with a little week-end bag. He was dressed in his white recital suit and had put on shoes and socks. There was a dagger buckled to his belt. John Henry had seen snow. Although he was only six years old, he had gone to Birmingham last winter and there he had seen snow. Frankie had never seen snow.

"I'll take the week-end bag," said Frankie. "You can start right in making a biscuit man."

"O.K."

John Henry did not play with the dough; he worked on the biscuit man as though it were a very serious business. Now and then he stopped off, settled his glasses with his little hand, and studied what he had done. He was like a tiny watchmaker, and he drew up a chair and knelt on it so that he could get directly over the work. When Berenice gave him some raisins, he did not stick them all around as any other human child would do; he used only two for the eyes; but immediately he realized they were too large—so he divided one raisin carefully and put in eyes, two specks for the nose, and a little grinning raisin mouth. When he had finished, he wiped his hands on the seat of his shorts, and there was a little biscuit man with separate fingers, a hat on, and even walking stick. John Henry had worked so hard that the dough was now gray and wet. But it was a perfect little biscuit man, and, as a matter of fact, it reminded Frankie of John Henry himself.

"I better entertain you now," she said.

They ate supper at the kitchen table with Berenice, since her father had telephoned that he was working late at his jewelry store. When Berenice brought the biscuit man from the oven, they saw that it looked exactly like any biscuit man ever made by a child—it had swelled so that all the work of John Henry had been cooked out, the fingers were run together, and the walking stick resembled a sort of tail. But John Henry just looked at it through his glasses, wiped it with his napkin, and buttered the left foot.

It was a dark, hot August night. The radio in the dining room was playing a mixture of many stations: a war voice crossed with the gabble of an advertiser, and underneath there was the sleazy music of a sweet band. The radio had stayed on all the summer long, so finally it was a sound that as a rule they did not notice. Sometimes, when the noise became so loud that they could not hear their own ears, Frankie would turn it down a little. Otherwise, music and voices came and went and crossed and twisted with each other, and by August they did not listen any more.

"What do you want to do?" asked Frankie. "Would you like for me to read to you out of Hans Brinker or would you rather do something else?"

"I rather do something else," he said.

"What?"

"Less play out."

"I don't want to," Frankie said.

"There's a big crowd going to play out tonight."

"You got ears," Frankie said. "You heard me."

John Henry stood with his big knees locked, then finally he said: "I think I better go home."

"Why, you haven't spent the night! You can't eat supper and just go on off like that."

"I know it," he said quietly. Along with the radio they could hear the voices of the children playing in the night. "But less go out, Frankie. They sound like they having a mighty good time."

"No they're not," she said. "Just a lot of ugly silly children. Running and hollering and running and hollering. Nothing to it. We'll go upstairs and unpack your week-end bag."

Frankie's room was an elevated sleeping porch which had been built onto the house, with a stairway leading up from the kitchen. The room was furnished with an iron bed, a bureau, and a desk. Also Frankie had a motor which could be turned on and off; the motor could sharpen knives, and, if they were long enough, it could be used for filing down your fingernails. Against the wall was the suitcase packed and ready for the trip to Winter Hill. On the desk there was a very old typewriter, and Frankie sat down before it, trying to think of any letters she could write: but there was nobody for her to write to, as every possible letter had already been answered, and answered even several times. So she covered the typewriter with a raincoat and pushed it aside.

"Honestly," John Henry said, "don't you think I better go home?"

"No," she answered, without looking around at him. "You sit there in the corner and play with the motor."

Before Frankie there were now two objects—a lavender seashell and a glass globe with snow inside that could be shaken into a snowstorm.

When she held the seashell to her ear, she could hear the warm wash of the Gulf of Mexico, and think of a green palm island far away. And she could hold the snow globe to her narrowed eyes and watch the whirling white flakes fall until they blinded her. She dreamed of Alaska. She walked up a cold white hill and looked on a snowy wasteland far below. She watched the sun make colors in the ice, and heard dream voices, saw dream things. And everywhere there was the cold white gentle snow.

"Look," John Henry said, and he was staring out of the window. "I think those big girls are having a party in their clubhouse."

"Hush!" Frankie screamed suddenly. "Don't mention those crooks to me."

There was in the neighborhood a clubhouse, and Frankie who was not a member. The members of the club were girls who were thirteen and fourteen and even fifteen years old. They had parties with boys on Saturday night. Frankie knew all of the club members, and until this summer she had been like a younger member of their crowd, but now they had this club and she was not a member. They had said she was too young and mean. On Saturday night she could hear the terrible music and see from far away their light. Sometimes she went around to the alley behind the clubhouse and stood near a honeysuckle fence. She stood in the alley and watched and listened. They were very long, those parties.

"Maybe they will change their mind and invite you," John Henry said.

"The son-of-a-bitches."

Frankie sniffled and wiped her nose in the crook of her arm. She sat down on the edge of the bed, her shoulders slumped and her elbows resting on her knees. "I think they have been spreading it all over town that I smell bad," she said. "When I had those boils and that black bitter smelling ointment, old Helen Fletcher asked what was that funny smell I had. Oh, I could shoot every one of them with a pistol."

She heard John Henry walking up to the bed, and then she felt his hand patting her neck with tiny little pats. "I don't think you smell so bad," he said. "You smell sweet."

"The son-of-a-bitches," she said again. "And there was something else. They were talking nasty lies about married people. When I think of Aunt Pet and Uncle Ustace. And my own father! The nasty lies! I don't know what kind of fool they take me for."

"I can smell you the minute you walk in the house without even looking to see if it is you. Like a hundred flowers."

"I don't care," she said. "I just don't care."

"Like a thousand flowers," said John Henry, and still he was patting his sticky hand on the back of her bent neck.

Frankie sat up, licked the tears from around her mouth, and wiped off her face with her shirttail. She sat still, her nose widened, smelling herself. Then she went to her suitcase and took out a bottle of Sweet Serenade. She rubbed some on the top of her head and poured some more down inside the neck of her shirt.

"Want some on you?"

John Henry was squatting beside her open suitcase and he gave a little shiver when she poured the perfume over him. He wanted to meddle in her traveling suitcase and look carefully at every thing she owned. But Frankie only wanted him to get a general impression, and not count and know just what she had and what she did not have. So she strapped the suitcase and pushed it back against the wall. "Boy!" she said. "I bet I use more perfume than anybody in this town."

The house was quiet except for the low rumble of the radio in the dining room downstairs. Long ago her father had come home and Berenice had closed the back door and gone away. There was no longer the sound of children's voices in the summer night.

"I guess we ought to have a good time," said Frankie.

But there was nothing to do. John Henry stood, his knees locked and his hands clasped behind his back, in the middle of the room. There were moths at the window—pale green moths and yellow moths that fluttered and spread their wings against the screen.

"Those beautiful butterflies," he said. "They are trying to get in."

Frankie watched the soft moths tremble and press against the window screen. The moths came every evening when the lamp on her desk was lighted. They came from out of the August night and fluttered and clung against the screen.

"To me it is the irony of fate," she said. "The way they come here. Those moths could fly anywhere. Yet they keep hanging around the windows of this house."

John Henry touched the gold rim of his glasses to settle them on his nose and Frankie studied his flat little freckled face.

"Take off those glasses," she said suddenly.

John Henry took them off and blew on them. She looked through the glasses and the room was loose and crooked. Then she pushed back her chair and stared at John Henry. There were two damp white circles around his eyes.

"I bet you don't need those glasses," she said. She put her hand down on the typewriter, "What is this?"

"The typewriter," he said.

Frankie picked up the shell. "And this?"

"The shell from the Bay."

"What is that little thing crawling there on the floor?"

"Where?" he asked, looking around him.

"That little thing crawling along near your feet."

"Oh," he said. He squatted down. "Why, it's an ant. I wonder how it got up here."

Frankie tilted back in her chair and crossed her bare feet on her desk. "If I were you I'd just throw those glasses away," she said. "You can see good as anybody."

John Henry did not answer.

"They don't look becoming."

She handed the folded glasses to John Henry and he wiped them with his pink flannel glasses rag. He put them back on and did not answer.

"O.K." she said. "Suit yourself. I was only telling you for your own good."

They went to bed. They undressed with their backs turned to each other and then Frankie switched off the motor and the light. John Henry knelt down to say his prayers and he prayed for a long time, not saying the words aloud. Then he lay down beside her.

"Good night," she said.

"Good night."

Frankie stared up into the dark. "You know it is still hard for me to realize that the world turns around at the rate of about a thousand miles an hour."

"I know it," he said.

"And to understand why it is that when you jump up in the air you don't come down in Fairview or Selma or somewhere fifty miles away."

John Henry turned over and made a sleepy sound.

"Or Winter Hill," she said. "I wish I was starting for Winter Hill right now."

Already John Henry was asleep. She heard him breathe in the darkness, and now she had what she had wanted so many nights that summer; there was somebody sleeping in the bed with her. She lay in the dark and listened to him breathe, then after a while she raised herself on her elbow. He lay freckled and small in the moonlight, his chest white and naked, and one foot hanging from the edge of the bed. Carefully she put her hand on his stomach and moved closer; it felt as though a little clock was ticking inside him and he smelled of sweat and Sweet Serenade. He smelled like a sour little rose. Frankie leaned down and licked him behind the ear. Then she breathed deeply, settled herself with her chin on his sharp damp shoulder, and closed her eyes: for now, with somebody sleeping in the dark with her, she was not so much afraid.

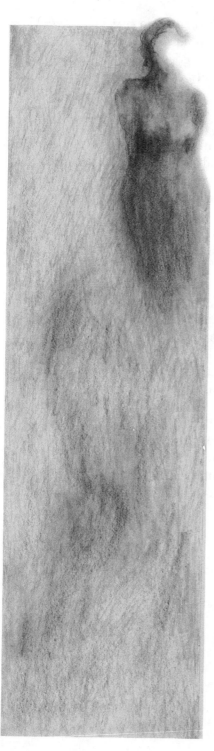

Looking for Love

WE begin to tire of our childhood games. Boys look at us in new sidelong ways. Hoping to guess what falling in love will be like, we spy on older girls who magically seem to have grasped it all.

In Joan Chase's "Celia's Time" three girl cousins push toward that first breathtaking glimmer of romantic love, as they watch the older Celia attract boys, who sprawl over every surface of the porch of their Indiana farmhouse. When she settles on her first boyfriend, Corley, the three cannot resist spying to learn what love will be like.

Sharon Olds's poem "First Boyfriend" celebrates our next step in looking for love, when we actually acquire a first love. And Mary McCarthy's Dottie, a Vassar graduate and proper Bostonian, rushes on toward her first sexual experience as she goes home with a man met at the wedding of classmate Kay—a handsome, slightly drunk, and defi-nitely unreliable actor, Dick.

As we gain experience—falling in love once, twice, and many times—we gradually see that high state of joy and anxiety is about more than finding the right man or even being "in love." Whether love is consum-mated gloriously or ignominiously, ends happily or painfully, is requited or unrequited, we are changed. By loving someone else, we begin to learn who *we* are, or long to be, or vow to change ourselves to be.

The next three heroines illustrate several possibilities for self-revela-tion through love. Terry McMillan's thirty-five-year-old Robin, a black professional woman, has just kicked out her unfaithful live-in lover, Rus-sell. Faced with the "New Men of the Nineties" who are not emotionally available for marriage, Robin tries to find out if she can make it with a man who is "not pretty" but is "available." Lee Smith's Sharon, on the other hand, thinks of herself as a happily married mother and wife—until she meets a sweet, romantic man over the Xerox machine and learns all she's left untapped in herself.

Jean Stafford's heroine is in love with a young engineer, thinking con-stantly of whether he'll like her hairdo or admire her eyes. In one momentous day she will discover whether she can turn her giddy roman-tic love into a deeper, more enduring love.

As we move from our first heart-stopping interest in the opposite sex, through failures in love that become funny in retrospect, to love that endures, we learn that loving is a tightrope act. Finding a lover requires us to have steady nerves, a taste for risk, and a good sense of internal bal-ance.

Celia's Time

JOAN CHASE

ONE EARLY spring evening when Celia was fourteen and the rest of us girls thirteen or nearly so, Uncle Dan came home, carrying the sack of groceries Aunt Libby had ordered over the phone, and saw a troop of boys sprawled around on the porch or hanging from the railings and balustrades. He stopped and asked them if there was some problem, had their mothers forgotten something at the market. They slunk off sideways and kicked the porch steps. But when Celia walked through the front door they came alive and in a fevered sprint backed away, running and hollering, to the far road, their speeding eyes in retreat still fastened on Celia, who smiled vaguely with a certain regal privilege. For a moment Uncle Dan's face was strange to us, unshielded by his bright mocking ironies. Then he recovered. Knew what was what. He appraised her long bare legs, asked if she had taken to going about half naked because of internal or external heat. She huffed, "Oh, Daddy! Don't be so old-fashioned," her face golden-lighted in the sun's reflection off her apricot hair, and she went inside tossing that mane, her legs slightly rigid at the knee, like a leggy colt. Uncle Dan flicked his gray, dust-colored eyes over the rest of us, who were dark-haired, with sallow complexions, or altogether too high-colored; he smiled outright, also an expression rare for him, and he seemed newly primed for the changed direction life was taking.

And after that we knew too that there was something different in Celia. It wasn't just that she was older. It was a confidence that came upon her, suddenly and entirely, so that it didn't matter that summer after summer her hair had swung out with more sun-riffled gleam or that her body had swelled here and tightened there into a figure that was at the same time voluptuous and lissome. Effortlessly she appealed to boys, boys who ever after seemed to wander our place with the innocent milling confusion of lambs for the slaughter. That was what Aunt Libby called them, gazing out. "Those poor souls. They don't know what's hit them." She shook her head and sometimes found fault with Celia as if she were too provocative. "Just look at that butt": she'd frown out toward where Celia was talking fifty miles an hour to some boy, leaning on a car window, her body swiveling, her hair swooping in dips, her smiles tossed like fanciful flowers. We couldn't tell for certain whether Aunt Libby was angry or proud.

Celia's change separated her from the rest of us. She seemed indifferent, didn't need us anymore. We fell back, a little in awe. Where she was bold we were unsure, wondering what Aunt Libby would say. Anxiously we tried for Celia's attention, wanted fiercely to be included. But it was no use, that desire; we could not reach her, or be content without her. So we watched her life ravenously while waiting for her to make some slip. . . .

Everything was changed. At the swimming pool Celia no longer entered the water unless she was thrown in by some boisterous youths, and then she let them, as eagerly, assist her in getting out, their hands now lingering and gentle on her. We peered out onto the front porch, the pack of boys more distant, even as we desired them more. It was seeing the way they waited, with a patient wistfulness for any attention Celia might chance to offer, boys who before had not wanted anything from a girl, that defeated us finally: Celia, in impartial imperious command, standing among them, her hands fixed like delicate fan clasps upon her jutting hips, her mouth small and yet full and piquant, like two sections of an orange. It seemed then that we were the intruders on our front porch, that everything belonged to Celia. We went into town, leaving her the porch while we sneaked into the swimming pool at night, or waited at the "Y" for the arrival of a few boys so that then we could walk the two miles home with our girl friends shadowed by the boys, who circled round us, calling out of the dark, fresh whoops coming nearer then moving further into the dark. Sometimes when we got home we'd stand behind the parlor drapes, up against the climbing roses of the wallpaper, and peek out onto the porch to watch Celia. Then we didn't laugh even to ourselves and there would be the run of saliva inside us, as though we were watching her eating steak. . . .

CELIA had him in the parlor. We stayed in the living room across the hall and were quiet, listening for any sounds they might make. We never heard any talking. This night Aunt Libby and Uncle Dan had gone out and Corley had come later, so we were the only ones who saw him go into the parlor with Celia and close the door.

The hall light was out. Across the darkness we could see the slight border of light under the double panel doors and between them where they pulled together. There was no hurry. We waited.

Going out of the room, Celia left the door open so we could see Corley waiting there while she was in the kitchen. She didn't even glance at us. Corley was her new boyfriend and already she was different with him. The other boys didn't come to the house now and she saw him every night Aunt Libby would allow it. Celia arguing nonstop all afternoon, then over supper. Corley wore his wavy hair in a slick ducktail, which he was constantly combing; we watched the muscles in his arms quivering even from that little bit of movement. When he smiled, his full lips barely lifted and there was no change in the expression of his thick-lidded eyes. Aunt Libby said he was lazy as the day is long, you could tell that by looking at him, and he wouldn't ever get out of bed once he'd got Celia into one. She said he dripped sex. To us that seemed to go along with his wet-looking hair.

Still we thought he was cute and Celia was lucky. He grinned now, combing his hair. "How you all doing?" His family had come up from Kentucky and he still talked that way, with a voice mushy and thick like his lips.

"Fine." We shrugged.

"Here's some money," he said. "You want to get some ice cream?" He must have thought we were still kids. There was a Dairy Delight now on the far lot beside the gas station; Gram spoke of her fields and meadows as lots now.

Sure, we said, knowing he wanted to get rid of us, knowing too what we'd do when we got back. We took our time walking there because there were a lot of cars driving in and out of the parking lot on a Saturday night and we knew some of the guys. Walking back, we felt the connection with the rest of the world sever as we left the high lamps and passed beyond the cedar hedge onto the dark gravel, the house shadowy too now, with only one small glow of light in the front hall.

We needed no words. We moved to the grass to quiet our walking. Through the gap in the honeysuckle we sneaked and climbed over the railing and stood to one side of the window, where we could see at an angle past the half-drawn drapes. At first we could scarcely make them out where they were on the floor, bound in one shape. We licked our ice cream and carefully, silently dissolved the cones, tasting nothing as it melted away down inside us. Tasting instead Corley's mouth on ours, its burning wild lathering sweetness. In the shaft of light we saw them pressed together, rolling in each other's arms, Celia's flowery skirt pulled up around her thighs. His hand moving there. Then she pushed him away, very tenderly, went to sit back on the couch while Corley turned his back and combed his hair. He turned and started toward her, tucking his shirt in. We stared at the unsearchable smile that lifted from Celia's face like a veil and revealed another self, as she began to unbutton her blouse, undressing herself until she sat there in the half-dark, bare to the waist, bare to the moon which had come up over the trees behind us. She drew Corley to her, his face after he'd turned around never losing its calm, kissed him forever, it seemed, as long as she wanted to. Then she guided his mouth to press into first one and then the other cone-crested breast, her own face lake-calm under the moon. Then she dressed again. Our hearts plunged and thudded. At that moment we were freed from Aunt Libby. We didn't care what it was called or the price to be paid; someday we would have it.

First Boyfriend

SHARON OLDS

(for D.R.)

WE WOULD park on any quiet street,
gliding over to the curb as if by accident,
the houses dark, the families sealed into them,
we'd park away from the street-light, just the
faint waves of its amber grit
reached your car, you'd switch off the motor and
turn and reach for me, and I would
slide into your arms as if I had been born for it,
the ochre corduroy of your sports jacket
pressing the inside of my wrist,
making its pattern of rivulets,
water rippling out like sound waves from a source.
Your front seat had an overpowering
male smell, as if the chrome had been
rubbed with jism, a sharp stale
delirious odor like the sour plated
taste of the patina on an old watch, the
fragrance of your sex polished till it shone in the night, the
jewel of Channing Street, of Benvenue Avenue, of
Panoramic, of Dwight Way, I
returned to you as if to the breast of my father,
grain of the beard on your umber cheeks,
delicate line of tartar on the edge of your teeth,
the odor of use, the stained brass
air in the car as if I had come
back to a pawnshop to claim what was mine —
and as your tongue went down my throat,

right down the central nerve of my body, the
gilt balls of the street-light gleamed like a
pawnbroker's over your second-hand Chevy and
all the toasters popped up and
all the saxophones began to play
hot riffs of scat for the return of their rightful owners.

Dottie Meets Dick

MARY McCARTHY

JUST at first, in the dark hallway, it had given Dottie rather a funny feeling to be tiptoeing up the stairs only two nights after Kay's wedding to a room right across from Harald's old room, where the same thing had happened to Kay. An awesome feeling, really, like when the group all got the curse at the same time; it filled you with strange ideas about being a woman, with the moon compelling you like the tides. All sorts of weird, irrelevant ideas floated through Dottie's head as the key turned in the lock and she found herself, for the first time, alone with a man in his flat. Tonight was midsummer's night, the summer solstice, when maids had given up their treasure to fructify the crops; she had that in background reading her *A Midsummer Night's Dream.* Her Shakespeare teacher had been awfully keen on anthropology and had had them study in Frazer about the ancient fertility rites and how the peasants in Europe, till quite recent times, had lit big bonfires in honor of the Corn Maiden and then lain together in the fields. College, reflected Dottie as the lamp clicked on, had been almost *too* rich an experience. She felt stuffed with interesting thoughts that she could only confide in Mother, not in a man, certainly, who would probably suppose you were barmy if your started telling him about the Corn Maiden when you were just about to lose your virginity. Even the group would laugh if Dottie confessed that she was exactly in the mood for a long, comfy discussion with Dick, who was so frightfully attractive and unhappy and had so much to give.

But the group would never believe, never in a million years, that Dottie Renfrew would come here, to this attic room that smelled of cooking fat, with a man she hardly knew, who made no secret of his intentions, who had been drinking heavily, and who was evidently not in love with her. When she put it that way, crudely, she could scarcely believe it herself, and the side of her that wanted to talk was still hoping, probably, to gain a little time, the way, she had noticed, she always started a discussion of current events with the dentist to keep him from turning on the drill. Dottie's dimple twinkled. What an odd comparison! If the group could hear that!

And yet when It happened, it was not at all what the group or even Mother would have imagined, not a bit sordid or messy, in spite of Dick's being tight. He had been most considerate, undressing her slowly, in a matter-of-fact way, as if he were helping her off with her outdoor things. He took her hat and furs and put them in the closet and then unfastened her dress, bending over the snaps with a funny, concentrated scowl, rather like Daddy's when he was hooking Mother up for a party. Lifting the dress carefully off her, he had glanced at the label and then back at Dottie, as though to match the two, before he carried it, walking very steadily, to the closet and arranged it on a wooden hanger. After that, he folded each garment as he removed it and set it ceremoniously on the armchair, looking each time at the label with a frown between his brows. When her dress was gone, she felt rather faint for a minute, but he left her in her slip, just as they did in the doctor's office, while he took off her shoes and stockings and undid her brassière and girdle and step-ins, so that finally, when he drew her slip over her head, with great pains so as not to muss her hairdo, she was hardly trembling when she stood there in front of him with nothing on but her pearls. Perhaps it was going to the doctor so much or perhaps it was Dick himself, so detached and impersonal, the way they were supposed to be in art class with the model, that made Dottie brave. He had not touched her once, all the time he was undressing her, except by accident, grazing her skin. Then he pinched each of her full breasts lightly and told her to relax, in just the tone Dr. Perry used when he was going to give her a treatment for her sciatica.

He handed her a book of drawings to look at, while he went into the closet, and Dottie sat there in the armchair, trying not to listen. With the book on her lap, she studied the room conscientiously, in order to know Dick better. Rooms told a lot about a person. It had a skylight and a big north window and was surprisingly neat for a man; there was a drawing board with some work on it which she longed to peek at, a long plain table, like an ironing table, monk's-cloth curtains, and a monk's-cloth spread on the single bed. On the chest of drawers was a framed photograph of a blonde woman, very striking, with a short, severe haircut; that must be "Betty," the wife. Tacked up on the wall, there was a snapshot that looked like her in a bathing suit and a number of sketches from the nude, and Dottie had the sinking feeling that they might be of Betty too. She had been doing her very best not to let herself think about love or let her emotions get entangled, for she knew that Dick would not like it. It was just a physical attraction, she had been telling herself over and over, while trying to remain cool and collected despite the pounding of her blood, but now, suddenly, when it was too late to retreat, she had lost her *sang-froid* and was jealous. Worse than that, even, the idea came to her that Dick was, well, *peculiar*. She opened the book of drawings on her lap and found more nudes, signed by some modern artist she had never heard of! She did not know, a second later, just what she had been expecting, but Dick's return was, by contrast, less bad.

He came in wearing a pair of white shorts and carrying a towel, with a hotel's name on it, which he stretched out on the bed, having turned back the covers. He took the book away from her and put it on a table. Then he made Dottie lie down on the towel, telling her to relax again, in a friendly, instructive voice; while he stood for a minute, looking down at her and smiling, with his hands on his hips, she tried to breathe naturally, reminding herself that she had a good figure, and forced a wan, answering smile to her lips. "*Nothing will happen unless you want it, baby.*" The words, lightly stressed, told her how scared and mistrustful she must be looking. "I know, Dick," she answered, in a small, weak, grateful voice, making herself use his name aloud for the first time. "Would you like a cigarette?" Dottie shook her head and let it drop back on the pillow. "All right, then?" "All right." As he moved to turn out the light, she felt a sudden harsh thump of excitement, right in *there*, like what had happened to her in the Italian restaurant when he said "Do you want to come home with me?" and fastened his deep, shadowed eyes on her. Now he turned and looked at her steadily again, his hand on the bridge lamp; her own eyes, widening with amazement at the funny feeling she noticed, as if she were on fire, in the place her thighs were shielding, stared at him, seeking confirmation; she swallowed. In reply, he switched off the lamp and came toward her in the dark, unbuttoning his shorts.

This shift gave her an instant in which to be afraid. She had never seen *that* part of a man, except in statuary and once, at the age of six, when she had interrupted Daddy in his bath, but she had a suspicion that it would be something ugly and darkly inflamed, surrounded by coarse hair. Hence, she had been very grateful for being spared the sight of it, which she did not think she could have borne, and she held her breath as the strange body climbed on hers, shrinking. "Open your legs," he commanded, and her legs obediently fell apart. His hand squeezed her down there, rubbing and stroking; her legs fell farther apart, and she started to make weak, moaning noises, almost as if she wanted him to stop. He took his hand away, thank Heaven, and fumbled for a second then she felt it, the thing she feared, being guided into her as she braced herself and stiffened. "Relax," he whispered. "You're ready." It was surprisingly warm and smooth, but it hurt terribly, pushing and stabbing. "Damn it," he said. "Relax. You're making it harder." Just then, Dottie screamed faintly; it had gone all the way in. He put his hand over her mouth and then settled her legs around him and commenced to move it back and forth inside her. At first, it hurt so that she flinched at each stroke and tried to pull back, but this only seemed to make him more determined. Then, while she was still praying for it to be over, surprise of surprises, she started to like it a little. She got the idea, and her body began to move too in answer, as he pressed *that* home in her slowly, over and over, and slowly drew it back, as if repeating a question. Her breath came quicker. Each lingering stroke, like a violin bow, made her palpitate for the next. Then, all of a sudden, she seemed to explode in a series of long, uncontrollable contractions that embarrassed her, like the hiccups, the moment they were over, for it was as if she had forgotten Dick as a person; and he, as if he sensed this, pulled quickly away from her and thrust that part of himself onto her stomach, where it pushed and pounded at her flesh. Then he too jerked and moaned, and Dottie felt something damp and sticky running down the hill of her belly.

Minutes passed; the room was absolutely still; through the skylight Dottie could see the moon. She lay there, with Dick's weight still on her, suspecting that something had gone wrong—probably her fault. His face was turned sideward so that she could not look into it, and his chest was squashing her breasts so that she could hardly breathe. Both their bodies were wet, and the cold perspiration from him ran down her face and matted her side hair and made a little rivulet between her breasts; on her lips it had a salty sting that reminded her forlornly of tears. She was ashamed of the happiness she had felt. Evidently, he had not found her satisfactory as a partner or else he would say something. Perhaps the woman was not supposed to move? "Damn it," he had said to her, when he was hurting her, in such a testy voice, like a man saying "Damn it, why can't we have dinner on time?" or something unromantic like that. Was it her screaming out that had spoiled everything? Or had she made a *faux pas* at the end, somehow? She wished that books were a little more explicit; Krafft-Ebing, which Kay and Helena had found at a secondhand bookstore and kept reading aloud from, as if it were very funny, mostly described nasty things like men making love to hens, and even then did not explain how it was done. The thought of the blonde on the bureau filled her with hopeless envy; probably Dick at this moment was making bitter comparisons. She could feel his breathing and smell the stale alcohol that came from him in gusts. In the bed, there was a peculiar pungent odor, and she feared that it might come from her.

The horrible idea occurred to her that he had fallen asleep, and she made a few gentle movements to try to extricate herself from under him. Their damp skins, stuck together, made a little sucking noise when she pulled away, but she could not roll his weight off her. Then she knew that he was asleep. Probably he was tired, she said to herself forgivingly; he had those dark rings under his eyes. But down in her heart she knew that he ought not to have gone to sleep like a ton of bricks on top of her; it was the final proof, if she still needed one, that she meant nothing to him. When he woke up tomorrow morning and found her gone, he would probably be glad. Or perhaps he would not even remember who had been there with him; she could not guess how much he had had to drink before he met her for dinner. What had happened, she feared, was that he had simply passed out. She saw that her only hope of saving her own dignity was to dress in the dark and steal away. But she would have to find the bathroom somewhere outside in that unlit hall. Dick began to snore. The sticky liquid had dried and was crusting on her stomach; she felt she could not go back to the Vassar Club without washing it off. Then the worst thought, almost, of all struck her. Supposing he had started to have an emission while he was still inside her? Or if he had used one of the rubber things and it had broken when she had jerked like that and that was why he had pulled so sharply away? She had heard of the rubber things breaking or leaking and how a woman could get pregnant from just a single drop. Full of determination, Dottie heaved and squirmed to free herself, until Dick raised his head in the moonlight and stared at her, without recognition. It was all true then, Dottie thought miserably; he had just gone to sleep and forgotten her. She tried to slide out of the bed.

Dick sat up and rubbed his eyes. "Oh, it's you, Boston," he muttered, putting an arm around her waist. "Forgive me for dropping off." He got up and turned on the bridge lamp. Dottie hurriedly covered herself with the sheet and averted her face; she was still timorous of seeing him in the altogether. "I must go home, Dick," she said soberly, stealing a sideward look at her clothes folded on the armchair. "*Must* you?" he inquired in a mocking tone; she could imagine his reddish eyebrows shooting up. "You needn't trouble to dress and see me downstairs," she went on quickly and firmly, her eyes fixed on the rug where his bare handsome feet were planted. He stooped and picked up his shorts; she watched his feet clamber into them. Then her eyes slowly rose and met his searching gaze. "What's the matter, Boston?" he said kindly. "Girls don't run home, you know, on their first night. Did it hurt you much?" Dottie shook her head. "Are you bleeding?" he demanded. "Come on, let me look." He lifted her up and moved her down on the bed, the sheet trailing along with her; there was a small bloodstain on the towel. "The very bluest," he said, "but only a minute quantity. Betty bled like a pig." Dottie said nothing. "Out with it, Boston," he said brusquely, jerking a thumb toward the framed photograph. "Does *she* put your nose out of joint?" Dottie made a brave negative sign. There was one thing she had to say. "Dick," and she shut her eyes in shame, "do you think I should take a douche?" "A douche?" he repeated in a mystified tone. "Why? What for?" "Well, in case . . . *you* know . . . birth control," murmured Dottie. Dick stared at her and suddenly burst out laughing; he dropped onto a straight chair and threw his handsome head back. "My dear girl," he said, "we just employed the most ancient form of birth control. *Coitus interruptus*, the old Romans called it, and a horrid nuisance it is." "I thought perhaps . . . ?" said Dottie. "Don't think. What did you think? I promise you, there isn't a single sperm swimming up to fertilize your irreproachable ovum. Like the man in the Bible, I spilled my seed on the ground, or, rather, on your very fine belly." With a swift motion, he pulled the sheet back before she could stop him. "Now," he said, "lay bare your thoughts." Dottie shook her head and blushed. Wild horses could not make her, for the words embarrassed her frightfully; she had nearly choked on "douche" and "birth control," as it was. "We must get you cleaned up," he decreed after a moment's silence. He put on a robe and slippers and disappeared to the bathroom. It seemed a long time before he came back, bringing a dampened towel, with which he swabbed off her stomach. Then he dried her, rubbing hard with the dry end of it, sitting down beside her on the bed. He himself appeared much fresher, as though he had washed, and he smelled of mouthwash and tooth powder. He lit two cigarettes and gave her one and settled an ashtray between them.

"You *came*, Boston," he remarked, with the air of a satisfied instructor. Dottie glanced uncertainly at him; could he mean that thing she had done that she did not like to think about? "I beg your pardon," she murmured. "I mean you had an orgasm." Dottie made a vague, still-inquiring noise in her throat; she was pretty sure, now she understood, but the new word discombobulated her. "A climax," he added, more sharply. "Do they teach that word at Vassar?" "Oh," said Dottie, almost disappointed that that was all there was to it. "Was that . . . ?" She could not finish the question. "That was it," he nodded. "That is, if I am a judge." "It's normal then?" she wanted to know, beginning to feel better. Dick shrugged. "Not for girls of your upbringing. Not the first time, usually. Appearances to the contrary, you're probably highly sexed."

Dottie turned even redder. According to Kay, a climax was something

very unusual, something the husband brought about by carefully studying his wife's desires and by patient manual stimulation. The terms made
Dottie shudder, even in memory; there was a horrid bit, all in Latin, in
Krafft-Ebing, about the Empress Maria Theresa and what the court doctor told her consort to do that Dottie had glanced at quickly and then
tried to forget. Yet even Mother hinted that satisfaction was something
that came after a good deal of time and experience and that love made a
big difference. But when Mother talked about satisfaction, it was not
clear exactly what she meant, and Kay was not clear either, except when
she quoted from books. Polly Andrews once asked her whether it was the
same as feeling passionate when you were necking (that was when Polly
was engaged), and Kay said yes, pretty much, but Dottie now thought
that Kay had been mistaken or else trying to hide the truth from Polly for
some reason. Dottie had felt passionate, quite a few times, when she was
dancing with someone terribly attractive, but that was quite different
from the thing Dick meant. You would almost think that Kay did not
know what she was talking about. Or else that Kay and Mother meant
something else altogether and this thing with Dick *was* abnormal. And
yet he seemed so pleased, sitting there, blowing out smoke rings; probably, having lived abroad, he knew more than Mother and Kay.

"What are you frowning over now, Boston?" Dottie gave a start. "To
be highly sexed," he said gently, "is an excellent thing in a woman. You
mustn't be ashamed." He took her cigarette and put it out and laid his
hands on her shoulders. "Buck up," he said. "What you're feeling is natural. 'Post coitum, omne animal triste est,' as the Roman poet said." He
slipped his hand down the slope of her shoulder and lightly touched her
nipple. "Your body surprised you tonight. You must learn to know it."
Dottie nodded. "Soft," he murmured, pressing the nipple between his
thumb and forefinger. "Detumescence, that's what you're experiencing."
Dottie drew a quick breath, fascinated; her doubts slid away. As he continued to squeeze it, her nipple stood up. "Erectile tissue," he said infor-
matively and touched the other breast. "See," he said, and they both
looked downward. The two nipples were hard and full, with a pink aure-
ole of goose pimples around them; on her breasts were a few dark hairs.
Dottie waited tensely. A great relief had surged through her; these were
the very terms Kay cited from the marriage handbooks. Down there, she
felt a quick new tremor. Her lips parted. Dick smiled. "You feel something?" he said. Dottie nodded. "You'd like it again?" he said, assaying
her with his hand. Dottie stiffened; she pressed her thighs together. She
was ashamed of the violent sensation his exploring fingers had discovered. But he held his hand there, between her clasped thighs, and
grasped her right hand in his other, guiding it downward to the opening

of his robe and pressed it over that part of himself, which was soft and limp, rather sweet, really, all curled up on itself like a fat worm. Sitting beside her, he looked into her face as he stroked her down there and tightened her hand on him. "There's a little ridge there," he whispered. "Run your fingers up and down it." Dottie obeyed, wonderingly; she felt his organ stiffen a little, which gave her a strange sense of power. She struggled against the excitement his tickling thumb was producing in her own external part; but as she felt him watching her, her eyes closed and her thighs spread open. He disengaged her hand, and she fell back on the bed, gasping. His thumb continued its play and she let herself yield to what it was doing, her whole attention concentrated on a tense pinpoint of sensation, which suddenly discharged itself in a nervous, fluttering spasm; her body arched and heaved and then lay still. When his hand returned to touch her, she struck it feebly away. "Don't," she moaned, rolling over on her stomach. This second climax, which she now recognized from the first one, though it was different, left her jumpy and disconcerted; it was something less thrilling and more like being tickled relentlessly or having to go to the bathroom. "Didn't you like that?" he demanded, turning her head over on the pillow, so that she could not hide herself from him. She hated to think of his having watched her while he brought *that* about. Slowly, Dottie opened her eyes and resolved to tell the truth. "Not quite so much as the other, Dick." Dick laughed. "A nice normal girl. Some of your sex prefer that." Dottie shivered; she could not deny that it had been exciting but it seemed to her almost perverted. He appeared to read her thoughts. "Have you ever done it with a girl, Boston?" He tilted her face so that he could scan it. Dottie reddened. "Heavens, no." "You come like a house afire. How do you account for that?" Dottie said nothing. "Have you ever done it with yourself?" Dottie shook her head violently; the suggestion wounded her. "In your dreams?" Dottie reluctantly nodded. "A little. Not the whole thing." "Rich erotic fantasies of a Chestnut Street virgin," remarked Dick, stretching. He got up and went to the chest of drawers and took out two pairs of pajamas and tossed one of them to Dottie. "Put them on now and go to the bathroom. Tonight's lesson is concluded."

Having locked herself into the hall bathroom, Dottie began to take stock. "Who would have thunk it?" she quoted Pokey Prothero, as she stared, thunderstruck, into the mirror. Her ruddy, heavy-browed face, with its long straight nose and dark-brown eyes, was just as Bostonian as ever. Somebody in the group had said that she looked as if she had been born in a mortarboard. There was something magistral about her appearance, she could see it herself, in the white men's pajamas with her sharp New England jaw protruding over the collar, like an old judge or a blackbird sitting on a fence—Daddy sometimes joked that she ought to have been a lawyer. And yet there was that fun-loving dimple lurking in her cheek and the way she loved to dance and sing harmony—she feared she might be a dual personality, a regular Jekyll and Hyde. Thoughtfully, Dottie rinsed her mouth out with Dick's mouthwash and threw back her head to gargle. She wiped off her lipstick with a bit of toilet tissue and peered anxiously at the soap in Dick's soap dish, thinking of her sensitive skin. She had to be awfully careful, but the bathroom, she noted with gratitude, was *scrupulously* clean and placarded with notices from the landlady: "Please leave this room as you would expect to find it. Thank you for your cooperation"; "Please use mat when taking shower. Thank you." The landlady, Dottie reflected, must be very broad-minded, if she did not object to women's coming to visit. After all, Kay had spent whole weekends here with Harald.

She did not like to think of what women guests Dick had, besides Betty, whom he had already mentioned. What if he had brought Lakey here the other night, after they took Dottie home? Breathing hard, she steadied herself on the washbasin and nervously scratched her jaw. Lakey, she argued, would not have let him do what he had done with *her*; with Lakey, he would not have dared. This line of thought, how-ever, was too unsettling to be pursued. How had he known that *she* would let him? There was one queer thing that her mind had been run-ning away from: he had not really kissed her, not once. Of course, there could be explanations; perhaps he did not want her to smell the liquor on his breath or perhaps she had hali herself . . . ? *No*, said Dottie firmly; she would have to stop thinking this way. One thing was clear; anyone could see it. Dick had been hurt, very much hurt, she repeated, nod-ding, by a woman or women. That made him a law unto himself, as far as she was concerned. If he did not feel like kissing her, that was *his* busi-ness. Her lustrous contralto rose humming as she combed out her hair with her pocket comb: "He's the kind of a man needs the kind of a woman like me-e." She did a gay dance step, stumbling a little in the long pajamas, to the door. Her fingers snapped as she pulled out the overhead light.

Once she was settled in the narrow bed, with Dick sleeping heavily beside her, Dottie's bird thoughts flew affectionately to Mother, Class of 1908. Urge herself as she would to get her beauty sleep after a *very* tiring day, she felt a craving to talk and share the night's experiences with the person whom she designated as the nicest person in the world, who never condemned or censured, and who was always so tremendously interested in young people's doings. Tracing back the steps of her initia-tion, she longed to set the scene for Mother: this bare room way west in

Greenwich Village, the moon's ray falling on the monk's-cloth bed-spread, the drawing table, the single wing chair with the neat slip cover, some sort of awning material, and Dick himself, of course, such an indi-vidual, with his restless chiseled face and incredible vocabulary. There were so many details of the last three days that would appeal to Mother: the wedding and going with him and Lakey that afternoon to the Whit-ney Museum and the three of them having dinner afterward in a dinky Italian restaurant with a billiard table in front and wine in white cups and listening to him and Lakey argue about art and then going to the Modern Museum the next day, again the three of them, and to an exhi-bition of modernistic sculpture, and how Dottie had never suspected that he was even thinking of her because she could see that he was fas-cinated by Lakey (who wouldn't be?) and how she was still sure of that when he turned up at the boat this morning to see Lakey off pretending that he wanted to give her some names of painters in Paris for her to meet. Even when he had asked *her*, at the dock, when the boat had sailed and there was a sort of a letdown, to have dinner with him tonight at that same restaurant (what a time she had finding it in a taxi, from the New Weston!), she had told herself that it was because she was Lakey's friend. She had been scared stiff at being alone with him because she was afraid he would be bored. And he *had* been rather silent and preoc-cupied until he looked straight into her eyes and popped that question. "*Do you want to come home with me?*" Would she ever, ever forget the casual tone of his voice when he said it?

What *would* startle Mother, undoubtedly, was the fact that there had been no thought of love on either side. She could hear her own low voice explaining to her pretty, bright-eyed parent that she and Dick had "lived together" on quite a different basis. Dick, poor chap, her voice announced coolly, was still in love with his divorced wife, and, what was more (here Dottie took a deep breath and braced herself), deeply attracted to Lakey, her *very* best friend this year. In Dottie's imagination, her mother's blue eyes widened and her gold curls trembled with the lit-tle palsied shake of her head, as Dottie leaned forward, impressively, and reiterated, "Yes, Mother, I would still swear it. Deeply attracted to Lakey, I faced the fact that night." This scene, which her fancy was rehearsing, was taking place in her mother's little morning room on Chestnut Street, though her mother, in actuality, had already left for the cottage at Gloucester, where Dottie was expected tomorrow or the day after: tiny Mrs. Renfrew was dressed in her tailored powder-blue Irish linen dress, with bare, tanned arms, from golfing; Dottie herself was wearing her white sharkskin sports dress and brown-and-white spectator pumps. She finished her piece, stared at her toes, and fingered the box pleats of her dress, waiting calmly for her mother to speak. "Yes, Dottie, I see. I *think*

I can understand." Both of them went on talking in low, even, musical voices, her mother a little more staccato and Dottie rumbling slightly. The atmosphere was grave and thoughtful. "You are sure, dear, the hymen was punctured?" Dottie nodded, emphatically. Mrs. Renfrew, a medical missionary's daughter, had been an invalid too in her youth, which gave her a certain anxiety about the physical aspect of things.

Dottie turned restlessly in the bed. "You'll adore Mother," she said to Dick in imagination. "She's a terrifically vital person and much more attractive than I am: tiny, with a marvelous figure, and blue eyes and yellow hair that's just beginning to go grey. She cured herself of being an invalid, by sheer will power, when she met Daddy, her senior year at college, just when the doctors said she'd have to drop out of her class. She decided that it was wrong for a sick person to marry and so she got well. She's a great believer in love; we all are." Here Dottie flushed and inked out the last few words. She must *not* let Dick think she was going to spoil their affair by falling in love with him; a remark like that one would be fatal. To let him see that there was no danger, it would be best, she decided, to frame a statement of some sort, clarifying her position. "I'm very religious too, Dick," she essayed with an apologetic smile. "But I think I' more pantheistic than most communicants of the Church. I love the Church for its ritual, but I believe God is everywhere. My generation is a little different from Mother's. *I* feel—all of us feel—that love and sex can be two separate things. They don't have to be, but they can be. You mustn't force sex to do the work of love or love to do the work of sex—that's quite a thought, isn't it?" she appended hurriedly, with a little nervous laugh, as her sources began to fail her. "One of the older teachers told Lakey that you have to live without love, learn not to need it, in order to live *with* it. Lakey was terrifically impressed. Do you agree?" Dottie's fancied voice had been growing more and more timid as she proffered her philosophy to the sleeping man by her side.

Her imagination had dared to mention Lakey's name to him in connection with love because she wanted to show that she was not jealous of the dark beauty, as he always called her; he did not like "Lakey" for a nickname. One thing Dottie had noticed was the way he absently straightened his tie whenever Lakey turned to look at him, like a man catching sight of himself in a subway mirror. And the way he was always serious with her, not mocking and saturnine, even when they disagreed about art. Yet when Dottie had murmured, several times, "Isn't she striking?" as they stood waving at her from the pier, in an effort to gain his confidence and share Lakey between them, he had merely shrugged his shoulders, as though Dottie were annoying him. "She has a mind," he retorted, the last time Dottie mentioned it.

Now that Lakey was on the high seas and *she* was in bed with Dick warm beside her, Dottie ventured to try out a new theory. Could it be, she asked herself, that Dick was attracted to Lakey platonically and that with herself it was more a physical thing? Lakey was awfully intelligent and knew a lot but she was cold, most people thought. Maybe Dick only admired her beauty as an artist and liked Dottie better the other way. The idea was not very convincing, in spite of what he had said about her body surprising her and all that. Kay said that sophisticated men cared more about the woman's pleasure than they did about their own, but Dick (Dottie coughed gently) had not seemed to be carried away by passion, even when he was exciting her terribly. A wanness crept over her as she thought of Kay. Kay would tell her bluntly that she did not have Lakey's "candle power," and that Dick obviously was using her as a substitute for Lakey, because Lakey was too much of a challenge, *too* beautiful and rich and fascinating for him to cope with in this bleak furnished room. "Dick wouldn't want a girl who would involve his feelings"—she could hear Kay saying it in her loud, opinionated, Western voice—"as Lakey would be bound to do, Renfrew. You're just an outlet for him, a one-night safety valve." The assured words crushed Dottie like a steamroller, for she felt they were true. Kay would probably say also that Dottie had wanted to be "relieved" of her virginity and was using Dick simply as an instrument.

Was that true too—awful thought? Was that how Dick had seen her? Kay meant well, explaining things so clearly and the terrible part was, she was usually right. Or at least she always *sounded* right, being so absolutely disinterested and unconscious of hurting your feelings. The moment Dottie let herself listen to Kay, even in imagination, she lost her own authority and became the person Kay decreed her to be: a Boston old maid with a "silver cord" tie to her mother. It was the same with all the weaker members of the group. Kay used to take their love affairs, as Lakey once said, away from them and returned them shrunk and labeled, like the laundry. That was what had happened to Polly Andrews' engagement. The boy she was supposed to marry had insanity in his family and Kay had shown Polly so many charts about heredity that Polly had broken off with him and collapsed and had to go to the infirmary. And of course Kay was right anybody would agree that Mr. Andrews was enough of a liability without marrying into another family with melancholia in the background. Kay's advice was for Polly to live with him, since she loved him, and marry someone else later, when she wanted to have children. But Polly did not have the courage, although she wanted to terribly. The whole group, except Lakey, had thought what Kay did, at least about not marrying, but none of them had had the heart to say it, straight out, to Polly. That was usually the case: Kay came right out and said to the person what the others whispered among themselves.

Dottie sighed. She wished that Kay would not have to find out about her and Dick. But it was probably pretty inevitable, Dick being Harald's friend. Not that Dick would tell, being a gentleman and considerate; more likely, Dottie would tell herself, for Kay was very good at getting things out of you. In the end, you told Kay wanting to hear her opinion more than you did *not* want to hear it. You were afraid of being afraid of the truth. Besides, Dottie saw, she could not really tell Mother or not for a long time, for Mother, being a different generation, would never see it as Dottie did, no matter how hard she tried, and the difference would just make her worried and unhappy. She would want to meet Dick, and then Daddy would meet him too and start wondering about marriage, which was utterly out of the question. Dottie sighed again. She knew she would have to tell someone—not the most intimate details, of course, but just the amazing fact that she had lost her virginity—and that someone was bound to be Kay.

Then Kay would discuss her with Dick. This was the thing Dottie shrank from most; she could not bear the idea of Kay dissecting and analyzing her and explaining her medical history and Mother's clubs and Daddy's business connections and their exact social position in Boston, which Kay greatly overestimated—they were not "Brahmins," horrid word, at all. A gleam of amusement appeared in Dottie's eye; Kay was such an innocent, for all her know-it-all airs about clubs and society. Someone ought to tell her that only tiresome people or, to be frank, outsiders were concerned about such things nowadays. Poor honest Kay: five times, Dottie recalled drowsily, before she was penetrated and so much blood and pain. Didn't Lakey say she had a hide like a buffalo? Sex, Dottie opined, was just a matter of following the man, as in dancing—Kay was a frightful dancer and always tried to lead. Mother was quite right, she said to herself comfily, as she drifted off to sleep: it was a *great* mistake to let girls dance together as they did in so many of the boarding schools of the second rank.

"Forget What I Just Said"

TERRY McMILLAN

ONCE it sunk in that he was really gone, it felt like there was this big hole in my life that needed to be filled. I was a mess. I lost eight pounds in two weeks, and still haven't been able to gain it back. I didn't have that much ass to begin with, and now it's *gone*. I don't know why I didn't get fired: I forgot about meetings I had with brokers and couldn't come up with quotes I'd promised. At night I sat by the phone, waiting for it to ring, and when it did, it was never him.

But I got tired of being depressed, so to make myself feel better, I went on an extended shopping spree: from July until right after Christmas. If somebody was having a sale, I was there when the doors opened. I also became the queen of mail order. At least two or three times a week the UPS man would ring my doorbell or leave the packages behind the big pot of jumping cholla outside my front door. It felt good coming home and finding these boxes waiting for me. Half the time I forgot what I ordered, but I made a game out of trying to guess what was underneath the tissue paper. I ran all of my credit cards up to their limit, which was why I had to get that consolidation loan last month. The bank made me cut all nine of them up, right there in that office, but thank God they let me keep my Visa and Spiegel cards. Russell still hasn't paid me back a dime.

I DID not like being by myself and wasn't used to it. I can't remember the last time I didn't have a man in my life. I needed some form of male stimulation and companionship before I went crazy or bankrupt, so I started making myself visible and accessible again. It didn't take long for me to find out that the pickings were slim, and I didn't know how rough it was "out there" until I found myself out there. But this time around, I

was determined to learn how to tell the difference between the Real
Thing and the Pretenders, and in the course of doing this, I spent many
an evening with quite a few understudies. I call it trial and error.

These New Men of the Nineties are scared of women like me. I
thought if I was honest and told them what I wanted, then all the cards
would be on the table. Silly me. All I did was tell a few of them I was
interested in having a serious relationship because I wanted to get married and have a baby. They ran like mice. What was the big deal?

I have always fantasized about what life would be like when I got married and had kids. I imagined it would be beautiful. I imagined it would
be just like it was in the movies. We would fall hopelessly in love, and
our wedding picture would get in *Jet* magazine. We would have a house-
ful of kids, because I hated being an only child. I would be a model
mother. We would have an occasional fight, but we would always make
up. And instead of drying up, our love would grow. We would be one
hundred percent faithful to each other. People would envy us, wish they
had what we had, and they'd ask us forty years later how we managed to
beat the odds and still be so happy.

I was this stupid for a long time.

Lately, though, I've had to ask myself some pretty tough questions,
like, What am I doing wrong? And why do I keep picking the wrong men
to fall in love with? I don't know what I'm doing wrong, to tell the truth,
but I do know that one of my major weaknesses has always been pretty
men with big dicks. And Russell definitely fit the bill. I've been trying to
figure out a way to get over this syndrome, but it's hard, especially when
that's all you're used to.

I should've paid closer attention to what Linda Goodman and the
Chinese astrologers have been saying all along. That I should stay away
from Pisceans, Virgos, Aries, Libras, and Geminis. They're a disturbed
group. And forget about those Boars, Cocks, Dragons, and Rats. I've had
it with men born under these signs, I don't care how good they look or
how big the bulge is in their pants. I've dated at least twenty or thirty of
these weirdos, enough to notice similar patterns in their behavior, and
it's taken me a long time to gain this astrological insight: Pisceans are
habitual liars, lazy, irresponsible, and have no willpower; Virgos are per-
fectionists, obsessive about *everything*, and freaks in bed; Aries are ego-
maniacs, narcissistic, and have run-for-your-life tempers, but they're
exquisite lovers; Libras are too sentimental and jealous, and so possessive you end up not wanting to sleep with them at all; and Geminis are
boring as hell, but they think they're deep, and I've never met one who
could fuck.

I can't say I haven't been tempted to take Russell back, especially since he's been bugging me these last couple of months to do just that. He said he missed me something fierce and had mended his ways. But he couldn't prove it. I admit that I made the mistake of letting him spend the night a few times during the siege of my first dry spell, but last week Gloria told me something that made me want to spit nails. Desiree, the girl down at Oasis Hair who does my weave, told Gloria she saw this woman named Carolyn driving Russell's car, the car I basically bought him, and if she wasn't mistaken, when she got out, the woman looked pregnant. I told Gloria that Russell wasn't the only one in Phoenix who drove a black Z. "I know that," she said, "but who else do you know whose license plates say SUAVE?"

Now I knew I didn't have dibs on him anymore, but I wanted to hear it from the horse's mouth, so I left an urgent message for him at his job. He didn't call me back until two days later. He said he didn't know anybody named Carolyn. And as far as he knew, no woman was carrying his baby. But I knew he was lying through his teeth. I called him a low-life, garbage-eating javelina and hung up on him. He called me right back and said he didn't know who was spreading all these lies about him, but I could believe it if I wanted to. He said he was still interested in marrying me, as soon as he got his finances together, which he hoped would be sometime this year. And maybe we could work on having a baby too. But he sounded like a damn fool. He had humiliated me for too long and now embarrassed me no end. What I *would* like to do is give his ass to the dog pound so they could make soap out of him, or call the FBI and tell them he's responsible for those ax murders I just read about in the paper. I wish there was some way I could give him life imprisonment, because he needs to be stopped. He needs to suffer for a while, long enough for him to realize that a woman's love is a privilege and not his right.

THERE's no sense in me lying about it. I'm desperate. I haven't been "out" with a man now in over a month. I've been trying to convince myself that I'm still a good catch, but I can't pass a mirror these days without staring at myself. All I do is look for new flaws, trying to forgive myself for not looking twenty-four anymore and apologizing for being a six instead of a ten. I know I've limited myself by only dealing with pretty boys, which is probably the main reason I'm going to the other extreme tonight.

Right now I'm sitting here waiting for Michael, this man who's coming over for dinner. Michael is not pretty, but he's available. He's also a half hour late, and you think he's called? Maybe something happened to him. I hope nothing's happened to him. This is our first date. We work at the same insurance company, but in different departments. To be honest, Michael never dredged up much in me until I'd gone through my old phone book and noticed that all the men I used to date had been crossed off: the ones who'd gotten married or moved or were so pitiful in bed that I didn't have any other choice but to draw a line through their name. So when I saw Michael's picture in our newsletter sitting at his desk, saying he'd been promoted to marketing rep, which was why I hadn't seen him on the elevator lately, and it was clear that he wasn't wearing a wedding ring anymore, and since I'd just finished this assertiveness training seminar at Black Women on the Move, I decided to be assertive and sent him a note of congratulations. It couldn't have been more than two hours after I'd put it in our interoffice mail that he called and invited me to lunch. In his office. Needless to say, I accepted his invitation without thinking of the consequences, because I've never dated anybody I worked with. Well, once, but he doesn't count.

Anyway, he had already ordered two turkey and Swiss sandwiches, diet Pepsis, and Doritos. I must admit that his presumptuousness turned me on in a weird sort of way. I like men who take control. His teeth were obviously all capped, so they were nice and white, and he had sleepy eyes, which some women would call sexy bedroom eyes, but he looked like he'd had too much to drink to me. I put him at about thirty-eight or thirty-nine, because he was starting to get those laugh lines when he wasn't even laughing. Michael also had the shortest, fattest little hands I'd ever seen on any man, and I've heard all the stories about short men with thick fingers before, but there's a whole lot of lies floating around in the world that have become myths that ignorant folks believe. I say make me a believer.

After the small talk about his two diseased marriages, two consequential children, dialing-for-dollars divorces, office politics, and what have you, it was clear to me that he was what teenagers call a nerd. But when Michael leaned forward in his chair and said, "So tell me, Robin, why isn't a beautiful woman such as yourself happily married?" he got my deepest attention, and all I could say was, "Because I haven't met a man I want to marry yet." I didn't dare tell him the truth, that no one had ever asked me, and Russell's phony little lightweight desperation plea doesn't even count. I couldn't believe Michael called me beautiful.

"What about you, Michael? Do you think you'll ever say 'I do' again?"

"Certainly," he said. "It's not that marriage itself is bad; it's the people we marry who give it a bad name." Then he sort of chuckled. "I think I'm wiser now, so I'll make a much better assessment the next time."

Assessment? Is that what you guys do, I thought, assess us? Well, if I had to *assess* him right now, on a scale of one to ten, I'd be generous in giving him a five. First of all, he's definitely not my type. He's light-skinned—pale when you get right down to it—and how about those freckles? His hair is that rusty reddish-brown, and he's about two inches shorter than I am, which would make him a whopping five foot seven. He's obviously not spending any time at the gym, because he's leaning toward pudgy. But I will say one thing. That baritone voice and those juicy lips could tip the scale in his favor.

So I had lunch with him again the next day, because he asked me. This time we went out to eat. Most men usually talk about themselves until you don't have any questions left to ask, but not Michael. He was actually curious about me.

"So, Robin," he said. "Tell me a little more about yourself."

I had already told him that I graduated from ASU and majored in anthropology, that I grew up in Sierra Vista because my daddy was in the army, and that I was an only child. "What else do you want to know?"

"How old are you?"

"How old do you think I am?"

"Twenty-seven. Twenty-nine at the most."

He got three points for that. "Thirty-five," I said.

"No kidding."

"No kidding," I said.

"Where's your family?"

"In Tucson."

"So at least you get to visit them."

"Yeah, I do, but it's not all that pleasant. My parents've been through living hell these last few years. My mother had to have a double mastectomy, and then two years ago my father was diagnosed with Alzheimer's."

"I'm sorry to hear that, Robin. Is he still able to be at home?"

"Yeah. Which is one reason why I try to get down there at least twice a month to help my mother out. He can't do too much for himself anymore. Look, can we talk about something else?"

"Okay," he said, and took a sip of his coffee. "Do you have any hobbies?"

"Hobbies?"

"You know, things you like to do on a regular basis."

"I used to sew a lot, make quilts, but I don't have much time for it anymore. I do collect black dolls, though."

"Really? What's your favorite color?"

"Orange."

"Favorite place?"

"Hawaii."

"Fruit?"

"Plums."

"Movie?"

"I don't know. What is this, *Jeopardy?*"

He laughed. "I'm just trying to make getting to know you more fun, that's all. If it bothers you, I can stop."

"No. Let me think. One of my favorite movies of all time was *Body Heat,* and I have to put *Raging Bull* in there and *Raiders of the Lost Ark.*"

Michael smiled. I didn't notice until now that he had a rather sexy, self-assured smile. "So do you have a steady?" he asked.

How corny, I thought, but at least he wanted to know, and for that reason I thought it would be smart not to tell the truth. "Well, I've been seeing someone on a regular basis, if that's what you mean, but how serious it is, I'm not sure yet. Why?"

"I just wanted to know if I was walking in on something."

Had I opened a door and said, "Michael, come on in," without knowing it, or was I projecting that hungry look? He looked me dead in the eye, and I noticed that they were a soft brown, the whites were milky white, and they *were* kind of dreamy. Maybe he had some other redeeming qualities that weren't so visible to the naked eye. But enough already, Robin. The last thing you need is to get yourself all tangled up with a chubby little dweeb from the office. However, since he'd started this conversation on hobbies and what have you, I felt obligated to ask him. "So, Michael. Do *you* have any hobbies?"

"As a matter of fact, I do. Drag racing, for one."

I almost choked on my diet Pepsi. Michael a drag racer?

"And deep-sea fishing and scuba diving."

"Where do you do all of these things?"

"Mexico. I also have a boat that I like to cruise around in when I can."

I swallowed hard. This was unreal. "Here in Phoenix?"

"No; I keep it up in the White Mountains."

"You're not making this up, are you, to impress me?"

"There's a whole lot of other things I'd be more inclined to lie about if I was just trying to impress you, Robin."

Then he started talking about the insurance business. He wanted to know how long I'd been in underwriting, but I didn't want to talk about insurance, so finally I just interrupted him and came right on out and asked him. "When's your birthday?"

"June second," he said, and sprinkled some salt on his french fries. "Why?"

"I was just curious." I found a slice of avocado in my salad, pierced my fork into it, and sighed. Another Gemini. By anybody else's standards, Michael would be considered a good catch — as catches go. He appears to be intelligent, tries hard to be witty, has a good job, and hell, he's available. So far he has been kind of charming and somewhat interesting and definitely a gentleman, which was a nice change of pace. I looked at him a few more minutes and didn't feel any disgust whatsoever. If I'm lucky, maybe his rising and moon signs are in Scorpio or Aquarius. Should I go ahead and give Michael a chance? I asked myself. Should I just forget all about astrology and try not to judge the man before I get to know him?

My questions were answered when I got to work the following morning and found a big bouquet of spring flowers on my desk. I hadn't decided if I actually liked Michael or not, and when I decided that I did like him a little bit I couldn't put my finger on why. I knew I wasn't attracted to him physically, but maybe that's what I needed: the kind of man every woman wouldn't be drooling over. Somebody decent and ordinary. But shoot, he could still turn out to be another Pretender. However, There was one way to find out.

So here I am, waiting.

I'm wearing bright orange tonight because I had my color chart done and Sunanda told me to wear warm colors if I want to emit warmth. I do. I definitely do. But maybe this color is too strong for Michael. Maybe he'll think I'm a hot number right off the bat and read me the wrong way. I ran into the bedroom and changed into a soft yellow sweater, then slipped a lace handkerchief into my skirt pocket. I was staring at myself in the mirror, trying to give myself approval, when Gloria and Bernadine popped into my mind. While I fastened all but the top three pearl buttons, I heard them cackling. They think I have poor taste in men (they despised Russell), and they also think I'm a nymphomaniac, which is why they jokingly refer to me as "the whore." But they're just envious. Bernadine has a husband she doesn't want to fuck, and Gloria doesn't know anybody who wants to fuck her. We fight like sisters, but I don't know what I'd do without them. When my mother was in the hospital, Bernadine and Gloria were right there. And when we found out that Daddy had Alzheimer's, my mother asked me when I could pay her back the three thousand dollars because they'd be needing that money real soon. Of course I didn't know when I'd have it, so Bernadine just wrote me a check and told me to forget about it. And when me and Russell broke up, it was Bernadine and Gloria who dragged me out of this apartment and treated me to a Beauty Day at Canyon Ranch and called me every three hours to make sure I was holding up okay. They're the ones who always send me flowers on my birthday, and we draw names at Christmas. They're both older than I am, which is why they're always offering me advice I don't need. And by their account, you'd swear I've slept with half the men in Phoenix, Scottsdale, and Tempe. But that's not true. I've slept with my share, mind you, but hell, this valley is pretty small.

I can't deny that before I met Russell and right after I broke up with him I was a little generous in the loose-sex department. And I admit that I sometimes find myself at parties and other social functions where I can count how many of the men in the room I've slept with. Unfortunately, in some rare instances, more than one is aware of the other. It's a small world.

I really have no business getting involved with somebody from my office, now do I? Especially since Michael already told me he thinks my being an underwriter is great, based on how fast I've moved up in the company. But he just doesn't know. I'm living from paycheck to paycheck and am scared to answer my phone sometimes because I know it might be the student-loan people. Since my daddy's been sick, the money he and my mother had put away for their retirement is dwindling fast, and I'm not in any position right now to help them out. And they need help. Plus, I'm tired of working ten- and twelve-hour days. I'll be the first to admit it: I would be content being a housewife if I could find the kind of man who wouldn't treat me like one. I want to know what it feels like to be pampered, to not have to worry about how high the phone bill is or if the rent is going up. I would like to have at least two kids before menopause sets in. I don't want to have to drag them to the Before School Program at seven-thirty in the morning and have to break my neck in rush hour to pick them up before six, like Bernadine and some of my other girlfriends do. Their kids spend more time away from home than they do at home. I'd also like to have some time to work on my quilting again and do laps and read books and take my kids to ballet or karate and piano lessons after school and still be home in time to grin in my husband's face. I'd like to go to the gym and work out when everybody else is at work. Shoot, I'd like to do some charity work. Take weekend trips. And I'd love to be able to go to the grocery store any weekday afternoon I choose instead of on Saturday mornings. And I want to live in a house, because now that I owe the IRS every year, I don't know when I'll ever have enough money for a down payment.

I just heard the doorbell.

Before I answered it, I checked to make sure the flowers I bought myself with the card signed by a man I made up were prominently displayed. I want Michael to think he's got some competition. I also took off Reba McEntire and put on Freddie Jackson. I'd already sprayed some Glade Spring Fresh throughout the whole apartment and sprinkled a few drops of Halston on all four of my pillows — just in case. I blotted my orange lips on a tissue so that when he kisses me it won't be smeared all over his. I opened the door. "Hi," he said.

Michael looked taller, and he didn't look quite so dorky, either. Why was that? I wondered. "Hi," I said.

"I'm sorry I'm late. I was stuck in traffic and couldn't call," he said, and walked right past me. What about my kiss?

His hair was different. It was slicked back and had little ripples of waves in it. Not bad, Michael. "I was getting worried that something had happened to you."

"Well, that was sweet," he said, and walked over and sat down on the couch. "Something sure smells good."

I'd almost forgotten about dinner and had to think for a minute what I'd bought. Stuffed shells from the Price Club, smothered in Classico basil and tomato sauce, along with Italian bread sticks. I had two bottles of wine and had opened one. I made the spinach salad myself.

"Your place is very nice," he said.

"Thank you, Michael."

"Beautiful flowers," he said, touching a gladiola petal. Then he looked at me with a smile on his face and said, "So, Robin, did you buy these for yourself, or do I have some fierce competition out there?" He winked at me. "You don't have to answer that," he said.

"Are you hungry?" I asked.

"Starving."

I betcha, I thought, but I just said, "Good, then let's eat!"

We ate. And went through a bottle of wine before I even thought to pull out the Price Club cheesecake. Freddie Jackson was sounding even better, now that Michael and I were both feeling pretty mellow. "Dessert?" I asked him.

"Yes," he said, but before I could get up from the table to get the cheesecake, he said, "I'd like to taste you." His bushy eyebrows moved up and down.

"Me?" I said, unable to think of anything better.

Michael got up from the table and took my hand, then led me to the couch.

"You're a great cook," he said, and I just said thank you, because I felt like taking the credit. Before I knew it, he was kissing me. For such a short man, he had an awfully long tongue, and a wild one at that. I pulled away, then pressed my lips on the side of his and tried not to let

the saliva running out the corners of my mouth distract me. I reposi-
tioned myself and went to put my tongue in his ear, but it was full of this
hard hair that made me change my mind. I rested my chin on his shoulder and pressed my breasts against his chest. For a minute there, I
thought I was hugging another woman. I felt these two soft spongelike
things on his chest. So I backed away, unbuttoned his shirt, and put my
hand inside, only to feel this fatty substance that should've been muscles
on his chest. Michael was about a 38B. I was repulsed, but I couldn't say
anything, because he was kissing me again and pulling me down on top
of him. When I looked at him, his eyes, of course, were closed, and I
closed mine for different reasons: I was trying to pretend that he was Russell. But Michael was too soft. What had I gotten myself into?

"You feel better than I thought you would," he said.

I didn't say anything, because I couldn't think of anything to say. I
would have loved to say, "Let go of me and go home and don't come
back, you tub of lard," but you just can't say that kind of thing without
hurting somebody's feelings.

The next thing I knew, Michael was lifting me up and carrying me
into the bedroom, just as I was entertaining the thought of how to stop
him altogether, but once I saw the sweat beads popping off his temples
and heard him panting like an asthmatic and what have you, I felt sort of
sorry for him. So when my foot crashed into the bathroom door, I just
said, "Wrong room," and pointed to my bedroom. The room was dark,
but after we got inside, he bumped into the bed and sort of dropped me
on it. I whispered, "Just a minute," and out of sheer habit, went to the
bathroom and put in my Today sponge. When I came back, I lit my fat
scented candle, and Michael was almost completely undressed, except
for his boxer shorts. Since he didn't look like he wanted to do it, I unbuttoned my own sweater and took off my bra. When I saw his eyes grow as
big as saucers, I worried about my breasts. With his shorts still on,
Michael slid under the covers before I got a chance to see what he had to
offer.

"I knew you were going to be beautiful all over," he said, after I got
under the covers. "And you smell so good." He put his little fat hand
over one of my breasts and squeezed. My nipples immediately deflated.

"Do you have protection, or should I get it?" I asked.

"Right here," he said, pulling it from the side of the bed. He took his
shorts off and threw them on the floor. Then he put his hands under the
covers, and his shoulders started jerking, which meant he was having a
rough time getting it on.

"Do you need some help?" I asked.

"No no no," he said. "There." He rolled over on top of me, and since

I could no longer breathe, let alone move, I couldn't show him how to get me in the mood. He started that slurpy kissing again, and I felt something slide inside me. At first I thought it was his finger, but no, his hands were on the headboard. Then he sort of pushed, and I was waiting for him to push again, so he could get it all the way in, but when he started moving, that's when I realized it was. I was getting pissed off about now, but I tried to keep up with his little short movements, and just when I was getting used to his rhythm he started moving faster and faster and he squeezed me tight against his breasts and yelled, "*God this is good!*" and then all of his weight dropped on me. Was he for real? I just kind of lay there, thinking: Shit, I could've had a V-8. I mean, did he really think he just did something here? A few minutes went by, and he lifted himself up, looked me in the eye, and said, "I knew you were somebody special. How do you feel?"

"About what?" I asked.

"Me. This. Everything?"

"I feel fine, except I feel like I could use a cigarette."

"I don't mind a woman who smokes," he said.

I wanted to say, "Did anybody ask you?" but instead I said, "It was just a compliment. I don't smoke," then I got out of the bed and went into the kitchen to get myself another glass of wine. I drank the whole thing, poured another one, and went back and stood in the bedroom doorway and stared at this human submarine sandwich sitting in my bed. How am I going to get rid of you? I wondered. And God, am I going to have to face you at work too?

"What are you thinking about?" he asked. He was smiling, of course.

"Oh, nothing," I said.

"You know what?" he said.

"No, what?"

"I like you, I like you a lot."

"You don't even know me, Michael."

"I like what I know so far."

"But you might not like me if you *really* got to know me."

"Tell me what you want, what you need."

"What?" He had this satisfied look on his face, like he had the goods on me or something.

"What's your fantasy?"

"What are you talking about, Michael?" I took another sip of my wine and found myself walking over toward the bed, which I had had no intention of doing. For some reason, this didn't feel real, it felt like . . . like a movie. I put my wineglass down and started running my hand through the few curls I had left, and all of a sudden I felt so sexy and aroused it was scary, because I was actually seeing myself outside myself, like I was on a big screen or something, and if I was, this is how I would act, this is what I'd do. So I licked my lips and looked down at Michael until he started to look like Russell, but then I remembered that I hated Russell. Denzel Washington would do, so I thought about him and gave him a wicked grin. The whole time I was rubbing my other hand up and down my thigh, and breathing so hard I could see my breasts rise and fall. This was just great.

"I mean, ideally, what do you want from a man? What would you want a man to be able to do for you?"

Michael was messing everything up, and I wished he would just be quiet. "Are you serious?" I said, snapping back to reality.

"Very."

"Everything," I said, trying to recapture my persona, but it was too late. It was gone.

"Be more specific."

I looked at him sitting up in my bed and realized that this man was dead serious. I moved the glass from the night table and put it on the floor, then sat down at the foot of the bed and said, "Are you sure you want to hear this?"

"It's the reason I asked."

He clasped his hands together and put them behind his head. For some weird reason, Michael was starting to look better. Why was that? I wondered. Since he was asking, I figured I should go ahead and tell the truth, because when I got right down to it, what did I have to lose? "I want to live in a house," I heard myself say.

"That's easy enough."

"In Scottsdale."

"I own a house in Scottsdale."

"You do?"

"Yep. What else?"

"I'd like to go away for long weekends." That's when I felt his foot ease under my crotch through the sheet, and then his big toe pushed up and made a tent inside me.

"What else?"

"I'd like to be able to eat out at least once or twice a week."

"And?"

"Get married and have a baby. Two or three."

"And?"

"Quit my job until the kids are at least seven."

"What else?"

"That's enough for now, don't you think?"

"You don't need much," he said, and motioned for me. Now I was slippery where I should've been earlier, and I sat up and walked on my knees toward the rest of him. I looked down at Michael hard, then harder, and he smiled at me. He's not *that* bad, I thought, and let's face it, Robin, he *is* a good catch, and hell, he's available. I lifted the covers and sat down on his now limp lump. Maybe I could get him to go on a diet. Maybe I could teach him how to fuck. How to use his tongue more efficiently. Maybe I could get him to go to a tanning salon, join the gym, and we could work out together. I could trim those hairs in his ears, couldn't I? I slid my hand between his legs and touched what he obviously assumed was a lethal weapon.

"I could sure get used to you," he said. He put his arms around me and closed his eyes. Then he fell asleep. I was thinking about waking him up and making him go home, but for some stupid reason, I changed my mind. It felt good having a man in my bed, even if he wasn't exactly my Dream Man.

I fell asleep too, and when I woke up, I decided that I wasn't letting him get out of here without at least giving me some iota of satisfaction. Too many of them get away with this shit as it is. So I rolled over, lifted my hips up, and reached underneath them until I found what I was looking for. I worked it until I got a rise out of it, then I sat down on it and pushed.

"What do *you* want?" I asked Michael, staring down at him and massaging my breasts so he could at least see how it's done.

"I think I've found it," he said, smiling.

"How can you say that, Michael?"

"Because I've been out here a long time, Robin, and I haven't felt like this in years."

"Like what?"

"This needed." After that, he nuzzled me in his arms, and for a minute I let my head rest on the cushion that was his chest. "I can give you everything you want, everything you need, if you'll let me," he said.

Without even thinking, I said, "Are you sure you know what you're saying?"

"I know exactly what I'm saying," he said. "I've been watching you for three years. Waiting for this opportunity. So yes, I'm sure."

I was so flattered that I didn't even realize what my body was doing. It pressed down hard and squirmed, then I leaned forward and whispered in his ear, "You want to make me happy right now?"

"Yes, I do," he said.

"Really really happy?"

"Really really happy," he said.

I leaned back and rocked forward again, this time gently pushing both nipples into his mouth. "You can start by sucking them gently and slowly." And he did. And he did it right, and I felt like silk, and for the next few minutes Michael wasn't fat or short or pale and I felt young and beautiful and sexy and desirable, and when I squeezed my pelvis and eyes real tight and my body exploded from the inside out, Michael felt just like the Real Thing and everything was just perfect. For once.

Me and My Baby View the Eclipse

LEE SMITH

SHARON SHAW first met her lover, Raymond Stewart, in an incident that took place in broad daylight at the Xerox machine in Stewart's Pharmacy three years ago—it *can't* be that long! Sharon just can't believe it. Every time she thinks about him now, no matter what she's doing, she stops right in the middle of it while a hot crazy ripple runs over her entire body. This makes her feel like she's going to die or throw up. Of course she never does either one. She pats her hair and goes right on with her busy life the way she did *before* she met him, but everything is different now, all altered, all new. Three years! Her children were little then: Leonard Lee was eleven, Alister was ten, and Margaret, the baby, was only three. Sharon was thirty-four. Now she's over the hill, but who cares? Since the children are all in school, she and Raymond can meet more easily.

"Is the *coast clear?*" Raymond will ask with his high nervous giggle, at her back door. Raymond speaks dramatically, emphasizing certain words. He flings his arms around. He wears huge silky handkerchiefs and gold neckchains and drives all the way to Roanoke to get his hair cut in what he calls a modified punk look. In fact Raymond is a figure of fun in Roxboro, which Sharon knows, and this knowledge just about kills her. She wants to grab him up and soothe him, smooth down his bristling blond hair and press his fast-beating little heart against her deep soft bosom and wrap him around and around in her big strong arms. Often, she does this. "Hush now, honey," she says.

For Raymond is misunderstood. Roxboro is divided into two camps about him, the ones who call him Raymond, which is his name, and the ones who call him Ramón, with the accent on the last syllable, which is what he *wants* to be called. "Putting on airs just like his daddy did," sniffs Sharon's mama, who works at the courthouse and knows everything. Raymond's daddy was a pharmacist who, according to Sharon's mama, never got over not being a doctor. She says this is common among pharmacists. She says he was a dope fiend too. Sharon doesn't know if this part is true or not, and she won't ask; the subject of his father—who killed himself—gives Raymond nervous palpitations of the heart. Anyway this is how Raymond came to be working at Stewart's Pharmacy, where he mostly runs the Xerox machine and helps ladies order stationery and wedding invitations from huge bound books which he keeps on a round coffee table in his conversation area—Raymond likes for things to be nice. A tall, sour-faced man named Mr. Gardiner is the actual manager—everybody knows that Raymond could never run a store. Raymond stays busy, though. He does brochures and fliers and handouts, whatever you want, on his big humming Xerox machine, and he'll give you a cup of coffee to drink while you make up your mind. This coffee is strong, sweet stuff. Sharon had never tasted anything quite like it before the day she went in there to discuss how much it would cost to print up a little cookbook of everybody's favorite recipes from the Shady Mountain Elementary School PTA to make extra money for art.

It was late August, hot as blazes outside, so it took Sharon just a minute to recover from the heat. She's a large, slow-moving woman anyway, with dark brown eyes and dark brown hair and bright deep color in her cheeks. She has what her mother always called a "peaches-'n'-cream complexion." She used to hear her mother saying that on the phone to her Aunt Marge, talking about Sharon's "peaches-'n'-cream complexion" and about how she was so "slow," and wouldn't "stand up for herself." This meant going out for cheerleader. Later, these conversations were all about how Sharon would never "live up to her potential," which meant marrying a doctor, a potential that went up in smoke the day Sharon announced that she was going to marry Leonard Shaw, her high school sweetheart, after all.

Now Sharon talks to her mother every day on the telephone, unless of course she sees her, and her mother still talks every day to Sharon's Aunt Marge. Sharon has worn her pretty hair in the same low ponytail ever since high school, which doesn't seem so long ago to her either. It seems like yesterday, in fact, and all the friends she has now are the same ones she had then, or pretty much, and her husband Leonard is the same, only older, heavier, and the years between high school and now have passed swiftly, in a strong unbroken line. They've been good years, but Sharon can't figure out where in the world they went, or tell much difference between them.

Until she met Raymond, that is. Now she has some high points in her life. But "met" is the wrong word. Until she saw Raymond with "new eyes" is how Sharon thinks of it now.

She went into Stewart's that day in August and showed Raymond her typed recipes and told him what she wanted. He said he thought he could do that. What kind of paper? he wanted to know. What about the cover? Sharon hadn't considered the cover. Raymond Stewart bobbed up and down before her like a jack-in-the-box, asking questions. It made her feel faint, or it might have been the sudden chill of the air-conditioning, she'd just come from standing out in her hot backyard with the hose, watering her garden. "What?" she said. Sharon has a low, pretty voice, and a way of patting her hair. "Sit right down here, honey," Raymond said, "and let me get you a cup of coffee." Which he did, and it was *so strong*, tasting faintly of almonds.

They decided to use pale blue paper, since blue and gold were the school colors. Sharon looked at Raymond Stewart while he snipped and pasted on the coffee table. "Aha!" he shrieked, and "Aha!" Little bits of paper went flying everywhere. Sharon looked around, but nobody seemed to notice: people in Stewart's were used to Raymond. She found herself smiling.

"Hmmm," Raymond said critically, laying out the pages, and "This sounds *yummy*," about Barbara Sutcliff's Strawberries Romanoff. Sharon had never heard a grown man say "yummy" out loud before. She began to pay more attention. That day Raymond was wearing baggy, pleated tan pants—an old man's pants, Sharon thought—a Hawaiian shirt with blue parrots on it, and red rubber flip-flops. "Oh, this sounds *dreadful*," Raymond said as he laid out Louise Dart's famous chicken recipe where you spread drumsticks with apricot preserves and mustard.

"Actually it's pretty good," Sharon said. "*Everybody* makes that." But she was giggling. The strong coffee was making her definitely high, so high that he talked her into naming the cookbook *Home on the Range* (which everybody thought was just darling, as it turned out), and then he drew a cover for it, a woman in a cowboy hat and an apron tending to a whole stovetop full of wildly bubbling pans. The woman had a funny look on her face; puffs of steam came out of some of the pots.

"I used to draw," Sharon said dreamily, watching him. Raymond has small, white hands with tufts of gold hair on them.

"What did you draw?" He didn't look up.

"Trees," Sharon said. "Pages and pages and pages of trees." As soon as she said it, she remembered it—sitting out on the porch after supper with the pad on her lap, drawing tree after tree with huge flowing branches that reached for God. She didn't tell him the part about God.

But suddenly she knew she *could*, if she wanted to. You could say any-thing to Raymond Stewart, just the way you could say anything to some-body you sat next to on a bus: *anything*.

He grinned at her. His hair stood up in wild blond clumps and behind the thick glasses his magnified eyes were enormous, the pale, flat blue of robins' eggs. "How's that?" He held up the drawing and Sharon said it was fine. Then he signed his name in tiny peaked letters across the bot-tom of it, like an electrocardiogram, which she didn't expect. Something about him doing this tugged at her heart.

Sharon drank more coffee while he ran off four copies of the recipe booklet; he'd do five hundred more later, if her committee approved. Raymond put these copies into a large flat manila envelope and handed it to her with a flourish and a strange little half-bow. Then somehow, in the midst of standing up and thanking him and taking the envelope—she was all in a flurry—Sharon cut her hand on the flap of the envelope. It was a long, bright cut—a half-moon curve in the soft part of her hand between thumb and index finger. "Oh!" she said.

"*Oh my God!*" Raymond said dramatically. Together they watched while the blood came up slowly, like little red beads on a string. Then Raymond seized her hand and brought it to his mouth and kissed it!—kissed the cut. When Sharon jerked her hand away, it left a red smear, a bloodstain, on his cheek.

"Oh, I'm sorry! I'm so sorry!" Raymond cried, following Sharon out as she fled through the makeup section of the pharmacy where Missy Har-rington was looking at lipstick and that older, redheaded lady was work-ing the cash register, and where nobody, apparently, had noticed *any-thing*.

"I'll call you about the recipe book," Sharon tossed back over her shoulder. It was only from years of doing everything right that she was able to be so polite . . . or was it? Because what *had* happened, anyway? Nothing, really . . . just not a thing. But Sharon sat in her car for a long time before she started back toward home, not minding how the hot seat burned the backs of her legs. Then, on the way, she tried to remember everything she had ever known about Raymond Stewart.

He was younger—he'd been three or four years behind Sharon in school. Everybody used to call him Highwater because he wore his pants so short that you could always see his little white socks, his little white ankles. He'd been a slight, awkward boy, known for forgetting his books and losing his papers and saying things in class that were totally beside the point. Supposedly, though, he was "bright": Sharon had had one class with him because he had advanced placement in something, she couldn't remember what now—some kind of English class. How odd that he'd never gone on to college. . . . What Sharon *did* remember, vividly, was Raymond's famous two-year stint as drum major for the high school, after her graduation. Sharon, then a young married woman sitting in the bleachers with her husband, had seen him in this role again and again. Before Leonard Lee was born, Sharon went to all the games with Leonard, who used to be the quarterback.

So she was right there the first time Raymond Stewart—wearing a top hat, white gloves, white boots, and an electric-blue sequined suit which, it was rumored, he had designed himself—came strutting and dancing across the field, leading the band like a professional. Nobody ever saw anything like it! He'd strut, spin, toss his baton so high it seemed lost in the stars, then leap up to catch it and land in a split. Sharon remembered remarking to Leonard once, at a game, that she could hardly connect this Raymond Stewart, the drum major—wheeling like a dervish across the field below them—with that funny little guy who had been, she thought, in her English class. That little guy who wore such high pants. "Well," Leonard had said then, after some deliberation—and Leonard was no dummy—"well, maybe it just took him a while to find the right clothes."

Raymond had a special routine he did while the band played "Blue Suede Shoes" and formed itself into a giant shoe on the field. Everybody in the band had showed more spunk and rhythm then, Sharon thought, than any of them had ever shown before—or since, for that matter. Under Raymond's leadership, the band won two AAA number-one championships, an all-time record for Roxboro High. They even went to play at the Apple Blossom Festival the year the governor's daughter was crowned queen, all because of Raymond Stewart.

And just what had Raymond done since? After his father's suicide, which must have happened around the end of his senior year, he had turned "nervous" for a while. He had gone to work at Stewart's Pharmacy and had continued to live with his mother in their big old nubby green concrete house on Sunset Street. Everybody said something should be done about the house, the shameful way Raymond Stewart had let it run down. Since the leaves had not been raked for years and years, all the grass had died—that carefully tended long sloping lawn which used to be Paul Stewart's pride and joy back in the days when he walked to work every morning in his gleaming white pharmacist's jacket with a flower in his buttonhole, speaking to everybody. Paint was peeling from the dark green shutters now, and some of them hung at crazy angles. The hedge had grown halfway up the windows. The side porch was completely engulfed in wisteria, with vines as thick as your arm. It was just a shame. Of course Raymond Stewart wouldn't notice anything like that, or think about raking leaves . . . and his mother!

Miss Suetta was as crazy as a coot. Raymond hired somebody to stay with her all the time. The Stewarts had plenty of money, of course, but Miss Suetta thought she was dirt poor. She'd sneak off from her companion, and hitchhike to town and go into stores and pick out things, and then cry and say she didn't have any money. So the salespeople would charge whatever it was to Raymond, and then they'd call him to come and get her and drive her home. Sharon had been hearing stories about Miss Suetta Stewart for years and years.

But about Raymond—what else? Every Sunday, he played the organ at the First Methodist Church, in a stirring and dramatic way. The whole choir, including Sharon's Aunt Marge, was completely devoted to him. They all called him Ramón. And he had had his picture in the paper last year for helping to organize the Shady Mountain Players, an amateur theatrical group which so far had put on only one show, about a big rabbit. Sharon saw that, but she couldn't remember if Raymond had had a part in it or not. Mainly you thought of Raymond in connection with weddings—everybody consulted Raymond about wedding plans—or interior decoration. Several of Sharon's friends had hired him, in fact. What he did was help you pick your colors through your astral sign. He didn't *order* anything for you, he just advised. In fact, come to think of it, Sharon herself had ordered some new business cards from Raymond Stewart several years ago, for Leonard when he got his promotion. Gray stock with maroon lettering, which Leonard hadn't liked. Leonard said they looked gay. When he found out where she got them, he said it figured, because Raymond Stewart was probably gay too. Sharon smiled at this memory now, driving home. How funny to find that she knew so much about him, after all! How funny that he'd been right here all along—that you could live in the same town with somebody all these years and just simply never notice them, never think of them once as a person. This idea made Sharon feel so weird she wished she'd never thought it up in the first place.

Then she pulled into her driveway and there was Margaret playing with the hose, pointing it down to drill holes in the soft black dirt of the flower bed. "Stop it! You stop it right now!" Sharon jerked her daughter's little shoulder much harder than she meant to, grabbing the hose.

Later, after Margaret had run in the house yelling and Sharon had turned off the water, she stood out in the heat with the dripping hose and stared, just stared, at the row of little pines that Leonard had planted all along the back of their property, noticing for the first time how much they had grown since he set them out there six years before, when they'd built the house. The pines were big now, as symmetrical as Christmas trees, their green needles glistening in the sun. Sharon thought she might try to draw them. Then she burst into tears, and when Raymond

Stewart came by her house in early September to deliver the PTA's five hundred recipe booklets, she went to bed with him.

RAYMOND was an ardent, imaginative lover. Sometimes he brought her some candy from the pharmacy. Sometimes he brought flowers. Once he brought her a butterfly, still alive, and kissed her on the mouth when she let it go. Sometimes he dressed up for her: he'd wear one of his father's pin-striped suits, or a Panama hat and army-green Bermuda shorts with eight pockets, or a dashiki and sandals, or mechanic's coveralls with "Mike" stitched on the pocket, or jeans and a Jack Daniel's cap. "Honestly!" Sharon would say. Because Raymond thought she was beautiful, she came to *like* her large soft body. She loved the way he made everything seem so special, she loved the way he talked—his high-pitched zany laugh—and how he stroked her tumbling hair. He was endlessly fascinated by how she spent her day, by all the dumb details of her life.

Oh, but there was no time, it seemed, at first, and no place to go—two hours once a week at Sharon's, once Margaret had been deposited at Mother's Morning Out—or late afternoon in the creepy old Sutton house, after the boys came home from school to watch Margaret, while Miss Suetta went to group therapy at the Senior Citizens' Center, with her companion. Miss Suetta hated both group therapy and her companion. Sharon lay giggling in Raymond's four-poster bed on these occasions, aware that if she'd ever acted so silly in her own house, Leonard would have sent her packing years ago. But Raymond gave her scuppernong wine in little green-stemmed crystal glasses. The strong autumn sun came slanting across his bed. The wine was sweet, Raymond was blind as a bat without his glasses. Oh, she could have stayed there forever, covering his whole little face, his whole body with kisses.

Raymond had a way of framing things with words that made them special. He gave events a title. For their affair, he had adopted a kind of wise-guy voice and a way of talking out of the side of his mouth, like somebody in *The Godfather.* "Me and my baby sip *scuppernong wine,*" he'd say—to nobody—rolling his eyes. Or, "Me and my baby *take in a show,*" when once they actually did this, the following summer when Sharon's kids spent the night with her mother and Leonard went to the National Guard. Raymond picked an arty movie for them to see, named *The Night of the Shooting Stars,* and they drove over to Greenville together to see it after meeting in a 7-Eleven at the city limits, where Sharon left her car. *The Night of the Shooting Stars* turned out to be very weird in Sharon's opinion and not anything you would really want to make a movie about. But Raymond thought it was great. Later, on the way back, he drove down a dirt road off the highway and parked in the warm rustling woods.

"Me and my baby *make out!*" Raymond crowed, pulling her into his arms. Oh, it was crazy!

And it got worse. They grew greedier and greedier. Several times, Raymond had just left by the back door when Leonard came in at the front. Several times, going or coming, Sharon encountered Raymond's mother, who never seemed to notice until the day Sharon picked her up hitchhiking downtown and drove her back to the house on Sunset Street. Just before Miss Suetta went in the front door, she stopped dead in her tracks and turned to point a long skinny finger back at Sharon. "Just who *is* this woman?" she asked loudly. And then her companion came and thanked Sharon and guided Miss Suetta inside.

By this time, of course, Sharon called him Ramón.

AFTER two years, he finally talked her into going to a motel, the new Ramada Inn in Greenville. Built on a grander scale than anything else in the county, this Ramada Inn was really more like a hotel, he told her, promising saunas and a sunken bar and an indoor pool and Nautilus equipment. "You know I wouldn't do any of that," said Sharon. Leonard had to go out of town on a selling trip anyway—Leonard can sell or trade anything, which is what he does for the coal company he works for. For instance, he will trade a piece of land for a warehouse, or a rear-end loader for a computer. Sharon doesn't know exactly what Leonard does. But he was out of town, so she let Alister and Leonard Lee spend the night with their friends and asked her mother to keep Margaret. "Why?" her mother had asked. "Well, I've been spotting between my periods," Sharon said smoothly, "and Dr. King wants me to go over to Greenville for some tests." She could lie like a rug! But before Sharon saw Raymond with new eyes, she had never lied in her whole life. Sharon felt wonderful and terrible, checking into the Ramada Inn with Raymond as Mr. and Mrs. John Deere. The clerk didn't bat an eye.

This Ramada was as fancy, as imposing as advertised. Their room was actually a suite, with a color TV and the promised sunken tub, and a king-size bed under a tufted velvet spread and a big brass lamp as large as Margaret. Sharon stifled a sob. She was feeling edgy and kind of blue. It was one thing to find an hour here and an hour there, but another thing to do this. "All I want for Christmas is to sleep with you *all night long,*" Raymond had said. Sharon wanted this too. But she hadn't thought it would be so hard. She looked around the room. "How much did this cost?" she asked. "Oh, not much. Anyway, I've got plenty of *money*," Raymond said airily, and Sharon stared at him. This was true, but she always forgot it.

Raymond went out for ice and came back and made two big blue drinks out of rum and a bottled mix. The drinks looked like Windex. "Me and my baby go Hawaiian," Raymond said gravely, clicking his glass against hers. Then they got drunk and had a wonderful time. The next morning Sharon was terrified of seeing somebody she knew, but it turned out that nobody at all was around. Nobody. Raymond joked about this as they walked down the long pale corridor. He made his voice into a Rod Serling *Twilight Zone* voice. "They think they're checking out of . . . the *ghost motel*," he said.

Then Sharon imagined that they had really died in a wreck on the way to the motel, only they didn't know it. When they turned a corner and saw themselves reflected in a mirror in the lobby, she screamed.

"She screams, but no one can hear her in . . . the *ghost motel*," said Raymond. He carried his clothes in a laundry bag.

"No, hush, I mean it," Sharon said.

She looked in the mirror while Raymond paid the bill, and it seemed to her then that she was wavy and insubstantial, and that Raymond, when he came up behind her, was nothing but air. They held hands tightly and didn't talk, all the way back to the 7-Eleven where Sharon had parked her car.

AND NOW, Raymond is all excited about the eclipse. He's been talking about it for weeks. He's just like a kid. Sharon's real kids, Leonard Lee and Alister and Margaret, have been studying eclipses at school, but they couldn't care less.

"I want to be with you, baby, to view the eclipse." Raymond has said this to Sharon again and again. He has made them both little contraptions out of cardboard, with peepholes, so they won't burn their retinas. Luckily, the eclipse is set for one-thirty on a Tuesday afternoon, so the children are at school. Leonard is at work.

Raymond arrives promptly at one, dressed in his father's white pharmacist's jacket. "I thought I ought to look scientific," he says, twirling around in Sharon's kitchen to give her the full effect. His high giggle ricochets off the kitchen cabinets. He has brought a bottle of pink champagne. He pops the cork with a flourish and offers her a glass. Which Sharon accepts gladly because in truth she's not feeling so good—it's funny how that lie she told her mother a couple of months ago seems to be coming true. Probably her uterus is just falling apart. The truth is, she's getting *old*—sometimes she feels just ancient, a hundred years older than Raymond.

Sharon sips the champagne slowly while Raymond opens all of her kitchen cabinets and pokes around inside them.

"What are you looking for?" she finally asks.

"Why—nothing!" When Raymond smiles, his face breaks into crinkles all over. He clasps her forcefully. "I like to see where you keep things," he says. "You're an endless mystery to me, baby." He kisses her, then pulls out a pocket watch she's never seen before. Perhaps he bought it just for the eclipse. "One-twelve," he says. "Come on, you *heavenly body* you. It's time to go outside."

In spite of herself, Sharon has gotten excited too. They take plastic lawn chairs and sit down right in the middle of the backyard, near the basketball goal but well away from the pines, where they can get the most open view. It's a cloudless day in early March. Sharon's daffodils are blooming. She has thought this all through ahead of time: the only neighbor with a view of her backyard, Mrs. Hodges, is gone all day. Raymond refills his glass with champagne. Sharon's lettuce is coming up, she notices, in crinkly green waves at the end of the garden. But Raymond is telling her what will happen next, lecturing her in a deep scientific voice which makes him sound exactly like the guy on *Wild Kingdom:* "When the moon passes directly between the earth and the sun so that its shadow falls upon the earth, there's a solar eclipse, visible from the part of the earth's surface on which the shadow lies. So it's the shadow of the moon which will pass across us."

I don't care! Sharon nearly screams it. *All I want,* she thinks, *honey, all I ever want is you.* Raymond sits stiffly upright in her plastic lawn chair, his head leaning to the side in a practiced, casual manner, lecturing about the umbra and penumbra. He has smoothed his spiky blond hair down for this occasion and it gleams in the early spring sun.

"A total solar eclipse occurs only once in every four hundred years in any one place. Actually this won't be a total eclipse, not where we are. If we'd driven over to Greensboro, we would have been right in the center of it." For a minute, his face falls. "Maybe we should have done that."

"Oh, no," Sharon assures him. "I think this is just fine." She sips her champagne while Raymond shows her how to look through the little box in order to see the eclipse. Raymond consults his watch—one-fifteen. Mrs. Hodges's golden retriever, Ralph, starts barking.

"Dogs will bark," Raymond intones. "Animals will go to bed. Pregnant women will have their babies. Birds will cease to twitter."

"*Twitter?*" Sharon says. "Well, they sure are twittering now." Sharon has a lot of birds because of the bird feeder Alister made in Shop II.

"*Trust me*. It's coming," says Raymond.

While Sharon and Raymond sit in her backyard with their boxes on their knees, waiting, Sharon has a sudden awful view of them from somewhere else, a view of how they must look, doing this, drinking champagne. It's so wild! Ralph barks and the birds twitter, and then, just as Raymond promised, they cease. Ralph ceases too. Raymond squeezes Sharon's hand. A hush falls, a shadow falls, the very air seems to thicken suddenly, to darken around them, but still it's not *dark*. It's the weirdest thing Sharon has ever seen. It's like it's getting colder too, all of a sudden. She bets the temperature has dropped at least ten degrees. "Oh, baby! Oh, honey!" Raymond says. Through the peephole in her cardboard box, Sharon sees the moon, a dark object moving across the sun's face and shutting more and more of its bright surface from view, and then it's really twilight.

"Me and my baby view the eclipse," says Raymond.

Sharon starts crying.

The sun is nothing now but a crazy shining crescent, a ghost sun. Funny shadows run all over everything—all over Sharon's garden, her house, her pine trees, the basketball goal, all over Raymond. His white jacket seems alive, dimly rippling. Sharon feels exactly like somebody big is walking on her grave. Then the shadows are gone, and it's nearly dark. Sharon can see stars. Raymond kisses her, and then the eclipse is over.

"It was just like they said it would be!" he says. "Just exactly!" He's very excited. Then they go to bed, and when Margaret comes home from school he's still there, in the hall bathroom.

"Hi, honey," says Sharon, who ran quickly into the kitchen when she first heard Margaret, so as to appear busy. Sharon moves things around in the refrigerator.

"Who's *that?*" Margaret drops her knapsack and points straight at Raymond, who has chosen just this moment to come out of the bathroom waving Sharon's new Dustbuster. Margaret is a skinny, freckled little girl who's mostly serious. Now she's in first grade.

"What's *this?*" Raymond waves the Dustbuster. He's delighted by gadgets, but whenever he buys one, it breaks.

"I'll show you," Margaret says. She demonstrates the Dustbuster while Raymond buttons his daddy's white pharmacy jacket.

"See?" Margaret says gravely.

"That's *amazing*," Raymond says.

Sharon, watching them, thinks she will die. But Raymond leaves before the boys get home, and Margaret doesn't mention him until the next afternoon. "He was nice," Margaret says then.

"Who, honey?" Sharon is frying chicken.

"That man who was here. Who was he?" Margaret asks again.

"Oh, just nobody," Sharon says. Because it's true. Her affair with Raymond Stewart is over now as suddenly and as mysteriously as it began. Sharon aches with loss. When she tells Raymond, he'll be upset, as she is upset, but he'll live, as she will. He'll find things to do. He has just been given the part of Ben in the Shady Mountain Players production of *The Glass Menagerie*, for instance, a part he's always wanted. He'll be okay. Sharon plans to say, "Raymond, I will never love anyone in the world as much as I love you." This is absolutely true. She loves him, she will love him forever with a fierce sweet love that will never die. For Raymond Stewart will never change. He'll grow older, more eccentric. People will point him out. Although their mothers will tell them not to, children will follow him in the street, begging him to talk funny and make faces. Maybe he'll have girlfriends. But nobody will ever love him as much as Sharon—he's shown her things. She knows this. And oh, she'll be around, she'll run into Raymond from time to time—choosing Leonard's new business cards, for instance, when Leonard gets another promotion, or making up the Art Guild flier, or—years and years from now—ordering Margaret's wedding invitations.

The Mountain Day

JEAN STAFFORD

WHEN I woke up that morning, in the fallow light before the sunrise, and remembered that the night before I had got engaged to Rod Stephansson, I could feel my blue eyes growing bluer; I could feel them becoming the color of the harebells that were blooming now in August all through the pasture beneath my window, and I thought, Will Rod notice this change and how will he speak of it? For weeks, like a leaf turning constantly to the sun for its sustenance, so my whole existence had leaned toward Rod's recognition and approval of me, as if without them I would fade and wither. When I was alone and he was miles away from me, not thinking of me at all, probably, as he catalogued botanical specimens at the Science Lodge, I nevertheless caused his eyes to take in the way I brushed my hair or mounted my horse or paddled my little brother Davy across our lake and back in the canoe. And going further, I would project us into the autumn, when our Western holiday would be over and he would come down from Harvard for a weekend in New York. I would, in my daydreams, receive him in a dozen different dresses and a dozen different countenances: now I was shy, now I was *soignée*, now unassailably cool and pure; sometimes I was talking in sparkling repartee on the telephone when he arrived, and sometimes I was listening to phonograph records; depending on my costume and my coiffure, the music was Honegger or Louis Armstrong or plainsong. Often, in the self-conceit of my love, I was so intent upon his image of me that I could not, for a moment, summon up an image of *him*. How was that possible! The mountain sun had turned him amber and had lightened his leonine hair; he was tall and lithe and sculptured and violet-eyed, and the bones of his intelligent face were molded perfectly. My sister Camilla, two years older than I and engaged to be married to a brilliant but distinctly batrachian Yale man, had, on first seeing Rod, said, "If he's

104

really going to be a doctor, the girl that marries him is in for trouble. What a practice he's going to have among women! Brother!"

I think I got this pressing need for high opinion from my father, who was a rich man of intellect and education but one of no vocation. Our life was sumptuous and orderly, and we lived it, in the winter, in New York and, in the summer, in the mountains of Colorado. The Grayson fortune, three generations old, founded on such tangibles as cattle, land, and cargo vessels, was now a complex of financial abstractions, the manipulation of which my father had turned over to bankers and brokers, since money, as a science, did not interest him. He had zeals and specialties, but I think he spent his whole life worrying about what people thought of him; a man of leisure had become an anachronism. One time, when he came to visit me at college and I had been telling him about a close friend of mine who was going on to study law after she finished at Bryn Mawr, he said, "D'you know, Judy, if I hadn't been rich, I'd have been a bum." He was not ashamed of his millions—they were no fault of his—but he *was* ashamed that his life was not consecrated; he had no fixed orbit. And, in a different way, this unease of his had come down to me, his middle child.

But I wasn't thinking of Daddy that morning—it was only years later that I was able to arrive at this analysis—and when I thought of Camilla's reaction to Rod, I went back to the first time I had met him and reviewed all the stages of growth that had culminated the night before in his asking me to marry him. I lay straight and still and smiling, my eyes wide open, hearing the pristine song of the first meadow larks on the fence posts, and hearing the famished, self-pitying coyotes wailing up in the sage.

One day late in June, soon after our arrival in Colorado, Daddy and Mother and Camilla and I had ridden our horses over to the Science Lodge to have lunch with a friend of Daddy's—Dr. Menzies, a geophysicist from Columbia, who taught there in the summers. It was an annual expedition, like the trip to the glacier, and the regatta at Grand Lake, and opening night at Central City; Daddy was a ritualist—each year, for example, he had the same four seats at Carnegie Hall for the Boston Symphony—and whether we liked it or not, we participated in his ceremonies. It had always bored Camilla and me terribly to go to the Science Lodge. The place was a dismal aggregate of log cabins, some of which were laboratories and lecture rooms and others Spartan living quarters for the faculty and for the dozen or so students—solemn, silent, myopic youths, who, we decided, must be even more solemn in the winter, at college, since coming to the Lodge to study high-altitude vegetation and the mineralogy of moraines was their notion of a holiday; the boys we knew bicycled through France or fooled around on boats off Martha's Vineyard. Everyone, staff and students and guests, sat at one long table in the mess hall and ate fried beefsteak, dehydrated potatoes, canned peas, and canned Kadota figs, and drank sallow coffee with canned milk. Daddy and Dr. Menzies would fervently discuss some such thing as the wisdoms and the follies of foundations. Mother, who was a beauty and had no intellectual class consciousness, would try to talk about flower arrangement with the ecologists and the systematic botanists, who blushed and addressed their eyes to their food. And Camilla and I would flounder through the maneuvers of "Do you know So-and-So at Dartmouth?" or "Have you been up to Troublesome Falls yet?," and, for our pains, got monosyllabic replies, usually in the negative. Not one time, until this summer, had she and I found any of these young men worthy of comment; they were, indeed, so much of a kind and so stunningly dull that in our private language we had a generic term, "a Science Lodge type," to designate nonentities we got stuck with at parties.

And then, this year, sitting directly across the table from me was Rod Stephansson, so sudden, somehow, so surprising, that I averted my eyes, as if his radiance would blind me. He was as serious as the other boys, but he was not solemn, and he and Mother, in a conversation about Boston, which she knew from visits to our aunts and cousins there and he knew because he went to Harvard, so charmed each other that long before we had reached the Nabiscos and the viscous figs, she had invited him to our house for Sunday supper. He was sophisticated and funny and acute, but he was gentle, too, and mannerly. His smile, in which the responsive eyes played the leading role, made me giddy, but I wanted, nevertheless, to remain within its sphere.

As soon as lunch was over, the scientists and their apprentices bolted for their microscopes and samples of pyrites—all except Dr. Menzies and Rod, who came with us to the hitching post where we had left the horses. As we sauntered through the red dust under the amazing alpine sky, I was breathless, filled with trepidation that I was going to do something clumsy and cause this paragon, who had not once looked in my direction, to despise me. So emphatic had been his immediate effect on me that, as if I had already committed the blunder and excited his disdain, I angrily shrugged my shoulders and said to myself, "Oh, to hell with him! He's nothing but a Science Lodge grind." But something quite else happened; when I had mounted Chiquita, my squatty little pinto cow pony, Rod took a blue bandanna handkerchief out of his pocket and, as if this were the most natural thing in the world, began to wipe the red dust off my boot and the edge of my jodhpurs, and when he was through—in my heady reveries later on I was to find it significant that he cleaned only *one* boot, so that my horse concealed him from the rest of the party—he looked up and gave me that inebriating smile and, in a secret voice, for my ears only, he said, "You'll be there on Sunday, won't you? You won't go off to Denver, or anything like that?" It never occurred to me to give him a flirtatious reply; I realized, with awe and with self-consciousness, that Rod had outgrown boyhood and the games of boyhood.

On the five-mile ride home, I was glad that Camilla and Daddy questioned Mother about him, because my voice would have come out as a croak or a squeak. Mother said he had told her that he was of Norwegian descent and came from Buffalo, and that he was going into his second year at Harvard Medical School. His family for generations had been landscape gardeners and horticulturists, and he had come out to the Science Lodge because, through his father, he had become interested in plant pathology ("He's very keen on viruses," said Mother), and Dr. Miles Houghton, eminent in the field, was on the staff this year. It was then that Camilla expressed her pity for the girl who married him, but Mother said, "I don't think he's in the least like that. His looks wouldn't mean a blessed thing if he weren't so awfully bright and nice. I think his character is very well put together."

It was a storybook summertime romance, woven in the mountain sun and mountain moonlight, beginning that first Sunday when he came to supper and delighted everyone. All my senses were heightened, as if I had been inoculated with some powerful, sybaritic drug: the aspen leaves were more brilliant than they had ever been before, the upland snow was purer, the pinewoods were more redolent, and the gentle winds in them were more mellifluous; the berries I ate for breakfast came from the bushes of Eden. In love with Rod, I seemed to love my parents more than ever, and Camilla and Davy, and my grandmother, who summered in a house across the lake from us; I adored the horses and the dogs and the barn cats and the wary deer that sometimes came at dusk down to the salt lick after the cows had been taken in.

Rod had never been West before, and because I had been coming here in the summer ever since my infancy, I was his cicerone, and took him to beaver dams and hidden waterfalls and natural castles of red rock, and to isolated, unmarked tombstones where God knew what murdered prospectors or starved babies were buried. We sifted the fool's gold of the cold streams through our fingers and we ate sweet piñon nuts; we rowed and rode and climbed and fished, and played doubles with Daddy and

Camilla. No other young man—not even Camilla's Fritzie Lloyd, whom Daddy liked enormously—had ever evoked from Daddy so much esteem, and once he said, "He plays at everything so well and handsomely, *besides* having medicine and virtue."

Rod rose at dawn to study ergot and potato blight, but in midafternoon he walked over to our house, in long, easy strides. When he got to the foot of the broad steps that led up to the veranda, he was not out of breath or hot or exhausted. I, trembling inwardly and greeting him with a falsely cool "Hey, Rod," would think, If I tell him I have been reading *War and Peace*, will he respect me?

For it was his respect, I suppose, that I wanted as much as I wanted his love. I wanted him to honor my judgments and my abilities as much as I honored his, but through some fortunate poise, inherited from my mother to counterbalance the doubt I had got from Daddy, I was not compelled to compete with him, as I often had to compete, to my grief, with boys whose unsureness of themselves made me arrogant. I must complement, not equal, Rod. Actually, I was not so uneasy with him as I sound; in his presence I was simply and naturally happy, and it was only when we were apart that I tried on different attitudes and opinions in search of the one he would like in me the best.

When August came and the holiday began to wane, I grew restive. In two weeks more, Rod would go back to Buffalo and I would go back to New York with my family, and soon after that we would be separated— we who had been inseparable since June—by a million light-years, he in Cambridge and I at Bryn Mawr. The night before, I had thought that if he did not speak in some way of the future, I would get sick. But I had set my sights so low that the most I had hoped for was an invitation to the Yale-Harvard game, and instead of that he had asked me to marry him! Is there anything on earth more unearthly than to be in love at eighteen? It is like an abundant spring garden. My heart was the Orient, and the sun rose from it; I could have picked the stars from the sky.

THE EVENING had started out badly. Fritzie Lloyd had come on from St. Louis for a week's visit, and at dinner he and Daddy had had an argument about Truman's foreign policy that had unsettled everyone. My father was, except in one particular, the very mildest of men: politically, he was a mad dog, and someone who disagreed with him became, temporarily, his mortal enemy. As I have said, he was very fond of Fritzie and highly approved of him for Camilla, but that night, over the Nesselrode, when Fritzie suggested, at considerable length, that the British attitude toward Communist China was more realistic than ours, Daddy protested so violently that you would have thought he might at any moment go and get a gun and shoot to kill. Everyone, and Fritzie most of all, was frightened by his fuming, stuttering rage, and after dinner Mother, to get us out of the house and calm Daddy down with a game of cribbage, proposed that Camilla and Fritzie and Rod and I take the station wagon and go somewhere to dance.

The only place within miles was a squalid, dusty honky-tonk in Puma, patronized by subhuman ne'er-do-wells and old wattled trollops who glared hostilely at us when we went in; at the bar an ugly customer, very drunk, spat on the floor as we walked by, and with feral hatred said, "Goddamn yearling dudes!" The reek of beer and green moonshine and nasty perfume, together with my grief that the summer was almost gone, harried me and made me hot and weak, and I was silent. Fritzie was morose and kept saying things like "I *know* which way the land lies with your old man, so why do I have to make him sore? Damn it, I like him so, what makes me pick the one thing that's going to make him take a scunner to me?" And Camilla kept stroking the back of his hand and consoling him, telling him that of *course* he didn't have to go back to Missouri the next day, and that while she knew it had been an awful experience, she was awfully proud of his sticking to his guns, and he must stop fretting, because Daddy honestly was probably dying of remorse this minute and was the *original* hatchet-burier. Rod and I danced once—speechless, except at the very end of the jukebox record, when he said, his lips in my hair, "I wish when we went out it would be snowing." Snowing! He wanted the winter to come? I gasped and whispered back, "Oh, no! I love the summer," and he replied, "I know, but I love the snow. I love the Public Garden in the snow. The swan-boat pond, those trees . . ." And he drifted off into a musing reverie that excluded me. Soon after that, we went back home, in melancholy silence.

Mother and Daddy had gone to see Grandmother, and Camilla and Fritzie, cheered by Daddy's absence, went into the house to drink Jack Daniels, which they had just discovered, and which they talked about as if their drinks of it, on the rocks, were the insignia of a particularly lofty secret society. Rod wanted to go out on the lake, and as I was helping him put the red canoe into the water, my mood of sorrow left, and I was abruptly dreadfully excited and felt that all my nerves were pulsing.

At its widest, Daddy's lake was just under a mile, and it was so deep in places that whenever I took Davy out on it, I put him in a Mae West. It was a wonderful lake—limpid, blue, shaped like a heart. Daddy stocked it each year, and the rainbow trout that came from it were so beautiful they looked like idealized paintings of trout. Not far from the pier at

Grandmother's house, there was a dense meadow of water lilies, and in the shallows near the shores tall cattails grew. But there were some horrid inhabitants of that lovely water, too—huge turtles and hellbenders, about which Davy sometimes had screaming nightmares. Rod and I paddled smoothly and languidly across to Grandmother's shore, and when we turned back, he said, "Let's sprint." The speed, our harmony, our skill, the spicy smell of the serviceberry bushes blooming along the bank, the stars, the lost, lorn, glamorous admonitions of far-off owls—these, and my love for Rod, required of me some articulation, for I could not bear the pressure and the tension of my experience. I might have screamed, I might have cried, but instead I began uncontrollably to laugh. It was my nervous system, not my mind at all, that initiated this uproarious giggling, which was immediately communicated to Rod. The lake had an echo, and we could hear our gagging, pealing ha-ha's coming back to us from all sides, but we managed, crippled as we were—aching, undone—to continue at the speed we had set and, still laughing, get the canoe to shore and up into the reeds and grass. We were spent. There had been no joke and I was a burst balloon. Now, in me, there was nothing but dejection, like a burden on my bones, and I lay down on the grass with my arms straight at my sides, as if I were lying in my casket.

And it was then, in the vast mountain hush, after our meaningless, visceral bout of mirth, that Rod asked me to marry him. Oh, the originality of my sensation! The uniqueness of this circumstance!

We heard Camilla and Fritzie talking on the veranda, and after a while we went up to join them, and to tell them that we were engaged. They seemed immeasurably old to me, for they had been through this delirious distemper so long ago, and they seemed kind and staid, as if they were our aunt and uncle, when, soothingly, they said that in this case we must have champagne.

Now, the next morning, the household was sleeping late, for it was Sunday, and there wasn't a sound except for the birds and an occasional moo or whinny; the sun had risen, and the derelict coyotes had slunk away, still hungry and pessimistic. While I was bewitched with my treasures—my memories were as new and crisp and astonishing as Christmas presents—I grew restless and could not wait for everyone to get up. I wanted to talk to Camilla and Mother, I wanted to hug Davy, I wanted to rush across the lake in the outboard to embrace my acerb, Dresden-doll grandmother and tell her what had happened to me; she would quiz me and tease me and insult me for being so young, and in the end she would rummage through the bottle-green velvet reticule she always carried and give me something antique and precious—a tiny perfume flask or a set of German-silver buttons.

Rod was coming over at eleven, and he and Fritzie and Camilla and I were going up to the glacier. We would ride as far as the ruin of the Bonanza silver mine, and go the rest of the way on foot and have our lunch on the summit of McFarland's Peak, above the mammoth slope of ice. But that was eleven and it was only six! Is he awake, I thought. Is he trying to imagine what I'm doing? With his eyes following me, I got up and put on my pink quilted peignoir and went to the window to see what sort of day we would have for our excursion. It was going to be perfect; it was what my father called "a mountain day." The air was so clear and rarefied it seemed to be an element superior to anything terrestrial—an unnamable essence that had somehow made its way to our valley and our range from another hemisphere. The violent violet peaks stood out against a sky of cruel, infuriated blue, and the snows at timberline shone like sun-struck mirrors. There was no wind; the field of harebells was motionless; the dark-blue lake was calm, and the red canoe, bottom up in the reeds, gleamed in the pure light like a bright, immaculate wound.

I dressed at last, changing a dozen times, trying first slacks, then Levi's, then khaki frontier pants, then jodhpurs, next a red shirt, a blue pullover, a black turtleneck, a striped apache jersey; I did my hair in a ponytail, in a pompadour, in pigtails, and finally I brushed it out straight and let it hang loose to my shoulders.

As soon as I decently could, I went across to Grandmother's and had breakfast with her and told her about Rod. She was pleased; she said that Rod was an Adonis and that she saw no point in marrying if one couldn't marry a handsome man. She opened up that vast, obsolete bag of hers and gave me a gold pin in the shape of two clasped hands.

My grandmother's house was, in these wildwoods of Colorado, a remarkable incongruity, for while she loved the West—she and my grandfather, who died when I was six, had started coming out here when my father, their son, was a baby, suffering from asthma—she despised roughing it. She could not bear crudity or imperfection, and she constantly implored Mother and Daddy to get rid of our cowhide rugs and our flawed, bubbly Mexican glassware and our redwood furniture. Her own house, though its exterior was the same as ours—rambling and made of logs—was furnished much as her apartment in New York was; the Oriental rugs were second-best and some of the tapestry chair-seat covers were machine-made, but the total effect, nonetheless, was that of an oasis of civilization in a barbaric waste. Each year she brought her maids with her, and for the past two or three summers they had been two red-haired Irish girls, Mary and Eileen, who looked down their pretty noses at Mother's servants—local mountain girls who wore ankle socks and cardigans when they served dinner.

Grandmother was not a snob. It was simply that her nature demanded continuity. Her maids today were going to Mass in Peaceful Glen, twenty miles away, and were to be driven there by Bandy, our horse-wrangler and general handyman. Mass was celebrated at the Glen only once a month, by an itinerant priest, who toured continually through the mountains and the plains to the sparse and widely separated settlements of Catholics. Like all such Sundays, it was a red-letter day for Mary and Eileen, and I could hear them in the kitchen, chattering as excitedly as girls going to a dance. Grandmother, a benign and understanding mistress, always gave them the day off after breakfast until it was time for them to prepare her tea, and she came to our house for lunch. After church, if the weather was good, the girls had a picnic beside the lake—an endearing, old-fashioned picnic, with a tablecloth and a wicker hamper. They were planning one for today, Mary said when she came in to clear away the breakfast things.

Grandmother told her that I was going to marry Rod. "That Viking lad," said Grandmother, and Mary, transfigured with happiness for anyone else's happiness, said, with her habitual lavish sentimentality, "It's as if it was my own wedding day. Oh, Miss Judy! May every saint and angel bless you!"

The rest of the morning somehow passed. Daddy had completely forgotten his wrath of the evening before and was talking baseball with Fritzie on the veranda while Mother and Camilla and I sat in Mother's bedroom and talked about engagements and marriage, and about Rod. Mother said, "What good girls I have, to pick out such extremely agreeable young men!" Finally, the last drop of the coffee in the pot on Mother's breakfast tray was gone, and she got up and went to the window and exclaimed, "What a day, what a day! How I envy you pretty girls going off up to McFarland's with your beaux! Do you realize how *important* love is at this time of your lives?" She was ragging us, of course, as Grandmother always did, but she partly meant what she said, for there was the faintest note of the disappointment of maturity in her voice. "What a mushy woman you are!" said Camilla affectionately, and Mother said, "And what a cold, critical woman you are! Now run, the pair of you, and have the grandest skylark ever."

CAMILLA and Fritzie rode ahead and carried on an enthusiastic conversation. Fritzie was studying architecture at Yale, and Camilla was studying art at Vassar, and they were both extremely ardent and in the know; they were, besides, after nearly a year of being engaged, so comfortable with each other that their relationship was no longer an *idée fixe*. But Rod and I were shy and strained, and, I suppose, in a sense we were wretched. These early stages of love are an egg-treading performance, and one is stiff and scared; the day after betrothal is made up almost equally of hell and heaven. He told me at length and feelingly, as if he were talking about the death of beloved kinsmen, how blight had all but obliterated the chestnut trees in the Northeast; so earnestly did I seek to maintain our concord of the night before that I nearly moaned to hear his facts, and languished with the roots of those afflicted trees, and turned my face away from the disease spores disseminated by the wind, and with my whole heart hoped that the attempt to cross the American species of chestnut with the blight-resistant Asiatic would be successful. After this, a leaden silence fell. But gradually, as we ascended the faint trail through Indian paintbrush and columbines, and the air began to make us drunk, we were infected by the glory and the grace of the day and we relaxed a little. I had, indeed, been so rigidly controlled that I had got cramps in the calves of both legs. Finally, ready to cry out with pain, I told Rod, who at once became my doctor and my protector. We dismounted in a field of volunteer timothy, and he massaged my legs until the knots were gone; the gesture, in itself utilitarian, served to return us to our rapture of the night before, and we were able to meet each other's eyes.

And now, much happier, we spurred our horses and came abreast of Camilla and Fritzie, and all the rest of the way to the mine the four of us had a general, factual conversation about New York restaurants, and Broadway musicals we had seen. To the unspoken relief of both Camilla and me, Rod and Fritzie obviously liked each other, and when they were hobbling the horses, we stood aside, praising them. Camilla said, "Rod really is a pet," and I said, "Fritzie grows on one. Last night when Daddy was being such a pain in the neck, I decided he was made of *steel*."

We had our lunch at the top of the world, sitting on saddle blankets spread out upon waxy yellow glacier lilies, which grew beside a snowdrift that some exotic bacteria had made the color of raspberry sherbet. We had cold fried chicken and tomato sandwiches and melon balls and lemony iced tea; it was unquestionably the best meal I had ever eaten in my life. I suddenly remembered Mary and Eileen and their picnic; they would be sitting among the wildflowers, eating dainty nasturtium sandwiches and telling each other spooky ghost stories in their delicious Dublin voices, and I thought, Everyone is happy today; this is the happiest day in the history of the world.

We dozed a little, all four of us, and drowsily watched an eagle banking and wheeling overhead as he scanned the earth for a jack rabbit for his lunch. We remained in this golden somnolence until a sharp wind riffled our hair and warned us that not long from now the sun would start going down. We gathered some of the lilies to decorate our bridles, and then we went slowly back to the horses, all of us quiet from our tranquil cat naps and our fulfillment and our unshakable faith in our future lives.

IN COLORADO, almost every afternoon in the summertime the Devil briefly beat his wife; the skies never darken but there is a short, prodigal fall of crystal rain. When it came today, we made for shelter in a stand of spruce, and when it was over, in only a few minutes, and we emerged, we found a vivid rainbow arched over the eastern sky. The pot of gold must be in the middle of our lake, I thought, exactly where my paroxysmal laughter had begun last night.

"This is too much," said Fritzie. "This is overdoing things. It's a cheap Chamber of Commerce trick."

"I know," said Camilla. "This is the most embarrassing, show-off place in the world. It's like advertisements for summer resorts. Strictly corn."

By the time we came in sight of the clearing where Grandmother's house stood, the shadows were beginning to lengthen and the air was turning cold. Camilla, shivering, said, "Let's stop at Grandmother's for tea. If we play our cards right, she'll give us rum in it."

"I want Jack Daniels," said Fritzie. "I feel so good I want to get loaded."

"You can't get loaded in my well-bred grandmother's drawing room," said Camilla. "She loathes oafs. But she won't mind if you get *comfy* with booze."

I was hesitant. "Grandmother won't like us to be dressed this way for tea," I said, but Camilla overrode my finicking objection, and we followed her lead, going the rest of the way at a lope and enthusiastically agreeing that we were hungry and that we wanted the indoor amenities of a hearth fire and soft sofas. After we had dismounted, leaving the horses free to crop the grass, and were walking up the path to the house, I heard, from our house, across the broad expanse of water, the sound of the phonograph playing Daddy's favorite Mozart quintet; every stimulus that my senses received intensified the enraptured condition of my heart, which was palpitating now in anticipation of Grandmother's regal greeting to Rod.

Tousled and dusty, we tramped through the foyer, where stood a venerable grandfather clock and two ponderous Spanish chairs, and into the

long, generous drawing room, where vases of columbines were everywhere. But there was no fire burning and the tea table had not been laid,
and Grandmother, dressed in Sunday-afternoon taffeta, with a fichu at
her throat, was pacing up and down, Grandfather's thin gold pocket
watch in her hand. She turned to us with a look of consternation and
appeal, and, forgetting, in her engrossing worry, to be a hostess, she said,
"Did you come round the lake? Did you see Mary and Eileen? They
were due back long ago!"

"No, we didn't come that way," said Camilla. "We've come down
from the glacier. Don't you suppose they're just off looking for puffballs?
They so love the nasty things."

Grandmother shook her head. "They're the most punctilious servants
I've ever had. They wouldn't go roaming off without letting me know. I
was taking a nap, but all the same they would have left a note."

"Maybe they went to sleep after their picnic," I said. "We did."

"Oh, I don't think they'd do a thing like that," said Grandmother.
"Still . . ."

"Bandy brought them home all right?" I said, and when Grandmother
nodded, Rod said, "Then they can't be far."

"We'll go and see if they went to sleep," said Camilla. "We'll find
them, darling, never you fear. They've got to make us an enormous tea,
because we're absolutely ravenous."

"We'll find them," echoed Rod reassuringly, and Fritzie said, "Don't
worry, Mrs. Grayson. We'll be back with your girls in a minute."

"Good children," said Grandmother, and smiled at us, but then she
looked fearfully out the window, where vermilion had begun to tinge
the western sky. "Hurry, my dears, it'll soon be dark."

My grandmother's anxiety had not really infected us, partly because,
being fearless ourselves, we were not afraid for anyone else, and partly
because we were unwilling to relinquish our earlier carefree mood, and
we started our walk around the lake in a spirit of sport, affectionately
making fun of Grandmother for sending us out as a posse, as if the West
were still wild and her maids had been scalped by Indians or were being
held as hostages by road agents. We took the trail around the lake that
was the longest way to our house, for Camilla and I knew that it was on
this side, on a favorite plot of grass, that the girls always had their picnic;
we had often seen them there. After they had come back from Mass, they
would take off their perky, beflowered, beribboned hats and their white
cotton gloves and their good shoes, but they would keep on their Sun-
day-best dresses for their light and ladylike collation. To Camilla and
me, whenever we spied on them, they looked like an illustration in an
old-fashioned romantic novel.

As we walked along, in single file, we discussed the many places they might be, safe and innocent, if we did not—as we were sure we would— find them snoozing in the dying day. Perhaps, all unknown to Grand- mother, they had beaux, who had flattered and cajoled them into being late; perhaps they were bird watchers and could not tear themselves away from some fascinating rite of magpies; perhaps they had strolled over to the dude camp nearby and were watching an amateur rodeo; perhaps a dozen things. Punctilious as Grandmother said they were, they were bound to lapse at least once in a blue moon.

PRESENTLY, halfway around the lake, we came to that favorite plot of grass, where, sure enough, the Irish girls had spread out their picnic. Its corners neatly held down with rocks, the tablecloth with a pattern of tulips was neatly set for two with blue willowware plates and kitchen sil- ver and jelly glasses; in the middle of the tablecloth there was a Dundee marmalade jar filled with Mariposa lilies. But the embossed-paper nap- kins had not been unfolded, the glasses had not been filled from the ther- mos, and the hamper had not been opened.

Perplexed and at last alarmed, we stood silent and unmoving for a minute, pointlessly scanning the immediate neighborhood, as if the maids were going to materialize before our eyes. It was Rod who spoke first.

"It does look queer," he said. "If they'd gone for a swim, they'd have come back by now. They'd have been starved after fasting for so long."

"Anyhow, they don't know how to swim," I said. "Neither one of them. Not a stroke."

"Then the lake's out, thank God," said Fritzie. "Or— They never use the boats, I suppose?"

Camilla and I exchanged a look of horror. Mary and Eileen were for- bidden to use the canoe, but, out of their ignorance, they could not, would not, believe in the perils of the lake, and over and over again someone would catch them paddling, grotesquely maladroit, through the shallow water under the willow trees that lined the shore on this side.

"Oh, God!" cried Camilla, and she and I, with the boys at our heels, plunged down through the bushes that hid the water from us here, stum- bling over the rocks and the willow suckers. When we got to the lake's edge, we saw the canoe immediately away to our right, riding upside down in the mild wind over a deep spot in the lake, not far from shore.

"Where do you keep the outboard?" asked Rod. His voice, though it was urgent, was controlled.

"There's one at Grandmother's," I said. "That's nearest."

"Then come on!" he said.

As Grandmother and Camilla and I stood by the dock watching the boys get into the outboard, it occurred to me suddenly that there was just possibly a chance that the poor, dear, clumsy girls had let the canoe go adrift after their guilty outing in it, and that—first debating for a while, dreading the scolding Daddy would give them for their carelessness—they had decided to go to our house to get help. Galvanized by this wild, ingenious hope, I ran off, saying nothing to the others, and this time I took the shorter path, on the other side of the lake. As I ran, I could hear the bee-buzz of the outboard and, faintly, from our house, the promise of peace of Bach's "Sheep May Safely Graze." Daddy seemed to be having a Roman holiday this afternoon, with all the music he fancied most. And as I ran, my mouth dry and my heart hurting, through the wavering, leafy patterns of sun and shade, my obsessed and egocentric mind began, in this crisis, to seek Rod's admiration, and I thought, What will he think of this practical, intelligent, well-thought-out act of mine? Dear God, let Mary and Eileen be there! Let nothing have happened to them but Daddy's dressing down! Just then I tripped and twisted my ankle, and the pain was so sharp that it took my breath away, and, pausing for a moment in my surprise and shock, I was seized with a passion of self-loathing for wanting the girls to be alive chiefly because their being so would set me up in Rod's eyes. I began to cry for the fair-skinned, green-eyed Dublin girls, and then I faltered on.

"Sheep May Safely Graze" still floated out serenely from our house, and a peaceful tower of smoke rose from our chimney. I prayed that in a minute I was going to see Mary and Eileen. But, instead, I saw Mother standing at our dock, and Daddy and Bandy starting out in our boat. The living-room windows of our house commanded a comprehensive view of the lake, as did Grandmother's directly opposite, and Mother told me later that she had seen Rod and Fritzie in the outboard by chance as she was watering the terrarium she kept on the sill; she had gazed at them idly for some time before she sensed that something was wrong and called my father. He had gone immediately down to the shore and shouted at the boys, who shouted back what they were doing.

"Have they—" I began, out of breath.

"They've found them, yes," said Mother. Out on the lake, I could see Rod and Fritzie diving from the boat. "Come, Judy, we must go and break the news to your grandmother. They're going to bring the bod— They're going to come back to this shore."

"Where's Davy?" I said. "Davy mustn't see!"

"Davy's all right. Luella will keep him busy. Come now." And Mother and I started out briskly, our eyes on the ground, not looking again, lest we see the boys bring two pitiful burdens to the surface of the water.

When we got to Grandmother's, we found Camilla and Grandmother in the drawing room. Even before the boys had sighted the bodies, Camilla had gone back there, to comfort Grandmother and to take her inside and persuade her not to look at the lake. We found them both in front of the fire, which Camilla had lit, Grandmother huddled in a big chair, looking terribly old and enervated. None of us could think of a word to say; we kept warming our hands at the fire and listening to the loud ticking of the grandfather clock. An age went by before we finally heard both outboards coming to this shore.

WHEN the three men came into this silent room, their faces were stricken and sickened. My father went to his mother and put his arm around her shoulder, and she looked up at him imploringly and said, "How ever shall I tell their poor families? Ah, Samuel, we should have destroyed that canoe." My father bent down and whispered something in her ear, and she got up, weakly, and went with him into the next room. Daddy had taken her away to tell her, as gently as he could, what Fritzie told us now. Mary and Eileen could not have been in the water for more than a few hours, but in that time the hellbenders and the ravenous turtles had eaten their lovely faces and their work-swollen hands; no one, certainly no kinsman, must see them.

A heavy hush and torpor fell on all of us after we had heard this new piece of frightful intelligence. I wanted to busy myself—to turn on the lamps and dispel the murk of twilight, to straighten a stalk of yucca that was leaning gracelessly out of a vase, to prod the logs and make the sparks scintillate and snap. But my flesh was leaden, and I sat still. Once, I looked at my mother, sagging in her chair as inertly as the rest of us, and I thought, with a rush of sympathy, that living did not insulate one against shock. What must my gentle, humane grandmother be going through there in the library! How was she going to write to the girls' distant families of their death? And how, without going into the ghastly details, could she enjoin them not to open the coffins?

After a long time, Grandmother came back into the room and, mistress of her house again (though the bright unshed tears in her eyes and the quivering of her thin old hands showed that she was not yet mistress of herself), flicked the master light switch and went to draw the curtains, saying, as she did so, "By this time of day, I have had enough of the wonders of Colorado." Strengthened by her example, I got up now and attended to the listing yucca. There was a general stir in the room, and our voices were restored to us. Fritzie asked Camilla if she thought our horses would be all right, and she assured him that by this time they would have gone back to the barn and one of the men would have unsaddled them; Mother, going to the fireplace, asked Rod to help her return to its proper place one of the andirons that had shifted. My grandmother came at last to the windows that gave on the lake, and she pulled the curtains shut quickly; she shuddered and for a moment stood still, confronting the blank expanse of wine-red velours. As if she were alone, as if she were speaking to herself or to God, she murmured, "I won't come here again with innocents."

She turned around then and said to my mother, "Samuel and I have agreed that under the circumstances someone should personally explain to the girls' families what happened—Samuel will go to Ireland at once."

My mother said only, "He'll have no trouble booking at this time of year," and my grandmother nodded, closing the subject of the sudden voyage.

My father came into the room carrying a tray of drinks, and Grandmother said, "It's cold; there's autumn in the air. Samuel and I decided that we all needed something to warm us on the inside."

It was the first time I had ever been given a real drink, and as Daddy handed me the glass, I thought, Is he being absentminded or does this mean I'm accepted as grown up? I didn't know which it was—the symbol of the whiskey, or my family's love for me and my love for them and my recognition of my security (I was thinking simultaneously of Mary's family and Eileen's, still ignorant of the crumbling of *their* solidarity as they lived through an ordinary day in Dublin), or whether it was my grandmother's moral majesty, which I saw for the first time and wanted to emulate. Whatever it was, I found myself just then standing firmly on my own, and I was able to see everyone clearly—even myself. Earlier, in my blinding cocoon, when I had thought so constantly about Rod's respect for me, I had lost, in a sense, my respect for myself, but now, at last, I was able to think of *him* and not of his opinion of *me*. Bedraggled, my hair all wild, beggar's-lice on my sweater and my trousers, I did not care at all how I looked. I cared only, looking at the green pallor of his face, that he had suffered. I wanted him to be as happy as he had been before we had started our search for the girls, and I thought, Love, real love, is just that: it is wanting the beloved to be happy. The simplicity of the equation surprised me, but only for a moment and then it was incorporated into me as naturally as if it had been there all along.

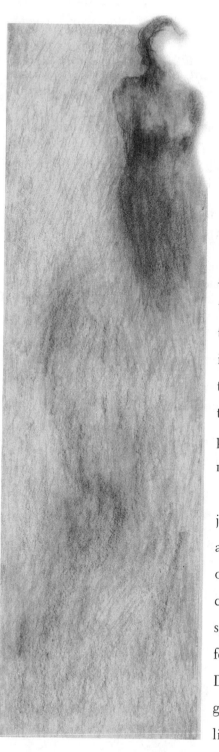

Finding Direction

A WOMAN may take a new direction in her life at age thirteen, twenty-eight, forty-five, or anywhere in between or beyond. That direction may be the vocation she finds, the past she leaves behind, or simply a deep, life-enhancing transformation in how she sees herself.

Many of us work competently at jobs or careers but secretly fear we are impostors in our roles, fooling others but not ourselves. Perri Klass chronicles the soul-testing year she spends as a pediatric intern caring for newborns at a Boston hospital. Despite months of her tending dangerously sick babies and making life-and-death choices for treatment, Klass discovers only when she is *out* of her doctor's whites whether she has indeed become a doctor.

Leaving home—either spiritually or physically—is always a perilous passage toward a new direction. At thirteen, Joyce Johnson sneaks away from her stuffy routine of girls' school and piano lessons to bohemian Greenwich Village to discover what she thinks is Real Life.

Far from being pushed by her parents to a specific future career, Annie Dillard describes her growing up in Pittsburgh in the 1950s with a wonderful number of choices. When she receives a microscope set for Christmas, the gift—paired with her parents' *un*interest—"hands me my life."

From girlhood up, we are pressured to value ourselves by how our faces and bodies match the current beauty ideal. Two essays show women pushing beyond this powerful pressure to conform to the freedom of being their full human selves. At nine Lucy Grealy was left by cancer of the jaw with a face that made people stare at her and children make fun of her. "Mirrorings" shows powerfully how Grealy finds the amazing grace to live through the ordeal of being ridiculed and in her twenties leaps forward beyond appearance to a magical transformation in how she relates to others. In "Striptease," Lauren Slater, a psychotherapist and former anorexic, is chagrined to be assigned a male client who prefers pornography to real women. Yet as their therapy exposes his fear of the natural female body, Slater looks anew at her own teenage obsession "to be thin thin thin."

Adversity is often the push that takes us in the direction we should have been going all along. When Molly—the shy middle-aged wife in J. California Cooper's ebullient story—is suddenly left by her selfish husband, Gravy, she is forced to shake up all her notions of who she is and discover what she can do.

Sometimes the push to change comes from within. At twenty-one Joan Didion came to New York City and fell in love with the city, discovering something interesting around every corner. How could she ever move on? She replies in "Goodbye to All That."

Flip-Flops

PERRI KLASS

I WAS in a little clothing store not far from my home when I heard a horrible noise out in the street—a crash of metal on metal followed by screams, automobile screeches, and general clamor. Without thinking, I ran out of the store and headed across the street; I had reached the island in the middle before it consciously occurred to me, *you're running to help because you're a doctor, you need to take charge.* Inevitably, I was wearing a tee shirt, ratty pants, and flip-flops; and I was particularly conscious of the flip-flops as I arrived at the crowd and pushed my way through. A motorcyclist had smashed into a pickup truck and been thrown far into the air; he lay now on the pavement with broken bones protruding through the skin of his wrists. I knelt down next to him and was relieved to see he was breathing, talking—he did not need cardiopulmonary resuscitation. What he was saying was this: "For God's sake, take my helmet off!" He gestured ineffectually with his wounded hands.

Helpful voices from the crowd immediately broke in: "He wants his helmet off, he said to take his helmet off." Someone else suggested that he be carried into the nearest shop, someone else that he shouldn't be moved.

I raised my voice. "I'm a doctor," I said, not sounding terribly convincing to myself. "I'm a doctor," I repeated. "The helmet stays on." I was shooing away a helpful bystander who was already working on the strap.

I had to say it maybe fifty times before the ambulance arrived. I didn't want to explain in detail, with this man already terrified and in pain, that a severe neck injury could be made worse if we moved his head, pulled off the helmet. I was also keeping an eye on his heart rate, on his breathing, on his general condition. And over and over I kept saying, "I'm a doctor. Please don't touch him. Please leave the helmet alone."

Do you know what I was wishing? Well, first and foremost that I wasn't wearing those flip-flops; they seemed to me to undercut my authority completely. But what I really wished was that I was six foot four, male, and an ex-football player, someone who could just bellow, "Stand back, everyone, I'm in charge here!" And, in my fantasy, everyone would immediately stand back, relieved to have someone in control.

Well, I did the right things. The ambulance arrived, and the EMTs splinted his broken bones and stabilized his neck, took him off to the hospital where X rays would show whether there was in fact an injury to his spinal cord. And I walked away feeling dissatisfied with myself, because I know perfectly well that you don't have to be an ex–running back to claim authority—when that authority is rightfully yours. You ought to be able to do it by force of character, manner, and self-confidence. But it isn't always easy.

Part of medical training is a rapid increase in authority; over a couple of years, you go from being a medical student—a novice in the hospital with no real power—to being an intern, a junior resident, a senior resident. You find yourself teaching medical students, supervising interns—you find yourself taking on, quite literally, responsibility for life-and-death decisions. And you have to come to terms with this authority. You have to accept it, learn to feel entitled to your own power. You have to develop a style for making decisions, giving orders, a style that works effectively with other doctors, with nurses, and with patients.

I've had a lot of trouble accepting my own authority over the past couple of years. It seems to me, in general, that women struggle with this whole question more than men do. Maybe men feel more entitled to power—or more unwilling to admit it if they are insecure. Also, there are time-honored styles of male authority in the hospital, and it often seems that men giving orders get immediate results—even if they aren't football players. But women may have to earn their authority, and it's just harder, in general, for women to use those commanding military tones that have traditionally gotten results for male doctors ("Scalpel!"). At the same time, women may not be easily forgiven for sounding brusque, or for taking control too assertively. We have to find our own way, develop our own special manner—and you can only do that if you feel entitled to your authority, if you are really ready to claim it.

In my training program, we have practice emergencies, situations where a group of doctors and nurses "resuscitate" a plastic dummy (the dummies come in baby, child, and adult sizes). At the beginning of my second year of residency, they told me it was my turn to run the resuscitation, give the orders. I said, quite honestly, that I wasn't ready, that I had no idea how to run a resuscitation. I knew how to follow orders—

how to do chest compressions, give the "patient" oxygen, or start the IV, but I couldn't run the damn thing. "That's the point," said the supervising doctor, gently. "You need to hear yourself say it. You'll hear your voice saying, 'Why don't we give him some—some—some—*epineph-rine!*' And there you'll be." Epinephrine, or adrenaline, is one of the drugs we give most commonly in resuscitations, since it acts as a cardiac stimulant. I had never ordered it before in such a situation. That night, I practiced saying it to my bathroom mirror. First I practiced Taking Control. "I'm in charge here, I'm running this resuscitation," I said firmly to the mirror. "Let's give him some epinephrine."

The next morning, at the resuscitation, a gang of interns and nurses looked at me expectantly, clustered around the plastic dummy. I heard my own voice, an octave higher than it had been when I talked to the mirror. "Why don't we give some—some—some—epinephrine!" I squeaked, and they did.

The authority of the "crash," the sudden life-and-death emergency, is the authority residents tend to fear most—a child will be found not breathing, and I'll be the only one there. Someone who was doing just fine will start to die before my eyes. But as residency moved along, I found that that authority did in fact come to me when I needed it. When I had to give those orders I gave them, though my voice still has a lamentable tendency to squeak. I find that I no longer automatically look around for a doctor when a sudden emergency occurs; it seems to have gotten through to me that I *am* a doctor. But there are other kinds of authority that may not loom quite so large, but which are even harder to assume, even harder to own. I remember once when a baby was brought to the emergency room essentially dead on arrival, a victim of sudden infant death syndrome, or crib death. We tried for half an hour to resuscitate that baby, not willing to admit that the small, perfect, still-warm body could really be beyond our help. But he was, and the senior doctor asked me to go out and tell the parents. And so I sat down with them and tried to explain, tried to give them answers they could believe, about a disease that nobody understands. I had to tell them, no, this did not happen because your apartment is too warm, no, it did not happen because you gave the baby a different brand of formula today—*it was not your fault.* I needed a particular mix of confidence, authority, and sympathy for that family, and I hope I found it.

As I have slowly claimed my authority as a doctor, I have worried that I may carry over some of those mannerisms into my life outside the hospital. I have learned to behave, in certain situations, as if I am the one with the final say, the one with the power. This does not go over particularly well on the home front. I have learned, when the going gets rough, to cut through the argument and give orders, make my choices, and accept the consequences. This is not a recommended technique for resolving arguments with one's significant other. The cliché of the surgeon's wife, who is constantly reminding her husband that he is no longer in the operating room, is relevant. Women cannot get away with this kind of behavior at home, by and large, and sometimes I think that the fear of sounding like I am trying to give orders has actually made me more wishy-washy in my personal life.

In a way, the most difficult authority for me to accept has been the responsibility in situations where I cannot help. A couple of months ago I was working in the newborn intensive care unit, it was the middle of the night, and a baby was getting sicker and sicker. I was working with the baby's nurse; together we did everything that could be done, increasing the help that the baby got from her respirator, adding one drug after another. It was becoming very clear that the baby was going to die, and I wondered whether I should wake up a more senior doctor and ask him to come help out. But the more I thought about it, the more I realized that there was nothing else he could do; I would be calling him in only so that he could be there to preside over our medical helplessness. The baby could not be saved. So I didn't call him. I just stayed there, with the nurse, doing what could be done. And toward morning, as I bent over the baby, I heard the nurse say, "You know, it's at moments like these that I'm really glad that I'm the nurse and you're the doctor." So I looked over my shoulder to see what doctor she was talking to—but there was no one else there. She was talking to me.

Greenwich Village

JOYCE JOHNSON

IT'S THE SPRING of 1949 and I'm thirteen and a half. With my best friend Maria, I am sitting in the very front seat of the top deck of a double-decker bus as it makes its way down lower Fifth Avenue toward Greenwich Village, which I've been assured is the very last stop—thus impossible to miss. Suddenly we see it, the famous arch that's supposed to be the entrance to Washington Square and to lots of other things— perhaps a life of romance and adventure—that I've heard about from four older, very knowledgeable Trotskyite girls whom I've met in the basement of Hunter College High School. Juniors who disdain the bourgeois cafeteria upstairs, they lunch secretly on yogurt deep in the locker room. They carry bags of knitting under which there are copies of the *Militant*, which they hawk around Fourteenth Street nearly every day after school. They have Trotskyite boyfriends whom they make sweaters and argyle socks for and endlessly discuss. They never quite explain to me what *Trotskyite* is, but it seems that if you are one, you're headed for trouble not only with the fascists but with detestable teen-age Stalinists who've been known to harass sellers of the *Militant* and even beat them up. I admire the daring of these girls tremendously, their whole style, in fact—dark clothes and long earrings, the cigarettes they smoke illicitly, the many cups of coffee they say they require to keep them going. Friendly as they are, however, they never invite me on their rounds. With Olympian disinterest, they delineate a territory that it's up to me to explore for myself.

As the bus lurches under the arch, Maria and I are leaning all the way forward in our seats, clutching hands. It's that moment when fantasy and expectation collide with reality, when what you've been told exists really turns out to be there—not quite as you've pictured it, but close enough. Here is the arch, as described by the Trotskyite girls, and there is the fountain, the circle in the square where, according to them, people gather every Sunday to sing folk songs. I'd imagined hordes of people, a whole guitar- and banjo-strumming population, their music ringing through the park—but hadn't trusted the glamour of that picture in my mind. I'd thought we mightn't find anyone at all.

Actually today there are about six of them—a few young men in old army jackets, a tall, blonde girl in faded jeans, a man in a wheelchair. They look a little drab, in fact—perhaps because it's also begun to rain. The drops fall on Maria and me as we rush over to them from the bus. Washington Square is emptying out fast. Wouldn't you know it—we've arrived just too late. In another moment they'll be packing up their instruments.

They stand their ground, however. The men turn up the collars of their jackets. As their audience vanishes, they launch into a new and appropriate song, "Let the Circle Be Unbroken," which they sing as loudly as possible into the wind that thins out their voices, disperses them like so much smoke. The rain rattles down harder. I wouldn't move out of it for anything.

I've fallen in love with them all. It's as though a longing I've carried inside myself has suddenly crystallized. To be lonely within a camaraderie of loneliness.

I watch them intently, especially the blonde girl, as if I could wish myself into her. She can't be *that* much older than I am, maybe sixteen, and yet she's been accepted by these grownup-looking men. (At that time in my life I have the strange conviction that the last person any adult male would be interested in is a young girl.) She has glasses and long pale stringy hair and a skinny body hidden inside a man's shirt several sizes too big for her that's torn at one shoulder—*my* mother would never let me out in anything that was torn. You'd think she was beautiful, the way she acts. And maybe she is. The more I watch her, the more I come to believe it.

She's shivering and laughing in the rain, twisting her hair into rope like wash she's wringing out. One of the men holds open his jacket and she ducks into the shelter of it, standing pressed against his side in a warmth I can only imagine with despair. Even now I only look eleven— that's my curse. My outside doesn't reflect my inside, so no one knows who I really am.

With my friend Maria, it's a different story. Maria's outside has that eerie agelessness some girls get so quickly and mysteriously, blooming overnight into child-women. Maria's baby fat has given way to definition—cheekbones, sharp little breasts; the slant of her eyes hints at experience she hasn't yet lived. It's Maria who connects us to this group of strangers.

The rain is getting serious, the sky is definitely black. Calling it a day, the young men snap their guitars into cases. Maria just walks up to one of them. "Where are you going now?" she says to him. "Are you going to sing somewhere else?" If it were left to me, I couldn't have gotten out one word.

He looks at her and smiles at this dark, eager, rather exotic, willowy kid. ("Did anyone ever tell you," more and more people keep telling Maria, "you look just like Gene Tierney?" "That's because my face is so Russian," she explains modestly. "Both my parents are Russian, you know.") "Are you going to come back next Sunday?" she asks. "My friend and I are learning the guitar."

"Is that so?" he says. "Maybe next time you'll bring yours."

"But we don't play very well yet."

This young man's still smiling at Maria in the most extraordinarily friendly way. "Why don't you come along and have some coffee? We're all going to the Art Center. Your friend, too," he says.

That's how easy it was.

I GOT home that first Sunday just in time for dinner. What did I tell my parents that night? Maria and I spent the afternoon doing homework? We went to the movies? Did my mind race guiltily through the current attractions, picking the one we saw? I knew the truth would be fatal. We took the Fifth Avenue bus to Washington Square. We talked to strange men. We went with them to the Art Center—which was not a center of all the arts, as I'd first thought, but a luncheonette on Eighth Street—a classic greasy spoon that would be rechristened The Griddle less misleadingly two years later. There we had coffee, which I was not allowed to drink at home. It seemed as wicked to drink coffee as to drink a martini. I had to put six sugars in mine to get it down. The men talked to Maria, really, rather than to me. Mostly they talked to each other about versions of folk songs that they wrote down in little notebooks, and someone called Pete Seeger, and there was a joke ending with the punchline "What's the party line on that?" which made them all laugh. The blonde girl necked with her boyfriend; she kicked off her shoes under the table. The man in the wheelchair was a doomed millionaire who lived on Park Avenue. He was a hemophiliac, which I had never heard of—Maria whispered to me it meant that if he got even a tiny scratch he'd bleed to death. He was bloated and greenish pale with brown circles under his eyes, and quite irritable, which seemed understandable under the circumstances. He collected—guitars, banjos, hundreds of folk and blues records; people, too, these people, for whom we heard he gave parties uptown, astonishing the snooty doormen with his guests. Would Maria and I ever go to any of these parties?

What all this seemed to promise was something I'd never tasted in my life as a child—something I told myself was Real Life. This was not the life my parents lived but one that was dramatic, unpredictable, possibly dangerous. Therefore *real*, infinitely more worth having. In trying to trace the derivations of this notion of experience, I come into blind alleys. It was simply there all of a sudden, full-fledged, like a fever I'd come down with. The air carries ideas like germs, infecting some, not others.

Real Life was not to be found in the streets around my house, or anywhere on the Upper West Side, for that matter, or in my school of girls grubbing joylessly for marks, hysterical about geometry exams and Latin homework, flirting ridiculously with the seventy-year-old elevator operator, the only male visible on the premises.

Real Life was sexual. Or rather, it often seemed to take the form of sex. This was the area of ultimate adventure, where you would dare or not dare. It was much less a question of desire. Sex was like a forbidden castle whose name could not even be spoken around the house, so feared was its power. Only with the utmost vigilance could you avoid being sucked into its magnetic field. The alternative was to break into the castle and take its power for yourself.

WE GO down to the Square the next Sunday and the one after that and the following one. The weather gets warmer; the fountain in the circle is finally turned on; people come out of cold-water flats and into the sun. New musicians arrive and either become regulars or make memorable one-shot appearances—like the man who came all the way down from Harlem with his washtub and broomstick one-string bass, or the old white-mustached Italian mandolinist who tremoloed his way one afternoon through "Oh Mary, don't you weep, don't you mourn" and "Take This Hammer" and "Put it on the ground / Spread it all around / If you dig it with a hoe, it will make your *flow*-ers grow." Proletarian musicians cause particular excitement. Although we sing the music of "The People," it is *they*, after all, who are the genuine article.

My whole being during the humdrum week is focused on these Sundays. At night I shut myself into my room and strum the guitar incessantly, singing the songs I've learned under my breath so as to escape my mother's critical ear. "Why are you spending so much time on that? You should be playing the piano more if you want to get anywhere." But the guitar, not the piano, is my passport to the world downtown.

Besides the music, I'm learning a great many other things very rapidly, such as the fact that America is a place of enormous injustice and inequality, where the little children of miners starve in shacks and where Negro men are lynched or jailed for crimes that are not even crimes, such as whistling at a white woman. . . . I learn that a picket line is something you never cross, lest you become a fink, and that espresso is black and bitter so it's much better to order cappuccino made with steamed frothy milk and cinnamon. . . . And that going crazy is not something frowned upon in the Village but sort of respected if done by artists.

I long to turn myself into a Bohemian, but lack the proper clothes. Oh, the belts I see in the Sorcerer's Apprentice, which is tucked away in a little courtyard off Eighth Street, like a cobbler's shop in a fairy tale. That's where everyone gets them. There are two styles that are popular. One laces up the front like the girdle of Lena the Goosegirl; the other fastens dramatically with a spiral made of brass about the size of a saucer. Such a belt—aside from enhancing your appearance, which I was sure it would immeasurably—is a badge, a sign of membership in the ranks of the unconventional. The way is smoothed for the wearer of this belt, or of the dirndl skirt of lumpy handwoven material that usually goes with it, not to mention the sandals crisscrossing up the ankle, or the finishing touch of a piece of freeform jewelry like a Rorschach test figure dangling down to the midriff by a thong. The way is smoothed because the problem of outside matching inside is so beautifully resolved by this simple means, which only costs money. I'd have been humiliated if anyone had told me that the desire to possess these items was, within a different context, like the desire to possess a certain kind of baseball jacket.

Somehow, early on, I do manage to acquire a pair of long copper earrings. They clank reassuringly against my neck in the slightest breeze, and pull at my ear lobes. I carry them with me at all times in case I need them. They constitute my downtown disguise. Peering into the dirty mirror of a gum machine in the West Fourth Street station of the IND to see how different they make me look, I put them on before I walk over to the Square.

I'm cool and clever as any double agent needs to be. No one on 116th Street would guess my destination. I have switched my route to the subway, so much faster than the bus. I can get to the Village a whole half-hour earlier, and wait till the very last minute to go home to make my seven o'clock curfew. Sunday by Sunday my "last minute" gets later, pushing the outer boundaries of safety. At 7:15 I can still walk in the door with some innocuous excuse for my mother. . . .

Nothing seems crueler than my curfew. I feel I'm missing Everything—whatever Everything it is that happens after seven o'clock. . . .

By 6:15 I start getting ready to tear myself away for another week. As the seconds bleed from the minutes, I'm in an odd state of heightened longing and anxiety. I feel much the same in later years whenever I part from a man I love. The anxiety is not so much over leaving as over an impending fading of identity.

# My Amoeba

ANNIE DILLARD

After I read *The Field Book of Ponds and Streams* several times, I longed for a microscope. Everybody needed a microscope. Detectives used microscopes, both for the FBI and at Scotland Yard. Although usually I had to save my tiny allowance for things I wanted, that year for Christmas my parents gave me a microscope kit.

In a dark basement corner, on a white enamel table, I set up the microscope kit. I supplied a chair, a lamp, a batch of jars, a candle, and a pile of library books. The microscope kit supplied a blunt black three-speed microscope, a booklet, a scalpel, a dropper, an ingenious device for cutting thin segments of fragile tissue, a pile of clean slides and cover slips, and a dandy array of corked test tubes.

One of the test tubes contained "hay infusion." Hay infusion was a wee brown chip of grass blade. You added water to it, and after a week it became a jungle in a drop, full of one-celled animals. This did not work for me. All I saw in the microscope after a week was a wet chip of dried grass, much enlarged.

Another test tube contained "diatomaceous earth." This was, I believed, an actual pinch of the white cliffs of Dover. On my palm it was an airy, friable chalk. The booklet said it was composed of the silicaceous bodies of diatoms—one-celled creatures that lived in, as it were, small glass jewelry boxes with fitted lids. Diatoms, I read, come in a variety of transparent geometrical shapes. Broken and dead and dug out of geological deposits, they made chalk, and a fine abrasive used in silver polish and toothpaste. What I saw in the microscope must have been the fine abrasive—grit enlarged. It was years before I saw a recognizable, whole diatom. The kit's diatomaceous earth was a bust.

All that winter I played with the microscope. I prepared slides from things at hand, as the books suggested. I looked at the transparent membrane inside an onion's skin and saw the cells. I looked at a section of cork and saw the cells, and at scrapings from the inside of my cheek, ditto. I looked at my blood and saw not much; I looked at my urine and saw long iridescent crystals, for the drop had dried.

All this was very well, but I wanted to see the wildlife I had read about. I wanted especially to see the famous amoeba, who had eluded me. He was supposed to live in the hay infusion, but I hadn't found him there. He lived outside in warm ponds and streams, too, but I lived in Pittsburgh, and it had been a cold winter.

Finally late that spring I saw an amoeba. The week before, I had gathered puddle water from Frick Park; it had been festering in a jar in the basement. This June night after dinner I figured I had waited long enough. In the basement at my microscope table I spread a scummy drop of Frick Park puddle water on a slide, peeked in, and lo, there was the famous amoeba. He was as blobby and grainy as his picture; I would have known him anywhere.

Before I had watched him at all, I ran upstairs. My parents were still at table, drinking coffee. They, too, could see the famous amoeba. I told them, bursting, that he was all set up, that they should hurry before his water dried. It was the chance of a lifetime.

Father had stretched out his long legs and was tilting back in his chair. Mother sat with her knees crossed, in blue slacks, smoking a Chesterfield. The dessert dishes were still on the table. My sisters were nowhere in evidence. It was a warm evening; the big dining-room windows gave onto blooming rhododendrons.

Mother regarded me warmly. She gave me to understand that she was glad I had found what I had been looking for, but that she and Father were happy to sit with their coffee and would not be coming down.

She did not say, but I understood at once, that they had their pursuits (coffee?) and I had mine. She did not say, but I began to understand then, that you do what you do out of your private passion for the thing itself.

I had essentially been handed my own life. In subsequent years my parents would praise my drawings and poems, and supply me with books, art supplies, and sports equipment, and listen to my troubles and enthusiasms, and supervise my hours, and discuss and inform, but they would not get involved with my detective work, nor hear about my reading, nor inquire about my homework or term papers or exams, nor visit the salamanders I caught, nor listen to me play the piano, nor attend my field hockey games, nor fuss over my insect collection with me, or my poetry collection or stamp collection or rock collection. My days and nights were my own to plan and fill.

WHEN I left the dining room that evening and started down the dark basement stairs, I had a life. I sat to my wonderful amoeba, and there he was, rolling his grains more slowly now, extending an arc of his edge for a foot and drawing himself along by that foot, and absorbing it again and rolling on. I gave him some more pond water.

I had hit pay dirt. For all I knew, there were paramecia, too, in that pond water, or daphniae, or stentors, or any of the many other creatures I had read about and never seen: volvox, the spherical algal colony; euglena with its one red eye; the elusive, glassy diatom; hydra, rotifers, water bears, worms. Anything was possible. The sky was the limit.

Mirrorings

LUCY GREALY

THERE was a long period of time, almost a year, during which I never looked in a mirror. It wasn't easy, for I'd never suspected just how omnipresent are our own images. I began by merely avoiding mirrors, but by the end of the year I found myself with an acute knowledge of the reflected image, its numerous tricks and wiles, how it can spring up at any moment: a glass tabletop, a well-polished door handle, a darkened window, a pair of sunglasses, a restaurant's otherwise magnificent brass-plated coffee machine sitting innocently by the cash register.

At the time, I had just moved, alone, to Scotland and was surviving on the dole, as Britain's social security benefits are called. I didn't know anyone and had no idea how I was going to live, yet I went anyway because by happenstance I'd met a plastic surgeon there who said he could help me. I had been living in London, working temp jobs. While in London, I'd received more nasty comments about my face than I had in the previous three years, living in Iowa, New York, and Germany. These comments, all from men and all odiously sexual, hurt and disoriented me. I also had journeyed to Scotland because after more than a dozen operations in the States my insurance had run out, along with my hope that further operations could make any *real* difference. Here, however, was a surgeon who had some new techniques, and here, amazingly enough, was a government willing to foot the bill: I didn't feel I could pass up yet another chance to "fix" my face, which I confusedly thought concurrent with "fixing" my self, my soul, my life.

TWENTY years ago, when I was nine and living in America, I came home from school one day with a toothache. Several weeks and misdiagnoses later, surgeons removed most of the right side of my jaw in an attempt to prevent the cancer they found there from spreading. No one properly explained the operation to me, and I awoke in a cocoon of pain that prevented me from moving or speaking. Tubes ran in and out of my body, and because I was temporarily unable to speak after the surgery and could not ask questions, I made up my own explanations for the tubes' existence. I remember the mysterious manner the adults displayed toward me. They asked me to do things: lie still for x-rays, not cry for needles, and so on, tasks that, although not easy, never seemed equal to the praise I received in return. Reinforced to me again and again was how I was "a brave girl" for not crying, "a good girl" for not complaining, and soon I began defining myself this way, equating strength with silence.

Then the chemotherapy began. In the seventies chemo was even cruder than it is now, the basic premise being to poison patients right up to the very brink of their own death. Until this point I almost never cried and almost always received praise in return. Thus I got what I considered the better part of the deal. But now it was like a practical joke that had gotten out of hand. Chemotherapy was a nightmare and I wanted it to stop; I didn't want to be brave anymore. Yet I had grown so used to defining myself as "brave" — i.e., *silent* — that the thought of losing this sense of myself was even more terrifying. I was certain that if I broke down I would be despicable in the eyes of both my parents and the doctors.

The task of taking me into the city for the chemo injections fell mostly on my mother, though sometimes my father made the trip. Overwhelmed by the sight of the vomiting and weeping, my father developed the routine of "going to get the car," meaning that he left the doctor's office before the injection was administered, on the premise that then he could have the car ready and waiting when it was all over. Ashamed of my suffering, I felt relief when he was finally out of the room. When my mother took me, she stayed in the room, yet this only made the distance between us even more tangible. She explained that it was wrong to cry *before* the needle went in; afterward was one thing, but before, that was mere fear, and hadn't I demonstrated my bravery earlier? Every Friday for two and a half years I climbed up onto that big doctor's table and told myself not to cry, and every week I failed. The two large syringes were filled with chemicals so caustic to the vein that each had to be administered very slowly. The whole process took about four minutes; I had to remain utterly still. Dry retching began in the first fifteen seconds, then the throb behind my eyes gave everything a yellow-green aura, and the bone-deep pain of alternating extreme hot and cold flashes made me tremble, yet still I had to sit motionless and not move my arm. No one spoke to me — not the doctor, who was a paradigm of the cold-fish physician; not the nurse, who told my mother I reacted much more violently than many of "the other children"; and not my mother, who, surely overwhelmed by the sight of her child's suffering, thought the best thing to do was remind me to be brave, to try not to cry. All the while I hated myself for having wept before the needle went in, convinced that the nurse and my mother were right, that I was "overdoing it," that the throwing up was psychosomatic, that my mother was angry with me for not being good or brave enough.

Yet each week, two or three days after the injection, there came the first flicker of feeling better, the always forgotten and gratefully rediscovered understanding that to simply be well in my body was the greatest thing I could ask for. I thought other people felt this appreciation and physical joy all the time, and I felt cheated because I was able to feel it only once a week.

BECAUSE I'd lost my hair, I wore a hat constantly, but this fooled no one, least of all myself. During this time, my mother worked in a nursing home in a Hasidic community. Hasidic law dictates that married women cover their hair, and most commonly this is done with a wig. My mother's friends were now all too willing to donate their discarded wigs, and soon the house seemed filled with them. I never wore one, for they frightened me even when my mother insisted I looked better in one of the few that actually fit. Yet we didn't know how to say no to the women who kept graciously offering their wigs. The cats enjoyed sleeping on them and the dogs playing with them, and we grew used to having to pick a wig up off a chair we wanted to sit in. It never struck us as odd until one day a visitor commented wryly as he cleared a chair for himself, and suddenly a great wave of shame overcame me. I had nightmares about wigs and flushed if I even heard the word, and one night I put myself out of my misery by getting up after everyone was asleep and gathering all the wigs except for one the dogs were fond of and that they had chewed up anyway. I hid all the rest in an old chest.

When you are only ten, which is when the chemotherapy began, two and a half years seem like your whole life, yet it did finally end, for the cancer was gone. I remember the last day of treatment clearly because it was the only day on which I succeeded in not crying, and because later, in private, I cried harder than I had in years; I thought now I would no longer be "special," that without the arena of chemotherapy in which to prove myself no one would ever love me, that I would fade unnoticed into the background. But this idea about *not being different* didn't last very long. Before, I foolishly believed that people stared at me because I was bald. After my hair eventually grew in, it didn't take long before I understood that I looked different for another reason. My face. People stared at me in stores, and other children made fun of me to the point that I came to expect such reactions constantly, wherever I went. School became a battleground.

Halloween, that night of frights, became my favorite holiday because I could put on a mask and walk among the blessed for a few brief, sweet hours. Such freedom I felt, walking down the street, my face hidden! Through the imperfect oval holes I could peer out at other faces, masked or painted or not, and see on those faces nothing but the normal faces of childhood looking back at me, faces I mistakenly thought were the faces everyone else but me saw all the time, faces that were simply curious and ready for fun, not the faces I usually braced myself for, the cruel, lonely, vicious ones I spent every day other than Halloween waiting to see around each corner. As I breathed in the condensed, plastic-scented air under the mask, I somehow thought that I was breathing in normality, that this joy and weightlessness were what the world was composed of, and that it was only my face that kept me from it, my face that was my own mask that kept me from knowing the joy I was sure everyone but me lived with intimately. How could the other children not know it? Not know that to be free of the fear of taunts and the burden of knowing no one would ever love you was all that anyone could ever ask for? I was a pauper walking for a short while in the clothes of the prince, and when the day ended I gave up my disguise with dismay.

I WAS LIVING in an extreme situation, and because I did not particularly care for the world I was in, I lived in others, and because the world I did live in was dangerous now, I incorporated this danger into my secret life. I imagined myself to be an Indian. Walking down the streets, I stepped through the forest, my body ready for any opportunity to fight or flee one of the big cats that I knew stalked me. Vietnam and Cambodia, in the news then as scenes of catastrophic horror, were other places I walked through daily. I made my way down the school hall, knowing a land mine or a sniper might give themselves away at any moment with the subtle metal click I'd read about. Compared with a land mine, a mere insult about my face seemed a frivolous thing.

In those years, not yet a teenager, I secretly read—knowing it was somehow inappropriate—works by Primo Levi and Elie Wiesel, and every book by a survivor I could find by myself without asking the librarian. Auschwitz, Birkenau: I felt the blows of the capos and somehow knew that because at any moment we might be called upon to live for a week on one loaf of bread and some water called soup, the peanut-butter sandwich I found on my plate was nothing less than a miracle, an utter and sheer miracle capable of making me literally weep with joy.

I decided to become a "deep" person. I wasn't exactly sure what this would entail, but I believed that if I could just find the right philosophy, think the right thoughts, my suffering would end. To try to understand the world I was in, I undertook to find out what was "real," and I quickly began seeing reality as existing in the lowest common denominator, that suffering was the one and only dependable thing. But rather than spend all of my time despairing, though certainly I did plenty of that, I developed a form of defensive egomania: I felt I was the only one walking about in the world who understood what was really important. I looked upon people complaining about the most mundane things—nothing on TV, traffic jams, the price of new clothes—and felt joy because I knew how unimportant those things really were and felt unenlightened superiority because other people didn't. Because in my fantasy life I had learned to be thankful for each cold, blanketless night that I survived on the cramped wooden bunks, my pain and despair were a stroll through the country in comparison. I was often miserable, but I knew that to feel warm instead of cold was its own kind of joy, that to eat was a reenactment of the grace of some god whom I could only dimly define, and that to simply be alive was a rare, ephemeral gift.

As I became a teenager, my isolation began. My nonidentical twin sister started going out with boys, and I started—my most tragic mistake of all—to listen to and believe the taunts thrown at me daily by the very boys she and the other girls were interested in. I was a dog, a monster, the ugliest girl they had ever seen. Of all the remarks, the most damaging wasn't even directed at me but was really an insult to "Jerry," a boy I never saw because every day between fourth and fifth periods, when I was cornered by a particular group of kids, I was too ashamed to lift my eyes off the floor. "Hey, look, it's Jerry's girlfriend!" they shrieked when they saw me, and I felt such shame, knowing that this was the deepest insult to Jerry that they could imagine.

When pressed to it, one makes compensations. I came to love winter, when I could wrap up the disfigured lower half of my face in a scarf: I could speak to people and they would have no idea to whom and to what they were really speaking. I developed the bad habits of letting my long hair hang in my face and of always covering my chin and mouth with my hand, hoping it might be mistaken as a thoughtful, accidental gesture. I also became interested in horses and got a job at a rundown local stable. Having those horses to go to each day after school saved my life; I spent all of my time either with them or thinking about them. Completely and utterly repressed by the time I was sixteen, I was convinced that I would never want a boyfriend, not ever, and wasn't it convenient for me, even a blessing, that none would ever want me. I told myself I was free to concentrate on the "true reality" of life, whatever that was. My sister and her friends put on blue eye shadow, blow-dried their hair, and spent interminable hours in the local mall, and I looked down on them for this, knew they were misleading themselves and being overly occupied with the "mere surface" of living. I'd had thoughts like this when I was younger, ten or twelve, but now my philosophy was haunted by desires so frightening I was unable even to admit they existed.

THROUGHOUT all of this, I was undergoing reconstructive surgery in an attempt to rebuild my jaw. It started when I was fifteen, two years after chemo ended. I had known for years I would have operations to fix my face, and at night I fantasized about how good my life would finally be then. One day I got a clue that maybe it wouldn't be so easy. An older plastic surgeon explained the process of "pedestals" to me, and told me it would take *ten years* to fix my face. Ten years? Why even bother, I thought; I'll be ancient by then. I went to a medical library and looked up the "pedestals" he talked about. There were gruesome pictures of people with grotesque tubes of their own skin growing out of their bodies, tubes of skin that were harvested like some kind of crop and then rearranged, with results that did not look at all normal or acceptable to my eye. But then I met a younger surgeon, who was working on a new way of grafting that did not involve pedestals, and I became more hopeful and once again began to await the fixing of my face, the day when I would be whole, content, loved.

Long-term plastic surgery is not like in the movies. There is no one single operation that will change everything, and there is certainly no slow unwrapping of the gauze in order to view the final, remarkable result. There is always swelling, sometimes to a grotesque degree, there are often bruises, and always there are scars. After each operation, too frightened to simply go look in the mirror, I developed an oblique method, with several stages. First, I tried to catch my reflection in an overhead lamp: the roundness of the metal distorted my image just enough to obscure details and give no true sense of size or proportion. Then I slowly worked my way up to looking at the reflection in someone's eyeglasses, and from there I went to walking as briskly as possible by a mirror, glancing only quickly. I repeated this as many times as it would take me, passing the mirror slightly more slowly each time until finally I was able to stand still and confront myself.

The theory behind most reconstructive surgery is to take large chunks of muscle, skin, and bone and slap them into the roughly appropriate place, then slowly begin to carve this mess into some sort of shape. It involves long, major operations, countless lesser ones, a lot of pain, and many, many years. And also, it does not always work. With my young surgeon in New York, who with each passing year was becoming not so young, I had two or three soft-tissue grafts, two skin grafts, a bone graft, and some dozen other operations to "revise" my face, yet when I left graduate school at the age of twenty-five I was still more or less in the same position I had started in: a deep hole in the right side of my face and a rapidly shrinking left side and chin, a result of the radiation I'd had as a child and the stress placed upon the bone by the other operations. I was caught in a cycle of having a big operation, one that would force me to look monstrous from the swelling for many months, then having the subsequent revision operations that improved my looks tremendously, and then slowly, over the period of a few months or a year, watching the graft reabsorb back into my body, slowly shrinking down and leaving me with nothing but the scarred donor site the graft had originally come from.

IT WASN'T until I was in college that I finally allowed that maybe, just maybe, it might be nice to have a boyfriend. I went to a small, liberal, predominantly female school and suddenly, after years of alienation in high school, discovered that there were other people I could enjoy talking to who thought me intelligent and talented. I was, however, still operating on the assumption that no one, not ever, would be physically attracted to me, and in a curious way this shaped my personality. I became forthright and honest in the way that only the truly self-confident are, who do not expect to be rejected, and in the way of those like me, who do not even dare to ask acceptance from others and therefore expect no rejection. I had come to know myself as a person, but I would be in graduate school before I was literally, physically able to use my name and the word "woman" in the same sentence.

Now my friends repeated for me endlessly that most of it was in my mind, that, granted, I did not look like everyone else, but that didn't mean I looked bad. I am sure now that they were right some of the time. But with the constant surgery I was in a perpetual state of transfiguration. I rarely looked the same for more than six months at a time. So ashamed of my face, I was unable even to admit that this constant change affected me; I let everyone who wanted to know that it was only what was inside that mattered, that I had "grown used to" the surgery, that none of it bothered me at all. Just as I had done in childhood, I pretended nothing was wrong, and this was constantly mistaken by others for bravery. I spent a great deal of time looking in the mirror in private, positioning my head to show off my eyes and nose, which were not only normal but quite pretty, as my friends told me often. But I could not bring myself to see them for more than a moment: I looked in the mirror and saw not the normal upper half of my face but only the disfigured lower half.

People still teased me. Not daily, as when I was younger, but in ways that caused me more pain than ever before. Children stared at me, and I learned to cross the street to avoid them; this bothered me, but not as much as the insults I got from men. Their taunts came at me not because I was disfigured but because I was a disfigured *woman*. They came from boys, sometimes men, and almost always from a group of them. I had long, blond hair, and I also had a thin figure. Sometimes, from a distance, men would see a thin blonde and whistle, something I dreaded more than anything else because I knew that as they got closer, their tune, so to speak, would inevitably change; they would stare openly or, worse, turn away quickly in shame or repulsion. I decided to cut my hair to avoid any misconception that anyone, however briefly, might have about my being attractive. Only two or three times have I ever been teased by a single person, and I can think of only one time when I was ever teased by a woman. Had I been a man, would I have had to walk down the street while a group of young women followed and denigrated my sexual worth?

Not surprisingly, then, I viewed sex as my salvation. I was sure that if only I could get someone to sleep with me, it would mean I wasn't ugly, that I was attractive, even lovable. This line of reasoning led me into the beds of several manipulative men who liked themselves even less than they liked me, and I in turn left each short-term affair hating myself, obscenely sure that if only I had been prettier it would have worked—he would have loved me and it would have been like those other love affairs that I was certain "normal" women had all the time. Gradually, I became unable to say "I'm depressed" but could say only "I'm ugly," because the two had become inextricably linked in my mind. Into that universal lie, that sad equation of "if only . . ." that we are all prey to, I was sure that if only I had a normal face, then I would be happy.

THE NEW surgeon in Scotland, Oliver Fenton, recommended that I undergo a procedure involving something called a tissue expander, followed by a bone graft. A tissue expander is a small balloon placed under the skin and then slowly blown up over the course of several months, the object being to stretch out the skin and create room and cover for the new bone. It's a bizarre, nightmarish thing to do to your face, yet I was hopeful about the end results and I was also able to spend the three months that the expansion took in the hospital. I've always felt safe in hospitals: they're the one place I feel free from the need to explain the way I look. For this reason the first tissue expander was bearable—just— and the bone graft that followed it was a success; it did not melt away like the previous ones.

The surgical stress this put upon what remained of my original jaw instigated the deterioration of that bone, however, and it became unhappily apparent that I was going to need the same operation I'd just had on the right side done to the left. I remember my surgeon telling me this at an outpatient clinic. I planned to be traveling down to London that same night on an overnight train, and I barely made it to the station on time, such a fumbling state of despair was I in.

I could not imagine going through it *again*, and just as I had done all my life, I searched and searched through my intellect for a way to make it okay, make it bearable, for a way to *do* it. I lay awake all night on that train, feeling the tracks slip beneath me with an odd eroticism, when I remembered an afternoon from my three months in the hospital. Boredom was a big problem those long afternoons, the days marked by meals and television programs. Waiting for the afternoon tea to come, wondering desperately how I could make time pass, it had suddenly occurred to me that I didn't have to make time pass, that it would do it of its own accord, that I simply had to relax and take no action. Lying on the train, remembering that, I realized I had no obligation to improve my situation, that I didn't have to explain or understand it, that I could just simply let it happen. By the time the train pulled into King's Cross station, I felt able to bear it yet again, not entirely sure what other choice I had.

But there was an element I didn't yet know about. When I returned to Scotland to set up a date to have the tissue expander inserted, I was told quite casually that I'd be in the hospital only three or four days. Wasn't I going to spend the whole expansion time in the hospital? I asked in a whisper. What's the point of that? came the answer. You can just come in every day to the outpatient ward to have it expanded. Horrified by this, I was speechless. I would have to live and move about in the outside world with a giant balloon inside the tissue of my face? I can't remember what I did for the next few days before I went into the hospital, but I vaguely recall that these days involved a great deal of drinking alone in bars and at home.

I had the operation and went home at the end of the week. The only things that gave me any comfort during the months I lived with my tissue expander were my writing and Franz Kafka. I started a novel and completely absorbed myself in it, writing for hours each day. The only way I could walk down the street, could stand the stares I received, was to think to myself, "I'll bet none of them are writing a novel." It was that strange, old, familiar form of egomania, directly related to my dismissive, conceited thoughts of adolescence. As for Kafka, who had always been one of my favorite writers, he helped me in that I felt permission to feel alienated, and to have that alienation be okay, bearable, noble even. In the same way that imagining I lived in Cambodia helped me as a child, I walked the streets of my dark little Scottish city by the sea and knew without doubt that I was living in a story Kafka would have been proud to write.

THE ONE good thing about a tissue expander is that you look so bad with it in that no matter what you look like once it's finally removed, your face has to look better. I had my bone graft and my fifth soft-tissue graft and, yes, even I had to admit I looked better. But I didn't look like me. Something was wrong: was *this* the face I had waited through eighteen years and almost thirty operations for? I somehow just couldn't make what I saw in the mirror correspond to the person I thought I was. It wasn't only that I continued to feel ugly; I simply could not conceive of the image as belonging to me. My own image was the image of a stranger, and rather than try to understand this, I simply stopped looking in the mirror. I perfected the technique of brushing my teeth without a mirror, grew my hair in such a way that it would require only a quick, simple brush, and wore clothes that were simply and easily put on, no complex layers or lines that might require even the most minor of visual adjustments.

On one level I understood that the image of my face was merely that, an image, a surface that was not directly related to any true, deep definition of the self. But I also knew that it is only through appearances that we experience and make decisions about the everyday world, and I was not always able to gather the strength to prefer the deeper world to the shallower one. I looked for ways to find a bridge that would allow me access to both, rather than riding out the constant swings between peace and anguish. The only direction I had to go in to achieve this was to strive for a state of awareness and self-honesty that sometimes, to this day, occasionally rewards me. I have found, I believe, that our whole lives are dominated, though it is not always so clearly translatable, by the question "How do I look?" Take all the many nouns in our lives—car, house, job, family, love, friends—and substitute the personal pronoun "I." It is not that we are all so self-obsessed; it is that all things eventually relate back to ourselves, and it is our own sense of how we appear to the world by which we chart our lives, how we navigate our personalities, which would otherwise be adrift in the ocean of *other* people's obsessions.

ONE EVENING toward the end of my year-long separation from the mirror, I was sitting in a café talking to someone—an attractive man, as it happened—and we were having a lovely, engaging conversation. For some reason I suddenly wondered what I looked like to him. What was he *actually* seeing when he saw me? So many times I've asked this of myself, and always the answer is this: a warm, smart woman, yes, but an unattractive one. I sat there in the café and asked myself this old question, and startlingly, for the first time in my life, I had no answer readily prepared. I had not looked in a mirror for so long that I quite simply had no clue as to what I looked like. I studied the man as he spoke; my entire life I had seen my ugliness reflected back to me. But now, as reluctant as I was to admit it, the only indication in my companion's behavior was positive.

And then, that evening in that café, I experienced a moment of the freedom I'd been practicing for behind my Halloween mask all those years ago. But whereas as a child I expected my liberation to come as a result of gaining something, a new face, it came to me now as the result of shedding something, of shedding my image. I once thought that truth was eternal, that when you understood something it was with you forever. I know now that this isn't so, that most truths are inherently unretainable, that we have to work hard all our lives to remember the most basic things. Society is no help; it tells us again and again that we can most be ourselves by looking like someone else, leaving our own faces behind to turn into ghosts that will inevitably resent and haunt us. It is no mistake that in movies and literature the dead sometimes know they are dead only after they can no longer see themselves in the mirror; and as I sat there feeling the warmth of the cup against my palm, this small observation seemed like a great revelation to me. I wanted to tell the man I was with about it, but he was involved in his own topic and I did not want to interrupt him, so instead I looked with curiosity toward the window behind him, its night-darkened glass reflecting the whole café, to see if I could, now, recognize myself.

Striptease

LAUREN SLATER

A PERSONALITY DISORDER is one of the more troubling diagnoses a mental health clinician can give to someone seeking relief from suffering, because unlike a neurosis, viewed as a set of curable symptoms, or a psychosis, increasingly believed to be the result of a trigger-happy brain in need of mere medication, the personality disordered individual is seen as close to hopeless, beyond the reach of either drugs or healing dialogue. The man or woman with such a diagnosis is thought of as a kind of blighted being, the udder of a cow on the belly of a gazelle, flippers on the side of a skunk. What can you do with this mishmash except try to soothe its confused cries?

George came to our clinic in early autumn and was diagnosed by the intake worker with an antisocial personality disorder—in short, a sociopath, a deviant—whom I, a newcomer to the field of psychology, was now assigned to work with in therapy for an undefined period of time. He looked almost ridiculously tough, sitting in a sleeveless leather vest in the clinic's lobby, hair scrunched back in a ponytail, a cigarette dangling from his mouth. Tattoos coiled over his arms, bloomed on his bare chest.

Immediately I felt awkward in his presence. Perhaps I was experiencing some throwback to my high-school days, when I longed to be liked by the cool and vicious popular kids who stared at the world slant-eyed and wagged their Winstons in the teachers' faces. Around such a crowd I have always felt stout and dumpy, the dust of my ancestors' Jewish shtetl still settled on my skin. The day I met George I was wearing my working garb, a sundress, a pair of falling-apart flats, legs stubbly from hair I'd only half shaved, and perhaps a swatch of slip showing from beneath my hem.

As a therapist, I think I should be beyond these silly social embarrassments. I think I should at least be beyond my own bodily insecurities enough to throw my full attention into the client's waiting lap, but I am not. Around George I am not, and the sense of shame he evokes in me, to this day, is part of our treatment story together.

My office at the time was windowless and so small we had to sit with our knees near brushing. I got ready to ask my usual orienting questions. Especially with a client like George, who makes rise in me my own archaic discomforts, these questions are like life rafts I throw myself, bright verbal floats I can cling to.

"Age?" I asked.

Instead of answering me, George gave a dramatic sigh. "Whew," he said, "have I been waiting for this day. I've seen six of you guys and so far no one's worked out. I need a doc who can really push me. I need to be challenged."

In my mind then I pictured a boxing ring, a hefty human in each corner, thick leather mitts poised for the punch.

"Challenged?" I asked. "Like how?"

"I've got my problems," George said, "and I can admit to them. The other six I went to just sat there and stared at me. I want someone who will give me feedback, make me see things in a new way."

"So what are these problems?"

George sat back, ran one hand over a large tattoo on his bicep. "Masturbation," he said gravely. "I can't stop."

"Can't—"

"Nope! Seven, eight, nine times a day. I have a strong drive." He shook his head in wonder. He looked proud, like a little boy opening a toy chest to show his speckled marbles and magnificent seven-sailed ship. Now he pulled a list out of his pocket and began to read. "Masturbation, pornography, aggression, defensiveness, pride, control. These are my character defects. Take porn. I love it, but the truth is I'd rather do it with a videotape than with my girlfriend Joanne. We have huge beefs, huge," George said. "My anger is just—" He paused. "Like I think I could kill her. I've killed a few people before so I wouldn't put it past me." George was staring straight at me when he said this, testing me for my reaction.

"So why do you think you prefer porn to people?" I said, keeping my voice even despite the fact that I suddenly felt like fleeing.

"Don't get me wrong," George said. "I like Joanne. She's a real smoker. But I'll be honest, a picture's just a lot easier. No one you gotta talk to. No one to perform for or try to please. Just a completely quiet and beautiful bod."

I thought of my own "bod" then and felt my breasts beneath my dress burn with shame.

FOR THE REST of that session I gathered background information. George is thirty-five years old, has lived seven of those years on the street, drugging, knife fighting, and stealing. During those years he slept beneath fire escapes and went in and out of prisons, where the beds were warmer, the dope cheaper. He has been clean now for a half-decade, a really remarkable achievement, which he attributes to his spirituality, a weird blend of mysticism and heavy metal. In his apartment, where he lived with Joanne, he has two special cupboards side by side. In one of them he keeps his incense and tarot cards, his books on palm reading; in the other he stores his collection of sadomasochistic videos and magazines. Oddly, this second cupboard is lined with floral contact paper left by a previous tenant.

They bring him satisfaction, these videos. A lot goes on for him each day. Joanne is, as he said, a beautiful woman, but she is also unpredictable and self-absorbed, a series of seismic cycles he cannot control. "Modern woman," he says, shaking his head. He tells me he is from the old school, expects his girl to cook and clean, to have fish on the table by six each night, expects dustless halls and sex where her moans are synchronized to his orgasms. When Joanne lets him down in any of these areas, he gets mad, really red-faced furious, so that he hauls her up against the wall, wallops her across the face; he feels so much sheer and irrational hate that he has to retreat to his room to watch his videos; they soothe him, images of female flesh cut into, female flesh controlled, the man pumping with pride above her.

Just by writing these words I can feel George's anger, his gut lust to control. It is real to me, this hate of the female form. In our first several sessions I tried to find the origins of his hate. For instance, George's father, a stonemason, dead now for ten years. He went to work at six in the morning, returned after eight each night, his face similar to the substances he worked with, features descending like ledges to a jutting chin nicked with a dimple. He would have been a handsome man except his expression was so stern and his breath smelled; when he was drunk, George imagined his father's breath took on the color of the liquor he swallowed, so he exhaled yellow on whiskey nights, neon green on Midora.

His father beat him, but the beatings were not as bad as the humiliation that went along with them. He remembers the strap, the hands that were like hatchets, but the intensity of his tale lies for me in this image: a small boy pressed against a refrigerator, white as a nuptial bedsheet, the man pressing against him, shouting at him; George could feel his father's groin, hot and hard, right in the nook between his thighs. He started to think of himself as having a nook there, a gross, gaping place.

One day, when he was outside playing, he had a terrible fantasy. George was twelve years old now; he imagined his body was a girl's. In his mind he took off his buttocks and put them on his flat chest, making breasts. Then he plucked off his penis and, peeling his mouth from his face, carefully placed it between his legs, tweaking the tongue so the red tip lapped over the lips. He could feel his father close by him, possibly right behind him, watching this and getting aroused. George was disgusted, horrified. A sheen of sweat broke out on his forehead. Soon afterward he learned to fight, started to lift weights, running from the softness that is the requisite for all rapes.

I HAD, at first, a hard time dealing with George because he offended me. I understood his pornography obsession as a deflection of his own anxieties. So he wouldn't have to feel his fear, his memories of helplessness, he tried to control women. He wanted to whittle my sex, and therefore me, down into a tiny teacup he could lift to his suddenly powerful lips and sip. Now understand, I am a woman who has spent much time aiming to please men. I am a woman who, in her adolescent days, denied herself food or threw it all up so I could fit into the airless image this man in my office was both struggling to possess and shed at the same time. I remember the smell of myself as an anorexic, a frail dry odor like scorched grass, my limbs coated with hair. Because of these memories, it was impossible for me to like George, but I did feel deeply for him. After all, hadn't I once striven for his same goals, to control the random, fleshy facets of female life, to eradicate the weak part of the self who hurts and bleeds and feeds? In a sense we were both murderers, and we were both crying out from our crimes.

During the first few weeks of our therapy together I began to feel the old shame about my body returning more strongly than it had in a while. Although George said he wanted help to overcome his pornography obsession (he was sometimes driven to watch five, six films a night), and to learn to understand and diffuse his rages, he used his sessions to vent about Joanne's latest transgressions and from there he would segue into paeans about "the perfect pussy," its size and smell. After a day during which I'd seen George had ended, I would go home and feel my flesh more heavily than ever. I often felt like weeping. And it was during this time I noticed small black pubes growing up around my nipples. On the one hand, I wanted to pluck them out. On the other hand, I wanted them to grow, lush like the marshweed that springs up in swamps.

MY PRESCRIPTION was for George to learn, somehow, that being soft does not mean being molested or murdered, necessarily. And also to learn that softness is not only a requisite for rape but also the texture of soil and sheets and the tender, almost melting skin that covers the penis. To that end, I thought he should explore his wounds and weaknesses and thereby gain the knowledge that feeling them now, in a safe place, would not bring the humiliation he feared but the enriched humanity he claimed he wanted. He would have none of it, of course. While he came to therapy stating he ached for change, he remained, in his actions, dedicated to defensiveness. He all but brought rifles to our sessions. He ranted, swore, swung the verbal muzzle left, now right; his neck was almost beautiful, strung with gut, with a trigger moving in his throat. . . .

MISTRUST is the fuel for so much mental pain, so many mental disorders. I am not here talking about the suspicions we sometimes have of one another, the distant but lurking sense that perhaps our lover lies to us, our best friend whispers behind our back. I am talking about a belief that betrayal inundates the atoms of the universe, is so woven into the workings of the world that every step is treacherous, and below the rich mud lies a mine.

George believed that the bodies outside him were missiles poised and poisonous. His aggressive slit-eyed stance is a typically male phenomenon. My eating disorder, the obsessive desire to be thin thin thin and perfectly poisonously poised, is typically a female phenomenon. But their shared themes must not go unnoticed if the sexes are ever to learn real compassion for one another. George and I were both victims of our culture's fear of the feminine, unable to lay down our system of weapons and spread out legs open to life because we learned that in this posture we will be shamed, not invigorated. We did not know how to trust what we could not dominate. In treating George, I came to remember with eerie clarity the years and years of my own hostile dieting—I am forcing myself to run ten miles under a broiling summer sun; I am climbing the sixty stories of my father's apartment building, footsteps slapping echoes in the clammy concrete stairwell. I believed my body was my enemy, every cell, unless vigilantly starved and stripped by exercise, eager to add layer upon layer of crude fat.

The culture that makes us afraid of the fat, the floppy, the soft and sap-sweet is the culture that kills us. And the recovering anorexic is not only in a particularly good position to articulate these truths, she is also, ironically, in a particularly good position, vis-à-vis therapy, to treat the misogynist male. She understands perhaps better than anyone the urge to whip and dominate, discipline and even delete the female form. I understand. I made my body a whitened bone, a pale blade. Like any real man, for years I lived with my fist and not with my flesh. I was hungry but could not risk the softness of surrender. I dreamt of letting down my guard, sitting at a table on which silver dishes steamed, and ingesting colors. Orange carrots, the soft wombs of tomatoes, the tangy dirt of chocolate cake. But I couldn't dare, couldn't trust enough to let myself go. My head was empty except for the willpower that drove me on, and the fear that I would fall through into life.

These are the memories that came to mind when I looked at George, rigid in his chair, his face set against the seepage of any emotion that wasn't cruel or lewd, his skin so tattooed I couldn't have found a plain limb to touch if I had wanted to. He told me about forcing himself to rise before dawn each morning, working out two hours a day, jogging barefoot in the snow. . . .

OF FRAYED rope and cracked sticks, a rickety bridge no doubt. But nevertheless, I did not feel we were strangers, only estranged. Ours was a lonely therapy. The more deeply I went into it with him, the more difficult he became. Except for the brief stories he had told me early on about his father's beatings, he absolutely refused to make himself vulnerable to me. Our therapy started to evolve so that I played a mostly silent role, while he went on and on—endlessly, it seemed—about Joanne's anatomy, her "tight little box," the "six-hour plow" (I got sore just thinking about that), her sagless "bags" with the nipple always hard in his hand. He spoke of split beavers and sucking dick *ad nauseam*.

"What about me?" I wanted to say to him. "Does it occur to you that I am a woman here, that you just might be *offending* me?" And beneath that another, smaller voice was crying, "What about me; am I not also attractive; do I not measure up to your standards; why not?"

I began to realize our sessions were a lot like porn, in which I, the silent subject, absorbed his fantasies and, in my featurelessness, reflected them back to him so that we both remained trapped in unalterable images of bondage. George let me know clearly what my role in our relationship was, by shifting impatiently whenever I spoke, by the quick brushing motions he made with his hands as though to sweep away my words, by interrupting me and then exploding in a tyrannical temper if I asserted my right to finish my own sentence.

"Quiet," he once roared at me, and I, like a little girl, sank back down in my seat and felt darkness grow up around me. At other times, I imagined myself in sequins, my crotch sprayed silver as I, nude, gyrated to the beat of his voice.

"I wonder if you ever think," I finally burst out to him one day, trying to chase the images of leopard skins and loincloths from my head as he spoke, "that I might be uncomfortable with your sexual talk, with the, uh, kinds of expressions you use."

"But you're a shrink," George said to me. "That's what you're here for, to listen to my expressions. That's your whole job."

"First of all," I said, "my whole job is not simply to sit and listen, but to go with you, as your coworker, codiscoverer, into the issues that make your life difficult, so we can *together* work them out. And second of all" (I felt a snarl creep into my voice), "not even in my office am I just a shrink. I am also a woman and the way you talk about my gender disgusts me." I wanted to reach out and slap him, see my palm, a tiny but powerful print on his white cheek.

"I wouldn't ever talk to a woman I was trying to make it with like that. But you're not supposed to—"

"Supposed to what?"

George looked uncomfortable. "Hallefuckinlujah," I thought. I imagined I saw the colors on his tattoo start to blur and bleed.

"Supposed to mind," he said.

"Surprise," I said. "I mind." Tapping the side of my head. "I have a mind."

George looked up at me, his expression confused. My face felt all red. For one moment then our masks dropped away. The stagnant stereotypes shifted, crumbled. I could tell by the way George was looking at me that he was, for maybe the first time, considering me not as a function but as a feeling. I smiled at him.

He nodded, hello.

SHORTLY after this encounter George left the state for six weeks to do a series of carpentry jobs in Arizona. During the time he was away I found myself thinking of him in the desert, in the small Indian towns with clumps of blowing tumbleweed. Was he lonely? Lost? I thought of him running his hands over the contours of rock, feeling within it the craggy father face; in my imagination he was there, with wood, long blond planks of it which, as he held them, turned to hanks of soft hair in his hands.

He returned to therapy in late May, deep spring in the North, the rose's red claw beginning to open. It was raining the day we resumed our sessions, and he stepped into my office soaking wet, beaded eyelashes, T-shirt stuck to his chest so the two tiny thorns of his nipples showed. His thick wavy hair was plastered down on a suddenly small skull; his shorts clung to buttocks I, for the first time, recognized as bony.

When I was a child I had a Shih Tzu dog, a high-blown, hairy canine with a fierce temper. I still have a small pale scar on my knee where he once tore out a hunk of my six-year-old skin. The first time my mother gave the dog a bath is etched in my memory as one of the most remarkable metamorphoses I've witnessed in my lifetime. She dunked him, struggling, into a tub of water; and he came up, fluffed hair now wet as a second skin, a thin little animal with the tracings of bone visible beneath his hide. Even his tail, that gorgeous caramel-colored flare of fur, was now no more than a piece of old raveled rope, hanging over a pitifully pink and naked anus.

George shivered in the air-conditioned building and goosebumps, like tiny buds, appeared on all the tattoos. I stared because I had never seen so much spontaneous movement in George's body before, any evidence that he wasn't willing, controlling. Wet George, I thought. I like you.

So it was a moment before I saw his expression. His eyes were hooded with exhaustion, ringed by blue, his face, untouched by the southern sun, too pale. He slumped down in his seat; looked at his lap.

"I was going to call you," he said in a low voice. I had never heard him use that voice before, a raw tone that brought to my mind a sapling branch stripped of its bark, and his voice elicited, for the first time, something gentle and even aching in me.

"What happened?" I asked.

"She left me," George said. He shook his head. "Just like that." He snapped his fingers in the air.

I was torn, surprised. I felt glad for Joanne. I had often worried about her safety with George, especially when he told me stories about shoving her, punching her, once even hauling her toward an open second-story window. I was glad she had finally gathered the courage to strike out on her own—this woman I had never met. But George looked awful.

"I came back from Arizona—the closets are empty, her picture's gone, not even a note. I called her at her parents', and she says it's completely finished. Gonzo. But I'm chasing her, I'm running after her like a goddamn desperate dog." George shook his head in confusion. "Me," he said, "I've never begged a bitch in my life; I can't stop; I'm making a fool of myself, phoning her ten, twenty times a day, bawling in her ear; but she's just wood. It doesn't matter what I do—"

"It doesn't matter what you do," I said. "Tell me more about that."

"I've never not been able to convince someone, to force someone if I needed to, into doing what I wanted. But I've been trying every ploy with this cunt for the past week and I',—"

"What? You're what?"

"Helpless." His mouth was a bitter line of tension but his eyes were wet.

"I think that's what upsets you the most about Joanne's leaving. That you have no control, that you feel helpless to get her back."

George, to my surprise, nodded in agreement. His own pain had made him flexible, open to vision and suggestion. I also wondered if, having seen me step out of my stereotype in our previous meeting, he now felt freer to step out of his.

"I've never, never felt this way before. I've been stabbed in the neck, but this is way worse. I'm afraid to go home. I'm afraid to be alone. I didn't know I could ever have pain like this. How can it be so bad? *This is not me.*"

"But it is you, only a part of you you've managed, until now, to ignore."

For the first time in six months of treatment I think we really talked. We exchanged. He had opened himself to me with his honest questions. Pain almost always does this, its intensity, like a hot spray, clearing away the dirt of denial. Perhaps this is one reason why, after we cry, we feel cleansed.

During this session, when George asked why and trembled, he brought up a lot of historical material, his relationship with his father, moments of abandonment, and all of this was important, but even more so was the intimacy now building between us, our voices low, our expressions intent, not masked.

"I feel we got something accomplished in this session," George said, "but I'm not sure what or how."

"I think it's that we really connected," I said. "I felt much closer to you in this session than I have before. I know you're really terrified of your openness, or weakness even, because you're afraid of being taken advantage of; but as far as I'm concerned, it's just the opposite. Your willingness to finally talk about your pain lets me see how complicated, and I guess colorful, you really are."

George smiled. "Of course," he said. "I'm no simple Joe Schmo. I'm quite a case, huh?" He looked at me proudly, thumped on his chest.

We laughed a little, and then the hour was up.

THE NEXT few weeks brought some changes in George. He found himself facing an emotion he could not defend himself against. No amount of swearing or swaggering could express mourning. The pain of Joanne's leaving so suddenly broke his shield with an intensity neither of us had anticipated, and brought up memories for him, as though, by going into a red wound, he had reached a new layer of his life. I was reminded of being in the Caribbean as a little girl and seeing, after a violent, sobbing storm, a school of dead sharks washed up on the beach, the silver bodies surprisingly lovely, laid out on the sand. George remembered touching his father's face once when the man was sleeping, pedaling to a pond in the summer, finding, one winter, a squirrel with something yellow dripping from its mouth, as now something yellow was dripping from his, some courage curdled and soured, some sadness. But to me he was not sour at all. The texture of our sessions altered. In his admission of pain, he was now naked; he had pressed himself against me, and I wanted to celebrate, not violate, this stance.

I was drawn in to George now, and I told him so, told him that for six months I had seen only a posture, and now I was seeing a person, and this person was brave.

"Brave?" George said to me. "I can't believe what a wreck I am. I can't believe that I am falling apart over some bitch. You call that brave?"

"You're a lot braver now than you were before," I said, "when you were too scared to face your own soul. To me," I said, "and these are just my own values, but to me, as a woman, I think of a man as someone who is strong enough to experience himself, not afraid of taking voyages instead of standing stuck in a block of cement."

I think he was a little grateful to me for saying that, for telling him I did find him masculine in the moments he considered his worst.

For the next few weeks George ricocheted between two ways of being. Outside of therapy he was his usual hostile and inappropriate self, fighting with people, threatening Joanne over the phone. But within the office, the combination of his now-surfaced suffering and the deepening level of trust between us made him open. In some moments I think I saw his real face, the flow of emotion across it like wind working on sand. Those days, early summer, the sounds of the city streets drifting up to us—the millions of languages of the modern world, the occasional roar of an airplane in its angle of ascent—we discussed the ancient myths and fairy tales, specifically the voyage of the archetypal hero who must leave his father's structured, cool castle and step into the messy wreckage of woods, the rotting leaves, in order to find a solid and secure authority within himself. It was crucial for George to be able to relate his painful journey to a mythic structure, to see that the rotting leaves of his soul were part of a socially sanctioned male odyssey. And I, well, I grew to love him and love the strength in his slow surrender.

IT IS AUGUST, I am twenty-three years old, I have never met George, I am just out of college. I weigh eighty-eight pounds. The heat of this month is thick as wet angora; the waxy leaves on the trees droop. When I look out my bedroom window I can see tulips; they are the most trust-

ing beings, they with their throats always open, their long gold tongues
hanging out. Nothing bad happens to them; the sun doesn't rape them;
they don't gag on the rain.

This day is really many months. I watch the world. I watch the natural
cycle of things. Cliché as it may be, this is what cures me.

There comes a moment when recovery is religious, when a person
says, "All right. I will have faith. I will lay down my sword and shield and
see what the world works in me."

It is a dangerous thing for us, we people who grow up suckling the
steel nipples of this country's missiles, men who think living in the world
is living in a war, women who think their bodies are Molotov cocktails
that must be detonated, destroyed, before they are munched up by their
own metabolisms. What symbols do we have of safety?

I look away from my bedroom window and go downstairs, out onto
the porch. Someone has set a table for me, my sister or an angel I don't
know. Sliced strawberries lie like the tongues of maidens on a platter.
Wedges of cheese and bread. I put food in my mouth; for the first time in
years I swallow the softness of ice cream. I want to see if my body will
blow up in disgusting fatness with this slow animal stupidity swelling in
my stomach. It doesn't. Letting down my guard, opening my many
mouths, does not bring about the ruin, the rape I had feared. On the
contrary. Food brings vitality back to me. I feel my hair take on its sheen,
grow longer, as though new stalks of thought are springing from my
brain; my brain, now nourished, thinks in colors instead of calories. I
can run harder, my eyes are moist enough to cry. It takes me years to
learn this, but in my memory just a day goes by. A sun sets. Food is fuel,
the weakness that makes us want it our greatest strength.

GEORGE started to taste—styles, voices, times. He reported allowing
himself to sleep late one morning, waking to a room where light quiv-
ered on the walls. He started going out some nights without his leather
vest or black boots, tried kissing a woman on the neck and "going no farther." He brought wood home with him at the end of working days,
stayed up late making small objects without any obvious functions—a
box, a mobile, a chiseled plaque. It turned out he was good not only at
nailing things together but also at carving out designs, the chisel nuz-
zling slowly into the pine, yellow shavings like the rinds of lemons littered around him.

One day he came to session and told he had met a woman—Lucky—
whom he thought he could fall in love with, "if only I could get over
Joanne."

"The other problem is," George said, "she's the greatest person, but she's heavy, maybe thirty pounds overweight. I've never made it with a fat woman before. You know me, I'm used to perfect curves, thighs I can grab ahold of, someone I can flip like a doll." He gave me one of his lewd George smiles.

I was enchanted by the idea of George with a fat woman, although, as often happens in therapy, his changes frightened him, and he retreated back into his shell, which was, nevertheless, not nearly as brittle as before. This leads me to believe that a personality disorder, even the most entrenched, is open to change. I had seen enough of George changed, naked, to imagine how his body would be within a fat woman's arms. I imagined her rocking him, and him kissing her face and mouth. I could not help but see her spread legs on a bed, and he, a little cowed by the sight of so much, trying to touch her, first with his fingers, then with his penis, allowing himself entry into the many layers of her life; he brushes her uterus, goes up past her hip, until he touches the curved rib bone, the hard male bone, taken a long time ago from the man, buried and found only in the full woman's body.

The Life You Live (May Not Be Your Own)

J. CALIFORNIA COOPER

LOVE, marriage, and friendship are some of the most important things in your life . . . if you ain't sick or dyin'! And, Lord knows, you gotta be careful, careful 'cause you sometimes don't know you been wrong 'bout one of them till after the mistake shows up! Sometimes it takes years to find out, and all them years are out of your own life! It's like you got to be careful what life you live, 'cause it may not be your own! Some love, marriage, or friend done led you to the wrong road, 'cause you trusted 'em!

Of course, I'm talkin' 'bout myself, but I'm talkin' 'bout my friend and neighbor, Isobel, too. Maybe you, too! Anyway, if the shoe don't fit, don't put it on!

I might as well start at the beginning. See, Isobel and I went to school together, only I lived in town and she came in from the country. Whenever she came. Her daddy was always keepin' her home from school to do work on that ol' broke-down farm of his. He was a real rude, stocky, solid, bearlike, gray-haired man with red-rimmed eyes. Can't lie about him, he worked all the time hisself. But that's what he wanted to do with his life. His kids, they didn't mind workin', but not ALL the time! He never gave them any money to spend on pleasure things like everybody need if they gonna keep workin' all the time.

He was even stingy at the dinner table. Grow it or don't get it! Even his horses and cows was thin. Everything on his farm didn't like him. All his kids he hadn't put out for not workin' left soon as they could, whether they was out of school yet or not! That finally left only Isobel. She did farm work and all the housework, small as she was. Her mother was sickly. I 'magine I'd get sick, too, if I knew that man was comin' home to me every day!

He ran all the boys off who came out to see Isobel. He either put them to work on some odd job or told 'em not to come back. I know, 'cause when we was 'bout sixteen and still in high school I rode out there with one boy who was scared to go by hisself. I wasn't scared of nothin' . . . then!

I saw that ol' man watchin' and waitin' for us to reach the house. Isobel was standing in the doorway, a pot in her hands and a apron on, getting ready to go slop some pigs. She looked . . . her face was all cracked, it seemed. Not 'cause she liked that boy so much, but because she wanted to be young, 'stead of old like her father. We left.

Now me, I grew up any which way in my parents' house, full of kids and everybody building their own world right there inside that house. We had the kind of family that when Mama and Daddy was gone off on some business or other and we s'posed to clean the house? we would slop soapy water all over the kitchen floor, put our skates on and have a skating rink party. Oh! That was fun, fun! Then as soon as Mama and Daddy drive up, them skates be off! We could mop, dust, wash dishes, make beds, whatever, before they got in the house! There! Poor, for sure, but happy!

Well, you know you grow up and forget everybody and everything 'cept your own special business. That's what I did. I was grown and married twelve years when Isobel came back into my life. She had been married 'bout seven years then herself.

Tolly was her husband's name, and he had done got to be a good friend of my husband. Tolly was a travelin' salesman, for true. He had traveled right on Isobel's daddy's farm and stole that girl right out from under her daddy's time clock she was still punching at. She was twenty-four years old then, still not ever married. We was both thirty-one or so when they moved next door to me and Gravy.

I was very glad to have a old school chum for a neighbor. I had just at that time left one of them ladies' clubs that ain't nothing but fussing, gossip, and keepin' up with the Joneses type of thing. Not doin' nothin' important! Just getting together to go to each other's houses to see how everybody else was livin'! Stuff like that. My usual best friend had moved away from this town, and I didn't have a new one I trusted. My mama had told me that I would look up one day and could count my friends on one hand and sometimes one finger! She was right . . . again.

One day, just before Tolly and Isobel moved in their new house, he was over to see Gravy, and I told him, "You all have dinner over here with us on your movin' day. Tell Isobel don't bother with no cookin'!"

He looked at me like I was in space. "Better not do that, Molly. I been puttin' off telling you that for some reason Isobel won't tell me, she does not like you . . . at all!"

I was honestly shocked. "Not like me? Why?"

He frowned and shook his head. "Won't tell me why. Just got awful upset when I told her you was going to be our neighbor."

I never heard of such a thing! "Upset?"

He nodded his head. "I mean she was! Almost didn't want to move here! There just ain't nowhere else I like right now, and the price is right."

I thought a minute. "Well, when you all move in, I'll find out what's wrong! I can't remember nothing I ever did to her. I was lookin' forward to having' you two close—"

He cut me off. "Don't count on it! Isobel is kinda sickly, and it makes her awful mean to get along with! Sometimes I want to give up, but we married and I'm gonna make it work, single-handed if I have to!"

I sat down, wondering. In all the time we knew him I never had guessed they had a problem marriage.

He turned to my husband. "Man, you lucky havin' a wife like Molly. Molly got sense. My woman think everybody always lyin' to her!" He turned to me. "If you ever run into her accident'ly don't mention nothin' 'bout my name! She b'lives every woman is after me! Anyway, she say you already done told all kinda lies on her when you all was in school."

I gasped, 'cause it wasn't true!

He kept talkin'. "She told me some terrible things about you! But I know how she lies, so I didn't pay them no mind."

Gravy was looking at him with a funny-lookin' frown on his face. I looked like I was being pushed out of a airplane.

Tolly ended up telling us, as he shook his head sadly, "She goes to bed . . . and every mornin' when she gets up, the pillowcase be just full of blood. Her mouth bleeds from rotten teeth. Her breath stinks! Bad! She don't never bathe. I have to make her! We don't have kids like you-all 'cause she hates 'em! Hates sex!" He looked at Gravy. "I have to *fight* her to get a little lovin'!"

Oh, he told us so many bad things about his own wife!

When they moved in, I pulled the shades down on that side of the house. And—don't this sound dumb?—we never hardly spoke for twelve years! Twelve years!

If I happen to come out to empty garbage or do something and see her over the hedge, we just did nod and sometimes we pretended we didn't see each other. At the market either, or . . . or anywhere!

Sometimes at some holiday gatherings when we all happen to be there I'd see Isobel. She'd be in a corner somewhere. Sad eyes, mouth always closed, and when she did talk, she put her hand over it. Which made what Tolly said seem true.

Sometimes when I had problems, I'd look over there and wish we

were friends. Tolly was gone 'bout four days out of every week. Even
when he was home they never went anywhere or had any company. So I
knew she had to get lonely sometime. But when Tolly would come over,
he always reminded me by some word or other that Isobel did not like
me . . . at all.

The twelve years passed without us ever getting together. Ain't that
dumb?

You remember I mentioned my problems? They didn't seem to be
big ones. All the ladies said I was lucky to have a husband like Gravy.
The fact is I got so many things to tell you that happened all at the same
time, I don't know how to start.

Now, Gravy was a good husband, good provider. We raised our kids
right. One went to college, one got married. Now we were home alone
together.

All down through our married years, he always liked me lookin' kinds
messy. Said it made me look homey and woman-warm. He urged me to
eat to get meat on my bones till you couldn't tell I had any bones! He
liked gray hair, so when mine started turning, he wouldn't let me dye it.
He didn't like makeup, so I didn't hardly wear none. Just liked my cooking, so we never went out to dinner, I always cooked! He liked me in
comfortable clothes, so I had a lot of baggy dresses. Didn't want me to
worry my "pretty head," so he took care of all the money.

I looked, by accident, in the mirror one day . . . and I cried! I was a fat,
sloppy-dressed, house-shoe wearin', gray-haired, old-lookin' woman! I
was forty-three and looked fifty-five! Now, ain't nothin' wrong with bein'
fifty-five years old if that's where you are. But I wasn't there yet! I had
been lookin' in mirrors through the years, and I could see myself then. I
felt bad, but I could take it if it made my husband happy. That last day
though, I couldn't take it!

That was the day I saw Gravy in the park. A Sunday. He had gone out
to do somethin'. Hadn't said what. I was sitting in the park, on a cold
bench, by myself. THEY was walkin', laughin' and holding hands. He
even peck-kissed her every once in a while, throwing his arm around her
shoulders and pulling her to his old slim body. Not a gray hair on his
head 'cause he said his job might think he was gettin' old. He dyed his
hair. He just liked mine gray.

Let me tell you, PLEASE! She was slim. Wasn't no potatoes, biscuits,
and pork chops sittin' on her hips! She had plenty makeup on. I'd say a
whole servin'! Black hair without a spot of gray in it! High-heeled shoes
and a dress that kept bouncing up so you could see that pretty underwear she had on. She was half his age! Why, she wasn't his type at all!
And I could tell by lookin' at her she didn't know how to cook . . . he
took her out!

Big as I was, I jumped behind the bushes and watched 'em slowly pass by, all my weight on my poor little bended knees. Cramped. By the time he got in front of me, I could have yelled a Tarzan holler and leaped on him and beat him into a ass pate.

But . . . I let them pass. I didn't want HER to see how bad I looked! I know I looked crazy, too, as well as ugly.

When they was well past me, I walked like a ape out of them bushes 'cause I couldn't stand up straight too fast! Some kids saw me come out them bushes and musta thought I had gone to the bathroom in there, 'cause they said something about a "swamp" and ran off laughin' . . . at me! I cried all the way home.

I'm telling you, I was hurt. Now, you hurt when somebody meets you and loves you up and in a few days you don't hear from them no more. But . . . this man been lovin' me up twenty-four years! Settin' my life, my looks, and my thoughts! I let him! Well, that hurt filled my whole body and drug my heart down past my toes, and I had to drag it home, forcin' one foot at a time. Going home? Wasn't no home no more. Chile, I hurt! You hear me?!

Now, I'm going to tell you somethin'. If you ain't ready to leave or lose your husband . . . don't get in his face and tell him nothin'! You wait till you got yourself together in your mind! You wait till you have made your heart understand . . . you can and will do without him! Otherwise, you may tell him you know what he's doin', thinking YOU smart and he's caught! And HE may say, "Well, since you know, now you know! I ain't giving her up!" Then what you gonna do?

Tell you what I did. But wait, let me tell you first things first. Gravy came home, sat in his favorite chair lookin' at TV, smokin' his pipe. I stared at him, waiting for him to see that I knew. He didn't see me so I got up, put my hands on my fat hips, nose flaring wide open, and I told him I KNEW!

Gravy put his pipe down, just as calm as I ever seen him in my life, turned off the TV, sat back down, put his hands on his knees, and told me . . . he wanted a divorce.

A DIVORCE?!

I felt like someone had dipped me in cement. I couldn't move. I couldn't speak. I couldn't do nothin' but stare at Gravy. My mind was rushin' back over our years together. Over the last months . . . looking for signs.

We had been so . . . comfortable.

He said to me, "You have let yourself go. You make me feel old. You ARE old."

I thought of answers, but my mouth wouldn't act right. He went on and on.

"I ain't got but one life, it ain't over! I got some good years left!" He patted his chest. "I need someone can move on with me. You don't and can't compete with nobody. You don't know how to do nothin' but cook and eat! You ain't healthy! All that fat! Look at your clothes! Look at your head! A lazy woman can't 'spect to keep a man! You been all right . . . but . . . I GOT to GO! You tell the kids."

My heart was twistin' around in my breast. I was struck!

He went on and on. "We'll sell this house and each get a new fresh start."

At last my lips moved. "Sell this house? My house? My home?"

His lips moved. "Ain't no home no more. Just a house." He got up talking, putting his foot down. "We gonna sell it and split the money and go each our own way."

I said to myself, This m— — f— —!

Then I said to him, "You m— — f— —!

He walked away. "Ain't no sense in all that. It's too late for sweet names now!"

Now, at first I had been feelin' smart, but that flew out the window. Chile, I lost all my pride, my good sense. Tell you what I did.

I fell out on the couch, cryin', beggin' him to think of our years together, our children, our home, our future, his promises, our dreams. I cried and I begged. Got on my knees, chile! Tears running down, nose running, mouth running, heart stopping. I fought in every way, using everything I could think of to say to hold that man! That man who did not want me! If I had waited till my sense was about me, I'd maybe begin to think of the fact of why was he so much I had to want him? After all, he wasn't no better, no younger than me! I had already had him twenty-four years . . . maybe that was enough! For him AND for me! But I didn't stop to think that. I just cried and begged.

I had heard some old woman say, "If your man 'bout to fight you or leave you, go somewhere, take your drawers off, go back where he is and fall out on the floor and kick your legs open when you fall back! That'll stop him!" Welllll, it don't always work! It don't always stop him as long as you want it to! Gravy stopped for 'bout thirty minutes, then that was over. I was back where I started.

He left, GOING SOMEWHERE. While I sat in my house that would soon be not mine.

Then I fought for that house like I had fought for him. Why, it stood for my whole life! It's all I had, 'sides my grown children, and they was gone on to live their own lives, have their own children, their own husband and wife.

I was alone.

Just yesterday I had a family. A home. I thought it was the worse moment in my life! But, you see, you never know everything till everything happens!

Then all this stuff started happenin' at the same time! Before my house was sold, when Isobel and Tolly had lived next door twelve years. Tolly died. Had a heart attack. A young man, too! Prove that by the fact that he had that attack in bed with a seventeen-year-old girl! Isobel was forty-three, like me. Now she was alone. I was half dead.

I decided to just go on over there, whether she liked me or not! I baked a cake and went to the wake. She was lookin' like a nervous wreck before Tolly died. Now she still looked a wreck but not so nervous. She looked like she was holdin' up quite well. So well I wished Gravy had died 'stead of getting a divorce. Anyway! She looked at me, her lip dropped, her eyes popped. I slammed the cake down as easy as I could, not to hurt that cake, you know, and said, "Yes, it's me! I'm doin' the neighborly thing whether you like me or not, and whether you eat it or not!" Then I turned to go and she grabbed my arm.

"Whether I like YOU?" she asked.

I turned to her. "Yeah! I don't care if you don't like me. I think all this mess is foolishness! I ain't never done nothin' to you!"

She looked kinda shocked. "Why . . . you're the one who does not like me! You didn't want to be friends with me! Tolly told me all those bad things you said about me!"

It was my turn to look shocked . . . again! You might say I was at the time of life where ever' which way I turned, I got shocked.

I gasped. "I never said anything bad about you! I wanted to be your friend."

Her eyes opened wide. "I wanted to be your friend. I needed a friend! I didn't never have nobody but Tolly."

We looked in each other's eyes till we understood that Tolly had planned all this no friendship stuff.

Well, we became friends again. She told me her new name was Belle, said, "Who wants to be named Is-so-bel!" Said, "Now that I am free, I can change my name if I want to! Change my whole life if I want to!" Now!

I learned a lot I did not know, just on account of my not stopping to think for myself. Listenin' to others, taking their words. Trusting them to THINK for me!

Tolly had told Belle the same thing he had told me. PLUS, he ruined that girl's mind! Just shit in it! Told her things like when she talked and opened her mouth, spit stretched from some teeth to some other teeth and just hung there. So she tried never to talk to people.

Told her all kinds of mean, violent things. Every time he went to the store alone, he would tell her stories, like someone was beatin' his wife 'bout tellin' lies. Or someone had killed his wife for lying! Sneaking out on the side! Every day he had things like these to tell her. He would slide out of bed and tell her she was the one left streaks of shit on it, 'cause she didn't wipe herself right! She got where she almost bathed when she went to the bathroom.

He had her believing nobody liked her! Everybody told lies on her! She was weak-minded. A fool about life. Was even ugly. Had a odor. Was very dumb and helpless. That she lost things.

He had taken her wedding rings once, for two years. Hid them. She found them in the bottom of a jar of cold cream. He told her she put them there. She knew she hadn't.

He told her she needed therapy and made her take—GAVE her— hot, hot baths, let the water run out and then he ran cold, cold water on her, holdin' her down in the tub. He threw her food out, said she was tryin' to poison him. Him! Complained he was sick after he would eat somethin' of hers. Whenever they was gettin' along all right and she wanted to go somewhere, he would dress, get to the door, then get very ill. If it was the show, he'd wait till he was in the line almost at the ticket window, then he'd get sick. If they went to the market together, he'd accuse her of talkin' and huggin' a man who had never even been there. He didn't allow her to spend any money except for the house note, food, and insurance. She bought plenty food, paid the house notes, and bought lots of insurance, 'cause that's all she could do!

Wouldn't let her join any clubs. Well, that mighta been good. I was in one at the time I needed to get out of. Tell you about that later!

He kept her up hundreds, thousands of nights, wouldn't let her sleep! Makin' her tell him about her past, and she really didn't have any. From her daddy to him. He had to know that. He did know that! He was sick, crazy. The kind of crazy that can walk around lookin' like everybody else and get away with it! I bet he told Gravy about all them ugly bleeding teeth, bad breath, oh, all them things to keep Gravy away from her when he was out of town!

I never did see her cry.

The slick bastard!

Well, you know. You know all about things like that.

We became friends again. I helped her settle her affairs and all. She said, "I'm gonna sell this prison."

I said, "Sell your only home?" Aghast.

She said, "Money buys another home."

I thought about that!

She said, "Some of the worst times of my life was spent here! First I was glad to leave my daddy's house. Now I'm glad to leave Tolly's! The next house I get is gonna be mine. MINE! I'll live in that one in peace."

I thought about that.

I went to the bank with her to get all the matters set straight. The lady at the desk heard the word *deceased* and looked up in sympathy. But Belle was smiling, a bright, happy smile. She was the happiest woman in the bank!

She sat there in front of that lady, a little ragged, hair undone but neat. Nervous breakdown just leavin', but still showing around the edges. Nails bit off. Lips bit up. Graying hair saying she was older, but bright future-lookin' eyes saying she was ready! MY friend!

That woman really had bought a lot of insurance! Over a hundred thousand dollars' worth! And insurance to pay the house off, the car she couldn't drive yet, off, and any furniture they owed for, off. That's one thing he did for her, he let her buy insurance. And she sure did!

Belle was gaining weight, lookin' way better as time went by. And she was going to the hairdresser, buying clothes, going to shows, nightclubs and restaurants. I went with her most times. I was still in my clubs, a reading club and a social club. I left the reading club 'cause they wanted us to make reports on what we read. I didn't want to make no report! I just wanted to read in peace . . . exchange books, eat, things like that. I dropped out that club and just started buying my own books.

Both Belle and me was lookin' better, healthier, and was more peaceful every day. She was taking painting lessons now and music appreciation. Tolly hadn't liked her to go to school; she might meet somebody. He always told her as he laughed at her, "What kinda thing you goin' over there to waste time doin'? Showing them people how clumsy and dumb you are! Girl, throw that mess out of your mind!" He put little holes in her plans, and her confidence just leaked out. The desire to go had stayed, though. She was the busiest widow I ever did see! Some people might turn over in their graves, but I knew if Tolly could see her he was spinning in his!

I looked at her livin' her life, and I began to really like what I saw. 'Stead of staying home in case Gravy called, I started goin' to a class to lose weight 'cause Belle said it was healthier and I would look better, too! I started goin' to the hairdresser. Not to dye my hair—that's too much work to keep up—but a natural ain't nothin' but a nappy if you don't take care of it! It's shaped and highlighted now. Belle was learning and showed me how to use a little makeup right. Don't try to hide nothin', just bring out what you got!

She gardened a lot, and I began to help her. We ate fresh vegetables and bought fresh fruit. Dropped them ham hocks and short ribs, chile, less we had a special taste for 'em sometime. I didn't miss 'em! Found out all that rice and gravy and meat was really for Gravy. Wondered how he was eatin' lately, but threw that out my mind 'cause I had to get to my financial-planning class or my jewelry-making class or my self-awareness class. The only one I dropped out of was self-awareness. I knew myself. I was learnin' my strength every day. I already was over my weakness.

I missed a man beside me at night, but I was so busy when I looked up six months had passed and I hadn't cried once.

I didn't fight for the house no more. I wanted it to be sold. I didn't fight for Gravy no more. I was glad he was gone. Mostly. He had done me a big favor by giving me MY life back. You hear me? He handed my life to me and I had fought him! Fought him to take it back! Keep it! Use me some more! Chile, chile, chile.

Gravy noticed when he dropped by to check on the house. He noticed a lot 'bout the new me. He slapped me on my behind. I didn't say nothin'; after all, he had been my husband. I sashayed it in front of him as I walked him to the door. I put him out 'cause I had to get to school or somethin'. Or maybe just lay down in peace and think of my new future. Or take a bath and oil and cream my skin for the next man in my life who I might love . . . anything! Whatever I want to do! Now!

I prayed for the house to sell. I wanted MY money! 'Cause I had plans.

Belle's house was sold. She moved in my spare rooms while she looked for somethin' she wanted to buy.

I asked her, "You gonna buy a smaller house this time? You don't need much room."

She looked at me thoughtfully. "You know, I been thinking. A house just sits you in one spot and you have to hold your life into that space and around the town it's in. I don't need much room in a house, but I need a lotta space around me."

I thought about that.

Soon after that, she told me she had bought five acres on the edge of a lake. She was goin' to buy a mobile home, nice, roomy, and comfortable. Live there with the lake on one side, the trees on the other, and the town where she could reach it if she wanted to.

I thought about that, liked it, but I couldn't afford that. I told her, "I like that. That's really gonna be nice."

She answered, "Well, come on with me then!"

I know I looked sad. "Girl, my money ain't that heavy. Not for land AND a mobile home. You got over a hundred thousand dollars; I MAY get twenty thousand."

She say, "I can't live all over my five acres. Get you a mobile home and live on my land!" I know I smiled big as she went on talkin'. "Better still, I'll buy your mobile home 'cause you gonna need your money to live on. You buy the landfill I want for the garden 'cause I want to grow my own food."

I thought only a minute; I wanted this to be MY life. So I told her, "The land is yours. If I buy landfill, if I ever leave. I ain't gonna take it with me so it will still be yours, too. Tell you what, I'll buy my mobile home and pay you rent for use of the land. Then if I ever move, you can buy my home, cheap."

She laughed. "Girl, the land is paid for. I don't need no rent for land that's gonna sit there anyway! You my friend! The only one I got now."

I was happy, said, "You my only friend, too!" I was happy 'cause friends are so hard to find. People count their money 'fore they count friends.

Then she was serious. "I want to be alone. Don't want no man, woman, chick or child tellin' me what to do no more!"

I shook my head. "Me neither! Lord, no!"

She went on. "But everybody need some company sometime. You keep me from gettin' lonely enough to run out there in them silly streets and bring somethin' home I don't want!"

I spoke. "You got me started on my new life . . . school and everything!"

She was still serious. "I trust you."

I got more serious. "I trust you."

She kept talkin'. "I'm going to try to pay for everything in cash. Pay it off! Don't want to owe nobody nothin'!"

I added, "And grow our own food."

She nodded. "Come into town for whatever we need or want."

I was eager. "Don't need no fancy clothes."

She smiled. "We can live on a little of nothin' . . . and be fine! Don't have to go to work or kiss nobody's behind for nothing!"

I laughed out loud. "NOTHIN'!"

You know what we did? We went downtown and bought cowboy jeans, hats, boots, and shirts! We was dressin' for our country life. We was sharp!

It was finally time for her to go, everything ready for her. She drove off with a car full of paints and canvases. I forgot to tell you, she had learned how to drive and had a little red sports car! She wore dark goggles and a long scarf around her neck, just a-flyin' in the wind.

One day, for a minute, just for a minute, she looked sad to me. I looked sad to me. Two older ladies lookin' for a future. Goin' around acting like we was happy. I felt like crying. Belle saw me and asked why, and I told her. Then I did cry.

She put her hands on my shoulders. "Molly? You 'bout forty-five years old."

I corrected her—"Forty-four"—as I sobbed.

She didn't laugh at me. "Well, s'pose you live to be eighty?"

Somethin' in my breast lifted.

She went on. "What you gonna do with them other thirty-five years? What you gonna call 'em if not your future?"

The tears stopped.

But she didn't. "Now, Molly, you my friend. But don't you move out there, away from all your clubs and people, if you gonna be sad. I don't want no sad, depressed killjoy for a neighbor, messin' up my beautiful days! Don't move!"

I could see she meant it. I thought of my clubs where I couldn't stand nobody hardly. I thought of my empty days of food with Gravy. I even thought of my kids who had their own families now. I shook my head so hard. Clearin' it! Shit!

She looked at me steady. "If you even THINK you might want to stay here, PLEASE stay! Till you get all of what you need. 'Cause if you get out there and you got a complaint, I don't want to hear it! 'Less it's 'cause you sick or somethin'!"

She left.

At last my house sold. I went and told the mobile-home man I was ready, gave him a check with no signature on it but mine!

Then I gave my last club meeting, 'cause I knew I was never gonna have to be bothered with them again!

One woman specially, Viola Prunebrough, always was talking 'bout me and laughin' at me. This meeting was specially for her, but the others deserved it, too.

In my reading class we had read Omar Khayyám, and I learned about wrapping food in grape leaves. At the last meeting before this one, I had served them, thinkin' it was some high-class stuff. I didn't know what to put in them, so I stuffed them with chitterlings. It was good to me! Viola had talked about me and laughed all over town. Made me look like a fool in front of everybody. Now you know why I wanted to pay her back. It's ugly, but it's true.

I let everybody in the club know the date for comin'. Then I went to try to find me some marijuana. It was hard to get! Didn't nobody know me that sells the stuff! But I finally got some. A quarter pound! When I prepared the food for that meetin', I mixed that stuff in everything I cooked. I put on a big pot of red beans. No meat, no salt, no onions, no nothin'! Just cooked. I had a plan, see?

When them ladies, all dressed up so nice to show off, got to eatin' all my good food, they went to talkin' loud, laughin', and jumpin' all over the place, saying stupid things. Eatin' and drinkin' everything in sight! I had to snatch some things right off the trays and hurry up and replace 'em 'cause them ladies was gonna eat my dishes and furniture if I didn't! Dainty painted lips just guzzled the wine.

Then I just happen to put on some records by Bobby Blubland. Chile! Them ladies was snapping their fingers, movin' around, shaking their behinds and everythin' else. Dancin' like they hadn't moved in years! Some was singing so loud they drowned Bobby Blubland out. They'd have got me put out if it wasn't my own house. We hadn't had no meeting yet, either!

Then all the food was gone 'cept the beans. Them women musta been still starved, 'cause B. B. King was singing when I looked up and ALL them ladies was bearing down, coming on me in the kitchen, lookin' for anything they could get their hands on to eat. That marijuana must be something!

They got hold of them beans and ate them all. Gobbled them, smacking their lips and ohhhhhing and ahhhhhing till every bean was gone. I laughed till I cried. Why, these were ladies! Beans were in their clothes, in their shoes, even in one lady's hair. I should felt 'shamed, but I didn't. I didn't eat anything myself! Some of them was getting sleepy. Well, they sure were full! Lou Rawls couldn't keep them up anymore. I told them they better go, and then I fixed something for Viola's stomach: a cup of hot tea with a little Black Draught in it. I rushed her out then. I know when she got home she didn't get no rest! I played music for her exit; she wanted to stay and talk and hug and cry between belches. She danced out the door with her fat self, cramps only beginnin' to hit them beans in her belly. Then they were all gone. When they came to theirselves, to ask me what I had cooked, I was gone, too!

I picked up all the supplies I would need for my jewelry makin'. I had found out I was very good at it. People always wanted to buy whatever I made. I was goin' to make a little livin' on the side!

I moved into my new two-bedroom mobile home with the little fireplace. I always wanted one. As I drove over there for the first time, the smile on my face liked to stretched from here to yonder! I laughed out loud, several times . . . and wasn't nobody in the car but me!

We each had a little sun porch built facing the lake. Just listen! 'Most every morning we wave to each other as we sit on that porch and watch the sun finish coming up, while we have coffee or tea or whatever! If it's warm, after the sun is up good, I always go for a swim. Belle usually comes out and sets up her painting stuff. Then maybe I fish and catch my lunch. I take her some, or if her sign is out that says "DON'T," then I don't!

Next, maybe I either put on some music I have learned to appreciate or go in my extra bedroom that is my workroom, 'less my kids are here visiting, and make jewelry to sell when I want to. Or I work in the garden, which is full and beautiful. Or I read. The main thing is I do whatever I want to, whenever I want to.

Sometimes I don't see Belle for days. I see her in the distance. We wave, but we don't talk. We ain't had a argument yet, except on where to plant the onions, tomatoes, or potatoes. Something like that.

I'm telling you, life can be beautiful! Peace don't cost as much as people think it does! It depends on what you want. Not money. People with plenty money don't get peace just 'cause they have money. I get lonely, but I never get sad or depressed. . . .

At that time, Belle's loneliness came out in another way. See, when you have all this space and beauty, it seems to bring you closer to God. Belle decided she ought to know Him better.

This is what she said: "I know the human race ain't no accident. Be 'bout three billion accidents now! And ain't no new kinda accident happenin' all by itself! Nowhere!"

I started to give my opinion, but she wasn't through.

"And another thing," she went on. "There has got to be some truth somewhere! Some of this stuff got to be lies! If we die and rush up to Heaven right away, what is the resurrection for? What is Judgment Day gonna be if everybody is already gone on to Heaven? And if everybody returns to God, then who is on that big, wide road Jesus said would be so packed full of people?"

She made good sense, and it felt warm talking 'bout it. She got some books, and pretty soon she had a Bible study man coming out here. They'd sit on that porch of hers and study, argue, and talk for two or three hours every week. Then she would teach me what she learned. Show it to me in the Bible even! I enjoyed it and was reading the books myself.

On one of Belle's trips to town in her little red sports car she ran into Gravy. He said he needed to see me. She called me and let him talk, 'cause it was my business to give out my own number. I told him he could come out and talk.

He came. He drove up early one morning in a very big, nice blue car. I know he came that early 'cause he wanted to see was anybody there with me. There was only me . . . and peace. I thought I'd be nervous, but I wasn't.

He stepped in the door, head way out in front of him, looking in and around. His shiny pointy-toe shoe slipped on one of my small steps and he went down on one knee. I know it hurt and he wanted to holler, but he held hisself together and limped on in.

Said, "Hot damn, Molly, you got to do somethin' 'bout that step! Shit!"

I told him, "I ain't never slipped on it. Come on in, sit down. Want some coffee?"

He set. "Yeah, bring me some of that good coffee of yours. You make the best coffee in the world!"

While I got everything together I was lookin' at him lookin' at my place, my home. I really looked at him tryin' to see my twenty-four years. I ain't gonna talk about him. He didn't make me do nothin'. I let everything that happened happen. Other than Mala, his girl. Maybe that, too. Remember, I begged to stay with him even when I knew he had her!

He had changed, naturally, a couple of years had gone by. I looked at his hair. He was letting it go, and it was pretty damn near all gray now. He saw me lookin' and patted his head, sayin', "Mala like this ol' gray hair, say it makes me look mature." He laughed a low, empty, scratchy laugh.

My eyes happen to look down at his stomach when I handed him the napkin. He saw that, too, and said, "Mala say she like a round, cozy stomach. Say it's a sign of satisfaction!"

I thought to myself, Or constipation.

He stirred his coffee. "She like all them hamburgers and hot dogs, boxes of candy, jelly rolls from the bakery. Say all that meat and gravy is too heavy to be healthy." His voice was tryin' to sound happy and young, but it still came out disgusted. He looked at me. I was a slim-plump. Meat all where it ought to be, and healthy!

I sat and crossed my legs, the ones he hadn't seen in twenty-four years. He looked, and took a swallow of hot coffee. It was too hot, but he couldn't spit it out. He finally got it down.

I asked, "How is Mala?"

He put the cup down. Said with a surprised look, "You know, I came down a little sick and she got mad at me for it! Like I could help it! One little ol' operation!"

I said, "For Heaven's sake!"

He said, "Yeah!" He started to take another swallow of the coffee, but put the cup back down.

I asked, "Well, things are better now since you up and all?"

He pursed his lips and rubbed that sore knee. Said, "I don't rightly know. She left me 'bout two months ago." He looked outraged. "Do you know, the judge ain't gonna make her sell that house I bought? 'Cause she got two kids! Them kids ain't mine! Mine is grown and got they own homes! Them some other man's children livin' in my house that she won't let me live in!"

I sat up. "Well, what happened, for God's sake?"

He looked like he could cry. "She told me she like this gray hair . . . this . . . this belly and my . . . my . . . 'scuse me, Molly—my lovin'! Then she got tired of my gray hair, my cozy belly, and my gas, and the way I cough in the bathroom in the mornings! Have you ever heard of such a thing?! You got to cough in the mornings to clear your throat! She crazy! That's what! Crazy!"

I sat back. "Well, I'll be damned!"

He was ready to really talk. "Ain't it a damn shame! And I have seen that man—that boy! She got him coming to MY house after dark! Nothin' but a kid! I could tell him something' 'bout what he is gettin' into! She ain't shit! She is a lyin' cracked-butt bitch!"

I sat up. "Don't talk like that in my house, Gravy. I got a special kind of vibration and atmosphere in my house. PEACE. I won't allow it to be disturbed."

He looked at me like I had just said, "Let's get in my flyin' saucer and go to Jupiter today!"

Well, I'm not goin' to bore you with what-all he said. He added up to him and me goin' back together, "like we always shoulda been in the first place." After all, I was the mother of his children. He missed me. When he got to the part where he had always thought of me, even in her arms, I gave him a look that he understood to mean "You are really killin' it!"

I didn't tell him, but I thought clearly. He don't have nothin' to show for twenty-six years of livin' now, 'cept gray hair, potbelly, and a blue car. I had a home . . . with atmosphere. I had a place where my children and grandchildren come spend the summer. I looked good. Because I was healthy. I ate right. Wasn't gonna go back to cookin' all that shit again!

I didn't need to say all those things. I didn't WANT him. No more, ever again, in this life, or no other life. I didn't love him.

I loved me.

Trying to hug me, he left, saying he'd be back bringing me something pretty. I told him, "Call first. I may be busy." As he drove away, he was the most sad, confused-lookin' man I had seen in a long, long time.

I never let him come back. He had done been free to pick and he had picked.

Belle got married to the Bible study man. She said to me, "Ain't it funny? People go to bars, be around purple-headed, shaved-headed, or even normal-lookin' people, lookin' for a mate. Why do they cry when things go wrong? What did they expect to find in a place like that? Moses?" That's the way she talks. Then she say, "How you doin', girl? Need anything?" That's what she says to me. My friend!

As a matter of fact, I'm doin' all right! I got a couple of fellows I go out with sometime. My jewelry makin' is so good I sell it fast as I can make it.

To think I fought this! Well, I don't know.

I don't have anyone I want to marry. Well, hell, I'm only goin' on fifty. I got a future if I live right. I got dreams. Now I swim in the lake. Maybe someday I'll try a ocean!

I get lonely sometime. But not loooooonely.

I might even get married again someday. That'd be nice, too. Only this time I know what kind of man I'd be lookin' for! 'Cause I have done found ME!

I love myself now . . . and everything around me . . . so much.

I know if I got a man there would be just that much more to love. But believe me, I'm going all right!

You hear me?

Goodbye to All That

JOAN DIDION

How many miles to Babylon?
Three score miles and ten —
Can I get there by candlelight?
Yes, and back again —
If your feet are nimble and light
You can get there by candlelight.

IT IS EASY to see the beginnings of things, and harder to see the ends. I can remember now, with a clarity that makes the nerves in the back of my neck constrict, when New York began for me, but I cannot lay my finger upon the moment it ended, can never cut through the ambiguities and second starts and broken resolves to the exact place on the page where the heroine is no longer as optimistic as she once was. When I first saw New York I was twenty, and it was summertime, and I got off a DC-7 at the old Idlewild temporary terminal in a new dress which had seemed very smart in Sacramento but seemed less smart already, even in the old Idlewild temporary terminal, and the warm air smelled of mildew and some instinct, programmed by all the movies I had ever seen and all the songs I had ever heard sung and all the stories I had ever read about New York, informed me that it would never be quite the same again. In fact it never was. Some time later there was a song on all the jukeboxes on the upper East Side that went "but where is the schoolgirl who used to be me," and if it was late enough at night I used to wonder that. I know now that almost everyone wonders something like that, sooner or later and no matter what he or she is doing, but one of the mixed blessings of being twenty and twenty-one and even twenty-three is the conviction that nothing like this, all evidence to the contrary notwithstanding, has ever happened to anyone before.

Of course it might have been some other city, had circumstances been different and the time been different and had I been different, might have been Paris or Chicago or even San Francisco, but because I am talking about myself I am talking here about New York. That first night I opened my window on the bus into town and watched for the skyline, but all I could see were the wastes of Queens and the big signs that said MIDTOWN TUNNEL THIS LANE and then a flood of summer rain (even that seemed remarkable and exotic, for I had come out of the West where there was no summer rain), and for the next three days I sat wrapped in blankets in a hotel room air-conditioned to 35° and tried to get over a bad cold and a high fever. It did not occur to me to call a doctor, because I knew none, and although it did occur to me to call the desk and ask that the air conditioner be turned off, I never called, because I did not know how much to tip whoever might come—was anyone ever so young? I am here to tell you that someone was. All I could do during those three days was talk long-distance to the boy I already knew I would never marry in the spring. I would stay in New York, I told him, just six months, and I could see the Brooklyn Bridge from my window. As it turned out the bridge was the Triborough, and I stayed eight years.

IN RETROSPECT it seems to me that those days before I knew the names of all the bridges were happier than the ones that came later, but perhaps you will see that as we go along. Part of what I want to tell you is what it is like to be young in New York, how six months can become eight years with the deceptive ease of a film dissolve, for that is how those years appear to me now, in a long sequence of sentimental dissolves and old-fashioned trick shots—the Seagram Building fountains dissolve into snowflakes, I enter a revolving door at twenty and come out a good deal older, and on a different street. But most particularly I want to explain to you, and in the process perhaps to myself, why I no longer live in New York. It is often said that New York is a city for only the very rich and the very poor. It is less often said that New York is also, at least for those of us who came there from somewhere else, a city for only the very young.

I remember once, one cold bright December evening in New York, suggesting to a friend who complained of having been around too long that he come with me to a party where there would be, I assured him with the bright resourcefulness of twenty-three, "new faces." He laughed literally until he choked, and I had to roll down the taxi window and hit him on the back. "New faces," he said finally, "don't tell me about *new faces.*" It seemed that the last time he had gone to a party where he had been promised "new faces," there had been fifteen people in the room, and he had already slept with five of the women and owed money to all but two of the men. I laughed with him, but the first snow had just begun to fall and the big Christmas trees glittered yellow and white as far as I could see up Park Avenue and I had a new dress and it would be a long while before I would come to understand the particular moral of the story.

It would be a long while because, quite simply, I was in love with New York. I do not mean "love" in any colloquial way, I mean that I was in love with the city, the way you love the first person who ever touches you and never love anyone quite that way again. I remember walking across Sixty-second Street one twilight that first spring, or the second spring, they were all alike for a while. I was late to meet someone but I stopped at Lexington Avenue and bought a peach and stood on the corner eating it and knew that I had come out of the West and reached the mirage. I could taste the peach and feel the soft air blowing from a subway grating on my legs and I could smell lilac and garbage and expensive perfume and I knew that it would cost something sooner or later—because I did not belong there, did not come from there—but when you are twenty-two or twenty-three, you figure that later you will have a high emotional balance, and be able to pay whatever it costs. I still believed in possibilities then, still had the sense, so peculiar to New York, that something extraordinary would happen any minute, any day, any month. I was making only $65 or $70 a week then ("Put yourself in Hattie Carnegie's hands," I was advised without the slightest trace of irony by an editor of the magazine for which I worked), so little money that some weeks I had to charge food at Bloomingdale's gourmet shop in order to eat, a fact which went unmentioned in the letters I wrote to California. I never told my father that I needed money because then he would have sent it, and I would never know if I could do it by myself. At that time making a living seemed a game to me, with arbitrary but quite inflexible rules. And except on a certain kind of winter evening—six-thirty in the Seventies, say, already dark and bitter with a wind off the river, when I would be walking very fast toward a bus and would look in the bright windows of brownstones and see cooks working in clean kitchens and imagine women lighting candles on the floor above and beautiful children being bathed on the floor above that—except on nights like those, I never felt poor; I had the feeling that if I needed money I could always get it. I could write a syndicated column for teenagers under the name "Debbi Lynn" or I could smuggle gold into India or I could become a $100 call girl, and none of it would matter.

Nothing was irrevocable; everything was within reach. Just around every corner lay something curious and interesting, something I had never before seen or done or known about. I could go to a party and meet someone who called himself Mr. Emotional Appeal and ran The Emotional Appeal Institute or Tina Onassis Blandford or a Florida cracker who was then a regular on what he called "the Big C," the Southampton–El Morocco circuit ("I'm well-connected on the Big C, honey," he would tell me over collard greens on his vast borrowed terrace), or the widow of the celery king of the Harlem market or a piano salesman from Bonne Terre, Missouri, or someone who had already made and lost two fortunes in Midland, Texas. I could make promises to myself and to other people and there would be all the time in the world to keep them. I could stay up all night and make mistakes, and none of it would count.

You see I was in a curious position in New York: it never occurred to me that I was living a real life there. In my imagination I was always there for just another few months, just until Christmas or Easter or the first warm day in May. For that reason I was most comfortable in the company of Southerners. They seemed to be in New York as I was, on some indefinitely extended leave from wherever they belonged, disinclined to consider the future, temporary exiles who always knew when the flights left for New Orleans or Memphis or Richmond or, in my case, California. Someone who lives always with a plane schedule in the drawer lives on a slightly different calendar. Christmas, for example, was a difficult season. Other people could take it in stride, going to Stowe or going abroad or going for the day to their mothers' places in Connecticut; those of us who believed that we lived somewhere else would spend it making and canceling airline reservations, waiting for weatherbound flights as if for the last plane out of Lisbon in 1940, and finally comforting one another, those of us who were left, with the oranges and mementos and smoked-oyster stuffings of childhood, gathering close, colonials in a far country.

Which is precisely what we were. I am not sure that it is possible for anyone brought up in the East to appreciate entirely what New York, the idea of New York, means to those of us who came out of the West and the South. To an Eastern child, particularly a child who has always had an uncle on Wall Street and who has spent several hundred Saturdays first at F. A. O. Schwarz and being fitted for shoes at Best's and then waiting under the Biltmore clock and dancing to Lester Lanin, New York is just a city, albeit *the* city, a plausible place for people to live. But to those of us who came from places where no one had heard of Lester Lanin and Grand Central Station was a Saturday radio program, where Wall Street and Fifth Avenue and Madison Avenue were not places at all but abstractions ("Money," and "High Fashion," and "The Hucksters"), New

York was no mere city. It was instead an infinitely romantic notion, the mysterious nexus of all love and money and power, the shining and perishable dream itself. To think of "living" there was to reduce the miraculous to the mundane; one does not "live" at Xanadu.

In fact it was difficult in the extreme for me to understand those young women for whom New York was not simply an ephemeral Estoril but a real place, girls who bought toasters and installed new cabinets in their apartments and committed themselves to some reasonable future. I never bought any furniture in New York. For a year or so I lived in other people's apartments; after that I lived in the Nineties in an apartment furnished entirely with things taken from storage by a friend whose wife had moved away. And when I left the apartment in the Nineties (that was when I was leaving everything, when it was all breaking up) I left everything in it, even my winter clothes and the map of Sacramento County I had hung on the bedroom wall to remind me who I was, and I moved into a monastic four-room floor-through on Seventy-fifth Street. "Monastic" is perhaps misleading here, implying some chic severity; until after I was married and my husband moved some furniture in, there was nothing at all in those four rooms except a cheap double mattress and box springs, ordered by telephone the day I decided to move, and two French garden chairs lent me by a friend who imported them. (It strikes me now that the people I knew in New York all had curious and self-defeating sidelines. They imported garden chairs which did not sell very well at Hammacher Schlemmer or they tried to market hair straighteners in Harlem or they ghosted exposés of Murder Incorporated for Sunday supplements. I think that perhaps none of us was very serious, *engagé* only about our most private lives.)

All I ever did to that apartment was hang fifty yards of yellow theatrical silk across the bedroom windows, because I had some idea that the gold light would make me feel better, but I did not bother to weight the curtains correctly and all that summer the long panels of transparent golden silk would blow out the windows and get tangled and drenched in the afternoon thunderstorms. That was the year, my twenty-eighth, when I was discovering that not all of the promises would be kept, that some things are in fact irrevocable and that it had counted after all, every evasion and every procrastination, every mistake, every word, all of it.

THAT is what it was all about, wasn't it? Promises? Now when New York comes back to me it comes in hallucinatory flashes, so clinically detailed that I sometimes wish that memory would effect the distortion with which it is commonly credited. For a lot of the time I was in New York I used a perfume called *Fleurs de Rocaille*, and then *L'Air du Temps*, and now the slightest trace of either can short-circuit my connections for the rest of the day. Nor can I smell Henri Bendel jasmine soap without falling back into the past, or the particular mixture of spices used for boiling crabs. There were barrels of crab boil in a Czech place in the Eighties where I once shopped. Smells, of course, are notorious memory stimuli, but there are other things which affect me the same way. Blue-and-white striped sheets. Vermouth cassis. Some faded nightgowns which were new in 1959 or 1960, and some chiffon scarves I bought about the same time.

I suppose that a lot of us who have been young in New York have the same scenes on our home screens. I remember sitting in a lot of apartments with a slight headache about five o'clock in the morning. I had a friend who could not sleep, and he knew a few other people who had the same trouble, and we would watch the sky lighten and have a last drink with no ice and then go home in the early morning light, when the streets were clean and wet (had it rained in the night? we never knew) and the few cruising taxis still had their headlights on and the only color was the red and green of traffic signals. The White Rose bars opened very early in the morning; I recall waiting in one of them to watch an astronaut go into space, waiting so long that at the moment it actually happened I had my eyes not on the television screen but on a cockroach on the tile floor. I liked the bleak branches above Washington Square at dawn, and the monochromatic flatness of Second Avenue, the fire escapes and the grilled storefronts peculiar and empty in their perspective.

It is relatively hard to fight at six-thirty or seven in the morning without any sleep, which was perhaps one reason we stayed up all night, and it seemed to me a pleasant time of day. The windows were shuttered in that apartment in the Nineties and I could sleep a few hours and then go to work. I could work then on two or three hours' sleep and a container of coffee from Chock Full O' Nuts. I liked going to work, liked the soothing and satisfactory rhythm of getting out a magazine, liked the orderly progression of four-color closings and two-color closings and black-and-white closings and then The Product, no abstraction but something which looked effortlessly glossy and could be picked up on a newsstand and weighed in the hand. I liked all the minutiae of proofs and layouts, liked working late on the nights the magazine went to press, sitting and reading *Variety* and waiting for the copy desk to call. From my office I could look across town to the weather signal on the Mutual of New York Building and the lights that alternately spelled out TIME and LIFE above Rockefeller Plaza; that pleased me obscurely, and so did walking uptown in the mauve eight o'clocks of early summer evenings and looking at things, Lowestoft tureens in Fifty-seventh Street windows, people in evening clothes trying to get taxis, the trees just coming into full leaf, the lambent air, all the sweet promises of money and summer.

Some years passed, but I still did not lose that sense of wonder about New York. I began to cherish the loneliness of it, the sense that at any given time no one need know where I was or what I was doing. I liked walking, from the East River over to the Hudson and back on brisk days, down around the Village on warm days. A friend would leave me the key to her apartment in the West Village when she was out of town, and sometimes I would just move down there, because by that time the telephone was beginning to bother me (the canker, you see, was already in the rose) and not many people had that number. I remember one day when someone who did have the West Village number came to pick me up for lunch there, and we both had hangovers, and I cut my finger opening him a beer and burst into tears, and we walked to a Spanish restaurant and drank Bloody Marys and *gazpacho* until we felt better. I was not then guilt-ridden about spending afternoons that way, because I still had all the afternoons in the world.

And even that late in the game I still liked going to parties, all parties, bad parties, Saturday-afternoon parties given by recently married couples who lived in Stuyvesant Town, West Side parties given by unpublished or failed writers who served cheap red wine and talked about going to Guadalajara, Village parties where all the guests worked for advertising agencies and voted for Reform Democrats, press parties at Sardi's, the worst kinds of parties. You will have perceived by now that I was not one to profit by the experience of others, that it was a very long time indeed before I stopped believing in new faces and began to understand the lesson in that story, which was that it is distinctly possible to stay too long at the Fair.

I COULD not tell you when I began to understand that. All I know is that it was very bad when I was twenty-eight. Everything that was said to me I seemed to have heard before, and I could no longer listen. I could no longer sit in little bars near Grand Central and listen to someone complaining of his wife's inability to cope with the help while he missed another train to Connecticut. I no longer had any interest in hearing about the advances other people had received from their publishers, about plays which were having second-act trouble in Philadelphia, or about people I would like very much if only I would come out and meet them. I had already met them, always. There were certain parts of the city which I had to avoid. I could not bear upper Madison Avenue on weekday mornings (this was a particularly inconvenient aversion, since I then lived just fifty or sixty feet east of Madison), because I would see women walking Yorkshire terriers and shopping at Gristede's, and some Veblenesque gorge would rise in my throat. I could not go to Times Square in the afternoon, or to the New York Public Library for any reason whatsoever. One day I could not go into a Schrafft's; the next day it would be Bonwit Teller.

I hurt the people I cared about, and insulted those I did not. I cut myself off from the one person who was closer to me than any other. I cried until I was not even aware when I was crying and when I was not, cried in elevators and in taxis and in Chinese laundries, and when I went to the doctor he said only that I seemed to be depressed, and should see a "specialist." He wrote down a psychiatrist's name and address for me, but I did not go.

Instead I got married, which as it turned out was a very good thing to do but badly timed, since I still could not walk on upper Madison Avenue in the mornings and still could not talk to people and still cried in Chinese laundries. I had never before understood what "despair" meant, and I am not sure that I understand now, but I understood that year. Of course I could not work. I could not even get dinner with any degree of certainty, and I would sit in the apartment on Seventy-fifth Street paralyzed until my husband would call from his office and say gently that I did not have to get dinner, that I could meet him at Michael's Pub or at Toots Shor's or at Sardi's East. And then one morning in April (we had been married in January) he called and told me that he wanted to get out of New York for a while, that he would take a six-month leave of absence, that we would go somewhere.

It was three years ago that he told me that, and we have lived in Los Angeles since. Many of the people we knew in New York think this a curious aberration, and in fact tell us so. There is no possible, no adequate answer to that, and so we give certain stock answers, the answers everyone gives. I talk about how difficult it would be for us to "afford" to live in New York right now, about how much "space" we need. All I mean is that I was very young in New York, and that at some point the golden rhythm was broken, and I am not that young any more. The last time I was in New York was in a cold January, and everyone was ill and tired. Many of the people I used to know there had moved to Dallas or had gone on Antabuse or had bought a farm in New Hampshire. We stayed ten days, and then we took an afternoon flight back to Los Angeles, and on the way home from the airport that night I could see the moon on the Pacific and smell jasmine all around and we both knew that there was no longer any point in keeping the apartment we still kept in New York. There were years when I called Los Angeles "the Coast," but they seem a long time ago.

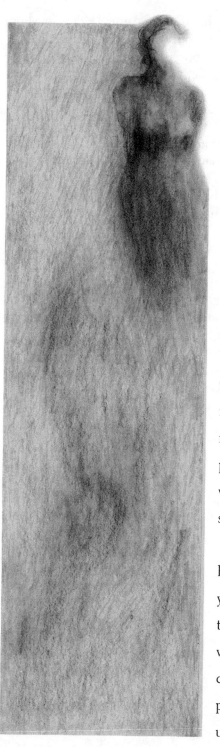

Love, Marriage, and in Between

THIS section title—"Love, Marriage, and in Between"—acknowledges that these days a couple may be deeply committed to each other without the official stamp of marriage. It also reflects the fact that more women are spending long periods of life as widows or divorced women—in between old relationships and others that may lie ahead.

Barbara Kingsolver's couple have been living together for seven years, but when they move from their roomy San Francisco house with many friends to an isolated cabin among conservative country people, their relationship reveals an unsuspected fragility.

"Breathing Lessons," on the other hand, from Anne Tyler's novel on marriage, stars a long-married couple journeying to a wedding. Like many couples, wife and husband are opposites. Maggie is warm, talkative, and emotional, while Ira is sensible, practical, and laconic. When they get lost on the drive, Maggie and Ira go through a complicated dance of anger before making up—an object lesson in how opposites manage to stay married.

How does a wife with a violent husband find the courage to escape? In " 'I Don't Believe This,' " Merrill Joan Gerber depicts a battered wife fighting a grueling battle of nerves to save herself and her children from a husband who practices emotional blackmail.

Second marriages carry a special brand of risk—and reward. After fifteen years of being a single mother, Phyllis Raphael married again, and in her essay she shares her own debate over remarrying in midlife, including the possibility that "If there is any period favorable to marriage, it is midlife."

Alison Lurie and Lynn Sharon Schwartz give two different scenarios for marriages that have lasted for some years. Lurie's Erica Tate considers herself quite happily married. Out of the blue, while her husband, a professor, is away lecturing, Erica finds her peaceful contentment threatened, and "The War Begins." In "Desire," Schwartz shows the continuing passion of a couple who have learned the secrets of happy married sex—and the tricky balance of simultaneous togetherness and separateness.

Widowhood is the subject of Joan Gould's moving essay on her living through her early bereavement. Though her husband has recently died, he hovers constantly in her mind and memory like a ghost, while Gould struggles not to turn him into a saint who will forever rule her life.

Blueprints

BARBARA KINGSOLVER

THE SOUP BOWLS slam against the sink, she's being careless, and Lydia wonders how it would feel to break something important on purpose. The crockery set would qualify. It has matching parts: the bowls, a large tureen, and a ladle in the elongated shape of a water fowl, all handmade by a woman in Sacramento named Earth, who gave it to Whitman last year as a solstice present. Lydia likes the crockery well enough. That isn't the problem.

"You sleep in the bathtub," she says to Whitman. "I'm sorry the light keeps you awake. But I'm not going to do my lesson plans in the bathroom."

The bathroom is the only part of the cabin that is actually a separate room, with a door. Lydia is standing at the kitchen sink and Whitman is still at the dining table and they are not very far apart at all.

"Last night you were up till eleven forty-five," he says.

"So sleep with the blanket over your head," she tells him in a reasonable voice. "For God's sake, Whitman, give me a break. It's not like you have to get up early to milk cows."

"I don't have to get up for any reason, you mean. And you do."

"That's not what I mean." She's about to say, "I respect your work," but instead decides she will just stop talking. Men do it all the time, she reasons, and men run the world.

What they told themselves last summer, when they moved from Sacramento to Blind Gap, was that the cabin would be romantic. Her mother pointed out that it's hard moving from a larger to a smaller place, that she and Hank did it once early in their marriage and the storage-space problem drove her insane. Lydia smiles into the dishwater, imagining her mother wild-haired and bug-eyed, stalking the house for a place to stash the punch bowl. Can this marriage be saved? Why, yes! By storage space. It's true, the Sacramento house had had plenty of it, closets gone to waste in fact, and bedrooms enough for an Indian tribe. But Whitman and Lydia had been living under the same roof for nine years and had reason to believe they were infinitely compatible. They figured they'd make it without closets.

They aren't making it, though. The couple they were then seems impossible to Lydia now, a sort of hippie Barbie and Ken sharing a life of household chores in that big, run-down house. Her memories from Sacramento smell like salt-rising bread—they used to do such wholesome, complicated cooking: Whitman with his sleeves rolled up, gregarious in a way that never came easily to Lydia, kneading dough and giving his kindest advice on copper plumbing and boyfriend problems to the people who gravitated endlessly to their kitchen. But when the Whitman-doll was removed from that warm, crowded place he'd hardened like a rock. Lydia would give her teeth right now to know why. She dries her hands and spreads papers over the table to prepare her lessons for the next day. Whitman hasn't surrendered his corner of the table. He leans on his elbows and works a spoon in his hands as if preparing to bend it double, and it occurs to Lydia that she can't predict whether or not he'll destroy the spoon. Certainly he is capable of it. Whitman is large and bearded and given to lumberjack flannel, and people often say of him that he has capable hands. The kitchen table is one of his pieces. He builds furniture without the use of power tools, using wooden pegs instead of nails. People in Sacramento were crazy about this furniture, and Lydia expected it would sell well up here too, but she was wrong. In Blind Gap, people's tastes run more along the lines of velveteen and easy-care Formica. They drive the hour to Sacramento to make their purchases in places like the Bargain Heaven Direct-2-U Warehouse. Whitman has to pile his pieces onto the truck and make the same drive, to show them on consignment in the Country Home Gallery.

David, the retriever, is pacing between the kitchen and bedroom areas. The click of his toenails on the wood floor is interrupted when he crosses the braided rug.

"Pantry," Whitman says, and David flops down in the corner behind the wood stove, sounding like a bag of elbows hitting the floor. David responds to eleven different commands regarding places to lie down. The house in Sacramento had eleven usable rooms, and the dog would go to any one of them on command. He was nervous after the move, circling and sniffling the walls, until Whitman and Lydia reassigned the names of eleven different areas of the new place. Now he's happy. Dogs like to know exactly what's expected of them.

Whitman is spinning the spoon on the table, some unconscious derivative of Spin the Bottle maybe. Or just annoyance. "We could just not talk to each other, that's always a good idea," says Lydia. "I heard about these two guys who lived in the same cabin and didn't talk to each other for fifty years. They painted a line down the middle."

"It was sixty-three years," he says. "You got that out of the *Guinness Book of Records*. The guys were brothers."

Whitman has an astonishing memory for details. Often he will draw out the plans for something he's building and then complete the whole piece without referring again to the blueprints. This talent once made Lydia go weak with admiration, but at this moment it doesn't. She looks up from her book, called *Hands-On Learning*, which is about teaching science to kids.

"Sometimes I think you try not to hear what I'm saying."

Whitman gets up and goes outside, leaving the spoon spinning on the table. When it stops, it's pointing at Lydia.

THE BEST part of her day is the walk home from school. From Blind Gap Junior High she takes a dirt road that passes through town, winds through a tunnel of hemlocks, and then follows Blind Creek up the mountain to their six acres. She could have used this in Sacramento—a time to clear her mind of the day's frustrations.

Even at the stoplight, the dead center of Blind Gap, Lydia can hear birds. She inhales deeply. A daily hike like this would be a good tonic for some of her students too, most of whom are obliged to spend a couple of hours a day behaving like maniacs on the school bus. The area served by the school is large; there are probably no more than a dozen kids of junior-high age in Blind Gap itself. The town's main claim to fame is a Shell station and a grocery store with a front porch.

She leaves town and walks through the hemlock forest, content to be among the mosses and beetles. "Bugs are our friends," Whitman says, mocking her, but Lydia feels this friendship in a more serious way than he imagines. The bugs, and the plants too, are all related to her in a complicated family tree that Lydia can describe in convincing detail. Back in college her friends were very concerned about the Existential Dilemma, and in the cafeteria would demand while forking up potatoes and peas, "Why are we here?" Lydia would say, "Because we're adapted for survival." The way she explained it, whatever ancestors were more dexterous and quick would live longer and reproduce more. Each generation got to be more like us, until here we were, "It's still going on," she would point out. "We're not the end of the line, you know." It all started with the blue-green algae, and if humans blew themselves off the map it would start all over again. Blue-green algae had been grow-ing on the inside of the nuclear reactors at San Onofre.

When she told this to her ninth grade class they just stared at her. None of them had ever been to San Onofre. They were waiting for the part about apes turning into men, so that according to their parents' instructions they could stop listening. Lydia thinks this is a shame. Evo-lution is just a way of making sense of the world, which is something she figures most ninth graders could use.

If they tell her to stop teaching evolution, she decides, she'll just call it something else. No one will be the wiser if she leaves out the part about ape-to-man. They couldn't seem to understand, ape-to-man was the least important part.

On her way up the last hill Lydia stops at Verna Delmar's. Verna is a sturdy woman of indeterminate age who owns the farm next to theirs. She has chickens and gives Lydia a good price on eggs because, she says, she had this same arrangement with the couple who owned the six-acre place before Whitman and Lydia bought it. Lydia is curious about how those people got along in the little cabin, and is tempted to ask, but does-n't because she's afraid of hearing something akin to a ghost story.

Today Verna details a problem she's having with chicken mites, and then asks after Lydia's garden and her husband's furniture business. Lydia tactfully doesn't correct Verna, but expects that eventually her neighbor will find out they aren't husband and wife. She has perpetu-ated this deception since their first conversation, when Verna asked how long they'd been married and Lydia, fearing the disapproval of her first acquaintance in Blind Gap, didn't lie outright but said they had "been together" for almost ten years, which was true. "We both turned thirty this year," she said.

"Lots of kids been married and divorced two or three times before they're your age," Verna had said, and Lydia agreed that ten years was longer than most people they knew. In Sacramento their friends referred to Lydia and Whitman as an institution. Now the word makes Lydia think of a many-windowed building with deranged faces pressing at the glass.

Whitman is building a bridge over Blind Creek, and she stops to watch him work. Their house is near the road, but the creek bank cuts steeply down from the shoulder, cutting off access to all the land on the left side of the road. Verna's farm has a front entrance bridge, but theirs doesn't; they have to continue on for a quarter mile to where the road passes over an old concrete bridge, then circle back by way of the orchard road at the back of their property. The new bridge will create a front entrance to their farm. Whitman is absorbed and doesn't see her.

The design of the bridge is unusual, incorporating a big old sycamore. Lydia likes the tree, with its knotty white roots clutching at the creek boulders like giant, arthritic hands. He's left a square hole in the bridge for the tree trunk to pass through, with just enough room on the side for the truck to get by. She watches his hands and arms and feels he's someone she's never talked with or made love to. She has no idea how this happened.

Whitman looks up. Possibly he did know she was watching. "Your friend Miss Busybody Delmar was up here earlier," he says.

"I know, she mentioned it. She doesn't think it's a good idea to build the bridge that way. She says that old tree is due to come down."

Whitman drives a nail too close to the end of a board and curses when it splits. Unlike his furniture construction, this project requires nails and a gasoline-powered table saw. "You tell her I admire her expertise in bridge building," he says. "Tell her I'd appreciate it if she would come up here and tell me how to build an end table."

Lydia can feel her bones dissolving, a skeleton soaking in acid. "It's a real nice bridge, Whitman. I like the design."

For the rest of the afternoon she tries to work on lesson plans so she won't keep him up late, but she can't concentrate on the families of the animal kingdom. She finishes the dishes she abandoned the night before. Whitman has gradually stopped doing housework, and Lydia has lost the energy to complain about it. For some reason she thinks of Whitman's mother. Lydia never met her, she has been dead a long time, but she wishes she could ask her what kind of little boy Whitman was. She used to imagine light brown curls, a woman's child, but now she pictures a tight-lipped boy waiting for his mother to guess where the hurt is and kiss it away. Whitman's story on his mother is that she was mistreated by his father, a Coast Guard man who eventually stopped coming home on leave. The martyred wife, the absent husband. Lydia's own mother is alive and well but equally martyred, in her way: the overly efficient, do-it-all-and-don't-complain type. Back when things were going well, when everybody was telling Whitman how evolved he was, the cliché of their parents' lives seemed like a quaint old photograph you'd hang on the wall. Now it's not so charming. Now it looks like one of those carnival take-your-picture setups with Lydia and Whitman's faces looking out through the holes. She realizes this with a physical shock, as if she's laid hands on a badly wired appliance. This is what's happened to them. They struck out so boldly as a couple, but the minute they lost their bearings they'd homed in on terra firma. It's frightening, she thinks, how when the going gets rough you fall back on whatever awful thing you grew up with.

THE MAIL brings in the usual odd assortment of catalogues: one with clever household items and one called "Ultimate Forester," which sells chainsaws and splitting mauls and handmade axes as expensive as diamond jewelry. Lydia hates the people who lived here before and calls them "Betty and Paul," for Betty Crocker and Paul Bunyan. There's also a catalogue for Lydia—Carolina Biological Supply—and some legal forms for Whitman. Of all things, he's changing his name: it's Walter Whitman Smith, and he's legally dropping the Walter, which he doesn't use anyway.

Lydia can't relate. People often find Bogtree—her own last name—humorous, but growing up with it has planted in her imagination a wonderful cypress tree spreading its foliage over a swamp at the dawn of the world. She believes now she got this image from a James Weldon Johnson poem containing the line "Blacker than a hundred midnights down in a cypress swamp." Lydia was the kind of child who knew "bog" meant swamp. The poem was about the creation of the earth. "I've always been a Bogtree and always will, don't blame me," she says, whenever her mother hints about Lydia and Whitman getting married. She knows, of course, that she could keep her own name, but even so, being married would sooner or later make her Mrs. Smith, she suspects.

Their old friends in Sacramento had gone through names like Kleenex. A woman she considered to be mainly Whitman's friend had christened herself Tofu, and actually named her children Maize, Amaranth, and Bean. In Lydia's opinion this was a bit much. "Aren't you kind of putting your own expectations on them?" she'd asked. "What if when they grow up they don't want to be vegetarians? What if your mother had named you Pot Roast?"

Lydia remembers this conversation, she realizes, with unusual bitterness. Tofu had what was called an open marriage, which became so open that it more or less lost its clasp. Her husband Bernard, as far as anyone knew, was still up in Washington picking apples. One of Tofu's numerous affairs was with Whitman during their brief experiment with non-monogamy. There was much talk about the complexity of human nature and satisfying different needs, but in the end Lydia sat on the bed and downed nearly a bottle of peppermint schnapps, and when Whitman came home she met him at the door demanding to know how he could have sex with a person named after a vegetable product. Lydia thinks of this as the low point of their relationship, before now.

OVER dinner they argue about whether to drive into Sacramento for the weekend. They should be thinking about firewood, but Whitman complains that they never see their friends anymore.

"Who'd have thought we'd *survive* without them," Lydia says, distressed at how much they sound like ninth graders. After so many years together it's as if they've suddenly used up all their words, like paper plates and cups, and are now using the last set over and over.

"If you didn't like my friends why didn't you say so? Why didn't you have your own friends?" Whitman swallows his dinner without comment. It's a type of chili Lydia invented, based on garbanzo beans, and it hasn't turned out too well.

"I don't know." She hesitates. "I don't think you ever understood how hard it was for me. All those people so absolutely sure they're right."

"That's your interpretation."

She tries salting her chili to see if this will help. Once Lydia was given a lecture on salt, the most insidious kind of poison, by a friend who'd come over for dinner. He would rather put Drano on his food, he said. She'd had half a mind to tell him to help himself, there was some under the sink.

"Whitman, I'm just trying to tell you how I feel," she says.

"Well you should have said how you felt back then."

"And you should have told me you didn't want to move here. Before I applied for the job. You sure seemed hot on the idea at the time."

Whitman scrapes his bowl. "It's only an hour. I didn't know we were going into seclusion."

Lydia goes to check the refrigerator, coming back with some carrots she harvested that morning. "I don't make the rules," she says. "The way your pals glorify the backwoods life, don't you think it's interesting they've never come up here for a visit?"

He picks up one of the carrots, its wilted tassel of leaves still attached, and bites off the tip. He looks like Bugs Bunny and she wishes to God he would say, "What's up, Doc?" Instead he says, "We don't have room for them to stay with us here. They're just being considerate."

Lydia laughs. As big as it was, the house in the city never seemed big enough for all the people passing through. Once for two months they put up a man named Father John and his "family," four women with seven children among them. They parked their school bus, in which they normally lived, in the backyard. The women did everything for Father John except drive the bus: they washed his clothes, bore his children, and cooked his meals in the bus on a wood stove with a blue mandala painted on it. They had to use their own stove because Lydia and Whitman couldn't guarantee the Karmic purity of their kitchen. At one time, in fact, Whitman and Lydia had been quite the carnivores, but Whitman didn't go into that. The people were friends of a friend and he didn't have the heart to throw them out until they got their bus fixed, which promised to be never. Lydia pitied the bedraggled women and tried to strike up cheery conversations about how pleasant it was that Whitman shared all the cooking and cleaning up. One night at dinner Lydia explained that she'd first fallen in love with Whitman because of his Beef Mongolian. Several members of Father John's family had to be excused.

But it was true. Whitman had been a rarity in their circle, the jewel in the crown, and Lydia understands now that most of the women they knew were in love with him for more or less the same reason. Really, she thinks, they ought to see him now. The water-fowl crockery set, hand-made by Earth, she's left sitting in the sink unwashed for days, as a sort of test. Not unexpectedly, Whitman failed. Without an audience the performance is pointless.

ON SATURDAY Lydia goes to see Verna. She carries two empty cartons which she'll bring back full of eggs. Verna's hens lay beautiful eggs: brown with maroon speckles and a red spot inside, where, as Verna puts it, the rooster leaves his John Henry. The food co-op in Sacramento sold eggs like these for $2.50 a dozen, a price Lydia thought preposterous and still does. She once had a huge argument with one of their friends, a woman named Randy, who acted like fertile eggs were everything short of a cure for cancer. "The only difference between a dozen fertile eggs and a dozen regular ones is twelve sperms," Lydia had explained to her. "That's what you're paying the extra dollar-fifty for. It comes to around twelve cents per sperm."

Later that same evening Randy had been in the kitchen helping Whitman make spaghetti, and Lydia overheard her complaining that she, Lydia, lacked imagination. Whitman had come to her defense, sort of. "Well, she's a science teacher," he said. "She probably knows what she's talking about."

"Don't I know *that*," Randy said. "She even dresses like a schoolteacher."

The next day Lydia had gone to the Salvation Army and bought some fashionably non-new clothes.

SHE'S surprised to find herself confiding in Verna about her problems with Whitman. Verna's kitchen has an extra refrigerator dedicated entirely to eggs, stacked carefully in boxes of straw. She listens to Lydia while she places eggs gently in cartons.

"I guess we're just getting on each other's nerves," she says. "The house we had before was a lot bigger."

Verna nods. They both know that isn't the problem. "Once you've got used to having more, it's hard to get by on less," she says.

Lydia is amazed that Verna can handle so many eggs without getting nervous.

On the way back she stops by the stone outbuilding Whitman has converted into his shop. It's lucky that his special kind of woodworking doesn't require electricity, although if the building were wired she could read out here at night without disturbing him. This strikes her as a provident idea, which she'll suggest when he's in a better mood.

She stands well out of his way and watches him plane the surface of a walnut board. She loves the dark, rippled surface of the wood and the way it becomes something under his hands. He's working on a coffee table that's a replica of an Early American cobbler's bench. In the niches where shoemakers used to keep their tools and leather, people can put magazines and ashtrays. These tables are popular in the city, and Whitman has sold six or seven. As a rule he makes each one of his pieces a little different, but he no longer changes this design, explaining that you can't beat success.

"I was talking to Verna this morning," Lydia says uneasily. "She thinks it's understandable that we'd have trouble living in such a small place." Whitman doesn't respond, but she continues. "She says we ought to forget the past, and pretend we're just starting out."

"So Verna's a psychologist, on top of being a civil engineer."

"She's my friend, Whitman. The only one I've got at the moment."

"These country people are amazing, all experts on the human condition." His back is to Lydia, and as he pushes the plane over the board in steady, long strokes, she watches the definition of the muscles through his damp T-shirt. It's as if the muscles are slipping from one compartment to another in his back.

"They don't knife each other in study hall," she says quietly. "Or take their neighbors hostage."

Whitman speaks rhythmically as his body moves forward and back. "With enough space between them anybody can get along. We ought to know that."

"There's more to it than that. They know what to expect from each other. It's not like that for our generation, that's our whole trouble. We've got to start from scratch."

The plane continues to bite at the wood, spitting out little brown curls. Whitman makes no sound other than this.

"I know it's not easy for you up here, Whitman. That everybody doesn't love you the way they did in Sacramento, but . . ." She intended to say, "I still do." But these are less than words, they're just sounds she's uttered probably three thousand times in their years together, and now they hang flat in the air before she's even completely thought them. It's going to take more than this, she thinks, more than talk, but she doesn't know what.

"But this is where we are now," she says finally. "That's all. We're committed to the place, so we have to figure out a way to go on from here."

"Fine, Lydia, forge ahead. It's easy for you, you always know exactly where you're headed." Every time he shoves the plane forward, a slice of wood curls out and drops to the floor, and she wonders if he's going to plane the board right down to nothing.

THE RAIN starts on Sunday night and doesn't let up all week. The old people in Blind Gap are saying it's because of those bomb tests, the weather is changing. It's too warm. If it were colder it would have been snow, rather than rain, and would come to no harm.

After Tuesday, school is shut down for the week. So many bridges are out, the buses can't run. One of the bridges washed away in the flood is the new one Whitman built on their farm. Lydia sees now that Verna was right, the design was a mistake. The flood loosened the ground under the roots of the sycamore and pulled it down, taking the bridge with it. Whitman blames the tree, saying that if it had been smaller or more flexible it wouldn't have taken out the whole bridge. Lydia can see that his pride is badly damaged. He's trapped inside the house now, despondent, like a prisoner long past the memory of fresh air. The rain makes a constant noise on the roof, making even the sounds inside her skull seem to go dead.

She wonders if everything would be all right if they could just scream at each other. Or cry. The first time she saw him cry was when David had parvo virus as a puppy and they expected him not to make it. Whitman sat up all night beside David's box on the kitchen floor, and when she found him the next morning asleep against the doorsill she told herself that, regardless of the fate of the puppy, this was the man she would be living with in her seventies. Forty years to go, she says aloud into the strange, sound-dead air. She can't begin to imagine it. Now Whitman doesn't even notice if David has food or water.

As she pads around the cabin in wool socks and skirt and down vest, Lydia develops a bizarre fantasy that they are part of some severe religious order gone into mourning, observing the silence of monks. Industrious out of desperation, she freezes and cans the last of the produce from the garden, wondering how it is that this task has fallen to her.

Their first week here they had spaded up the little plot behind the cabin, working happily, leaning on each other's shoulders to help dig the shovel in, planting their garden together. But by harvest time it's all hers. Now Whitman only comes into the kitchen to get his beer and get in the way, standing for minutes at a time with the refrigerator door open, staring at the shelves. The distraction annoys her. Lydia hasn't canned tomatoes before and needs to concentrate on the instructions written out by Verna.

"It's cold enough, we don't have to refrigerate the state of California," she shouts above the roar of the rain, but feels sorry for him as he silently closes the refrigerator. She tries to be cheerful. "Maybe we ought to bring back the TV next time we go into the city. If Randy would give it back. Think she's hooked on the soaps by now?"

"Probably couldn't get anything up here," he says. He stands at the windows and paces the floor, like David.

"Bedroom," she commands, wishing Whitman would lie down too.

On Monday it's a relief for both of them when school starts again. But the classroom smells depressingly of damp coats and mildew, and after nearly a week off, the kids are disoriented and wild. They don't remember things they learned before. Lydia tried to hold their attention with stories about animal behavior, not because it's part of the curriculum but because it was her subject in graduate school and she's now grasping at straws. She tells them about imprinting in ducks.

"It's something like a blueprint for life," she explains. "This scientist named Konrad Lorenz discovered that right after they hatched the baby birds would imprint on whatever they saw. When he raised them himself, they imprinted on him and followed him around everywhere he went. Other scientists tried it with cats or beach balls or different shapes cut out of plastic and it always worked. And when the baby ducks grew up, they only wanted to mate with those exact things."

The kids are interested. "That's too weird," one of them says, and for once they want to know why.

"Well, I don't know. Nobody completely understands what's going on when this happens, but we understand the purpose of it. The animal's brain is set up so it can receive this special information that will be useful later on. Normally the first thing a baby duck sees would be an adult duck, right? So naturally that would be the type of thing it ought to grow up looking for. Even though it's less extreme, we know this kind of behavior happens in higher animals too." She knows she's losing her audience as she strays from ducks, but feels oddly compelled by the subject matter. "Most animals, when they're confused or under stress, will fall back on more familiar behavior patterns." As she speaks, Lydia has a sudden, potent vision of the entire Father John family, the downtrodden women at their mandala woodstove and the ratty-haired children and the sublime Father John himself. And standing behind him, all the generations of downtrodden women that issued him forth.

A girl in the back speaks up. "How did the scientists get the ducks to, um, go back so they were normal?"

"I'm sorry to say they didn't. It's a lifetime commitment." Lydia really is sorry for the experimental ducks. She has thought of this before.

"So they go around wanting to make it with beach balls all the time?" one boy asks. Several of the boys laugh.

Lydia shrugs. "That's right. All for the good of science."

SHE WAKES UP furious, those women and ducks still on her mind. Instead of boiling the water for coffee and oatmeal, she goes to the sink and picks up the handmade soup tureen. "Do you like this bowl?" she asks Whitman, who is standing beside the bed buttoning his shirt.

He looks at her, amazed. They haven't been asking lately for each other's opinions. "I don't know," he says.

"You don't know," she says. "I don't either. I'm ambivalent, that's my whole problem." She holds it in front of her at arm's length, examining it. Then she lifts it to chin level, shuts her eyes, and lets it fall on the stone hearth. The noise is remarkable and seems to bear no relation to the hundreds of pieces of crockery now lying at her feet, cupped like begging palms, their edges as white and porous as bone. Lydia, who has never intentionally broken anything in her life, has the sudden feeling she's found a new career. She goes to the cabinet and finds the matching duck-shaped ladle and flings it overhand against the opposite wall. It doesn't explode as she'd hoped, but cracks like a femur and falls in two pieces. David gets up and stands by the door, looking back over his shoulder, trembling a little. Whitman sits back down on the bed and stares, speechless and bewildered.

"I never applied for this job I'm doing here," she says. "I don't know how I got into it, but I know how to get out." With shaky hands she stacks her papers into neat piles, closes her briefcase, and goes to work.

THE WALK home from school is not pleasant. The mud sticks to her boots, making her feet heavy and her legs tired. Tonight she'll have a mess to clean up, and she'll have to talk to Whitman. But his silent apathy has infected her and she's begun to suspect that even screaming won't do it. Not talking, and not screaming; what's left but leaving? She can see why people scramble to get self-help books, the same way David falls over his own feet to be obedient. Things are so easy when someone else is in charge.

She decides she's a ripe target for a book called *How to Improvise a Love Affair That's Not Like the Failures You've Already Seen.* That would sell a million, she thinks. Or *How to Live with a Man After He's Stopped Talking.*

David runs down the hill to greet her as she passes the fence separating Verna's farm from theirs. "Come on, David, come on boy," she says, and because of the creek between them David is frantic, running back and forth along the bank. He raises his head suddenly, remembering, and takes off up the hill for the long way around by the orchard road.

Farther up on the opposite bank she can see Whitman's table saw where he set it up above the wrecked bridge. He is salvaging what lumber he can, and cutting up the rest for firewood. At the moment the saw isn't running and Whitman isn't around. Then she sees him, halfway down the bank below the table saw. He is rolled up in such an odd position that she only recognizes him by his shirt. A hot numbness runs through her limbs, like nitrous oxide at the dentist's office, and she climbs and slides down the slick boulders of the creek bed opposite him. She can't get any closer because of the water, still running high after the flood.

"Whitman!" She screams his name and other things, she can't remember what. She can hardly hear her own voice over the roar of the water. When he does look up she sees that he isn't hurt. He says something she can't hear. It takes awhile for Lydia to understand that he's crying. Whitman is not dead, he's crying.

"God, I thought you were dead," she yells, her hand on her chest, still catching her breath.

Whitman says something, gesturing, and looks at her the way the kids in school do when she calls on them and they don't know the answer. She wants to comfort him, but there is a creek between them.

"Hang on, I'm coming," she says. She begins to climb the bank, but Whitman is still saying something. She can only make out a few words: "Don't leave."

She leans against the mossy face of a boulder, exhausted. "I have to go over there." She screams the words one at a time, punctuating them with exaggerated gestures. "Or you can come here. Or we can stay here and scream till we hyperventilate and fall in the river." She knows he isn't going to get the last part.

"Don't dive into the river," he says, or "I'm not going to throw myself in the river," or something along those lines, spreading his arms in the charade of a swan dive and shaking his head "no." He indicates a horizontal circle: that he will come around to where she is. She should stay there. He seems embarrassed. He points both his hands toward Lydia, and then puts them flat on his chest.

They are using a sign language unknown to humankind, making it up as they go along. She understands that this last gesture is important, and returns it.

David, who had a head start, has already made it to the road. Risking peril without the slightest hesitation, he gallops down the slick creek bank to Lydia. Her mind is completely on Whitman, but she takes a few seconds to stroke David's side and feel the fast heartbeat under his ribs. It's a relief to share the uncomplicated affection that has passed between people and their dogs for thousands of years.

Breathing Lessons

ANNE TYLER

MABEL tore the bill off a pad and handed it to Ira. He paid in loose change, standing up to root through his pockets. Maggie, meanwhile, placed her damp Kleenex in the empty chip sack and made a tidy package of it so as not to be any trouble. "Well, it was nice talking to you," she told Mabel.

"Take care, sweetheart," Mabel said.

Maggie had the feeling they ought to kiss cheeks, like women who'd had lunch together.

She wasn't crying anymore, but she could sense Ira's disgust as he led the way to the parking lot; it felt like a sheet of something glassy and flat, shutting her out. He ought to have married Ann Landers, she thought. She slid into the car. The seat was so hot it burned through the back of her dress. Ira got in too and slammed the door behind him. If he had married Ann Landers he'd have just the kind of hard-nosed, sensible wife he wanted. Sometimes, hearing his grunt of approval as he read one of Ann's snappy answers, Maggie felt an actual pang of jealousy.

They passed the ranch houses once again, jouncing along the little paved road. The map lay between them, crisply folded. She didn't ask what he'd decided about routes. She looked out the window, every now and then sniffing as quietly as possible.

"Six and half years," Ira said. "No, seven now, and you're still dragging up that Fiona business. Telling total strangers it was all my fault she left. You just have to blame someone for it, don't you, Maggie."

"If someone's to blame, why, yes, I do," Maggie told the scenery.

"Never occurred to you it might be your fault, did it."

"Are we going to go through this whole dumb argument again?" she asked, swinging around to confront him.

"Well, who brought it up, I'd like to know?"

"I was merely stating the facts, Ira."

"Who asked for the facts, Maggie? Why do you feel the need to pour out your soul to some waitress?"

"Now, there is nothing wrong with being a waitress," she told him. "It's a perfectly respectable occupation. Our own daughter's been working as a waitress, must I remind you."

"Oh, great, Maggie; another of your logical progressions."

"One thing about you that I really cannot stand," she said, "is how you act so superior. We can't have just a civilized back-and-forth discussion; oh, no. No, you have to make a point of how illogical I am, what a whifflehead I am, how you're so cool and above it all."

"Well, at least I don't spill my life story in public eating places," he told her.

"Oh, just let me out," she said. "I cannot bear your company another second."

"Gladly," he said, but he went on driving.

"Let me out, I tell you!"

He looked over at her. He slowed down. She picked up her purse and clutched it to her chest.

"Are you going to stop this car," she asked, "or do I have to jump from a moving vehicle?"

He stopped the car.

Maggie got out and slammed the door. She started walking back toward the café. For a moment it seemed that Ira planned just to sit there, but then she heard him shift gears and drive on.

The sun poured down a great wash of yellow light, and her shoes made little cluttery sounds on the gravel. Her heart was beating extra fast. She felt pleased, in a funny sort of way. She felt almost drunk with fury and elation.

She passed the first of the ranch houses, where weedy flowers waved along the edge of the front yard and a tricycle lay in the driveway. It certainly was quiet. All she could hear was the distant chirping of birds — their *chink! chink! chink!* and *video! video! video!* in the trees far across the fields. She'd lived her entire life with the hum of the city, she realized. You'd think Baltimore was kept running by some giant, ceaseless, underground machine. How had she stood it? Just like that, she gave up any plan for returning. She'd been heading toward the café with some vague notion of asking for the nearest Trailways stop, or maybe hitching a ride back home with a reliable-looking trucker; but what was the point of going home?

She passed the second ranch house, which had a mailbox out front shaped like a covered wagon. A fence surrounded the property — just

whitewashed stumps linked by swags of whitewashed chain, purely orna-
mental—and she stopped next to one of the stumps and set her purse on
it to take inventory. The trouble with dress-up purses was that they were
so small. Her everyday purse, a canvas tote, could have kept her going for
weeks. ("You give the line 'Who steals my purse steals trash' a whole new
meaning," her mother had once remarked.) Still, she had the basics: a
comb, a pack of Kleenex, and a lipstick. And in her wallet, thirty-four
dollars and some change and a blank check. Also two credit cards, but
the check was what mattered. She would go to the nearest bank and
open the largest account the check would safely cover—say three hundred dollars. Why, three hundred dollars could last her a long time!
Long enough to find work, at least. The credit cards, she supposed, Ira
would very soon cancel. Although she might try using them just for this
weekend.

She flipped through the rest of the plastic windows in her wallet, passing her driver's license, her library card, a school photo of Daisy, a folded
coupon for Affinity shampoo, and a color snapshot of Jesse standing on
the front steps at home. Daisy was double-exposed—it was all the rage
last year—so her precise, chiseled profile loomed semitransparent
behind a full-face view of her with her chin raised haughtily. Jesse wore
his mammoth black overcoat from Value Village and a very long red
fringed neck scarf that dangled below his knees. She was struck—she
was almost injured—by his handsomeness. He had taken Ira's one drop
of Indian blood and transformed it into something rich and stunning:
high polished cheekbones, straight black hair, long black lusterless eyes.
But the look he gave her was veiled and impassive, as haughty as Daisy's.
Neither one of them had any further need of her.

She replaced everything in her purse and snapped it shut. When she
started walking again her shoes felt stiff and uncomfortable, as if her feet
had changed shape while she was standing. Maybe they'd swollen; it was
a very warm day. But even the weather suited her purposes. This way
she could camp out if she had to. She could sleep in a haystack. Provid-
ing haystacks still existed.

Tonight she'd phone Serena and apologize for missing the funeral.
She would reverse the charges; she could do that, with Serena. Serena
might not want to accept the call at first because Maggie had let her
down—Serena was always so quick to take offense—but eventually she'd
give in and Maggie would explain. "Listen," she would say, "right now I
wouldn't mind going to Ira's funeral." Or maybe that was tactless, in view
of the circumstances.

The café lay just ahead, and beyond that was a low cinderblock building of some sort and beyond that, she guessed, at least a semblance of a

town. It would be one of those scrappy little Route One towns, with much attention given to the requirements of auto travel. She would register at a no-frills motel, the room scarcely larger than the bed, which she pictured, with some enjoyment, as sunken in the middle and covered with a worn chenille spread. She would shop at Nell's Grocery for foods that didn't need cooking. One thing most people failed to realize was that many varieties of canned soup could be eaten cold straight from the tin, and they made a fairly balanced meal, too. (A can opener: She mustn't forget to buy one at the grocery.)

As for employment, she didn't have much hope of finding a nursing home in such a town. Maybe something clerical, then. She knew how to type and keep books, although she wasn't wonderful at it. She'd had a little experience at the frame shop. Maybe an auto-parts store could use her, or she could be one of those women behind the grille at a service station, embossing credit card bills and handing people their keys. If worst came to worse she could punch a cash register. She could wait tables. She could scrub floors, for heaven's sake. She was only forty-eight and her health was perfect, and in spite of what some people might think, she was capable of anything she set her mind to.

She bent to pick a chicory flower. She stuck it in the curls above her left ear.

Ira thought she was a klutz. Everybody did. She had developed a sort of clownish, pratfalling reputation, somehow. In the nursing home once, there'd been a crash and a tinkle of glass, and the charge nurse had said, "Maggie?" Just like that! Not even checking first to make sure! And Maggie hadn't been anywhere near; it was someone else entirely. But that just went to show how people viewed her.

She had assumed when she married Ira that he would always look at her the way he'd looked at her that first night, when she stood in front of him in her trousseau negligee and the only light in the room was the filmy shaded lamp by the bed. She had unbuttoned her top button and then her next-to-top button, just enough to let the negligee slip from her shoulders and hesitate and fall around her ankles. He had looked directly into her eyes, and it seemed he wasn't even breathing. She had assumed that would go on forever.

In the parking lot in front of Nell's Grocery & Café two men stood next to a pickup, talking. One was fat and ham-faced and the other was thin and white and wilted. They were discussing someone named Doug who had come out all over in swelters. Maggie wondered what a swelter was. She pictured it as a combination of a sweat and a welt. She knew she must make an odd sight, arriving on foot out of nowhere so dressed up and citified. "Hello!" she cried, sounding like her mother. The men stopped talking and stared at her. The thin one took his cap off finally and looked inside it. Then he put it back on his head.

She could step into the café and speak to Mabel, ask if she knew of a job and a place to stay; or she could head straight for town and find something on her own. In a way, she preferred to fend for herself. It would be sort of embarrassing to confess she'd been abandoned by her husband. On the other hand, maybe Mabel knew of some marvelous job. Maybe she knew of the perfect boardinghouse, dirt cheap, with kitchen privileges, full of kindhearted people. Maggie supposed she ought to at least inquire.

She let the screen door slap shut behind her. The grocery was familiar now and she moved through its smells comfortably. At the lunch counter she found Mabel leaning on a wadded-up dishcloth and talking to a man in overalls. They were almost whispering. "Why, *you* can't do nothing about it," Mabel was saying. "What do they think *you* can do about it?"

Maggie felt she was intruding. She hadn't counted on having to share Mabel with someone else. She shrank back before she was seen; she skulked in the crackers-and-cookies aisle, hoping for her rival to depart.

"I been over it and over it," the man said creakily. "I still can't see what else I could have done."

"Good gracious, no."

Maggie picked up a box of Ritz crackers. There used to be a kind of apple pie people made that contained no apples whatsoever, just Ritz crackers. What would that taste like, she wondered. It didn't seem to her there was the remotest chance it could taste like apple pie. Maybe you soaked the crackers in cider or something first. She looked on the box for the recipe, but it wasn't mentioned.

Now Ira would be starting to realize she was gone. He would be noticing the empty rush of air that comes when a person you're accustomed to is all at once absent.

Would he go on to the funeral without her? She hadn't thought of that. No, Serena was more Maggie's friend than Ira's. And Max had been just an acquaintance. To tell the truth, Ira didn't have any friends. It was one of the things Maggie minded about him.

He'd be slowing down. He'd be trying to decide. Maybe he had already turned the car around.

He would be noticing how stark and upright a person feels when he's suddenly left on his own.

Maggie set down the Ritz crackers and drifted toward the fig newtons.

One time a number of years ago, Maggie had fallen in love, in a way, with a patient at the nursing home. The very notion was comical, of course. In love! With a man in his seventies! A man who had to ride in a wheelchair if he went any distance at all! But there you are. She was fascinated by his austere white face and courtly manners. She liked his stiff turns of speech, which gave her the feeling he was keeping his own words at a distance. And she knew what pain it caused him to dress so formally each morning, his expression magnificently disengaged as he worked his arthritic, clublike hands into the sleeves of his suit coat. Mr. Gabriel, his name was. "Ben" to everyone else, but "Mr. Gabriel" to Maggie, for she guessed how familiarity alarmed him. And she was diffident about helping him, always asking his permission first. She was careful not to touch him. It was a kind of reverse courtship, you might say. While the others treated him warmly and a little condescendingly, Maggie stood back and allowed him his reserve.

In the office files, she read that he owned a nationally prominent power-tool company. Yes, she could see him in that position. He had a businessman's crisp authority, a businessman's air of knowing what was what. She read that he was widowed and childless, without any close relations except for an unmarried sister in New Hampshire. Until recently he had lived by himself, but shortly after his cook started a minor grease fire in the kitchen he'd applied for admission to the home. His concern, he wrote, was that he was becoming too disabled to escape if his house burned down. Concern! You had to know the man to know what the word concealed: a morbid, obsessive dread of fire, which had taken root with that small kitchen blaze and grown till not even live-in help, and finally not even round-the-clock nursing care, could reassure him. (Maggie had observed his stony, fixed stare during fire drills—the only occasions on which he seemed truly to be a patient.)

Oh, why was she reading his file? She wasn't supposed to. Strictly speaking, she shouldn't read even his medical record. She was nothing but a geriatric nursing assistant, certified to bathe her charges and feed them and guide them to the toilet.

And even in her imagination, she had always been the most faithful of wives. She had never felt so much as tempted. But now thoughts of Mr. Gabriel consumed her, and she spent hours inventing new ways to be indispensable to him. He always noticed, and he always thanked her. "Imagine!" he told a nurse. "Maggie's brought me tomatoes from her own backyard." . . .

. . . Mr. Gabriel . . . declared her tomatoes smelled like a summer's day in 1944. When she sliced them they resembled doilies—scalloped around the edges, full of holes between intersections—but all he said was: "I can't tell you how much this means to me." He wouldn't even let her salt them. He said they tasted glorious, just as they were.

Well, she wasn't stupid. She realized that what appealed to her was the image he had of her—an image that would have staggered Ira. It would have staggered anyone who knew her. Mr. Gabriel thought she was capable and skillful and efficient. He believed that everything she did was perfect. He said as much, in as many words. And this was during a very unsatisfactory period in her life, when Jesse was just turning adolescent and negative and Maggie seemed to be going through a quarrelsome spell with Ira. But Mr. Gabriel never guessed any of that. Mr. Gabriel saw someone collected, moving serenely around his room straightening his belongings.

At night she lay awake and concocted dialogues in which Mr. Gabriel confessed that he was besotted with her. He would say he knew that he was too old to attract her physically, but she would interrupt to tell him he was wrong. This was a fact. The mere thought of laying her head against his starched white shoulder could turn her all warm and melting. She would promise to go anywhere with him, anywhere on earth. Should they take Daisy too? (Daisy was five or six at the time.) Of course they couldn't take Jesse; Jesse was no longer a child. But then Jesse would think she loved Daisy better, and she certainly couldn't have that. She wandered off on a sidetrack, imagining what would happen if they did take Jesse. He would lag a few steps behind, wearing one of his all-black outfits, laboring under his entire stereo system and a stack of record albums. She started giggling. Ira stirred in his sleep and said, "Hmm?" She sobered and hugged herself—a competent, adventurous woman, with infinite possibilities.

Star-crossed, that's what they were; but she seemed to have found a way to be star-crossed differently from anyone else. How would she tend Mr. Gabriel and still go out to a job? He refused to be left alone. And what job would she go to? Her only employment in all her life had been with the Silver Threads Nursing Home. Fat chance they'd give her a letter of reference after she'd absconded with one of their patients.

Another sidetrack: What if she didn't abscond, but broke the news to Ira in a civilized manner and calmly made new arrangements? She could move into Mr. Gabriel's room. She could rise from his bed every morning and be right there at work; no commute. At night when the nurse came around with the pills, she'd find Maggie and Mr. Gabriel stretched out side by side, staring at the ceiling, with their roommate, Abner Scopes, in the bed along the opposite wall.

Maggie gave another snicker.

This was turning out all skewed, somehow.

Like anyone in love, she constantly found reasons to mention his name. She told Ira everything about him—his suits and ties, his gallantry, his stoicism. "I don't know why you can't act that keen about my father; he's family," Ira said, missing the point entirely. Ira's father was a whiner, a user. Mr. Gabriel was nothing like him.

Then one morning the home held another fire drill. The alarm bell jangled and the code blared over the loudspeaker: "Dr. Red in Room Two-twenty." This happened in the middle of activity hour—an inconvenient time because the patients were so scattered. Those with any manual dexterity were down in the Crafts Room, knotting colored silk flowers. Those too crippled—Mr. Gabriel, for instance—were taking an extra session of P.T. And of course the bedridden were still in their rooms. They were the easy ones.

The rule was that you cleared the halls of all obstructions, shut stray patients into any room available, and tied red cloths to the doorknobs to show which rooms were occupied. Maggie closed off 201 and 203, where her only bedridden patients lay. She attached red cloths from the broom closet. Then she coaxed one of Joelle Barrett's wandering old ladies into 202. There was an empty tray cart next to 202 and she set that inside as well, after which she dashed off to seize Lottie Stein, who was inching along in her walker and humming tunelessly. Maggie put her in 201 with Hepzibah Murray. Then Joelle arrived, wheeling Lawrence Dunn and calling, "Oops! Tillie's out!" Tillie was the one Maggie had just stashed in 202. That was the trouble with these drills. They reminded her of those pocket-sized games where you tried to get all the silver BBs in their nooks at once. She captured Tillie and slammed her back in 202. Disturbing sounds were coming from 201. That would be a fight between Lottie and Hepzibah; Hepzibah hated having outsiders in her room. Maggie should have dealt with it, and she should also have gone to the aide of Joelle, who was having quite a struggle with Lawrence, but there was something more important on her mind. She was thinking, of course, about Mr. Gabriel.

By now, he would be catatonic with fear.

She left her corridor. (You were never supposed to do that.) She zipped past the nurses' station, down the stairs, and made a right-angle turn. The P.T. room lay at the far end of the hall. Both of its swinging doors were shut. She raced toward them, rounding first a folding chair and then a canvas laundry cart, neither of which should have been there. But all at once she heard footsteps, the squeak of rubber soles. She stopped and looked around. Mrs. Willis! Almost certainly it was Mrs. Willis, her supervisor; and here Maggie was, miles from her proper station.

She did the first thing that came to mind. She vaulted into the laundry cart.

Absurd, she knew it instantly. She was cursing herself even as she sank among the crumpled linens. She might have got away with it, though, except that she'd set the cart to rolling. Somebody grabbed it and drew it to a halt. A growling voice said, "What in the world?"

Maggie opened her eyes, which she had closed the way small children do in one last desperate attempt to make herself invisible. Bertha Washington, from the kitchen, stood gaping down at her.

"Hi, there," Maggie said.

"Well, I never!" Bertha said. "Sateen, come look at whoall's waiting for the laundry man."

Sateen Bishop's face arrived next to Bertha's, breaking into a smile. "You goofball, Maggie! What will you get up to next? Most folks just takes baths," she said.

"This was a miscalculation," Maggie told them. She stood up, batting away a towel that draped one shoulder. "Ah, well, I guess I'd better be—"

But Sateen said, "Off we goes, girl."

"Sateen! No!" Maggie cried.

Sateen and Bertha took hold of the cart, chortling like maniacs, and tore down the hall. Maggie had to hang on tight or she would have toppled backward. She careened along, dodging as she approached the bend, but the women were quicker on their feet than they looked. They swung her around handily and started back the way they'd come. Maggie's bangs lifted off her forehead in the breeze. She felt like a figurehead on a ship. She clutched the sides of the cart and called, half laughing, "Stop! Please stop!" Bertha, who was overweight, snorted and thudded beside her. Sateen made a *sissing* sound through her teeth. They rattled toward the P.T. room just as the all-clear bell sounded—a hoarse burr over the loudspeaker. Instantly the doors swung open and Mr. Gabriel emerged in his wheelchair, propelled by Mrs. Inman. Not the physical therapist, not an assistant or a volunteer, but Mrs. Inman herself, the director of nursing for the entire home. Sateen and Bertha pulled up short. Mr. Gabriel's jaw dropped.

Mrs. Inman said, "Ladies?"

Maggie laid a hand on Bertha's shoulder and climbed out of the cart. "Honestly," she told the two women. She batted down the hem of her skirt.

"Ladies, are you aware that we've been having a fire drill?"

"Yes, ma'am," Maggie said. She had always been scared to death of stern women.

"Are you aware of the seriousness of a fire drill in a nursing home?"

Maggie said, "I was just—"

"Take Ben to his room, please, Maggie. I'll speak with you in my office later."

"Yes, ma'am," Maggie said.

She wheeled Mr. Gabriel toward the elevator. When she leaned forward to press the button, her arm brushed his shoulder, and he jerked away from her. She said, "Excuse me." He didn't respond.

In the elevator he was silent, although that could have been because a doctor happened to be riding with them. But even after they arrived on the second floor and parted company with the doctor, Mr. Gabriel said nothing.

The hall had that hurricane-swept appearance it always took on after a drill. Every door was flung open and patients were roving distractedly and the staff was dragging forth the objects that didn't belong in the rooms. Maggie wheeled Mr. Gabriel into 206. His roommate hadn't returned yet. She parked the chair. Still he sat silent.

"Oh, land," she said, giving a little laugh.

His eyes slid slowly to her face.

Maybe he could view her as a sort of *I Love Lucy* type—madcap, fun-loving, full of irrepressible high spirits. That was one way to look at it. Actually, Maggie had never liked *I Love Lucy*. She thought the plots were so engineered—that dizzy woman's failures just built-in, just guaranteed. But maybe Mr. Gabriel felt differently.

"I came downstairs to find you," she said.

He watched her.

"I was worried," she told him.

So worried you took a joyride in a laundry cart, his glare said plainly.

Then Maggie, stopping to set the brake on his wheelchair, was struck by the most peculiar thought. It was the lines alongside his mouth that caused it—deep crevices that pulled the corners down. Ira had those lines. On Ira they were fainter, of course. They showed up only when he disapproved of something. (Usually Maggie.) And Ira would give her that same dark, sober, judging gaze.

Why, Mr. Gabriel was just another Ira, was all. He had Ira's craggy face and Ira's dignity, his aloofness, that could still to this day exert a physical pull on her. He was even supporting that unmarried sister, she would bet, just as Ira supported *his* sisters and his deadbeat father, a sign of a noble nature, some might say. All Mr. Gabriel was, in fact, was Maggie's attempt to find an earlier version of Ira. She'd wanted the version she had known at the start of their marriage, before she'd begun disappointing him.

She hadn't been courting Mr. Gabriel; she'd been courting Ira.

Well, she helped Mr. Gabriel out of his wheelchair and into the armchair next to his bed, and then she left to check the other patients, and life went on the same as ever. In fact, Mr. Gabriel still lived at the home, although they didn't talk as much as they used to. Nowadays he seemed to prefer Joelle. He was perfectly friendly, though. He'd probably forgotten all about Maggie's ride in the laundry cart.

But Maggie remembered, and sometimes, feeling the glassy sheet of Ira's disapproval, she grew numbly, wearily certain that there was no such thing on this earth as real change. You could change husbands, but not the situation. You could change *who*, but not *what*. We're all just spinning here, she thought, and she pictured the world as a little blue teacup, revolving like those rides at Kiddie Land where everyone is pinned to his place by centrifugal force.

She picked up a box of fig newtons and read the nutrition panel on the back. "Sixty calories each," she said out loud, and Ira said, "Ah, go ahead and splurge."

"Stop undermining my diet," she told him. She replaced the box on the shelf, not turning.

"Hey, babe," he said, "care to accompany me to a funeral?"

She shrugged and didn't answer, but when he hung an arm around her shoulders she let him lead her out to the car.

"I Don't Believe This"

MERRILL JOAN GERBER

AFTER it was all over, a final detail emerged, one so bizarre that my sister laughed crazily, holding both hands over her ears as she read the long article in the newspaper. I had brought it across the street to show to her; now that she was my neighbor, I came to see her and the boys several times a day. The article said that the crematorium to which her husband's body had been entrusted for cremation had been burning six bodies at a time and dumping most of the bone and ash into plastic garbage bags, which went directly into their dumpsters. A disgruntled employee had tattled.

"Can you imagine?" Carol said, laughing. "Even that! Oh, his poor mother! His poor *father*!" She began to cry. "I don't believe this," she said. That was what she had said on the day of the cremation, when she had sat in my back yard in a beach chair at the far end of the garden, holding on to a washcloth. I think she was prepared to cry so hard that an ordinary handkerchief would never have done. But she remained dry-eyed. When I came outside after a while, she said, "I think of his beautiful face burning, of his eyes burning." She looked up at the blank blue sky and said, "I just don't believe this. I try to think of what he was feeling when he gulped in that stinking exhaust. What could he have been thinking? I know he was blaming me."

She rattled the newspaper. "A dumpster! Oh, Bard would have loved that. Even at the end he couldn't get it right. Nothing ever went right for him, did it? And all along I've been thinking that I won't ever be able to go in the ocean again, because his ashes are floating in it! Can you believe it? How that woman at the mortuary promised they would play Pachelbel's Canon on the little boat, how the remains would be scattered with 'dignity and taste'? His mother even came all the way down with that jar of his father's ashes that she had saved for thirty years, so father and son could be mixed together for all eternity. Plastic garbage baggies! You know," she said, looking at me, "life is just a joke, a bad joke, isn't it?"

BARD had not believed me when I'd told him that my sister was in a shelter for battered women. Afraid of *him*? Running away from *him*? The world was full of dangers from which only *he* could protect her! He had accused me of hiding her in my house. "Would I be so foolish?" I had said. "She knows it's the first place you'd look."

"You better put me in touch with her," he had said, menacingly. "You both know I can't handle this for long."

It had gone on for weeks. On the last day, he called me three times, demanding to be put in touch with her. "Do you understand me?" he shouted. "If she doesn't call here in ten minutes, I'm checking out. Do you believe me?"

"I believe you," I said. "But you know she can't call you. She can't be reached in the shelter. They don't want the women there to be manipulated by their men. They want them to have space and time to think."

"*Manipulated?*" He was incredulous. "I'm checking *out*, this is *IT*. Good-bye forever!"

He hung up. It wasn't true that Carol couldn't be reached. I had the number. Not only had I been calling her but I had also been playing tapes for her of his conversations over the phone during the past weeks. This one I hadn't taped. The tape recorder was in a different room.

"Should I call her and tell her?" I asked my husband.

"Why bother?" he said. He and the children were eating dinner; he was becoming annoyed by this continual disruption of our lives. "He calls every day and says he's killing himself and he never does. Why should this call be any different?"

Then the phone rang. It was my sister. She had a fever and bronchitis. I could barely recognize her voice.

"Could you bring me some cough syrup with codeine tomorrow?" she asked.

"Is your cough very bad?"

"No, it's not too bad, but maybe the codeine will help me get to sleep. I can't sleep here at all. I just can't sleep."

"He just called."

"Really," she said. "What a surprise!" But the sarcasm didn't hide her fear. "What this time?"

"He's going to kill himself in ten minutes unless you call him."

"So what else is new?" She made a funny sound. I was frightened of her these days. I couldn't read her thoughts. I didn't know if the sound was a cough or a sob.

"Do you want to call him?" I suggested. I was afraid to be responsible. "I know you're not supposed to."

"I don't know," she said. "I'm breaking all the rules anyway."

The rules were very strict. No contact with the batterer, no news of him, no worrying about him. Forget him. Only female relatives could call, and they were not to relay any news of him—not how sorry he was, not how desperate he was, not how he had promised to reform and never do it again, not how he was going to kill himself if she didn't come home. Once, I had called the shelter for advice, saying that I thought he was serious this time, that he was going to do it. The counselor there—a deep-voiced woman named Katherine—had said to me, very calmly, "It might just be the best thing; it might be a blessing in disguise."

My sister blew her nose. "I'll call him," she said. "I'll tell him I'm sick and to leave you alone and to leave me alone."

I hung up and sat down to try to eat my dinner. My children's faces were full of fear. I could not possibly reassure them about any of this. Then the phone rang again. It was my sister.

"Oh, God," she said. "I called him. I told him to stop bothering you, and he said, *I have to ask you one thing, just one thing. I have to know this. Do you love me?*" My sister gasped for breath. "I shouted *No*—what else could I say? That's how I *felt*. I'm so sick, this is such a nightmare; and then he just hung up. A minute later I tried to call him back to tell him that I didn't mean it, that I did love him, that I *do*, but he was gone." She began to cry. "He was gone."

"There's nothing you can do," I said. My teeth were chattering as I spoke. "He's done this before. He'll call me tomorrow morning, full of remorse for worrying you."

"I can hardly breathe," she said. "I have a high fever and the boys are going mad cooped up here." She paused to blow her nose. "I don't believe any of this. I really don't."

AFTERWARD she moved right across the street from me. At first she rented the little house, but then it was put up for sale, and my mother and aunt found enough money to make a down payment so that she could be near me and I could take care of her till she got her strength back. I could see her bedroom window from my bedroom window—we were that close. I often thought of her trying to sleep in that house, alone there with her sons and the new, big watchdog. She told me that the dog barked at every tiny sound and frightened her when there was nothing to be frightened of. She was sorry she had got him. I could hear his barking from my house, at strange hours, often in the middle of the night.

I remembered when she and I had shared a bedroom as children. We giggled every night in our beds and made our father furious. He would come in and threaten to smack us. How could he sleep, how could he go to work in the morning, if we were going to giggle all night? That made us laugh even harder. Each time he went back to his room, we would throw the quilts over our heads and laugh till we nearly suffocated. One night our father came to quiet us four times. I remember the angry hunch of his back as he walked, barefoot, back to his bedroom. When he returned for the last time, stomping like a giant, he smacked us, each once, very hard, on our upper thighs. That made us quiet. We were stunned. When he was gone, Carol turned on the light and pulled down her pajama bottoms to show me the marks of his violence. I showed her mine. Each of us had our father's handprint, five red fingers, on the white skin of her thigh. She crept into my bed, where we clung to each other till the burning, stinging shock subsided and we could sleep.

CAROL'S sons, living on our quiet, adult street, complained to her that they missed the shelter. They rarely asked about their father and only occasionally said that they wished they could see their old friends and their old school. For a few weeks they had gone to a school near the shelter; all the children had had to go to school. But one day Bard had called me and told me he was trying to find the children. He said he wanted to take them out to lunch. He knew they had to be at some school. He was going to go to every school in the district and look in every classroom, ask everyone he saw if any of the children there looked like his children. He would find them. "You can't keep them from me," he said, his voice breaking. "They belong to me. They love me."

Carol had taken them out of school at once. An art therapist at the shelter held a workshop with the children every day. He was a gentle, soft-spoken man named Ned, who had the children draw domestic scenes and was never once surprised at the knives, bloody wounds, or broken windows that they drew. He gave each of them a special present, a necklace with a silver running-shoe charm, which only children at the shelter were entitled to wear. It made them special, he said. It made them part of a club to which no one else could belong.

While the children played with crayons, their mothers were indoctrinated by women who had survived, who taught the arts of survival. The essential rule was *Forget him, he's on his own, the only person you have to worry about is yourself.* A woman who was in the shelter at the same time

Carol was had had her throat slashed. Her husband had cut her vocal cords. She could speak only in a grating whisper. Her husband had done it in the bathroom, with her son watching. Yet each night she sneaked out and called her husband from a nearby shopping center. She was discovered and disciplined by the administration; they threatened to put her out of the shelter if she called him again. Each woman was allowed space at the shelter for a month, while she got legal help and made new living arrangements. Hard cases were allowed to stay a little longer. She said that she was sorry, but that he was the sweetest man, and when he loved her up, it was the only time she knew heaven.

CAROL felt humiliated. Once each week the women lined up and were given their food: three very small whole frozen chickens, a package of pork hot dogs, some plain-wrapped cans of baked beans, eggs, milk, margarine, white bread. The children were happy with the food. Carol's sons played in the courtyard with the other children. Carol had difficulty relating to the other mothers. One had ten children. Two had black eyes. Several were pregnant. She began to have doubts that what Bard had done had been violent enough to cause her to run away. Did mental violence or violence done to furniture really count as battering? She wondered if she had been too hard on her husband. She wondered if she had been wrong to come here. All he had done—he said so himself, in the taped conversations, dozens of times—was to break a lousy hundred-dollar table. He had broken it before, he had fixed it before. Why was this time different from any of the others? She had pushed all his buttons, that's all, and he had gotten mad, and he had pulled the table away from the wall and smashed off its legs and thrown the whole thing out into the yard. Then he had put his head through the wall, using the top of his head as a battering ram. He had knocked open a hole to the other side. Then he had bitten his youngest son on the scalp. What was so terrible about that? It was just a momentary thing. He didn't mean anything by it. When his son had begun to cry in fear and pain, hadn't he picked the child up and told him it was nothing? If she would just come home, he would never get angry again. They'd have their sweet life. They'd go to a picnic, a movie, the beach. They'd have it better than ever before. He had just started going to a new church that was helping him to become a kinder and more sensitive man. He was a better person than he had ever been; he now knew the true meaning of love. Wouldn't she come back?

ONE DAY Bard called me and said, "Hey, the cops are here. You didn't send them, did you?"

"*Me?*" I said. I turned on the tape recorder. "What did you do?"

"Nothing. I busted up some public property. Can you come down and bail me out?"

"How can I?" I said. "My children . . ."

"How can you *not?*"

I hung up and called Carol at the shelter. I said, "I think he's being arrested."

"Pick me up," she said, "and take me to the house. I have to get some things. I'm sure they'll let me out of the shelter if they know he's in jail. I'll check to make sure he's really there. I have to get us some clean clothes, and some toys for the boys. I want to get my picture albums. He threatened to burn them."

"You want to go to the house?"

"Why not? At least we know he's not going to be there. At least we know we won't find him hanging from a beam in the living room."

We stopped at a drugstore a few blocks away and called the house. No one was there. We called the jail. They said their records showed that he had been booked, but they didn't know for sure whether he'd been bailed out. "Is there any way he can bail out this fast?" Carol asked.

"Only if he uses his own credit card," the man answered.

"I *have* his credit card," Carol said to me, after she had hung up. "We're so much in debt that I had to take it away from him. Let's just hurry. I hate this! I hate sneaking into my own house this way."

I drove to the house and we held hands going up the walk. "I feel his presence here, that he's right here seeing me do this," she said, in the dusty, eerie silence of the living room. "Why do I give him so much power? It's as if he knows whatever I'm thinking, whatever I'm doing. When he was trying to find the children, I thought that he had eyes like God, that he would go directly to the school where they were and kidnap them. I had to warn them, 'If you see your father anywhere, run and hide. Don't let him get near you!' Can you imagine telling your children that about their father? Oh, God, let's hurry."

She ran from room to room, pulling open drawers, stuffing clothes in paper bags. I stood in the doorway of their bedroom, my heart pounding as I looked at their bed with its tossed covers, at the phone he used to call me. Books were everywhere on the bed—books about how to love better, how to live better; books on the occult, on meditation; books on self-hypnosis for peace of mind. Carol picked up an open book and looked at some words underlined in red. "*You can always create your own experience of life in a beautiful and enjoyable way if you keep your love turned on within you—regardless of what other people say or do,"* she read aloud. She tossed it down in disgust. "He's paying good money for these," she said. She kept blowing her nose.

"Are you crying?"

"No!" she said. "I'm allergic to all this dust."

I walked to the front door, checked the street for his car, and went into the kitchen.

"Look at this," I called to her. On the counter was a row of packages, gift-wrapped. A card was slipped under one of them. Carol opened it and read it aloud: "I have been a brute and I don't deserve you. But I can't live without you and the boys. Don't take that away from me. Try to forgive me." She picked up one of the boxes and then set it down. "I don't believe this," she said. "God, where are the children's picture albums! I can't *find* them." She went running down the hall.

In the bathroom I saw the fishbowl, with the boys' two goldfish swimming in it. The water was clear. Beside it was a piece of notebook paper. Written on it in his hand were the words *Don't give up, hang on, you have the spirit within you to prevail.*

TWO DAYS later he came to my house, bailed out of jail with money his mother had wired. He banged on my front door. He had discovered that Carol had been to the house. "Did *you* take her there?" he demanded. "*You* wouldn't do that to me, would you?" He stood on the doorstep, gaunt, hands shaking.

"Was she at the house?" I asked. "I haven't been in touch with her lately."

"Please," he said, his words slurred, his hands out for help. "Look at this." He showed me his arms; the veins in his forearms were black and blue. "When I saw that Carol had been home, I took the money my mother sent me for food and bought three packets of heroin. I wanted to OD. But it was lousy stuff; it didn't kill me. It's not so easy to die, even if you want to. I'm a tough bird. But please, can't you treat me like regular old me? Can't you ask me to come in and have dinner with you? I'm not a monster. Can't anyone, *anyone*, be nice to me?"

My children were hiding at the far end of the hall, listening. "Wait here," I said. I went and got him a whole ham I had. I handed it to him where he stood on the doorstep and stepped back with distaste. Ask him in? Let my children see *this*? Who knew what a crazy man would do? He must have suspected that I knew Carol's whereabouts. Whenever I went to visit her at the shelter, I took a circuitous route, always watching in my rearview mirror for his blue car. Now I had my tear gas in my pocket; I carried it with me all the time, kept it beside my bed when I slept. I thought of the things in my kitchen: knives, electric cords, mixers, graters, elements that could become white-hot and sear off a person's flesh.

He stood there like a supplicant, palms up, eyebrows raised in hope, waiting for a sign of humanity from me. I gave him what I could—a ham, and a weak, pathetic little smile. I said, dishonestly, "Go home. Maybe I can reach her today; maybe she will call you once you get home." He ran to his car, jumped in it, sped off. I thought, coldly, *Good, I'm rid of him. For now we're safe.* I locked the door with three locks.

Later Carol found among his many notes to her one that said, "At least your sister smiled at me, the only human thing that happened in this terrible time. I always knew she loved me and was my friend."

He became more persistent. He staked out my house, not believing I wasn't hiding her. "How could I possibly hide her?" I said to him on the phone. "You know I wouldn't lie to you."

"I know you wouldn't," he said. "I trust you." But on certain days I saw his blue car parked behind a hedge a block away, saw him hunched down like a private eye, watching my front door. One day my husband drove away with my daughter beside him, and an instant later the blue car tore by. I got a look at him then, curved over the wheel, a madman, everything at stake, nothing to lose, and I felt he would kill, kidnap, hold my husband and child as hostages till he got my sister back. I cried out. As long as he lived he would search for her, and if she hid, he would plague me. He had once said to her (she told me this), "You love your family? You want them alive? Then you'd better do as I say."

ON THE DAY he broke the table, after his son's face crumpled in terror, Carol told him to leave. He ran from the house. Ten minutes later he called her and said, in the voice of a wild creature, "I'm watching some men building a house, Carol. I'm never going to build a house for you now. Do you know that?" He was panting like an animal. "And I'm coming back for you. You're going to be with me one way or the other. You know I can't go on without you."

She hung up and called me. "I think he's coming back to hurt us."

"Then get out of there," I cried, miles away and helpless. "Run!"

By the time she called me again, I had the number of the shelter for her. She was at a gas station with her children. Outside the station were two phone booths. She hid her children in one; she called the shelter from the other. I called the boys in their booth and I read to them from a book called *Silly Riddles* while she made arrangements to be taken in.

She talked for almost an hour to a counselor at the shelter. All the time I was sweating and reading riddles. When it was settled, she came into her children's phone booth and we made a date to meet in forty-five minutes at Sears, so that she could buy herself some underwear and her children some blue jeans. They were still in their pajamas.

Under the bright fluorescent lights in the department store we looked at price tags, considered quality and style, while her teeth chattered. Our eyes met over the racks, and she asked me, "What do you think he's planning now?"

My husband got a restraining order to keep him from our doorstep, to keep him from dialing our number. Yet he dialed it, and I answered the phone, almost passionately, each time I heard it ringing, having run to the room where I had the tape recorder hooked up. "Why is she so afraid of me? Let her come to see me without bodyguards! What can happen? The worst I could do is kill her, and how bad could that be, compared with what we're going through now?"

I played her that tape. "You must never go back," I said. She agreed; she had to. I took clean nightgowns to her at the shelter; I took her fresh vegetables, and bread that had substance.

Bard had hired a psychic that last week, and had gone to Las Vegas to confer with him, taking along a $500 money order. When Bard got home, he sent a parcel to Las Vegas containing clothing of Carol's and a small gold ring that she often wore. A circular that Carol found later under the bed promised immediate results: *Gold has the strongest psychic power—you can work a love spell by burning a red candle and reciting "In this ring I place my spell of love to make you return to me." This will also prevent your loved one from being unfaithful.*

Carol moved in across the street from my house just before Halloween. We devised a signal so that she could call me for help if some maniac cut her phone lines. She would use the antique gas alarm our father had given to me. It was a loud wooden clacker that had been used in the war. She would open her window and spin it. I could hear it easily. I promised her that I would look out my window often and watch for suspicious shadows near the bushes under her windows. Somehow neither of us believed he was really gone. Even though she had picked up his wallet at the morgue, the wallet he'd had with him while he breathed his car's exhaust through a vacuum-cleaner hose and thought his thoughts, told himself she didn't love him and so he had to do this and do it now; even though his ashes were in the dumpster; we felt that he was still out there, still looking for her.

Her sons built a six-foot-high spider web out of heavy white yarn for a decoration and nailed it to the tree in her front yard. They built a graveyard around the tree, with wooden crosses. At their front door they rigged a noose and hung a dummy from it. The dummy, in their father's old blue sweat shirt with a hood, swung from the rope. It was still there long after Halloween, swaying in the wind.

Carol said to me, "I don't like it, but I don't want to say anything to them. I don't think they're thinking about him. I think they just made it for Halloween, and they still like to look at it."

First Thoughts on My Second Marriage

PHYLLIS RAPHAEL

WHEN after fifteen years of divorce, single parenthood, and other char-
acter-building experiences, I met, began to love and several years later to
live with a man who wanted me to marry him, I was at first resistant.
What do we need it for? I asked. Why should two middle-aged people
with six children, two ex-spouses, and an accountant named Rochelle
who says marriage is a dumb idea get married? I explained that I wasn't
ambivalent about him. I wasn't going anywhere. As a matter of fact, I
would have been hard pressed to come up with a fantasy of anything I
wanted more than what I had.

On our first vacation together we had flown to Rome and driven south
along the Amalfi Coast to Positano. High in the hills, in a white hotel
room where cerulean blue louvered doors opened to a view of red-tile
rooftops and the Mediterranean Sea, I awoke in the middle of the night
surprised by the fierceness of remembering what it had been like to visit
beautiful places alone. I didn't want to change what I had. But marriage,
I had learned, guaranteed nothing. Why bother? What would be the reason for it?

It took me awhile to get past my own two minds on the subject. And
then it was time to tell the children. While they were growing up, I had
always thought of the four of us as allies. Surely they would be happy for
me. They were, in fact, ecstatic. My son, an aspiring filmmaker with
whom I had always enjoyed what I believed to be a particularly close
mother-son relationship, threw a paternal arm around my shoulder and
confided his elation. It was such a big relief to him not to have to worry
about me anymore. He pumped the hand of the man who was to
become his stepfather and admonished, "Take good care of her." My

eldest daughter came to dinner that very night to celebrate. The festivi-
ties were delayed, however, when she received a telephone call from her
father, my ex-husband ("I told him to call me here. You don't mind, do
you?"), with whom she enjoyed a leisurely chat while the pasta cooled.
My youngest child was the most direct. She said the news was "great,
just great." Then she told me a harrowing story about a girl she knew at
college whose father, after a long courtship, married a woman who was
killed a month later in an airplane crash in the Rocky Mountains.

My mother, I assumed, would be genuinely delighted by my news.
For years she had been asking pointed questions about even my most
casual dates and remarking that life must be lonely for me, that she did-
n't know how I "did it." She was, I thought, particularly fond of the man
who was to become her son-in-law, for as a member of the medical pro-
fession he had been extremely helpful in a recent and tragic family
upheaval when my father had to enter a nursing home. On the evening
we told her our plans, she recommended we scrap our idea for a small
wedding and "just go somewhere and get married." Then she reminisced
fondly about how much my first husband had loved her pot roast. She
tidied up the evening with a few revelations of family insanity, case his-
tories even I hadn't known. As I left for home, she pulled me aside and
whispered that she hoped I would keep my own name—and my "independence."

After spending an evening with us, my sister boasted that she and her
husband could tell our relationship was the genuine article. "True love,
the real thing," she chimed. Her clue? "It was so sweet the way you never
made a peep all those times he interrupted while you were talking."
Upon learning of my marriage plans, one dear friend was quick to supply
me with the name of an attorney skilled in writing prenuptial agreements. A second praised me for my "courage." Still another, a buddy
from consciousness-raising days, said she knew I would be "just fine."
The most positive aspect of marriage at our age, she said in all seriousness, was that I would have no worries about my identity. "If you're not
secure by now," she imparted, "when will you be?"

Eventually it began to sink in. All the world does not love middle-aged
lovers—at least not my part of the world. The notion of late-life marriage,
so appealing as a concept, aroused, when it became a reality, something
disquieting, even frightening in me and the people who cared about me.
Change, and what we all stood to lose by it, were the culprit. In
announcing that I was about to exchange formally an old self for the one
I'd become, I threatened who I was to others and the comfortable way I
viewed myself. Unlike snakes that shed their skins, we humans tend to
cling to the familiar long past the point of usefulness or suitability.

Despite the turmoil, I have come to my own conclusion on the matter: If there is any period favorable to marriage, it is midlife. Colette, the French writer and "last word" on affairs of the heart, as well as the compulsively married Henry VIII, were both fifty-two years old when they embarked upon their only happy unions. Colette's third husband, Maurice Goudeket, was seventeen years younger than she, but the only man she'd ever known with the wisdom not to try to change her. For his last bride Henry chose Catherine Parr, the only one of his six wives who was his equal in education and duly possessed of a talent for keeping him interested.

Friends—many, like me, having coped with first-time disappointments and the fears that failure engenders—exhibit in midlife marriage the characteristics that sages have told us for centuries are the secret to contented lives: a sense of humor, the willingness to let go of the unimportant, and an awareness of the fleeting nature of time. These can't guarantee a successful marriage, but they almost certainly tilt the odds. The ability to live in concert with another human being may be a skill we learn not at first but at last.

It was over a bowl of hot and sour soup in a neighborhood Chinese restaurant on a rainy night in March that I finally decided, Why not? We were discussing summer plans when it dawned on me that the time had come. We had been together nearly five years, had lived together for three of them, and had eaten dinner in this particular restaurant about half a dozen times a year (double that if you include takeout) for a total of sixty Chinese meals together. It began to feel crazy not to marry a man with whom I shared so much of my life. And although I never came up with a reason for marriage beyond wanting to, my conclusion was to hell with it, maybe I didn't have to have a reason.

We got married on January 1, to celebrate the start of the year and the dawn of the decade. My children, mother, sister, other family members, and friends all attended. Rochelle, my accountant, wished us the best. We flew to Paris on our honeymoon, then to Cairo and one dark Egyptian night rode a bus into the desert. At a sound-and-light show at the base of the pyramids I congratulated my new husband on our accomplishment. "Why did you want to get married?" I asked. Now that we'd done it, it seemed such a brilliant idea. "What can I say?" he shrugged, as strobes danced on and off the face of the Sphinx. "To live is to risk."

The War
Begins

ALISON LURIE

MARCH 20. A cold spring morning. It rained last night, perforating the crusted snow of the Tates' front lawn, and everything is wet and glitters: the fine gravel of the drive, the ice in the ditch beside it, the bare elm twigs outside the bathroom window. The sun shines sideways at the house, brilliantly, impartially. Seeing it through the kitchen window when she comes down to make breakfast, Erica Tate feels her emotional temperature, which has been unnaturally low of late, rise several degrees.

"Tomorrow's the beginning of spring," she says to Jeffrey Tate, aged fifteen, as he stumbles into the room fastening his shirt.

"What's for breakfast?"

"Eggs, toast, jam—"

"Any sausages?"

"No, not today." Erica tries to keep her voice cheerful.

"There's never anything to eat in this house," Jeffrey complains, falling heavily into his chair.

Suppressing several possible answers to this remark, Erica sets a plate before her son and turns toward the stairs. "Matilda! It's twenty minutes to eight."

"All right! I heard you the first time."

"Look at that sun," Erica says to her daughter a few minutes later. "Tomorrow's the first day of spring."

No reply. Erica sets a plate in front of Matilda, who will be thirteen next month.

"I can't eat this stuff. It's fattening."

"It's not fattening, it's just an ordinary breakfast, eggs, toast . . . Anyhow, you're not fat."

"Everything has gobs of butter on it. It's all soaked in grease."

"Aw, shut up, Muffy, you'll make me barf."

Again Erica suppresses several rejoinders. "Would you like me to make you a piece of toast without butter?" she asks rather thinly.

"Okay. If you can do it fast."

The sun continues to shine into the kitchen. Standing by the toaster, Erica contemplates her children, whom she once thought the most beautiful beings on earth. Jeffrey's streaked blond hair hangs tangled and unwashed over his eyes in front and his collar in back; he hunches awkwardly above the table, cramming fried egg into his mouth and chewing noisily. Matilda, who is wearing a peevish expression and an orange tie-dyed jersey which looks as if it had been spat on, is stripping the crusts off her toast with her fingers. Chomp, crunch, scratch.

The noises sound loud in Erica's head; louder still, as if amplified: CHOMP, CRUNCH, SCRATCH—No. That is coming from outside. She goes to the window. In the field beyond the orchard, something yellow is moving.

"Hey, the bulldozer's back," Jeffrey exclaims.

"I guess they're going to put up another ranch house," his sister says.

The tone of both these remarks is neutral, even conversational; yet they strike Erica as more coarse and cold than anything that has yet been said this morning. "You don't care what's happening to our road!" she cries. "How can you be so selfish, so unfeeling? You don't really mind at all, either of you!"

Her children go on eating. It is evident that they do not.

Chomp; smash. The hands of the clock over the sink move toward eight. Jeffrey and Matilda rise, grumbling, grab their coats and books, and leave to catch the bus for junior high. Alone in the kitchen, Erica clears the table. She pours herself a cup of coffee, puts the buttered toast Matilda refused on a clean plate, and sits down. She starts to reach for the sugar bowl, and stops. Then she puts her head down on the table beside a splash of milk and some blobs of cherry jam, and weeps painfully. Tears run sideways across her small, slightly worn, delicate features, and into her crisp dark hair.

There is no one to hear her. Her friend and husband, Brian Tate, is away lecturing on foreign policy at Dartmouth. If he were there, she thinks, he would understand why she had screamed at the children, and not blame her (as he sometimes does lately) for being unable to handle them. He would listen to her, share her feelings, and console her afterward—possibly back in bed. Lately the Tates have taken to making both love and conversation on weekday mornings before Brian leaves for the university. In the evening there is always the suspicion that the children might be listening—at first from the sitting room for the unguarded exclamation, the raised voice; later, overhead, for the thump and squeak of bedroom furniture.

Once, Erica had liked the acoustical permeability of this old house, because it meant that she could always hear Muffy or Jeffo if they should wake crying with an upset tummy or a bad dream. Now, at night, she and Brian dare not either laugh or cry. In the dark, in their pajamas, they may begin to speak or move: "They were so rude today," Erica will sigh. "That ass McGruder, my grader, you know what he's done—" Brian will begin. Then upstairs the floor will creak, and he will fall silent; or will remove his hand from her breast. "We live in the same house and we sleep in the same bed and we never see each other any more," Erica had whispered once recently.

But now it is eight-fifteen. Brian is in Hanover, New Hampshire, and she is sitting with her head on the kitchen table, weeping, trying to understand her situation. How has it all come about? She is—or at least she was—a gentle, rational, even-tempered woman, not given to violent feelings. In her whole life she cannot remember disliking anyone as much as she now sometimes dislikes Jeffrey and Matilda. In second grade she had briefly hated a bulky girl named Rita who ate rolls of pastel candy wafers and bullied her; in college freshman year a boy with a snuffle and yellowed nylon shirts who followed her around everywhere asking her to go out with him. She had, in the abstract, hated Hitler, Joseph McCarthy, Lee Harvey Oswald, etc., but never anyone she had to live with and should have loved—had for years and years warmly loved.

They were a happy family once, she thinks. Jeffrey and Matilda were beautiful, healthy babies; charming toddlers; intelligent, lively, affectionate children. There are photograph albums and folders of drawings and stories and report cards to prove it. Then last year, when Jeffrey turned fourteen and Matilda twelve, they had begun to change; to grow rude, coarse, selfish, insolent, nasty, brutish, and tall. It was as if she were keeping a boarding house in a bad dream, and the children she had loved were turning into awful lodgers—lodgers who paid no rent, whose leases could not be terminated. They were awful at home and abroad; in company and alone; in the morning, the afternoon and the evening.

But the worst moments for Erica were at night, when they were asleep. She would go into a bedroom to close the window against wind and rain, or make sure they were covered. In the filtered light from the hall, the childish features she remembered so well could be recognized again beneath the coarsening acned masks. Her dear Muffy and Jeffo were still there, somewhere inside the monstrous lodgers who had taken over their minds and bodies, as in one of Jeffrey's science-fiction magazines.

One windy evening not long ago, after this had happened, Erica got back into bed and asked Brian if he had ever thought that they might try to have another child before they were too old. But Brian replied that they were already too old. If they conceived a baby now, for example, he would be past retirement when it finished college. Besides, they had to remember the population problem. He forbore to mention what the babies they already had, had turned into, which was just as well, for Erica would probably have cried out, "Yes, but before that happens we would have at least twelve good years."

Though equally awful, the children are awful in somewhat different ways. Jeffrey is sullen, restless and intermittently violent. Matilda is sulky, lazy and intermittently dishonest. Jeffrey is obsessed with inventions and space; Matilda with clothes and pop music. Matilda is extravagant and wasteful; Jeffrey miserly and ungenerous. Jeffrey is still doing all right in school, while his sister's grades are hopeless; on the other hand, Matilda is generally much cleaner than Jeffrey.

Erica knows and remembers that Jeffrey and Matilda had once loved her. They had loved Brian. Now they quite evidently do not like either of their parents. They also do not like each other: they fight constantly, and pick on each other for their respective failings.

The worst part of it all is that the children are her fault. All the authorities and writers say so. In their innocent past Erica and Brian had blamed their own shortcomings on their parents while retaining credit for their own achievements. They had passed judgment on the character of acquaintances whose young children were not as nice as Muffy and Jeffo— But everyone did that. To have had disagreeable parents excused one's faults; to have disagreeable children underlined them. The parents might not look especially guilty; they might seem outwardly to be intelligent, kind and charming people—but inside were Mr. and Mrs. Hyde.

It was agreed everywhere, also, that Mrs. Hyde was the worse; or at least the more responsible. A father might possibly avoid blame for the awfulness of his children—a mother never. After all, they were in her "area of operations," to use Brian's term. An admirer of George Kennan's early writings, he had long subscribed to the doctrine of separate spheres of influence, both in national and domestic matters; he attributed the success of their marriage partly to this doctrine. He might advise Erica on important policy decisions, but ordinarily he would not question her management of the home, nor would she ever try to intervene in his professional life. If he lost his job (which had never been very likely and was now impossible, since he had tenure), it was his fault. If the children became uncontrollable, it was hers.

The fact that they had been quite all right until last year was no excuse. Erica has read widely on the subject and knows that there are several unpleasant explanations of this. Only last week she came across an article which spoke of the tendency of women who marry older men to remain, and wish to remain, children. (Brian is now forty-six, seven years older than she.) It was pointed out that such women tended to identify closely, "even symbiotically" with their children. The author of this article would probably say that Jeffrey and Matilda are now struggling to break out of a symbiotic neurosis. Other experts might maintain that Erica has bewitched them out of spite and envy of their youth, energy and "developing sexuality," while still others would assert that the children have been assigned to work out her and Brian's repressed antisocial drives. And any or all of these experts might be right. Erica is not aware of these motives in herself, but that does not prove anything; naturally, they would not be conscious.

It is all academic by now, because now she consciously dislikes her children, and this alone would be enough to poison them spiritually, morally and emotionally. She dislikes them for being what they now are, and for having turned her into a hateful, neurotic, guilty person. For if the truth were known, that would and must be her reputation in the world.

Outside, the bulldozer continues to operate. Crack; crunch; smash. Blackberry and sumac bushes are uprooted; wide muddy wounds are scraped in the long pale winter grass. What is happening to Jones Creek Road seems to Erica all of a piece with what is happening to Jeffrey and Matilda: natural beauty and innocence are being swallowed up in ugly artificial growth, while she watches helplessly.

Eight years ago, when the Tates first moved to Corinth, they found on this back road a big deserted, sagging gray farmhouse smothered in broken dark pines. It had been for sale for over a year, but they were the first to see its possibilities. The trees were thinned, the house remodeled and painted yellow; suddenly they owned a beautiful, even a rather grand place, only a few miles from campus.

Not far enough, as it turned out. Three years ago Jones Creek Road was widened and resurfaced, and the first ranch homes began crawling toward them over the hill to the west, blocking their sunset. Brian and Erica, realizing what was happening, tried to buy more land around their half-acre. But it was too late; the developer was not interested. Each subsequent year the bulldozers have moved nearer; soon they will be surrounded.

The Tates have talked about moving farther out, of course; but to be safe now they would have to go ten or fifteen miles, beyond the school district. Besides, Erica cannot bear to abandon her house: the chestnut woodwork she has scraped and scrubbed and refinished; the double daffodils and white narcissus she has planted under the old trees; the asparagus and strawberry beds—hours, years of loving labor.

It is not only the ruin of the landscape which is so painful, but also the redefinition of this part of town, now renamed "Glenview Heights" — what it means now to live there. Not that their new neighbors are poor white trash — indeed, most of them are richer than the Tates. The Glenview Home to their left, a "Charleston" model with false white pillars and wrought-iron balconies glued to the façade, costs twice as much as their house; the "Paul Revere" next to it not much less. The Homes are full of expensive built-in appliances; their carports bulge with motorboats and skimobiles. The children who live there watch 25-inch color TV every evening, their eyes reflecting the artificial circus lights. Jeffrey and Matilda watch with them when they are allowed. "You're not against television on principle; you just don't want to spend the money. You want us to freeload off the Gobrights and the Kaisers," Jeffrey had accused recently, voicing an opinion which Erica suspects is shared by her neighbors. She knows that the Glenview Homeowners, who are mostly not university people, regard her as unfriendly and a little odd, though she has tried to maintain cordial relations, and has never mentioned aloud that she believes them partly responsible for the awful change in her children. And even if they are, she is not exonerated, because it means that the heredity and environment provided by the Tates were faulty or ineffective. Anyhow, why mention it? It is already too late, and it will go on being even later.

Jeffrey will be living at home for nearly four more years. Matilda will be with them for nearly six more years. As Erica is contemplating these facts, with her head on the damp table, the telephone rings.

She sits up, rubs her eyes dry, and answers.

"Hello, this is Helen in the Political Science office, how are you today? . . . Oh, I'm very well too . . . There's a letter here for Brian, it's marked 'Urgent — Personal,' and I wondered . . . Well, if he's going to call you tonight, that's fine . . . That's a good idea. I'll phone Mrs. Zimmern in the French department now and ask her to pick it up . . . You're welcome."

This conversation, though banal, raises Erica's morale. It reminds her that she is successfully married, whereas Helen is a widow, and her best friend Danielle Zimmern a divorcée; that Brian is an important professor who receives urgent business letters; and that he calls home every evening when he is out of town.

She is encouraged to stand up, to clear the table and do the dishes and start her day's work. She picks up the house, skipping the children's rooms; washes out two sweaters; draws for an hour and a half; and makes herself a chicken sandwich. After lunch she goes shopping and to the bank, driving cautiously, for the sky has darkened again and an icy drizzle is falling from it. Her morale has fallen also, and a parody of Auden, composed by her friend Danielle some years ago, keeps running tediously in her head:

> Cleopatra's lips are kissed
> while an unimportant wife
> writes, "I do not like my life"
> underneath her shopping list.

She drives home, puts away the groceries, makes a raspberry mousse, and is mixing some lemon cookies when Danielle's VW pulls into the driveway.

"What a hell of a day, huh? Spring, it says on the calendar . . . Oh, here's that letter for Brian, before I forget," Danielle says, stepping out of her slushy boots on the back porch and coming into the kitchen in purple tights.

"Thank you. How is everything?" Erica puts the letter on a shelf in front of her cookbooks without looking at it. "Would you like some coffee?"

"Love it. The kids won't be home till four, thank God." Danielle pulls off her coat with the careless, angry energy that has lately marked all her actions, and flings it toward a chair. Twenty years ago, when Erica first met her, she had a similar energy—only then it was not angry, but joyful.

Erica and Danielle had known each other at college, though not intimately—Danielle being a year ahead, and in a different set. After graduation they lost touch; in the autumn of 1964, when Danielle's husband joined the English department and the family moved to Corinth, Erica was not aware of it; nor did Danielle realize that Erica already lived there. But a few weeks after their accidental meeting at Atwater's Supermarket, each accompanied by a nine-year-old daughter, it was as if they had remained friends uninterruptedly.

Danielle, like Erica, has been described by her admirers as tall, dark-haired and beautiful. But where Erica is narrow, in the shoulders and hips, Danielle is broad; she is deep-bosomed, and stands on sturdy baroque legs. Her hair is long, heavy and straight, with a russet overtone; her skin has a russet glow even in the northern winter, when Erica bleaches to the color of cream. People who do not much like Erica admit that she is pretty, while those (a larger number) who do not much like Danielle admit that she is good-looking.

In college they had avoided each other slightly, as women who are attractive in conflicting styles often do—for the same motive that prevents Atwater's Supermarket from placing cases of ice cream and sherbet next to cartons of beer. But now that they had both been purchased and brought home, this ceased to matter.

That first day Erica accompanied Danielle back to her house and stayed there, drinking coffee and talking, for two hours. Soon they met or telephoned almost daily. Erica recommended to Danielle her pediatrician, her garage, her cleaning woman, and those of her acquaintances she thought worthy of the privilege. They lent each other books, and went with their children to fairs and matinées and rummage sales. Muffy Tate and Ruth Zimmern (known as Roo) also became inseparable.

Equally agreeable, and more surprising, was the friendship that developed between Brian and Leonard Zimmern. For years, both Erica and Danielle had had the problem that their husbands did not get on very well with any of their friends' husbands. Now they realized, with relief, that this was not due to prejudice or character defects. It was merely that men of their age (Leonard was then forty-three, Brian forty-one) could not be expected to become intimate with the fledgling editors, lawyers, artists, teachers, etc., whom their wives' friends had married.

Since they were in different divisions of the university Leonard and Brian could not share the concerns of colleagues; but this very fact prevented competitive jockeying and the tendency to talk shop on social occasions, so tiresome to wives. Neither could hinder or further the other's career; so they were able to risk disagreement, to speak their minds freely. The differences of temperament and background which had made Erica and Danielle fear they would quarrel actually endeared the men to each other—and to themselves. Leonard congratulated himself on a range of interests and sympathies that allowed him to get on with a WASP political scientist, while Brian felt the same in reverse. Moreover, the existence of the friendship proved to both men that any revulsion they might feel from some of the pushy New York Jews or fat-ass goyim bastards they ran up against professionally was *ad hominem* and not *ad genere.*

Even the fact that Danielle did not really care for Brian; and that Erica, though she liked Leonard, found him physically unattractive (too thin, and with too much wiry black hair all over his body) helped to stabilize the relationship. The sort of complications which often occur when two couples spend much time together were avoided almost unconsciously, by mutual consent.

"I see they're at it again." Danielle gestures with her head at the field next door. The bulldozer has now made what looks like an incurable muddy wound there, with the white roots of small trees sticking up from it like broken bones. "I thought maybe they wouldn't come back this year, the way building costs are rising."

"That's what I hoped, too."

"What you should do, you should plant some evergreens; then you won't have to look at it."

"I'd still know it was there." Erica smiles sadly.

"Or you could put up a redwood fence," continues Danielle, who has learned since Leonard's departure to take a practical view of things and cut her losses. "That'd be faster. And if you did it now, before the people moved in, they couldn't take it personally."

"Mm," Erica says noncommittally, pouring her friend a cup of coffee. Redwood fences, in her view, are almost as bad as ranch houses.

"Thanks." Danielle sits down, spreading her full purple tweed skirt. "You've been drawing," she remarks, glancing into the pantry, where Erica's pad lies open on the shelf. "Let's see."

"Just sketching. I was trying to work out something for the Ballet Group; Debby asked me to do a program for their spring show. Freezy, of course."

"That's slick." When alone, Danielle and Erica use the language of their college years; the once enthusiastic phrases have become a sort of ironic shorthand.

"Virginia Carey is doing the poster, but she told them she hadn't time for the program."

"Yeah, man." Among the old slang, Danielle, since she started teaching, mixes that of the present generation.

"I don't mind really. I'm better on a small scale. I know that."

"There's one thing about posters: they get thrown away," Danielle says encouragingly. "People save their programs for years." Erica does not reply or smile. "Maybe you should do another book."

"I don't know." Erica sighs, stirs her coffee. In the past she had written and illustrated three books dealing with the adventures of an ostrich named Sanford who takes up residence with an American suburban family. These books had been published and had enjoyed a mild success. ("Gentle and perceptive fun for the 4–6 age group"; "The drawings are lively, delicate, and colorful.") But the last of the series had appeared over two years ago. Erica does not want to write any more about Sanford. For one thing, she cannot think of anything else for him to do. And she does not want to write any more about Mark and Spencer, the children with whom Sanford lives. She knows that they would have grown up by now, and what they would be like.

A silence, broken only by the regular humming of the new refrigerator. Aware that she is being dull, even unfriendly, Erica rouses herself. "How's your class going?" she asks.

"Oh, okay. Hell, you know I really love teaching; the only thing that gets me down is De Gaulle." This refers to the head of the French department, whose name is not De Gaulle. "He asked me again today how my thesis was getting along, in this smiling threatening way. You know I can't do any work on it until I have some time off, and I can't afford time off. But he has no conception of what my life is like. I ought to be at the grocery right now, there's nothing to eat at home."

"Would you like to have supper with us? You could bring Roo and Silly. Brian's not coming back till Friday."

"Well . . . yes, why not? Or you could all come to my house. I've got to shop anyhow."

"No, let's eat here. I ought to be home when Brian calls."

"All right."

For a few moments both women are silent, thinking the same thing: that Danielle now has to come to dinner behind Brian's back, and how uncomfortable that is. Danielle, however, blames the discomfort wholly on Brian, while Erica blames it partly on Danielle and partly on her ex-husband.

It is nearly two years now since the trouble between Danielle and Leonard Zimmern started. At first, as often happens, their disagreements brought them closer to their best friends. Danielle confided in Erica, and Leonard in Brian; the Tates spent hours discussing the rights and wrongs of the case, and more hours conveying their decisions to the Zimmerns. It was their often-expressed conviction that Danielle and Leonard were both intelligent, serious, decent people who had deep affection for each other, and that they would, with help, be able to work out their difficulties.

As time dragged on, however, it became more and more clear that the difficulties were not being worked out. This was very depressing and annoying to Erica and Brian, who had put so much thought and effort into the case, and whose opinions and advice had been neglected. Finally they declared to Leonard and Danielle that there was no point in talking about the problem any more; they just had to wait and hope. The result of this prohibition was to make relations between the couples strained and artificial. Whenever they met, it was as if they were actively supporting rival parties, Marriage and Divorce, but had agreed not to discuss politics. The agreement, however, did not preclude wearing campaign buttons and carrying signs. Brian and Erica, without intending it, found themselves silently demonstrating their support of Marriage in a rather theatrical way: smiling fondly more often than necessary, deferring to each other's opinion, holding hands at the movies, etc.; while Leonard and Danielle, more noisily, demonstrated the opposite.

After Leonard left home, early last year, things got even worse. The superior political qualifications of Divorce was the last matter the Zimmerns agreed upon. Bitter quarrels over money and objects began; recrimination and self-justification; deception and self-deception. Friends and acquaintances of the couple began to choose up sides, declaring that Leonard (or Danielle) had after all behaved pretty unforgivably, and that it would therefore really be wrong to forgive him (or her).

The Tates, however, refused to choose sides. They announced that they still loved and respected both the Zimmerns and intended to remain friends with both of them. This high-minded and generous impartiality naturally irritated everyone. Each party suspected that the Tates were really on the other side, and were only pretending sympathy for theirs. Possibly they were even conscious spies. At the very least, Leonard finally admitted, he was hurt and surprised that Brian and Erica could still feel the same toward Danielle after what she had done to him and the children. Danielle thought the same in reverse; and she said so whenever they met, which was beginning to be rather less often.

The attachment between Erica's and Danielle's husbands, which had once helped to cement their friendship, now threatened to drive them apart. The continual recital by Danielle of Leonard's many faults and crimes did not move Brian. Leonard was his friend, he finally told her outright, and he refused to judge Leonard's character and behavior—or, presently, even to discuss it.

There were also social difficulties. If the Tates had Danielle to a party, they could not have Leonard, and vice versa. Moreover, if it was a dinner party, there was the problem of finding an extra man whom Danielle would not resent being paired with, or suspect of having been asked "for" her, or both. Danielle despised the idea of her friends' matchmaking: she could take care of that problem herself, she declared. It became easier to have her alone, or with her children, to family suppers where such suspicions could not arise.

If Leonard was invited to dinner, on the other hand, he usually asked if he might bring along some girl, always a different and hateful one. Most of these girls were not intrinsically hateful; but the way they sat in Danielle's place at the table all evening, their eyes fixed proudly upon Leonard as he spoke about politics and the arts—just as Danielle's once had been—was horrible to Erica. She ceased having Leonard to dinner at all, and only asked him to large parties where she would not have to notice his girl friends.

But when Danielle heard of these large parties from mutual acquaintances she became upset, and since it was not her nature to conceal her feelings, the next time she came to supper she mentioned them. She also asked what Leonard's current girl friend was like, which was not quite fair. On one occasion she remarked bitterly that she understood quite well why the Tates had asked Leonard to their last such party instead of her: it was because he was an important professor and literary critic, while she was just a deserted housewife and underpaid French instructor.

That night after Danielle had left, Brian announced that he was tired of seeing her. Erica replied that she was tired of seeing Leonard and his girl friends. After considerable discussion, it became apparent that it might be better to let both relationships cool off for a while.

In effect, this turned out to mean that Brian went on seeing Leonard and Erica went on seeing Danielle, but both avoided mentioning it. A fog of silent discomfort settled over that area, and was not much dissipated last fall when Leonard went back to New York alone.

Erica and Danielle are still best friends, but their friendship now is full of Swiss-cheese holes in which sit things which cannot be discussed, which have to be edged around. Brian is in one of these holes, a rather large one. He has moved onto Leonard's side: he resents Danielle because her obstinate and promiscuous behavior has driven his friend out of Corinth. Erica, on the other hand, sympathizes with Danielle's view, which is that Leonard had taken her and the children to a distant provincial town and abandoned them there, probably on purpose, to live on macaroni and cheese, while he has returned to New York and eats every night in gourmet restaurants.

Danielle breaks the silence. "Is there more coffee?"

"What?"

She repeats the question.

"Yes, of course. I'm sorry." Erica stands up. In slow motion, she tests the white Pyrex pot with her slim pale hand, lifts it, and pours, off-center. An umber lukewarm stream runs across the blue-sprigged oilcloth. "Oh, how clumsy. I'm sorry." She reaches for a sponge and slowly wipes the table, wrings the sponge out into the sink, and sits down again.

Danielle looks at Erica, registering her appearance, which is dim today, even washed-out. Characteristically, she meets the problem head-on. "Hey. Are you feeling low about something?"

"Not especially. Sort of betwixt-between. I think it's the weather, and . . ." Erica pauses. The local climate, the encroachment of Glenview Homes, the fact that she has been asked to do elaborate artwork without remuneration, are too familiar to explain her mood. "And Brian's being away, that—" She swallows the rest of the phrase, recalling that Leonard is now always away; that from Danielle's point of view she has little to complain about. "And the children."

"Oh?"

"They were rather tiresome this morning. So loud. And rude too, really. It used to be fun getting up and having breakfast with them, but now— Whatever I cook, they don't like it; they want something else. They're so awful to each other; and they don't like me much either. And I don't always like them. Sometimes I think I hate them." Erica laughs to take the weight off this declaration, which she had not intended to make. The fact that she hates her own children is her darkest, most carefully guarded secret. Even to Danielle she has never fully revealed it. In public she speaks of them as everyone else does, with proud concern or humorous mock despair. Her acquaintances protest that on the contrary they have always found Jeffrey and Matilda most polite (as apparently they can sometimes pretend to be). Then, in a light, humorous tone, they complain amusingly of John's room or Jerry's attitude toward homework, which makes Erica wonder if they too might be harboring monstrous lodgers. When Susan says, smiling, that her children are "quite dreadful," does she mean in reality that she dreads them? When Jane exclaims that her daughter is "hopeless," has she indeed lost hope?

"Adolescents ought not to be allowed to live at home. There ought to be a law against it," she says, hopping back into the convention.

"You're telling me. I thought last night, when we were arguing about what to do with those mud turtles, how I'd love to give Roo to Reed Park along with them, and the hamsters and the chameleon and Pogo. They could all live in a cage there together and kind people could feed them through the bars."

Danielle, unlike Erica, can afford to be frank about how awful her children are. It is self-evident, at least to Danielle's self, whose fault it is: that of their father, who has deserted them and given them neuroses, so that now Roo prefers animals to people, including her former best friend Matilda Tate, and Celia, age eight, has become shy and withdrawn.

Erica laughs. "I'd like to send mine there too sometimes. Both of them." She looks around guiltily at the kitchen clock, but it is only three: Jeffrey and Matilda won't be home for half an hour. "It's not really that I don't like them any more," she lies. "It's just that I don't know how to cope with them. And I know it's my fault if they're difficult."

"Your fault? Why shouldn't it be Brian's fault?"

"Well, because I'm their mother. I must be doing something wrong—Oh, I know I am. This morning, for instance. They were late for school and they started shouting at me, and I shouted back at them."

"Hell, everyone loses his temper sometimes. You can't always be right."

"Mm," Erica replies, not expressing agreement. Her greatest ambition is to be right: seriously and permanently in the right. Until recently, that was where she usually felt she was. "It's the same with the house. Lately it's as if everything I do goes wrong." She laughs consciously.

"But you're the best housekeeper I know."

"Not any more. I keep forgetting to buy detergent and I leave the parking lights on in the car and I lose the library books. Brian keeps asking what's wrong with me."

"There's nothing wrong with you," Danielle pronounces. "Everyone forgets things like that sometimes. Brian's just making you feel guilty."

"Oh, I don't think so. Certainly not consciously."

"It doesn't have to be conscious," Danielle says impatiently. "Men can make you feel guilty, and stupid and incompetent, without even trying. Because that's how they really believe women are."

"Uh." Erica makes a deprecating noise. She wishes she had never mentioned Brian. But it is too late: Danielle is already off again on her new hobby-horse, the awfulness of men. Erica sees this horse as a large gray-white wooden nag mounted on red rockers, unattractively and aggressively female.

"It's the truth. And what's worse is, we accept that judgment. They get us to believe at one and the same time that we can't do anything right and that everything is our fault because we don't."

"You make it sound like an international conspiracy." Erica smiles.

Danielle shakes her head. "There doesn't have to be any conspiracy. It's all been going on so many hundreds of years that it's automatic with them." She leans forward; Erica imagines her urging the old gray mare on, its coarse white hair and tail, and her own dark mane, flowing roughly in the wind. "You know that conference I had Monday with Celia's teacher? Well, at first, like I told you, I felt Mrs. Schmidt was being over-anxious. Celia didn't mind her nickname, I thought. She knew we meant it fondly, that nobody thought she was really silly, any more than they thought her sister was a kangaroo. But yesterday I was talking to Joanne — you know, the woman I met at that last WHEN meeting . . ."

"Mm." Recently Danielle has been going to a campus discussion group called Women for Human Equality Now; Brian refers to them as the Hens.

"Well, Joanne said that if Celia were a boy, nobody would dream of calling her Silly. Men don't have nicknames like that. Even in college they aren't called things like Bubsey and Ducky and Sliver, the way our friends were."

"No," Erica agrees.

"But you know, our names, yours and mine — they're just as bad. They're not real names, only the feminine diminutives of men's. Little Eric and Little Daniel."

"I never thought of it that way," Erica says.

"No, neither did I. But once I had, it really bothered me. I don't like the idea of being called Little Daniel all my life." She laughs. "I was thinking, maybe I should change my name."

"What would you change it to?"

"I suppose to Sarah. My middle name."

"I don't know if I could get used to that. I have a conviction that your name is Danielle."

"I don't know either . . . Oh damn. I've got to go, Silly'll be coming home. I mean Celia. You're right: it's not going to be easy. Well, we'll be over later."

As she stands by the kitchen window, watching her friend drive off into the wet, chilly afternoon, Erica thinks of Leonard Zimmern with irritation. It is one more thing to hold against him that he has turned Danielle against men in general—since women judge men in general by the behavior of their husbands.

But, after all, Danielle's open dislike of men is better than what Erica had grown up with: the lies and subterfuges with which her own mother tried to cope with the same situation, the desperate playacting, the feinting and flattery—Erica frowns, staring out into the empty yard. She does not think of her mother very often any more; Lena Parker has been dead for seven years. Even when she was alive Erica thought of her as seldom as possible. She thinks of her now: a tall, slim, bony woman with a distinguished face and slightly protruding eyes; always well-dressed and carefully made up; unconventional, intelligent but ill-read, impulsively and effusively affectionate. Since adolescence Erica had not cared for her very much. Perhaps that was unfair: Lena Parker certainly had her troubles; perhaps Erica's old dislike is now being dreadfully revenged through Jeffrey and Matilda.

It had not always been like that, of course. For the first ten years of Erica's life everything was peaceful and ordinary. Like Dick and Jane in the reader, she lived with her Daddy and Mommy and her baby sister and her dog Brownie in a nice house on a nice street in Larchmont. Things began to change in 1940 when Daddy, motivated perhaps as much by restlessness as by political sympathy, enlisted in the Canadian Army. He revisited Larchmont in the following years, but less and less often. Presently he did not revisit it at all. He had not been killed in the war, reported missing, or even injured—although Lena Parker later sometimes allowed these things to be supposed. Actually he had married a Canadian lady and gone to live with her in Ontario though it was some time before Lena admitted this even to her own daughters. She never admitted to anyone, possibly including herself, that she had been unilaterally deserted, but took equal or greater responsibility for the separation ("Harold agreed with me that it would be best . . ."). Even now Erica is not absolutely sure that it had not been Lena's idea, or at least her secret intention.

In any case, her adjustment was rapid. Within a month of her divorce she had a job at Manon's, a local dress shop; in two years she was assistant manager, in five manager. She developed a special effusive manner—half ingratiating, half domineering—which was successful in flattering or bullying well-to-do women into buying clothes. She learned to suggest that the imported blouses and scarves and "frocks" in which Manon's specialized were at once more fashionable and more timeless, more delicate and more durable than American-made goods. She learned to believe this, and also all that, in the largest sense, it implied.

As time passed, Lena Parker's preference for the foreign increased and spread, like an exotic imported plant which at first merely survives, then flourishes, crowds out the native flowers, and at length jumps the garden wall to become a pestilential weed. As they wore out, Lena replaced first her own and her children's clothes, then her books and furnishings, and finally her friends with those of alien origin. She began to sprinkle her professional conversation with French phrases ("*Magnifique!*" "*Mais non!*") and ended by speaking English, even at home, with a foreign intonation.

To Erica, entering junior high school in a mood of "Ballad-for-Americans" patriotism and in the wrong sort of clothes, it was all false, disgusting and hateful. Her mother made Erica wear shopworn rejects, but she hoarded sugar and canned goods in a cupboard in the basement. She collected extra gas coupons; she cheated her customers in small ways, cutting off labels and passing part rayon as pure silk—Erica had heard her boast of it. Worst of all, she justified herself for doing all these things. If she only hadn't justified herself, it wouldn't have been so bad.

Erica did not excuse Lena because of her financial difficulties. She would rather have had one plain ordinary American sweater and skirt than all her elaborate dowdy hand-hemmed and silk-lined foreign dresses, and she said so. But Lena could not bear to waste money on "shoddy factory stuff"—besides, it was against her principles. Determined to go on living in her nice house on the nice street, but on half the income, she had made the discovery that foreign things do not so easily proclaim their price. The Mexican equivalent of wicker chairs and dime-store china, the Indian equivalent of badly printed bedspreads and thin frayed rugs, can be seen as bohemian and chic rather than cheap. A French name and some squares of dry toast will disguise vegetable soup as a meal, and costs even less than hot dogs.

Visitors praised Lena to her daughters for the marvelous way she managed, and called her a remarkable woman—meaning among other things one about whom remarks are made. Erica hated these remarks, and the men who made them. They were mostly foreign too, often from obscure stamp-album countries like Guatemala and Estonia, refugees from what her mother called The Fascist Persecution. They ate the vegetable soup and sat on the wicker furniture. Some borrowed the clothes Erica's father had left behind and did not bring them back, and one from Albania who smelled of onions tried to hug her in the corner behind the piano.

Erica was also embarrassed by the fact that her father had left home and her mother worked in a store. The hours after school which she and her sister Marian spent in the cluttered back room at Manon's, because Lena did not trust them alone at home and could not afford a sitter, were among the worst she had ever passed. She hated everything about it: the backside of the beige velvet curtains, like the belly of a scruffy old cat; the stained and scratched plywood of the cutting table, on one end of which she did her homework; the racks of dresses which crowded against her like pushy women (it was the sort of shop where most of the clothes are kept hidden, to be brought out a few at a time with dramas of appreciation).

Marian, being some years younger and of a more docile temperament, did not mind Manon's. She played on the floor among the cartons of painted wooden hangers, the piles of bags printed with beige and pink roses, and the stacks of cardboard glazed beige and pink on one side, ready to be folded into dress boxes; she dressed her dolls in the scraps left from alterations. Marian did not mind going into the showroom to be displayed like a dress to some favorite customer, being introduced to them as "Marianne." But for Erica it was shameful, hideous, to have her name called out in Lena's penetrating phony-foreign voice; to try to pretend not to hear; finally to be dragged, or pushed from behind by Lena's assistant, through the scruffy cat-fur curtains—lanky, awkward, silent, in her traditional junior-high saddle shoes and knee socks and one of those wrong, awful, tucked and scalloped dresses. "*Voyez*, this great overgrown child, *si jolie*, but I can do nothing with her!" Lena would cry—mock despairing, false—while Erica glanced rapidly around the room to see if the worst thing of all had occurred and some girl she knew was there watching the scene.

During those hours in the back room Erica resolved to become as much unlike her mother as possible. Whatever happened to her in life, she would be honest and straightforward about it. She would avoid and suspect everything and everyone foreign.

This prejudice persisted for years, and had far-reaching effects. It was

partly responsible for her initial coolness to Danielle, who was legiti-
mately half-French. And it was certainly not the least of Brian's original
attractions that his family had been in this country for generations and
that he was studying American government. Moreover, he had not (like
so many of Erica's other friends) been charmed by Lena or found her
remarkable. It was even in his favor that Lena was not charmed by him.
She pretended to be, of course: she smiled and flattered and posed and
deferred to his opinion, as she did with all men; and after Erica
announced her engagement she did so even more. But Erica knew that
her mother disliked in Brian exactly the qualities she liked: she thought
him humorless, solemn, unsympathetic, overcritical.

Her true opinion came out the morning of the wedding day. It suddenly started to pour, so that they could not have the ceremony under a
striped awning in the garden, but would all have to crowd inside among
the shabby wicker furniture and burlap curtains. Erica, standing in her
long white satin slip looking out the window into the heavy rain, just as
she is doing now, began to weep with nerves and vexation. And Lena,
who was already dressed for the occasion (apricot pleated silk and real
lace), put her hand on her daughter's bare shoulder and said, "Don't cry.
Suppose it doesn't work out, you can always get a divorce."

Well, there is no use being angry about that now: Lena has been dead
for seven years. Erica takes the cookie dough out of the refrigerator,
arranges it on a baking sheet, and puts it into the oven. She is going into
the other room to start the ironing when her glance falls on Brian's letter
from the university. Probably what she should do is open it now and see
what they want so that when he calls tonight she won't have to waste any
time.

Inside the long official-looking envelope, marked URGENT — PERSONAL
in mercurochrome red, are several awkwardly folded sheets of typing
paper covered edge to edge with large round manuscript, written with
the same vermilion marking pen.

Saturday

Dear Mr. Professor Tate!

I came round to see you this a.m. before I left town but no answer too bad. I
mean bad. I left yr. J. S. Mill with Mr. Cushing next door, sorry not to return
it sooner.

I keep thinking of you, how are you doing up there? I am not doing that well
here; this scene is really bringing me down. It was juicy the first couple days
with me and Ma, the Good Relationship, but neither of us could keep it up.
Friday night Linda & Ralph came by with a couple of friends and kind of
took over the place. Ma went upstairs which I thought showed real under-

standing but next morning we had the whole generation drama again. Of course she wouldn't admit she was pissed at being turned out of Her Own Living Room, and how grungy we left the kitchen, we had to talk about Larger Issues. You know Wendee Ma says to me smiling anxiously I am worried about the kind of boys you are seeing so much of these days, and Linda too, I wonder what her parents think of them. Their long hair no I don't mind that she says smiling tolerantly as long as they keep it washed. It is the rudeness the loudness the total lack of consideration for Others and well their unkempt dirty appearance that too. I sometimes try to imagine how it must be for your professors having to face a class full of students looking like that, I really feel sorry for them she says smiling pityingly.

By now Erica has determined that the red letter is neither official nor urgent—merely the chatter of some eager, confiding student, such as Brian frequently receives. She reads on only out of inertia, plus mild curiosity and some sympathy with Ma.

I guess you would like it better if I was seeing a professor, I said. Well maybe Ma said smiling ruefully. I am a mother after all and naturally I want to feel that my child is safe and well taken care of. You may laugh now but you just wait until you are a mother and you will see. Okay, I said, I can wait. Mother! I thought, what if I told her. Don't worry Ma I have already taken your advice and I am seeing a professor. Oh good Wendee are you seeing a lot of him. Oh yeh I am Ma I am seeing his face and his hands and his arms and his legs and his ass and his cock. But not right now, which is a big drag. Dear Brian, I just hope it is for you too. I want to lie down on your floor again. I need very bad to be with you and talk and argue with you and think and learn and grow and fuck.

> yours yours yours yours you

Erica returns to page one and reads this letter over again. She begins to feel hot and cold as she reads, as if she were running a fever; she holds the contagious paper farther from her, by its extreme edges, not touching the writing. The last blood-red word has been written over the margin so that part of it is missing. Erica supplies the rest: rs yours yours yours . . . an endless train of this word, steaming off the page into her kitchen and out the window across space and time; over the wet snow-crusted front lawn, the ice-pocked road, the cold fields and hills beyond.

Slowly, methodically, she refolds the letter and replaces it in its envelope. There is a peculiar burning odor in the room, like explosives. For a moment Erica thinks she is having a hallucination. Then she opens the oven door: at once the kitchen fills with smoke and the hot, sweet, ashy smell of scorched cookies. The war has begun.

 # Desire

LYNNE SHARON SCHWARTZ

WASN'T it miraculous, that she could feel this way after so long? Desire, she meant, and its fulfillment. Ivan lay collapsed on her, slipping out in a protracted slowness. She made no effort to keep him. In a moment she would open her eyes to the bedroom ceiling, an off-white marked by grainy, old imperfections of the surface. She would repossess identity, a structure chiseled by circumstance. Till then she would yield to this larger existence: the breadth of oceans, the reach of continents! A dupe, of course, yet what a fine geographical extravaganza, sponsored by Ivan. Caroline smiled.

He moved, and left her. They lay side by side for a while, till Ivan sat up and announced, "I have to go jogging."

Caroline sighed. "I suppose it's only fair that you should exercise other parts as well. Legs."

"It's heart and lungs, actually."

"I see. So you'll have taken care of the reproductive, circulatory and respiratory systems. Very thorough. Then you can come home and eat, for the digestive."

"Come on," he pleaded, and aimed a feinting blow at her jaw. She stretched flat so he could climb over her to get out of bed, and observed his body vaulting through space.

"I should be back in a half hour or so," he said, "I'll ring. Will you hear me?" How discreet he was, this lover. Decoded, the question meant, was she going to get up or go back to sleep? Ivan felt that too much of life's precious time was spent in sleep. He rang because he claimed the weight and jingle of keys would disturb the delicate euphoria of his jogging.

"I'll hear you. I'll be out of the shower by the time you're back."

Just the other day she had found some lines about love quoted in the morning paper. " 'Love,' " she had read to Ivan, who stood soberly before the glass pane of the china closet, holding his tie, " 'Love is the word used to label the sexual excitement of the young, the habituation of the middle-aged, and the mutual dependence of the old.' " She paused. "Is that what we have? Habituation?"

"We're still in the young category," Ivan said with a smile, his eyes, not his head, veering in her direction. A pleasant leer. Good. She didn't care for the writer's attitude anyway. She leered back and bit into her bread and cheese with a youthful appetite. Ivan flipped the long end of the royal blue tie over the short, pulled it up from under, and negotiated the knot with pained jerking motions of the neck, as though his head, dark and pensive, were striving to escape from captivity. He hated business clothes and maintained he would be most happy living in a loincloth, but he was going to meet with the sources of money. He was in a position of power at the Metropolitan Museum, where at last his particular virtues had found their niche: impeccable taste, a learned eye, and a brilliant, apparently artless diplomacy in regard to the sources of money. Watching the manoeuvres of the tie, Caroline thought impassively, He makes this sacrifice of comfort to earn our daily bread. She earned it too, but the higher mathematics could be taught in slacks and pullover, so innately elevated were they. Ivan worked his way into a suit jacket.

"Beautiful," she commented from the kitchen table. "They'll never guess you abhor the corporate structure."

He grimaced, ran a finger under his collar and left the room.

Were they? Were they really among the young?

She was out of the shower and halfway through her exercises when she realized Ivan was not back. He always came straight home after jogging since he was too sweaty to go anywhere else. She had never been possessive about his time—freedom was part of their tacit pact, their longevity. But she feared the dangers of the park, especially on deserted weekdays, gray mornings. It was a gray Tuesday. Ivan was on vacation and would have dismissed her fears as nonsense. Probably he had met a neighbor and been enticed into one of his errands of mercy, fixing warped keys for helpless children, pulling shopping carts up the street for elderly widows, sweat notwithstanding.

She forced her attention to the exercises, strenuous ballet warm-ups to keep her body young and pliant. (For whom? she occasionally wondered. Herself? Ivan? Some future imperative?) She had the notion that the exercises could hold back the incursions of time, as a disciplined army holds back a destructive horde. She also believed in the story of the boy who could lift a cow. He began the day it was born and lifted it daily. There could be no one day when she would wake up old and find it impossible to do the lifts and swings and balances she had done easily the day before. In Zeno's paradox, which boggled the minds of her freshmen, the arrow never reached its mark, the intermediate steps being an infinitely divisible succession. Speeding by, time moved in tiny increments. Caroline was forty-five, but as her friends sometimes told her and she believed, she looked years younger.

When she was finished she checked the kitchen clock. He had been gone more than an hour. Suddenly, overlaid on the clock's square face there came to her a vision of Ivan attacked on an abandoned lane by three swaggering boys with knives. That he carried no money enraged them; they cut him up and left him bleeding on the limp July grass. Transfixed, she reran the scene in greater detail. They approached him, skinny dark boys in dark clothes walking close together with their shoulders almost touching, and blocked his path. How poignant was Ivan's surprise, he who lacked the imagination of disaster. They surrounded him, pinned his arms back, felt his white shorts for money. When he tried to break away, as he surely would, they pulled out their knives and slashed at him: face, arms, chest. Few people walked down that lane; he would bleed to death, slowly. Or else be discovered and brought back to her breathing his last. Perhaps he would live on, an invalid. There was a man in the next building in a wheelchair. He stopped neighbors to tell jokes and they suffered his advances out of pity, for he had been mugged and was paralyzed as a result. The vision flashed again, Ivan lying on his back on the lonesome path, stretched out as if crucified, this time the front of his white shorts a bloody hole. Caroline pressed her fists to her eyes in a surge of self-hate. How could she even imagine such a thing? Dead would be better than that. For his own sake, she would rather have him brought back to her dead.

She shook herself as if to throw off a web. He disappeared, he had no sense of time; that was his way. Last summer he took the girls to the beach and didn't reappear till nine-thirty at night. She had pictured trawlers dragging the ocean floor for their bodies, if it was possible to drag ocean floors, especially in the dark. When they walked in, brown, sandy and laughing, she blanched as if at a trio of revenants. She had vowed that minute to waste no more of her ebbing vitality worrying over him. Very well, then. Back in the bedroom she pulled her jeans from a bottom drawer and tugged them up with satisfaction. You didn't have to run to stay young, she thought savagely as she reached for the hairbrush.

It was a terribly hot day. Just last week a neighbor, fifty-two, a mere couple of years older than Ivan, dropped down on the tennis court, stone dead, after three games in extreme heat. Precisely. Ivan was not the mugging-victim type: too big and arrogant. He might be sprawled in the same pose as Jeff Tate, felled by heat exhaustion and heart failure. She should have warned him not to go—Jeff's wife said she had warned him, not that it helped—but Caroline tried to avoid a wifely tone, even in middle age. That was part of their tacit pact too, never to adopt the mannerisms of "husband" and "wife." Besides, given the nature of Ivan, solicitude would evoke a contrary response. So out of their joint perversity, he was dead.

The children, away at camp! How could she possibly tell them? They were too young for such a loss—Greta a mere baby and Isabel nearly full-grown in body but a child still when it came to grief. Poor Greta—her first summer away. Ivan had been so devoted to them. When Isabel was small a glow surrounded the two of them, as if they were lovers. Then Greta was born, and he found he could be in love with two girls at once, the lithe pre-pubescent and the rosy infant. Caroline had had to accept the dispersion of his love. Isabel at fourteen pretended to a coolness she thought was mature; her grief would be enormous but restrained. Caroline would writhe inside with the need to see her weep. Greta, transparent as glass, would be all tears and talk, defying any attempts at distraction. Caroline would look at her and see straight through to the shattered heart.

She laid down her hairbrush with a sharp bang. This was carrying the game too far. He would return safe. He had to. Fate might be cruel and thoughtless—her own life, God knows, had been buffeted by time and chance—but there were some things that simply could not be permitted to happen, even in fantasy: the suffering of children. . . . And yet it happened all the time, in real life. She herself had been barely older than Isabel when her mother died. She remembered the torment vividly, though she no longer felt it. Why should her children be exempt?

Sinking into the enveloping easy chair in the bedroom, she closed her eyes and recalled the odious packing ahead of her. They were setting off tomorrow for a three-week camping trip in Canada. A vision of cold mountain lakes and the soft splash of canoe paddles with an arc of droplets gleaming off their length transported her into a shaded green peace. This hour would be forgotten. Any second, Ivan would ring the bell. They would pack up, go to bed early, and rise at dawn to slip into their jaunty white car, its motor humming a promise of space and solitude. She jerked to her feet. The car! He had mentioned last night, just as she was falling asleep, that he needed to bring the car in this morning to have Angel look it over before the trip. He had forgotten to remind her as he left. Ah well, that was Ivan. Her relief was immediate, like an inner flood of light.

She ought to make sure, though. She approached Ivan's desk drawer with a faint sense of violation. They were very careful about privacy: regarding desk drawers, mail, telephone calls, a minimum of questions was asked. Discretion had helped them stay married. But this was different. She pulled open the drawer. The car keys lay there, splayed out like an open, three-fingered hand. Never mind, he must have taken her set again. Like a child, he liked using her things—towels, fountain pens, scissors, camera. She reached up to the high shelf where she kept them. Her fingertips touched the jagged edge of cold metal, and she fell back in the chair, numbed at this horrible betrayal by her own emotions, by life itself.

He had simply vanished, like Gauguin. She allowed the crazy notion to settle over her gently, like a blanket. Like someone dragging about with flu, who finally surrenders and goes to bed, she felt the relief of giving in. Yes, after all these years, and yes, in his white jogging shorts, idiotic as it seemed. He could always borrow clothes from his younger brother Vic, who was the same size and lived only a mile downtown. There was a streak of the unpredictable in Ivan; it was one of his charms. From the beginning, he had had the yearnings of pioneers, explorers, adventurers. He longed to discover landscapes and make them his own by striding through them and imprinting his foot. Were he living in another age he might have driven stakes into the ground or hoisted his country's flag. She, rooted to the spot, adventurous only within the confines of her self, was what held him back. Something within him had finally revolted.

Why, after all, should Ivan want to spend his entire life joined to her? He had thought at first that he would want to, but now he had changed his mind, and with good reason. She was difficult. Though no more so than he—their difficulties, alas, were perfectly complementary. And she was not astonishingly beautiful, nor brilliant (except in her own obscure and narrow work), nor even particularly kind. There was nothing spectacular about her. Though there had been moments, with him, when she felt spectacular, so illumined she might glow in the dark. But in truth even the common glow of youth had left her. Wasn't it true despite all the exercising, hadn't she seen but pretended not to, that in certain bends and twists the skin on the outside of her upper thighs crinkled like parchment? She squeezed her eyes shut in resistance. Of course she had seen, this morning, and the morning before, many mornings before, but she had made believe it was nothing, an accident of the light that could happen to anyone in those contorted positions. But it would not happen to Isabel, or to Isabel's taut friends. Ivan was a courtly lover; he would have pretended not to notice. He knew she could not forever remain as she was the day he first saw her. He had also grown abstracted—he might indeed not have noticed. Other men would. Eventually she would become like Blanche DuBois, making love only in the murky shade of lanterns.

This was no time for levity. She crouched deeper in the uncritical embrace of the chair, her arms huddled round herself though the room was warm. He was gone, then. She would have to accept it somehow. What she would never accept was his timing. Just after they made love— that was the most unkindest cut. Had he been planning it all along? This is the last time, baby, you better enjoy it! No, no, Ivan could not think like that. More likely it was with lordly benevolence, condescension. I grace you one last time . . .

It was not any failing in her that had decided him. He was quite aware of her flaws, and abundantly tolerant: they had both tolerated a great deal. What he could tolerate no longer was his own love of a flawed object. A secret perfectionist: not from her but from love, from his own vast and undiscriminating devotion, had he run in his white shorts and blue shoes, run out of the park to the tip of the island, across a bridge to the mainland, out to the hinterlands, out, out, away from love. Love the dark victor whom no one outwits, as a young poet said. Ivan would outwit it. At the very start, in Rome, he had tried to outwit it. He was more skilled now, at evasion. Oh yes, she could see it radiantly, tall broad Ivan against the flat morning horizon, running steady and swift towards a purer region.

Well, it was a pretty picture, but it could not soothe the fury pervading her like bloat. Who did he think he was, running out on her after so many years, running out on their children for some metaphysical indulgence? Had he coerced her into marriage, then, only to desert her? Had he weathered the strife of two decades only to leave now when they were more calm? Of Isabel and Greta she could not even think any more; a ring congealed around her heart at the unspoken sound of the names. Who did he think she was, to have spent years of her life accommodating him in more ways than she wished to remember, and then be left bereft in middle age, so that no one else could ever see her as she once was, in her beauty. And the perversity of him, to leave on the very eve of their vacation. All winter, through the grease fire in the oven and the break-down of the plumbing, through Greta's broken arm, her own bitter fight for the Women's Studies program, the theft of the Volvo—through all the abominations they had dreamed of a time alone. He had made a mockery of their dream. Of their whole lives.

She felt tears coming, but she would not weep for him, the bastard. There had always been something elusive about him. Let him go, then. Let it all go. Comforting visions of her life without him sprang up like magic flowers, unfurling as she watched. She would have the bedroom all to herself. It would have Renaissance prints of her own choosing— nothing past 1650 except maybe Matisse—and not a plant in sight. With Ivan's crowds of plants, their living room was an alien green jungle, permeated with the smell of soil. Flowers instead; fresh flowers every day, graceful and mortal, in wine flasks. At night she could finally sleep diagonally without the pressure of his palm on her spine, her shoulders, her ribs: seeking, touching. Always touching. Her clothes could overflow into the empty drawers, for she would gather up his socks and handkerchiefs and underwear, his plastic shirt stays and foreign coins and spare shoelaces, and throw it all away. Burn it. It was a pity they were not still living in the old house—she could have tossed the lot into the fireplace and watched his socks turn to ashes. The shirt stays would not burn, stupid little things, so out of date. But he liked relics. Suddenly she could see the tight impatience in Ivan's lips as he struggled to insert them, and her heart fell into an abyss, with an intimation of the frozen solitude preparing for her.

She refused it. She rejected it, shuddering. If only to defy him, she would not be solitary. There were opportunities, and she had by no means forgotten how to seize them. The world was full of them: the blond smiling man in the administration office whose eyes strafed her body crossing the room. And the one who owned the bookstore and always tried to detain her, showing her new texts. Even the young Greek in the pizzeria who twirled the dough so splendidly that it danced between his fingers. "You busy Saturday night, lady? You and me, we go dancing!" Well, no, not him. There were limits. But all the others: she would like to run her fingers down all those hairy chests.

She was relaxing in the chair, mildly dazed in her fantasies. Things of no substance. But Ivan was real! Her heart thumped once, so hard it left an ache in the bones of her chest. He had been gone two hours. He might really be in pain somewhere. Waiting, wondering why she didn't come. They always, always came to each other's aid, even in the worst of times. She rushed from the apartment and down the four flights of stairs.

In the lobby Mr. Abrey, the malcontent superintendent of the building, hacked at a broken mailbox with the handle of a screwdriver. She and Ivan had thought him sinister when they first moved to New York ten months ago, because he never smiled and spoke only to warn of various impending perils. But now for some reason, perhaps his mortality— he was dying of cancer—Caroline trusted him.

"Good morning, Mr. Abrey. You haven't seen my husband around, by any chance?"

"Why, off and left you at last?" His chuckle was like a rake dragged along concrete.

"He went out jogging a couple of hours ago. I thought maybe you'd seen him around the building." She swallowed hard her abandoned pride. Mr. Abrey would be dead soon anyway.

"Jogging. Ha! Run themselves into the ground. The park ain't what it used to be, either. They hide in the bushes and wait for people to come by. I ain't seen him." He coughed, spit into a handkerchief, and turned away to tap his screwdriver against the hollow metal of the box. His frame was wasted from disease and radiation treatments — x-rays, he called them. There were no contours discernible beneath the dingy gray of his work pants; the fabric hung as if suspended on bone. In the presence of a dying man her visions of disaster did not seem far-fetched at all. She stood a moment longer, mesmerized by Mr. Abrey's tapping and the mortifications of his flesh, then darted out the door, around moving cars and into the lonesome park.

An occasional jogger passed with a salute. They must take her for one of their legion, even without the uniform. Perhaps she could stop one and ask if he had seen a tall man in blue running shoes and white shorts. But their eyes were glazed and they stopped for nothing. After a few minutes she had to slow down to a walk. Ivan was nowhere, not on the path or the narrow shaded lanes branching off, nor lying in the clumps of trees beyond. No tire tracks from ambulance or police car. When Caroline finished her search there came the quiet satisfaction of obligations discharged. Nothing more could be expected of her. She walked slowly home. The truth was nothing, a gap; not crime, nor sudden illness, nor abandonment. Her mind, filled before with extravagant fancies, was hollowed out, as when a show of fireworks is scraped from the dome of the sky, leaving a black arc.

Back home, the bedroom was too light. It seemed night should have fallen, she had ranged through such vastnesses of time. But it was not quite one-thirty. She drew the shades. Sitting down in the soft chair, she let her head drop and her eyelids fall closed. In the darkness, the ordeal she had put herself through seemed gross, and inappropriate at her age. Was that love? She made herself recollect viscerally Ivan making love to her this morning, and was not surprised to be touched by longing. But the longing was remote. She could regard herself and her reflexive longing with a large, condescending indifference. Ivan had said their love was not the habituation of the middle-aged because they were still on the other side, in the sexual excitement of the young. Very likely he had been mistaken; very likely she had skipped right from the sexual excitement of the young to the pathetic dependence of the old, with never any relaxing habituation in between.

She must have fallen asleep. At the touch of his hand on her head she gasped and the breath stuck in her throat.

He was grinning. "Sleeping again. As soon as I go out, you sink into decadence."

He was unaltered save for the dripping sweat of exertion, while she felt years older, dry. "My God! Where the hell have you been? I thought you dropped dead or something. Why couldn't you call, at least?"

"You know I don't carry any change." He waved at the pocketless white front of his shorts.

"How did you get in?"

"I met Mr. Abrey out front. He told me you went out, so I borrowed his keys. What's the trouble?"

"What's the trouble! Didn't it occur to you I might be curious? I went out to look for you! I didn't know what became of you."

Ivan was quite calm. "I thought you would realize I had things to do. I brought the car in to Angel's, and I had to wait there. The carburetor's clogged. I have to go pick it up later."

"But you didn't even take the car keys."

"Oh. I met Vic running at the south end of the reservoir. So I figured, rather than come back home I would take his keys. He still had that spare set. Anyway, I stayed at Vic's awhile."

"But why couldn't you call me from there?"

"I didn't know the car would take so long. Come on, Caroline, you sound like the Spanish Inquisition." A private joke—she was expected to laugh on cue. Ivan reached for her hand but she folded her arms.

"How are things at Vic's?" she asked dully.

"Not so good. There's a problem with Cindy's leg. You remember that knee injury she had in the winter? It seems the bones didn't knit together properly. She's in a lot of pain. She'll probably need a leg brace or maybe an operation."

The intrusion of other people's troubles was revitalizing. "You know, it really kills me how you can walk in blithely after three hours and tell me all about the carburetor and Cindy's knee and whatnot. People don't just disappear like that, in shorts, dammit. Don't give me that crap about money. I'm sure Angel would have loaned you a dime—you're one of his best customers."

"Shut up!" he yelled. "Shut up!" A powerful assault of sound. What did he do with all that power, where did he keep it trapped, all the hours he was not shouting? "I will not have you keeping track of my comings and goings! I don't do it to you. I can remember days at a stretch when I barely saw you. If you have to worry, that's your business!"

He stopped short and gazed around the room blinking, as if he had stunned himself as well. The silence was heavy. At least she had left him notes, she thought, so that he knew she was alive. Ivan raised the shade and opened the window wide. He leaned out and looked over the park. "As a matter of fact," he said in an ordinary tone, turning to her once more, "I was concerned about Cindy, and then I was thinking about Greta and Isabel, away. What a risk it all is. I didn't think of calling you. I thought you were busy packing." He tossed the car keys over to the dresser. They struck the edge and landed at her feet. As Caroline picked them up and handed them to him their fingers touched; she pressed his.

"I'm concerned about Cindy too," she said quietly. "And you know I don't keep track. But Ivan. More than three hours just for a quick run around the park? I thought you were bleeding to death on the grass."

"This is sweat, not blood." He pulled her to her feet, beginning to smile. "Blood is red. Sweat is colorless. I jogged back from Angel's too. Feel." He grabbed her hand.

He knew she hated clammy clothes. Caroline tried to pull away but he held her wrist tightly, forcing her hand to his cold, wet shirt, where the sweat made a grayish arc on his chest. "Stop! You're disgusting," she cried, but she laughed. He had both her wrists in his hands; she struggled in vain.

"Come on, show some affection. Sweat is very good for you. You know you love it." He tried to force her arms around him, but she kicked and twisted in his grasp. They were laughing wildly, but suddenly Caroline went limp and silent.

"Let me be. I'm not in the mood," she said.

He released her and pulled the T-shirt off. "I'm going to take a shower."

"That's an excellent idea."

Ivan threw the wet shirt at her. She caught it in one hand and threw it back at his head. "Mr. Abrey said you probably left me at last."

"I wouldn't leave you right before we go camping. I'm scared to sleep in the woods all by myself." He picked up the shirt, rolled it in a ball and stalked off to the bathroom.

Only when she heard the steady stream of the shower did she feel full relief, a protean relief that took the eerie shapes of disappointment. What high drama it would have been: his funeral, her grief, the shock and sympathy of friends; or his hospital stay and her saintly nursing; or even his sudden abandonment and her rectitude in the face of despair. Now she would have the packing instead, while he attended to the carburetor. Drama indeed.

In fifteen minutes he was back, wearing the red kimono she bought him for their last anniversary. He was addicted to Japanese kimonos. When they wore out she bought him new ones, in vibrant colors. He had washed his hair too. She watched him brush it with rhythmic, energetic strokes. His father had told him, when he was a small boy, that if he brushed his hair vigorously twice a day he would never become bald, and Ivan still believed it. For as long as she had known him, over twenty years, morning and night he brushed his hair with unflagging vigor. No doubt he would brush it in the woods as well, outside their tent. And in fact his hair had thinned only a bit since the days of his youth. He must have felt her eyes on him, for he turned midstroke, caught her gaze and lowered his lids momentarily, as if in code. When he was quite finished brushing, he knelt down beside her chair. "My sins are washed away," he said.

She leaned forward and put her arms around his neck, and he rested his head on her lap.

"Move over." He got into the chair with her. She loosened the front of the red kimono.

"I thought for a while you had decided to disappear."

"What did you say?" he mumbled.

"I thought you had finally had it."

"Had what?"

"You know. With us, I mean."

"Don't be ridiculous." He was fumbling with her clothes. "Why are women's things constructed in such an infernal manner?"

"I should think you could manage by now, with all your experience. Let me do it."

"Much obliged." He kissed her. "You have strange lapses, you know, Caroline? If I didn't leave before, why would I now?"

"I don't know. I thought it, though. Don't you ever have fantasies like that, about me?"

It was pointless to ask such a question of Ivan. He never lied to her; he only abstained. Instead he moved his hands over her body, lovingly. It was not true that there was no progress. Progress seeped through as slowly and secretly as exposed wood darkened with age. Five years ago she would have shouted much longer, and Ivan would have mocked her fears. There would have been days of gelid silence before they came close again. Now none of that had happened. All that had happened was that he had forced her to discover, one more time out of many, the great reaches of inner space. Just as she shifted in the chair to accommodate Ivan, she would accommodate the repetitions of the future.

Perhaps he noticed a wandering of her attention, for he opened his eyes and stared hard at her face, all of him concentrated and given to that gaze. Nothing elusive about him now. "You're not going to cry over this, are you?" he asked.

"Oh no," she replied. "Oh no, I don't cry so easily these days."

"These days? That's funny. I remember when I first saw you, you seemed pretty tough even then."

"Did I?" She laughed dryly. "Back then? That was nothing, Ivan."

His hand on her breast stopped moving, and he looked at her with a sad frown. "Am I that bad?"

"I didn't say that. No."

There had been a quiver of recognition when they first met. Not love at first sight, but bowing to destiny. Since then, periodically she would fall in love with him over again, and in cooler phases, knowing it would recur, anticipated it almost as some transcendent ordeal. Living with him, she had come to believe that men and women are given, or seek unawares, the experience they require for their own particular ignorance, that pain is not random. She thought often about Michelangelo's statues that they had seen years ago in Florence in the first excitement of their love, figures hidden in the block of stone, uncovered only by the artist's chipping away the excess, the superficial blur, till smooth and spare, the true shape is revealed. She and Ivan were hammer and chisel to each other . . .

My Ghost

JOAN GOULD

HOW RICH, strange and tumultuous are the romances we conduct after death. I see myself—even before the condolence letters are acknowledged—crouching in the corner of what I still call our bedroom, pawing through my files, reassuring myself over and over again about the subject that intrudes like flesh among the funeral flowers: money. Time and time again, without cause, I add up the figures, as if some of them may have vanished during the night. I cannot stop myself from doing it.

And there, among checkbooks, bankbooks, partnership agreements, carbons of impeccably prudent letters, while looking for surety for the life that lies ahead of me, I find instead (I should say, in addition)— something. Never mind what. Surely checkbooks are the diaries of our time, and bank tellers our biographers!

It is nothing much, I add hastily, only a trifle. But it exists nonetheless, and what's more, it was meant to remain secret. The seamless wall is no longer seamless. Water can seep through this chink. A few moments ago, I was a widow, but suddenly I am transformed to wife again, an outraged wife at that. It feels good, this anger of mine, and, canny in the ways of grief by this time, I apply bellows to it, having discovered that anger is the only analgesic guaranteed to work every time.

All widows were married to saints, all divorcées to devils, a friend counsels me; but for me, it is no longer so. Where there was an empty space in the bed beside me, I summon a ghost whose shape I know so well, and try to flesh him out with more knowledge than I possessed in all those years. Well, we have plenty of time to get to know each other better, now that life no longer parts us.

Let me look back. Twenty-eight years is a long time that vanishes in the instant of a diagnosis. When my husband left the hospital after the operation, we entered a land where time is a liquid, rich and thick like honey, to be tasted drop by drop, for it is very probable there will not be enough of it to cloy the palate. We took our boy out to dinner; we took a Sunday walk through the Lower East Side; my husband took two months off from work for the first time since he left school over three decades earlier.

And all during that honeymoon, unable to help myself, I was having the roof fixed, getting the plumbing overhauled, taking care of things that had been neglected for years. Why? I'm not sure. Perhaps I was keeping myself, literally, from going to pieces; perhaps I was equipping myself with a dowry for widowhood.

Strange days, stranger nights. I remember one, not far from the end, when he awoke with his wound leaking over his bandage, pajamas, bed. I changed his bandage, changed the linens, gave him the urinal and cough medicine, tried to arrange his pillows since he could no longer sit up. Finally, I asked if there was anything else I could bring him. Asleep or nearly so, from the depth of his nature he answered, "Only my dancing shoes."

Did I delude myself, then, because there were moments of heroism and devotion, that we were heroic? Did I forget the fundamental enmity of the sick and the well, at 4 A.M., when the sick one needs to be heard and the well one needs to sleep, when the sick one knows this is it, and the well one knows this is not it, there are years ahead and someone has to fight with the plumber in the morning?

Of course I forgot.

And then there was the bit of folly that I discovered among the financial records. We quarreled, my ghost and I, and as usual his reasonableness won all the points. You kept a secret, I accused him. If so, there's proof I didn't choose to wound you, he answered. But a secret, deceit between *us*, I railed. You think you have the right to know every part of another human being, he countered, turn another person inside out? Is that what you'll do someday to our son? But that means you weren't completely happy in the marriage, I let out the truth at last. Only happy enough to sacrifice anything else for it, he said, and silenced me.

In that silence I heard a final lesson: If a secret existed, however small, then we two were not really one, and I was not in the grave as I imagined.

BUT my partner, my ghost, wasn't the only one with the right to reveal a new aspect during this late-blooming romance. I, too, was changing. Death is a great awakener.

Within this self of mine that had grown spiritually flabby during years of love and joint returns, I have discovered another self, one that I remember dimly from half a lifetime ago. It is leaner, more alert, warier, but at the same time more grateful for friendship, more suspicious of change and yet more convinced of the necessity to embrace it. It is a more supple self. Somehow it seems younger. When he left me, I was a middle-aged housewife. Now I am an adolescent widow, emotionally volcanic like all adolescents and convinced at times that I'm unnecessary, but alive, definitely alive.

I remember the day when one of my husband's clients who was divorced called for advice because he was worried. He had met a wonderful woman and wanted to remarry. Then why on earth was he worried? my husband asked. It seemed that she had been widowed twice. Both husbands had committed suicide, both by jumping out of windows, as it happened. "Get married, get married!" my husband counseled exuberantly. "But just to play safe, take an apartment on a low floor."

NOT bad advice, it seems to me, this tempered buoyancy, though it needn't take the form of remarriage in my case. All of us over the age of forty, I find, suffer from bouts of self-pity. All of us, not just widows and divorcées, waste strength regretting the past, either because it was so good or because it was so bad, but only widows bear the special burden of our friends' pity, which implies that we're no longer the personages we used to be.

Of course we're not. We've changed, and so will our friends. The truth is that all of us—divorcées, widows and those whose time has not yet come—are going to have more than one life to live. Sooner or later we discover that we only rent our happiness or unhappiness, we don't own it, and we'd better be prepared to move out on short notice, carrying our own suitcases at that. After all, who ever promised us perpetual care?

That can be found in only one place, my ghost in dancing shoes tells me.

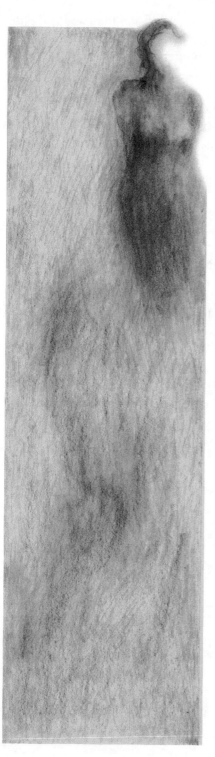

Motherhood

ONLY recently have women been allowed to demystify motherhood and write not only of the deep and life-enhancing love they feel for their children but also the rage, ambivalence, sorrow, and regrets that bearing children brings.

The intense but mixed emotions of childbirth are dramatized in Abby Frucht's "Are You Mine?" Cara gives birth to her second child and is troubled by the fact that five hours later—still thinking loyally of her firstborn—she hasn't fallen in love with the new baby.

Fran Castan's poem "The Adoption" lyrically brings to life a joyously *un*ambivalent moment of love between baby and mother, as the mother gives the baby its bottle and they seem "a single body joined in a ceremony of light." And Mary Gordon's "A Mother's Love" evokes a mother's amazed discovery, on an ordinary day, of her love for her children—"as physically rooted as sexual desire."

Adrienne Rich broke the silence about the darker side of motherhood, writing of the immense range of feelings that crowd a mother's heart. In "Anger and Tenderness" Rich's journal and comments searingly explore "the murderous alternation between bitter resentment and raw-edged nerves, and blissful gratification and tenderness" that a mother may feel within the span of one single day.

The tragedy and regret that mothers risk by loving their children are dealt with—first in Gloria Naylor's "Luciela Louise Turner," which shows a mother working through the greatest of losses, and then in Tillie Olsen's "I Stand Here Ironing." Olsen's tired working-class mother sadly measures how her struggles against poverty robbed her eighteen-year-old daughter of love and security.

Ntozake Shange's "Mama" is a black mother in Charleston, South Carolina, who shares an up-and-down Christmas with her three exuberant daughters and lays to rest some of her own fears for them.

Kelly Cherry's "Not the Phil Donahue Show" rounds out "Motherhood." When her twenty-year-old daughter makes an startling announcement about her love life, Cherry's heroine must wrestle with that painful passage: accepting with good grace that her daughter is taking charge of her own life.

Are You Mine?

ABBY FRUCHT

IT WAS early evening on the day of the birth of Cara's second child, Max. Max was born at noon, and at suppertime Cara was still waiting to fall in love with him. She didn't love him the very instant he was born, as many women say they love their babies, or during pregnancy, as other women do. In fact her inclination all along had been to ignore him entirely, so that the changes in her body during pregnancy seemed to her to be just that, changes in *her* body, not in anyone else's. She barely thought of the baby at all until the labor began, and then her recognition of him was clouded by pain. By suppertime, she hadn't forgotten the pain, as women say they do, but she was trying to forget it. Still, she kept hearing someone down the hall in the throes of it, screaming, "I can't do it, I can't do it, I can't do it," until Cara's entire body clenched in agonized, convulsive sympathy, and only on reflection could Cara say to herself, "I did do it, I did do it, I did do it, it's over."

Cara's gown did not fit properly. Either that or she was wearing it wrong, because it didn't cover her. She couldn't have cared less. She had license to be half-naked, lazy, depraved, steeped in strange, uncommon relief. She was feeling quite pleased with herself, and she was pleased with her baby twitching in sleep on the high, wheeled, glassed-in cart at the foot of her bed, where she could gaze at him as if through a window. He was knobby and pink, unconscious, detached. She hadn't counted his fingers or toes, as mothers are said to do, but she knew they were all there because the nurses would have said something if they weren't, and she knew he was breathing. She could see the uneven rhythm of it through the blanket, unless that was his heartbeat, so fierce in so tiny a body. No matter what, he was alive. She had said to Douglas several times since the delivery, "He's alive, he's alive," meaning, *I'm alive, I'm alive, I'm alive.*

CARA had been out of bed just once all day and knew she'd be expected to get out again soon, to go to the bathroom. The nurses insisted she move her bowels. Now that the labor was done, that was what scared her the most. She might split apart, pushing it out. She had stitches where she tore and where they cut her. Besides, she felt shaky even now but nothing like when he was born. Then she'd been afraid to hold him she was shaking so hard, and her breath had thumped under her ribs. She could see that they were holding the baby above her, still wet and unwashed, bloody, with the white, pasty stuff still on him, but it had not occurred to her to take him into her own long arms even when her fingers parted as if to receive him. When the nurses lowered him onto her chest she said to Douglas, "Hold him there, don't let me hold him." The baby was warm and wet, and she didn't welcome the feel of him the way women are said to. It was too distracting. She wanted only the sensation of the pain being shaken off of her, limb by limb.

"I feel like I'm going to die," she had said.

Douglas had smiled. "Well, you're not."

"Yes, I am. Look at this." She held up a hand that was shaking so hard its outline was blurred. Beyond it she could see the nurses clustered around the baby on the cart against the wall, cleaning him, clipping him, tapping here and there and examining. Then the doctor was sitting between Cara's propped-apart legs with a needle and thread, peering critically at the ragged edges needing to be mended. So calmly, so confidently did the doctor thread her needle that she might have been sewing on a button. She gave Cara a shot of novocain meant to last five minutes, but the stitching took five and a half. Douglas held Cara's hand, but how eerie it was, because the hand was not part of her body. Rather, she *had* no body. She was all system, no flesh, all blood rushing this way and that in narrow, endless, humming channels that seemed never to reach her brain. When someone cranked up the head of her bed, it was only like a change in the weather as if after a rain, when the air thins out. Cara thought she might stay that way forever, all effect and no substance, even while the nurse palpated her belly to make sure her uterus was shrinking.

"That's very good," the nurse had commended, as if Cara had anything to do with it. This is not a bad way to be, Cara had thought—buzzing, buzzing—but already it was starting to fade. For a while she was all pins and needles, and then she was only someone lying on a too-small bed in a hospital room. One elbow stuck out past the edge of the mattress, and both feet did, too, when her knees weren't bent. Now the pain was like a ball of yarn unraveling, as if the nurse across the room were drawing it to her to be wrapped up and taken to the neighboring room, where the next woman lay in labor. Cara's room was large and pleasant, with salmon-hued walls and a dense mauve carpet. Over the sink, a mirror reflected Cara propped up on pillows, and she could see the baby there, too, looking more remote than ever. There was the bathroom, which she avoided looking at, and just next to the bed a table with a water pitcher on it. She was reaching for a cup when Douglas said, "I can get you some ginger ale or juice from the hall," startling her because she hadn't seen him in the mirror. He was sitting in the armchair with his newspaper and pencil, solving the Cryptoquip.

"You were asleep," he said.

"No, I wasn't."

He raised his eyebrows.

"Ginger ale," she said, "and a toothbrush, please."

Douglas said he'd help her to the bathroom.

"Never mind," Cara said.

"It's okay. I can walk you."

"It's not that."

"What?"

"It's what I'm supposed to do when I get there. I can't."

"That's okay. You don't have to."

Her feet were bare, and she laid them flat on the floor all at once, just to feel the ground against the soles, before putting any weight on them. In the bathroom she didn't look at the toilet but took a moment to look in the mirror, where she noticed how vivid she looked; how dark her lips, how red her hair, how pale her skin, like an electric Snow White, only her gown had fallen wide open so you could see her pubic hair and the elastic belt around her hips, which held the sanitary pad. It would have to be changed. It was heavy with blood and hung loose between her thighs, and as she took it off she got blood on her fingers and on the toilet seat. She rolled the pad into a ball, wrapped it in a strip of toilet paper, and was dropping it into the garbage when she realized that she didn't have another. She called out of the bathroom to Douglas, but he was getting the ginger ale. Instead there was a nurse in the room, hovering near the bathroom door.

"I don't have any pads," said Cara.

"Did you go?" said the nurse.

"What?"

"Did you go to the bathroom? Have you moved your bowels?"

"I don't have to," said Cara.

The nurse brought in a stack of pads and a squirt bottle, which she filled with warm water at the sink.

"You clean yourself with this," said the nurse, gesturing with the bottle, "and then pat yourself dry with these," holding up a bag of cotton balls.

Cara said nothing. She was in awe of all the blood, as she had been years ago after Georgie was born, when they had made her wash herself with Betadine. Now water was the thing, apparently. It had run down her legs, and when she wiped it, the soaked cotton turned immediately scarlet. No man can ever bleed like this and still be healthy, she thought, but she didn't say it to Douglas when he came in carrying the can of soda. He would think she was insulting him, and maybe she was. She climbed gingerly back up on the bed, then took the straw in her mouth and sipped, concentrating hard until she thought she could feel in her body the very spot from where the blood began to flow, like the start of a river. It was like sun beating down on ice, and the ice clopping off in big chunks that released just a drop, then trickled, then gushed. It was like sitting on hot ice. She was reveling in this when a nurse approached the baby and stood hovering over the cart. The baby was waking, the edges of his blanket beginning to tremble, a high wail escaping. Douglas reached the baby first and brought him to Cara, but the nurse had started taking Cara's temperature. After that there was the blood pressure to be taken again, and the palpating of the uterus, the baby mewing all the while as Douglas rocked him. Cara hadn't put him on the breast yet and thought of letting Douglas feed him with a bottle; they made a snug-looking pair, and she would keep a safe distance and watch them together, today, and maybe tomorrow as well, and maybe the day after. But Douglas put him in her arms before she had a chance to speak. What a shock it was; Max was practically weightless, yet in a moment he managed to find her nipple, all by himself.

"He has a strong suck," Cara said after a while.

Douglas bent close to the nipple and said he could hear the stuff coming out of it; it made a sound like the fizz of champagne.

"I could go buy us some champagne," he said. "But I'd rather stay here if you don't mind."

"I don't mind. I want you to. Can you bring me a couple of pillows? Put your finger in his hand; see how he grabs hold."

"He's really cute."

"He's so small. When's the doctor going to come and look at him? He's tinier than Georgie ever was. And look how dark his hair is."

"So was Georgie's. It'll change."

"He looks like Georgie as a baby. He's so red all over. I wish . . . Oh, look, he's opened his eyes."

"He's looking at you," said Douglas.

"You take him and feed him with a bottle and then he'll look at you," Cara said boldly.

"I'm not worried," said Douglas.

"I am."

"What?"

"I am worried," said Cara.

"Because why?"

"I don't want to say it."

"Don't worry. It'll happen."

"What will?"

"You'll fall in love with him," said Douglas. "Soon enough. You said the same thing with Georgie."

"I'm not just saying it," said Cara.

"I know. I mean the same thing happened. It took a while."

"It's already been an hour!"

"No, it hasn't. It's been five. You're exhausted, Cara. You're too tired to fall in love."

"But what if I don't?"

"You will," said Douglas.

"You will," said the nurse, who had been there all along, stacking towels at the edge of the sink.

THE timing of this second labor had been the same as the first; Cara had wakened at three in the morning and given birth at noon. At three-fifteen the first time, she woke up Douglas; now she'd waited until quarter to four.

"How far apart?" Douglas had asked, both times.

"Fifteen minutes."

"What do they feel like?"

"Like fists clenching and unclenching." She got up on one elbow and looked at the clock. "I don't know. Fourteen minutes that time. And they don't really hurt. It's just pressure. It's just a squeeze." She was thinking it was probably false.

"That's what it felt like the last time," said Douglas. "It didn't hurt at the beginning."

"It's premature."

"It's two days before the delivery date," said Douglas.

"I know. But I was planning on being late. Remember?"

"Well, doesn't look like you're going to be late."

"I don't know. I don't think this is it. Fourteen minutes again. Shit."

"Did that hurt?"

"No. Listen."

It was the dog. Whenever anyone woke up in the middle of the night, she woke up, too, and needed to go out. She was sitting at the base of the steps, shaking, tail thumping on the floor. Douglas sighed and climbed out of bed. Cara made a fist and hit the pillow, her way of kicking the dog.

"You'll be okay for a couple of minutes?"

"Sure," Cara said, and then she watched him get dressed in the light from the hall. Half in and half out of it, his nakedness glowed and dissolved, glowed and dissolved. He had a flat, narrow belly and pale, gangly legs, yet a way of stepping gracefully into his jeans, toes pointed, a little wiggle to the hips when he pulled them up. Last night there'd been a party in the park down the street—high school was out for the year—and she knew he'd try to gather up the thrown-around beer cans and then drop them, get mad, give up, then collect them again.

"Don't hurry up," she told him. "Just have a good walk."

The dog yelped excitedly when Douglas started downstairs, and Cara thought she heard their other child stirring in the room across the hall.

Other child, she thought, horrified, already I said *other child*.

There was a window above the headboard of the bed, and when she pulled herself up and looked out, she felt the fist again, sharper than before. She nearly yelled. But she looked at the clock instead. Fourteen minutes, same as always. Not much later, she heard Douglas drop the empty beer cans on the porch outside the door, then kick his sandals off his feet. "There's some water in your bowl," he said reasonably, and the dog tick-ticked to her bowl in the kitchen. Not since the birth of their first child had Cara said even that to Kato. Long ago she used to sing to her, and lie on the floor with her head on the dog's soft ruff while stroking her paws. Now Kato was just an animal needing meager helpings of affection that Cara doled out begrudgingly if she had a little extra. Cara wasn't one of those big-hearted women like the one who lived just down the block. If you knocked on her door it was opened by children and dogs all sizes, shapes, and colors, not one at a time but all at once, ten or eleven of them, crowding the steps and front hall. After visiting there, Cara felt stingy with love. She was worried she would use it up. Pregnant, she kept looking at her son, thinking, what will happen to us? Even then she kept getting lost staring at him. He was already four, already a ponderer, already learning to read, and she needed to examine him in order to know whom he was changing into, so she would love him for who he was now, and not who he had been before. These days he was Bilbo Baggins on his way to Murkwood. Despite the summer heat, he wore Cara's giant fuzzy slippers and a magic ring she had made out of foil. The ring was supposed to make him invisible, so she would pull him onto her lap and pretend she didn't know he was there. "Bilbo! Bilbo Baggins!" she'd call, and set him down in the chair and get up and go from room to room looking for him, from closet to closet, all the while hearing him giggling against the arm of the chair until she came back in and sat down right on top of him saying, "Forget it, I can't find him, he must have gone to Murkwood." Ordinarily he was playful, but once he grew very still and worried there underneath her so that at last she got up and took his head in her hands, exclaiming in an adoring voice, "Oh, you're back, I've found you," taking a risk and calling him not Bilbo but by his name, Georgie. He didn't want to let go. They stayed in the chair as the room glowed with sunset, and let the rice scorch on the stove. She could feel the baby hiccupping inside her in jumps and starts as it did every day at this time. Her son seemed unaware of them. Cara conducted an experiment; she told herself the hiccups were a baby that she needed to love, and she sat there and loved it and felt how much love was left over for her son in her arms. Almost none. It was terrible. When she wanted to start loving Georgie again, she had to stop loving the hiccups.

"I called Georgie our *other child*," she said to Douglas when he'd come upstairs.

"How are you feeling?" he asked.

"I don't know. It's still every fourteen minutes."

"You still think it's fake?"

"No."

He unbuttoned his shirt and in that same graceful, unconscious fashion let it slide from his body. In bed, he put his hand on her belly so the cool temperature of it was like a balm on top of the next contraction. She took his hand in her own and moved it in widening circles around her navel and then up over her breasts to her neck and chin. She was scared about the labor because she hadn't read any books this time and had forgotten the breathing techniques. Throughout this pregnancy—early on when she was tired, then later when she'd felt so high and buoyant—Cara had insisted, had believed, that this delivery wouldn't hurt. But now she knew that it would. She was being made to prepare herself. It was like some hand reaching in, grabbing hold of her guts, squeezing hard, withdrawing, only later it wouldn't withdraw, it would knead and twist, it would dig in with knuckles and nails.

"That was nine minutes," she said after a while. "They're getting harder. I think we should call the doctor. I'm taking a shower. You should wash your hands, they smell like beer."

In the shower she shaved her armpits and her legs although that was difficult because her belly was in the way and because she didn't want to be already doubled over when the contraction came. Soon her son padded into the bathroom, unfastened his drawstring pajamas, stepped to the toilet, peed, climbed up on his step stool, washed his hands, climbed down to dry them, climbed up again to get a drink of water out of his cup, all this with his pajamas down around his ankles.

"You're all grown up," said Cara, who was drying herself while standing in the tub.

"I know."

"Get Daddy!" said Cara, but Douglas was in the room already with a pile of clothes that he helped her get into.

"What should I put in the bag?" he said breathlessly.

"Get breakfast for Georgie. Call Deena and tell her to come by for him. I'll get the bag. I'm okay. I should call my mother," said Cara, who when the contraction faded felt cool, organized, able. She packed her caftan, two books, three pairs of socks, and the engraved silver hair clip she always meant to wear and never did because no matter what, it never seemed appropriate. She forgot underpants, a toothbrush, and everything else. The next contraction took the breath out of her and forced her to stand absolutely still as if to acknowledge its presence.

"Okay, okay," Cara said to it, and then, to herself, "If they stay like this I can make it. I can deal with this."

The hospital was just down the street five blocks, and she imagined she and Douglas might stroll it together in their almost-matching sunglasses, arm in arm along the sidewalks, stopping every seven minutes to look at the pigeons on the telephone wires. But then she found she'd put her sandals on and was standing at the door, waiting, her hands on her belly, her bag packed but upstairs where she'd left it. She was like someone trying to stay calm in an air raid. But for the sake of what? It was only going to get worse. When Georgie had kissed her three times goodbye, she made straight for the car without so much as a glance at Deena leading him away. In the car she announced, "I'm not going to do up my seat belt." There was nobody else on the road just then, and Cara had the feeling that everything in the world was being put on hold so that she could have her baby. She felt singled out. The windshield was free of the bird droppings that always fell on it during the night, but she didn't think about her husband having found a minute in their hectic morning to clean it. She only stared at the glittering hood of the car as it brought her closer to the hospital.

"This might not be the real thing," Cara said to the nurse examining her. "They seem to be subsiding. I think if I go home and rest, get in my own bed, read a little or something, clean up a little, do some . . ."

The nurse said that Cara was four centimeters dilated, that it was certainly the real thing, that the baby might hold on till evening, and that if Cara felt she would be more comfortable at home in her own bed or on a lawn chair in the shade, then she could leave the hospital and come back around five.

"What do you think?" said Douglas, in such a way that Cara knew he was thinking of Georgie and of how fast that had happened, faster than the nurses had predicted.

"I don't know," said Cara. "Why don't I sit down a minute and we can wait a while and get my breath and see how things go, and if I'm okay for a while we'll go. You can make lemonade."

There was an armchair recliner in the corner of the room, big and sturdy-looking with just the right amount of yield when she put her weight in it. Just as she relaxed there was a contraction long and painful, not like the ones before it.

"This is a really bad one," Cara said, and no sooner had she said it then she felt something pop and then a gush of fluid. Cara was astonished, but the nurse was unconcerned.

"Well then. You better go to Admitting," she said to Douglas before mopping it up, then changing Cara's gown. "Here. You're okay. But it will speed things up if you walk around a little."

"I don't need to speed things up," said Cara.

"It distracts you a little, if you walk around."

The nurse fitted some paper slippers onto Cara's feet, then took her arm and led her slowly out into the ward. It had been a busy weekend, so the ward was nearly full. The nurse led Cara to the window of the nursery, where together they looked in at the babies, all sleeping except for one, who stared back through the glass.

"I'll take that one," said Cara. "Oh, no."

"Just relax. Breathe deep. Look at me." The nurse took a long breath, then let it out just as slowly.

Cara inhaled, her eyes on the nurse's eyes, her arm linked through the nurse's arm. When it was over she could remember from the other delivery this same childlike awe she felt for the nurses, who looked wise and even lovely in their white costumes, and whose sensible calm was their greatest virtue along with the fact that they all seemed to know precisely how much it hurt. They never made apologies or told you to be brave or said it would be over soon if it wasn't going to be. They said things like, *Let me know if you think you're about to faint,* or if you urinated on the delivery table, *Don't worry about that, that's nothing compared to what's coming.* They never showed worry or impatience, and they might at any minute walk straight up to you and stick a thermometer under your tongue in such a way that you didn't even flinch. Then there you'd be with the thermometer in your mouth while a second nurse began taking your blood pressure and a third cranked the headrest one notch higher. They were like Gypsies, Cara thought as she lay there among them; one of them could pick your pocket in a second. Except the gown didn't have any pockets. It was white with black medallions, so soft and loose she barely noticed it was there, which was fine because then she didn't notice so much when it wasn't. Twice it had slipped off her shoulders, and now as she lay on the delivery bed, it fell open over her breasts. She didn't know for how long she had been lying on the bed, knees up, head raised, Douglas stroking her arm the way she liked during foreplay, shoulder to wrist with just the barest touch of his fingernails. The contractions were back-to-back with no more than a minute between them in which to drink a little water and tell him to keep doing what he was doing, although she knew very well he would keep doing it anyway. Another thing she said, when she had the time, was, "You don't have any idea what this is like."

"You're right," said Douglas. "But I can imagine."

"No, you can't imagine," said Cara.

"We called the doctor," said one of the nurses. "She said she needed to do a few things and then she'd be on her way over to check up on you. Hang in there."

"A few things!" said Cara.

"Shhh," said the nurse. "Breathe. Good. Slow. Slow. That baby won't be out for another two hours."

"Yes, it will," said Cara.

"You're doing fine," said Douglas.

"I'm doing terribly," said Cara.

"You'll forget about it when it's over," said one of the nurses, which was as close as they ever came to downplaying the pain. Serene as glass, Cara thought reproachfully, looking at the nurse. It was a challenge.

At once she yelled, "I'm pushing!" and gripped the edges of the mattress.

"No pushing!" said the nurse and Douglas at once.

"I have to," said Cara.

"You won't."

"I'm going to!" she yelled. She had to. If she didn't she would split apart. Rather, the thing that had become her would split apart. For it was no longer her body. It was hers and the baby's together. The two of them were like a padlock trying to get itself open. And there wasn't a key. They were steel. The nurse had taken hold of Cara's wrists and was staring her straight in the eyes saying, "No, you *will not push. It is not time to push.*"

"It *is* time to push," Cara protested, knowing all the while that she wouldn't push, that if she did, she would split apart, just as surely and horribly as she would split apart if she *didn't* push, so that the only thing to do was scream at the nurse and thrash at her husband and so keep herself locked in this noisy limbo between not-pushing and pushing, between pushing and not-pushing, between splitting apart and splitting apart again.

The nurse was no longer serene; that battle was won, anyway.

Near eleven-thirty the doctor came, tugging on some gloves and whipping her hair up into a cap. Then she was between Cara's knees, pushing them gently apart while gazing firmly and sympathetically at Cara's face. Cara screamed, "I can't do it!" and then, "I want drugs, I want drugs, I want drugs. Douglas, I want drugs," turning victoriously toward him as if he were the reason she hadn't said anything about drugs in the first place. He wasn't. Cara had had no thought of drugs, ever, during either this pregnancy or the last, and the very idea of drugs now was so amazing and so surprisingly, unexpectedly welcome that she nearly burst out laughing in the middle of her screams.

"Demerol!" she cried. "Demerol, Demerol, Demerol," while Douglas raised his eyebrows at the doctor. The doctor frowned. She pulled her hand out of Cara, then stood up and called for a gown.

"Not quite," she said, and then something that Cara didn't hear because Cara was screaming again at the words *not quite.* Not quite *what?* she wanted to know, screaming and screaming, in the back of her mind still thinking about the breathing that had worked a bit with Georgie's delivery and that had seemed, for a while, to be working with this one except that the screaming seemed more responsible, somehow. It was like being hit by a train; you didn't lie there deep-breathing if you'd had your legs run over, did you? No, you screamed, and everybody accepted it, and if you didn't they'd be begging you to do it.

"I want Demerol!" she yelled. "I can't do it! I'm pushing!" and then something happened, at least Cara thought that it happened, although she couldn't quite believe it. That is, the doctor did or didn't place the tip of her index finger directly and purposefully on Cara's clitoris creating such a shock of pleasure, like a slap in the face of the pain, that Cara quit screaming all at once for the second that it lasted and locked eyes with the doctor in a gaze so intense that between them it made a tightrope that the baby might walk across from one to the other. Then the doctor said, "Okay, Cara, you can push."

"I HAVE to tell you all that I screamed," Cara confessed to her friends during visiting hours that evening. Elizabeth had opened a box of chocolates, and they were passing it around.

"You're excused."

"You look beautiful."

"You're glowing. Your hair, it's like a halo, and your face is so pale. Translucent, practically."

"I mean I didn't just shout. I *screamed*. The breathing didn't work, or else I didn't want to be bothered. I couldn't help it. I wasn't even embarrassed."

"Oh, they don't care."

"They're used to it."

"Did you have an episiotomy?"

"I tore, and then I had an episiotomy."

"I've never heard of anyone who hasn't had an episiotomy, personally."

"Oh, I have."

"Really, Cara, he's so beautiful. He was the only one in the nursery who wasn't asleep."

"He was the only one who wasn't crying."

"He was the only one who really seemed to know what was going on."

Her friends all laughed giddily. Cara laughed, too, but she knew that her friends didn't understand quite how loudly and persistently she had screamed during the labor. That was okay, only she didn't know if she should be ashamed or not. Maybe just a little. From down the hall where that other woman was in labor came screams more guttural than Cara's but with that same shocked pulse as if every second of pain were somehow unexpected. Cara could hear through the wall the way the moaning reached a pitch and then tabled out, and then the other moments when the woman began arguing as if with the pain itself, with the clutching, tearing hand, saying, "Oh no, oh no, oh no." How perplexing it was, to be listening like this, and to be sympathizing but not feeling, as she had before, that sympathetic, agonized contraction. For a moment, for the third or fourth time that evening, she considered describing for her friends what the doctor had done, or what the doctor hadn't done although it felt like she did it. Cara could swear that she did it. But then again . . . it was unbelievable. Wasn't it? One of her friends would believe it, one of them wouldn't, the third would be entirely skeptical. And Cara didn't feel up to a debate about it or an analysis of why, since the doctor was a woman, the gesture was magnificent, but had the doctor been a man, it would have been obscene. She was happy being chattered at and admired. She got nervous when the nurse came in announcing visiting hours were over, because that meant she would get the baby back. Visiting hours he had to stay in the nursery, the rest of the time he could stay with her. Not that she wasn't impatient for him. She was, for his tiny soft warmth right up against her through the thin cotton of the gown, and for his strange smell so similar to the smell of sex. But she wasn't in love with him yet, at all. In fact, after Douglas went home to eat supper with Georgie, Cara fully resigned herself to the notion of not ever really loving this child but getting simple comfort from his smell and proximity. "I'll be a good mother to him," she supposed. He'd never know. No one ever would. She'd stroke him, nurse him, teach him, show him. But not as she did with Georgie. Never in a whirlwind of need and sensation. Inside her would be only patience, and fortitude, and this same, resigned magnanimity.

Cara's bed was equipped with padded metal armrests that could be pulled up on either side of the mattress or dropped down. Cara had pulled both of them up. She'd asked the nurse for extra pillows to be propped against the armrests, although their bulk made it harder to get in and out of bed. Indeed, when the baby awakened needing to be held, she had to pull herself down to the foot of the mattress before sliding off the edge of it, her stitches tugging at her crotch, and when she'd picked the baby up gently and carried him back to the bed, she found it impossible to pull herself back up the length of the mattress while holding onto him. But if she put the baby down at the top of the bed and then shimmied up after, she'd have to swivel around and pick him up without falling on top of him first or knocking off the pillows, and then she'd be stuck halfway up and half down, anyway. It all seemed so impossible. And the baby was wailing. Down she sat in the armchair to nurse him, hoping that one of the nurses would come take him away from her so she could get back into bed. But the nurse didn't come. Through the wall, Cara heard the heavy, angry panting of the woman in labor, but the sound left her curiously empty and unimpressed by anything but her own after-pains spreading over her inch by inch. She began to cry, purposefully at first and then helplessly so her tears fell on the baby's arm and slid under the loose plastic of the bracelet printed with his name.

Max, Cara read, in a moment of lucidity.

"Look at me, Max," she instructed.

But the baby didn't look. Instead he grunted, squeezed his eyes shut, and defecated. The stuff filled his diaper then oozed like tar into the folds of his blanket and onto Cara's arm. When at that moment Douglas walked into the room, Cara held the baby out to him with every bit of strength saying, "Here. This was a mistake. This was a terrible mistake."

WIDE awake at last, the baby gazed at Douglas, who explained to him who and where he was and how he got there.

"Your name is Max," said Douglas. "You have a brother, who isn't here right now. And a dog. This is a room in the hospital. Your mother did all of the work, and that's why she's so exhausted and disoriented that she forgot how to get back in bed."

"I didn't forget how to get back in bed. I told you that. I just can't get back in bed when I'm holding him because I won't be able to grab hold of the armrests and pull myself up without splitting myself open, Douglas. I want the doctor. Oh, God I haven't talked to my mother."

"Cara, I've never heard of a single woman splitting open from having a baby. I'll stay with him, you go take a sitz bath. You remember how good it felt last time."

"I know," said Cara, chastised, because this was the first time since she'd gone into labor that Douglas appeared to find it safe to infuse, into his usual measure of tenderness, his smaller dose of sarcasm. She got out of the chair, then climbed slowly, ever so slowly, onto the bed, knee by knee, hand over hand, like someone climbing onto an inflated raft in a swimming pool. "That hurt," she said, just as the nurse came in with a fluted paper cup. Cara downed her medication before reaching out her arms for the baby. Holding him, she found that the head of the bed was too high, so she gave the baby back, lowered the bed, then took him into her arms again. He was cross-eyed. If Cara moved an index finger back and forth above his upturned face, one eye stayed put while the other tried to follow, lagging behind and then skipping ahead. Gradually he closed his eyes and was asleep in such a way that he appeared to be just hovering on the surface of his own unformed consciousness. Cara watched him awhile, aware of her own eyes closing and of Douglas getting up out of the armchair, kissing both her and the baby, shutting the light, and leaving for home.

"Douglas," she said.

"What?"

A pause.

"When can I see Georgie?"

"Tomorrow at lunch, I'll bring him," he answered.

"Douglas."

"Yes."

Another pause.

"I'm still not in love with him."

"Just go to sleep, Cara."

"Good night."

"Good night."

"Good night, Max," said Cara, relieved that the room was not totally dark, that there was still a dim light over the sink and a little from the hallway through the half-closed door. Then she slept, too. First she felt the pleasant warm weight of the baby on top of her, but soon she was spinning in a dizzy fatigue that made their two bodies seem to clasp each other equally as if falling together through space.

AT THREE O'CLOCK that morning, when the nurse came for Max to check his heartbeat and temperature, Cara wouldn't give him up from his place against her under the blankets. There was a sleepy tug-of-war before the nurse finally took hold of Cara's fingers and gently but forcibly dislodged them from their hold on the baby. "Go back to sleep," she said. "When I'm finished with him I'll bring him back all clean and diapered and you can wake up and nurse him. He's due for a feeding. When did you feed him last?"

"Eleven," Cara guessed.

"How long on each side?"

"Five minutes," Cara answered, although in fact she had no idea. The nurses insisted on five minutes per breast and that you had to rub lanolin onto the nipples to keep them from cracking.

"Have you been using the lanolin?" asked the nurse.

"Yes," said Cara. She hadn't at all, but now she found it in its tube on her night table, next to the ginger ale. It smelled like sheep in a barn, and when the baby was brought back for nursing, he first nibbled at the breast experimentally, licking and tasting. Then when he tried latching on, he slipped off, over and over again. It's like getting a rocky start on sex, Cara thought, before they finally settled into a good rhythm. At last he sucked firmly and hungrily. The nurse told her to please put the baby back in his bassinet after feeding and not to sleep like that with him lying against her chest, and Cara nodded gamely but knew she'd keep him with her. For one thing, in order to put him back in his bassinet she'd have to climb out of bed again, and then, once out, she knew she would have to go to the bathroom. If she stayed put, she'd be able to hold it in. For how long she couldn't calculate. She might talk to the doctor about it. She was wondering about this when the baby stopped sucking and lifted his face openly toward hers as if to say, *Here I am.* He was utterly, unfathomably calm.

THROUGHOUT the very early part of the second day, the nurses kept bustling in to ask if she was alright and occasionally to take the baby away from her. Each time before giving him back they took pains to make some comment about the soaps and shampoos and lotions in the basket in the bathroom, but by nine in the morning they had stopped coming in so much. Cara ate breakfast while the baby observed blissfully and then blankly and then thoughtfully every move of her hand as it traveled from plate to mouth.

"This is orange juice," she explained. "This is a muffin. I'm taking a bite."

Max lay in a thin kimono on a pillow on her lap, and she imagined that to remain like this and watch him drifting in and out of awareness would be enough for the rest of the day if she didn't need to learn how to bathe him. She'd forgotten how to do it. There were parts of him—his umbilicus, for one, his fresh circumcision—that seemed too vulnerable even to be looked at. Also, his breathing was somewhat uneven: one-two, one-two, giving way all at once to a speedy vibration or else stopping altogether for two or three seconds during which Douglas placed the palm of her hand on his rib cage and waited, patiently. In the mirror across the room she watched herself unmoving under the blanket—knees up, hair brilliant and uncombed, one shoulder unclothed. Then one arm snaked out and found the silver hair clip on the table near the bed. She swept her hair into a knot and clipped it in place, then undid the knot and refastened the clip behind an ear. It looked romantic either way, but in the end she took it out and laid it back on the table with care. Her eyes were bright, her face was pale, she wore a coy, cool, secretive smile. She hadn't mentioned to the nurses that her baby stopped breathing occasionally. Simply, there was no way to say it without making it sound horrible when really there was something delicate and necessary about it, as if it were his way of coming to grips with the fact that he was now, whether he liked it or not, part of the world.

Just before noon, the nurse drifted in and asked hopefully if Cara had moved her bowels.

"I haven't had to," Cara lied.

"It would be a good idea. You don't want to get constipated. We might give you an enema in an hour or so if nothing happens, before the doctor shows up. Are you planning on having a shower before your husband comes?"

Cara said no, thank you, she was perfectly comfortable.

"I'll change the linens, then," continued the nurse, who held a stack of fresh sheets already in her hand, white as could be, and a thin yellow blanket.

"Oh, really, don't bother," said Cara, sliding deeper into the bed until she no longer could look past her knees to the mirror. The nurse, making a face, dropped the clean sheets onto the armchair and, before turning to go, pulled open the blinds on a window revealing a damp-looking courtyard with nothing in it. Only then did Cara begin to wonder, and to notice the smell. She'd grown accustomed to it, sitting in the middle of it for so long; in fact, it had become rather interesting in the way certain wild animal smells are interesting if you can be objective about them. Cara sat for a while just taking it in before she noticed the strange texture of the sheets underneath her, which were sodden and crusty at once, while between her thighs the big sanitary pad felt as dense as a sausage. Looking under the blanket, she could see that the pad was black all through but no blacker than the sheets she'd been sitting on. Everything was saturated with blood, and everything smelled. Even a corner of the blanket was stiff with blood, while the hems of the pillowcases propped here and there were soaked through as well with a fresher, redder color. The only thing not stained was her ill-fitting gown, which had ridden up completely over her hips. Now she pressed a corner of it gingerly between her thighs, and having satisfied herself that the blood was thick and crimson, she held the baby desperately, kissing him and kissing him.

The Adoption

FRAN CASTAN

I REMEMBER the quiet room, the dark
green chair where we sat afternoons,
the sun—no matter how tightly shuttered out—
coming in and curving across us
as if we were not separate, but a single body
joined in a ceremony of light.
My legs beneath you, my arms around you,
my breast under the glass bottle with rubber nipple,
I talked to you and sang to you,
No one interrupted us.
The dog sat quietly in the corner.
If I could have given birth to you,
I would have. I would have taken you
inside me, held you
and given birth to you again.
All the hours we spent in that room. Then,
one day, with your eyes focused on mine, you
reached up and stroked my cheek. Your touch
was that of the inchworm on its aerial thread
just resting on my skin, a larval curve
a lighting and lifting off, a lightness
practicing for the time it will have wings.
I like to think wherever you go, you will
keep some memory of sunlight in the room
where I first loved you, and you first loved.

A Mother's Love

MARY GORDON

SHE LOOKED at the clock. It was two-thirty; soon the children would be home. She waited for the sound of their arrival as if she were dressed for a party, listening for a taxi. No one had told her what it would be like, the way she loved her children. What a thing of the body it was, as physically rooted as sexual desire, but without its edge of danger. The urge to touch one's child, she often thought, was like, and wasn't like the hunger that one felt to touch a lover: it lacked suspense and greed and the component parts of insecurity and vanity that made so trying the beloved's near approach. Once they were in the house, the air became more vivid and more heated: every object in the house grew more alive. How I love you, she always wanted to say, and you can never know it. I would die for you without a thought. You have given to my life its sheerest, its profoundest pleasure. But she could never say that; instead, she would say, "How was school?" "Was lunch all right?" "Did you have your math test?"

They ran into the kitchen, opened the refrigerator. Peter began telling her about his science project. He and Daniel Greenspan were going to build a solar clock. It had begun already, that queer thing: her son knew more about some things than she did. He was trying to explain something about a pendulum; she didn't understand. Impatiently, he shoved the cookie he was eating into his mouth and fiddled in his school things for a pen and paper. He began to sketch things: here is the sun, here is the clock, this is the force of gravity. For years, she felt, males had been impatiently making sketches of the world for uncomprehending females. But his sketch was good; he made her see something, and he was proud of her pride in him, she could see it: his teaching had given him a courtliness so he could drop favor over his mother's shoulders like the mantle of a king. He was impatient, though, to get on with things, to leave her. He ran when he heard Daniel knocking at the door.

It shocked her when she'd learned how much she could like or dislike other children depending on their treatment of her own. She'd always adored Daniel, she'd known him all his life. He shared with Peter a precocious, dry, intellectuality, a pointed energy, and an unpopularity with other children, but he added to it an irony that Peter could never approach.

"I'm going to get dressed for ballet class," said Sarah. Then she was gone, they were both gone. Anne was alone again, but this time she felt lonely. No one would ever know the passion she felt for her children. It was savage, lively, volatile. It would smash, in one minute, the image people had of her of someone who lived life serenely, steering always the same sure, slow course. As it was, as they would never know, she was rocked back and forth, she was lifted up and down by waves of passion: of fear, of longing, and delight.

It was such an odd thing, motherhood. She didn't understand how people could say, "She's a good mother," in the same way they said, "She's a good neurosurgeon," or "She sings well." It wasn't a skill; there was no past practice to be consulted and perfected by strict application and attention to detail; there was no wisdom you could turn to; every history was inadequate, for each new case was fresh—each new case was a person born, she was sure of it, with a nature more fixed than modern thought led people to believe. She loved that, that her children were not tabulae rasae, but had been born themselves. She loved the intransigence of their nature, all that could never be molded and so was free from her. She liked to stand back a little from her children—it was why some people thought her, as a mother, vague. But she respected the fixity of her children's souls, what they were born with, what she had, from the first months, seen. She admired, for example, Peter's fastidiousness—it wasn't only physical although it had its roots in the physical—she admired it even when it exhausted her and made her feel quite futile. Since he could talk, he had come to her in positions of outraged justice with questions that had no answers, although she agreed with him, they should have had: "Why did Jessica's father go away and never see her?" "Why does Amanda like to play with Oliver better than me when I share all my toys and he hogs his?" He was always ardent; he took things to heart, and she was proud of his seriousness, his suffering, his fine, inflexible standards, but she wished she could protect him from himself. He would not be easily beloved, she could see that, but perhaps he would be honored. Perhaps, she had often thought, with a thrill of atavistic pride, an ancient, probably ignoble pride, open only to the mothers of sons, he would one day be feared.

Sarah was nothing like him. She stood back from life, found it amusing, looked on it with a slant, ironic gaze that judged, particularly the actions of adults, *de haut en bas*, with kindness, but with condescension. She had more hidden life than Peter, her dramas were inward, sometimes only to be guessed at, or eavesdropped upon.

Anne worried that Sarah's evenness excluded her from too much maternal concern; perhaps in apportioning her worries toward her son, she was depriving her daughter. But when she thought of Sarah's future she could only imagine the two of them—she and her daughter—sitting across from each other, drinking coffee, having wonderful conversations, full and calm and rich. She could only imagine a good life for her daughter; it was for her son alone she feared. But it was absurd, these fears and these imaginings. There was no way of knowing what would happen to them, and, she often felt, not much that you could do to influence the course of things determined so much by their natures and their fates. All you could do was, while they were still children, keep them safe.

Anger and Tenderness

ADRIENNE RICH

. . . to understand is always an ascending movement; that is why comprehension ought always to be concrete. (one is never got out of the cave, one comes out of it.)
— Simone Weil, First and Last Notebooks

ENTRY FROM MY JOURNAL, NOVEMBER 1960

My children cause me the most exquisite suffering of which I have any experience. It is the suffering of ambivalence: the murderous alternation between bitter resentment and raw-edged nerves, and blissful gratification and tenderness. Sometimes I seem to myself, in my feelings toward these tiny guiltless beings, a monster of selfishness and intolerance. Their voices wear away at my nerves, their constant needs, above all their need for simplicity and patience, fill me with despair at my own failures, despair too at my fate, which is to serve a function for which I was not fitted. And I am weak sometimes from held-in rage. There are times when I feel only death will free us from one another, when I envy the barren woman who has the luxury of her regrets but lives a life of privacy and freedom.*

And yet at other times I am melted with the sense of their helpless, charming and quite irresistible beauty—their ability to go on loving and trusting—their staunchness and decency and unselfconsciousness. *I love them.* But it's in the enormity and inevitability of this love that the sufferings lie.

APRIL 1961

A blissful love for my children engulfs me from time to time and seems almost to suffice—the aesthetic pleasure I have in these little, changing crea-

---

*The term "barren woman" was easy for me to use, unexamined, fifteen years ago. As should be clear throughout this book, it seems to me now a term both tendentious and meaningless, based on a view of women which sees motherhood as our only positive definition.

tures, the sense of being loved, however dependently, the sense too that I'm not an utterly unnatural and shrewish mother—much though I am!

MAY 1965

To suffer with and for and against a child—maternally, egotistically, neurotically, sometimes with a sense of helplessness, sometimes with the illusion of learning wisdom—but always, everywhere, in body and soul, *with* that child—because that child is a piece of oneself.

To be caught up in waves of love and hate, jealousy even of the child's childhood; hope and fear for its maturity; longing to be free of responsibility, tied by every fibre of one's being.

That curious primitive reaction of protectiveness, the beast defending her cub, when anyone attacks or criticizes him—And yet no one more hard on him than I!

SEPTEMBER 1965

Degradation of anger. Anger at a child. How shall I learn to absorb the violence and make explicit only the caring? Exhaustion of anger. Victory of will, too dearly bought—far too dearly!

MARCH 1966

Perhaps one is a monster—an anti-woman—something driven and without recourse to the normal and appealing consolations of love, motherhood, joy in others . . .

Unexamined assumptions: First, that a "natural" mother is a person without further identity, one who can find her chief gratification in being all day with small children, living at a pace tuned to theirs; that the isolation of mothers and children together in the home must be taken for granted; that maternal love is, and should be, quite literally selfless; that children and mothers are the "causes" of each others' suffering. I was haunted by the stereotype of the mother whose love is "unconditional"; and by the visual and literary images of motherhood as a single-minded identity. If I knew parts of myself existed that would never cohere to those images, weren't those parts then abnormal, monstrous? And—as my eldest son, now aged twenty-one, remarked on reading the above passages: "You seemed to feel you ought to love us all the time. But there *is* no human relationship where you love the other person at every moment." Yes, I tried to explain to him, but women—above all, mothers—have been supposed to love that way.

From the fifties and early sixties, I remember a cycle. It began when I had picked up a book or began trying to write a letter, or even found myself on the telephone with someone toward whom my voice betrayed eagerness, a rush of sympathetic energy. The child (or children) might be absorbed in busyness, in his own dreamworld; but as soon as he felt me gliding into a world which did not include him, he would come to pull at my hand, ask for help, punch at the typewriter keys. And I would feel his wants at such a moment as fraudulent, as an attempt moreover to defraud me of living even for fifteen minutes as myself. My anger would rise; I would feel the futility of any attempt to salvage myself, and also the inequality between us: my needs always balanced against those of a child, and always losing. I could love so much better, I told myself, after even a quarter-hour of selfishness, of peace, of detachment from my children. A few minutes! But it was as if an invisible thread would pull taut between us and break, to the child's sense of inconsolable abandonment, if I moved—not even physically, but in spirit—into a realm beyond our tightly circumscribed life together. It was as if my placenta had begun to refuse him oxygen. Like so many women, I waited with impatience for the moment when their father would return from work, when for an hour or two at least the circle drawn around mother and children would grow looser, the intensity between us slacken, because there was another adult in the house.

I did not understand that this circle, this magnetic field in which we lived, was not a natural phenomenon.

Intellectually, I must have known it. But the emotion-charged, tradition-heavy form in which I found myself cast as the Mother seemed, then, as ineluctable as the tides. And, because of this form—this microcosm in which my children and I formed a tiny, private emotional cluster, and in which (in bad weather or when someone was ill) we sometimes passed days at a time without seeing another adult except for their father—there *was* authentic need underlying my child's invented claims upon me when I seemed to be wandering away from him. He was reassuring himself that warmth, tenderness, continuity, solidity were still there for him, in my person. My singularity, my uniqueness in the world as *his mother*—perhaps more dimly also as Woman—evoked a need vaster than any single human being could satisfy, except by loving continuously, unconditionally, from dawn to dark, and often in the middle of the night.

2

IN A LIVING ROOM in 1975, I spent an evening with a group of women poets, some of whom had children. One had brought hers along, and they slept or played in adjoining rooms. We talked of poetry, and also of infanticide, of the case of a local woman, the mother of eight, who had been in severe depression since the birth of her third child, and who had recently murdered and decapitated her two youngest, on her suburban front lawn. Several women in the group, feeling a direct connection with her desperation, had signed a letter to the local newspaper protesting the way her act was perceived by the press and handled by the community mental health system. Every woman in that room who had children, every poet, could identify with her. We spoke of the wells of anger that her story cleft open in us. We spoke of our own moments of murderous anger at our children, because there was no one and nothing else on which to discharge anger. We spoke in the sometimes tentative, sometimes rising, sometimes bitterly witty, unrhetorical tones and language of women who had met together over our common work, poetry, and who found another common ground in an unacceptable, but undeniable anger. The words are being spoken now, are being written down; the taboos are being broken, the masks of motherhood are cracking through.

For centuries no one talked of these feelings. I became a mother in the family-centered, consumer-oriented, Freudian-American world of the 1950s. My husband spoke eagerly of the children we would have; my parents-in-law awaited the birth of their grandchild. I had no idea of what I wanted, what I could or could not choose. I only knew that to have a child was to assume adult womanhood to the full, to prove myself, to be "like other women."

To be "like other women" had been a problem for me. From the age of thirteen or fourteen, I had felt I was only acting the part of a feminine creature. At the age of sixteen my fingers were almost constantly ink-stained. The lipstick and high heels of the era were difficult-to-manage disguises. In 1945 I was writing poetry seriously, and had a fantasy of going to postwar Europe as a journalist, sleeping among the ruins in bombed cities, recording the rebirth of civilization after the fall of the Nazis. But also, like every other girl I knew, I spent hours trying to apply lipstick more adroitly, straightening the wandering seams of stockings, talking about "boys." There were two different compartments, already, to my life. But writing poetry, and my fantasies of travel and self-sufficiency, seemed more real to me; I felt that as an incipient "real woman" I was a fake. Particularly was I paralyzed when I encountered young children. I think I felt men could be—wished to be—conned into thinking I was truly "feminine"; a child, I suspected, could see through me like a shot. This sense of acting a part created a curious sense of guilt, even though it was a part demanded for survival.

I have a very clear, keen memory of myself the day after I was married: I was sweeping a floor. Probably the floor did not really need to be swept; probably I simply did not know what else to do with myself. But as I swept that floor I thought: "Now I am a woman. This is an age-old action, this is what women have always done." I felt I was bending to some ancient form, too ancient to question. *This is what women have always done.*

As soon as I was visibly and clearly pregnant, I felt, for the first time in my adolescent and adult life, not-guilty. The atmosphere of approval in which I was bathed—even by strangers on the street, it seemed—was like an aura I carried with me, in which doubts, fears, misgivings, met with absolute denial. *This is what women have always done.*

Two days before my first son was born, I broke out in a rash which was tentatively diagnosed as measles, and was admitted to a hospital for contagious diseases to await the onset of labor. I felt for the first time a great deal of conscious fear, and guilt toward my unborn child, for having "failed" him with my body in this way. In rooms near mine were patients with polio; no one was allowed to enter my room except in a hospital gown and mask. If during pregnancy I had felt in any vague command of my situation, I felt now totally dependent on my obstetrician, a huge, vigorous, paternal man, abounding with optimism and assurance, and given to pinching my cheek. I had gone through a healthy pregnancy, but as if tranquilized or sleep-walking. I had taken a sewing class in which I produced an unsightly and ill-cut maternity jacket which I never wore; I had made curtains for the baby's room, collected baby clothes, blotted out as much as possible the woman I had been a few months earlier. My second book of poems was in press, but I had stopped writing poetry, and read little except household magazines and books on child-care. I felt myself perceived by the world simply as a pregnant woman, and it seemed easier, less disturbing, to perceive myself so. After my child was born the "measles" were diagnosed as an allergic reaction to pregnancy.

Within two years, I was pregnant again, and writing in a notebook:

NOVEMBER 1956

Whether it's the extreme lassitude of early pregnancy or something more fundamental, I don't know; but of late I've felt, toward poetry,—both reading and writing it—nothing but boredom and indifference. Especially toward my own and that of my immediate contemporaries. When I receive a letter soliciting mss., or someone alludes to my "career," I have a strong sense of wanting to deny all responsibility for and interest in that person who writes—or who wrote.

If there is going to be a real break in my writing life, this is as good a time for it as any. I have been dissatisfied with myself, my work, for a long time.

My husband was a sensitive, affectionate man who wanted children and who—unusual in the professional, academic world of the fifties—was willing to "help." But it was clearly understood that this "help" was an act of generosity; that *his* work, *his* professional life, was the real work in the family; in fact, this was for years not even an issue between us. I understood that my struggles as a writer were a kind of luxury, a peculiarity of mine; my work brought in almost no money: it even cost money, when I hired a household helper to allow me a few hours a week to write. "Whatever I ask he tries to give me," I wrote in March 1958, "but always the initiative has to be mine." I experienced my depressions, bursts of anger, sense of entrapment, as burdens my husband was forced to bear because he loved me; I felt grateful to be loved in spite of bringing him those burdens.

But I was struggling to bring my life into focus. I had never really given up on poetry, nor on gaining some control over my existence. The life of a Cambridge tenement backyard swarming with children, the repetitious cycles of laundry, the night-wakings, the interrupted moments of peace or of engagement with ideas, the ludicrous dinner parties at which young wives, some with advanced degrees, all seriously and intelligently dedicated to their children's welfare and their husbands' careers, attempted to reproduce the amenities of Brahmin Boston, amid French recipes and the pretense of effortlessness—above all, the ultimate lack of seriousness with which women were regarded in that world—all of this defied analysis at that time, but I *knew* I had to remake my own life. I did not then understand that we—the women of that academic community—as in so many middle-class communities of the period—were expected to fill both the part of the Victorian Lady of Leisure, the Angel in the House, and also of the Victorian cook, scullery maid, laundress, governess, and nurse. I only sensed that there were false distractions sucking at me, and I wanted desperately to strip my life down to what was essential.

JUNE 1958

These months I've been all a tangle of irritations deepening to anger: bitterness, disillusion with society and with myself; beating out at the world, rejecting out of hand. What, if anything, has been positive? Perhaps the attempt to remake my life, to save it from mere drift and the passage of time . . .

The work that is before me is serious and difficult and not at all clear even as to plan. Discipline of mind and spirit, uniqueness of expression, ordering of daily existence, the most effective functioning of the human self—these are the chief things I wish to achieve. So far the only beginning I've been able to make is to waste less time. That is what some of the rejection has been all about.

By July of 1958 I was again pregnant. The new life of my third—and, as I determined, my last—child, was a kind of turning for me. I had learned that my body was not under my control; I had not intended to bear a third child. I knew now better than I had ever known what another pregnancy, another new infant, meant for my body and spirit. Yet, I did not think of having an abortion. In a sense, my third son was more actively chosen than either of his brothers; by the time I knew I was pregnant with him, I was not sleepwalking any more.

August 1958 (Vermont)

I write this as the early rays of the sun light up our hillside and eastern windows. Rose with [the baby] at 5:30 A.M. and have fed him and breakfasted. This is one of the few mornings on which I haven't felt terrible mental depression and physical exhaustion.

. . . I have to acknowledge to myself that I would not have chosen to have more children, that I was beginning to look to a time, not too far off, when I should again be free, no longer so physically tired, pursuing a more or less intellectual and creative life. . . . The *only* way I can develop now is through much harder, more continuous, connected work than my present life makes possible. Another child means postponing this for some years longer—and years at my age are significant, not to be tossed lightly away.

And yet, somehow, something, call it Nature or that affirming fatalism of the human creature, makes me aware of the inevitable as already part of me, not to be contended against so much as brought to bear as an additional weapon against drift, stagnation and spiritual death. (For it is really death that I have been fearing—the crumbling to death of that scarcely-born physiognomy which my whole life has been a battle to give birth to—a recognizable, autonomous self, a creation in poetry and in life.)

If more effort has to be made then I will make it. If more despair has to be lived through, I think I can anticipate it correctly and live through it.

Meanwhile, in a curious and unanticipated way, we really do welcome the birth of our child.

There was, of course, an economic as well as a spiritual margin which allowed me to think of a third child's birth not as my own death-warrant but as an "additional weapon against death." My body, despite recurrent flares of arthritis, was a healthy one; I had good prenatal care; we were not living on the edge of malnutrition; I knew that all my children would be fed, clothed, breathe fresh air; in fact it did not occur to me that it could be otherwise. But, in another sense, beyond that physical margin, I knew I was fighting for my life through, against, and with the lives of my children, though very little else was clear to me. I had been trying to give birth to myself; and in some grim, dim way I was determined to use even pregnancy and parturition in that process.

Before my third child was born I decided to have no more children, to be sterilized. (Nothing is removed from a woman's body during this operation; ovulation and menstruation continue. Yet the language suggests a cutting- or burning-away of her essential womanhood, just as the old word "barren" suggests a woman eternally empty and lacking.) My husband, although he supported my decision, asked whether I was sure it would not leave me feeling "less feminine." In order to have the operation at all, I had to present a letter, counter-signed by my husband, assuring the committee of physicians who approved such operations that I had already produced three children, and stating my reasons for having no more. Since I had had rheumatoid arthritis for some years, I could give a reason acceptable to the male panel who sat on my case; my own judgment would not have been acceptable. When I awoke from the operation, twenty-four hours after my child's birth, a young nurse looked at my chart and remarked coldly: "Had yourself spayed, did you?"

The first great birth-control crusader, Margaret Sanger, remarks that of the hundreds of women who wrote to her pleading for contraceptive information in the early part of the twentieth century, all spoke of wanting the health and strength to be better mothers to the children they already had; or of wanting to be physically affectionate to their husbands without dread of conceiving. None was refusing motherhood altogether, or asking for an easy life. These women—mostly poor, many still in their teens, all with several children—simply felt they could no longer do "right" by their families, whom they expected to go on serving and rearing. Yet there always has been, and there remains, intense fear of the suggestion that women shall have the final say as to how our bodies are to be used. It is as if the suffering of the mother, the primary identification of woman *as* the mother—were so necessary to the emotional grounding of human society that the mitigation, or removal, of that suffering, that identification, must be fought at every level, including the level of refusing to question it at all.

Luciela Louise Turner

GLORIA NAYLOR

THE CHURCH was small and dark. The air hung about them like a stale blanket. Ciel looked straight ahead, oblivious to the seats filling up behind her. She didn't feel the damp pressure of Mattie's heavy arm or the doubt that invaded the air over Eugene's absence. The plaintive Merciful Jesuses, lightly sprinkled with sobs, were lost on her ears. Her dry eyes were locked on the tiny pearl-gray casket, flanked with oversized arrangements of red-carnationed bleeding hearts and white-lilied eternal circles. The sagging chords that came loping out of the huge organ and mixed with the droning voice of the black-robed old man behind the coffin were also unable to penetrate her.

Ciel's whole universe existed in the seven feet of space between herself and her child's narrow coffin. There was not even room for this comforting God whose melodious virtues floated around her sphere, attempting to get in. Obviously, He had deserted or damned her, it didn't matter which. All Ciel knew was that her prayers had gone unheeded—that afternoon she had lifted her daughter's body off the kitchen floor, those blank days in the hospital, and now. So she was left to do what God had chosen not to.

People had mistaken it for shock when she refused to cry. They thought it some special sort of grief when she stopped eating and even drinking water unless forced to; her hair went uncombed and her body unbathed. But Ciel was not grieving for Serena. She was simply tired of hurting. And she was forced to slowly give up the life that God had refused to take from her.

AFTER the funeral the well-meaning came to console and offer their dog-eared faith in the form of coconut cakes, potato pies, fried chicken,

and tears. Ciel sat in the bed with her back resting against the headboard; her long thin fingers, still as midnight frost on a frozen pond, lay
on the covers. She acknowledged their kindness with nods of her head
and slight lip movements, but no sound. It was as if her voice was too
tired to make the journey from the diaphragm through the larynx to the
mouth.

Her visitors' impotent words flew against the steel edge of her pain,
bled slowly, and returned to die in the senders' throats. No one came
too near. They stood around the door and the dressing table, or sat on
the edges of the two worn chairs that needed upholstering, but they
unconsciously pushed themselves back against the wall as if her hurt was
contagious.

A neighbor woman entered in studied certainty and stood in the middle of the room. "Child, I know how you feel, but don't do this to yourself. I lost one, too. The Lord will . . ." And she choked, because the
words were jammed down into her throat by the naked force of Ciel's
eyes. Ciel had opened them fully now to look at the woman, but raw
fires had eaten them worse than lifeless—worse than death. The woman
saw in that mute appeal for silence the ragings of a personal hell flowing
through Ciel's eyes. And just as she went to reach for the girl's hand, she
stopped as if a muscle spasm had overtaken her body and, cowardly,
shrank back. Reminiscences of old, dried-over pains were no consolation in the face of this. They had the effect of cold beads of water on a
hot iron—they danced and fizzled up while the room stank from their
steam.

Mattie stood in the doorway, and an involuntary shudder went
through her when she saw Ciel's eyes. Dear God, she thought, she's
dying, and right in front of our faces.

"Merciful Father, no!" she bellowed. There was no prayer, no bended
knee or sackcloth supplication in those words, but a blasphemous fireball
that shot forth and went smashing against the gates of heaven, raging and
kicking, demanding to be heard.

"No! No! No!" Like a black Brahman cow, desperate to protect her
young, she surged into the room, pushing the neighbor woman and the
others out of her way. She approached the bed with her lips clamped
shut in such force that the muscles in her jaw and the back of her neck
began to ache.

She sat on the edge of the bed and enfolded the tissue-thin body in
her huge ebony arms. And she rocked. Ciel's body was so hot it burned
Mattie when she first touched her, but she held on and rocked. Back
and forth, back and forth—she had Ciel so tightly she could feel her
young breasts flatten against the buttons of her dress. The black mam-

moth gripped so firmly that the slightest increase of pressure would have cracked the girl's spine. But she rocked.

And somewhere from the bowels of her being came a moan from Ciel, so high at first it couldn't be heard by anyone there, but the yard dogs began an unholy howling. And Mattie rocked. And then, agonizingly slow, it broke its way through the parched lips in a spaghetti-thin column of air that could be faintly heard in the frozen room.

Ciel moaned. Mattie rocked. Propelled by the sound, Mattie rocked her out of that bed, out of that room, into a blue vastness just underneath the sun and above time. She rocked her over Aegean seas so clean they shone like crystal, so clear the fresh blood of sacrificed babies torn from their mother's arms and given to Neptune could be seen like pink froth on the water. She rocked her on and on, past Dachau, where soul-gutted Jewish mothers swept their children's entrails off laboratory floors. They flew past the spilled brains of Senegalese infants whose mothers had dashed them on the wooden sides of slave ships. And she rocked on.

She rocked her into her childhood and let her see murdered dreams. And she rocked her back, back into the womb, to the nadir of her hurt, and they found it—a slight silver splinter, embedded just below the surface of the skin. And Mattie rocked and pulled—and the splinter gave way, but its roots were deep, gigantic, ragged, and they tore up flesh with bits of fat and muscle tissue clinging to them. They left a huge hole, which was already starting to pus over, but Mattie was satisfied. It would heal.

The bile that had formed a tight knot in Ciel's stomach began to rise and gagged her just as it passed her throat. Mattie put her hand over the girl's mouth and rushed her out the now-empty room to the toilet. Ciel retched yellowish-green phlegm, and she brought up white lumps of slime that hit the seat of the toilet and rolled off, splattering onto the tiles. After a while she heaved only air, but the body did not seem to want to stop. It was exorcising the evilness of pain.

Mattie cupped her hands under the faucet and motioned for Ciel to drink and clean her mouth. When the water left Ciel's mouth, it tasted as if she had been rinsing with a mild acid. Mattie drew a tub of hot water and undressed Ciel. She let the nightgown fall off the narrow shoulders, over the pitifully thin breasts and jutting hipbones. She slowly helped her into the water, and it was like a dried brown autumn leaf hitting the surface of a puddle.

And slowly she bathed her. She took the soap, and, using only her hands, she washed Ciel's hair and the back of her neck. She raised her arms and cleaned the armpits, soaping well the downy brown hair there. She let the soap slip between the girl's breasts, and she washed each one separately, cupping it in her hands. She took each leg and even cleaned under the toenails. Making Ciel rise and kneel in the tub, she cleaned the crack in her behind, soaped her pubic hair, and gently washed the creases in her vagina—slowly, reverently, as if handling a newborn.

She took her from the tub and toweled her in the same manner she had been bathed—as if too much friction would break the skin tissue. All of this had been done without either woman saying a word. Ciel stood there, naked, and felt the cool air play against the clean surface of her skin. She had the sensation of fresh mint coursing through her pores. She closed her eyes and the fire was gone. Her tears no longer fried within her, killing her internal organs with their steam. So Ciel began to cry—there, naked, in the center of the bathroom floor.

Mattie emptied the tub and rinsed it. She led the still-naked Ciel to a chair in the bedroom. The tears were flowing so freely now Ciel couldn't see, and she allowed herself to be led as if blind. She sat on the chair and cried—head erect. Since she made no effort to wipe them away, the tears dripped down her chin and landed on her chest and rolled down to her stomach and onto her dark pubic hair. Ignoring Ceil, Mattie took away the crumpled linen and made the bed, stretching the sheets tight and fresh. She beat the pillows into a virgin plumpness and dressed them in white cases.

And Ciel sat. And cried. The unmolested tears had rolled down her parted thighs and were beginning to wet the chair. But they were cold and good. She put out her tongue and began to drink in their saltiness, feeding on them. The first tears were gone. Her thin shoulders began to quiver, and spasms circled her body as new tears came—this time, hot and stinging. And she sobbed, the first sound she'd made since the moaning.

Mattie took the edges of the dirty sheet she'd pulled off the bed and wiped the mucus that had been running out of Ciel's nose. She then led her freshly wet, glistening body, baptized now, to the bed. She covered her with one sheet and laid a towel across the pillow—it would help for a while.

And Ciel lay down and cried. But Mattie knew the tears would end. And she would sleep. And morning would come.

I Stand Here Ironing

TILLIE OLSEN

I STAND here ironing, and what you asked me moves tormented back and forth with the iron.

"I wish you would manage the time to come in and talk with me about your daughter. I'm sure you can help me understand her. She's a youngster who needs help and whom I'm deeply interested in helping."

"Who needs help." Even if I came, what good would it do? You think because I am her mother I have a key, or that in some way you could use me as a key? She has lived for nineteen years. There is all that life that has happened outside of me, beyond me.

And when is there time to remember, to sift, to weigh, to estimate, to total? I will start and there will be an interruption and I will have to gather it all together again. Or I will become engulfed with all I did or did not do, with what should have been and what cannot be helped.

She was a beautiful baby. The first and only one of our five that was beautiful at birth. You do not guess how new and uneasy her tenancy in her now-loveliness. You did not know her all those years she was thought homely, or see her poring over her baby pictures, making me tell her over and over how beautiful she had been—and would be, I would tell her—and was now, to the seeing eye. But the seeing eyes were few or nonexistent. Including mine.

I nursed her. They feel that's important nowadays. I nursed all the children, but with her, with all the fierce rigidity of first motherhood, I did like the books then said. Though her cries battered me to trembling and my breasts ached with swollenness, I waited till the clock decreed.

Why do I put that first? I do not even know if it matters, or if it explains anything.

She was a beautiful baby. She blew shining bubbles of sound. She loved motion, loved light, loved color and music and textures. She would lie on the floor in her blue overalls patting the surface so hard in ecstasy her hands and feet would blur. She was a miracle to me, but when she was eight months old I had to leave her daytimes with the woman downstairs to whom she was no miracle at all, for I worked or looked for work and for Emily's father, who "could no longer endure" (he wrote in his good-bye note) "sharing want with us."

I was nineteen. It was the pre-relief, pre-WPA world of the depression. I would start running as soon as I got off the streetcar, running up the stairs, the place smelling sour, and awake or asleep to startle awake, when she saw me she would break into a clogged weeping that could not be comforted, a weeping I can hear yet.

After a while I found a job hashing at night so I could be with her days, and it was better. But it came to where I had to bring her to his family and leave her.

It took a long time to raise the money for her fare back. Then she got chicken pox and I had to wait longer. When she finally came, I hardly knew her, walking quick and nervous like her father, looking like her father, thin, and dressed in a shoddy red that yellowed her skin and glared at the pockmarks. All the baby loveliness gone.

She was two. Old enough for nursery school they said, and I did not know then what I know now—the fatigue of the long day, and the lacerations of group life in nurseries that are only parking places for children.

Except that it would have made no difference if I had known. It was the only place there was. It was the only way we could be together, the only way I could hold a job.

And even without knowing, I knew. I knew the teacher that was evil because all these years it has curdled into my memory, the little boy hunched in the corner, her rasp, "why aren't you outside, because Alvin hits you? that's no reason, go out, scaredy." I knew Emily hated it even if she did not clutch and implore "don't go Mommy" like the other children, mornings.

She always had a reason why we should stay home. Momma, you look sick, Momma. I feel sick. Momma, the teachers aren't there today, they're sick. Momma, we can't go, there was a fire there last night. Momma, it's a holiday today, no school, they told me.

But never a direct protest, never rebellion. I think of our others in their three-, four-year-oldness—the explosions, the tempers, the denunciations, the demands—and I feel suddenly ill. I put the iron down. What in me demanded that goodness in her? And what was the cost, the cost to her of such goodness?

The old man living in the back once said in his gentle way: "You should smile at Emily more when you look at her." What *was* in my face when I looked at her? I loved her. There were all the acts of love.

It was only with the others I remembered what he said, and it was the face of joy, and not of care or tightness or worry I turned to them—too late for Emily. She does not smile easily, let alone almost always as her brothers and sisters do. Her face is closed and sombre, but when she wants, how fluid. You must have seen it in her pantomimes, you spoke of her rare gift for comedy on the stage that rouses a laughter out of the audience so dear they applaud and applaud and do not want to let her go.

Where does it come from, that comedy? There was none of it in her when she came back to me that second time, after I had had to send her away again. She had a new daddy now to learn to love, and I think perhaps it was a better time.

Except when we left her alone nights, telling ourselves she was old enough.

"Can't you go some other time, Mommy, like tomorrow?" she would ask. "Will it be just a little while you'll be gone? Do you promise?"

The time we came back, the front door open, the clock on the floor in the hall. She rigid awake. "It wasn't just a little while. I didn't cry. Three times I called you, just three times, and then I ran downstairs to open the door so you could come faster. The clock talked loud. I threw it away, it scared me what it talked."

She said the clock talked loud again that night I went to the hospital to have Susan. She was delirious with the fever that comes before red measles, but she was fully conscious all the week I was gone and the week after we were home when she could not come near the new baby or me.

She did not get well. She stayed skeleton thin, not wanting to eat, and night after night she had nightmares. She would call for me, and I would rouse from exhaustion to sleepily call back: "You're all right, darling, go to sleep, it's just a dream," and if she still called, in a sterner voice, "now go to sleep, Emily, there's nothing to hurt you." Twice, only twice, when I had to get up for Susan anyhow, I went in to sit with her.

Now when it is too late (as if she would let me hold and comfort her like I do the others) I get up and go to her at once at her moan or restless stirring. "Are you awake, Emily? Can I get you something?" And the answer is always the same: "No, I'm all right, go back to sleep, Mother."

They persuaded me at the clinic to send her away to a convalescent home in the country where "she can have the kind of food and care you can't manage for her, and you'll be free to concentrate on the new baby." They still send children to that place. I see pictures on the society page of sleek young women planning affairs to raise money for it, or dancing at the affairs, or decorating Easter eggs or filling Christmas stockings for the children.

They never have a picture of the children so I do not know if the girls still wear those gigantic red bows and the ravaged looks on the every other Sunday when parents can come to visit "unless otherwise notified"—as we were notified the first six weeks.

Oh it is a handsome place, green lawns and tall trees and fluted flower beds. High up on the balconies of each cottage the children stand, the girls in their red bows and white dresses, the boys in white suits and giant red ties. The parents stand below shrieking up to be heard and the children shriek down to be heard, and between them the invisible wall "Not To Be Contaminated by Parental Germs or Physical Affection."

There was a tiny girl who always stood hand in hand with Emily. Her parents never came. One visit she was gone. "They moved her to Rose Cottage" Emily shouted in explanation. "They don't like you to love anybody here."

She wrote once a week, the labored writing of a seven-year-old. "I am fine. How is the baby. If I write my letter nicely I will have a star. Love." There never was a star. We wrote every other day, letters she could never hold or keep but only hear read—once. "We simply do not have room for children to keep any personal possessions," they patiently explained when we pieced one Sunday's shrieking together to plead how much it would mean to Emily, who loved so to keep things, to be allowed to keep her letters and cards.

Each visit she looked frailer. "She isn't eating," they told us.

(They had runny eggs for breakfast or mush with lumps, Emily said later, I'd hold it in my mouth and now swallow. Nothing ever tasted good, just when they had chicken.)

It took us eight months to get her released home, and only the fact that she gained back so little of her seven lost pounds convinced the social worker.

I used to try to hold and love her after she came back, but her body would stay stiff, and after a while she'd push away. She ate little. Food sickened her, and I think much of life too. Oh she had physical lightness and brightness, twinkling by on skates, bouncing like a ball up and down up and down over the jump rope, skimming over the hill; but these were momentary.

She fretted about her appearance, thin and dark and foreign-looking at a time when every little girl was supposed to look or thought she should look a chubby blonde replica of Shirley Temple. The doorbell sometimes rang for her, but no one seemed to come and play in the house or be a best friend. Maybe because we moved so much.

There was a boy she loved painfully through two school semesters. Months later she told me how she had taken pennies from my purse to buy him candy. "Licorice was his favorite and I brought him some every day, but he still liked Jennifer better'n me. Why, Mommy?" The kind of question for which there is no answer.

School was a worry to her. She was not glib or quick in a world where glibness and quickness were easily confused with ability to learn. To her overworked and exasperated teachers she was an overconscientious "slow learner" who kept trying to catch up and was absent entirely too often.

I let her be absent, though sometimes the illness was imaginary. How different from my now-strictness about attendance with the others. I wasn't working. We had a new baby, I was home anyhow. Sometimes, after Susan grew old enough, I would keep her home from school, too, to have them all together.

Mostly Emily had asthma, and her breathing, harsh and labored, would fill the house with a curiously tranquil sound. I would bring the two old dresser mirrors and her boxes of collections to her bed. She would select beads and single earrings, bottle tops and shells, dried flowers and pebbles, old postcards and scraps, all sorts of oddments; then she and Susan would play Kingdom, setting up landscapes and furniture, peopling them with action.

Those were the only times of peaceful companionship between her and Susan. I have edged away from it, that poisonous feeling between them, that terrible balancing of hurts and needs I had to do between the two, and did so badly, those earlier years.

Oh there are conflicts between the others too, each one human, needing, demanding, hurting, taking—but only between Emily and Susan, no, Emily toward Susan that corroding resentment. It seems so obvious on the surface, yet it is not obvious. Susan, the second child, Susan, golden- and curly-haired and chubby, quick and articulate and assured, everything in appearance and manner Emily was not; Susan, not able to resist Emily's precious things, losing or sometimes clumsily breaking them; Susan telling jokes and riddles to company for applause while Emily sat silent (to say to me later: that was *my* riddle, Mother, I told it to Susan); Susan, who for all the five years' difference in age was just a year behind Emily in developing physically.

I am glad for that slow physical development that widened the difference between her and her contemporaries, though she suffered over it. She was too vulnerable for that terrible world of youthful competition, of preening and parading, of constant measuring of yourself against every other, of envy, "If I had that copper hair," "If I had that skin. . . ." She tormented herself enough about not looking like the others, there was enough of the unsureness, the having to be conscious of words before you speak, the constant caring—what are they thinking of me? without having it all magnified by the merciless physical drives.

Ronnie is calling. He is wet and I change him. It is rare there is such a cry now. That time of motherhood is almost behind me when the ear is not one's own but must always be racked and listening for the child cry, the child call. We sit for a while and I hold him, looking out over the city spread in charcoal with its soft aisles of light. "*Shoogily*," he breathes and curls closer. I carry him back to bed, asleep. *Shoogily*. A funny word, a family word, inherited from Emily, invented by her to say: *comfort*.

In this and other ways she leaves her seal, I say aloud. And startle at my saying it. What do I mean? What did I start to gather together, to try and make coherent? I was at the terrible, growing years. War years. I do not remember them well. I was working, there were four smaller ones now, there was not time for her. She had to help be a mother, and housekeeper, and shopper. She had to set her seal. Mornings of crisis and near hysteria trying to get lunches packed, hair combed, coats and shoes found, everyone to school or Child Care on time, the baby ready for transportation. And always the paper scribbled on by a smaller one, the book looked at by Susan then mislaid, the homework not done. Running out to that huge school where she was one, she was lost, she was a drop; suffering over the unpreparedness, stammering and unsure in her classes.

There was so little time left at night after the kids were bedded down. She would struggle over books, always eating (it was in those years she developed her enormous appetite that is legendary in our family) and I would be ironing, or preparing food for the next day, or writing V-mail to Bill, or tending the baby. Sometimes, to make me laugh, or out of her despair, she would imitate happenings or types at school.

I think I said once: "Why don't you do something like this in the school amateur show?" One morning she phoned me at work, hardly understandable through the weeping: "Mother, I did it. I won, I won; they gave me first prize; they clapped and clapped and wouldn't let me go."

Now suddenly she was Somebody, and as imprisoned in her difference as she had been in anonymity.

She began to be asked to perform at other high schools, even in colleges, then at city and statewide affairs. The first one we went to, I only recognized her that first moment when thin, shy, she almost drowned herself into the curtains. Then: Was this Emily? The control, the command, the convulsing and deadly clowning, the spell, then the roaring, stamping audience, unwilling to let this rare and precious laughter out of their lives.

Afterwards: You ought to do something about her with a gift like that—but without money or knowing how, what does one do? We have left it all to her, and the gift has as often eddied inside, clogged and clotted, as been used and growing.

She is coming. She runs up the stairs two at a time with her light graceful step, and I know she is happy tonight. Whatever it was that occasioned your call did not happen today.

"Aren't you ever going to finish the ironing, Mother? Whistler painted his mother in a rocker. I'd have to paint mine standing over an ironing board." This is one of her communicative nights and she tells me everything and nothing as she fixes herself a plate of food out of the icebox.

She is so lovely. Why did you want me to come in at all? Why were you concerned? She will find her way.

She starts up the stairs to bed. "Don't get me up with the rest in the morning." "But I thought you were having midterms." "Oh, those," she comes back in, kisses me, and says quite lightly, "in a couple of years when we'll all be atom-dead they won't matter a bit."

She has said it before. She *believes* it. But because I have been dredging the past, and all that compounds a human being is so heavy and meaningful in me, I cannot endure it tonight.

I will never total it all. I will never come in to say: She was a child seldom smiled at. Her father left me before she was a year old. I had to work her first six years when there was work, or I sent her home and to his relatives. There were years she had care she hated. She was dark and thin and foreign-looking in a world where the prestige went to blondeness and curly hair and dimples, she was slow where glibness was prized. She was a child of anxious, not proud, love. We were poor and could not afford for her the soil of easy growth. I was a young mother, I was a distracted mother. There were the other children pushing up, demanding. Her younger sister seemed all that she was not. There were years she did not want me to touch her. She kept too much in herself, her life was such she had to keep too much in herself. My wisdom came too late. She has much to her and probably nothing will come of it. She is a child of her age, of depression, of war, of fear.

Let her be. So all that is in her will not bloom—but in how many does it? There is still enough left to live by. Only help her to know—help make it so there is cause for her to know—that she is more than this dress on the ironing board, helpless before the iron.

Mama

NTOZAKE SHANGE

"MAMA, this gumbo is ridiculous." Sassafrass was eating so fast she could barely get the words out of her mouth. "Mama, you know if I told them white folks at the Callahan School that I wanted some red sauce & rice with shrimp, clams, hot sausage, corn, okra, chicken & crab meat, they'd go round the campus saying, 'You know that Negro girl overdoes everything. Can you imagine what she wanted for dinner?' " Cypress was at the side board of the sink doing *pliés* which Sassafrass' story had interrupted.

"Hey S., don't tell no more jokes. I can't do my exercises."

"I helped Mama make that gumbo, Sassafrass. I'm so glad you like it," chirped Indigo at the table, working on a doll for some little girl her mother said Santa wouldn't be visiting.

Hilda Effania was ecstatic. All her girls were home. Cypress was back from studying dance in New York. Sassafrass had made that terrible bus trip from New England. As much as they'd changed she still recognized them as her children. Spinning in the kitchen, while her girls did whatever they were going to do, was her most precious time.

From her corner view, she could see everyone. Sassafrass was still eating & still heavy hipped. If the white folks' food was so awful, you sure couldn't tell it. On the other hand, Cypress was too thin round her waist. It was as if she was rejecting the body the Lord gave her. There is nothing can be done with a colored behind. Hilda knew Cypress was so determined to be a ballet dancer she'd starve, but never lose that backside. Indigo was making every effort to be in on the big girls' talk. Hilda spun her fleece. Later, they'd all help her dye, warp, & weave. They always did.

"Sassafrass, it's 'those' white folks, not 'them.' Cypress, your sister's name is Sassafrass, not 'S.' "

In the midst of an *arabesque penché* Cypress retorted, "So tell me something I don't know."

Hilda Effania took a deep breath, sighed quite loudly. These northern ways would haveta be quieted. "I'm sorry, Cypress, I don't think I heard what you said." Cypress returned to first position, *bras en répos*.

"Aw, Mama, that's a turn of phrase. You know, some slang."

"Sounded like a fresh somebody to me," Hilda said, without loosing the gait of her spinning.

"Vocabulary is simply a way of knowing & letting others know your intentions. That's what Madame says." Cypress executed a *croisé devant*, balanced, smiled.

"& does Madame encourage you to insult your mother?" Hilda went on. Sassafrass was looking very bored, though Cypress kept trying to impress them with her new skills: *rond de jambe en l'air*; *gargouillade*; *cabriole, brisé*. Repeating the words, with each movement.

"Cypress, do you speak English anymore? Or has everyone in New York learned French in deference to the ballet?" Indigo laughed. Hilda smiled inside. Cypress relaxed her body & looked more like herself to Hilda.

"Mama, would you explain to my sister from the woods that I was trying to offer her some culture."

"She's right there. You can tell her."

"Cypress, I am going to a school where culture is never mentioned, per se, because all those white folks up there is 'culture,' or so they'd like us to believe." Sassafrass leaned back in her chair. Cypress was right. What she was doing was so pretty. Cypress was in her own way offering a gift.

"Cypress, could you show me some of that? I mean, how you do that? Those WASPs don't look like you when they do it. You make it look so easy."

"Show me too. I wanta know too." Indigo stuck a needle in the bosom of the dollie & stood up, ready for her first lesson at the *barre*.

Hilda wisht her husband Alfred could see the girls lined up by the kitchen sink, taking a ballet lesson from Cypress, while Sassafrass recited Dunbar. They were so much his children: hard-headed, adventurous, dreamers. Hilda Effania had some dreams of her own. Not so much to change the world, but to change her daughters' lives. Make it so they wouldn't have to do what she did. Listen to every syllable come out that white woman's mouth. It wasn't really distasteful to her. She liked her life. She liked making cloth: the touch, the rhythm of it, colors. What she wanted for her girls was more than that. She wanted happiness, however they could get it. Whatever it was. Whoever brought it.

"Oh. I can't imagine how I forgot. I think that Skippie Schuyler boy is having a party on Christmas Eve. & I do believe there's an invitation on the table by the front door."

"Skippie Schuyler, the doctor's son, invited us, Mama?"

"Well, I don't see why not. You're getting better training & education than anybody else in Charleston. You certainly are the prettiest girls I've seen round here for a long time."

Sassafrass ran to get the invitation. Firm white paper with gold printing.

Eugene Alphonso Schuyler, III

invites

Sassafrass, Cypress & Indigo

to a

Christmas Eve Wassail

Six to Nine O'Clock   Chaperoned/R.S.V.P.

Indigo jumped up & down. "Mama, Mama, he invited me! Me! He doesn't even know me!"

"No, but he might have heard there was a beautiful child gone astray with those Geechee Capitans," Hilda remarked.

Sassafrass & Cypress looked hard at Indigo. "You've been being a what?" Cypress screeched.

"A Jr. G.C., but I resigned. I resigned."

"Well, I don't see anything so bad about it, Mama. She'll never meet those kinds of fellas at Eugene Alphonso Schuyler III's house. Thank God for the colored people."

"Sassafrass, are you crazy? Indigo can't be runnin' the streets with those hoodlums." Cypress was incensed with her sister's cavalier attitude. Those kinds of fellas killed people, maimed people. She'd seen it where she lived on the Lower East Side.

"Look, Cypress, except for some rich little colored boys just like Skippie at our 'Brother' school, I haven't seen any Negroes in over 5 months. Any Negro whose color don't wash off is a treasure now. Believe me."

"But, I said I had resigned. I want to go to Skippie's party. Really I do." Indigo couldn't understand the tension between her sisters. What was the matter? They were all going. Then Indigo remembered the Wheeler girls. Those skinny yellow girls.

They were more like honey in a wolf's body, arsenic in a chocolate. As a Jr. G.C., Indigo'd put those children in their places. What would they do, if she were at a party with them?

Sassafrass just wanted to go. Some Negroes. Three hours of solid Negro conversation. Not having to explain to anybody what it was she actually meant. A dance. A dance with somebody who knew the rhythm of the song. A hand that was not afraid to touch hers. She wanted to go. . . .

INDIGO'S freshly curled & pressed hair was standing all over her head when she came in the door. "Mama, I danced with Charlie, Edward, Butch, Skippie himself, and Philip."

"That's not all she did, Mother. She invited Spats & Crunch into the Schuyler's house," Cypress slurred. "They seemed to have a good time, with their hats on."

"Oh, they did. We all did. Didn't we, Sassafrass?" Sassafrass was on the porch tongue-kissing Skippie Schuyler's second cousin from Richmond, who was also a doctor's son.

"Mama, you know none of the Wheeler girls had on a specially made for them dress. Can you believe that?"

Hilda Effania gave Cypress one of those looks that means you-&-I-will-talk-later. That child had gotta hold of some liquor somewhere. In the meantime, Hilda Effania was experiencing being tickled. Her girls were great successes. They knew. Everybody else knew it. She knew it. She tried to be very serious as she called Sassafrass in from the porch, but it was all so exciting. Sassafrass finally came in from the cold.

"Aw, Mama, isn't love wonderful?"

Cypress stood in the corner doing *battements* with the grace of a panther. "Mama, I want to go back to New York."

"Mama, I think I need to go see Aunt Haydee. She tol' me one time that all I had to do was watch the moon. & I couldn't even see the moon tonight."

"Don't worry 'bout that, darling. Tomorrow we'll all have our Christmas. We'll see what we have to do, after Santa pays us a visit."

"Aw Mama, not Santa Claus." All three together.

"Yes. Santa Claus." Hilda Effania gave a hot toddy & a piece of pound cake to each & every one. She listened to the five & ten minute courtships her daughters recounted.

"& then he said . . . you know what Billy said to me, I know I was chosen . . . Go on, Mama, guess what happened then . . ."

HILDA EFFANIA couldn't wait till Christmas. The Christ Child was born. Hallelujah. Hallelujah. The girls were home. The house was humming. Hilda Effania just a singing, cooking up a storm. Up before dawn. Santa's elves barely up the chimney. She chuckled. This was gonna be some mornin'. Yes, indeed. There was nothing too good for her girls.

Matter of fact, what folks never dreamt of would only just about do. That's right, all her babies home for Christmas Day. Hilda Effania cooking up a storm. Little Jesus Child lyin' in his Manger. Praise the Lord for all these gifts. Hilda Effania justa singin':

> Poor little Jesus Child, Born in a Manger
> Sweet little Jesus Child
> & they didn't know who you were.

Mama's breakfast simmering way downstairs drew the girls out of their sleep. Indigo ran to the kitchen. Sassafrass turned back over on her stomach to sleep a while longer, there was no House Mother ringing a cow bell. Heaven. Cypress brushed her hair, began her daily *pliés* & leg stretches. Hilda Effania sat at her kitchen table, drinking strong coffee with Magnolia Milk, wondering what the girls would think of her tree.

"Merry Christmas, Mama." Indigo gleamed. "May I please have some coffee with you? Nobody else is up yet. Then we can go see the tree, can't we, when they're all up. Should I go get 'em?" Indigo was making herself this coffee as quickly as she could, before Hilda Effania said "no." But Hilda was so happy Indigo could probably have had a shot of bourbon with her coffee.

"Only half a cup, Indigo. Just today." Hilda watched Indigo moving more like Cypress. Head erect, back stretched tall, with some of Sassafrass' easy coyness.

"So you had a wonderful time last night at your first party?"

"Oh, yes, Mama." Indigo paused. "But you know what?" Indigo sat down by her mother with her milk tinged with coffee. She stirred her morning treat, serious as possible. She looked her mother in the eyes. "Mama, I don't think boys are as much fun as everybody says."

"What do you mean, darling?"

"Well, they dance. & I guess eventually you marry 'em. But I like my fiddle so much more. I even like my dolls better than boys. They're fun, but they can't talk about important things."

Hilda Effania giggled. Indigo was making her own path at her own pace. There'd be not one more boy-crazy, obsessed-with-romance child in her house. This last one made more sense out of the world than either of the other two. Alfred would have liked that. He liked independence.

"Good morning, Mama. Merry Christmas." Sassafrass was still tying her bathrobe as she kissed her mother.

"Merry Christmas, Indigo. I see Santa left you a cup of coffee."

"This is not my first cup of coffee. I had some on my birthday, too."

"Oh, pardon me. I didn't realize you were so grown. I've been away, you know?" Sassafrass was never very pleasant in the morning. Christmas was no exception. Indigo & her mother exchanged funny faces. Sassafrass wasn't goin' to spoil this day.

"Good morning. Good morning. Good morning, everyone." Cypress flew through the kitchen: *coupé jeté en tournant.*

"Merry Christmas, Cypress," the family shouted in unison.

"Oh, Mama, you musta been up half the night cooking what all I'm smelling." Cypress started lifting pot tops, pulling the oven door open.

"Cypress, you know I can't stand for nobody to be looking in my food till I serve it. Now, come on away from my stove."

Cypress turned to her mama, smiling. "Mama, let's go look at the tree."

"I haven't finished my coffee," Sassafrass yawned.

"You can bring it with you. That's what I'm gonna do," Indigo said with sweet authority.

The tree glistened by the front window of the parlor. Hilda Effania had covered it, of course, with cloth & straw. Satin ribbons of scarlet, lime, fuchsia, bright yellow, danced on the far limbs of the pine. Tiny straw angels of dried palm swung from the upper branches. Apples shining, next to candy canes & gingerbread men, brought shouts of joy & memory from the girls, who recognized their own handiwork. The black satin stars with appliqués of the Christ Child Cypress had made when she was ten. Sassafrass fingered the lyres she fashioned for the children singing praises of the little Jesus: little burlap children with lyres she'd been making since she could thread a needle, among the miniatures of Indigo's dolls. Hilda Effania had done something else special for this Christmas, though. In silk frames of varied pastels were the baby pictures of her girls, & one of her wedding day: Hilda Effania & Alfred, November 30, 1946.

Commotion. Rustling papers. Glee & Surprise. Indigo got a very tiny laced brassiere from Cypress. Sassafrass had given her a tiny pair of earrings, dangling golden violins. Indigo had made for both her sisters dolls in their very own likenesses. Both five feet tall, with hips, & bras. Indigo had dressed the dolls in the old clothes Cypress & Sassafrass had left at home.

"Look in their panties," Indigo blurted. Cypress felt down in her doll's panties. Sassafrass pulled her doll's drawers. They both found velvet sanitary napkins with their names embroidered cross the heart of silk.

"Oh, Indigo. You're kidding. You're not menstruating, are you?"

"Indigo, you got your period?"

"Yes, she did." Hilda Effania joined, trying to change the subject. She'd known Indigo was making dolls, but not that the dolls had their period.

"Well, what else did you all get?" Hilda asked provocatively.

Cypress pulled out an oddly shaped package wrapped entirely in gold sequins. "Mama, this is for you." The next box was embroidered continuously with Sassafrass' name. "Here, guess whose?" Cypress held Indigo's shoulders. Indigo had on her new bra over her nightgown. Waiting for her mother & sister to open their gifts, Cypress did *tendues*. "Hold still, Indigo. If you move, my alignment goes off."

"Oh, Cypress, this is just lovely." Hilda Effania didn't know what else to say. Cypress had given her a black silk negligée with a very revealing bed jacket. "I certainly have to think when I could wear this. & you all won't be home to see it."

"Aw, Mama. Try it on," Cypress pleaded.

"Yeah, Mama. Put that on. It looks so nasty." Indigo squinched up her face, giggled.

"Oh, Cypress, these are so beautiful. I can hardly believe it." Sassafrass held the embroidered box open. In the box lined with beige raw silk were 7 cherrywood hand-carved crochet needles of different gauges.

"Bet not one white girl up to the Callahan School has ever in her white life laid eyes on needles like that!" Cypress hugged her sister, flexed her foot. "Indigo, you got to put that bra on under your clothes, not on top of 'em! Mama, would you look at this little girl?"

Hilda Effania had disappeared. "I'm trying on this scandalous thing, Cypress. You all look for your notes at the foot of the tree." She shouted from her bedroom, thinking she looked pretty good for a widow with three most grown girls.

Hilda Effania always left notes for the girls, explaining where their Christmas from Santa was. This practice began the first year Sassafrass had doubted that a fat white man came down her chimney to bring her anything. Hilda solved that problem by leaving notes from Santa Claus for all the children. That way they had to go search the house, high & low, for their gifts. Santa surely had to have been there. Once school chums & reality interfered with this myth, Hilda continued the practice of leaving her presents hidden away. She liked the idea that each child experienced her gift in privacy. The special relationship she nurtured with each was protected from rivalries, jokes, & Christmas confusions. Hilda Effania loved thinking that she'd managed to give her daughters a moment of their own.

My Oldest Darling, Sassafrass,
In the back of the pantry is
something from Santa. In a red box
by the attic window is something your
father would want you to have. Out
by the shed in a bucket covered with
straw is a gift from your Mama.
                              Love to you,
                                  Mama

Darling Cypress,
Underneath my hat boxes in the
2nd floor closet is your present from
Santa. Look behind the tomatoes I
canned last year for what I got you
in your Papa's name. My own choice
for you is under your bed.
                              XOXOX,
                                  Mama

Sweet Little Indigo,
This is going to be very simple.
Santa left you something outside your
violin. I left you a gift by the outdoor
stove on the right hand side. Put your
coat on before you go out there. And
the special something I got you from
your Daddy is way up in the china
cabinet. Please, be careful.
                    I love you so much,
                                  Mama

In the back of the pantry between the flour & rice, Sassafrass found a necklace of porcelain roses. Up in the attic across from Indigo's mound of resting dolls, there was a red box all right, with a woven blanket of mohair, turquoise & silver. Yes, her father would have wanted her to have a warm place to sleep. Running out to the shed, Sassafrass knocked over the bucket filled with straw. There on the ground lay eight skeins of her mother's finest spun cotton, dyed so many colors. Sassafrass sat out in the air feeling her yarns.

Cypress wanted her mother's present first. Underneath her bed, she felt tarlatan. A tutu. Leave it to Mama. Once she gathered the whole thing out where she could see it, Cypress started to cry. A tutu *juponnage*, reaching to her ankles, rose & lavender. The waist was a wide sash with the most delicate needlework she'd ever seen. Tiny toe shoes in white & pink graced brown ankles tied with ribbons. Unbelievable. Cypress stayed in her room dancing in her tutu till lunchtime. Then she found *The Souls of Black Folks* by DuBois near the tomatoes from her Papa's spirit. She was the only one who'd insisted on calling him Papa, instead of Daddy or Father. He didn't mind. So she guessed he wouldn't mind now. "Thank you so much, Mama & Papa." Cypress slowly went to the 2nd floor closet where she found Santa'd left her a pair of opal earrings. To thank her mother Cypress did a complete *port de bras*, in the Cecchetti manner, by her mother's vanity. The mirrors inspired her.

Indigo had been very concerned that anything was near her fiddle that she hadn't put there. Looking at her violin, she knew immediately what her gift from Santa was. A brand-new case. No second-hand battered thing from Uncle John. Indigo approached her instrument slowly. The case was of crocodile skin, lined with white velvet. Plus, Hilda Effania had bought new rosin, new strings. Even cushioned the fiddle with cleaned raw wool. Indigo carried her new case with her fiddle outside to the stove where she found a music stand holding *A Practical Method for Violin* by Nicolas Laoureux. "Oh, my. She's right about that. Mama would be real mad if I never learned to read music." Indigo looked thru the pages, understanding nothing. Whenever she was dealing with something she didn't understand, she made it her business to learn. With great difficulty, she carried her fiddle, music stand, & music book into the house. Up behind the wine glasses that Hilda Effania rarely used, but dusted regularly, was a garnet bracelet from the memory of her father. Indigo figured the bracelet weighed so little, she would definitely be able to wear it every time she played her fiddle. Actually, she could wear it while conversing with the Moon.

Hilda Effania decided to chance fate & spend the rest of the morning in her fancy garb from Cypress. The girls were silent when she entered the parlor in black lace. She looked like she did in those hazy photos from before they were born. Indigo rushed over to the easy chair & straightened the pillows.

"Mama, I have my present for you." Hilda Effania swallowed hard. There was no telling what Indigo might bring her.

"Well, Sweetheart. I'm eager for it. I'm excited, too."

Indigo opened her new violin case, took out her violin, made motions of tuning it (which she'd already done). In a terribly still moment, she began "My Buddy," Hilda Effania's mother's favorite song. At the end, she bowed to her mother. Her sisters applauded.

Sassafrass gave her mother two things: a woven hanging of twined ikat using jute and raffia, called "You Know Where We Came From,

Mama"; & six amethysts with holes drilled thru, for her mother's creative weaving.

"Mama, you've gotta promise me you won't have a bracelet, or a ring or something made from them. Those are for your very own pieces." Sassafrass wanted her mother to experience weaving as an expression of herself, not as something the family did for Miz Fitzhugh. Hilda Effania was still trying to figure out where in the devil she could put this "hanging," as Sassafrass called it.

"Oh, no dear. I wouldn't dream of doing anything with these stones but what you intended."

When the doorbell rang, Hilda Effania didn't know what to do with herself. Should she run upstairs? Sit calmly? Run get her house robe? She had no time to do any of that. Indigo opened the door.

"Merry Christmas, Miz Fitzhugh. Won't you come in?" Hilda sank back in the easy chair. Cypress casually threw her mother an afghan to cover herself. Miz Fitzhugh in red wool suit, tailored green satin shirt, red tam, all Hilda's design, and those plain brown pumps white women like, wished everyone a "Merry Christmas." She said Mathew, her butler, would bring some sweetbreads & venison over later, more toward the dinner hour. Miz Fitzhugh liked Sassafrass the best of the girls. That's why she'd sponsored her at the Callahan School. The other two, the one with the gall to want to be a ballerina & the headstrong one with the fiddle, were much too much for Miz Fitzhugh. They didn't even wanta be weavers. What was becoming of the Negro, refusing to ply an honorable trade.

Nevertheless, Miz Fitzhugh hugged each one with her frail blue-veined arms, gave them their yearly checks for their savings accounts she'd established when each was born. There be no talk that her Negroes were destitute. What she didn't know was that Hilda Effania let the girls use that money as they pleased. Hilda believed every family needed only one mother. She was the mother to her girls. That white lady was mighty generous, but she wasn't her daughters' mama or manna from Heaven. If somebody needed taking care of, Hilda Effania determined that was her responsibility; knowing in her heart that white folks were just peculiar.

"Why Miz Fitzhugh, that's right kindly of you," Hilda honeyed.

"Why Hilda, you know I feel like the girls were my very own," Miz Fitzhugh confided. Cypress began a series of violent *ronds de jambe*. Sassafrass picked up all the wrapping papers as if it were the most important thing in the world. Indigo felt some huge anger coming over her. Next thing she knew, Miz Fitzhugh couldn't keep her hat on. There was a wind justa pushing, blowing Miz Fitzhugh out the door. Because she had blue blood or blue veins, whichever, Indigo knew Miz Fitzhugh would never act like anything strange was going on. She'd let herself be blown right out the door with her white kid gloves, red tailored suit, & all. Waving good-bye, shouting, "Merry Christmas," Miz Fitzhugh vanished as demurely as her station demanded.

Sucha raucous laughing & carrying on rarely came out of Hilda Effania's house like it did after Miz Fitzhugh'd been blown away. Hilda Effania did an imitation of her, hugging the girls.

"But Miz Fitzhugh, do the other white folks know you touch your Negroes?" Hilda responded, "Oh, I don't tell anyone!"

Eventually they all went to their rooms, to their private fantasies & preoccupations. Hilda was in the kitchen working the fat off her goose, fiddling with the chestnut stuffing, wondering how she would handle the house when it was really empty again. It would be empty, not even Indigo would be home come January.

"Yes, Alfred. I think I'm doing right by 'em. Sassafrass is in that fine school with rich white children. Cypress is studying classical ballet with Effie in New York City. Imagine that? I'm sending Indigo out to Difuskie with Aunt Haydee. Miz Fitzhugh's promised me a tutor for her. She doesn't want the child involved in all this violence 'bout the white & the colored going to school together, the integration. I know you know what I mean, 'less up there's segregated too.

"No, Alfred I'm not blaspheming. I just can't imagine another world. I'm trying to, though. I want the girls to live the good life. Like what we planned. Nice husbands. Big houses. Children. Trips to Paris & London. Going to the opera. Knowing nice people for friends. Remember we used to say we were the nicest, most interesting folks we'd ever met? Well, I don't want it to be that way for our girls. You know, I'm sort of scared of being here by myself. I can always talk to you, though. Can't I?

"I'ma tell Miz Fitzhugh that if she wants Indigo in Difuskie that tutor will have to be a violin teacher. Oh, Alfred, you wouldn't believe what she can do on that fiddle. If you could only see how Cypress dances. Sassafrass' weavings. I wish you were here sometimes, so we could tell the world to look at what all we, Hilda Effania & Alfred, brought to this world."

Once her Christmas supper was organized in the oven, the frigerator, the sideboard, Hilda Effania slept in her new negligée, Alfred's WWII portrait close to her bosom.

Not the Phil Donahue Show

KELLY CHERRY

THIS is not the Phil Donahue show; this is my life. So why is my daughter, who is 20 years old and, to me, so heartbreakingly beautiful that I think that for the sake of the health of the entire world and probably universe she shouldn't be allowed out of the house without a cardiologist at her side, why is my daughter standing in my doorway telling me she's a lesbian?

She hangs in the doorway, her face rising in the warm air like a bloom in a hothouse. (I have been cooking.) She has chin-length blonde hair, straight as a pin, side-parted. Her skin is bare of makeup. Her blue eyes are like forget-me-nots in an open field. She has a superficial scratch on her cheek, a deep resentment that pulls her head down and away from me.

I'm standing here with a wooden spoon in my hand like a baton and I feel like there is some music that should be playing, some score that, if I only knew it, I ought to be conducting.

If I say it's a phase, that she'll outgrow it, she'll peel herself from the wall like wallpaper and exit, perhaps permanently, before I can even discern the pattern.

If I say honey, that's great, nonchalant and accepting as history, I could be consigning her to a life that I'm not sure she really wants — maybe she's just testing me. Maybe this *is* just a phase.

I can't help it, for just a moment I wish her father were here. I want him to be as shocked and stuck as I am, here in this blue-and-white room with steam rising from the stove, enough garlic in the air to keep a host of vampires at bay. But I remind myself: he would have been glad to be here. I am the one who walked out on him. As Isabel, in her posture, her sullen slouch, her impatient, tomboy gestures, never lets me forget. *Daddy would know how to handle this*, she seems to be saying, defiant as a rebel with a cause. *I dare you to try.*

It is five o'clock. It's already been a long day, which I have spent as I spend most of my days—nursing patients to whom I have let myself get too close. And sometimes I feel a kind of foreclosure stealing into my heart, sometimes I feel like an S & L, sometimes I feel overextended. But I'm always home from my shift at the hospital by four-thirty, while Ian stays late after school to devise lesson plans, tutor the sluggardly, confer with parents.

Now the front door swings open and it's Ian. He's taller than I, who am tall, so tall his knees seem to be on hinges, and he unlatches them and drops into one of the dining-room chairs. I can watch him over the dividing counter that connects the dining room with the kitchen, one of the results of our renovation last summer. Isabel has not moved from her post in the doorway (there's no door) between us.

"Hi, Shel," Ian says to me. "Hi, Belle," he says to my daughter. "Nice to see you."

He wants so much for her to let him enter her life. He has no children of his own—he wants to be, if not a second father, at least a good friend. "Shelley," he says, "What are we drinking tonight?"

"Isabel has an announcement," I say, waving my wooden wand. I turn around and start stirring, the steam pressing the curl out of my hair like a dry cleaner.

"I'm in love," I hear her say behind my back.

"Hey, that's great," Ian responds and I realize how unfair we have been to him, we have set him up for this.

"With a woman," she says.

Girl, I want to correct her. With a *girl*.

Marlo Thomas would kill me.

"Oh," Ian says. "Well, why isn't she here? When do we get to meet her?"

And I remember: this is why I married him. Because he puts people ahead of his expectations for them, even though his expectations can be annoyingly well defined. Because he doesn't create a crisis where there isn't one.

But this is a crisis. If she were *his* daughter, he'd realize that.

ENTIRELY without meaning to, entirely illogically, I am suddenly angry with Ian for not being the father of my daughter. Why wasn't he around when I was 20—her age, I realize, startled—and looking for something to do with my life, which I had begun to understand stretched before me apparently endlessly like an unknown continent, one I was afraid to explore by myself? Why did I have to wait for most of my life before he showed up?

We are seated at the table from my first marriage, now located under the dining-room window overlooking the leaf-strewn front lawn and Joss Court. It is September in Wisconsin, and the home fires have begun to burn, smoke lifting from the chimneys like an Ascension. The maple and walnut trees are a kaleidoscope of color; the bright orange-red berries of the mountain ash are living ornaments. Soon it will be Halloween, Thanksgiving, Christmas. Across the street, abutting Joss but facing Highland, is my friend Nina's house, in which I lived for a year while making up my mind to divorce Isabel's father. Directly across from me, behind Nina, lives Sophie, recently widowed. She pushes a hand mower, the last lawncut of the season before raking starts.

"You should go over and offer to rake for her sometime soon," I say to Ian.

"I will," he agrees, drilling a corkscrew into the unopened wine.

Isabel says, "I think she likes doing things for herself."

"I can still offer," Ian says. "She can say no."

During this conversation, a fourth party has been silent; Judy, Isabel's friend. As soon as Ian suggested we meet, Isabel raced out of the house and brought her back for supper.

Judy is not what I expected. For one thing, she's pretty—almost as pretty as my daughter. She has long wavy honey-blonde hair so perfectly cut it falls with mathematical precision, like a sine-curve, around her glowing face. She has this generation's white, even teeth, a kittenish face. It is easy to see why Isabel has fallen in love with her; in fact, I don't see how anyone could *not* fall in love with either of them—so why shouldn't they fall in love with each other?

Thinking these thoughts, I am swept by a sense of déjà-vu. I have lived this scene before—but where? In another life?

Then I figure it out: not lived but read, in all the contemporary novels Nina lends me. Again and again, a mother is visited over the holidays by her college-going son, who arrives with a male lover in tow to explain that he is now out of the closet. Sometimes the father seizes this opportunity to declare that he, too, has all along been a homosexual. I glance at Ian suspiciously. He is in his gracious mode, entertaining the two girls with tales from his life in the Peace Corps, following the fall of Camelot. These stories now have the lustre of legend about them; they are tales from far away and long ago. The girls listen to them, enthralled and cynically condescending at the same time, in both their lovely faces the question, *But how could anyone have ever been so innocent and hope-ful?* And I am filled with the furious rush of my love for Ian, my heart pumping, powerful as hydrology, and I want to say to them, *That's the kind of innocence you learn, it takes age and experience to be able to shake off your self-protective defenses and give yourself over to helping someone else.* But I don't say anything, I just look at Ian, reminding myself that later the girls will be gone and we can indulge our heterosexual sexual preferences on the water bed, and he says, "Passez-moi le salt, s'il vous plaît."

Ian teaches French at West High.

Two sky-blue tapers burn driplessly next to wildflowers I brought back from the farm a few weeks ago. The wildflowers have dried—it was a delicate transition from life to death, so shaded it would have been impossible to say exactly when death occurred: at what point did these flowers become what they are now?

The candlelight projects a silhouette of the wildflowers onto the wall; it polishes the real gold of Judy's hoop earrings, casts a mantle of light over Isabel's bent head.

I'm not losing a daughter, I tell myself, I'm gaining a daughter.

"THEY are children," I say to Ian in the kitchen, after they have vanished into the night.

I remember those college nights, full of adventure, philosophy, midnight desperation in the diner over coffee and cigarettes. I had two years of them before I decided to go to nursing school, where nihilism was not part of the curriculum.

I peer out the window as if the children, or my youth, might still be out there, in the dark.

Through the window, which we have opened slightly to cool off, comes an autumnal aroma of fallen apples, bitter herbs. Already, the birds have started south.

"Isabel's almost 21," he says. "You've got to start getting used to the idea that she's grown up. She has her own life to live."

When he says "life to live," I of course think of one of my patients, only a few years older than Isabel and like her gay, who, however, has but a death to die.

Noting parallels and contrasts to patients' lives in this way is, I discovered a long time ago, an occupational hazard of nursing, and I don't allow myself to be sidetracked. I just say, "That's easy for you to say."

He slams the silverware drawer shut. "No, it isn't, Shelley. As a matter of fact, it's very hard for me to say, because I know you're upset and you're going to take it out on me. It would be much easier for me not to say anything, but someone has to keep you from making a big mistake here."

He's right, but I don't have to be happy about that.

I'm elbow-deep in hot water—literally. I rinse the last dish and he hands me a dishtowel. When we remodeled this kitchen, we made it comfortable for both of us to work in at the same time. We both like to cook. When I think of Ian, I naturally think of spices—"a young stag upon the mountains of spices." Old deer, I have called him, teasing; old dear.

Sometimes he sits at the dining-room table, marking papers, while I make something that can be stored in the freezer for the following day, and as I scoop and measure, doing the Dance of the Cook, I look at him through the rectangular frame created by the counter and cabinets. He is a year younger than I am. His eyes are small, his cheeks ruddy. He would have made a great British colonel, except that he would have liberated all the colonials, at the same time forcing them at gunpoint to call in their pledges to public radio. He is a born and bred Wisconsinite, and I love every contradiction his un-French mind so blithely absorbs. For him, I left a husband who was equally good-hearted but incapable of such contradiction, paradox, surprise.

"Maybe I'm not the one to do that in this case," he continues. "Call Nelson. Maybe *he* can keep you from going off the deep end."

I look at Ian; I pick up the phone; I dial. It rings. "Nel?" I say.

"Shel."

God, we were young. We were young for so long—longer than we should have been. We were still so young even by the time our daughter was born that we thought, amazingly, that the family that rhymed together would stay together.

"I need to talk to you. Can you meet me at Porta Bella?"

"In 20 minutes," he says. "Listen, I know what it's about. Everything's going to be all right."

"SHE told you first?" I ask. I can't help it, I'm hurt.

Nelson leans back in the booth, and the leather seat creaks. His white hair—it started turning white when he reached forty—looks pink in the red haze of the table lamp, a stubby candle in a netted hurricane shield.

At the bar, male and female lawyers and professors bump against one another, pushing, as if hoping to annoy someone into noticing them. When you are young, you're a sex object because you're *sexy*, but then you reach an age when you have to make someone aware of you as an *object* before it will occur to him or her that you just might possibly be a *sex object.* This is one of the few places near State Street that the students tend to leave to an older crowd.

Nelson's pink beard looks like spun sugar, and for a moment, I remember being a child, wanting to go to the circus and buy cotton candy. My parents said no. It was the polio scare—people thought perhaps children contracted polio from being in crowds. No circus, no swimming lessons, no—

"It's hard on her, our divorce," he says. "I'm happy things have worked out for you with Ian, but you must realize she senses a barrier there now. There's not the same unimpeded access to you that she had."

Unimpeded access. Do I detect smugness in his voice, the way he drapes one arm over the back of the booth like a long, sly, coat-sleeved cat?

"Do you think she's doing this just to get back at me? Will she grow out of it?"

"I think it's the real thing, Shelley," he says. He smiles. "As real as Coke." He means Coca-Cola, I know. We are not the kind of people who would ever mean anything else, I realize, wondering if this is insight, boast, or lament. It could be an elegy. "I think she's in love."

He has brought his arm down, shifted closer to the table. Whatever he wanted to say about my behavior, he feels he has said. Now we can talk about hers. "She's still our little girl," he says.

"She always will be," I agree. "And she's *free to be herself.*" I start to tell him that I'm quoting Marlo Thomas, then don't. The guy has enough to deal with without his ex-wife quoting Marlo Thomas. "It's just that, well, weren't you counting on grandchildren someday?"

"I wouldn't rule out the possibility yet," he says. "A lot of lesbians have children, one way or another. I think she wants to have children someday."

He leans back again, the thick, pink beard like a strawberry milkshake glued to his face. "That wasn't the only thing I was counting on," he says sadly.

WE WAKE to FM. Ian and I lightly touch our mouths together on the corner of Joss and Highland, walking in opposite directions to our respective places of work.

All day at the hospital, I dispense meds, take temps, rig I-V's. I draw blood, turn or ambulate patients, record BP's. It's an unexceptional day—people are dying. September sunlight, that last hurrah of brightness already muted by the foreknowledge of winter, slips across the islanded rooms, making watery squares of shadow on the white sheets of so many, many single beds, in all of which people are dying. Some will go home first; some will have remissions; some will live long lives; all are dying.

In the hall, I pass Nelson, his white coat flapping behind him like a sail, a tail. If he hurried any more, he would lift off, airborne, a medical kite, a human Medflight. We nod to each other, the way we did before we were married, while we were married.

In the fluorescent glow of the hospital hallways, his beard no longer looks like peppermint. It is as white as surgical gauze.

Gloved and gowned, I duck into Reed's room.

Reed has AIDS. He has been here before, during two other episodes of acute infection. This time he has pneumonia. This time, when he leaves here, he will go to a nursing home to die.

It seems to me that his single bed is like a little boat afloat in the sea of sunlight that fills the room. Reed lies there on his back, with his eyes shut, as if drifting farther and farther from shore.

"Reed," I say to call him back.

He opens his eyes and it takes him a moment to process the fact that I am here, that it is I. I believe the dementia that occurs in 80 percent of AIDS patients has begun to manifest itself, but it's hard to say. I don't know what Reed was like before he became an AIDS patient.

I pull up a chair and sit beside him. The skinnier he gets, the more room his eyes take up in his face. He winks at me, a thin eyelid dropping over a big brown eye that seems, somehow, just a little less sharp than it did the last time he was here.

"Hello, Shelley," he says.

"I thought for a minute you'd forgotten me."

"I still have my *mind*, Shelley," he says, too quick, I think, to assume I mean more than my surface statement. "It's just my body that's going."

I don't contradict him. He knows everything there is to know at this point about his disease. He knows more about it than I do—like many AIDS victims, he has read the research, questioned the doctors, exchanged information. At the limits of knowledge, the issue becomes belief, and I figure he has a right to choose his beliefs. Reed believes he will lick his illness.

I look at the *body that's going*: He has lost more weight since his last hospitalization, despite a rigorous fitness plan. His cheekbones are as pointy as elbows. His brown eyes have lost some of their laughter. When I pick up his hand to hold it, it doesn't squeeze back. There are sores on his arms—the giveaway lesions of Kaposi's Sarcoma. K.S., we say around here. I take his pulse, the wrist between my fingers and thumb not much bigger than a sugar tube.

"Reed," I ask him, "are you sorry you're gay?" I almost say *were*. As in *were gay*. Or *sorry you were gay*.

"Because of this?" He withdraws his hand.

"No. Just—if there were no such thing as AIDS, if nobody ever died from it, would you be glad to be gay?"

"How can I answer that? How can I pretend Eddie never died?"

Eddie was his lover; he died of AIDS two years ago, in California. Reed came back home, but his parents, small dairy farmers in northern Wisconsin, have been unable, or perhaps unwilling, to look after him.

He's not having trouble talking; his lungs are much better now, he is off oxygen, and he'll surely leave us in a day or two. I'll never see him again—this former social worker, still in his twenties, now dying more or less alone, whose gentleness is reflected in the sterling silver-framed photo portraits of Eddie and his parents and sister that he brings here with him each time and props on the night-table, next to the telephone and water tray.

In my imagination, I try to read—Reed!—the dinner scene from the story of *his* life: His parents are seated at either end of the old oak table that has been the heart of their family life for 25 years. Would they place Reed next to his sister, across from Eddie? Or would they put the two boys together, facing their only daughter? The former, I think: Eddie is an outsider in this scene.

I know what they look like, gathered around that table, because of the portraits. Reed's sister is dark, a little overweight; she is the mediator, the one who tries to make all the emotional transactions among the family members run smoothly. His mother looks like a blueberry pie—dark and creamy-skinned, round-faced, plumply bursting out of her Sears slacks and top. His father is shy, turning away from the camera, turning away from Eddie not out of any dislike in particular for him but because he always turns, always has turned, away from even the merest implicative reference to sex, and Eddie's presence is an implication. And Eddie— Eddie is healthy. Eddie is broad-faced and big-shouldered, Eddie is the one who looks like a farmhand, who looks like he could do chores all day under a midwestern sun and drink Stroh's at night, fish for muskie and shingle the roof on Sunday. He does not look like he will be dead anytime soon.

I wonder how the family took it, how explicit Reed was or how much they guessed or refused to understand. Reed would have been sensitive about everyone's feelings, wanting not to hurt either his parents or his lover, wanting his sister not to be disappointed in her big brother but eager for her to understand Eddie's importance in his life. I wonder how Reed felt when, after dinner, they all rose from the table and said, not impolitely, goodnight, taking him and Eddie up on their offer to do the dishes, and retired to their rooms—not condemning him but also, not, not—what did he expect from them? he asked himself. Had he hoped they would embrace Eddie as their own, that they would feel, when they looked at Eddie, the warmth of emotion that sometimes suddenly welled up in him so intensely he could almost cry, a cup overflowing? When he turned the dial on the dishwasher, a red light came on like a point of reference.

While I am musing, Reed is busy fighting off an invisible force that wants to pull his mouth down, wants to yank tears out of his eyes. When he wins, his face falls into place again, at rest, the exhausted victor of yet another round in an intramural boxing match against grief.

"How are Ian," he asks me, "and Isabel?"

We are talking together in low voices, telling each other about our lives, when Dr. Feltskog stops in with a couple of residents following in his wake. They are all using universal precautions. This is a teaching hospital. He introduces them to Reed, explains Reed's situation, the presenting pneumocystic pneumonia, our methodology for managing the disease.

Dr. Feltskog finishes his spiel, and I am looking at Reed, trying to measure its impact, when one of the young doctors steps forward. "Reed," she says—even the youngest doctors no longer use patients' last names—"how do you feel?"

Reed winks at me again, though so slowly I am not sure the others in the room recognize it as a wink. They may just think he is tired, fighting sleep.

"Okay," he says.

The young doctor nods as if she understands exactly what he is doing: He has said that he feels okay because he doesn't want to burden them with details about how he really feels. It doesn't occur to her that maybe he just doesn't want to burden himself with the attention he can tell she is dying to give him.

"Now, Reed," she says, leaning over him so close it is as if he has no boundaries at all, leaning into his face, "we know you have feelings you want to talk about. It's natural. If you like, we can ask a staff psychiatrist to stop in to see you."

There is a silence in which I learn to feel sorry even for her—not just Reed, not just Isabel, not just Ian and my ex, and not just myself but even this jejune, over-helpful (and unconsciously manipulative), too-well-intentioned doctor in pearls and Hush Puppies, the white coat, though she doesn't know it, a symbol of all that she owes to women my age, who made it possible for her to do what she does, have what she has—as I watch Dr. Feltskog register, on his mental ledger sheet, her lack of sensitivity.

To Reed, the suggestion that he see a psychiatrist means he really is losing his mind. It means he will be defeated after all: if his mind is not on his side, how can he combat what is happening to his body? It means he really is going to die before he has had a chance to live.

"I don't want a psychiatrist," he says softly, the tears he had beaten back earlier now overtaking him.

They leap to his eyes, those tears, and others to mine, as he says, with as much exclamatory emphasis as he can command, a look on his face like that of a child who has been unfairly trapped into protesting his innocence even after he knows that everyone knows he is guilty, "Why are you interrogating me about my feelings like this? This is not the Phil Donahue show! This is my life!"

When he says this, I lose track of which one of us is me. It seems to be *me* in that bed, it is *my* body going, *my* mind that's no longer to be trusted. This is the opposite of a near-death out-of-body experience, this experience of being in *someone else's* body near *someone else's* death. Those are my tears on his face, surely; surely, these are his tears on mine.

At first I think he has read my mind. As I begin to regain my ontological footing, I understand that, all over America, people are struggling to prove to themselves that their lives are more than television, that their lives are real, the real thing.

Assembled like this, we have all entered a world outside time, it is as if a collective catastrophe has carried us into a place of silence and immobility, we are a mass accident, a tragedy.

Thus: a moment of stasis, a moment like cardiac arrest, and then we all come to life again, a jumpstart, a fibrillation. And a fluttering, too, a fluttering is going on here: a fluttering of hands, of hearts, of eyelids too nervous to lift themselves all the way up. There is this swift, generalized occupation, and I have a sense as of tents being taken down and away quickly and quietly, a stealth of tents, and yes, now everyone has scattered and I am alone again with Reed. I think of all the things he might have said, the true profanity of his condition, and it seems to me that no words could ever be as shocking as "Phil" and "Donahue" and "Show," words that have brought America into this hospital room, the dream of an essential empowerment so at odds with the insomniac knowledge of our own helplessness, our midnight desperation over coffee and cigarettes.

"Please," I say to Reed, and I am intrigued to note how my voice supplicates, my voice, which is, really, pretty good at both giving and accepting orders and not accustomed to hovering in between like this, "get some rest now, Reed."

He doesn't answer. He turns his face away from me and I wait, but he still doesn't answer or look at me. I am left staring at the back of his head, the bald spot that is the tonsure of early middle age and was once the fontanelle of an infant, and I think—what else could I think—that I don't care what kind of life Isabel leads, so long as she gets to lead one.

I think of my beautiful daughter, her grumpy spirit caged by the circumstances of her own sexuality and her mother's, and of how it will one day—soon, I think—be freed, *free to be itself*, and how, when it is, her sweetly curved profile will disclose the inner strength I know is there, how her blue, blue eyes, deep and true as columbine, will sparkle with the triumph that integrity is.

Not that I wouldn't prefer things to be otherwise; not that I am exactly happy about my daughter's choice. I wouldn't go so far as that—not yet. But what I know, almost annoyed with myself for knowing it because I wish I could surprise myself, but then that is why I married Ian, isn't it, to be surprised, is that I'm going to. I love her too much not to know that the day will come when I will feel however I must feel in order to keep her in my life. This, I realize, was never in doubt, no matter how much I may have been in doubt. The issue always becomes belief.

But back out in the hallway I stop short, confused, almost dizzied, feeling I have lost my place in some book or other. They are paging Nelson— *Dr. Lopate, Dr. Lopate!*—and I remember how I used to call him that our first year together in Detroit. We were the same height, and I'd launch his newly earned title in a low whisper from the rim of his ear, a little raft afloat on the sea of ego. And he loved it, at least for that first year.

I find my way to the locker room and change out of my work shoes into Nikes. Walking home on Highland, I see that we are having what I secretly think of as a Code Blue sky—alarmingly bright, the kind of sky that can galvanize you. A sky like emergency medicine, needing to be attended to on the spot. So when I get home I call Ian at the school. The secretary has to go get him, of course, because he's in his classroom, grading papers. *Nous aimons, vous aimez, ils aiment.*

Elles aiment.

"Let's spend the night at the farm," I tell him. "I'll swing by and pick you up."

AFTER supper we go for a walk and wind up down by Beaver Pond. The pond is as round as a smiling cheek, the setting sun a blush on it like rouge, and in the sky a thin crescent moon, the squinty eye of it, the shut eye of it, is already risen, as if it just can't wait, it has things it wants to see, it won't be kept in the dark any longer. Ian and I straddle a log, and we're glad, given the late-day chill, that we are wearing flannel shirts.

Let's face it, things are not exactly quiet out here in the country.

Things are going on even out here. We can hear the beavers working away in a scramble against winter. Every so often, there's a crash or a cry, and no way of knowing whether the sound means life or death. There are so many creatures out here, deer and owls and just so many, and the prairie grass, and the abandoned orchard, and wildflowers.

Sometimes I think of the whole world as a kind of hospital, the earth itself as a patient.

There are days, now, when so much seems to be slipping away. Even the things one tends not to think of, like the walnuts. The walnuts are slipping away, going off to be stockpiled by squirrels. The green of summer is slipping away, hiding its light under a bush or a bushel of autumn leaves. There are dreams that slip away in the middle of the night, losing themselves forever in some dark corner of the subconscious. There are stars that are disappearing even as we look at them. There are mothers and fathers and children, all of them slipping away like the fish in the pond, going down deeper for winter. And you reach out to hold on to your child, and she is slipping away, going off into some life that is not your life, and you are afraid to see her go because you know, you know how far it is possible to go, how far it is possible for things to slip away.

"You're thinking," Ian says. "What about?"

But I don't know how to say what I'm thinking, because it seems to me I am thinking of everything there is to think of and of nothing at all, at the same time. "I don't know how to put it into words," I confess. "You have to remember, I had only two years of Liberal Arts."

"I've often wondered," Ian says, "what the Conservative Arts would be. Anything Jesse Helms likes, I guess."

We hear a noise like a senator. "Did you hear that?" I ask. "That must have been a frog."

We listen to two or three frogs bandying croaks back and forth. They're more subdued than they are during the spring, but they still have something to say. "There are throats in those frogs," I say. "Those frogs are talking to one another."

"In French," Ian says. "Frogs always talk in French."

I let out a whoop and get up from the log, but when I do I trip and Ian jumps up to catch me, and he holds me, and my face is buried against his right arm, and my left ear is over his heart, which is making its own happy racket through the walls of his chest, as loud as a neighbor living it up.

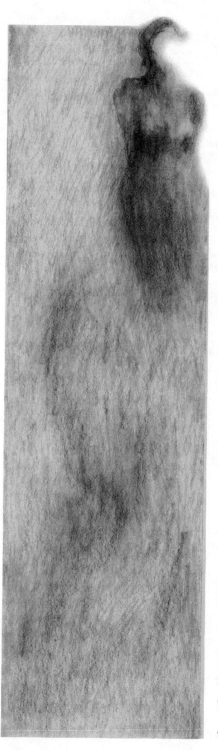

Family and Friends

THROUGH all the seasons of a woman's life, our love and history with our original families and our friends sustain us. They also drive us crazy. Every woman wrestles with the universal passage of separating from her early family world to become her own person. Three stories explore how the painful tug among family, love, and independence can work out. Shirley Abbott's autobiographical "On the Road" recalls the youthful Shirley's making her escape from Hot Springs, Arkansas, though her father, a bookie in the local gambling establishment, does all he can to keep her home.

Amy Tan's Waverly lunches with her mother, who is, by Waverly's weary description, "A Horse, born in 1918, destined to be obstinate and frank to the point of tactlessness." Waverly, unhappily, is "a Rabbit, born in 1951, supposedly sensitive, with tendencies toward being thin-skinned and skittery at the first sign of criticism."

Judith Ortiz Cofer's personal essay gives a different twist to a woman's realizing how much she still feels tied to her family. Cofer watches an old silent home movie of her Puerto Rican family party and sadly sees how much of her family history she has missed by becoming Americanized.

Dorothy Allison's powerful memoir, "Skin, Where She Touches Me," illuminates her nearly lifelong struggle not to lose the two people she loved most: her mother and her first woman lover. She shows how love shapes whom we become—both in the loving and the letting go.

A long-term woman friend of mine says, "Lovers come and go, children grow up and leave you, but my women friends stay on forever." The friendships we form with other women *are* different from relations with family or male friends. Sisters, rivals, stalwart comforters, and supporters—all are part of the friendships we forge with our own sex. In "Cathy, Now and Then," Jill McCorkle celebrates a friendship that has endured from grade school and college to grown-up years. Pam Houston's haunting "In My Next Life" reveals the deep emotional exchange of two young women, whose love for each other is intensified by being cut short. And Grace Paley's "Ruthy and Edie" begins with a friendship on the stoop of a brownstone and extends through ups and downs of the years to grandmotherhood. Now *that's* a friendship.

Cathy, Now and Then

JILL McCORKLE

SOMETIMES I think my punishment for being a social organization dropout is an unerring memory for their oaths and pledges, secret handshakes and songs. I remember every stanza of "We've a Story to Tell to the Nation" from GAs (Girls' Auxiliary) at the Baptist Church (where I never made it past the bottom rung of a rather lengthy climb leading to Queen Regent in Service), and the Phi Mu Sorority's secret knock and *na nu na nu*, Mork from Ork-style handshake. But the oath that reverberates most often is that little ditty in the front of the Brownie and Girl Scout handbooks: "Make new friends, but keep the old. One is silver and the other's gold." I'm not sure that's the exact wording but it's certainly close enough and I regret that I'm unable to get the little singsongy tune that accompanies it onto the page for full effect.

I hate the song and yet I see people shining in such a way: aluminum and bronze, silver today and gold tomorrow. Certainly making new friends these days is an entirely different process. No one has time for all-night phone calls and pajama parties; no one has time to ruminate over those stories from the past that have made me who I am. New friendships rely on quick meetings for lunch where I practically burst with excitement at seeing another adult and then spend much of the time talking about my husband, the children, my work. I don't have time to tell about the summer after third grade when I accidentally bleached my hair orange and then had to get a severe pixie, or about when a boy in the fourth grade told me that my legs looked like a chimpanzee's legs and I went home, snuck a razor, and shaved my kneecaps. I don't have time to tell that I barely graduated from college or that I once, while trying to make up for basic laziness in a literature class, rambled on and on about the bird imagery in a particular poem only to have the professor say: "Swan? What swan? I said *swine*." Somehow these things just never seem to come up. It's hard enough to give the good parts of ourselves to new friends; who has time for those moments of humiliation, heartbreak, and poor mental health? And though I really like meeting people as the person I am *now*, and though I look forward to years of slowly filling in details and stories and hearing theirs in exchange — seeing the elemental values of a relationship grow with each visit — there's nothing that can ever take the place of someone who knew you when and likes you, loves you, in spite or because of it. When that someone is a part of the present, then you have the rarest of all friendships; you speak your own language, a kind of shorthand only available to childhood friends, where a word or phrase conjures up major portions of your life. With such a friendship you know and accept all of the changes that have occurred over time; you know the past history that shapes the present, and you know the surface appearance and all that lies underneath. When a writer talks about having a strong sense of place he or she is talking about such encompassing knowledge — knowledge directly tied to one's roots. In the same way, the friendship that offers a strong sense of person does not happen suddenly but is one you grow with and into.

I HAVE known Cathy Lewis for as long as I can remember. Our hometown, Lumberton, North Carolina, was small enough when we were growing up that it seemed everyone knew everyone. Though we were never in the same class at Tanglewood Elementary School, we shared the same history and had witnessed the same events. We remember when Cindy Barnes broke her arm (white face, protruding bone, a circle of screaming fourth-graders) while doing the slide-to-slide on the playground; we recall with great detail the time Jim Connelly threw up in the cafeteria and set off a chain reaction down the yellow Formica table; we knew who got paddled in the hall and who had to stay after school beating erasers. We realize now that we were even in the same Brownie troop; we wore brown uniforms and beanies while eating stale Lorna Doones and drinking Hawaiian Punch; we wrapped cracked marbles in remnant pieces of net to make corsages for our mothers and sewed little squares of oilcloth into "sit-upons." I quit when the troop leader said that we could not take our sit-upons home, that they belonged to the troop. Cathy endured a bit longer.

In the seventh grade we finally landed in the same homeroom. This year is marked in my mind with songs like "Na Na Hey Hey Kiss Him Goodbye," lovebeads, Indian moccasins which we all purchased at The Hodge Podge (a used shoe store), and by a boy in our class, Raymond Weston, who, knowing Cathy's dad was a veterinarian, provoked her to fury by saying, "Your daddy's a dog killer." Good old Raymond, a little piece of rawhide tied around his plump neck, talked nonstop about his minibike and his future plans of owning a Harley, and said things like "That girl's so ugly they could throw her in the Lumber River and skim ugly for weeks," or "Your mama had to tie pork chops around your neck to get the dogs to play with you." Raymond pressed my button by flashing big fake smiles my way and saying in an annoyingly sweet voice, "Aren't you so nice? All the time smiling. Ain't you just the teacher's pet?" On those excruciatingly hot afternoons when the sun baked through the big wavy windows of our dilapidated school (the ceiling of our math class crashed in one day while everybody was at recess), Raymond killed flies with rubber bands and lined them up in his pencil tray.

I think Cathy and I were first united by the mutual aggravation supplied by the likes of Raymond, but it was really in high school when our friendship as we know it began. Since our last names began with the letters L and M, we always shared homeroom and we quickly chose seats next to each other. It was natural that first thing every morning we had a lot to discuss (who was talking to whom out in the smoking area, who was wearing so-and-so's blue jeans jacket even though he hadn't officially broken up with what's-her-name, who was "grubbing"—the term that year for making out—up against the lockers before first bell, and so on). We had everything in the world in common: we both loved plants, and we both loved Elton John's "Madman across the Water" album. We both knew a lot about everything even though we hadn't *done* anything. We were both tall brunettes, always in the back row in every group shot, we both hated cafeteria food and algebra and loved English. We were the types who would decorate for school dances and build the floats for the homecoming parade. If there are proms in the afterlife she'll be hanging old parachutes, Spanish moss, and crepe paper flowers in the celestial gym and I'll be tying balloons and maroon and gold pom-poms to the pearly gates. We both loved to talk about and analyze books and stories, songs and movies. As the editor of the high school paper she published my lousy poetry and I was grateful.

During senior year we even shared a job. We were sales clerks at the Smart Shop in downtown Lumberton, a clothing store owned by some of the kindest, most generous women I have ever known. They were interested in selling, yes, but they were more interested in honesty: "Lord now, child, I believe you need more bosom than you've got for a dress cut like that," or "No, honey, I can't let you buy that dress with it looking that way."

We learned to tell someone tactfully that she was too old, fat, young, or skinny for this or that. On Christmas Eve when husbands came in desperate to buy something, we were told not to think of a quick sale, but "to think of that poor sweet wife sitting there by the tree with the baby, stars in her eyes as she wonders what her husband will give her. She probably ordered him some nice things from the L. L. Bean catalog. Keep her in mind when he's trying to buy something that doesn't match." We heard our mentors say, "Now, I know your wife and I know she's no size six. Uh-uh, no, not a fourteen either. What about some costume jewelry or a nice pair of gloves?" and we also heard customers discuss their husbands and boyfriends and body parts. We never forgot the woman who patted her lower abdomen and referred to it as her "cooter." There was a lengthy discussion as to what constituted a plump, pretty cooter (an abdomen that rounded into the material) and a poor one (concave).

Cathy and I alternated afternoon hours but then on Saturdays we were both there, changing the clothes of the mannequins in the window and helping people decide what to buy. Mainly we spent our time adorning ourselves, putting things on layaway until we had used up everything we'd earned. Truth be told we probably both lost money while working there, but I can remember every piece of 1970s polyester that we purchased, especially my safari pantsuit complete with a shirt that had a lion's face on the front and his tail on the back. Cathy's taste was more conservative, her jumpsuit was yellow instead of orange, for example; her leisure-style pantsuit forest green instead of orange.

I admired the certainty with which she gave her opinions and the way she seemed to know instantly whether or not she liked something or someone. There was a self-assurance about her that I did not possess. She never buckled under the peer pressure to start smoking or to do anything else unless she *wanted* to do it. She decided who she wanted to date and it didn't matter what anybody else might think about him. I envied these traits. I tried to figure out why she had them and I didn't. For a long while I believed that she had escaped severe self-consciousness and guilt by growing up Methodist instead of Baptist. If only I'd never gone to Girls' Auxiliary at the church. The Methodist Youth Center on Sunday nights was much livelier than Baptist Training Union; they shot pool in a room they had been allowed to paint black and played loud music while pondering the larger questions of life; they smoked cigarettes and made out behind the building. Surely this exposure was what had given her such confidence. Surely if I hung around with her long enough I, too, could say "I *don't* want to go" (instead of "well, let's see, let me think about it") or "I *love* this" without all of the lengthy pauses and second guesses and musings.

We graduated from Lumberton High School in 1976 and that fall we were roommates at the University of North Carolina at Chapel Hill. We arrived on a hot August afternoon, our dads sweating as they carried box after box up to our lime green room on the third floor of an un-air-conditioned dorm, our mothers making sure we had toothpaste and soap and plenty of stamps. It was almost like going off to camp (a compressed social organization) except that I was happy to be there. Neither of us could stand for things not to match so we had a color scheme; everything we bought that year was bright yellow and green, except for my wardrobe which, despite Cathy's encouragement to branch out with color, was (aside from my orange items) in shades of basic brown and tan.

We still hated the thought of institutional food and the rules and order that accompanied a meal plan, so our domestic habits started early. We cooked canned goods on a little two-burner stove. It was going down to the hall bathroom to wash the dishes that posed problems, so freshman year we threw out enough Tupperware to have a king-size party. My contributions to roommate living were a love for television and junk food, things that both Cathy and now my husband claim they didn't indulge in before living with me. Cathy brought the stereo and the ability to shag. She gave dancing lessons to people on our hall, the beach music blasting as we took turns learning to twirl and dip. I was the local cosmetologist; I spent a lot of time trimming, perming, and coloring hair, and plucking eyebrows. I sat out in the hall smoking cigarettes while she sat under a space-age hair dryer and asked me if I liked the idea of having cigarette breath. We looked forward to football Saturdays, and neither of us ever went to the library, but we read our English papers aloud to each other. We took a math course that was filled to capacity by much of the football team; the course was the mathematical equivalent of the geology course I was also taking known as "rocks for jocks." But the worst course that I talked Cathy into was Geography 38. "How hard can it be?" I asked. "A few plateaus and mountains, maybe a bit of weather," but it was the hardest class we had ever encountered. The questions on the first little quiz went something like: "In Jakarta, Indonesia, on May twenty-second, 1900, at what angle was the sun to the horizon at 2:35 P.M." We couldn't even skip class to sit in the student union and do the crossword puzzle in the campus paper because this professor had a troop of graduate students who took the roll.

The night before our final, sympathetic friends wished us luck. We tried to study but we got so hungry we had to walk over to Roy Rogers for burgers and fries. Then we decided that maybe our minds would be loosened by just a little television. Then we opted to go down to the dorm basement and bake cookies for somebody we knew who was in prison.

Finally, Cathy said she was going to hang it up and go to bed. When my parents called at ten to wish us luck, we were both asleep.

When we went to take the exam the next day, Cathy's Toyota was already packed to go home for the holidays. I looked at the exam and knew that my best option was just to eenie-meenie it. I got past the professor and the graduate assistants and then I ran. I was leaning against the car, smoking cigarettes as fast as I could, when I discovered that Cathy was right behind me. "Why did I let you talk me into this course?" she said. " 'Little plateaus, an island or two.' " She was so upset she didn't even complain that I was chain-smoking in her car. Thirty minutes out of town and we were laughing—nervous, but laughing. We returned to scan the grades, standing side-by-side in the darkened hallway of the geography department, our fingers frantically seeking out our social security numbers. "D"s. We had "D"s. I was exhilarated; Cathy was relieved. This was not my first or last "D," but it was her only one.

I was not soaring academically, so I decided to take some time off from school. Come July, while lifeguarding at the Lumber River, I knew this had been a dumb idea, but by then Cathy had been assigned a new roommate who would live on my side of that lime green room and I had to find a new place to live. The good thing to come of that separated year was that because I had not preregistered for classes, I had to pick up a whole schedule at drop-add. At the time I had no ideas for a major. I thought it likely that I'd major in physical education and try to coach a women's swim or tennis team or something. I signed up for English 23W (beginning fiction writing) because I liked to write and assumed it would be an easy course.

When Cathy and I were reunited for apartment life junior year, our color scheme of green and yellow still with us, I had both a major and goals for what I wanted to do with my life, as well as a brand-new Smith-Corona typewriter humming on the kitchen table. Cathy was equally involved in her journalism courses and the various romantic interests (photographers, news writers, copyeditors) that had evolved therein. That fall I joined her sorority and was formally taught all the secret hand-shakes and songs and codes that she had already divulged. We went to mixers and toga parties; I took care of the cooking and she did the cleaning. We called ourselves Alice and Theresa after two maiden sisters from our hometown who lived together and split the chores in a similar way. Really, though, we were more like Laverne and Shirley—Cathy with her zest for going out and wearing monograms on her clothes, and me with a neurosis about everything except school.

Although red polyester was not even our idea of a bad joke, come summer that's what we found ourselves wearing. If we had been at the

Smart Shop, we would have said, "Lord, girl, you do not have a butt for red polyester." And yet there we were, pushing slices at the Pizza Hut. Unfortunately, the owners knew that we tended to talk a lot, so they always put us on separate shifts on different nights. Our only time to see each other was while we lay out in the sun or in the wee hours when one of us came home, smelling of pepperoni, with a free large Super Supreme. These were given to us by Brent, the cook, a former reform school student who confessed to us that he had burned down his room there. In fact, he insisted that we take home large Super Supreme pizzas, and he also insisted—once the doors to the Hut were locked at midnight—that we play the jukebox with quarters from our tips and dance with him. He had long, greasy, black hair that fell forward when he bent to unzip his shiny boots so he could *disco* in his ratty socked feet.

Cathy and I often sat in our apartment at one A.M. eating pizza, one of us in a nightgown the other in the red suit, talking about Brent. We could complain that he made us dance with him but then he'd tell that we took home Super Supremes every night. Besides, we were scared of meeting up with Brent outside of work. One night, when my brother-in-law's Chevrolet Biscayne wouldn't go into reverse, I pressed harder on the accelerator and jiggled the gears; all of a sudden Brent jumped up from behind where he had been holding the bumper. Incidents like this reminded us that two of our friends from high school had been locked in the walk-in freezer at a Pizza Hut in Winston-Salem by a gun-toting man in a ski mask just two weeks before. It reminded us that people like Ray Weston were now *out there*, all grown up, with tattoos and Harleys and saying things far worse than "Your daddy kills dogs."

We were desperate to quit our jobs. Cathy was on the waiting list for a position at a clothing store at the mall and I had applied at a kennel and cattery. She liked clothes and I liked animals; by then we both hated pizza. It was while all of this was going on that we befriended our neighbor, the young woman who lived above us. Within the first afternoon of chatting she revealed that she was pregnant and that her boyfriend frequently beat her up. Now, during our carefree summer, beer in the fridge, Jimmy Buffett blasting from our apartment windows, we became therapists. Cathy has always had the great ability to ask just the right questions; people will tell her everything. I oftentimes get the same results by saying nothing. Together we were hearing more than we wanted. We were supportive and comforting, we encouraged her to seek help, to leave. We sat up in the wee hours waiting to hear if anything was happening.

A week or so passed and we were still at the Hut. We had begun coming in from the sun earlier to enjoy the luxury of an afternoon nap. One afternoon we both sat up at the same time, having just dreamed that we heard our door slam. We then heard the monotonous bass beat booming from the upstairs stereo and realized that the boyfriend was home. It seemed our neighbor, now noticeably pregnant, stopped by more and more frequently. We came home one day in the pouring-down rain to find her standing outside our door with a big trash bag that she had used to shield her head. Her boyfriend had locked her out and we invited her in to wait for him to get home. The conversation turned to one we liked discussing: clothes and how they fit people, outrageous examples of poor taste, and the kinds of things we'd heard and said at the Smart Shop ("MmmmMmmmmMmmmm, that's pitiful isn't it? Somebody ought to tell her that a bigger size would do wonders"). We talked sizes and shapes and then the neighbor shyly disappeared. We whispered about how sorry we felt for her. What could we do?

I was midway through my shift a few nights later, having been stiffed on tips at least twice already, when Brent loped his greasy way over with an occasional disco turn—shades of what I had to look forward to—to tell me I had a phone call; "The other one of you," he said. I barely answered before Cathy was asking if I'd borrowed the tip money on her dresser.

"I wouldn't do that," I told her. "Not without telling you."

"Well, I know that," she said with that little laugh that emerges when she gets nervous. "But it would be okay if you did." She was clearly stalling. "My watch is gone, too," she whispered and I could hear her beginning to open and close drawers. All of her earrings were gone. "My clothes!" she was shouting. "My clothes are gone!"

The owners were furious that I was leaving. "You girls don't take work seriously," the man said. Brent watched me longingly; he was going to have to use his own quarter to hear "Disco Inferno" and dance by himself. "Well, you don't get robbed every day!" I said. "It's not like we knew." But then I did know who had done it and I ran back to the phone. Cathy had the same thought at the same time. It all made sense. We *had* heard our door slam that day; someone had stood in the doorway of our room and watched us there on our matching little patchwork bedspreads, both of us in gym shorts and tee shirts. I drove home as fast as I could. I was sure that my typewriter was gone and Cathy's stereo and the small black-and-white television that my mother had won as a bridge party door prize years earlier.

When I arrived, Cathy and her date were in the living room with the policeman. The policeman eyed me and my attire and then went back to his little pad. "So," he said. "You girls have some grass?"

"What?" We both looked at him like he might be the idiot he was.

Did he really think we'd give it to him if we did? Cathy told him that we had beer in the refrigerator.

"Most of these break-ins are drug related," he said and stared hard at us. "So I'll ask again if you're housing anything."

"No," Cathy said. Her hands were on her hips and her eyebrows were raised as they were in the seventh grade when Ray Weston barked at her. She was just about ready to take this guy out, and even in her Maleia sundress, bright green espadrilles, and add-a-beads, she could have done it. We tried to tell him that we knew who had robbed us. We went to look her up in the phone book but our robber had taken that, too. Maybe she thought we wouldn't know how to call the police without it. The officer said there was really nothing that he could do since we had no proof. I went on Cathy's date with her (a very brief date) and then we spent the rest of the night rehashing our clues. I was so relieved to see my typewriter that I hadn't even done a full inventory, so we sat up late going through our things. That's when I discovered that that woman had not taken any of my clothes! She had taken all of my shoes, bathing suits, and underwear, but she had not taken one damn article of clothing! There hung my brown sundress and my safari pantsuit. "I've been trying to tell you," Cathy said. "Haven't I been trying to tell you?"

The next day, every time we came or went, the crooked neighbors were watching us from above, hands holding back the curtains. We thought about faking an exit, parking on the other side of the building and then waiting inside for them, but we chickened out. We asked to borrow their phone book, thinking that they'd accidentally give us ours, the one with the sorority house and various friends and family members' numbers scribbled inside, but of course they weren't that stupid.

When the weekend came, we decided to take action. We went to the super of our complex and requested a solid door with a dead bolt instead of the standard glass door. He refused. Fire regulations, he said. So we said we were moving and needed our deposit back. We hadn't told our parents about the robbery. We were afraid they'd make us come home to Lumberton for the rest of the summer. We decided we'd tell them after we were settled in a new place. Once we made up our minds, we were out of there in twenty-four hours. We rented a U-Haul, packed Cathy's car to the gills, and were gone before the neighbors got home. By suppertime that night we were settled into a cute little duplex-type apartment on a wooded road. We had a deck, our own rooms, and were paying less rent. I had one pair of sneakers and no bathing suits but things were definitely looking up.

The good luck continued. We told our parents what had happened and they were more relaxed than we had expected. We badgered our former manager until he returned our fifty-dollar deposit. We turned in our red polyester and Cathy spent her days selling clothes (and steadily replacing her losses) and I spent mine joyfully hosing down dog runs. It seemed we were finally back on track. We had our nights off to go downtown or leisurely eat our Swanson frozen Mexican dinners while watching reruns of "The Andy Griffith Show." We drank enough Tab to sail a ship. I still smoked like a fiend either in my room or out on the deck. While nothing was going on at the kennel, I began writing what I called "The Jillzette," a paper I designed purely for Cathy's amusement. I wrote social columns describing our most recent dates (hers in great detail) and a "Horrorscopes" column where I profiled and drew pictures of people we didn't like.

One Saturday afternoon we unplugged the phone and went to take naps. I was asleep in my room, dreaming I was at a party and wearing this shirt I had loved. It was a nondescript sort of buff-colored Qiana oversized shirt that I had purchased at the Smart Shop and had worn with a pair of matching Candies that made me about six feet tall. I opened my eyes, wondering how tall Miss Crook—who now must have been about nine months pregnant—stood in my Candies, when all of a sudden I realized that one thing of mine had been stolen—that very shirt. I felt a momentary surge of pride and then an avalanche of fury. I ran to Cathy's room and woke her. I even lit a cigarette in the main room and she didn't say anything about it. "This is it," I told her. "We are *mad.*"

We called our former neighbors and asked to speak to the woman. He said she wasn't there, could he help me?

"We know you robbed us," I said. "My roommate's daddy hired a PI who's been tracking you and now we've got all the evidence we need. The PI has asked us to take out a warrant but we thought we'd give her one last chance seeing as how she's about to have a baby and all." I know now that we must have been scared to death because we sat there looking at each other while I delivered that mouthful of garbage without one laugh. Finally, all those years watching "Kojak" were paying off. The woman came to the phone and said, "What do you want?"

"Return everything to us and we'll drop it. Otherwise you and your baby are going to jail."

"Why don't you come upstairs?"

"We don't live there anymore." I paused while she acted surprised. "Meet us in front of University Mall," I said, thinking we'd have a policeman there with us. Although they had fallen for the ridiculous story, they didn't fall for that. We finally got her to say that she would take everything downstairs to another neighbor.

When it was all over and we were safely back in our apartment going through labelless clothes, Cathy called the police to tell them that we had solved our own case. They said we were stupid, foolish girls but, of course, we knew better.

After that experience, we felt older and wiser. We felt too old and wise for secret handshakes and knocks; we were about to become Phi Mu dropouts. For the rest of the summer, we sat out on our teeny tiny deck and played albums. We read cheap trashy fiction aloud and we read good fiction aloud. We drank cheap champagne and practiced various shag moves. We played word games and had contests to see who could come up with the most outrageous stories about people we knew and deliver them without laughing. We talked about what we wanted to do, where we wanted to go.

The only disturbing incident after our move was when I accidentally killed an orphaned cat. I dipped it for fleas as you would a dog and the result was immediate poisoning. For nights after I couldn't close my eyes without seeing that convulsing cat. Today, in the midst of a group of people, Cathy will turn to me and with a blank face say "Tell about when you killed that cat. Tell about how none of your clothes got stolen."

That fall my first short story was published in the university literary magazine. Cathy and I had already celebrated this event many times over. We celebrated when it was accepted, celebrated when the issue came out. But the biggest celebration of all came when there was a very good review of the issue in the school newspaper with a whole paragraph devoted to my story. I know I didn't go to class that day; I just sat in the student union staring at the review. I remember getting to the apartment door and finding the review taped to it, that paragraph highlighted in yellow.

We shared everything that year. She read all of the manuscripts for my writing class and I brainstormed with her on ad campaigns for her journalism course. We could almost smell graduation, but it seemed the closer it came the less we talked about moving away; she had a job in Raleigh and I was going to graduate school for writing. We both knew that some things are just understood. There's no reason to say it or talk it to death, no need for little social hugs and kisses. If you've got it, you know it, it's that simple. I knew as our senior year was drawing to a close that we were about to experience a great loss. Oh sure, we'd always be there for each other; we'd live on the telephone. But what about the way we told each other everything that happened? What about the jokes other people didn't think were funny because they hadn't been in that seventh-grade classroom? What about our great album collection?

But there was no need to worry. We are still taping albums to fill in the gaps. Now we talk and tell everything that has happened during the week. We call to complain ("the baby has an ear infection," or "it's too damn hot to go outside"); to get reassurance ("who has time to just lie around in the sun and get skin cancer?"); to get that totally biased opinion that we all need from time to time (she always reads all of my work in manuscript); or simply to gossip (between the two of us we know all of the hometown news even though neither of us lives there). When I quit smoking we talked constantly, her cigarette cracks strengthening my resolve; and when her son was born I was there to assure her that she would (in a year or so) sleep a full night and get to take a shower by herself. I have learned to say *no* much more often and have improved my wardrobe. She relies on me to remember and entertain, to dredge up and record the kinds of sordid details from adolescence that most people choose to forget. We have huge phone bills but we always rationalize that they aren't as much as an hour with a really good shrink.

I've been surprised to learn that everyone doesn't have a Cathy, and every month or two—phone cords twisting as we pause and turn into our separate homes to say things like "get that out of your mouth"—one of us will remind the other how very lucky we are. The silver friend knows your present and the gold friend knows all of your past dirt and glories. Once in a blue moon there's someone who knows it all, someone who knows and accepts you unconditionally, someone who's there for life. I shudder to think how different my life would have been if I'd wound up in another homeroom.

On the Road

SHIRLEY ABBOTT

*There is an aloneness which is common to us all. There are rooms in
every heart where no one else can ever enter.*
—A letter from my father, June 24, 1956

MY ESCAPE PLAN materialized nicely, as neatly as if I had tunneled
out of jail. Having dreamed of New York throughout my college years, I
had decided to settle there, though I had no money, and my parents certainly had none to give me, not for that purpose at least. But at the end of
my senior year, I actually won a trip to New York in a contest for college
girls sponsored by a woman's magazine. On June 1, I set off for a month
as a guest editor for *Mademoiselle,* but then, according to the promise I
had given my parents, I returned home. The magazine paid its guest editors a small salary and gave us airline tickets back to wherever we came
from; I pocketed the salary, traded the plane ticket for round-trip train
fare, and even had a little cash to spare. I went home only for a week, to
collect a few possessions and say goodbye.

My parting with my father, when the moment came, took place at the
train station—inevitable as the departure itself. Only three trains a week
left Hot Springs now from the Missouri-Pacific depot. (The service was
canceled shortly afterward, and the old station fell into decay. People had
to bid one another farewell at the Little Rock airport from then on.) It
was a humid July evening, still over a hundred degrees at twilight, and
the three of us trembled in the heat. The grime of the waiting room gave
off the smell of tracks, gravel, and coal—the fragrance of travel when you
come from a small town. I had my ticket, fifty dollars in cash, the promise
of a place to stay—on Perry Street, just off Seventh Avenue—for a month
when I got there, and a city map. I already knew how to get from Grand
Central Station to Greenwich Village on the subway. I was not afraid.

I had spent the day not looking into my father's eyes, meticulously ironing every garment that was to be folded in my suitcase, polishing my shoes, taking an endless shower, doing all that I could do to make the hours go by. "You can't live in Greenwich Village," he had said. "I won't have it. It's full of dope fiends. You'll become a dope fiend too." But after a month's exposure, I was drunk on New York, and dizzily in love with it. Perhaps this was what my father was trying to combat, with every allegation he could think of.

Sometimes he argued from a statesmanlike stance. "I have a great deal to say to you as you start out in life, and I intend to do so," he had written to me just before I returned home. "Don't start to man your defenses, because I have no intention of trying to run your life. I love you and want you to be happy and successful, but how to attain that I surely do not know. If it is your firm desire to be a career girl in New York, you have a few qualities that might bring success. You have a great deal of natural ability. You have looks and poise (often quaking inwardly). You can bluff your way through a difficult situation, and you have a substantial reserve of the 'old con.' On the other side of the ledger you have no money, no wardrobe, no reserves. Lots of people are smarter and shrewder than you, and as you say your education has a lot of blind spots in it. And you belong here with your family. Your mother and I need you. Neither of us are well, and though we dread doing so, we may have to call on you sooner than we think."

But seeing that reason would not deter me, he descended to threats. "High prices." "White slavery." "Low wages." "Exorbitant rent." "Beatniks in beards." "You don't own a warm coat, and the temperature stays at zero for three months in the winter." "Nobody will marry a poor girl like you. Men marry to advance themselves." "New Yorkers are rude, rough folks." "The subways are dangerous. Will you promise me you'll never go into the subways?" "Who will look after my little girl if she gets sick?" Growing tired of his own barrage, he would subside into anger at one moment and grief the next.

I endured all this as best I could. My mother didn't want me to go, but at least admitted she knew very little about New York. I hadn't met any dope fiends yet, though the thought did make me anxious. But I was confident that there weren't any more of them south of Fourteenth Street than north. I knew the rents were high. I was frightened of hunting for a job. I'd no idea what I'd do when my month's sublet ran out. And I knew my father was right about the coat and the freezing winters. But I was leaving, drawing the line. I am my own creature, I said to myself. "Daughter" is not a lifelong assignment. I am not Athena, born from your head. Athena is not my goddess anymore. I will not aid the ladies in their spinning. I'll answer to myself. And my anger and terror would gnaw away at me like an impending nervous breakdown, until I too wept.

What would you say, I asked him silently, if I were leaving to be married, to become a wife? Would we dance our final waltz before you delivered me to my husband's arms, wrapped in white satin and tied with a bow? Would you have permitted me to leave in that manner, so that I at least belonged to another man, not to myself, and was not leaping into this maelstrom of independence and enterprise all on my own? No, you would be worse off than you are if I were getting married. This is what you designed me for, the mandate you gave me. How can I ride the top of the fast freight and serve as your caretaker at the same time? You fitted me out for this journey. And he replied, as silently as I, traitor, traitor, traitor. But the hour finally came, and we drove the long way to the station without speaking.

One shabby alcove was still marked COLORED, and the one dirty drinking fountain said WHITES. Such things were illegal now, but there were so few passengers that it hadn't seemed worth the trouble to remove the signs. The railroads were dying, Jim Crow was dying, gambling was dying, and it was a toss-up what to tear down first—the signs, the station, or the town.

"You'll be sorry," said my father for the hundredth time. "We always let you do what you wanted. You were a spoiled child. When we're dead and gone, you will wish you had stayed with us. No one will ever think as much of you as we do."

When had my father started saying "dead and gone"?

"Hat, hush. She's going. She deserves her chance. Can't we act like decent people?" My mother fanned herself with a newspaper, aiming small breezes in my direction when she could, smiling a crooked little smile, her face set, as on so many other occasions, with the effort of not weeping.

"At least," I said, indicating the WHITES sign, "I won't have to look at stuff like that anymore."

"Yeah, and niggers will be pushing you off the sidewalk."

"Don't say that word to me. Don't ever say that to me again." My anger kicked on as if by pilot light. We eyed each other with rage.

"You've got fifty dollars in your purse. That won't last long. You must not expect us to finance this foolishness. We can't do it."

"I don't expect anything. I never intend to ask you for a dime."

"Please, please, hush, the both of you. You know we'll help you out if we can."

I turned my face toward the door, more than ready for the conductor's "All aboard." So many pilgrims had arrived here, often on stretchers, with every joint bent and aching, and then departed upright, or maybe never departed at all, throwing in their lot with this small society where the law of the land did not apply. I thought of the old gunfighters and con men who'd been unceremoniously ushered out of town, given their one-way ticket to Malvern on this very railroad. Now I was an outlaw, too. A ship-jumper. I ought to stay, I thought, and somehow go out on Central Avenue and do something constructive. But my home was no longer my home, and I could no longer comply with its demands. I had begun to see that what this society did to black people, it did to white women too, but requiring your full submission and collusion until you believed in Big Brother, until you became a collaborator and turned into a white male supremacist yourself.

The train had to back into the station from Little Rock, this being a branch line without any roundhouse. It clanged and puffed, this prehistoric beast, pulling its two musty day coaches, surely the last steam locomotive service. "Big choo-choo, all dark," I recollected myself saying years before. But this time my father wouldn't be waiting to collect me at the next junction. Only two other people were boarding that evening, and I was eager to join them, as panic overtook me and I wondered whether I'd be able to make the break. "Don't love me so much," I wanted to say to my mother. "I'm grown up now. You should have your own life. You should stop thinking about me." But I couldn't say it. A life at Candle's Drugstore? A life taking care of my father? If only they would say goodbye and leave, but they clung sweatily and desperately to each other and to me, mounting the steps with me, choosing the best seat for me, stowing my luggage on the rack. This ancient, straight-backed, day coach was grimier even than the waiting room. "Now you'll have quite a layover in Little Rock," my father was saying. "But I would-n't go outside on the streets if I were you. Just stay in the station and have a cup of coffee. Be sure you check with the ticket agent. The train to St. Louis may be late. Be sure you check the track number."

I sat down, my knees weakening, and my parents perched briefly on the seat opposite. Images tumbled through my mind. The Tabu ad, that woman's fingers leaving the piano keyboard as she succumbed to the violinist's embrace. The red shoes, and the wicked old man in the tree, beckoning. Will Flanders wandering the corridors of an aircraft carrier with his bloodied head. I was by now convinced that this was happening to someone else. Out the filthy window, the small town beyond the station looked stripped, sacked by barbarians. An old hotel once teeming with traveling salesmen was now boarded up. The picture show had taken on a seedy look. The black community nearby showed every sign of decay. My God, was this what the South was doomed to?

My father's face suddenly flooded with tears, and he took my hands in his. "You mustn't do this to me, my darling. You mustn't leave me. You're all I've got. Who will I talk to now?"

"Stop, Daddy, don't." I put my arms around him. I felt deep sorrow for my mother. He could talk to her, if only he would ever try.

She began to cry, and I put my arms around her, too.

"I have to go. I'm going. That's all there is to it. You have to let me go. I can't live here any longer. It has nothing to do with you. You mustn't carry on like this. Honest to God, I'll phone, I'll write. I'll come home every chance I get. You'll come and visit me. Mama, Daddy, I'll take care of myself. I won't get sick." And I babbled words of comfort to them, thinking, my father has led me to this moment; why does he tell me I cannot go?

The conductor called at last, and they kissed me and descended as the doors closed and the ancient locomotive clanged and screamed and began slowly rolling out of the station. I watched them go, my mother's arm around my father, and I loved them so much that I began to weep. In my purse, when I searched for a handkerchief, I found an envelope containing a hundred dollars. Which of them had put it there? The train rolled down through the ghetto, and bars lowered at the crossing, lights flashing like police cars in an emergency, and then we were out of town and gaining speed. Wet with tears and sweat, I wrestled the window open and thrust my head out into the oncoming breeze. The pain in my chest, the feeling of being stunned, the gathering migraine in my left temple, even the guilt, eased off in a few moments. The roadbed was ancient and the train rocked precariously, just coasting along until the track improved around Malvern. As we rounded the curves I could see the locomotive up ahead, its eye searching the darkening twilight. We lumbered past Malvern, where Daddy had come to claim me and take me home again eighteen years before, and the engineer opened up the whistle in the wind, loosened the throttle. We've got the right of way. Only some lingering sense of the ridiculous kept me from bursting into song, dancing in the vestibule, kissing my fellow passenger, a lady about my mother's age on her way to Little Rock. I wasn't riding the top of the train like my father, but I was free.

I didn't have to choose between self-ownership and death. I didn't even have to look for a job as a saleslady. I need not yearn for a proper young businessman to marry me and house me in a heavily mortgaged buff brick ranch. I could skip Sears, Roebuck and the washer-dryer. I need not wear my hair in a beehive! I alone have escaped alive to tell thee! I began to laugh, no matter what the lady thought. My father had forbidden me to go to New York, but so what? I was gone. I could live without my father's approval, maybe. The old pantheon had fallen down. If I broke Athena's bargain, as my father construed it, to love him and serve him forever, I at least had a chance to make good on the larger contract—to become some sort of bookmaker myself. And to stand on my feet and depend on no man, another segment of the bargain I made with him, for better or for worse.

Four Directions

AMY TAN

I HAD TAKEN my mother out to lunch at my favorite Chinese restaurant in hopes of putting her in a good mood, but it was a disaster.

When we met at the Four Directions Restaurant, she eyed me with immediate disapproval. *"Ai-ya!* What's the matter with your hair?" she said in Chinese.

"What do you mean, 'What's the matter,' " I said. "I had it cut." Mr. Rory had styled my hair differently this time, an asymmetrical blunt-line fringe that was shorter on the left side. It was fashionable, yet not radically so.

"Looks chopped off," she said. "You must ask for your money back."

I sighed. "Let's just have a nice lunch together, okay?"

She wore her tight-lipped, pinched-nose look as she scanned the menu, muttering, "Not too many good things, this menu." Then she tapped the waiter's arm, wiped the length of her chopsticks with her finger, and sniffed: "This greasy thing, do you expect me to eat with it?" She made a show of washing out her rice bowl with hot tea, and then warned other restaurant patrons seated near us to do the same. She told the waiter to make sure the soup was very hot, and of course, it was by her tongue's expert estimate "not even *lukewarm."*

"You shouldn't get so upset," I said to my mother after she disputed a charge of two extra dollars because she had specified chrysanthemum tea, instead of the regular green tea. "Besides, unnecessary stress isn't good for your heart."

"Nothing is wrong with my heart," she huffed as she kept a disparaging eye on the waiter.

And she was right. Despite all the tension she places on herself—and others—the doctors have proclaimed that my mother, at age sixty-nine, has the blood pressure of a sixteen-year-old and the strength of a horse. And that's what she is. A Horse, born in 1918, destined to be obstinate and frank to the point of tactlessness. She and I make a bad combination, because I'm a Rabbit, born in 1951, supposedly sensitive, with tendencies toward being thin-skinned and skittery at the first sign of criticism.

After our miserable lunch, I gave up the idea that there would ever be a good time to tell her the news: that Rich Schields and I were getting married.

"WHY are you so nervous?" my friend Marlene Ferber had asked over the phone the other night. "It's not as if Rich is the scum of the earth. He's a tax attorney like you, for Chrissake. How can she criticize that?"

"You don't know my mother," I said. "She never thinks anybody is good enough for anything."

"So elope with the guy," said Marlene.

"That's what I did with Marvin." Marvin was my first husband, my high school sweetheart.

"So there you go," said Marlene.

"So when my mother found out, she threw her shoe at us," I said. "And that was just for openers."

MY MOTHER had never met Rich. In fact, every time I brought up his name—when I said, for instance, that Rich and I had gone to the symphony, that Rich had taken my four-year-old daughter, Shoshana, to the zoo—my mother found a way to change the subject.

"Did I tell you," I said as we waited for the lunch bill at Four Directions, "what a great time Shoshana had with Rich at the Exploratorium? He—"

"Oh," interrupted my mother, "I didn't tell you. Your father, doctors say maybe need exploratory surgery. But now, now they say everything normal, just too much constipated." I gave up. And then we did the usual routine.

I paid for the bill, with a ten and three ones. My mother pulled back the dollar bills and counted out exact change, thirteen cents, and put that on the tray instead, explaining firmly: "No tip!" She tossed her head back with a triumphant smile. And while my mother used the restroom, I slipped the waiter a five-dollar bill. He nodded to me with deep understanding. While she was gone, I devised another plan.

"*Choszle!*"—Stinks to death in there!—muttered my mother when she returned. She nudged me with a little travel package of Kleenex. She did not trust other people's toilet paper. "Do you need to use?"

I shook my head. "But before I drop you off, let's stop at my place real quick. There's something I want to show you."

MY MOTHER had not been to my apartment in months. When I was first married, she used to drop by unannounced, until one day I suggested she should call ahead of time. Ever since then, she has refused to come unless I issue an official invitation.

And so I watched her, seeing her reaction to the changes in my apartment—from the pristine habitat I maintained after the divorce, when all of a sudden I had too much time to keep my life in order—to this present chaos, a home full of life and love. The hallway floor was littered with Shoshana's toys, all bright plastic things with scattered parts. There was a set of Rich's barbells in the living room, two dirty snifters on the coffee table, the disemboweled remains of a phone that Shoshana and Rich took apart the other day to see where the voices came from.

"It's back here," I said. We kept walking, all the way to the back bedroom. The bed was unmade, dresser drawers were hanging out with socks and ties spilling over. My mother stepped over running shoes, more of Shoshana's toys, Rich's black loafers, my scarves, a stack of white shirts just back from the cleaner's.

Her look was one of painful denial, reminding me of a time long ago when she took my brothers and me down to a clinic to get our polio booster shots. As the needle went into my brother's arm and he screamed, my mother looked at me with agony written all over her face and assured me, "Next one doesn't hurt."

But now, how could my mother *not* notice that we were living together, that this was serious and would not go away even if she didn't talk about it? She had to say something.

I went to the closet and then came back with a mink jacket that Rich had given me for Christmas. It was the most extravagant gift I had ever received.

I put the jacket on. "It's sort of a silly present," I said nervously. "It's hardly ever cold enough in San Francisco to wear mink. But it seems to be a fad, what people are buying their wives and girlfriends these days."

My mother was quiet. She was looking toward my open closet, bulging with racks of shoes, ties, my dresses, and Rich's suits. She ran her fingers over the mink.

"This is not so good," she said at last. "It is just leftover strips. And the fur is too short, no long hairs."

"How can you criticize a gift!" I protested. I was deeply wounded. "He gave me this from his heart."

"That is why I worry," she said.

And looking at the coat in the mirror, I couldn't fend off the strength of her will anymore, her ability to make me see black where there was once white, white where there was once black. The coat looked shabby, an imitation of romance.

"Aren't you going to say anything else?" I asked softly.

"What I should say?"

"About the apartment? About *this?*" I gestured to all the signs of Rich lying about.

She looked around the room, toward the hall, and finally she said, "You have career. You are busy. You want to live like mess what I can say?"

MY MOTHER knows how to hit a nerve. And the pain I feel is worse than any other kind of misery. Because what she does always comes as a shock, exactly like an electric jolt, that grounds itself permanently in my memory. I still remember the first time I felt it.

I WAS ten years old. Even though I was young, I knew my ability to play chess was a gift. It was effortless, so easy. I could see things on the chessboard that other people could not. I could create barriers to protect myself that were invisible to my opponents. And this gift gave me supreme confidence. I knew what my opponents would do, move for move. I knew at exactly what point their faces would fall when my seemingly simple and childlike strategy would reveal itself as a devastating and irrevocable course. I loved to win.

And my mother loved to show me off, like one of my many trophies she polished. She used to discuss my games as if she had devised the strategies.

"I told my daughter, Use your horses to run over the enemy," she informed one shopkeeper. "She won very quickly this way." And of course, she had said this before the game—that and a hundred other useless things that had nothing to do with my winning.

To our family friends who visited she would confide, "You don't have to be so smart to win chess. It is just tricks. You blow from the North, South, East, and West. The other person becomes confused. They don't know which way to run.

I hated the way she tried to take all the credit. And one day I told her so, shouting at her on Stockton Street, in the middle of a crowd of people. I told her she didn't know anything, so she shouldn't show off. She should shut up. Words to that effect.

That evening and the next day she wouldn't speak to me. She would say stiff words to my father and brothers, as if I had become invisible and she was talking about a rotten fish she had thrown away but which had left behind its bad smell.

I knew this strategy, the sneaky way to get someone to pounce back in anger and fall into a trap. So I ignored her. I refused to speak and waited for her to come to me.

After many days had gone by in silence, I sat in my room, staring at the sixty-four squares of my chessboard, trying to think of another way. And that's when I decided to quit playing chess.

Of course I didn't mean to quit forever. At most, just for a few days. And I made a show of it. Instead of practicing in my room every night, as I always did, I marched into the living room and sat down in front of the television set with my brothers, who stared at me, an unwelcome intruder. I used my brothers to further my plan; I cracked my knuckles to annoy them.

"Ma!" they shouted. "Make her stop. Make her go away."

But my mother did not say anything.

Still I was not worried. But I could see I would have to make a stronger move. I decided to sacrifice a tournament that was coming up in one week. I would refuse to play in it. And my mother would certainly have to speak to me about this. Because the sponsors and the benevolent associations would start calling her, asking, shouting, pleading to make me play again.

And then the tournament came and went. And she did not come to me, crying, "Why are you not playing chess?" But I was crying inside, because I learned that a boy whom I had easily defeated on two other occasions had won.

I realized my mother knew more tricks than I had thought. But now I was tired of her game. I wanted to start practicing for the next tournament. So I decided to pretend to let her win. I would be the one to speak first.

"I am ready to play chess again," I announced to her. I had imagined she would smile and then ask me what special thing I wanted to eat.

But instead, she gathered her face into a frown and stared into my eyes, as if she could force some kind of truth out of me.

"Why do you tell me this?" she finally said in sharp tones. "You think it is so easy. One day quit, next day play. Everything for you is this way. So smart, so easy, so fast."

"I said I'll play," I whined.

"No!" she shouted, and I almost jumped out of my scalp. "It is not so easy anymore."

I was quivering, stunned by what she said, in not knowing what she meant. And then I went back to my room. I stared at my chessboard, its sixty-four squares, to figure out how to undo this terrible mess. And after staring like this for many hours, I actually believed that I had made the white squares black and the black squares white, and everything would be all right.

And sure enough, I won her back. That night I developed a high fever, and she sat next to my bed, scolding me for going to school without my sweater. In the morning she was there as well, feeding me rice porridge flavored with chicken broth she had strained herself. She said she was feeding me this because I had the chicken pox and one chicken knew how to fight another. And in the afternoon, she sat in a chair in my room, knitting me a pink sweater while telling me about a sweater that Auntie Suyuan had knit for her daughter June, and how it was most unattractive and of the worst yarn. I was so happy that she had become her usual self.

But after I got well, I discovered that, really, my mother had changed. She no longer hovered over me as I practiced different chess games. She did not polish my trophies every day. She did not cut out the small newspaper item that mentioned my name. It was as if she had erected an invisible wall and I was secretly groping each day to see how high and how wide it was.

At my next tournament, while I had done well overall, in the end the points were not enough. I lost. And what was worse, my mother said nothing. She seemed to walk around with this satisfied look, as if it had happened because she had devised this strategy.

I was horrified. I spent many hours every day going over in my mind what I had lost. I knew it was not just the last tournament. I examined every move, every piece, every square. And I could no longer see the secret weapons of each piece, the magic within the intersection of each square. I could see only my mistakes, my weaknesses. It was as though I had lost my magic armor. And everybody could see this, where it was easy to attack me.

Over the next few weeks and later months and years, I continued to play, but never with that same feeling of supreme confidence. I fought hard, with fear and desperation. When I won, I was grateful, relieved. And when I lost, I was filled with growing dread, and then terror that I was no longer a prodigy, that I had lost the gift and had turned into someone quite ordinary.

When I lost twice to the boy whom I had defeated so easily a few years before, I stopped playing chess altogether. And nobody protested. I was fourteen.

"YOU KNOW, I really don't understand you," said Marlene when I called her the night after I had shown my mother the mink jacket. "You can tell the IRS to piss up a rope, but you can't stand up to your own mother."

"I always intend to and then she says these little sneaky things, smoke bombs and little barbs, and . . ."

"Why don't you tell her to stop torturing you," said Marlene. "Tell her to stop ruining your life. Tell her to shut up."

"That's hilarious," I said with a half-laugh. "You want me to tell my mother to shut up?"

"Sure, why not?"

"Well, I don't know if it's explicitly stated in the law, but you can't *ever* tell a Chinese mother to shut up. You could be charged as an accessory to your own murder."

I wasn't so much afraid of my mother as I was afraid for Rich. I already knew what she would do, how she would attack him, how she would criticize him. She would be quiet at first. Then she would say a word about something small, something she had noticed, and then another word, and another, each one flung out like a little piece of sand, one from this direction, another from behind, more and more, until his looks, his character, his soul would have eroded away. And even if I recognized her strategy, her sneak attack, I was afraid that some unseen speck of truth would fly into my eye, blur what I was seeing and transform him from the divine man I thought he was into someone quite mundane, mortally wounded with tiresome habits and irritating imperfections.

This happened to my first marriage, to Marvin Chen, with whom I had eloped when I was eighteen and he was nineteen. When I was in love with Marvin, he was nearly perfect. He graduated third in his class at Lowell and got a full scholarship to Stanford. He played tennis. He had bulging calf muscles and one hundred forty-six straight black hairs on his chest. He made everyone laugh and his own laugh was deep, sonorous, masculinely sexy. He prided himself on having favorite love positions for different days and hours of the week; all he had to whisper was "Wednesday afternoon" and I'd shiver.

But by the time my mother had had her say about him, I saw his brain had shrunk from laziness, so that now it was good only for thinking up excuses. He chased golf and tennis balls to run away from family responsibilities. His eye wandered up and down other girls' legs, so he didn't know how to drive straight home anymore. He liked to tell big jokes to make other people feel little. He made a loud show of leaving ten-dollar tips to strangers but was stingy with presents to family. He thought waxing his red sports car all afternoon was more important than taking his wife somewhere in it.

My feelings for Marvin never reached the level of hate. No, it was worse in a way. It went from disappointment to contempt to apathetic boredom. It wasn't until after we separated, on nights when Shoshana was asleep and I was lonely, that I wondered if perhaps my mother had poisoned my marriage.

Thank God, her poison didn't affect my daughter, Shoshana. I almost aborted her, though. When I found out I was pregnant, I was furious. I secretly referred to my pregnancy as my "growing resentment," and I dragged Marvin down to the clinic so he would have to suffer through this too. It turned out we went to the wrong kind of clinic. They made us watch a film, a terrible bit of puritanical brainwash. I saw those little things, babies they called them even at seven weeks, and they had tiny, tiny fingers. And the film said that the baby's translucent fingers could *move*, that we should imagine them clinging for life, grasping for a chance, this miracle of life. If they had shown *anything else* except tiny fingers—so thank God they did. Because Shoshana really was a miracle. She was perfect. I found every detail about her to be remarkable, especially the way she flexed and curled her fingers. From the very moment she flung her fist away from her mouth to cry, I knew my feelings for her were inviolable.

But I worried for Rich. Because I knew my feelings for him were vulnerable to being felled by my mother's suspicions, passing remarks, and innuendos. And I was afraid of what I would then lose, because Rich Shields adored me in the same way I adored Shoshana. His love was unequivocal. Nothing could change it. He expected nothing from me; my mere existence was enough. And at the same time, he said that he had changed—for the *better*—because of me. He was embarrassingly romantic; he insisted he never was until he met me. And this confession made his romantic gestures all the more ennobling. At work, for example, when he would staple "FYI—For Your Information" notes to legal briefs and corporate returns that I had to review, he signed them at the bottom: "FYI—Forever You & I." The firm didn't know about our relationship, and so that kind of reckless behavior on his part thrilled me.

The sexual chemistry was what really surprised me, though. I thought he'd be one of those quiet types who was awkwardly gentle and clumsy, the kind of mild-mannered guy who says, "Am I hurting you?" when I can't feel a thing. But he was so attuned to my every movement I was sure he was reading my mind. He had no inhibitions, and whatever ones he discovered I had he'd pry away from me like little treasures. He saw all those private aspects of me—and I mean not just sexual private parts, but my darker side, my meanness, my pettiness, my self-loathing—all the things I kept hidden. So that with him I was completely naked, and when I was feeling the most vulnerable—when the wrong word would have sent me flying out the door forever—he always said exactly the right thing at the right moment. He didn't allow me to cover myself up. He would grab my hands, look me straight in the eye and tell me something new about why he loved me.

I'd never known love so pure, and I was afraid that it would become sullied by my mother. So I tried to store every one of these endearments about Rich in my memory, and I planned to call upon them again when the time was necessary.

AFTER much thought, I came up with a brilliant plan. I concocted a way for Rich to meet my mother and win her over. In fact, I arranged it so my mother would want to cook a meal especially for him. I had some help from Auntie Suyuan. Auntie Su was my mother's friend from way back. They were very close, which meant they were ceaselessly tormenting each other with boasts and secrets. And I gave Auntie Sue a secret to boast about.

After walking through North Beach one Sunday, I suggested to Rich that we stop by for a surprise visit to my Auntie Su and Uncle Canning. They lived on Leavenworth, just a few blocks west of my mother's apartment. It was late afternoon, just in time to catch Auntie Su preparing Sunday dinner.

"Stay! Stay!" she had insisted.

"No, no. It's just that we were walking by," I said.

"Already cooked enough for you. See? One soup, four dishes. You don't eat it, only have to throw it away. Wasted!"

How could we refuse? Three days later, Auntie Suyuan had a thank-you letter from Rich and me. "Rich said it was the best Chinese food he has ever tasted," I wrote.

And the next day, my mother called me, to invite me to a belated birthday dinner for my father. My brother Vincent was bringing his girlfriend, Lisa Lum. I could bring a friend, too.

I KNEW she would do this, because cooking was how my mother expressed her love, her pride, her power, her proof that she knew more than Auntie Su. "Just be sure to tell her later that her cooking was the best you ever tasted, that it was far better than Auntie Su's," I told Rich. "Believe me."

The night of the dinner, I sat in the kitchen watching her cook, waiting for the right moment to tell her about our marriage plans, that we had decided to get married next July, about seven months away. She was chopping eggplant into wedges, chattering at the same time about Auntie Suyuan: "She can only cook looking at a recipe. My instructions are in my fingers. I know what secret ingredients to put in just by using my nose!" And she was slicing with such a ferocity, seemingly inattentive to her sharp cleaver, that I was afraid her fingertips would become one of the ingredients of the red-cooked eggplant and shredded pork dish.

I was hoping she would say something first about Rich. I had seen her expression when she opened the door, her forced smile as she scrutinized him from head to toe, checking her appraisal of him against that already given to her by Auntie Suyuan. I tried to anticipate what criticisms she would have.

Rich was not only *not* Chinese, he was a few years younger than I was. And unfortunately, he looked much younger with his curly red hair, smooth pale skin, and the splash of orange freckles across his nose. He was a bit on the short side, compactly built. In his dark business suits, he looked nice but easily forgettable, like somebody's nephew at a funeral. Which was why I didn't notice him the first year we worked together at the firm. But my mother noticed everything.

"So what do you think of Rich?" I finally asked, holding my breath.

She tossed the eggplant in the hot oil and it made a loud, angry hissing sound. "So many spots on his face," she said.

I could feel the pinpricks on my back. "They're freckles. Freckles are good luck, you know," I said a bit too heatedly in trying to raise my voice above the din of the kitchen.

"Oh?" she said innocently.

"Yes, the more spots the better. Everybody knows that."

She considered this a moment and then smiled and spoke in Chinese: "Maybe this is true. When you were young, you got the chicken pox. So many spots, you had to stay home for ten days. So lucky, you thought."

I couldn't save Rich in the kitchen. And I couldn't save him later at the dinner table.

He had brought a bottle of French wine, something he did not know my parents could not appreciate. My parents did not even own wineglasses. And then he also made the mistake of drinking not one but two frosted glasses full, while everybody else had a half-inch "just for taste."

When I offered Rich a fork, he insisted on using the slippery ivory chopsticks. He held them splayed like the knock-kneed legs of an ostrich while picking up a large chunk of sauce-coated eggplant. Halfway between his plate and his open mouth, the chunk fell on his crisp white shirt and then slid into his crotch. It took several minutes to get Shoshana to stop shrieking with laughter.

And then he had helped himself to big portions of the shrimp and snow peas, not realizing he should have taken only a polite spoonful, until everybody had had a morsel.

He had declined the sautéed new greens, the tender and expensive leaves of bean plants plucked before the sprouts turn into beans. And Shoshana refused to eat them also, pointing to Rich: "He didn't eat them! He didn't eat them!"

He thought he was being polite by refusing seconds, when he should have followed my father's example, who made a big show of taking small portions of seconds, thirds, and even fourths, always saying he could not resist another bite of something or other, and then groaning that he was so full he thought he would burst.

But the worst was when Rich criticized my mother's cooking, and he didn't even know what he had done. As is the Chinese cook's custom, my mother always made disparaging remarks about her own cooking. That night she chose to direct it toward her famous steamed pork and preserved vegetable dish, which she always served with special pride.

"Ai! This dish not salty enough, no flavor," she complained, after tasting a small bite. "It is too bad to eat."

This was our family's cue to eat some and proclaim it the best she had ever made. But before we could do so, Rich said, "You know, all it needs is a little soy sauce." And he proceeded to pour a riverful of the salty black stuff on the platter, right before my mother's horrified eyes.

And even though I was hoping throughout the dinner that my mother would somehow see Rich's kindness, his sense of humor and boyish charm, I knew he had failed miserably in her eyes.

Rich obviously had had a different opinion on how the evening had gone. When we got home that night, after we put Shoshana to bed, he said modestly, "Well. I think we hit it off *A-o-kay.*" He had the look of a dalmatian, panting, loyal, waiting to be petted.

"Uh-hmm," I said. I was putting on an old nightgown, a hint that I was not feeling amorous. I was still shuddering, remembering how Rich had firmly shaken both my parents' hands with that same easy familiarity he used with nervous new clients. "Linda, Tim," he said, "we'll see you again soon, I'm sure." My parents' names are Lindo and Tin Jong, and nobody, except a few older family friends, ever calls them by their first names.

"So what did she say when you told her?" And I knew he was referring to our getting married. I had told Rich earlier that I would tell my mother first and let her break the news to my father.

"I never had a chance," I said, which was true. How could I have told my mother I was getting married, when at every possible moment we were alone, she seemed to remark on how much expensive wine Rich liked to drink, or how pale and ill he looked, or how sad Shoshana seemed to be.

Rich was smiling. "How long does it take to say, Mom, Dad, I'm getting married?"

"You don't understand. You don't understand my mother."

Rich shook his head. "Whew! You can say that again. Her English was *so* bad. You know, when she was talking about that dead guy showing up on *Dynasty*, I thought she was talking about something that happened in China a long time ago."

THAT NIGHT, after the dinner, I lay in bed, tense. I was despairing over this latest failure, made worse by the fact that Rich seemed blind to it all. He looked so pathetic. *So pathetic*, those words! My mother was doing it again, making me see black where I once saw white. In her hands, I always became the pawn. I could only run away. And she was the queen, able to move in all directions, relentless in her pursuit, always able to find my weakest spots.

I woke up late, with teeth clenched and every nerve on edge. Rich was already up, showered, and reading the Sunday paper. "Morning, doll," he said between noisy munches of cornflakes. I put on my jogging clothes and headed out the door, got into the car, and drove to my parents' apartment.

Marlene was right. I had to tell my mother—that I knew what she was doing, her scheming ways of making me miserable. By the time I arrived, I had enough anger to fend off a thousand flying cleavers.

My father opened the door and looked surprised to see me. "Where's Ma?" I asked, trying to keep my breath even. He gestured to the living room in back.

I found her sleeping soundly on the sofa. The back of her head was resting on a white embroidered doily. Her mouth was slack and all the lines in her face were gone. With her smooth face, she looked like a young girl, frail, guileless, and innocent. One arm hung limply down the side of the sofa. Her chest was still. All her strength was gone. She had no weapons, no demons surrounding her. She looked powerless. Defeated.

And then I was seized with a fear that she looked like this because she was dead. She had died when I was having terrible thoughts about her. I had wished her out of my life, and she had acquiesced, floating out of her body to escape my terrible hatred.

"Ma!" I said sharply. "Ma!" I whined, starting to cry.

And her eyes slowly opened. She blinked. Her hands moved with life. "Shemma? Meimei-ah? Is that you?"

I was speechless. She had not called me Meimei, my childhood name, in many years. She sat up and the lines in her face returned, only now they seemed less harsh, soft creases of worry. "Why are you here? Why are you crying? Something has happened!"

I didn't know what to do or say. In a matter of seconds, it seemed, I had gone from being angered by her strength, to being amazed by her innocence, and then frightened by her vulnerability. And now I felt numb, strangely weak, as if someone had unplugged me and the current running through me had stopped.

"Nothing's happened. Nothing's the matter. I don't know why I'm here," I said in a hoarse voice. "I wanted to talk to you. . . . I wanted to tell you . . . Rich and I are getting married."

I squeezed my eyes shut, waiting to hear her protests, her laments, the dry voice delivering some sort of painful verdict.

"*Jrdaule*"—I already know this—she said, as if to ask why I was telling her this again.

"You know?"

"Of course. Even if you didn't tell me," she said simply.

This was worse than I had imagined. She had known all along, when she criticized the mink jacket, when she belittled his freckles and complained about his drinking habits. She disapproved of him. "I know you hate him," I said in a quavering voice. "I know you think he's not good enough, but I . . ."

"Hate? Why do you think I hate your future husband?"

"You never want to talk about him. The other day, when I started to tell you about him and Shoshana at the Exploratorium, you . . . you changed the subject . . . you started talking about Dad's exploratory surgery and then . . ."

"What is more important, explore fun or explore sickness?"

I wasn't going to let her escape this time. "And then when you met him, you said he had spots on his face."

She looked at me, puzzled. "Is this not true?"

"Yes, but, you said it just to be mean, to hurt me, to . . ."

"Ai-ya, why do you think these bad things about me?" Her face looked old and full of sorrow. "So you think your mother is this bad. You think I have a secret meaning. But it is you who has this meaning. Ai-ya! She thinks I am this bad!" She sat straight and proud on the sofa, her mouth clamped tight, her hands clasped together, her eyes sparkling with angry tears.

Oh, her strength! her weakness!—both pulling me apart. My mind was flying one way, my heart another. I sat down on the sofa next to her, the two of us stricken by the other.

I felt as if I had lost a battle, but one that I didn't know I had been fighting. I was weary. "I'm going home," I finally said. "I'm not feeling too good right now."

"You have become ill?" she murmured, putting her hand on my forehead.

"No," I said. I wanted to leave. "I . . . I just don't know what's inside me right now."

"Then I will tell you," she said simply. And I stared at her. "Half of everything inside you," she explained in Chinese, "is from your father's side. This is natural. They are the Jong clan, Cantonese people. Good, honest people. Although sometimes they are bad-tempered and stingy. You know this from your father, how he can be unless I remind him."

And I was thinking to myself, Why is she telling me this? What does this have to do with anything? But my mother continued to speak, smiling broadly, sweeping her hand. "And half of everything inside you is from me, your mother's side, from the Sun clan in Taiyuan." She wrote the characters out on the back of an envelope, forgetting that I cannot read Chinese.

"We are a smart people, very strong, tricky, and famous for winning wars. You know Sun Yat-sen, hah?"

I nodded.

"He is from the Sun clan. But his family moved to the south many centuries ago, so he is not exactly the same clan. My family has always live in Taiyuan, from before the days of even Sun Wei. Do you know Sun Wei?"

I shook my head. And although I still didn't know where this conversation was going, I felt soothed. It seemed like the first time we had had an almost normal conversation.

"He went to battle with Genghis Khan. And when the Mongol soldiers shot at Sun Wei's warriors—heh!—their arrows bounced off the shields like rain on stone. Sun Wei had made a kind of armor so strong Genghis Khan believed it was magic!"

"Genghis Khan must have invented some magic arrows, then," I said. "After all, he conquered China."

My mother acted as if she hadn't heard me right. "This is true, we always know how to win. So now you know what is inside you, almost all good stuff from Taiyuan."

"I guess we've evolved to just winning in the toy and electronics market," I said.

"How do you know this?" she asked eagerly.

"You see it on everything. Made in Taiwan."

"Ai!" she cried loudly. "I'm not from Taiwan!"

And just like that, the fragile connection we were starting to build snapped.

"I was born in China, in *Taiyuan*," she said. "Taiwan is not China."

"Well, I only thought you said 'Taiwan' because it sounds the same,"

I argued, irritated that she was upset by such an unintentional mistake.

"Sound is completely different! Country is completely different!" she said in a huff. "People there only dream that it is China, because if you are Chinese you can never let go of China in your mind."

We sank into silence, a stalemate. And then her eyes lighted up. "Now listen. You can also say the name of Taiyuan is Bing. Everyone from that city calls it that. Easier for you to say. Bing, it is a nickname."

She wrote down the character, and I nodded as if this made everything perfectly clear. "The same as here," she added in English. "You call Apple for New York. Frisco for San Francisco."

"Nobody calls San Francisco that!" I said, laughing. "People who call it that don't know any better."

"Now you understand my meaning," said my mother triumphantly.

I smiled.

And really, I did understand finally. Not what she had just said. But what had been true all along.

I saw what I had been fighting for: It was for me, a scared child, who had run away a long time ago to what I had imagined was a safer place. And hiding in this place, behind my invisible barriers, I knew what lay on the other side: Her side attacks. Her secret weapons. Her uncanny ability to find my weakest spots. But in the brief instant that I had peered over the barriers I could finally see what was really there: an old woman, a wok for her armor, a knitting needle for her sword, getting a little crabby as she waited patiently for her daughter to invite her in.

Skin, Where She Touches Me

DOROTHY ALLISON

Skin, the surface of skin, the outer layer protecting the vulnerable inside, the boundary between the world and the soul, what is seen from the outside and hides all the secrets. My skin, my mama's skin, my sisters' skin. Our outer layer hides our inner hopes. White girls, tough-skinned and stubborn, born to a family that never valued girls. I am my mama's daughter, one with my tribe, taught to believe myself of not much value, to take damage and ignore it, to take damage and be proud of it. We were taught to be proud that we were not Black, and ashamed that we were poor, taught to reject everything people believed about us—drunken, no-count, lazy, whorish, stupid—and still some of it was just the way we were. The lies went to the bone, and digging them out has been the work of a lifetime.

DEATH changes everything. The death of someone you love alters even the boundaries of the imagination. The dead become fiction, myth, and legend. The two most important women in my life—my mother and my first lover—are dead. Because I cannot stop talking about them, retelling their stories and making them mine, turning their jokes to parables and their stubborn endurance to legend, I can feel them changing, in my own mind and in the imaginations of those who know them only through me. Writing about them, I have been holding on to them, even as I was when they were alive. Telling stories about people very like them, but not really them, has been a way to save what they and I have lost. But death is more than the closing of a life. Death is the point at which people begin to sum up, to say what things meant, what the life was about, what was accomplished and what was not. Death is the point at which, if it has not already been claimed, vindication becomes possible. Death changes everything.

No matter what I say about my mother or my first lover, you cannot know if it is true. You cannot go and see them, hear their versions of my stories. You cannot watch my mama laugh with her hand drawn up before her mouth to hide her loose teeth. You cannot look into her eyes and see what half a century of shame and grief did to her. You cannot ask Cathy what she meant when she told everyone that it was I who was the lesbian, not her.

Two women, as complicated and astonishing as any women can be, have shaped who I have become. I can look down at my hands and see their hands touching mine, imagine their voices, things they said or might have said, things they wanted to do but never got a chance to. I think sometimes that I have been driven to write fiction because of those I have lost, the first woman I ever fell passionately in love with, and my mother, the first woman I ever understood to be deeply hurt and just as deeply heroic. I have written stories about people like them out of my need to understand them and reimagine their lives. Better to mythologize them, I have told myself, than to leave them with their fractured lives cut off too soon.

MY MOTHER died of cancer, twenty minutes before I could reach her bedside, just before midnight on November 11, 1990. She was fifty-six years old and had had cancer for thirty of them—a hysterectomy when I was a child, two mastectomies five years apart, and finally the tumors in her lung, brain, and liver that she could not survive. For half my life I had been separated from her, unable to be in her home while she lived with my stepfather, but talking to her every few weeks, sending her copies of everything I wrote, and always knowing that whatever else was uncertain in our lives, her love for me was like mine for her—unquestioning, absolute, and painful.

When I was in my twenties, my mother and I had come to an exacting agreement: I would come home very rarely, but not talk about why that was so. The promise I made her was that I would not cause trouble, would not fight with my stepfather or even be cold to him on the phone, that I would cooperate in the family effort to keep the peace. She would not demand more of me. Through all the years, we rarely talked about my stepfather and the violence Mama always believed to have been her responsibility. She had never been able to stop it, and she had never left him. Only toward the end of her life did she begin to ask me to forgive her, and no matter how much I assured her that I loved her and understood what she had done, she never forgave herself.

ON THE afternoon my mama was buried, my sisters and I went through her photographs with our aunt Nuell, who came the morning after Mama died and stayed with us for the next three days—through the first grief and the awful funeral. We let her take over caring for our stepfather, feeling only a moment's hesitation because we knew her so slightly. She was not one of the Gibson sisters, only our aunt by marriage. She had married Mama's little brother, Tommy, and moved with him to Alabama in the late 1950s. All our lives we had been hearing stories about her but had seen her only a few times. Still, when she got the call about Mama, she drove through the night to be with us for the funeral, and her presence made things easier. It was as if she had taken on the mantle of our legendary aunts, hugging us like we were children, telling us what to do, making it easier to do as she wanted than to argue. She sat down with us to go through the torn and faded pictures as if that were just one more part of being the oldest living woman in the family. Some of the vaguely recognizable faces she knew instantly.

"Your great-aunt," she said, pointing to an almost washed-out image of a woman standing in front of a gas station storefront. "Don't think I ever knew her name, but she was the one moved off to Oklahoma before your mama married your daddy. And oh, this one, this one is Tommy and Jack when they were boys, that's David and Dan, and those—those look like some boys from the air base. Don't know if you're related or not."

My sister Barbara rolled her eyes over to my sister June. June looked at me. I tried politely to interrupt Aunt Nuell, to ask if she could maybe write down the names she remembered on the photos themselves.

"Oh, I suppose," she murmured, bending over the big pile and pulling out one picture after another. Her eyes were soft and wet. Though she could only remember a few names, and fewer incidents, the impact of the features was unmistakable. "All these people are gone," she said once, in a voice so taut and pained I didn't dare ask more of her.

MY UNCLE JACK arrived the night before the funeral. When I saw him in the morning, his face was awestruck, horrible. He couldn't smile at me, only grimaced, his mouth pulled back and the loose skin of his face falling into folds. The creases running down from his cheeks were gullies, his eyes were peach-pit hollows, black seeds unable to face the morning sun. He stayed out on the grass, refusing to go inside the funeral home or come to the grave site. When I walked over to put some flowers on the casket, I looked back and saw him standing rigid and tall on a little rise near the memorial to the veterans of American wars. The sun glinted off the wet on his face, the face itself so anguished I could not stand to look at him.

He was the last, though one of Mama's sisters was hanging on—
Maudy with the colostomy bag hidden under her housedress, her raging temper still flaring at the nieces and nephews who prowled her
porch. She had sent a message, a spray of flowers Cousin Bobby had
probably arranged.

"Bobby's the one gets things done," everyone told me the last time I
visited Greenville. Aunt Dot was still alive then, playing the role my
grandmother Mattie Lee had played before her death—telling everyone's
secrets and coaxing you out of yours so she could say she knew everything first. Dot said it was Bobby who got her sister to check into a motel
when she was dying of breast cancer, this after some of her children had
been caught stealing her painkillers for their own use.

"Little sons-a-bitches," Aunt Dot had mouthed around her false teeth.
"Should have drowned those little bastards while they were still small
enough for us to get away with it." I had never had a chance to ask Bobby
if the story was true, and Mama wouldn't talk about it, just told me that,
yes, my cousin had spent the weeks before she died in a motel out on
the edge of Greenville where the Highway 85 overpass cut south of the
city.

"Now that's a mean story," I had said to Mama. "Worse than anything
I've even thought of writing."

"That imply you an't gonna think about it now?" Mama had looked at
me with a patient, almost martyred expression. I had flushed with embar-
rassment, nodding reluctantly, agreeing that I might write about it someday. There were many things we did not talk about, but we both tried
never to lie to each other knowingly. Some of what I wrote had been
painful for my mama to read, but she had never suggested I should not
write those stories and publish them. "I've never been afraid of the
truth," she told me after my book of short stories came out. She spoke
in the blunt, stubborn tone that meant she was saying something she
wanted to be true.

My mama had been ashamed too often in her life, ashamed of things
she could not have managed differently, and more ashamed of being
ashamed than of the original sins. Shame was one of the things my
mama hated, one of the things she tried to root out of herself and us.
And shame was the constant theme of my childhood.

"Never back down," my mama taught me. "Never drop your eyes.
People look at you like a dog, you dog them." I had laughed and tried to
emulate her, to stare back at hatred and stare down contempt. Like
Mama, I learned to stand tall when confronted by my sins, to say, All
right, so what? Like Mama, I learned to gaze at the world with my scars
and outrage plainly revealed, determined not to hide, not to drop my

head or admit defeat. It was good training for a child of the Southern working poor, better training for an adolescent lesbian terrified of what her desires might mean, who she might become and what she might learn about herself.

"The truth won't kill me," Mama said, but I wasn't sure I believed her. Truth seemed to me a very dangerous, tricky concept. Was truth only what we agreed it to be, or was there a book somewhere that would show me the real truth, the rules of right and wrong? A complicated system of vindication and judgment hid behind the small truths everyone presented as Truth. "What's going on here?" my stepfather would shout at us some evenings, and we would all freeze and drop our heads, knowing that he did not really want to know, knowing that to tell him the truth about what we were thinking or feeling or planning was the most foolish choice we could make. No, the truth was something to keep to ourselves and protect—when we knew what it was, when we could be sure of anything.

Skin fear, pulling back, flinching before the blow lands. Anticipating the burn of shame and the shiver of despair. Conditioned to contempt and reflexive rage, I am pinned beneath a lattice, iron-hard and locked down. Believing myself inhuman, mutant, too calloused to ever love deeply or well.

MY FIRST lover had been beaten by her father. Everybody who knew Cathy had heard how her daddy caught her at sixteen with her blouse open and her hands in her boyfriend's jeans. He called her a whore and threw her out on the street. She repaid him by going back a few nights later to smash the windows in his truck and smear shit on his radiator coils. When she told me that story I smiled, admiring wholeheartedly any woman strong enough to have taken that particular revenge on a truck-loving Southern man. But by the time I met her, Cathy was three years past her revenge, three years of living hand to mouth with one boyfriend after the other, doing heroin when she could get it and shivering sick when she could not. She wasn't charming. She was so deeply scored by anger that there was no measuring where the anger left off and a woman you could love might begin. Most people were afraid of her, and so was I, some, especially when she looked at me and laughed, knowing at a glance what none of the other would-be hippies in our little community had figured out—that I was a lesbian, and the flush on my face was not only self-consciousness but lust.

Why does anyone fall passionately in love? Does the beloved have to know something, have something, be something you do not know, or have, or cannot be yourself? I had no idea. But from the moment Cathy put her palm flat on my breast and her teeth close to my ear, I knew that I could go mad with love for her. She smelled strong and dangerous and marvelous. When she crawled naked into the bed where I had been lying, hoping she would come to find me, her skin was burning hot, scorching mine at every surface. Still, instead of flinching away I pushed up into her, wanting that heat, wanting her more than I had ever wanted anything.

WITHIN our family it was astonishingly difficult to sort out the truth from the lies. If you did not think about things—and there were so many things all of us tried not to think about—you tended to lose track of what you really thought or felt. We had been raised on public contempt and private outrage, been told every day of our lives that there was something intrinsically wrong with us. Our stepfather shouted it at us, the Baptist ministers said it in soft, sad voices, and the girls at school made it plain with their laughter and comments on how we dressed. Mama's response to that chorus was rage and stubborn insistence that we act as if we didn't believe any of it. But we knew that the power of public opinion wounded her too. She was never as confident as she tried to pretend. I could look into my mama's exhausted grey features and see just how painful, how dangerous the truth could be. The truth might vindicate us, but then again it might destroy us. We might as easily find that all those hateful faces turned to us were right and we were damned from birth, helpless to escape the trap that had ground down our mama. It was never simple. It was never easy to know what was true.

I found ever more complicated truths as I grew up. There was, for example, the fact that Mama told me to my face that she was proud of my writing and "didn't give a rat's ass if I married puppy dogs so long as I was happy." But even as I let her hold me close and say it, I knew that the magazines and stories I sent her disappeared into one box or another, that she never showed what I wrote to anyone, not even my sisters, and certainly never talked about it.

Aunt Dot told me once that the thing Mama regretted most about my life was that I had not had a child. "She don't mind you keeping company with women," Aunt Dot said. "She just wishes you would marry some man long enough to make a couple of babies." I had never discussed with my aunt or my mama the fact that I couldn't have children, and even at twenty-five did not feel capable of talking about why that was so, anymore than I had been able, at the age of eleven, to tell them how badly I hurt "down there," or what had really happened to me. Would it have been "the truth" to hold my aunts and my mama responsible for the venereal infection that was never treated when I knew how hard I had tried to hide my pain from them at the time? Before I could be angry at them, I had to get past being angry at myself and dig my way down to who really hurt me, and why we had worked so hard to pretend nothing was happening. No, it was not the truth to say my mama was at fault, not the truth to blame the child I had been, not even the whole truth to blame my stepfather.

I worried it out over years and years, and finally, I broke the silence, not by going home to hold a massive family confrontation, but by writing a story in which I told everything that had happened to that child and the cost of it, the children that child would never have, the break in the family that could never be fully mended. Some days still, I think about how I wrote that story and gave it to my mama to read, and I know that doing that says more about truth and the depth of my own sense of shame than I could ever say in an explicit conversation.

BEFORE Cathy I had thought myself a kind of chrome nun, armored and dispassionate. I had known myself a lesbian, had loved or thought I loved, but I had always felt an icy distance from the emotional excesses and vulnerabilities all around me. I considered myself cynical, wise beyond my years, knowledgeable about the world's cruelties, and a connoisseur of the risks of any kind of physical or sexual contact. I didn't need that, I told myself. I was different. Perhaps I wasn't a real woman, but some kind of alien mutant creature crafted by sexual abuse and natural resilience — a monster.

Cathy was the first woman with whom I fell in love. Every crush, every close friendship, every momentary rush of desire or fear that came before or after was made understandable by what I felt for her, simply because nothing else was as intense and overpowering. Lying in her arms, I felt crazy and willingly so, eager to give my life to make her happy, to suffer if suffering would ease her misery, to shame myself or look silly if that would make her smile. Breathing in the aura of her, that salty smoky taste of soapy skin and bitter cigarettes, made my heart swell and tightened my throat until it ached. Dreaming about her woke me up. Cathy proved to me that I was my mother's daughter, my sisters' equal.

IT WAS Aunt Dot who told me that Aunt Maudy and Uncle Jack didn't speak, that after years of arguing and cursing, pot throwing and blue streaks, Jack had sworn she could die on her own, that he'd "never darken her door again."

"He said that?" I was amused that he'd use that particular phrase, so melodramatic and emphatic.

"Oh, he cursed her to her face same as she cursed him. They've been going on since they were kids. Never could stand each other." Aunt Dot had smiled then in pleasure, her face wrinkling up like damp laundry pulled out of the bottom of the refrigerator. "Jack's always been a pisser, you know."

I knew. I had always loved that in him, the way he would come in and do anything he pleased, never mind what anybody thought. And I loved the way he moved that long, lanky body, as if there was music playing in his head, blues or rock 'n' roll, his hips jiggling gently or gliding as smoothly as butter melting. My uncle Jack was the man who made it possible for me to understand how women fell in love with men.

That day at the funeral, Mama's loss ached in me as if a central part of my body had been stolen. I had wanted Jack to comfort me, wanted his smile and his charm, his loose way of reaching around and pulling you up into his big, wide shoulders, the spread of his love and confidence. But he looked as if he, too, had been robbed, as if the meat of his confidence, the deepest, richest part of his life was gone, the sweet stuff of him evaporated in the Florida heat.

"Lord," he said once, and I knew all he meant—the curse and the prayer.

"Who are all those people in Mama's photos?" I asked him just before he left my sister's house.

He barely glanced at the pile on the dining room table. "Family," he grunted, "all kinds of family. Flesh and blood sons-a-bitches." His hands were shaking. He fought with Aunt Nuell and my stepfather, refused to sleep in Mama's house another night, even on the floor as he had the night before. The shadows under his eyes were more cruel than the grey in his hair. "There's lots of dead people in there," he said, pointing at the pictures, "people you girls should have known but didn't. And damn it, it's too late now."

"BETTER watch out for me," Cathy was always saying. "I'm Fedayeen." And then she would toss her dark hair and bare her teeth in a fierce almost-angry smile.

"You're Arab?" I asked her once, naively.

Her answer was sudden and harsh. "No, I'm a Nigger. Can't you tell?"

The people standing around us laughed, and I quickly backed away in confusion. At the time, I had no idea if Cathy was Black, Arab, Cuban, or just another mean white girl making fun of me. No one I knew made jokes about color. No one talked about it, except to announce occasionally that they were not racist crackers like their parents, and to insist somewhat nervously that they got along fine with all the Cubans who had moved into Central Florida.

"Yeah, right!" Cathy would bark, laughing.

"Liars and cowards," she would sneer at half the people we knew. She had an unfailing instinct for people who could be teased into betraying their prejudices, girls who would back up and withdraw if they thought she wasn't just like them, boys who were reduced to tears when she would not tell them if she was really a colored girl.

"Look at me," she insisted once when we sat up talking into the early dawn. I smiled and told her she was pretty, but she held my hands and insisted. "No, really look at me."

So I did. I looked close, very close—at the dark mass of hair that sprang out from her head like a great cloud of electrically charged wool, the smooth tanned skin only a few shades darker than my own, the fine scar at the outside of her left eye, the mouth that was always pulled back as if she were about to sneer or curse. Her eyes were black and angry, but as I looked closely I realized that she might have been afraid.

"You see?" she demanded. But I shook my head, not knowing what she wanted me to see, not knowing what I was willing to admit I did see.

"They all think it. They look at me and wonder if I'm not some Black bitch from the projects getting over on them. So I say it before they can whisper it to each other. I say it so they have to think about how they're gonna talk to me, how they're gonna behave. I say it so they can't pretend nothing. I make them think about who they are."

"But what about who you are?"

"Yeah, what about it?"

I looked at her hands, the fingers curled into the palms, the knotted fists pressing down on her thighs so hard the knuckles stood out pale and sharp. My words surprised me. "You're just about the scariest person I've ever met," I told Cathy, and waited for her anger to flare. Instead she looked almost pleased.

"Yeah," she agreed. "Damn right."

"THE way you talk about your mama is extraordinary," women would tell me, and I would blush, knowing that sometimes they meant not "extraordinary" but "strange," that I talked about my mama with the passion of a lover, obsessively, proudly, angrily, tenderly, insistently. I knew, too, that what it sounded like was not what it was, that I did not want to possess her but to free her. The touch of my mother was always a reminder that she was caught in a trap I could not have survived one day more than I did.

Write me a love story, my girlfriends asked. Write a political story, the women in my consciousness-raising group told me, and I wondered what that would be. Should I use words like *patriarchy* and *male madness* and *class oppression*? I tried. But every time, I found myself stopped, the words sour and mean.

What I began with was the story of my mother's life, my mother as a girl of fourteen, dropping out of school and pregnant with me, proud and stubborn and ashamed. I began with my mother's family—my family—the Gibsons and Yearwoods and Campbells and Hendersons. "Poor white trash," we had been called when I was a girl back in Greenville, "dirty fucking trash." When they were saying it to our faces there was no need for anything but the curse.

As I began to show people what I was writing, I kept the stories about my family back. It was too complicated to explain the mix of pride and shame, easier to write about being a lesbian and figuring that out, about falling in love or not, or about politics, the simple politics of having grown up female in the South. I hadn't a clue how to write the complicated story, the story of growing up female in our particular family, the daughter of the youngest of the Gibson girls, that trashy family where the boys all went to jail and the women all made babies when they were still girls themselves. My mama was one month past fifteen when I was born, her attempt at marriage annulled by my grandmother before anyone knew I was on the way. I worked my way back to that story, knowing it was the one I needed to tell to be able to write. I had to believe in the use of writing, and the primary use was to reject hatred, simple categories, shame. The first rule I learned in writing was to love the people I wrote about—and loving my mama, loving myself, was not simple in any sense. We had not been raised to love ourselves, only to refuse to admit how much we might hate ourselves.

Skin hunger. Sometimes it seemed that my skin ached like an empty belly. The fine hairs below my navel seemed to reach up, wanting to touch something. My mouth would open when I slept and my tongue would push at the air, reaching, reaching. I would wake from dreams of rising like yeast into an embrace that welcomed and satisfied that hunger, an embrace I wanted desperately.

WHEN Cathy called me a dyke, she made it sound like something to be proud of. She was gripping my fingers tight and laughing into my neck. Her whole body was stretched along mine, open and easy and warm against me. "You're such a tough dyke," she growled, and heat went all through me. "So touch," she repeated, in a softer, breathier voice, and in that moment I understood all the teenage boys I had seen blush and preen under a girl's teasing. I felt for all the world like a teenage boy, proud and nervous and anxious to please. I wanted to make her smile. I wanted to make her proud of me. I wanted to lie forever with her strong hand cupping my shoulder and her whisper against my neck.

"I love you," I said. But she only shook her head.

WRITE funny stories, my mama told me. That's what people need and want to hear. Mama told funny stories all her life, charming strangers out of quarters across a diner counter, teasing a little more time out of bill collectors, coaxing a discount out of repairmen or car salesmen, and always, and most important, distracting my stepfather out of his rages so that his hands would fall less heavily on her daughters. My mama used charm, funny stories, and that seemingly easy confidence to fight off a world of hurt and deprivation. It dismayed her that her daughters grew up angry, that all of us grimaced when she would have smiled, that none of us had her way with a funny story—and even more terrible was that we did not want it. Of all the things about our mama that we were supposed to find shameful—the poverty, lack of education or steady work— the only thing we hesitated to admire was the ingratiating, desperate charm that had eased her life.

"Mama's something, ain't she?" my little sister would say, tempering admiration with uncertainty. I would agree, knowing that this was not a simple statement but a host of contradictory ones. Write mean stories, my sister dared me one night. "Go ahead and tell the world what really happened," she taunted, then just as fast as she had spoken the words, she withdrew them. "No, better not." I knew what she was thinking. I too have that voice inside me, the one that murmurs continually. *Maybe we shouldn't say anything*, it whispers. *Maybe if we are real quiet, the world will leave us alone.* If I told as much of the truth as I knew, what would happen? The world would know what he had done, who we had become to survive him. People would think I was a lesbian because he raped me, a pervert because he beat me, a coward because I had not killed him, and worse: I still went home like a well-trained puppy dog keeping my head down and never challenging him.

Sometimes I look into my little sister's eyes and I see those warring demands: the one that wants to take somebody by the throat and choke out answers for all the grief she has survived, and the other, that wounded figure, still a child wanting only to be left alone. Sometimes I don't have to look at my sisters to see that expression. It is in the mirror surface of my own pupils.

WE HAD BEEN brutal with each other. *Smart-mouthed sluts, whores, bitches.* He had called us those names so often, we used the same words on each other. But it is his voice I hear in my dreams, like a wave of burning liquid breaking over me. "Think you're so good, think you're so special, you're nothing, nothing." Dark, dark wave of curse and contempt. "Stupid bitch."

He never called me a dyke, but my sisters did, and from them it was unbearable. They seemed to believe that my being a lesbian meant I was not sexual at all. Like everyone else, they thought that lesbians were women who were afraid of sex, which was something that only happened with men. Only in the last few years have my sisters begun to see me as both a lesbian and sexual in the same way they are—complicated and romantic and prone to entangled, difficult relationships. I have lived with the same woman for six years now, introduced her as my partner, had a child with her, adopted that child, and loved her more than I can sometimes understand. It is this relationship, so like their marriages, this woman, so like their husbands, that has begun to be real to my sisters. Only recently have I glimpsed how important it is for me to have that shared sense of the quality of daily life, the same sense of meaning in what we do sexually. More than just tolerance.

The worst thing either of my sisters ever said to me was spoken one evening on a wave of fury and whiskey, resentment and jealousy, all of it peaking a few hours after he had raged and screamed what a slut she was. "He don't have to worry about some man stealing you away from him, and it an't as if he gave a shit about women." I wanted to kill her for saying it, even while I knew she had it right. My stepfather, who considered women dogs, probably thought about it just that way—that I was his meat, and as long as no other man had me, I still belonged to him. When I had finally straddled a man's hips and settled myself down on a man's cock, I realized it was only partly an experiment to prove to myself I could do it if I wanted to. I never imagined telling my stepfather, who got no access to any of my life, but I made a point of letting my sisters know.

WHAT Mama taught us was to keep our heads up and refuse to *act* ashamed. She could not teach us how not to *feel* ashamed. She didn't know how to do that herself. No one in our family did. What they knew most deeply was the power of rage and silence. Don't tell nobody nothing, my aunts would have insisted if they had lived. Telling the truth is too dangerous, too expensive. I know I am the child of my family on the days when I hear their voices echoing inside me, telling me to keep my mouth shut and give no one a weapon to use against us, those days when I cannot help but think that they were right.

"YOU'RE the real thing," Cathy told me once, though I hadn't a clue what she meant. I did not know enough to realize how rare it was for one woman to pursue another unafraid. I could only imagine the kind of romance I had read in paperbacks. Before Cathy, I thought I was the only woman in the world who so desperately wanted sex with another woman. But Cathy's desires were so sudden, so explicit and so powerful, I would flush every time I imagined her skin touching mine. I would go home from Cathy to my mama's house, drunk with pleasure.

"I'm in love," I wanted to say to my mama, but I would see something, some tremor in her hands, and I would stop. It was not the fact that I was in love with a woman; it was my mama's life, the madness that love had thrown at her, the violence, the grief, and the shame.

"GODDAMN, your mama must have been crazy about your stepfather!" my friend Marge told me after reading some of the stories in *Trash*. Oddly, that was the first time I really thought about it. Had Mama ever been genuinely happy with my stepfather? Way back, had she loved him with a girl's love, full of hope and faith? Before he started storming through the house breaking doors and waving his fists in the air, before he began to beat us, before we grew into teenagers and he cursed us with every breath, before he started acting like a crazy man all the time, sitting in the living room with his hands moving rhythmically inside his loose shorts, or going for weeks not speaking to anyone, and when he did, talking only about how we were driving him crazy, how it would be our fault when he killed us all, killed us in the night after we'd pushed him too far, the way he was always threatening? Had there been a time when my mama had been safe to feel love for that man?

I tried to remember when our home had not been a madhouse, when my stepfather had not been that scary, scary man who careened through my childhood. It seemed to me things had deteriorated slowly over the years. In the beginning the beatings had been spankings that went on just a little too long or were a little too harsh. Always there had been a reason, one he would force Mama to admit. I broke a glass and hid the evidence. One of my sisters stole change left on the dresser. Another lied about where she had been playing. Little things became enormous, evidence that we were bad, like his beatings were evidence that he loved us. Everyone spanked their kids, everyone had to if they wanted them to grow up right. When was a spanking too much? When did it become a beating? How could you know? How could my mama know? She couldn't even ask anyone. How was she supposed to be able to tell? How were we?

Hadn't he loved her? Hadn't there been a time when everyone knew that he loved her? For my own life, I tried to remember and understand if that had been so.

I HAD never really believed my mama would die.

That had been the worst nightmare of my childhood, an omnipresent fear that Mama would disappear, and with her the shelter and protection she gave us. I lived in terror not only of our stepfather's rages, but of being left to face the world's contempt without my mama. The fear was not fantasy. Death stalked the women of my family. My granny died just after turning fifty-nine, and only one of my aunts lived long enough to qualify for social security—Aunt Dot, who still managed to die at sixty-three. Cancer went through us like a fire leaping from one to the next, my mama, my aunts, my cousins.

I have been a student of cancer for half my life. I lost friends to it a half dozen times over, and I was the one Mama talked to at the first mastectomy. I was the one who persuaded her to continue the chemotherapy after the second mastectomy and the recurrence that followed. I brought her books, articles clipped out of magazines, pages of testimonies from other survivors. I even went back with her to Greenville to visit her sisters, reading her a prose poem I called "Deciding to Live" on the way. Mama and all of us, we practiced positive thinking, living our lives as if cancer were not something we all dreamed about, nightmares in which people disappeared before you could get home to see them again.

When the call came and my sister Barbara told me that no, it wasn't that viral infection, this time the cancer was really back—for a moment I prayed it was just another terrible dream. But I was staying in a cabin up in Vermont, and to take the call I had to walk a quarter of a mile to the phone. I did it at a run, my nervous system flaring the whole way.

Barbara cried and asked me please could I get home quickly.

I sat down in the dirt, cradled the phone between my shoulder and my ear, clenched my hands together, and said to my sister, "It's all right. Just tell me everything." When I hung up, I found I had rubbed a blister under the ring on my left hand. I took off my ring and called my lover. Alix was waiting for me. Her voice was deep and reassuring. She said, "It's all right. Just tell me everything." All around me the ashy scent of a New England fall drifted through the trees. My mama was dying. I was a thousand miles away. After a few minutes I stopped crying and we started to make plans.

Alix took a leave from her job, and in two days we were both in Orlando sitting at my mama's kitchen table eating biscuits she had insisted on baking. She had a few days free before she had to check into the hospital and start chemotherapy, or decide not to do it at all and get ready to die.

"There's a tumor on my lung," she said, a cigarette in the ashtray in front of her. I let her explain everything Barbara had already told me, watching her face tighten and then relax as she talked. "It's going to be all right, baby," she said, laying her hand on mine. "I'll go in, they'll make these tests. Ten days from now we'll know a lot more. It's going to be all right."

Mama kept smiling at Alix, flirting lightly the way she had done with every woman I ever brought home. Mama looked good, a little thin and tired, but better than I expected. She would start chemo on Thursday and radiation soon after, and maybe it wasn't as bad as they said. Maybe she could fight it off again. She certainly didn't look like a woman about to die as she smiled at me, hugged Alix, and went to pull another tray out of the oven. I took a deep breath and held on to Alix's hand.

Mama was, at that moment, less than a month from her death.

There is delight in this. The skin flushes and shines. Heat rises and the fine skim of curls beneath my navel lifts. When I laugh, my skin sings, a music of blood and bone in perfect meter, a body that has learned the worth of endurance, passion, and release. Put your hand here. Hear the echo of my mama's pulse, her laugh, her songs. While I live and sing she does not die.

IT GOT so bad so fast. I was never sure of all the ways that my love for Cathy had begun to break down. I told myself it was mostly about drugs.

"Don't start telling no lies about me," Cathy complained once when I was talking about applying for a job with the Social Security Administration, talking about how Cathy, too, could get better work, how I would help her pass the exams offered now and then for county jobs. Cathy was having none of it, but she was stoned on something, as she was almost all the time then. I looked at her, not knowing what she had taken, only knowing that it was no use to talk at all when she was in that condition, but I couldn't stop myself.

"Why?" I demanded. "Why do you do it?"

" 'Cause I have to," she told me. " 'Cause it stops the noise in my head, and it's the only damn thing that does."

I stood there, not moving, while she walked away. I knew what she meant. I knew that noise. It was in my head too, that constant dragging fearful chorus of uncertainty and confusion. But I had never used drugs to stop it. The only time that noise in my head had ceased was when I lay spent in Cathy's arms.

WE STAYED for three weeks. We went with Mama to schedule the radiation and afterward to look at the free wigs they offered cancer patients. Mama teased about shaving her head, but blushed when the woman helping her commented on the ink stains the doctors had left on her neck.

"Be careful not to wash those off," the woman said.

"What does she think? I've got cancer, I'm not stupid," Mama whispered at me when the woman stepped away. Both of us grinned then, united as we always had been in dealing with the world of bureaucratic strangers.

It was one of the last good days we had, for the chemo seemed more brutal than any she had survived before. Was she weaker than I had imagined? The doctor wouldn't say much, and Mama couldn't. "It'll be all right," she kept murmuring, even while the chemicals flowed into her arm and her skin turned yellow-pale and her cheeks sank in to leave the bones standing out plain and sharp.

I sat with her in the hospital, told her stories, and hummed old tunes whose words I no longer remembered. Mama's hands would clench at mine occasionally while her mouth opened and closed, and her eyes moved constantly under the translucent membranes of her eyelids. With my sisters at work and Alix running interference with my stepfather, I tried to keep Mama distracted while the nausea rocked her from side to side in the bed.

"BE CAREFUL," my mama whispered to me that last week while she was lying in her hospital bed. Her words were like an echo caught in the folds of my brain, the one phrase she had been repeating all my life. *Be careful, baby.* Things that might not be dangerous for other people were terribly dangerous for us. And if I knew that to be true, and I did, how could I ever be the person I wanted to be? What chance did I have to understand enough to write what I wanted to write? And whose story do I tell, hers or mine? There was no certainty, no reassurance.

"I LOVED it when you came up to visit me at Fire Island," I whispered to Mama one afternoon when she seemed weaker than ever.

With her eyes closed, she smiled and whispered back, "All those beautiful boys, and that hat."

I pulled her palm up to my mouth and kissed it. Her eyes opened then and looked at me. The pupils were dark. Her smile had disappeared.

"Baby," she said in a voice even softer than her whisper. Moisture appeared in the fine lines at the corners of her eyes. Her pupils looked strange, the irises cloudy, her expression confused. "I never meant for you to be hurt," she said. "I thought I was doing the right thing."

It was as if she had hit me. I jerked back and almost dropped her hand, then grabbed it fiercely, pressing it to my neck. Ancient habit took over and my voice dropped to a husky undertone, something no one standing more than a foot or so away could hear. I said, "Mama, there is nothing to forgive. You were not the one who did anything wrong."

"I should have left him." Her head turned on the pillow while her mouth worked and she worried her lips with her teeth. "But every time I thought I would, something happened." Her hand in mine shook, the fingers broke free and grabbed my wrist. "Something always happened."

"I know." I said it softly, looking into her eyes. I said, "I know, Mama. I know. Don't do this. There's no use to it. You did what you had to do."

"All those years," she said. "At first I just wanted to protect you, then I wanted a way to make it up to you. I wanted you to know you were never any of the things he called you." Her face was wet, no discrete tears coursing along her cheeks, just a tide of grief slowly slipping down to her chin.

MY STEPFATHER almost always came with Mama when she visited me. Each time I just barely managed, tight-lipped and stubbornly silent, or polite and carefully noncommittal. But in 1984 when they came to New York, he put his hand on my arm and my eyesight went black. I leaned over and vomited on the sidewalk. I could not stop retching until I was in a taxi moving away from him. That time they left the next day.

The following year they came back. Mama was sick again, one of the chemo years. I took her out to Fire Island with her old friend Mab, who tried to flirt with the gay men in the Ice Palace, and kept asking me if it was really true that they were all of them homosexual.

"Such beautiful boys," Mab said. She had mothered half a dozen sons through four marriages and never saw any of them anymore.

"Yes," I agreed, and did not smile at the hungry, lonely way she watched those beautiful boys.

Mama lay on our rented deck in a lounge chair, face turned away from the sun. My stepfather joined us on the third day, and I walked down to the beach to throw up in the ocean. "We'll leave," Mama told me. I started to cry. It was like cancer, that throwing up, the body suddenly betraying me, not letting me go on pretending nothing was wrong. He would reach to touch me, and years of practice, years of hatred would keep my face still and expressionless. But now my stomach battered at the back of my throat, refusing to allow any compromise, robbing me of my last chances to see my mother. They left before sunset, Mama looking at me over the side rail of the ferry with a rigid, pained expression.

I had bought Mama a sun hat with a hot pink ribbon. She put it on at an angle, waving at me. My stepfather told her to take it off loudly, said the ribbon was a "faggy pink." On either side of him two tall gay men stood, as muscled and powerful as football players. At his words, they reached over his head to put their arms around each other's shoulders. Ramona laughed. Mama just looked at me. My stepfather flushed dark purple, so dark the veins on his neck stood out in pale relief. I looked down at his hands and saw they had become fists. I was thirty-six years old. The last time he beat me with those hands I was sixteen. Twenty years. I said the words, but no one could hear me over the sudden roar of the ferry engine. I looked into his face, his empty eyes. My nausea receded, and the boat pulled away from the dock.

I WAS never sure how Cathy died, did not know what to believe of all the stories that went around afterward. The rumors swore it was an overdose, and I could believe that easily enough. What was certain was that her family had not wanted to pay to have her body shipped back from Arizona, where she had died, but when a collection was taken up everyone insisted her mother contributed a share. There was a memorial service, one attended by a few people who had really known her—the handful who had somehow gotten clean or weren't in jail at the time.

"You should have been there," the ones who had known us together told me when they saw me. "You could have spoken for her," they said, and I just shook my head. For years after I would wake up thinking about it, what I would have said if I had gone back to stand up in front of those people who had seen us as friends rather than lovers. Could I have said anything equal to the grief of her loss? Had there been anything I could have done to mute the roar in her head?

MY SISTERS and I divided Mama's pictures among us. I took away a pile of her snapshots—faded, torn, stained sepia-toned images of her brothers, sisters, cousins, family—people whose faces we had not recognized, even those Aunt Nuell had been able to name. Strong-faced women with high cheekbones and dark eyes looked out from most of Mama's photos, all of them clearly related. Like Joan Crawford or Barbara Stanwyck, I thought, when I held one up to see it better in the light of the lamp my sister June set up on the dining room table. They had favored dark lipstick, thick, arched eyebrows, and engaged the camera directly. Most of the extended family pictures were from the forties or early fifties, while the mass of snapshots of us were taken before and just after 1962 when we moved to Florida. The Florida pictures all seemed to have been shot at the beach, and many featured Mama lying back like a bathing beauty with us playing at the edge of the water behind her. I could barely stand to look at those, and let my sisters take most of them.

I kept the old pictures, particularly the ones of Mama and her sisters, and in the months after Mama's death returned to them again and again. Aunt Maudy and Aunt Dot were in most of the photos, gazing from Barbara Stanwyck's eyes, clenching Joan Crawford's jaw. Mama, younger and more beautiful, had Grace Kelly's chin and eyes. Looking away and down, she seemed posed for the vulnerable line of her neck and the soft slope of her cheek, slightly mysterious but not traditionally pretty. *Film noir* heroines, I thought, every time I shifted through the pile. I kept fingering the snapshot that made my young Aunt Dot look like Maureen O'Hara with that full dark-red hair framing her strong features. Not tragic, though. Flirtatious. She crossed her arms below her breasts and stared at the world forthrightly and unafraid, denying my memories of a stooped, squinting woman with thin grey hair and hands that always lay loosely in her lap. I had known my aunts were strong, determined women, but I had never imagined them as burning, hopeful girls. I had always thought Aunt Dot a woman without vanity, wearing the same housedresses year after year, shunning makeup and laughing at how fat she had grown with her nine children. But the pictures proved that even she had been different as a girl, making herself up to heighten her resemblance to a movie star. Maybe it had been like that for all the sisters, for a year or two in their youth, trying to look like those strong-willed fantasy heroines, not realizing yet what real strength was, their stubborn capacity to endure all that fate would throw at them.

CATHY taught me that I was just like everyone else, capable of emotional and erotic obsessions, deeply needy and hungry for affection, and as talented as my mother and sisters at falling in love with someone who could break my heart. My love for her proved to me that I was female and feminine in the most traditional sense, foolish and damaged and hopeful. That knowledge, the human insight I gained from discovering myself passionate, capable of great joy, vulnerability, and love, had been astonishing. The outrage and despair I experienced in so desperately loving a woman who did not need me as much as she needed the needle in her arm was simply appalling. It took me years to see that falling in love with an addict who did not trust love in any way was a part of proving that I was not a monster, not the sexless creature I had imagined. Cathy showed me that I was humanly fragile. I found in myself the heroine of every heartbreak song I had ever laughed at but played again. I was not completely calloused. My skin was as thin as anyone's.

WHEN I was eleven years old I loved my mama more than my life. When I was twenty-six I was so angry at her I could not even speak to her on the telephone. When I was thirty-six I could no longer pretend that my stepfather, her husband, had not broken me, body and soul. Years between and after, I bargained for every quiet moment she and I could steal. I was forty-one the year Mama died, and sometimes I was angry, sometimes not. We had gone past bargains and lies, past talking about it or not, even past agreeing on what had happened and what had not. I no longer needed that, if I ever had. All I knew was that I loved my mama and that she had always loved me, and that most of what was strong and healthy and hopeful in my life was possible because of her.

OUR lives are not small. Our lives are all we have, and death changes everything. The story ends, another begins. The long work of life is learning the love for the story, the novels we live out and the characters we become. In my mama's photos is a world of stories never told: my stolid aunt a teasing girl, my sisters with their mouths open to laugh, and hidden in the pile, a snapshot of me at twenty-two, dark and furious, with Cathy's pale face solemn over one shoulder. Disappeared, anonymous, the story we might have told then remade. She has become legend, I human in grief, and full of the need to grab what I can and hold on, to remake death and begin another tale.

I WEAR my skin only as thin as I have to, armor myself only as much as seems absolutely necessary. I try to live naked in the world, unashamed even under attack, unafraid even though I know how much there is to fear. What I have always feared is being what people have thought me — my stepfather's willing toy, my mother's betrayer, my lover's faithless tease, my family's ultimate shame, the slutty, racist, stupid cracker dyke who doesn't know what she is doing. Trying always to know what I am doing and why, choosing to be known as who I am — feminist, queer, working class, and proud of the work I do — is as tricky as it ever was. I tell myself that life is the long struggle to understand and love fully. That to keep faith with those who have literally saved my life and made it possible for me to imagine more than survival, I have to try constantly to understand more, love more fully, go more naked in order to make others as safe as I myself want to be. I want to live past my own death, as my mother does, in what I have made possible for others — my sisters, my son, my lover, my community — the people I believe in absolutely, men and women whom death does not stop, who honor the truth of each other's stories.

Silent Dancing

JUDITH ORTIZ COFER

WE HAVE a home movie of this party. Several times my mother and I have watched it together, and I have asked questions about the silent revellers coming in and out of focus. It is grainy and of short duration but a great visual aid to my first memory of life in Paterson at that time. And it is in color—the only complete scene in color I can recall from those years.

WE LIVED in Puerto Rico until my brother was born in 1954. Soon after, because of economic pressures on our growing family, my father joined the United States Navy. He was assigned to duty on a ship in Brooklyn Yard, New York City—a place of cement and steel that was to be his home base in the States until his retirement more than twenty years later.

He left the Island first, tracking down his uncle who lived with his family across the Hudson River, in Paterson, New Jersey. There he found a tiny apartment in a huge apartment building that had once housed Jewish families and was just being transformed into a tenement by Puerto Ricans overflowing from New York City. In 1955 he sent for us. My mother was only twenty years old, I was not quite three, and my brother was a toddler when we arrived at *El Building*, as the place had been christened by its new residents.

My memories of life in Paterson during those first few years are in shades of gray. Maybe I was too young to absorb vivid colors and details, or to discriminate between the slate blue of the winter sky and the darker hues of the snow-bearing clouds, but the single color washes over the whole period. The building we lived in was gray, the streets were gray with slush the first few months of my life there, the coat my father had bought for me was dark in color and too big. It sat heavily on my thin frame.

I do remember the way the heater pipes banged and rattled, startling all of us out of sleep until we got so used to the sound that we automatically either shut it out or raised our voices above the racket. The hiss from the valve punctuated my sleep, which has always been fitful, like a nonhuman presence in the room—the dragon sleeping at the entrance of my childhood. But the pipes were a connection to all the other lives being lived around us. Having come from a house made for a single family back in Puerto Rico—my mother's extended-family home—it was curious to know that strangers lived under our floor and above our heads, and that the heater pipe went through everyone's apartments. (My first spanking in Paterson came as a result of playing tunes on the pipes in my room to see if there would be an answer.) My mother was as new to this concept of beehive life as I was, but had been given strict orders by my father to keep the doors locked, the noise down, ourselves to ourselves.

It seems that Father had learned some painful lessons about prejudice while searching for an apartment in Paterson. Not until years later did I hear how much resistance he had encountered with landlords who were panicking at the influx of Latinos into a neighborhood that had been Jewish for a couple of generations. But it was the American phenomenon of ethnic turnover that was changing the urban core of Paterson, and the human flood could not be held back with an accusing finger.

"You Cuban?" the man had asked my father, pointing a finger at his name tag on the Navy uniform—even though my father had the fair skin and light brown hair of his northern Spanish family background and our name is as common in Puerto Rico as Johnson is in the U.S.

"No," my father had answered looking past the finger into his adversary's angry eyes "I'm Puerto Rican."

"Same shit." And the door closed. My father could have passed as European, but we couldn't. My brother and I both have our mother's black hair and olive skin, and so we lived in El Building and visited our great-uncle and his fair children on the next block. It was their private joke that they were the German branch of the family. Not many years later that area too would be mainly Puerto Rican. It was as if the heart of the city map were being gradually colored in brown—café-con-leche brown. Our color.

The movie opens with a sweep of the living room. It is "typical" immigrant Puerto Rican decor for the time: the sofa and chairs are square and hard-looking, upholstered in bright colors (blue and yellow in this instance, and covered in the transparent plastic) that furniture salesmen then were adept at making women buy. The linoleum on the floor is light blue, and if it was subjected to the spike heels as it was in most places, there were dime-sized indentations all over it that cannot be seen in this movie. The room is full of people dressed in mainly two colors: dark suits for the men, red dresses for the women. I have asked my mother why most of the women are in red that night, and she shrugs, "I don't remember. Just a coincidence." She doesn't have my obsession for assigning symbolism to everything.

The three women in red sitting on the couch are my mother, my eighteen-year-old cousin, and her brother's girlfriend. The "novia" is just up from the Island, which is apparent in her body language. She sits up formally, and her dress is carefully pulled over her knees. She is a pretty girl but her posture makes her look insecure, lost in her full skirted red dress which she has carefully tucked around her to make room for my gorgeous cousin, her future sister-in-law. My cousin has grown up in Paterson and is in her last year of high school. She doesn't have a trace of what Puerto Ricans call "la mancha" (literally, the stain: the mark of the new immigrant—something about the posture, the voice, or the humble demeanor making it obvious to everyone that that person has just arrived on the mainland; has not yet acquired the polished look of the city dweller). My cousin is wearing a tight red-sequined cocktail dress. Her brown hair has been lightened with peroxide around the bangs, and she is holding a cigarette very expertly between her fingers, bringing it up to her mouth in a sensuous arc of her arm to her as she talks animatedly with my mother, who has come to sit between the two women, both only a few years younger than herself. My mother is somewhere halfway between the poles they represent in our culture.

IT BECAME my father's obsession to get out of the barrio, and thus we were never permitted to form bonds with the place or with the people who lived there. Yet the building was a comfort to my mother, who never got over yearning for la isla. She felt surrounded by her language: the walls were thin, and voices speaking and arguing in Spanish could be heard all day. Salsas blasted out of radios turned on early in the morning and left on for company. Women seemed to cook rice and beans perpetually—the strong aroma of red kidney beans boiling permeated the hallways.

Though Father preferred that we do our grocery shopping at the supermarket when he came home on weekend leaves, my mother insisted that she could cook only with products whose labels she could read, and so, during the week, I accompanied her and my little brother to La Bodega—a hole-in-the-wall grocery store across the street from El

Building. There we squeezed down three narrow aisles jammed with various products. Goya and Libby's—those were the trademarks trusted by her Mamá, and so my mother bought cans of Goya beans, soups and condiments. She bought little cans of Libby's fruit juices for us. And she bought Colgate toothpaste and Palmolive soap. (The final *e* is pronounced in both these products in Spanish, and for many years I believed that they were manufactured on the Island. I remember my surprise at first hearing a commercial on television for the toothpaste in which Colgate rhymed with "ate.")

We would linger at La Bodega, for it was there that mother breathed best, taking in the familiar aromas of the foods she knew from Mamá's kitchen, and it was also there that she got to speak to the other women of El Building without violating outright Father's dictates against fraternizing with our neighbors.

But he did his best to make our "assimilation" painless. I can still see him carrying a Christmas tree up several flights of stairs to our apartment, leaving a trail of aromatic pine. He carried it formally, as if it were a flag in a parade. We were the only ones in El Building that I knew of who got presents on both Christmas Day and on *Dia de Reyes,* the day when the Three Kings brought gifts to Christ and to Hispanic children.

Our greatest luxury in El Building was having our own television set. It must have been a result of Father's guilt feelings over the isolation he had imposed on us, but we were one of the first families in the barrio to have one. My brother quickly became an avid watcher of Captain Kangaroo and Jungle Jim. I loved all the family series, and by the time I started first grade in school, I could have drawn a map of Middle America as exemplified by the lives of characters in "Father Knows Best," "The Donna Reed Show," "Leave It to Beaver," "My Three Sons," and (my favorite) "Bachelor Father," where John Forsythe treated his adopted teenage daughter like a princess because he was rich and had a Chinese houseboy to do everything for him. Compared to our neighbors in El Building, we were rich. My father's Navy check provided us with financial security and a standard of life that the factory workers envied. The only thing his money could not buy us was a place to live away from the barrio—his greatest wish and Mother's greatest fear.

In the home movie the men are shown next, sitting around a card table set up in one corner of the living room, playing dominoes. The clack of the ivory pieces is a familiar sound. I heard it in many houses on the Island and in many apartments in Paterson. In "Leave It to Beaver," the Cleavers played bridge in every other episode; in my childhood, the men started every social occasion with a hotly debated round of dominoes: the women would sit around and watch, but they never participated in the games.

Here and there you can see a small child. Children were always brought to parties and, whenever they got sleepy, put to bed in the host's bedrooms. Babysitting was a concept unrecognized by the Puerto Rican women I knew: a responsible mother did not leave her children with any stranger. And in a culture where children are not considered intrusive, there is no need to leave the children at home. We went where our mother went.

Of my pre-school years I have only impressions: the sharp bite of the wind in December as we walked with our parents towards the brightly lit stores downtown, how I felt like a stuffed doll in my heavy coat, boots and mittens; how good it was to walk into the five-and-dime and sit at the counter drinking hot chocolate.

On Saturdays our whole family would walk downtown to shop at the big department stores on Broadway. Mother bought all our clothes at Penny's and Sears, and she liked to buy her dresses at the women's specialty shops like Lerner's and Diana's. At some point we would go into Woolworth's and sit at the soda fountain to eat.

We never ran into other Latinos at these stores or eating out, and it became clear to me only years later that the women from El Building shopped mainly at other places—stores owned either by other Puerto Ricans, or by Jewish merchants who had philosophically accepted our presence in the city and decided to make us their good customers, if not neighbors and friends. These establishments were located not downtown, but in the blocks around our street, and they were referred to generically as *La Tienda, El Bazar, La Bodega, La Botánica.* Everyone knew what was meant. These were the stores where your face did not turn a clerk to stone, where your money was as green as anyone else's.

On New Year's Eve we were dressed up like child models in the Sears catalogue—my brother in a miniature man's suit and bow tie, and I in a black patent leather shoes and a frilly dress with several layers of crinolines underneath. My mother wore a bright red dress that night, I remember, and spike heels; her long black hair hung to her waist. Father, who usually wore his Navy uniform during his short visits home, had put on a dark civilian suit for the occasion: we had been invited to his uncle's house for a big celebration. everyone was excited because my mother's brother, Hernán—a bachelor who could indulge himself in such luxuries—had bought a movie camera which he would be trying out that night.

Even the home movie cannot fill in the sensory details such a gathering left imprinted in a child's brain. The thick sweetness of women's perfume mixing with the ever-present smells of food cooking in the kitchen: meat and plantain *pasteles,* the ubiquitous rice dish made special with pigeon peas—*gandules*—and seasoned with the precious *sofrito* sent up from the island by somebody's mother or smuggled in by a recent traveler. *Sofrito* was one of the items that women hoarded, since it was hardly ever in stock at La Bodega. It was the flavor of Puerto Rico.

The men drank Palo Viejo rum and some of the younger ones got weepy. The first time I saw a grown man cry was at a New Year's Eve party. He had been reminded of his mother by the smells in the kitchen. But what I remember most were the boiled *pasteles*—plantain or yucca rectangles stuffed with corned beef or other meats, olives, and many other savory ingredients, all wrapped in banana leaves. Everyone had to fish one out with a fork. There was always a "trick" pastel—one without stuffing—and whoever got that one was the "New Year's Fool."

There was also the music. Long-playing albums were treated like precious china in these homes. Mexican recordings were popular, but the songs that brought tears to my mother's eyes were sung by the melancholic Daniel Santos, whose life as a drug addict was the stuff of legend. Felipe Rodríguez was a particular favorite of couples. He sang about faithless women and broken-hearted men. There is a snatch of a lyric that has stuck in my mind like a needle on a worn groove: "De piedra ha de ser mi cama, de piedra la cabecera . . . la mujer que a mi me quiera . . . ha de quererme de veras. Ay, Ay, corazón, ¿por qué no amas . . . ?" I must have heard it a thousand times since the idea of a bed made of stone, and its connection to love, first troubled me with its disturbing images.

The five-minute home movie ends with people dancing in a circle. The creative filmmaker must have asked them to do that so that they could file past him. It is both comical and sad to watch silent dancing. Since there is no justification for the absurd movements that music provides for some of us, people appear frantic, their faces embarrassingly intense. It's as if you were watching sex. Yet for years, I've had dreams in the form of this home movie. In a recurring scene, familiar faces push themselves forward into my mind's eye, plastering their features into distorted close-ups. And I'm asking them: "Who is she? Who is the woman I don't recognize? Is she an aunt? Somebody's wife? Tell me who she is. Tell me who these people are."

"No, see the beauty mark on her cheek as big as a hill on the lunar landscape of her face—well, that runs in the family. The women on your father's side of the family wrinkle early; it's the price they pay for that fair skin. The young girl with the green stain on her wedding dress is *La Novia*—just up from the island. See, she lowers her eyes as she approaches the camera like she's supposed to. Decent girls never look you directly in the face. *Humilde*, humble, a girl should express humility in all her actions. She will make a good wife for your cousin. He should consider himself lucky to have met her only weeks after she arrived here. If he marries her quickly, she will make him a good Puerto Rican-style wife; but if he waits too long, she will be corrupted by the city, just like your cousin there."

"She means me. I do what I want. This is not some primitive island I live on. Do they expect me to wear a black *mantilla* on my head and go to mass every day? Not me. I'm an American woman and I will do as I please. I can type faster than anyone in my senior class at Central High, and I'm going to be a secretary to a lawyer when I graduate. I can pass for an American girl anywhere—I've tried it—at least for Italian, anyway. I never speak Spanish in public. I hate these parties, but I wanted the dress. I look better than any of these *humildes* here. My life is going to be different. I have an American boyfriend. He is older and has a car. My parents don't know it, but I sneak out of the house late at night some-times to be with him. If I marry him, even my name will be American. I hate rice and beans. It's what makes these women fat."

"Your *prima* is pregnant by that man she's been sneaking around with. Would I lie to you? I'm your great-uncle's common-law wife—the one he abandoned on the island to marry your cousin's mother. I was not invited to this party, but I came anyway. I came to tell you that story about your cousin that you've always wanted to hear. Remember that comment your mother made to a neighbor that has always haunted you? The only thing you heard was your cousin's name and then you saw your mother pick up your doll from the couch and say: 'It was as big as this doll when they flushed it down the toilet.' This image has bothered you for years, hasn't it? You had nightmares about babies being flushed down the toilet, and you wondered why anyone would do such a horrible thing. You didn't dare ask your mother about it. She would only tell you that you had not heard her right and yell at you for listening to adult conversations. But later, when you were old enough to know about abor-tions, you suspected. I am here to tell you that you were right. Your cousin was growing an *Americanito* in her belly when this movie was made. Soon after she put something long and pointy into her pretty self, thinking maybe she could get rid of the problem before breakfast and still make it to her first class at the high school. Well, *Niña*, her screams could be heard downtown. Your aunt, her Mamá, who had been a mid-wife on the Island, managed to pull the little thing out. Yes, they proba-bly flushed it down the toilet, what else could they do with it—give it a Christian burial in a little white casket with blue bows and ribbons? Nobody wanted that baby—least of all the father, a teacher at her school with a house in West Paterson that he was filling with real children, and a wife who was a natural blond.

"Girl, the scandal sent your uncle back to the bottle. And guess where your cousin ended up? Irony of ironies. She was sent to a village in Puerto Rico to live with a relative on her mother's side: a place so far away from civilization that you have to ride a mule to reach it. A real change in scenery. She found a man there. Women like that cannot live without male company. But believe me, the men in Puerto Rico know how to put a saddle on a woman like her. *La Gringa*, they call her. ha, ha. ha. *La Gringa* is what she always wanted to be . . ."

The old woman's mouth becomes a cavernous black hole I fall into. And as I fall, I can feel the reverberations of her laughter. I hear the echoes of her last mocking words: *La Gringa, La Gringa!* And the conga line keeps moving silently past me. There is no music in my dream for the dancers.

When Odysseus visits Hades asking to see the spirit of his mother, he makes an offering of sacrificial blood, but since all of the souls crave an audience with the living, he has to listen to many of them before he can ask questions. I, too, have to hear the dead and the forgotten speak in my dream. Those who are still part of my life remain silent, going around and around in their dance. The others keep pressing their faces forward to say things about the past.

My father's uncle is last in line. He is dying of alcoholism, shrunken and shriveled like a monkey, his face is a mass of wrinkles and broken arteries. As he comes closer I realize that in his features I can see my whole family. If you were to stretch that rubbery flesh, you could find my father's face, and deep within *that* face—mine. I don't want to look into those eyes ringed in purple. In a few years he will retreat into silence, and take a long, long time to die. *Move back, Tío,* I tell him. *I don't want to hear what you have to say. Give the dancers room to move, soon it will be midnight. Who is the New Year's Fool this time?*

In My Next Life

PAM HOUSTON

THIS is a love story. Although Abby and I were never lovers. That's an odd thing for me to have to say about another woman, because I've never had a woman lover, and yet with Abby it would have been possible. Of course with Abby anything was possible, and I often wonder if she hadn't gotten sick if we would have been lovers: one day our holding and touching and hugging slipping quietly into something more. It would have been beside the point and redundant, our lovemaking, but it might have been wonderful all the same.

That was the summer I was organic gardening for a living, and I had a small but steady clientele who came to me for their produce and kept me financially afloat. I had a trade going with Carver's Bakery, tomatoes for bread, and another with the farmers' market in Salt Lake City, fresh herbs for chicken and groceries. I grew wheat grass for my landlord Thomas and his lover, who both had AIDS. I traded Larry, at the Purina Mill, all the corn his kids could eat for all the grain I needed for my mare. She was half wild and the other half stubborn, and I should have turned her out to pasture like most of my friends said, or shot her like the rest recommended, but I had an idea that she and I could be great together if we ever both felt good on the same day.

Abby had long black hair she wore in a single braid and eyes the color of polished jade. Her shoulders were rounded like a swimmer's, although she was afraid of the water, and her hands were quick and graceful and yet seemed to be capable of incredible strength.

I met her at a horse-handling clinic she was teaching in Salt Lake that I'd gone to with my crazy mare.

"There are no problem horses," Abbey said. "Someone has taught her to be that way."

In the middle of explaining to her that it wasn't me who taught my horse her bad habits, I realized it could have been. Abby had a way of

388

looking at me, of looking into me, that made everything I said seem like the opposite of the truth.

"There are three things to remember when working with horses," Abby said to the women who had gathered for the class. "Ask, Receive, Give." She said each word slowly, and separated them by breaths. "Now what could be simpler than that?"

I rode as hard as I knew how that day at the clinic. Abby was calm, certain, full of images. "Your arms and hands are running water," she said. "Let the water pour over your horse. Let the buttons on your shirt come undone. Let your body melt like ice cream and dribble out the bottom of your bones."

My mare responded to the combination of my signals and Abby's words. She was moving with confidence, bending underneath me, her back rounded, her rhythm steady and strong.

"Catch the energy as if you were cradling a baby." Abby said. "Grow your fingers out to the sky. Fly with your horse. Feel that you are dancing." She turned from one woman to another. "Appeal to the great spirit," she said. "Become aware, inhibit, allow."

At the end of the day while we were walking out the horses Abby said, "You are a lovely, lovely woman. Tell me what else you do."

I told her I played the banjo, which was the other thing I was doing at the time, with a group that was only marginally popular with people my age but a big hit with the older folks in the Fallen Arches Square Dance Club.

Abby told me she had always been intimidated by musicians.

She told me I had medieval hair.

ON THE first day after the clinic that Abby and I spent together I told her that meeting her was going to change my whole life. She seemed neither threatened nor surprised by this information; if anything, she was mildly pleased. "Life gives us what we need when we need it," she said. "Receiving what it gives us is a whole other thing."

We were both involved with unavailable men, one by drugs, one by alcohol, both by nature. There were some differences. She lived with her boyfriend, whose name was Roy. I lived alone. Roy was kind, at least, and faithful, and my man, whose name was Hardin, was not.

I said to Thomas, "I have met a woman who, if she were a man, I would be in love with." But of course Abby could have never been a man, and I fell in love anyway. It's not the kind of definition Abby would have gotten mired in, but I think she may also have been a little in love with me.

Once, on the phone, when we weren't sure if the conversation was over, when we weren't sure if we had actually said goodbye, we both held our receivers, breathing silently, till finally she had the guts to say, "Are you still there?"

"We are a couple of silly women," she said, when we had finally stopped laughing. "A couple of silly women who want so badly to be friends."

Although only one-sixteenth Cherokee, and even that undocumented, Abby was a believer in Native American medicine. Shamanic healing, specifically, is what she practiced. The healing involved in shamanic work happens in mind journeys a patient takes with the aid of a continuous drumbeat, into the lower or upper world, accompanied by his or her power animal. The power animal serves as the patient's interpreter, guardian, and all number of other things. The animals take pity on us, it is believed, because of the confusion with which we surround ourselves. The learning takes place in the energy field where the animal and the human being meet.

A guided tour into the lower world with a buffalo is not the kind of thing a white girl from New Jersey would discover on her own, but for me, everything that came from Abby's mouth was magic. If she had told me the world was flat, I'd have found a way to make it true.

When Abby taught me the methods of shamanic healing I started to try to journey too. Abby played the drum for me. She shook the rattle around my body and blew power into my breastbone and into the top of my skull. The drumming altered my mental state, that was for certain, but I couldn't make myself see anything I could define. If I pressed my arm hard enough against my eyeballs I could start to see light swirling. But a tunnel? another world? Animals and spirits I couldn't muster.

"People have different amounts of spiritual potential," she said, "and for some people it takes a while. Don't be discouraged by a slow start."

So I would try again and again to make forms out of the shapes inside my eyelids, and I'd stretch the truth of what I saw in the reporting. I wanted to go all of the places that Abby could go. I was afraid she might find another friend with more spiritual potential than me.

"You're seeing in a way you've never seen before," Abby said. "You just don't know how to recognize it. It isn't like cartoons on your eyelids. It's not like a big-screen TV."

Finally, my mind would make logical connections out of the things I was seeing. "It was a bear," I would say, "running away and then returning." Abby's green eyes never let mine falter. "A big white bear that could run on two legs." As I said the words, it seemed, I made it so. "It was turning somersaults, too, and rolling in the blueberries." It didn't feel like I was lying, but it also didn't feel like the truth.

One thing was certain. I believed what Abby saw. If she said she rose into the stars and followed them to South Africa, if she danced on the rooftops of Paris with her ancestors, if she and her power animal made love in the Siberian snow, I believed her. I still believe her. Abby didn't lie.

But it wasn't only the magic. Abby was gentle and funny and talked mostly with her hands. She made great mashed potatoes. She had advanced degrees in botany, biology, and art history. And the horses, Abby loved her horses more than any power animal her imagination could conjure up.

"The Indians don't believe in imagination," she told me. "They don't even have a word for it. Once you understand that fully this all becomes much easier."

We had climbed the mountain behind my house, way above the silver mine, and were lying in a meadow the moon made bright. Abby threw handfuls of cornmeal on the ground. "I'm feeding my power animal," she said. "When I do this he knows that I need him around."

I MADE Abby batches of fresh salsa, pesto, and spaghetti sauce. I brought her squash blossoms, red peppers, and Indian corn to make a necklace her power animal told her to wear.

She told me about her college roommate, Tracy, her best friend, she said, before me. Tracy's marriage had broken up, she said, because Tracy had been having an affair with a woman, and her husband, Steve, couldn't handle it. They had tried going to therapy together, but Tracy eventually chose the woman over Steve.

"She said she never expected to have an affair with a woman," Abby said, "but then they just fell in love."

I thought about my friend Thomas, about how he gets so angry whenever anybody says that they respect his sexual choice. "Choice has nothing to do with it," I can hear him saying. "Why would I ever have done this if I had had a choice?"

But I wonder if it's not a question of choice for a woman. Aren't there women who wake up tired of trying to bridge the unbridgeable gap, who wake up ready to hold and be held by somebody who knows what it means?

"In my next life," Thomas was famous for saying, "I'm coming back as a lesbian."

"THAT'S what I did," my friend of five years, Joanne, said, when I asked her opinion, as if her lesbian affair was something I'd known about all along, "with Isabelle. And it was wonderful, for a while. But what happens too often is that somewhere down the line you are attracted to a man and want to go back, and then it's a whole new kind of guilt to deal with. You're hurting somebody who's on your team, who really knows you, who really is you, I suppose, if you stop and think."

"There are so many more interesting things to do than fall in love," Abby said. "If Roy and I split up, I want to live in a house full of women, old women and young women, teenagers and babies. Doesn't falling in love sound boring, compared to that?"

I had to admit, it didn't. We were both fighting our way out of codependency. I wasn't as far as she was yet.

"The problem with codependency," Abby said, "is that what you have to do to be codependent, and what you have to do to not be codependent, turn out so often to be the same thing."

"So what would you do about sex, in this house full of women?" I said. We were sitting sideways on her sofa like kids on a Flexible Flyer. She was braiding and unbraiding my medieval hair.

"Frankly," she said, "that's the least of my concerns."

"That's what you say now," I said, "but I think after a few years without, you would start to feel differently."

"Yeah, maybe you're right," she said, giving the short hairs at the nape of my neck a tug. "Maybe sex would turn out to be the big snafu."

IT WAS only the third or fourth time we were together when Abby told me about the lump in her breast. "It's been there a long time," she said, "about two years, I guess, but my power animal says it's not cancer, and besides it gets bigger and smaller with my period. Cancer never does that."

Even the doctor, when she finally did go, said he was ninety-nine percent sure that the lump was not a "malignancy" (doctors apparently had stopped using the "C" word), but he wanted to take it out anyway, just to make sure.

On the night before Abby's biopsy, I made her favorite thing: three kinds of baked squash, butternut, buttercup, and acorn.

"Sometimes I'm jealous of Hardin," I said. "He lives right on the surface and he's happy there. Who am I to tell him how to live his life? I should be that happy in all my depth."

"I had a friend in grade school named Margaret Hitzrot," Abby said. "Once on our way to a day of skiing we were the first car in a twenty-one-vehicle pile up. Our car spun to a stop, unharmed against the snowbank, but facing back the way we had come, and we watched station wagons, delivery trucks, VW buses, collide and crash, spin and smash together. Mrs. Hitzrot said, 'Margaret, do you think we should wait for the police?' And Margaret said, 'If we don't get to the ski area before the lift opens the whole day will be ruined,' so we got in our car and drove away."

"It's not the worst way to live," I said.

"The problem with the surface," Abby said, "is that it's so slippery. Once you get bumped off, it's impossible to climb back on."

Abby's arms bore scars on the white underside, nearly up to the elbows, thin and delicate, like an oriental script. "It was a long, long time ago," she said. "And I wasn't trying to kill myself either. My stepfather had some serious problems. There was a good bit of sexual abuse. I never even thought about dying. I just wanted to make myself bleed."

After dinner we rode the horses up to our favorite meadow. She had been riding my horse, who had turned to putty in her hands. I was riding one of hers, a big gray gelding who was honest as a stone. We kept saying we were going to switch back, now that my horse had been gentled, but I didn't push the issue. I was afraid my mare would go back to her old habits and Abby would be disappointed. It was something I'd never felt with a woman, this giant fear of looking bad.

I was depressed that night. Hardin was in another state with another woman, and it made me so mad that I cared.

"You have given all your power away to Hardin," Abby said. "You need to do something to get it back."

We sat under the star-filled sky and Abby said she would journey beside me, journey, she said, on my behalf. This was accomplished by our lying on the ground side by side. We touched at the shoulders, the knees, and the hips. We both tied bandannas around our heads, and Abby pulled her Walkman and drumming tape out of the saddlebags.

"Don't feel like you need to journey," she said. "I'll do all the work for you, but if you feel yourself slipping into a journey, go ahead and let it happen."

For a long time I watched the white spots turn on the inside of my bandanna while Abby's breathing quickened, and leveled and slowed. Then I saw a steady light, and reflections below it. It was my first real vision, nothing about it questionable or subject to change. It was moonlight over granite, I think, something shiny, and permanent and hard.

Abby came back slowly, and I turned off the tape.

"Your power source is the moon," she said. "It was a bear who told me. A giant bear that kept getting smaller and smaller. He was multicolored, like light, coming through a prism. The full moon is in five days. You must be out in the moonlight. Drink it in. Let it fill you. Take four stones with you and let them soak the moonlight. This is one of them."

She pressed a tiger's-eye into my hand. "It is up to you to find the other three."

I CARRIED flowers with me into the short-stay surgery wing. I saw Abby in a bed at the end of the hall. She was wide awake and waving.

"You brought flowers," she said.

"Store-bought flowers, made to look wild," I said. "How do you feel?"

"Good," Abby said. "Not too bad at all."

The doctor came in and leaned over the bed like an old friend.

"Your lump was a tumor, Abby," he said.

"What kind of tumor?" she said. "What does it mean?"

"It was a malignancy," he said. "A cancer." (Sweet relief.) "I have to tell you, of all the lumps I did today, and I did five, yours was the one I expected least of all to be malignant."

His pager went off and he disappeared through the curtain. It took a few seconds, but Abby turned and met my eyes.

"Cancer, huh?" she said. "My power animal was wrong."

When I had Abby tucked into her own bed I drove home the long way, over the mountain. It was the day that would have been John Lennon's fiftieth birthday, and on the radio was a simulcast, the largest in history, a broadcast reaching more people than any other broadcast had ever done. It was live from the United Nations. Yoko Ono read a poem, and then they played "Imagine." It was the first time I cried for John Lennon.

Abby called me in the middle of the night.

"I know it sounds crazy," she said, "but I can't sleep without my lump. I should have asked the doctor for it. I should have brought it home and put it under my pillow," she said. "Where do you think it has gone?"

BEFORE her second surgery, a double mastectomy and lymph-node exploration, I took Abby down to southern Utah, to the piece of land I'd bought in the middle of nowhere because I loved it there and because having it seemed a little bit like security. My six acres is in the high desert, where it never rains except too much and more often it snows and freezes cherry blossoms or hails hard enough to make bruises on uncovered flesh. It was sage and juniper mostly, a few cacti.

Abby put her feet into the ground like she was planting them. Two ravens flew overhead in pursuit of a smaller bird, gray and blue. There was squawking, the rustle of wings, and then a clump of feathers floated down and landed at Abby's feet. Three feathers stuck together, and on each tip, a drop of blood.

Abby started singing and dancing, a song she made up as she went along, directed toward the east.

"Why do you sing and dance?" she'd once asked me. "To raise your spirits, right?" she laughed. "That is also why I sing and dance," she said. "Precisely."

She sang the same song to each of the four horizons, and danced the same steps to each with the gray bird's feathers in her hair. The words elude me now, half-English, half-Navajo. It was about light, I remember, and red dirt, and joy. When she finished dancing and turned back toward the eastern horizon the full moon rose right into her hands.

ABBY looked tiny and alone in the giant white bed and among the machines she was hooked to.

"How are you?" I said.

"Not bad," she said. "A little weak. In the shamanic tradition," she said, "there is a certain amount of soul loss associated with anesthesia. Airplane travel too," she said. "Your soul can't fly fast enough to keep up. How are you?" she said. "How's Hardin?"

"He left for the Canadian Rockies this morning," I said. "He'll be gone six weeks. I asked him if he wanted to make love. He was just lying there, you know, staring at the ceiling. He said, 'I was just trying to decide whether to do that or go to Ace Hardware.' "

"I don't want you to break up with him because he would say something like that," Abby said. "I want you to break up with him because he'd say something like that and not think it was funny."

The doctor came in and started to say words like "chemotherapy," like "bone scan" and "brain scan," procedures certain to involve soul loss of one kind or another.

Simply because there was no one, I called Hardin in Canada. "That's too bad," he said, when I told him the cancer was extensive in the lymph nodes. And as usual, he was right.

The nights were getting colder, and the day after Abby got out of the hospital we picked about a thousand green tomatoes to pickle in Ball jars.

"I don't know where I want Roy to be in all of this," she said. "I know it would be too much to ask him for things like support and nurturance, so I thought about asking for things he would understand. I'd like him to stop smoking around me. I'd like him to keep our driveway free of snow."

"Those sound like good, concrete things," I said.

"I love him very much, you know," she said.

And God help me, I was jealous.

We took a walk, up towards the Uintas, where the aspen leaves had already fallen, making a carpet under our feet.

"You know," I said, "if you want to go anywhere, this year, I'll come up with the money and we'll go. It's just credit cards," I said. "I can make it happen."

"I know why my power animal lied," Abby said. "It was the intent of my question. Even though I said 'Do I have cancer?' what I meant was 'Am I going to die?' That's what I was really asking, and the answer was no."

"I'm glad you worked that out," I said.

"I've made a decision," she said. "I'm going to stop seeing the doctors."

Something that felt like a small bomb exploded in my ribs. "What do you mean?" I said.

"I'm not going to have the chemotherapy," she said. "Or any more of the tests. My power animal said I don't need them, they could even be *detrimental*, is what he said."

The sound of the dead leaves under my boots became too loud for me to bear. "Is that what he really said, Abby?" I faced her on the trail. "Did he open his mouth and say those words?"

She walked around me and went on down the trail. "You won't leave me," she said after a while. "Even if things get real bad."

I leaned over and kissed her, softly, on the head.

"I WANT to support her decision," I told Thomas. "I even want to believe in her magic, but she's ignoring hundreds of years of medical research. This ugly thing is consuming her and she's not doing anything to stop it."

We were walking in the moonlight on our way up to the old silver mine not far above my house. It was the harvest moon, and so bright you could see the color in the changing leaves, the red maple, the orange scrub oak, the yellow aspen. You could even tell the difference in the aspen that were yellow tinged with brown, and the ones that were yellow and still holding green.

"She is doing something," Thomas said. "She's just not doing what you want her to do."

"What, listening to her power animal?" I said. "Waiting for the spirits from the lower world to take the cancer away? How can that mean anything to me? How can I make that leap?"

"You love Abby," he said.

"Yeah," I said. The bright leaves against the dark evergreens in the moonlight were like an hallucination.

"And she loves you," he said.

"Yeah," I said.

"That's," he said, "how you make the leap."

I DON'T want to talk about the next few months, the way the cancer ambushed her body with more and more powerful attacks. The way she sank into her own shadow, the darkness enveloping what was left of her hair and skin. Her vitality slipping. Maybe I do want to talk about it, but not right now.

With no doctor to supply the forecasts and explanations, watching Abby's deterioration was like reading a book without a narrator, or seeing a movie in another language. Just when you thought you knew what was going on, the plot would thicken illogically.

When it all got to be too much for Roy, he moved out and I moved in. I even thought about trying to find some old ladies and teenagers, of calling some of the ladies from the Fallen Arches, thinking I could create the household Abby had wished for. It wasn't really as pathetic as it sounds. We ate a lot of good food. We saw a lot of good movies. I played my banjo and Abby sang. We laughed a lot those last days. More, I'll bet, than most people could imagine.

Abby finally even refused to eat. The world had taken everything from her she was going to let it take, and she died softly in her room one day, looking out the window at her horses.

Once I hit a rabbit in the highway, just barely hit it, I was almost able to swerve out of its way. It was nighttime, and very cold, and I stopped the car on the side of the road and walked back to where it lay dying. The humane thing, I'm told, would have been to shoot it or hit it in the head with the tire jack or run over it again. But I picked it up and held it under my coat until it died, it was only a few minutes, and it was the strangest sensation I know of, when the life all at once, it seemed, slipped away.

Abby and I didn't talk at all the day she died. She offered me no last words I could use to make an ending, to carry on with, to change my life. I held her hands for the last few hours, and then after that till they got colder than hell.

I sat with her body most of the night, without really knowing what I was looking for. An eagle, I guess, or a raven, some great huge bird bursting in a shimmer of starlight out of her chest. But if something rose out of Abby at the end, it was in a form I didn't recognize. Cartoons, she would have said, are what I wanted. Disneyland and special effects.

For two days after her death I was immobile. There was so much to be done, busy work, really, and thank goodness there were others there to do it. The neighbors, her relatives, my friends. Her stepfather and I exchanged glances several times, and then finally a hug, though I don't know if he knew who I was, or if he knew that I knew the truth about him. Her mother was the one I was really mad at, although that may have been unfair, and she and I walked circles around the house just to avoid each other, and it worked until they went back to Santa Cruz.

The third day was the full moon, and I knew I had to go outside in it, just in case Abby could see me from wherever she was. I saddled my mare for the first time in over a year and we walked up high, to the place where Abby and I had lain together under our first full moon not even a year before. My mare was quiet, even though the wind was squirrelly and we could hear the occasional footsteps of deer. She was so well behaved, in fact, that it made me wish I'd ridden her with Abby, made me hope that Abby could see us, and then I wondered why, against all indications, I still thought that Abby was somebody who had given me something to prove. *Your seat feels like a soft glove*, Abby would have said, *your horse fills it.*

I dismounted and spread some cornmeal on the ground. *Become aware, inhibit, allow.* I laid my stones so they pointed at each of the four horizons. Jade to the west, smoky quartz to the north, hematite to the south, and to the east, Abby's tiger's-eye. *Ask, receive, give.* I sang a song to the pine trees and danced at the sky. I drank the moonlight. It filled me up.

Ruthy and Edie

GRACE PALEY

ONE DAY in the Bronx two small girls named Edie and Ruthy were sitting on the stoop steps. They were talking about the real world of boys. Because of this, they kept their skirts pulled tight around their knees. A gang of boys who lived across the street spent at least one hour of every Saturday afternoon pulling up girls' dresses. They needed to see the color of a girl's underpants in order to scream outside the candy store, Edie wears pink panties.

Ruthy said, anyway, she liked to play with those boys. They did more things. Edie said she hated to play with them. They hit and picked up her skirt. Ruthy agreed. It *was* wrong of them to do this. But, she said, they ran around the block a lot, had races, and played war on the corner. Edie said it wasn't *that* good.

Ruthy said, Another thing, Edie, you could be a soldier if you're a boy.

So? What's so good about that?

Well, you could fight for your country.

Edie said, I don't want to.

What? Edie! Ruthy was a big reader and most interesting reading was about bravery—for instance Roland's Horn at Roncevaux. Her father had been brave and there was often a lot of discussion about this at supper-time. In fact, he sometimes modestly said, Yes, I suppose I was brave in those days. And so was your mother, he added. Then Ruthy's mother put his boiled egg in front of him where he could see it. Reading about Roland, Ruthy learned that if a country wanted to last, it would require a great deal of bravery. She nearly cried with pity when she thought of Edie and the United States of America.

You don't want to? she asked.

No.

Why, Edie, why?

I don't feel like.

Why, Edie? How come?

You always start hollering if I don't do what you tell me. I don't always have to say what you tell me. I can say whatever I like.

Yeah, but if you love your country you have to go fight for it. How come you don't want to? Even if you get killed, it's worth it.

Edie said, I don't want to leave my mother.

Your mother? You must be a baby. Your mother?

Edie pulled her skirt very tight over her knees. I don't like it when I don't see her a long time. Like when she went to Springfield to my uncle. I don't like it.

Oh boy! said Ruthy. Oh boy! What a baby! She stood up. She wanted to go away. She just wanted to jump from the top step, run down to the corner, and wrestle with someone. She said, You know, Edie, this is *my* stoop.

Edie didn't budge. She leaned her chin on her knees and felt sad. She was a big reader too, but she liked *The Bobbsey Twins* or *Honey Bunch at the Seashore*. She loved that nice family life. She tried to live it in the three rooms on the fourth floor. Sometimes she called her father Dad, or even Father, which surprised him. Who? he asked.

I have to go home now, she said. My cousin Alfred's coming. She looked to see if Ruthy was still mad. Suddenly she saw a dog. Ruthy, she said, getting to her feet. There's a dog coming. Ruthy turned. There *was* a dog about three-quarters of the way down the block between the candy store and the grocer's. It was an ordinary middle-sized dog. But it *was* coming. It didn't stop to sniff at curbs or pee on the house fronts. It just trotted steadily along the middle of the sidewalk.

Ruthy watched him. Her heart began to thump and take up too much space inside her ribs. She thought speedily, Oh, a dog has teeth! It's large, hairy, strange. Nobody can say what a dog is thinking. A dog is an animal. You could talk to a dog, but a dog couldn't talk to you. If you said to a dog, STOP! a dog would just keep going. If it's angry and bites you, you might get rabies. It will take you about six weeks to die and you will die screaming in agony. Your stomach will turn into a rock and you will have lockjaw. When they find you, your mouth will be paralyzed wide open in your dying scream.

Ruthy said, I'm going right now. She turned as though she'd been directed by some far-off switch. She pushed the hall door open and got safely inside. With one hand she pressed the apartment bell. With the other she held the door shut. She leaned against the glass door as Edie started to bang on it. Let me in, Ruthy, let me in, please. Oh, Ruthy!

I can't. Please, Edie, I just can't.

Edie's eyes rolled fearfully toward the walking dog. It's coming. Oh, Ruthy, please, please.

No! No! said Ruthy.

The dog stopped right in front of the stoop to hear the screaming and banging. Edie's heart stopped too. But in a minute he decided to go on. He passed. He continued his easy steady pace.

When Ruthy's big sister came down to call them for lunch, the two girls were crying. They were hugging each other and their hair was a mess. You two are nuts, she said. If I was Mama, I wouldn't let you play together so much every single day. I mean it.

MANY YEARS later in Manhattan it was Ruthy's fiftieth birthday. She had invited three friends. They waited for her at the round kitchen table. She had been constructing several pies so that this birthday could be celebrated in her kitchen during the day by any gathered group without too much trouble. Now and then one of the friends would say, Will you sit down, for godsakes! She would sit immediately. But in the middle of someone's sentence or even one of her own, she'd jump up with a look of worry beyond household affairs to wash a cooking utensil or wipe crumbs of flour off the Formica counter.

Edie was one of the women at the table. She was sewing, by neat hand, a new zipper into an old dress. She said, Ruthy, it wasn't like that. We both ran in and out a lot.

No, said Ruth. You would never have locked me out. You were an awful sissy, sweetie, but you would never, never have locked me out. Just look at yourself. Look at your life!

Edie glanced, as people will, when told to do that. She saw a chubby dark-haired woman who looked like a nice short teacher, someone who stood at the front of the schoolroom and said, History is a wonderful subject. It's all stories. It's where we come from, who we are. For instance, where do you come from, Juan? Where do your parents and grandparents come from?

You know that, Mizz Seiden. Porto Rico. You know that a long-o time-o, Juan said, probably in order to mock both languages. Edie thought, Oh, to whom would he speak?

For Christsakes, this is a party, isn't it? said Ann. She was patting a couple of small cases and a projector on the floor next to her chair. Was she about to offer a slide show? No, she had already been prevented from doing this by Faith, who'd looked at the clock two or three times and said, I don't have the time, Jack is coming tonight. Ruth had looked at the clock too. Next week, Ann? Ann said O.K. O.K. But Ruthy, I want to say you have to quit knocking yourself. I've seen you do a million good things. If you were such a dud, why'd I write it down in my will that if anything happened to me, you and Joe were the ones who'd raise my kids.

You were just plain wrong. I couldn't even raise my own right.

Ruthy, really, they're pretty much raised. Anyway, how can you say an awful thing like that? Edie asked. They're wonderful beautiful brilliant girls. Edie knew this because she had held them in her arms the third or fourth day of life. Naturally, she became the friend called aunt.

That's true, I don't have to worry about Sara anymore, I guess.

Why? Because she's a married mommy? Faith asked. What an insult to Edie!

No, that's O.K., said Edie.

Well, I do worry about Rachel. I just can't help myself. I never know where she is. She was supposed to be here last night. She does usually call. Where the hell is she?

Oh, probably in jail for some stupid little sit-in or something, Ann said. She'll get out in five minutes. Why she thinks that kind of thing works is a mystery to me. You brought her up like that and now you're surprised. Besides which, I don't want to talk about the goddamn kids, said Ann. Here I've gone around half of most of the nearly socialist world and nobody asks me a single question. I have been a witness of events! she shouted.

I do want to hear everything, said Ruth. Then she changed her mind. Well, I don't mean everything. Just say one good thing and one bad thing about every place you've been. We only have a couple of hours. (It was four o'clock. At six, Sara and Thomas with Letty, the first grandchild, standing between them would be at the door. Letty would probably think it was her own birthday party. Someone would say, What curly hair! They would all love her new shoes and her newest sentence, which was Remember dat? Because for such a long time there had been only the present full of milk and looking. Then one day, trying to dream into an afternoon nap, she sat up and said, Gramma, I boke your cup. Remember dat? In this simple way the lifelong past is invented, which, as we know, thickens the present and gives all kinds of advice to the future.) So, Ann, I mean just a couple of things about each country.

That's not much of a discussion, for Christsake.

It's a party, Ann, you said it yourself.

Well, change your face, then.

Oh. Ruth touched her mouth, the corners of her eyes. You're right. Birthday! she said.

Well, let's go, then, said Ann. She stated two good things and one bad thing about Chile (an earlier visit), Rhodesia, the Soviet Union, and Portugal.

You forgot about China. Why don't you tell them about our trip to China?

I don't think I will, Ruthy; you'd only contradict every word I say.

Edie, the oldest friend, stripped a nice freckled banana she'd been watching during Ann's talk. The thing is, Ruth, you never simply say yes. I've told you so many times, *I* would have slammed the door on you, admit it, but it was your house, and that slowed me down.

Property, Ann said. Even among poor people, it begins early.

Poor? asked Edie. It was the Depression.

Two questions—Faith believed she'd listened patiently long enough. I love that story, but I've heard it before. Whenever you're down in the dumps, Ruthy. Right?

I haven't, Ann said. How come, Ruthy? Also, will you please sit with us.

The second question: What about this city? I mean, I'm kind of sick of these big international reports. Look at this place, looks like a toxic waste dump. A war. Nine million people.

Oh, that's true, Edie said, but Faith, the whole thing *is* hopeless. Top to bottom, the streets, those kids, dumped, plain dumped. That's the correct word, "dumped." She began to cry.

Cut it out, Ann shouted. No tears, Edie! No! Stop this minute! I swear, Faith said, you'd better stop that! (They were all, even Edie, ideologically, spiritually, and on puritanical principle against despair.)

Faith was sorry to have mentioned the city in Edie's presence. If you said the word "city" to Edie, or even the cool adjective "municipal," specific children usually sitting at the back of the room appeared before her eyes and refused to answer when she called on them. So Faith said, O.K. New subject: What do you women think of the grand juries they're calling up all over the place?

All over what place? Edie asked. Oh, Faith, forget it, they're going through something. You know you three lead such adversarial lives. I hate it. What good does it do? Anyway, those juries will pass.

Edie, sometimes I think you're half asleep. You know that woman in New Haven who was called? I know her personally. She wouldn't say a word. She's in jail. They're not kidding.

I'd never open my mouth either, said Ann. Never. She clamped her mouth shut then and there.

I believe you, Ann. But sometimes, Ruth said, I think, Suppose I was in Argentina and they had my kid. God, if they had our Sara's Letty, I'd maybe say anything.

Oh, Ruth, you've held up pretty well, once or twice, Faith said.

Yes, Ann said, in fact we were all pretty good that day, we were sitting right up against the horses' knees at the draft board—were you there, Edie? And then the goddamn horses started to rear and the cops were knocking people on their backs and heads—remember? And, Ruthy, I was watching you. You just suddenly plowed in and out of those monsters. You should have been trampled to death. And you grabbed the captain by his gold buttons and you hollered, You bastard! Get your goddamn cavalry out of here. You shook him and shook him.

He ordered them, Ruth said. She set one of her birthday cakes, which was an apple plum pie, on the table. I saw him. He was the responsible person. I saw the whole damn operation. I'd begun to run—the horses—but I turned because I was the one supposed to be in front and I saw him give the order. I've never honestly been so angry.

Ann smiled. Anger, she said. That's really good.

You think so? Ruth asked. You sure?

Buzz off, said Ann.

Ruth lit the candles. Come on, Ann, we've got to blow this out together. And make a wish. I don't have the wind I used to have.

But you're still full of hot air, Edie said. And kissed her hard. What did you wish, Ruthy?" she asked.

Well, a wish, some wish, Ruth said. Well, I wished that this world wouldn't end. This world, this world, Ruth said softly.

Me too, I wished exactly the same. Taking action, Ann hoisted herself up onto a kitchen chair, saying, ugh my back, ouch my knee. Then: Let us go forth with fear and courage and rage to save the world.

Bravo, Edie said softly.

Wait a minute, said Faith . . .

Ann said, Oh, you . . . you . . .

But it was six o'clock and the doorbell rang. Sara and Thomas stood on either side of Letty, who was hopping or wiggling with excitement, hiding behind her mother's long skirt or grabbing her father's thigh. The door had barely opened when Letty jumped forward to hug Ruth's knees. I'm gonna sleep in your house, Gramma.

I know, darling, I know.

Gramma, I slept in your bed with you. Remember dat?

Oh sure, darling, I remember. We woke up around five and it was still dark and I looked at you and you looked at me and you had a great big Letty smile and we just burst out laughing and you laughed and I laughed.

I remember dat, Gramma. Letty looked at her parents with shyness and pride. She was still happy to have found the word "remember," which could name so many pictures in her head.

And then we went right back to sleep, Ruth said, kneeling now to Letty's height to kiss her little face.

Where's my Aunt Rachel? Letty asked, hunting among the crowd of unfamiliar legs in the hallway.

I don't know.

She's supposed to be here, Letty said. Mommy, you promised. She's really supposed.

Yes, said Ruth, picking Letty up to hug her and then hug her again. Letty, she said as lightly as she could, She *is* supposed to be here. But where can she be? She certainly is supposed.

Letty began to squirm out of Ruth's arms. Mommy, she called, Gramma is squeezing. But it seemed to Ruth that she'd better hold her even closer, because, though no one else seemed to notice—Letty, rosy and soft-cheeked as ever, was falling, already falling, falling out of her brand-new hammock of world-inventing words onto the hard floor of man-made time.

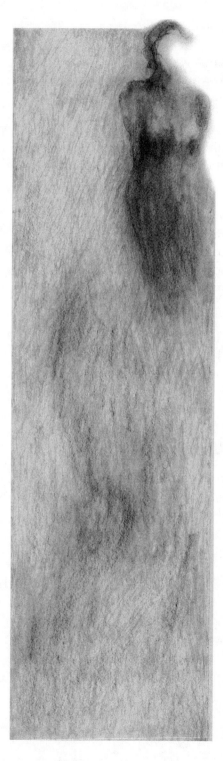

The Fullness of Life

WOMEN are redefining the way they think of themselves and the possibilities for the last one third of life. Indeed, the writings in this section are among the most revolutionary in the book, for they blow holes in many of our own fears of aging. Gloria Steinem's "Fifty Is What Forty Used to Be" sounds the theme as she writes about the significance of her own fiftieth birthday—a comfortable age for her at last, Steinem says.

Abigail Thomas's Louise is "pushing down the tall grasses near the land of menopause." But when a young carpenter asks her out for a date, Louise has an adventure that is both comic and poignant. Here is a woman who dares to take risks but lands on her feet.

Mona Van Duyn, who was poet laureate of the United States, evokes in "Late Loving" the difference between new love and that seasoned by many shared years: " 'Love' is finding the familiar dear. / 'In love' is to be taken by surprise."

Carolyn Heilbrun (also known as Amanda Cross, author of mysteries about a woman detective who is a university professor, as was Heilbrun) gives a brilliantly convincing scenario in "Coming of Age" of how she and other women are redefining this time when we are "neither young nor old." Once we give up the fight to look and act eternally young, we discover new powers of attractiveness and sources of pleasure.

The grace to forgive and heal old wounds is one of the blessings of long life. Cynthia Kadohata's short story "Miracles in the Sky and on the Road" shows a Japanese-American woman who doesn't object when her former husband, who left her for another woman, is asked to join her family Christmas party in California. She sees on the drive the miracle of her own life compared to his.

Helen Norris writes of an elderly woman who is losing her memory. She fears that her daughter, though loving and well-meaning, will soon send her to a nursing home. This story of how Mrs. Moonlight reaches out to an old lover evokes the suspense we usually feel reading about the youngest lovers. Norris manages to show the healing powers of love without being in the slightest bit sentimental.

May Sarton's "At Seventy: A Journal" attracts readers of all ages for this remarkable novelist-poet chronicles a life that is busy with both friends and creative work. With a steady eye she sets down moments of solitude, friendship, loneliness, and the feeling that "My life at the moment is like a little game of solitaire that is coming out. . . . The long hard work is bearing fruit. . . ."

Fifty Is What Forty Used to Be

GLORIA STEINEM

FOR MOST of the first 20 years of my life, I pretended to be older. Because I had reached my current height by the time I was 11 or 12, the deception was easy, and because I was working as a dancer in anything from supermarket openings and Eagles Club dances to operettas, makeup and costumes added to the illusion and money to the incentive. At 12, I was passing for 16. At 15, I was entering talent contests pretending to be 21.

Then came college, and the unimportance of age: we were all within four years of each other anyway. This obsession didn't raise its head again until I was in my mid-thirties in New York and being constantly told, in those prefeminist days, that no woman over 30 in her right mind ever told her real age. When one friend and one relative both said in print that I was two years younger as a kindly gesture, I maintained that wrong figure for a while, and learned a big lesson. Unlike my earlier adventures with breaking age taboos, this deception was actually giving in to one: the taboo against women as grown-ups. Falsifying one small fact made me feel foolish and false about everything else. Finally, worrying about how dumb I would feel if discovered became a far more immediate penalty than growing older. I went back to my real age with relief.

At the same time, I often had an odd and opposite thought that I didn't really analyze. I was fantasizing pleasurably about being very old. I must have concluded that only as an acerbic and independent old lady would I finally be free of the vulnerability and lack of seriousness and humiliations of the "feminine" role that focuses on women in the child-bearing years. Only then would I stop being treated like that interchangeable moving part: "a pretty girl." The craziness of the role was actually making me wish my life away.

Fortunately, by the time I got to my late thirties, feminism had helped me understand that you could change the role instead of shortening life. Only then did I see the disease of which my old-age fantasy had been just a symptom.

By the time I turned 40, this wave of feminism had been around long enough to encourage rebellion against all double standards. A contagion of truth-telling on everything from rape and abortion to unequal pay and marriages had turned out to be the major way we could give one another the strength of knowing we were neither wrong nor alone. It occurred to me that going very public with a fortieth birthday might help other women come out of the closet about age, too, and thus give a nudge to the prejudice that allowed men to be considered young and vital after 40 while women were over the hill. So, instead of inviting only friends to dinner at a woman-owned restaurant where my colleagues at *Ms.* were giving me a party, I also sent announcements to a couple of journalists.

It was one of those reporters who kept insisting that I didn't *look* 40. And it was in reply that I explained, "This is what forty looks like. We've been lying so long, who would know?"

Only the public reaction to this accidental exchange made me understand how much more age is still a psychic barrier for women than for men. The quote was widely reported, with clippings coming back from Europe as well as here—even some translated into Hindi and Japanese. I'm still asked more about that one statement than any of the more serious facts I've tried to report.

But the truth was that I kept right on making assumptions about what being 50 would be like. Fifty was serious, grown-up, and finally old: a year that would be a rite of passage, a transformation, and a proof of mortality.

I'm not saying that I gave my own birthday real thoughtfulness as it finally approached. Growing up in the pragmatic Midwest still makes me choose action over introspection. . . . Activist friends also helped make this occasion useful in a way additional to truth-telling by suggesting that the occasion be turned into a fund-raiser for the foundation that publishes *Ms.* Magazine, as well as for the Ms. Foundation for Women, which is the magazine's parent; thus giving me extra time to lead up to this landmark . . . as well as the big present of having the chance to see many friends.

Nonetheless, I am still trying to work up a healthy sense of panic or at least concern about this birthday: behaving as if I were immortal may cause me to plan poorly, to say the least. Furthermore, lots of friends and strangers have been giving me advice about what I should do now, from running for political office (which I wouldn't be good at) to writing more (which I want very much to do); from having a baby (a very popular suggestion from gynecologists who see a chance to expand the late-birth market) to being sure *not* to get married (contrary to myth, many women seem proud that I and others can get through life both happy and single).

Though I know very well that my own conclusions depend greatly on the luck and luxury of having good health, good friends, and work I care about, I offer the following thoughts:

Fifty is what forty used to be. I mean that literally. Between 1970 and 1982 alone, life expectancy for white women increased from 75.6 years to 78.3; and, though any race gap is unacceptable, black women's life expectancy has increased even more, from 69.4 years to 74.5. Revolution seems to be good for our health. Furthermore, surveys show that middle-aged women in the paid labor force—in spite of problems of bad pay and job ghettoization—report being in better physical and mental health than do homemakers; a comment not on the worth of homemaking itself but on the isolation and low esteem that goes along with it. Contrary to the notion that women in "men's jobs" will get "men's diseases"—perhaps just a backlash argument that success will make us sick—the truth seems to be that self-esteem and a measure of success keep us going: not just in our heads but in our bodies.

The frontier of sexuality is being pushed back, too. From Angie Dickinson to Cicely Tyson, from Sophia Loren to Shirley MacLaine, women who already have passed or are about to reach 50 are remaining whole and sexual people in the public eye. It's true that the double standard is still cruel and effective: an over-50 Dan Rather is regarded as the young replacement for Walter Cronkite, for instance, but at the same age, Barbara Walters is treated as a miracle of longevity. Nonetheless, the 1940s Helen Trent soap opera question, "Can a woman over thirty-five find love and romance?" is now clearly a joke. And a handful of women like Lena Horne, Lauren Bacall, and Dinah Shore are pushing the public boundaries of womanliness past 60.

Women's ability to choose younger men is beginning to nibble away at the Insecurity Gap. I don't mean to oversell this point: there are still millions more bald and paunchy men with younger (and usually less prosperous) women than there are even the fittest women with younger men. But the slight increase in economic and social security that allows some women to choose men they actually like and share interests with, even if those men are younger or less established, is beginning to make some older men insecure in a way previously reserved exclusively for older women. Perhaps progress for women is becoming a little more sure of ourselves and for men, it's becoming a little less so.

All of the above may be separable from the question of mortality. The only real age *schreck* I've managed to produce occurred while I was brushing my teeth during my book tour and suddenly realized that, in about the same amount of time *Ms.* Magazine has been alive, I will be 60. This spelled closeness to death, even though the current state of medical arts could produce a life expectancy of 100 if actually applied. For me, it meant a sudden and heightened sense of how very, very much I still have to do before I die.

The truth is that defiance seems to be the best psychic way of lengthening our lives—and I am feeling more and more joyfully defiant. On the other hand, recognizing mortality is the best way to celebrate and maximize our lives in the present.

But at least now I know that fear of aging is not the same as fear of no longer living, as women especially have been encouraged to believe. I hope I can diminish the first and increase the second—for time is all there is.

A Tooth for Every Child

ABIGAIL THOMAS

LOUISE, who is pushing down the tall grasses near the land of menopause, accepts an invitation from Mona, who is not that far behind. Mona could use the sight of Louise. "I need a drinking companion," she says. Louise can hear the twins wailing in the background.

"We don't drink anymore," Louise reminds her.

"But we can talk about it, can't we? Remember pink gins?"

"That wasn't us, Mona, pink gins. That was our grandmothers."

"Don't quibble. Just get off the bus in Portland. I'll pick you up."

"I'll come Friday. Thursday I've got my teeth."

THE ONLY man in Louise's life right now is her Chinese dentist. Her entire sex life consists of his warm fingers in her mouth, against her cheek. She thinks of them as ten slender separate animals, so dexterous is he. She is undergoing root canal, paying the coward's price for years of neglect. Every Thursday she settles herself in his chair and he sets up what he calls the rubber dam. Eyes closed, Louise imagines a tent stretched from tree to tree. Under this canopy he sets to work chipping and drilling, installing a system of levees and drains. He stuffs tendrils of gutta-percha in the hollowed-out roots of her teeth and sets them on fire, reminding Louise of the decimation of the tropical rain forests. She imagines bright green parrots flying squawking out of her mouth, lizards running up the fingers of her dentist. Loves may come and loves may go, but dental work goes on forever, thinks Louise.

"You owe me nine thousand dollars," says Dr. Chan.

"WE'RE having a lot of work done," says Mona apologetically, as they pull off the country road and onto the rough dirt path that leads to the house Mona and Tony have built overlooking the lake.

"Aren't you embarrassed to be so successful?" asks Louise.

"It's not me, Louise. Blame Tony. All I've been recently is fertile. Wait till you see little Joe. He is anxious to see you."

Mona and Louise have been friends for thirty years. Louise had her babies first, four of them; she has been married twice, divorced twice. Her children have all grown up and gone except the baby, who at seventeen is in Italy this summer. Mona's first child, Joe, is five years old. She has twins, Ernie and Sue, eleven months. Louise wishes she had had her children later, when she knew better; Mona wishes she had done it when she was young. The two women are comfortable together, and Louise is planning to spend the week playing with the kids, sunning herself on the porch, reading.

Tony is off supervising the tennis court ("the tennis court?" Louise has repeated, incredulous), and Mona and she and little Joe are in the kitchen, Joe nestled in Louise's lap. Joe is learning about where babies come from. Mona is horrified to discover he thinks babies and peepee come from the same place, and Louise has taken it upon herself to explain about the three holes. A hole for peepee, a hole for poopoo, and the babyhole. "The babyhole is just for babies," Louise explains, proud of her succintness. She had told her own children, years ago, that she had made them all by herself, out of a special kit. "What is the babyhole used for when there aren't any babies?" asks little Joe, not unreasonably. Louise looks mournfully at Mona. "Well, not really much of anything," Louise says, "in a bad year." Mona bursts out laughing, and the two women cackle until their noses turn pink.

"The place is crawling with workmen," says Mona later. "You always wanted a guy who worked with his hands, remember? And the roofer is really quite choice. Fifty-three. Good hands."

"Do you talk like this in front of Tony?" asks Louise.

But it is the boy who catches Louise's eye first. Standing beside the path leading to the lake, he is bent over a snapping turtle the size of a Thanksgiving turkey. Louise doesn't know which to look at first, the long brown back of the boy or the spiky ridged shell of the turtle. So she stands there in the middle of the road looking from one to the other. Then the boy straightens up and turns toward Louise. "Oh my God," is what she says. She hopes he will think she is talking about the turtle.

"Ever see one this big?" he asks, nudging the shell with the toe of one work-booted foot and hitching his belt slightly so the hammer hangs down his left hip. His upper body is bare, his shoulders smooth and deeply muscled. His eyes and hair are almost black, and he has a red bandanna tied around his head. He is smiling at her.

"Not for a long time." Louise notices the turtle's head come poking out of its shell. "Careful," she warns him, "he might bite you." She is a mother, first and foremost.

"Nah, he wouldn't dare. I'm so mean I have to sleep with one eye open so I don't kick myself in the ass." He laughs, seeming to find himself vastly entertaining. His teeth are remarkably white, and there is a fine powdering of sawdust on his right cheekbone that she would like to brush off. "Don't you come too close, is all," he says to her. "This baby take you in his mouth, no telling when he'd turn you loose." He grins at Louise, who is oddly flustered. She feels fourteen years old. The boy shows no sign of boredom, of turning away from her, no sign of having anything better to do than to stand there and talk to her. She looks around to see who it is he is really talking to. Some young girl somewhere he is trying to impress.

"You up here for the whole summer?" he is asking her now. She shakes her head. "Friend of Mrs. Townshend's?" She nods. "Nice lady," the boy says, "very nice lady." He pauses. "So how long are you staying?"

"Just a week," she says. "I'm from New York."

"Figured that," he says, pulling a crumpled pack of Marlboros out of the back pocket of his jeans. "Smoke?" He offers her one.

"No, I quit. Three packs a day I used to do." Louise is bragging. She watches him cup his hands around the cigarette he is lighting, shake out the match and flick it in the dirt.

"No, I mean do you *smoke*," he says, making the quick sucking sounds of a joint.

"Oh, do I smoke. No," she says firmly, "I hate to smoke. I get paranoid."

He cocks his head to one side. "No kidding?" he says. "Not me. Hey, know what I call paranoia? Heightened awareness," and he cracks himself up again. He takes another drag and says after a moment's hesitation, "Would you like to see the countryside around here? I can take you for a drive later. That's my truck," he says proudly, pointing to a black Ford pickup parked a little down the road. It has a bumper sticker that reads TOO CUTE TO STAY HOME.

In one of those moments Louise is famous for, when she decides to do something without thinking, she says, "Yes, sure. Thank you very much." And then regrets it. "Well," she says, "see you," and hurries into her cabin where she goes directly to the bathroom and peers at herself in the mirror.

"Who was he talking to?" she asks out loud.

"So when is he picking you up?" Mona asks. The twins are having lunch in their highchairs.

"I don't know," says Louise. "I ran away. I'm not going."

"Of course you're going," says Mona, cutting up a hot dog for the twins. "You're doing it for me," she says. "If you don't, we'll both get old. Now go sit out there on that porch and wait for him to tell you what time."

"I can't. I feel like an enormous piece of bait," says Louise. "I feel like a ridiculous elderly baby bird."

"Out," says Mona firmly. "I'm going to ask Bridget to clean in here, and you have to be outside in the sun," she says, spooning mashed potato into Ernie's little mouth.

Louise sits tilted back in her chair. She has Auden face down in her lap, her own face turned toward the sun. Her legs and feet are bare against the railing of the deck. The house is built on a wooded hill above a lake, and through the trees Louise can see water glittering in the sun. She has been remembering the first time a boy opened her clothes. It was 1957 or '58, she and Tommy Morell were leaning against the scaffolding of what was to become the Loeb Student Center in Washington Square. She was wearing a new blue coat from the now-long-defunct De Pinna, it was freezing cold and they were standing out of the wind, kissing. She can remember today the taste of his mouth: decay and wintergreens. Every time somebody walked past, she would hide her face against his shoulder. And then she felt his hands on the front of her coat, the sensation taking a moment to travel through the many layers of her clothes, like light from a star; and his fingers were working at the buttons, the many small difficult buttons of this coat, and she was not pushing his hands away. Louise sighs. Amazing what else she has forgotten, but this scrap of memory is real as yesterday. This morning.

Louise is deep in daydream when hammering begins under the porch, startling her. Sitting in her thin cotton dress, the hammering directly beneath feels particularly intimate. She hears murmuring of men's voices, and the next thing she knows the boy has swung himself up over the railing, defying God knows what laws of physics, and is hunkering down next to her on the porch.

"So I'll pick you up at seven-thirty? I need to go home and get a shower first. Okay?"

"Well, sure," she says, "that's fine. Sure."

"See you later," and he grins and bounds back off the deck. His head reappears a moment later. "I'm Donny," he says. "You're—?"

"Louise."

"JUST wear what you have on," advises Mona, after Louise has changed her clothes three times. "That nice dress that buttons down the front."

"You don't think I look as if I'm trying to look like Little Bo-Peep?"

"Louise, that's the last thing I'd say you looked like. You look fine. You look really good, in fact. No wonder he asked you."

"Mona, what are we going to talk about? What am I going to say to this boy? I'm forty-fucking-six years old. I certainly can't talk about my kids. They're probably older than he is."

"I don't think you're going to be doing a whole lot of talking," says Mona. "I don't think talk is Donny's specialty."

Donny comes to the door to pick her up just like a real date. He is wearing a shirt tonight, which has the odd effect of making him seem even younger. Louise feels awkward when he says hello to Mona, calls Tony "sir." Louise can't get out of there fast enough. "Take my sweater, Louise," calls Mona. "It's outside there on the rocker."

Donny opens the door of the truck and closes it behind her when she is safely inside. Then he runs around and hops up on the driver's side. "Do you have any idea how old I am?" asks Louise when they are both sitting in the truck. She feels she should get this over with right away.

"Well, I know you're older than me." Donny turns to look at her. "I figure you're twenty-eight or so." Twenty-eight or so? Dear God. Twenty-eight or so?

"Oh," says Louise, "how old are you?"

"I'll be twenty-one next month."

"You're twenty," says Louise, closing her eyes briefly. "You're twenty years old."

"Yeah, but I'll be twenty-one next month," he repeats, and turns the key in the ignition and the truck starts to vibrate pleasantly, reminding Louise, not surprisingly, of an enormously powerful animal just barely held in check. "Ready?" he asks.

She is looking at how loosely his hand rests on the stick shift. She nods, watching his hand tighten on the stick, the muscles in his arm bulging slightly as he puts the truck in first and they begin lurching down the steep path that leads to the highway.

"Wahoo!" he yells, thrusting his body half out the window, then he ducks back in and grins at Louise. "Couldn't help it," he says sheepishly. "I just feel good." She smiles at him.

Louise is now completely at ease. As soon as the truck started moving she felt something inside her click into place. She knows exactly who she is and what she is doing. She is a blond-headed woman in the front seat of a moving vehicle, she is nobody's mother, nobody's former wife, nobody's anything. Louise is a girl again.

A mile down the highway Donny fishes around under his seat and comes up with a Sucrets box, which he hands her. "Can you light me up the joint? Matches on the dash." Louise opens the box and picks the joint up. It is lying next to loose grass and on top of a bunch of rolling papers. Louise hasn't smoked a joint in a long time. The last time she did, she became convinced that she was about to become dinner: about to be minced, put in a cream sauce, and run under the broiler. She was at a party being given by her then-new husband's old friends.

"I don't really smoke," she begins, and then, "Oh, what the hell," she says, shrugging, and lights the joint. "Maybe I've changed," she says, talking mostly to herself.

"Maybe the company has changed," says Donny, and she can't imagine what he thinks he means by that, but they are passing the joint back and forth, and Louise is beginning to feel pretty good. Something lovely is happening deep in her throat, some awareness she has never experienced before. "God, I've got such an interesting *throat*," she says, and Donny laughs.

"You're getting high," he says.

"I am?" Louise sits up straight.

"You okay? Feeling okay?"

"I think I feel good," she says, taking stock. "Yes," she announces rather formally, "I feel really quite good." Donny slows down and takes a right turn into what he calls a sand pit. It is a parking area off the road, behind a kind of berm. "Let's roll another," he says, proceeding to do so. Louise watches fascinated; she has always loved watching people use their hands. When he licks the paper to seal the cigarette she sees his tongue is pink. This kid's tongue is actually pink, oh lordy lordy, thinks Louise.

"Why don't you have a girlfriend?" she wants to know.

"I had a girlfriend. She moved out three months ago. She left me a note saying she was going to Wyoming." Donny snaps the Sucrets box shut now and looks for the matches.

"Oh. Crummy. Were you sad?"

"For a while. Thing that made it easier was she took my damn stereo. Hard to be sad and pissed at the same time. But yeah, we had some good times. Bummed me out she couldn't tell me to my face she was going."

"She probably wouldn't have been able to leave, then."

"Yeah. That's what she said in her note." He offers her the new joint to light, but she shakes her head.

"What was her name?"

"Robin. But anybody asks me now 'how's Robin?' know what I say? 'Robin who?' I say, 'Robin who?' " Donny laughs and then turns his head to look out the window. "Company," he says, as a red Toyota pulls in. "Let's go somewhere a little less public. Want to see the lake?"

"Sure," says Louise. "Anything." What a nice state Maine is to provide sand pits and lakes for its citizens to park in, Louise is thinking. They head off and stop along the way to see the school Donny was kicked out of. It is a plain, one-story brick building that Louise thinks privately looks pretty depressing, but Donny is driving around it slowly, almost lovingly. "You had a good time here?" she asks him.

"Yep. I had a good time here."

"How come they kicked you out?"

"Oh, this and that. I was a hothead then, I guess. I'm a lot calmer now, though you might not believe it. Straightening myself out. Full-time job in itself," he laughs. "Full-time job in itself."

"I like hotheaded," says Louise. "I always did."

Donny, who has been circling the school building, pulls over to the far end of the lot and parks under a tree. Turns the engine off and they look at each other in the fading light of the summer evening, a little moon starting to show between the trees; a street light blinks on thirty feet away. They look at each other, and then he reaches quite frankly for her, or perhaps she reaches for him, but his hands are on her dress, the front of her dress at the buttons, and his dark head is against her neck, his breath everywhere. Her hands are in his hair, under his shirt, feeling the tight muscles of his belly above his belt. Fumbling. Then they are kissing, and, because his window does not close completely, the truck fills with mosquitoes, and they are kissing and slapping and slapping and cursing and laughing and kissing and kissing and kissing. Donny drags a blanket out from behind his seat, and they stumble out of the truck and onto the grass, and Louise is lying down under a million or so stars. "I wanted to fuck you the first time I saw you, to tell you the truth," Donny is whispering as he lowers his body down on hers.

They sleep in the truck that night, parked near the lake that seems to be everywhere. Or rather, Donny sleeps, his head in Louise's lap. Louise is awake all night, watching the woods drain of moonlight and fill up again slowly with a misty brightness that seems to rise from the ground. Donny's body is arranged somehow around the gearshift, his head and shoulders resting on Louise. He sleeps like a baby. She looks at his closed eyes, dark lashes, his straight black brows. His skin is beautiful, like silk. Dear God, how came this beautiful wild child to be asleep in my lap, thinks Louise. At six, she jiggles his shoulder. "Time to wake up," she says. "We've been gone all night."

"What if I refuse to take you back?" he asks sleepily. "Suppose I just decide to keep you?"

MONA is up, of course, when Louise gets in. The twins are out with Bridget; little Joe and Tony are down by the lake doing something with boats. "Don't let Tony see you," says Mona. "I told him you got in late last night. You know Tony." Tony has never approved of Louise, not since she asked him if she could upend herself in his laundry hamper. "For the pheromones," she had explained. "It's been so long since the last good kiss." Louise had read somewhere that women who lived without the company of men were apt to age more quickly.

"Why can't she just ride the subway at rush hour?" Tony had asked irritably. "Plenty of nice hair tonic and body sweat in there. Why does it have to be my laundry?"

"So?" says Mona now, pouring two cups of coffee. "Or don't I really want to know?"

"I'll say one word," says Louise, "to satisfy your curiosity, because I know it's on your mind. Hung."

"*Comme* zee horse?" Mona is leaning forward.

"*Comme* zee horse."

"Ahhhh."

"And you know what else? I like him, I actually like him. He's working so hard to grow up. His girlfriend left him, and he had to move back with his parents because he couldn't afford the rent by himself. He works his ass off. I like him."

"Yeah? Well, great, but don't start taking this seriously."

"He's picking me up again tonight. You know what? Staying up all night makes me feel young again, isn't that weird? I haven't been this tired since I was young."

"Go lie down. I'll wake you up at lunch."

"Mona? I loved not talking about my kids. It was like being twenty myself, you know? It was like not having a tail I had to fit everywhere. I'm never going to tell anyone about my kids again."

"Louise, you're delirious. Go upstairs and lie down."

"Good night."

"Louise?" calls Mona, as Louise disappears up the stairs. "You're being careful? I'm not talking about babies, you know what I'm talking about."

Louise's head appears around the corner. "Mona," she says, "Do you think I was born yesterday?"

Two days later Donny takes off work. "I've got vacation time coming," he says. "I'm taking you four-wheeling. That is if you want to drive around with me for a few days."

Mona is worried. "I hope you're not taking this seriously," she keeps saying. "I know how you can get, Louise, and I don't want you to get involved with a twenty-year-old boy who lives with his parents."

"Come on, Mona, I haven't had this much fun in my whole life," says

Louise. "I'm twenty years old myself this week. The last time I was twenty I had two children and an ex-husband in the making."

Mona's expression relaxes. "All right, but I don't want to hear a word of complaint out of you for eighteen months, and I hope you have plenty of raw meat for the trip."

LOUISE feels like a summer house this kid has broken into, pushing his way through doors that haven't been opened in years, snapping up blinds, windows, pulling dust covers off furniture, shaking rugs, curtains, bouncing on the beds. A fine, honorable old house, and he appreciates the way it has been made, the way it has lasted, the strength of its structure, noble old dimensions. It has been a long time since Louise was put to such good use.

"What's the longest you've ever gone without making love?" she asks him.

"Fifteen years," he answers.

Louise loves his raw energy, and the lavish way he squanders it on pointless undertakings, impossible feats, such as driving the truck directly up the steep woodside of a mountain whenever he thinks he spies faint tracks. (Louise sees only dense woods.) He screeches the truck to a stop, leaps down to lock the front wheels, jumps back inside to do something sexy to the gears, pausing to kiss Louise for five minutes, and then he coaxes, bullies, cajoles the truck off the road and into the trees. Louise loves it. She loves everything about him by now. She loves the muscles in his shoulders, the veins in his forearms. "I like how you touch me," he whispers. She wants him to explain everything he knows, the difference between a dug and an artesian well, how to build a ladder, hang a door, put a roof on. "You're really interested?" he asks her. "You really want to know?" She nods. "The plumb line is God," he begins gravely.

Louise is as close to carefree as she has ever been. There is nothing behind her, her past is not part of this trip, and nothing in front but a dashboard full of music and the open road. They like the same music, sing the same songs. Stevie Ray Vaughn, the Georgia Satellites, Tom Petty and the Heartbreakers. "Break Down" is their favorite song and they blast it all week, yelling it out the windows, singing it to each other in the truck, and then they collapse laughing, this forty-six-year-old woman and this twenty-year-old boy, who are having the time of their lives. They rent a room in a motel when they get tired of fighting off the mosquitoes. Louise uses her Visa card expecting any minute the long arm of the law to grab her by the collar, bring her to her senses. Donny is bent over the register saying, "You'll want an address?" and Louise hears the manager saying, "Oh, just put anything," with a knowing snicker. For just a second, she feels gawky, naked. How many good years does she have left, she wonders, before she appears pathetic. Right now she can still get away with it, but fifty approaches, the hill she will one day be over is looming in the distance. So when the manager shows them the room and it contains two double-decker beds, one cot, and a king-size four-poster, Louise rubs her hands together largely for his benefit and says, "Good. We can really use the room."

They order Chinese take-out that night from an improbable place down the road, and Louise bites down into something hard in her moo shu pork and, spitting it into her hand, she sees it is a human tooth. She hurries into the bathroom and locks the door. "You all right in there?" asks Donny, knocking. It is Louise's tooth, her temporary cap, and she rinses it off and jams it back in her mouth praying to God it will stay. "Donny," she says, coming out of the bathroom. "I've got to tell you how old I am. Guess what, I'm forty-six." He doesn't seem particularly interested. "I'm forty-six, did you hear me?"

"Yeah?" He is lying down on the big bed, his hands behind his head. "So?"

"And what's more I have four kids, and three of them are older than you, and I have two grandchildren on top of that." Louise seems out of breath all of a sudden. He just looks at her.

"Come here," he says. She goes there. He grabs her hand. "I guess that makes me some kind of motherfucker," he says with a lazy grin, pulling her down on the bed. "Stick with me, I won't let you get old," he says, into her hair. "But I am old," she wants to moan, "I already am old."

"Why are a woman's breasts always softest in the evening?" he wants to know, pulling her toward him.

Louise is awake all night. "You can't kiss all the time," a friend of hers once said, by way of explaining having picked up a few words of Italian one summer. "You can't kiss all the time." Louise thinks she knows this, she knows it is time to go back to the grown-ups, back to New York, her office. Back to real life. This isn't real life, this relationship relies too heavily on rock 'n' roll and the open road. Real life is not this dream come true, it is long winter nights with nothing to talk about. You can't kiss all the time. "I'll build you a house," Donny said yesterday. "Stay. I'll build you a house."

He knows before she tells him that she is going home. He is quiet all morning, sullen even. "What's the matter?" she asks, but he shakes off her hand.

"You're leaving."

"But I'm coming back. I'm coming back for your birthday."

"But you're leaving, right?"

She nods.

"Well, I'm bummed."

She tells him about the office, the mail, her apartment, bills unpaid, her daughter coming home from Europe soon.

"What do you want for your birthday?" she asks him.

"You."

"You've got me. What else?"

"More of you."

"You've got me. What else?"

"Am I asking too much?"

BACK in New York, Louise is lonelier than she expected to be. New York is gritty, dirty, sad. Her apartment is so empty, quiet. Louise is of an age now when most of the men in her life are former lovers who fly in from nowhere for a couple of days every six years or so; they sit on her chairs, eat at her table, sleep in her bed, and when they leave they leave a kind of half-life behind, an absence so palpable it is almost a presence. The furniture rebukes Louise on these occasions. "So where'd he go?" asks the white sofa, the pink chair. The bed. But Donny has never been here, so she has to conjure up his memory out of whole cloth, so to speak. And she misses him more than she thought she would.

In fact, she talks of little else. She is as apt to pull pictures of Donny out of her wallet as of her grandsons. "You're in luck," she might have said a month ago, "I have fifty-three new pictures of my grandsons." Now she takes seven photographs out of her wallet, they are all of Donny, and she lays them out on the table like a row of solitaire. "So," she says, to anyone who will listen. "You know that poem by Auden? 'Lay your sleeping head my love'?" Her friends are respectful, for the most part silent. They let her play it out.

"Do we sleep with the young to stay young ourselves or just to lie down next to all that beauty?" Louise wants to know. Mona is irritated. They are together in Riverside Park with the kids. Joe is in the sandbox, Mona and Louise are pushing the twins in the little swings. "Neither," says Mona. "How should I know?" she snaps. Then, more gently, "To lie down next to all that beauty."

"I knew it," says Louise, hopping. "I knew it!"

"I'm worried about you," says Mona. "I mean, I hope you're not being faithful to him or anything."

Louise bursts out laughing. "Come on, Mona. Who am I going to go out with? The dry cleaner?"

"I'm just concerned you might get hurt. You let your emotions get involved."

"Well, of course I let my emotions get involved. What the hell is the point if you don't let your emotions get involved? But it's not like going out for ice cream and coming home and saying, 'Gee, I wish I hadn't had that ice cream.' I liked the kid. I loved the kid, if you want to know."

"Just what I was afraid of. And I certainly don't think you should go back up there for his birthday. Enough is enough."

"I promised him I'd go. I promised him."

BUT LOUISE has not heard from Donny, and though she has left messages with his mother (an exquisitely humiliating experience), he has not returned her calls. The night before she is supposed to get on the bus she finally gets him on the phone. She does not want to keep her end of the bargain and wind up sitting on a suitcase in a parking lot in Portland waiting for Godot. It is a bad connection, and she can barely hear him, and she has to keep repeating "What?" into the telephone like an old woman with an ear trumpet.

"Are we still on for tomorrow?" she shouts, although she already knows the answer.

"Things have changed around here," Donny says. His voice sounds so foreign, so young.

"So do you still want me to come up tomorrow?" Louise is amazed at how painful this is.

"I guess now is not a good time," he says, but she can barely hear him.

"What?"

"No," he says, "not this time."

"Well, Happy Birthday to you," she says, hanging up the phone.

"WOULD you mind removing your lipstick?" asks Dr. Chan, handing Louise a tissue. He always makes this request, but Louise wears it to his office just the same. She likes to look her best for the dentist. Dr. Chan wears his hair cut short except for three very long, very skinny braids, and Louise has always been too shy to inquire as to their significance.

"Today we put in your permanent tooth," says Dr. Chan, setting out his instruments, mixing his little pots of cement.

"That's good," says Louise, "because this one fell out over the summer and I had to put it back myself. 'A tooth for every child,' " she adds, but Dr. Chan does not ask after her meaning.

She settles back in her chair. The land of menopause stretches out behind her closed lids, as Dr. Chan easily removes the temporary cap. It seems to be a quiet place, resembling a kind of savannah. There are mountains in the distance. There doesn't appear to be much activity beyond a certain amount of flank-nuzzling, as far as Louise can tell. But who knows? She has heard some odd cries at night, down by the water hole.

Late Loving

MONA VAN DUYN

What Christ was saying, what he meant [in the story of Mary and Martha] was that the pleasures of that hair, that ointment, must be taken. Because the accidents of death would deprive us soon enough. We must not deprive ourselves, our loved ones, of the luxury of our extravagant affections. We must not try to second-guess death by refusing to love the ones we loved. . . .

MARY GORDON, *Final Payments*

If in my mind I marry you every year
it is to calm an extravagance of love
with dousing custom, for it flames up fierce
and wild whenever I forget that we live
in double rooms whose temperature's controlled
by matrimony's turned-down thermostat.
I need the mnemonics, now that we are old,
of oath and law in re-memorizing that.
Our dogs are dead, our child never came true.
I might use up, in my weak-mindedness,
the whole human supply of warmth on you
before I could think of others and digress.
"Love" is finding the familiar dear.
"In love" is to be taken by surprise.
Over, in the shifty face you wear,
and over, in the assessments of your eyes,
you change, and with new sweet or barbed word
find out new entrances to my inmost nerve.
When you stand at the stove it's I who am most stirred.
When you finish work I rest without reserve.
Daytimes, sometimes, our three-legged race seems slow.
Squabbling onward, we chafe from being so near.
But all night long we lie like crescents of Velcro,

turning together till we re-adhere.
Since you, with longer stride and better vision,
more clearly see the finish line, I stoke
my hurrying self, to keep it in condition,
with light and life-renouncing meals of smoke.
As when a collector scoops two Monarchs in
at once, whose fresh flights to and from each other
are netted down, so in vows I re-imagine
I re-invoke what keeps us stale together.
What you try to give is more than I want to receive,
yet each month when you pick up scissors for our appointment
and my cut hair falls and covers your feet I believe
that the house is filled again with the odor of ointment.

 Coming of Age

CAROLYN HEILBRUN

SIGNS OF AGE come upon women in our society like marks of the devil in earlier times. And it seems that we must either fight them by inflicting painful and irreversible acts upon our bodies or allow ourselves to be captured by regret, resentment and despair. For no one, certainly not for any woman, do the marks of age come easily, or without terror. "They are all young, these people who suddenly find that they are old," Simone de Beauvoir has said. "One day," she continues, "I said to myself: 'I'm forty!' By the time I recovered from the shock of that discovery I had reached fifty." The shock of that discovery is a choice: whether to live as a different woman or die as an old woman pretending to be young.

Old is a dirty word in our culture. If I say I am old, outrage is heard from all quarters. But you are not old, they say, you are vigorous, powerful, doing wonderful things. Exactly. And I am (thank God) no longer young. "But you don't look your age," they argue, in a last-ditch stand. "Yes, I do," I say. "I look the way I feel at the age I am."

But I cannot redeem the word old. It is a down word, a depressant, a doom. So we speak of midlife, a neologism to suggest the time when we can be called neither young nor old. This is the span I want to recover for women, the extended moment that can become a new rite of passage, an initiation. The only occasion I can think of to match it is the swearing in of a federal judge: She has ascended to a new position, a new rank, a new chance for effectiveness, and she can remain there until she dies or turns her mind to something else. No one asks where the male gaze would place her on a scale of one to ten. She lives outside the male gaze. Her value is not determined by whether she turns men on, whether their eyes light up on beholding how she looks. Their eyes light up when they recognize the person she is.

As a person, however, the judge, or any woman, faces more than the threat of not looking young, of drowning in a raftless sea of sunken flesh. Age, De Beauvoir has told us, changes the individual's relationship to time and therefore her relationship to the world. De Beauvoir has been there. "I loathe my appearance now: the eyebrows slipping down toward the eyes, the bags underneath, the excessive fullness of the cheeks and that air of sadness around the mouth that wrinkles always bring." But she did nothing to her body to change it, and her biographer Deirdre Bair writes of her wonderful new life in her fifties, sixties and seventies. Many people now sought her out for her help and advice. Instead of trying to recapture the old life, designed in the hope that men would look at her with desire, she moved into the new world of age where her voice, her ability to affect events, increased. She did not die back into youth; she lived in her age.

De Beauvoir moved from anger at aging to the discovery of a new life. Men were still there. Younger men might be lovers. But she had undergone the rite: She had passed from youth to age without trying artificially to keep her youth. She bemoaned it as all passing pleasures are bemoaned. But she allowed herself to be transformed, not by cosmetic surgery, or the infusion of silicone, or the removal of ribs or fat, but by looking to another country, a foreign country, where they do things differently. (In *The Go-Between*, L. P. Hartley said that of the past; I say it of the future.)

Neither the gaze of men nor her former need for them to gaze will define the life of a woman who has undertaken this rite of passage. John Berger has said all that is finished: "*Men act* and *women appear. Men look at women. Women watch themselves being looked at. This determines not only most relations between men and women but also the relation of women to themselves. The surveyor of woman in herself is male: the surveyed female. Thus she turns herself into an object—and most particularly an object of vision: a sight.*" As she ages, a woman must escape (if and for a time in camouflage) from that gaze. She may love men, cherish them as friends and comrades, sons, husbands, fathers. But they will not define how she will look. Men will still say, "If I am not turned on just by looking at you, you are no longer woman." She will answer, "Only youth has that talent, and I will not impersonate youth; I will not live in drag for your sake. I will not try to pass as young."

Women athletes and dancers, like their male counterparts, know they must prepare for a life when the youthful confidence of their bodies has deserted them. None believes she can imitate youth. All women should live as dancers: recognizing physical facts, eschewing the tricks that promise, but cannot deliver, extended youth. We must learn to move with confidence into a new, as yet unnamed, life. A life, birth and not death, where we live by what we do, not by how we look or who looks at us. In the disguise of age, we explore and then live in this new world. As real as the men in the world we formerly occupied, we will take the reality we recognized only in them and claim it for ourselves.

This rite of passage is no easier than most initiations, and it takes longer. It recognizes stages. The first is often hair, because for too many, our body tells us our life is ready to move on. I am asked by most of the women around forty I know (and, more and more, most of the women I know are around forty), Should I dye my hair? I suppose we all begin by plucking out the gray hairs, combing them from sight. And then comes the question. My answer is: Dye it if you feel more comfortable that way. My own random sample suggests that many women will stop dyeing their hair after a few years, but a few will persist even on their deathbeds. It doesn't really matter; so long as we do not think that we can successfully impersonate youth, we should do, with hair dye and makeup, what offers us the chance to take our bodies for granted. For as women enter this new phase of life, this new landscape, they should not underestimate the importance of camouflage. One wears camouflage in the jungle, I understand, so as to be overlooked by snipers: The same protection is recommended for our risky journey. But camouflage is only skin deep; its salient characteristic is that it can be shed when in safety. To make actual changes in the body, as with cosmetic surgery, is to go unsuccessfully into the jungle in a disguise assuring defeat.

No one finds it easy to overlook the fact that as older women we will have to be what we do; we will watch ourselves grow invisible to youth worshipers, and to the male gaze. Despair is inevitable but must be wrestled with. The hardest initiation lies ahead, an initiation as in a fairy tale, readying one for a quest: To get to that new place, a woman must pass through the stage of invisibility. We will be mysteriously unseen. We will not be noticed immediately upon entering a store, a party, a meeting. We will move invisibly for a time, to relearn seeing and to forget being seen. As we grow slowly visible, we will be heard more and seen less. Our voices will ramify, our bodies will become the house for our new spirit.

The alternative to escaping the male gaze is trying to hold it, and the measures are desperate: surgical intrusions on the body that cannot be undone, and that are only briefly if at all effective. Worse, they increase the fear of age, enhancing its intensity. I once met a woman who had had her face lifted, breasts injected with silicone, fat removed by operations on thighs and stomach and bottom ribs cut out to give her an apparent waist. I looked at her with interest. Thin and brittle, she was a midlife woman embalmed in youth. On a stage, an actress may get away with it; in life, never. In life, one should encourage youth, not try to be it.

I have recently been amused, reading the many new biographies of women, at how unhappy the biographer becomes with a subject who has allowed herself to grow fatter in later years. Yet these very women — Margaret Mead, for example — had no problem living a full life, fat or not. I remember years ago seeing Mead dining at a table full of attentive men in a restaurant where I sat with someone devoted to the old female script: Make men admire my looks. Clout and a passion for accomplishment, perhaps for a cause, count more than a waistline in keeping the attention of the world. Power and influence are discovered not under the surgeon's knife but in the world of that other country, where they do things differently.

Colette comes to mind here, triumphant into her last, long years. "I am merely alone and not abandoned," she wrote. To men she said, "What you see emerging from a confused heap of feminine castoffs, still weighed down like a drowned woman by seaweed . . . is your sister, your comrade: a woman who is escaping from the age when she is a woman. She has, like you, rather a thick neck, bodily strength that becomes less graceful as it weakens and that authority which shows you that you can no longer make her despair, or only dispassionately."

Many women hovering near fifty have whispered to me and I to them of how the world opens up, of the mysterious change, the surge of freedom, the possibility of new adventures, indeed of birth, when they can say, "I am not young, I do not want to be young, I do not want men to look at me as though I were young. My life no longer starts with my body, with how I look. In the spectrum of camouflage, I am now at the far end with no camouflage whatever. I have gray hair that I keep in a bun and I wear glasses, but who I am is what I do, what I say, and whom I love. I have passed through the magic circle of invisibility into a new life."

In Gabriel García Márquez's novel *Love in the Time of Cholera*, someone accuses a character of being rich. "No," he answers, "not rich. I am a poor man with money, which is not the same thing." So when someone tries to complement us who have been initiated into this special time of life by telling us we look young, we must say, "No, not young. I am an older woman with pizzazz, which is not the same thing."

Miracles in the Sky and on the Road

CYNTHIA KADOHATA

A MIRACLE is in the eye of the beholder, thought Hisako. She'd just seen a westbound jet fly nearly across the sky and then, with a sudden turn, fly back to the east. When the jet flew out of sight, she sat down at a table in her small living room. Fifteen years earlier, shortly before her second husband died, one of her daughters had given her the table. Hisako lived in one of the best Japanese retirement homes in Los Angeles; the management let you keep your own things.

A commercial came on the television as she tapped a pen on a pad of paper. A dog dressed as Santa Claus started singing and kittens in green caps danced around him.

A couple of blocks over, hundreds of homeless and drug addicts sat on the sidewalks, but here in Little Tokyo Hisako felt insulated. Except to see her doctor, she never left the area unless one of her kids or grandkids came to pick her up.

She wrote "jetliner" on a piece of paper. Every week she listed strange things she'd seen. Hisako's kids thought she was eccentric, thought the odd things she saw in clusters were random, but Hisako knew the world always gave you signs, and you were responsible for figuring out what they meant.

For instance, once on the way to an art class at the senior center she passed two boys spray-painting graffiti in red, and when she got to class several students were wearing red sweaters. On the way home, she saw a young boy, strikingly beautiful except for his bloodshot right eye. She decided all the red meant the devil was chasing her and she should drop her class. She didn't know why fate wouldn't want her to take the art class, but she took one instead called "Improving Your Vocabulary." She thought with pride of how she'd gotten 100 on the final exam. To her that proved she'd been correct about the signs.

Since her life consisted mostly of habits, it was easy to figure out what the signs she saw meant—they usually referred to one of the uncommon events going on in her life. The most unusual recent event was that her first husband, Satoru, whose second wife, Fumi, had died in her sleep a few weeks earlier, had called from his nursing home to ask whether he could spend Christmas with her family, since he had no family of his own left. Even before he'd gotten sick, he'd lived in the home to be with Fumi, who'd had Alzheimer's.

Over the years, he'd called Hisako once in a while—that is, whenever he wanted a favor. Sat and Fumi had been married on Christmas, which for a long time had made the holiday an unhappy one for Hisako. She'd loved her first husband, and he'd broken her heart, but she still couldn't escape a sense of obligation to him as his former wife. She turned up the TV, just for some extra noise. "Why did the jet turn around?" she wrote on her paper.

ONE of Hisako's granddaughters was a happy, lovely girl only too glad to spend time with her, but the girl wasn't free to help pick up Sat at his home. It was Hisako's other granddaughter, her glum one, who helped her out. Lorraine was almost 30, the only Japanese girl Hisako had ever seen with stringy hair. She did have an extraordinary complexion, but she needed to pluck her eyebrows and shave the hair over her lips.

Lorraine picked her up at noon on Christmas Eve and they headed to central California and Sat's home. It was a warm day, the horizon misty but clear of smog. Lorraine silently drove along the highway blowing smoke into the car as Hisako smothered coughs. Even Lorraine's car was glum, a tiny messy thing that smoked, hissed and growled. As they rode along a particularly barren stretch of interstate, Hisako tried to start a conversation. "It would be nice to live in the wide open, though I'd miss having neighbors."

Lorraine lit a cigarette before replying. "Neighbors are pigs. They should all be killed."

Goodness. Goodness. Hisako didn't say another word until they arrived at the nursing home several hours later.

Sat was sitting on the outside steps, a bag at his side, looking like a boy running away from home. He bowed extravagantly, the way a white person might, and kissed their hands. "Lovely girl, very pretty, like her grandmother," he said to Lorraine, as charming a liar as always. But when he was young the charming lies seemed effortless and natural.

Now Hisako could see the effort it took this bony old man to lie.

The last time Hisako had been here she'd seen Fumi scratching with a pen on a sheet of paper as a nurse looked on bored. Fumi had possessed neither beauty nor particular intelligence, but she'd been gifted with a gentleness such as Hisako had never seen before or since.

Satoru pushed at Lorraine with his cane. "Time is short, dear. I don't want to push you, but maybe just encourage."

"Whatever," she mumbled. Behind the wheel of the car, she said, "Where's he staying, anyway?"

"At your aunt's," said Hisako.

THEY ate fast food for dinner and set off for Los Angeles. It got dark as Lorraine sped down the interstate. The scenery seemed unfamiliar to Hisako as she drifted in and out of sleep. After a while Lorraine mumbled something about being lost and turned hard left, across one of the dirt pathways the Highway Patrol used to cross the median. Hisako watched sleepily as they drove in the opposite direction. Opposite . . . same as the jet . . . another sign? She dozed off and woke to hear Sat talking.

"Gee, you're a wonderful driver," he said. "But when do we stop?"

Lorraine didn't answer, just tugged at the skin on her lips.

Hisako pulled her sweater closer around herself, becoming aware that she was cold and that her back was starting to hurt. "A motel?" she said.

Lorraine stared blankly out the windshield.

"I need to pee bad," Sat said. Lorraine pulled off the highway and down a back road, the car bouncing precariously.

When she stopped she left the parking lights on so they could see. Sat, seeming embarrassed to have to pee in front of them, started making conversation. "This is grade-A prime nature! It's good to go out into nature and do some kind of thing once in a while." No one replied and he set off. He walked perhaps 100 yards, feeling with his cane as if he were blind.

His dark form looked like a cutout against the stars. He'd shrunk a few inches over time. Hisako had seen him probably once a year for the past 55 years. How she had cried when he'd left her, left her not because he was having an affair with Fumi, not because he'd ever even kissed her, but because he hoped to, and he knew Fumi wouldn't accept the attentions of a married man.

In the distance he zipped up his pants. She felt a pang in her back. "We should find a motel," she said firmly.

"Whatever," said Lorraine.

They checked into a place with beds that creaked like coffin lids. Outside, the swimming pool was full of leaves and surrounded by a chain-link fence. It was only 9 o'clock. Hisako lay on the floor for a bit, to help her back. Right before Sat had gone into his room, he'd scratched shyly at the ground with his cane. "Thanks, wonderful lady," he said to Lorraine. To Hisako he said, apropos of nothing, "Fumi would have been miserable if she'd outlived me."

Lorraine's bed creaked as she turned over. Hisako loved her granddaughter, but she didn't understand her at all, didn't understand, for example, why she wouldn't shave her mustache the way Hisako had always religiously shaved her own. She fell asleep and, later, from a dream, thought she heard Lorraine crying.

Everyone woke early, when it was still dark, and set off for the San Fernando Valley, where Sat would be staying. It was not really night and not really morning. In Los Angeles, Lorraine drove up through the Hollywood Hills rather than taking a direct route. Even this early, a waterfall of car lights spilled over a freeway down below and a still fog rimmed the hills. "I always do this," Lorraine said suddenly, then turned off the headlights and put the car in neutral. They floated down a hill. The car was low on gas, and the orange fuel light flickered in the dark. When they passed a street lamp, it was odd to see the shadow from their car jump out in front of them. Hisako felt she should suggest to her granddaughter that this was an unsafe way to drive, but she didn't because the ride was so enjoyable.

It surprised her that the glum girl beside her should have discovered this new way of driving. Lorraine's face held a contradictory expression, sort of a furious serenity. In the dim light she wasn't pretty but she possessed an unearthly quality that was astounding. Hisako had never noticed that quality before, but now it seemed like the most obvious thing about her.

A white coyote sprang through the trees and turned to watch them. Christmas lights sparkled in the houses as they passed quietly by. Finally Lorraine turned on the lights and began driving normally. When they reached her aunt's house, Sat got out of the car. They were quiet for a moment. "Where did you learn to drive like that?" Hisako said.

"Well, it's like this," Lorraine answered. "Do you think the face on Mars is real?" Hisako didn't know why she'd asked that; indeed, she herself couldn't see a single star in the sky, let alone a face on Mars. "I do," said Lorraine with unusual animation. "And you know how scientists crossed a firefly and a flower? Well, I think on other planets they don't have to do that because it's natural for flowers to glow like fireflies. And I think somewhere, right here in this city, there's a place for me. So one night when I was thinking about finding that place, I started driving like that." She stopped talking abruptly, then said, "He told me something when you fell asleep in the car."

"What?"

"He told me to tell you he smothered Fumi in her sleep. He said he did it because he's going to die and there was no one to take care of her."

"I know," Hisako was surprised to hear herself say. She hadn't known until now that she knew, and had known from the moment Sat told her of Fumi's death. She'd known two couples who'd decided to die together, and she wondered what Fumi would have decided had she been able. When she'd last seen Fumi at the nursing home, Sat had still been enraptured by her and her gentleness, though she could no longer recognize him. But Hisako wondered whether Fumi had still been able to feel a soft breeze, or hear the sound of leaves. Sat had always been a user, but he'd loved Fumi alone among everyone in the world—friends, family, neighbors, girlfriends—whom he could have loved, should have loved.

IN THE END, his life had been Fumi and only Fumi. And now she was gone, as he soon would be. In her own life Hisako had seen many sad things, and after they were over she'd walked away from them the way she imagined a man must walk away from a battlefield, without faulting either friend or enemy. If fault should be found, that was for later, and probably for her.

Cool wind seeped through the car window. Lorraine started the engine. Hisako turned to look at Sat sitting expressionless with his bag as they drove off. She remembered how when she and her second husband had driven off to their new life, she'd felt hopeful and desperate, hopeful she could trust this man she now loved, and desperate to hold on to her signs. As years passed, she'd felt only hopeful and not desperate, and, finally, she'd become happy. She'd trusted her second husband deeply in the end. By then, thinking about signs had become a habit.

Lorraine drove into the hills and put the car in neutral again, her face taking on that contradictory expression as they began to glide. Hisako's second husband had once said that everything beautiful was a contradiction, like the way lightning in a rainstorm lit up the sky like fire in a sea; also the way, Hisako thought now, her first Christmas without Sat had been one of her hardest days, but today Christmas was the only time she saw all her family in one place. She thought about how long it had taken her to trust her second husband; about how she'd never felt close to Lorraine until this moment; and about how, someday, Lorraine would realize that her place in the city was exactly here, gliding through the dark streets, her face aglow with hope and desperation as she searched for a world that was right in front of her eyes.

Mrs. Moonlight

HELEN NORRIS

DURING the night she would forget about the treehouse. In the morning when she heard the hammering, like a woodpecker gone just a little wild, she would go outside and look at Mr. Snider halfway up the tree and say to him, "What are you building?" And he would stop and tell her gravely, "Ma'am, I'm making you this treehouse like you ast me to do." And then she would remember. To forget and then remember made a wonderful surprise at the start of each day. Sometimes she remembered without having to be told. But whichever way it was, she was happy about the treehouse.

She didn't tell him that she planned to live in it. She knew better than that. She told him that she wanted it for her granddaughter Mitzi. He didn't guess she would live there to be out of her daughter's hair once and for all so the question of the nursing home would disappear.

Her daughter was to be away from home for two weeks; she sold cosmetics on the road. And Mrs. Gideon figured she could get the treehouse ready in that length of time and be all moved in when her daughter got back. So she asked Mr. Snider what his charge would be. He added up numbers in his little gray notebook with the stub of a pencil he kept hanging from it on a piece of string. He told her he could do it for four hundred if she wanted the best. If she wanted less than that, he could make it three-fifty. "I want the best," she said.

"What about plumbing?" she inquired.

"Plumbing? Oh, ma'am, they got restrictions."

"It's all right," she said. "I can come down for that."

"You planning on being up here some yourself?"

"I might," she said. "You can't tell."

He looked at her slantwise. "I wouldn't recommend it."

"What about a stove?"

"A stove?"

"For cooking."

"That ain't exactly possible. Unless . . ." He consulted the sky, the tree, and the ground. He turned and spat with care on the far side of her. "Unless a 'lectrician could run a line up the trunk. You might could have a little hot plate, something of that nature. I said might. They got restrictions."

"That's what I'll do," she said.

"I said he might could do it, ma'am."

"It's all right either way. I can fix sandwiches. And I'm very fond of junk food."

Sometimes the way he looked at her she thought he might have guessed her plans, but she didn't care. He was being paid and that was that. She was sick to death of everybody dabbling in her business. Mattie the maid was always snooping. She had been told to do it. "Miss Fanny, you ain't et a bite a lunch." "Miss Fanny, I wouldn't walk that far if I was you." Her daughter was gone all day and Mitzi was in school till three o'clock. So Mattie trailed her. "Mattie, don't you have some cleaning you can do?"

Mrs. Gideon had a special treehouse in mind. She drew the plan for Mr. Snider on a paper napkin. "It has to look this way. I had a treehouse once and it was just like this. I want a window here, and just a little platform where I can sit and watch the moon."

He looked slantwise again. "I wouldn't recommend a person being up here after dark. A ladder ain't that safe."

"Make it safe," she said.

When the house was well along, she looked up one morning and was amazed to see that it was like the treehouse she had had when she was young. "Mr. Snider, this is wonderful! This is just the way my treehouse looked when I was young, the little porch and all."

"Ma'am, I'm building it the way you ast me to do."

"Did I?" she said in wonder. "Well, I'm glad." She had forgotten all about it.

But the treehouse of the past was very clear in her mind. It had been built when she was ten, and there the best years of her life had been spent. Sometimes she had slipped up to watch the sunrise. She had watched the moonrise too, heard the wind in the leaves and the treefrogs after rain and the chatter of the squirrels and birds going to sleep, all as if she had belonged to the world of the tree. Especially she remembered how clear her mind had been. Everything that happened seemed to fall into a crystal pool and she could look down and see it lying on the bottom whenever she chose. Not like it was today. Not like that at all.

Again she asked Mr. Snider what his charge would be. Then she wrote him out a check and pinned it to the leaf of the tree he was in. "I might forget it later on. Things slip my mind." She thought of telling him that she was seventy-eight. Or was she older than that? Or maybe she was younger. She would have to look it up, but it didn't matter.

She waited till one day when the house was almost finished. All it needed was the ladder and a second coat of fern green paint. Then she made a phone call. Just dialing made her happy.

He answered her at once, as if he had been waiting. He sounded just the same, but older of course.

"Robert, this is Fanny Gideon."

"Fanny Gideon!" he said, as if they shared something precious, which of course they did.

"I know it's a long way, but I got something to show you."

"Have you, now?"

"I know it's a long way."

"Not for me. Ten miles is not far. I got wheels." And he laughed. "That's what my grandson says."

"They let you drive?" she said. "That's wonderful, Robert. They took my wheels away."

"They wouldn't try it with me. I can outdrive 'em all."

"Can you come right away?"

"You bet I can." He sounded happy about it.

She made a little note for herself and put it on the door, just in case she forgot, which she didn't think she would. It said: "Robert is coming over to see the treehouse."

But she didn't need the note. She was waiting in the swing on the porch. And when he drove up and got out of his car, she knew again that they had made the big mistake of their lives when they hadn't gotten married when they were fifteen, hadn't run away again when they were caught and brought back, hadn't told the family just to go to hell.

She had seen him the last time, oh, she couldn't remember when. She would have to ask him. He came toward her, not as tall as then, not as steady on his feet, but just as straight. All his hair. All his teeth, as far as she could tell. A beautiful man.

She stood up to greet him. "I see you got both eyes and both hands and both feet."

He looked down at his feet and then he held up his hands. "So I have," he said, surprised. And with his hands he took hers.

"But we have to wear glasses," she said, gay and happy.

"No, we don't. But they tell us to do it, and we humor 'em."

She led him out to the treehouse. Mr. Snider was standing on his painting ladder. The ladder for the house he was going to build last. Only his paint-speckled shoes could be seen.

"What do you think?" she said.

His eyes misted over. He circled the tree. Leaves were winking in the sunlight.

"What do you think?"

"It's perfect," he said, moved. "It's just the way it was."

"I thought you would like it."

"Like it! It's the best thing been built in the last sixty years. Maybe sixty-five. How old are we, Fanny?"

"I can't remember. But I know how old we were. We were fifteen then. It was the best year of my life."

He gazed up at the treehouse, narrowing his eyes. He took off his glasses and sighted through one lens. "Mine too. The best."

"You see the little porch where we used to watch the moon?"

"I do," he said.

"You used to call me Mrs. Moonlight. You said it was because my hair was like moonlight."

"It still is," he said.

"Of course it's not. It never was . . . I wanted you to see what I was up to here."

"Why you doin' it, Fanny?"

"Well, because I have a little trouble remembering things. But I remember that, up there, things were clear as ice. I could look down on things and see the way they were. And I was closer to the sun and it warmed up my brain and made it work fine, and the moon cooled it off so it didn't overheat."

He laughed out loud. "You gonna climb up and heat up and cool off and recall things?"

She laughed along with him. "I aim to do just that."

"I might come and join you."

"Do you think your wife would mind?"

"She died," he said.

"Did I know that?" she said.

"You came to the funeral."

She was silent for a bit. "You see what I mean?" It must have been at the funeral that she had seen him last. She added, "I'm sorry . . . I'm sorry again."

He put his arm around her. "It was five years ago."

"Did you grieve a lot?"

He thought about it for a while. "She didn't like me very much."

She touched his hand lightly. "How could she not?"

HER DAUGHTER came back before the ladder was made. She stood and looked up at the treehouse in the early sun. She was smartly dressed.

Her face was made up with some of the cosmetics she'd been selling on the road. A purplish shade of lipstick that was catching on. Eye shadow to match. Nail polish to match. She wore white sandals, a white pleated skirt, a silk and linen sweater in a fuchsia shade, and a little white scarf to hide the lines in her throat. She left to talk with Mattie. She came out again and lay in wait for Mr. Snider. She told him she was sorry but it had to come down. He shook his head from side to side.

"Don't worry, you'll be paid."

"I done been paid," he said. "It's a shame to knock it down. I done my best work."

"Mr. Snider, I'm surprised at you. You should have known better."

"Better 'n what?" he said, indignant. "I work for hire."

Mrs. Gideon kept to her room. Through her door she heard the murmur of Mattie telling on her. When her daughter knocked, she stiffened every muscle in her body. "Come in," she said, although she didn't want to say it. She hardly knew her daughter with the purple lipstick on and her purple lids.

"Mama, I hope you know we can't leave it there."

"Why? Why?" said Mrs. Gideon. "I had it built to live in."

"To live in!" said her daughter. "When you have a nice room in a comfortable house?" She tore off her scarf as if she couldn't breathe.

"But I get in your way. You talk of putting me somewhere." She would not say the word. "I should think you'd be happy to have me out of the house."

Her daughter dropped to Mrs. Gideon's bed and thrust her face into her purple-tipped fingers. "Mama, I want to keep you here, but you make it very hard when you do things like this. I have to work. I have to travel. I have to leave you alone. And Mattie can't keep up with you every minute of the day. How could you imagine you could live in a treehouse?"

"Well, I didn't," said Mrs. Gideon, seeing how the wind was blowing. "I thought it would be nice for Mitzi to play in."

"Mitzi is seventeen. She doesn't want a treehouse. She wants clothes and a car."

"I had a treehouse when I was fifteen, but maybe times have changed."

"It has to come down."

Mrs. Gideon was holding back the tears. "Why does it? Why does it? It looks lovely in the tree."

"Because, Mama, if I leave it you'll be climbing up some day."

"How could I when it doesn't have a ladder made?"

"You will find one somehow and you will fall and I will be to blame."

"No one would blame you if I fell."

"I would blame myself."

Mrs. Gideon thought tearfully that many of the wretched things that happen in the world grow out of people's saying that they don't want the blame for something that in the first place is totally not their business. She said with dignity, "I've never even seen what it is like inside, but if you like I'll promise you I won't go up."

"Mama, you'll forget. You always forget. You light the stove and forget. You plug in the iron and then you forget. You almost burn the house down once a week. You took the bus to town and forgot to come home."

"I didn't forget. I wasn't ready."

"Mama, you forgot. You've even forgotten now that you forgot."

"I can't win," said Mrs. Gideon. She blew her nose and looked through the window. "About the treehouse, I paid for it," she said at last, "entirely with my money. I remember that quite clearly. I wrote a check."

"Your money. Well, Mama, it's your money and it isn't. Because when you spend it up it's mine that keeps you going."

"I have enough to last me."

"Not at this rate you don't."

Afterward Mrs. Gideon lay on the bed and thought that she was tired of being treated as if she were too young to have sense and at the same time too old to have sense. She wouldn't let herself believe that they would tear the treehouse down . . .

But late in the morning she heard the sound of hammering and splintering wood. And she cried into her pillow as if her heart would break.

She would not come out for lunch, so Mattie left a tray on the floor outside her room. When her daughter had gone to work in the afternoon she ventured from the room, stepping over the tray of food, and looked out the back door. In the tree there was nothing. It was as if the treehouse had never been. It was just the way the other one had gone when she was young. Gone in an hour. Nothing left.

She turned away, tears blinding her eyes. Mattie was working in the bedroom upstairs. She passed the telephone and thought of calling Robert, for he would grieve too. But what could he do? The phone book was opened to the yellow pages, and there she saw marked the name of a nursing home, the number outlined.

She was cold all over. Her fingers were numb, but she found Robert's number. "I need you," she said.

He heard the cry in her voice. "I'm coming," he said.

When he came she was sitting in the swing on the porch. "Go look at the treehouse." She did not want to see its ruination again.

He returned in a moment. "What happened?" he asked.

"She had it torn down. That's what happened."

He saw her eyes red from weeping. After a while he said, "But we can remember it. She can't tear that down."

She swung for a little, while he stood below her in the grass. "I didn't tell you, Robert, but I was planning to live there. Be out of her way. Get all moved in by the time she got back . . . It's not crazy," she said. "I was going to have a little hot plate put in. Be out of her way . . ." The chain creaked as she swung. "But now you know what? I made the thing happen I didn't want to happen. The reason I did it was to keep it away. She called a nursing home. I saw the number by the phone. I'm so afraid, Robert. I'm so afraid."

He climbed the steps then and sat down beside her. They swung together. He held her hand.

"I'm so tired of being treated like I don't have sense enough to live here."

"I know," he said. "I get it too. But when he gets too out of line I tell my son off."

"You do? I wish I could."

"You gotta have guts, the older you get." He thought of it, swinging. "It takes more guts than it does when you're young."

"If we had got married when we tried then . . . If we had been faster so they couldn't have caught us . . ."

He squeezed her hand.

"I don't ever think about my husband," she said. "Isn't that strange? I never think about him. It was like when he died I had got that over with. I must have been sad, though. I can't recall."

They swung in silence.

"I wish I could start my life over again. I'd fix it so I wouldn't have to be afraid."

"I'm thinking," he said. "I'm thinking now. You wanta live in a tree-house? My kid brother has a little house in the woods. You remember Alfie. It's in the next county. Trees around it. You can't hardly see it for all the trees. Nothing fancy inside. He goes there to hunt in the winter-time."

She was suddenly so happy she began to cry. "You mean we could go?"

"Why not?" he said. "I slipped around and saw where he hides the key."

Her eyes were shining as she thought of it.

"You go in and leave a note for your daughter. Say you're with me and we've gone to the woods. I'll be in the car."

"I'll do it," she said. She went inside but didn't write the note. She grabbed her purse from the dresser and a sweater from the bed and slipped out when Mattie was running water in the sink. She climbed in beside him in the Pontiac.

Down the road a ways he said, "Did you leave her the note?"

"I think I forgot it."

"You didn't forget. You just didn't want to do it. I know you, Fanny Gideon, from way, way back."

"I was afraid she'd come and get me. Are you mad with me, Robert?"

"Hell, no, I'm not mad. She deserves what she gets."

"You didn't tell your son."

"I never tell him a thing. Once you start leaving notes it's like asking permission."

She couldn't remember when she had been so happy. "This is like when we were young and ran away to get married." She was smiling at him.

He was smiling too but looking hard at the road. Drivers everywhere were getting crazier all the time. Just stay out of their way. If he lost his license now he wouldn't get it back.

"Robert," she said, "can you remember things?"

"Not as well as I did, but well enough I guess."

"Good," she said. "You take care of the past and I'll handle the present."

"Who's in charge of the future?"

"Oh, it's in charge of itself."

It seemed to him a very funny thing for her to say. "So should we finish what we started back then and get married?" He hadn't planned to say it, but it was said and he was glad.

"What about your wife?"

He tensed to make a turn. "She died."

". . . I'm truly very sorry."

"It's all right," he said. "It's over and done. So do you want to get married?"

"I sort of like the idea of living in sin. Don't you?"

"I do," he said.

At length he put it to her gravely, "If you married me I think they'd leave us alone. We could live somewhere."

"It's too late for that."

"Too late? Like you said, the future is in charge of itself."

A shade passed over her. "I'm too late."

They left the pavement. They drove into the country and now he relaxed. Beside them were fields of greening oats crosshatched with shadows from the passing clouds. Swarms of keening birds swept out of the sky. A whirl of wind whipped out of a tunnel beneath the road. It raked the pasture grasses and combed them all backward and followed the road. The willows in the ditches bridled and dipped.

She tied her sweater loosely in a knot about her throat. "It was raining before. We were driving through rain."

"The windshield misted up. I had to go slow."

"I remember everything about that day." They passed cattle standing knee deep in a lake. "We're running from them now like we did before."

"We're not running from them. Don't think about running. Don't think about them. Think about they're young, with the memories they're proud of crammed with junk, plain junk. There's not much about them we could recommend."

"They're faster," she said. "The people who come after you are always faster. Or they wouldn't win."

He turned into the trees and shifted gears. With a howl from the engine they drove up, up on a pine-needled road. And soon, very soon he pointed to the house tucked away in trees. She exclaimed with delight. There was a series of steps they must climb to reach it. Like a ladder, she laughed. He wanted to help her, but she waved him away. "I've still got my legs." "So you have," he observed her. "You're like a mountain goat. I've gotten slower."

Inside was a small and airless room with a hearth at one end and a bed at the other. There was a smell of ash. Against one wall was a rusting stove. "I told you not fancy."

"I didn't come for fancy." It made her think of an acorn, brown and secret, the way a room should be that lives in trees. She could feel the swaying of her childhood treehouse when the wind blew at dusk and she pulled her long hair over her head to match the birds snug in their rippling feathers.

"It's got a bathroom off that door by the bed."

"And a porch," she whispered, knowing it was there on the other side of another door. She pulled it open and walked out slowly. The sun was nesting in a giant maple full of summer. The lowest branches swept the weathered boards. The massive trunk fell out of sight below. She dropped her purse and settled like a wren among the leaves.

He watched her from the doorway. Then he joined her, stepping through the branches to inspect what lay beneath. The floor of the forest dropped sharply away. The porch had the look of being blown into the hillside and the house that followed it propped on piles. Fanny's own treehouse had been better made.

He returned to her and stood among the mammoth branches, their leaf clusters hanging like fruit in the motionless air. He smiled at her but he could not speak. He had lost the power and the spell of a tree, lost how it was to feel himself all gone into the green . . . to desire it so much . . . to climb anything, to swing from anything, a rope, a vine, daring death to get it . . . a craving so strong it was strange it wasn't called immoral or illegal. But then the moralists were all grown up. He had been young and full of the craving and Fanny Gideon had given him her tree. If she hadn't had a treehouse, would they have loved?

She looked up at him with happiness. "We have always been married."

He held out his hand. She pulled it down and kissed it and kept it in hers. "Your hand is just the way I need a hand to be. Not young and not old. Take care of it," she said.

"I will," he said, moved, and knowing he would have loved her without her tree. "Are you hungry?" he asked. "There might be something in there."

She shook her head. "I'm too happy to eat. This is the happiest I've ever been. I've forgotten the rest."

Her happiness began to make him afraid. Like the tree before them, it was larger than life. There was nothing to tell him if it was real, or if she had made it to hide her fear. Her fear was real, for he felt it stir in the deep of his throat, in the palm of his hand, the way he would know whatever was wrong when she was a girl. When they climbed the ladder it was always there for the tree to know. For him to know if he knew the tree. He had learned the tree. On the calmest day he could feel it wanting to circle and toss, have some fun, give them something to think about. On a windy day he would spin with it, going green inside, getting into its marrow, feeling within it the way she was, knowing he would marry the way she was, the way he felt the way she was . . . And now he was troubled with the empty years. They turned in his bones where they must have lain but he hadn't known. What he dreaded most at this time of his life was to live through anything over again. The flight they'd begun being ended again, the door they had opened being shut once more. Life had come to seem like a series of things that repeated themselves, until one day he had closed his heart. It was better perhaps to forget . . . like Fanny. He could feel something break like a bough in the woods.

Her eyes had never left the tree. The air was stirring. A shudder swept through the leaves and into her. "How long will we be here?"

"Till we want to leave."

"Till they find us, you mean?"

He did not reply. He was aware that the tree was growing dark within. Only the tips of branches were still green-gold. Somewhere deep within it was a whir of wings. He went inside and found some coffee to brew in a pan. There were crackers in a tin, but they seemed too stale. He came out with her coffee. "It's the best we have."

She took the cup absently and drank a little. "It's very good, Robert." She laid the cup on the floor. Her voice, it seemed to him, was just as it had been. In the failing light he saw her face again young and kindling the treehouse they had never let go. Her hair was the color it had been in the moonlight . . .

He found a weathered chair that had been tipped against the wall. He drew it across the floor and sat beside her in the dusk. It was dark in the tree. They could hear the birds within settling into the night, and somewhere an owl. And a wind came from nowhere to sleep in the woods, bedding down in the leaves but restless, turning, sighing, troubled with dreams, sleepwalking in leaf mold, crouching in the chimney, falling into the ravine . . . It was turning cooler. "Where is the moon?" she asked with longing in her voice.

"It isn't time, Mrs. Moonlight. Give it time." He stroked her hair while they sat between the tree dark and the dark of their room, between two darks with an equal claim, and neither would release them into the other. But fireflies wove the darks into night . . . He took her hand and led her, it seemed to her, into the tree, but it must have been the room. For she lay on the bed and he took off her glasses and then her shoes. He covered her with a blanket that smelled of smoke.

"I want you near me," she said.

So he lay down beside her. "There isn't a light," he whispered. "Do you mind the dark?"

"Not when you are with me."

He found her hands and kissed them. They were trembling and cold. He drew the blanket closely about her throat.

She said, "I won't think about anything but now. Or remember . . . I won't remember anything but then. I fight all the time to keep from losing myself. They try to make me remember the things they want me to remember. Why do I have to remember *their* things? Never mine. My things. Go to a nursing home because I left my coat in the park? Such a fuss she made. I didn't care about the coat. I never liked it. I didn't try to remember it. I don't have room in my mind for all the things they want me to remember. I just have room for when you kissed me in the treehouse . . . and I was Mrs. Moonlight. It fills up my brain. There's no room for the rest."

"Don't think about the rest." He kissed her hair.

"I have to think of it. I have to," she said.

He could feel that she was losing all the joy of the tree, as if the wind they heard were blowing it away and blowing her with it away from him. "Don't think," he begged her.

"I have to think of it," she said. He could feel her pain. "When she tore down the treehouse it was like she tore me down. Like she tore down the things of mine I need to remember. I can't forgive her for that. And now I want to forget her . . . along with the rest. She will put me in that home so I might as well forget her . . . Help me do it," she said. She was weeping now. "Help me forget her and just remember you."

He held her face in his hands. "I would if I could but I don't know how. I have never known how." He took his hands away. His mind was heavy with the chirring of the crickets round their bed. Birds had flown in and were muttering in the gloom above the open door. After a time he said through her weeping, as if to himself. "Whiskey is a good thing but it doesn't last. I tried it for a while when my wife stopped loving me . . . It doesn't last."

"I need something to last."

"I know," he said. "I know. But it always comes back. I closed myself up for most of my life. Till today when you called . . ."

She turned to embrace him. "You will be always in my mind. All the rest will go but you. Do you believe it?" she said.

"I believe it, Mrs. Moonlight. I truly do."

She lay quietly beside him, sleeping a little, waking to find him sleeping, then waking again to find him waking too. A full moon had risen behind the tree. The churning leaves were frothing the light that struck the bed. "I'm trying to forget her. It's hard, so hard. It's like your own children get stuck in your mind. Maybe when they're born to you they aren't all born. Maybe a part of them is left inside . . . Hold me," she said.

He folded his arms about her.

"When you hold me I can almost . . . There's so much . . . so much. She would run and always open her little hands to fall. They were full of stone bruises and splinters and cuts . . . I would look at her hands and I'd kiss them and cry . . ."

"Try to sleep," he said.

"Red flowers made her smile . . ." It was a while before she asked, "Do you think they'll come?"

"My son is smart enough to figure this out."

"But not before morning?"

He felt the brush of a moth upon his lips. "Not before then."

"So we have tonight. We mustn't fall asleep."

But they did. When he woke she was gone. He sat up in panic. His fear was so strong his heart was beating in his throat. He could not hear a sound but the wind in the tree. Suppose she had forgotten where she was and fallen down the steps or walked into the woods and fallen into the ravine . . .

He stumbled to the porch, where he found her in the moonlight among the moving leaves. He did not trust his voice to speak. He drew her up to him and held her. She was as soft as a girl. As small as she had been. As yielding as then.

"Robert?" she said. "Robert?" Her voice was breaking with bewilderment. "Why are we here?" She pulled away from his arms. "This isn't our treehouse. Who does it belong to? My daughter tore it down . . . the one I had made. Why are we here?" she said again. "Are we running away?"

"There's no reason," he said. "Come inside," he begged.

"Don't let them take us back."

"No," he whispered. "No."

She caught her breath. "I forget . . . But the old things are there." She reached a hand to the tree. "New things that happen are so hard to keep. They fall through the leaves . . . Unless they break your heart. Unless they're what she did." She turned to search his face. "How did we get here? There's a room . . . and a bed."

"Yes, inside. Come inside."

"There's one way," she said.

"Tell me," he said, hardly hearing her words. She was trembling in his arms.

"Then I have to tell you this one thing you never knew. After they brought us back, they tore down our treehouse."

"I knew that," he said. "I went to see it one night and it was gone."

"But you didn't know that after that I tried to kill myself. I was crazy with grief. I didn't want to live. I cut my wrist. I wanted that much to die. When you're fifteen you're crazy like a fox, they said. I was ashamed of it later."

After a moment she pulled back her sleeve and showed him the scar. He found it in the moonlight and kissed it slowly.

"What if they hadn't found me and made me live?"

"What are you saying?"

"I want to go back and die to the rest of my life. I want to go back and die before my daughter came."

"But you went on living."

"What if I hadn't?"

"Then what are we now tonight?" he asked in despair.

"This is another life. Don't you feel it?" she said.

"You're saying it isn't real?"

"Oh, no, it's the realest thing that's ever been."

He was stroking her hair. "Your hair is like moonlight . . . Come back to bed."

He led her inside and they lay down together, side by side, hands touching, eyes closed against the dark. "I love you, Mrs. Moonlight." He heard her breath growing faint. "Please don't die," he pled. Her hair was like smoke. He drew the smoke of their blanket to cover them both.

"No, I'm only going backward. A part of me will die." She was weeping. They wept together. He held her in his arms.

"Don't go to sleep," she said. "I need you to help me."

"I don't know how," he wept. "I don't know what you're doing."

"I'm making it that she never happened to me."

"Are you sure it's what you want?"

"Yes, I am. I'm sure. You're the only one ever that belonged in my life . . . Think about the way we were. Think about the moon."

He could hear the owl. Beyond her hair, through the door he could see how the wind was slicing the moonlight, tossing it with leaves, thrusting it deep . . . and deeper into the tree. "You never let me kiss you but once a day, even though we said that we were going to be married. You were that shy."

"I'm not now," she said. "Kiss me now."

He kissed her long and gently, like an echo of the way it used to be. And the way it used to be reechoed till at last she was hearing nothing else, not the wind in the leaves, not the owl, not her daughter's voice . . . After a time she whispered, "It all slips away unless I hold on. It's like I am singing and the words blow away."

"Marry me," he said, "and I'll remember for you." Beneath his hand her head was tracing a refusal. "Everything you need to keep I'll keep for you."

"There's just a little bit and I can keep it myself and let go the rest."

He was losing his breath in the smoke of her hair. "If you do she'll put you in the home all the sooner."

"I know it," she said. "But this way it will be like a stranger has done it. Nothing a stranger does to you can make any difference."

IT WAS morning when they woke to a thrasher's song. Beyond the door the tree was like another country in another season. It glistened. It unfolded. Light and shadow flew about in it like restless birds.

They heard the car outside. He rose and went to the window. "Well, they're here," he said. "It's my son's gray car."

Then her daughter entered, hair disheveled, eyes wild with reproach. "Mama, why have you done this? Why are you here?"

Fanny Gideon looked up at her serenely. "Do I know you?" she said.

The birdsong throbbed in the maple tree and circled the bed where Fanny Gideon lay with her hair on the pillow like a bridal veil. Her daughter turned upon him her shocked, accusing face. "How dare you take her?"

Long ago, when he was still a boy who swung from trees, before she was born, someone who was like her had asked him the same. It seemed to him that now he had grown into the answer. He summoned all his force to make a stand against her and against all the ones who ride you down to take you back and stash you in some corner, flush you down some snakehole, throw you away.

"Not this time," he said to her, calling up the memory of that ancient flight and capture. "This time we're married."

He saw her face give way . . . He found Fanny's glasses and put them on her.

She sat up in bed and looked past the strange woman standing beside her. The tree itself seemed to sing with the bird. She had only to rise to belong to the tree world, belong to its mystery, the mystery of greenness, her own sweet youth. She smiled at him, seeing him deep in the green, seeing him already shadowed with leaves. On this first morning of the rest of their life she remembered him. As she always would.

At Seventy: A Journal

MAY SARTON

Monday, May 3rd, 1982

Such a peaceful, windless morning here for my seventieth birthday—
the sea is pale blue, and although the field is still brown, it is dotted with
daffodils at last. It has seemed an endless winter. But now at night the
peepers are in full fettle, peeping away. And I was awakened by the car-
dinal, who is back again with his two wives, and the raucous cries of the
male pheasant. I lay there, breathing in spring, listening to the faint
susurration of the waves and awfully glad to be alive.

The table is set downstairs, all blue and white, with a tiny bunch of
miniature daffodils, blue starflowers, and, glory be, two fritillaries. They
always seem unreal with their purple-and-white-checkered bells, and I
have never succeeded with a real show of them. . . .

What is it like to be seventy? If someone else had lived so long and
could remember things sixty years ago with great clarity, she would seem
very old to me. But I do not feel old at all, not as much a survivor as a
person still on her way. I suppose real old age begins when one looks
backward rather than forward, but I look forward with joy to the years
ahead and especially to the surprises that any day may bring.

In the middle of the night things well up from the past that are not
always cause for rejoicing—the unsolved, the painful encounters, the
mistakes, the reasons for shame or woe. But all, good or bad, painful or
delightful, weave themselves into a rich tapestry, and all give me food
for thought, food to grow on.

I am just back from a month of poetry readings, in and out through all
of April. At Hartford College in Connecticut I had been asked to talk
about old age—"The View from Here," I called the reading—in a series
on "The Seasons of Womanhood." In the course of it I said, "This is the

best time of my life. I love being old." At that point a voice from the audience asked loudly, "Why is it good to be old?" I answered spontaneously and a little on the defensive, for I sensed incredulity in the questioner, "Because I am more myself than I have ever been. There is less conflict. I am happier, more balanced, and" (I heard myself say rather aggressively) "more powerful." I felt it was rather an odd word, "powerful," but I think it is true. It might have been more accurate to say "I am better able to use my powers." I am surer of what my life is all about, have less self-doubt to conquer, although it has to be admitted that I wrote my new novel *Anger* in an agony of self-doubt most of the year, the hardest subject I have attempted to deal with in a novel since *Mrs. Stevens Hears the Mermaids Singing*. There I was breaking new ground, giving myself away. I was fifty-three and I deliberately made Mrs. Stevens seventy, and now here I am at what then seemed eons away, safely "old." . . .

Perhaps the answer is not detachment as I used to believe but rather to be deeply involved in something, is to be attached. I am attached in a thousand ways—and one of them compels me now to leave this airy room high up in the house to go down and get ready for my guests.

TUESDAY, MAY 4TH

FOR breakfast at five I had a fresh egg from Anne and Barbara's chickens, a piece of homemade bread Donna brought last night with strawberry jam she had made, and I felt extraordinarily blessed by all that happened yesterday as I started to read a big manuscript on fathers and daughters that I promised to say something about. The price of being attached "in a thousand ways" is that there is never even twenty-four hours free of pressure, but this year I am clear in my mind that just this is what my life is all about, and what I have to learn (so late!) is to accept the multiple demands and understand that a rich life is bought at a high price in energy. . . .

The house is full of amazing flowers, among them huge pink rhododendrons flown from California, marvelous dark-red roses, yellow lilies in the blue and white Belgian jar, and a vase of pink African daisies and white chrysanthemums that Bob, the florist, brought as his birthday present. He read *Recovering* some weeks past and was so moved he has been bringing me flowers. Happy the writer who has a florist for a fan! . . .

SUNDAY, MAY 16TH

. . . [I]t is the business of the journalist to record a mood as it comes, as exactly as possible, knowing that life is flux and that the mood must change. Today I am suffering from deprivation in spite of all the friends who made my birthday memorable, suffering because there is no central person. I laugh about it and say that the sea is to be my final muse, but one cannot fill a well with an ocean.

And that is the problem. A life extended in a thousand directions risks dispersion and madness. A kite can fly only when it is held taut by a string in a hand and then catches the wind. Today I am a kite entangled in a tree, and there is no one to free me for flight. Let us hope the garden will do it!

MONDAY, MAY 17TH

IT would be fine if now, after two weeks of it, the east wind that has been coming in every afternoon, cold and enervating, subsided. Later on in summer it is a blessing, and we are often ten degrees cooler than the town of York, but now when the ocean is still icy cold, the wind comes like a death blast and shrivels some flowers—though not the tough daffodils—and blows the seeds out of my hands. I did get in three rows yesterday and planted a box of Chinese and Connecticut Yankee delphiniums in the terrace border, because they never grow to great heights and should work well there. I'm also trying blue erigeron, but these plants are so small, the chances are slight that they will take hold. I just keep on ordering in the middle of winter in an intoxication of hope.

Every day now something new is happening in the woods when I take Tamas on our morning walk. The wood anemones are full out, shining like stars above their delicate shower of fine-cut leaves, so that each one is a tiny bouquet in itself. I hope the nymphs are happily transforming themselves into dragonflies, for the mosquitoes have already begun to buzz in my ears and the horrible blackflies are back. At least the east wind does keep them down when I am working outdoors these days.

Peace flows in, now there is a little less pressure. But I must write letters.

I begin to feel the fatigue of the runner when a race is over, but I am quite pleased that I managed that month of public appearances, and all that has happened since because of my birthday, and felt happy and more or less in control. I am far better able to cope at seventy than I was at fifty. I think that is partly because I have learned to glide instead of to force myself at moments of tension. It doesn't always work, of course, but I am far less nervous before a poetry reading now than I used to be and so enjoy doing it. I used to be in a hard knot of nerves for days.

I realize that seventy must seem extremely old to my young friends, but I actually feel much younger than I did when I wrote *The House by the Sea* six years ago. And younger than I did in Nelson when I wrote the poem "Gestalt at Sixty." Those previews of old age were not entirely accurate, I am discovering. And that, as far as I can see, is because I live more completely in the moment these days, am not as anxious about the future, and am far more detached from the areas of pain, the loss of love, the struggle to get the work completed, the fear of death. I have less guilt because there is less anger. Perhaps before I die I shall make peace with my father and be able to heal the wound that Leonard's book has forced me to think about again.

SUNDAY, JUNE 6TH

. . . I have been meaning to speak of the television play on Golda Meir that was aired sometime last week with Ingrid Bergman as Golda. I saw only the second part. It is good that we are forced to remember the absolute peril that Israel has been in from the start, for it explains what often looks like intransigence. I was moved by all of it, and by Bergman's authentic, honest performance. The only trouble is that part of Golda's power was in her worn, lined, very plain face and grizzled, untidy hair. Bergman is too beautiful. So I missed the real face—it had in it all the suffering, tension, and courage demanded to overcome impossible odds that made Golda what she was. Neither she nor Eleanor Roosevelt was beautiful, but in both the spirit triumphed over plain features and shone out. So why do we worry about lines in our faces as we grow old? A face without lines that shows no mark of what has been lived through in a long life suggests something unlived, empty, behind it. I think of Lotte Jacobi's face, a mass of wrinkles, now she is well over eighty, but so full of wisdom that *that* is what one sees, and she is still enchanting.

Still, one mourns one's young face sometimes. It has to be admitted. I now use a night cream for the first time in my life. At the same time, as I went over photographs yesterday for a children's book of biographies in which I am included, I felt that my face is better now, and I like it better. That is because I am a far more complete and richer person than I was at twenty-five, when ambition and personal conflicts were paramount and there was a surface of sophistication that was not true of the person inside. Now I wear the inside person outside and am more comfortable with my self. In some ways I am younger because I can admit vulnerability and more innocent because I do not have to pretend. . . .

WEDNESDAY, JULY 28TH

I had it on my mind to telephone my adopted daughter, Georgia, who had called while Royce and Frances were here. I had checked in with her at ten, after dinner, but by then she was too tired to talk. So this was the time to communicate at some length. My life sometimes amuses me it is so packed with such a variety of things that summon me out of myself. While we talked, I heard loud scrabbling and thumping in the cupboard where I keep birdseed. A red squirrel, of course! Almost every day one turns up somewhere in the kitchen to scare the daylights out of me, as they are lightning-quick and stop the breath as a snake does. . . . I am proud to see how Georgia recaptures her composure after times of stress and how well able she is then to analyze herself and come to terms with the very real anxieties she has to handle. We are on the same beam, each needing to say things out in words, and she is a true pelican, nurturing her two small children as I hope I am nurturing a lot of people I hardly know. So we call ourselves the Pelicans and can laugh and weep together. But all the time we talked the noises erupted in the cupboard, and I knew I would have to cope with this unwanted, terrified stranger as soon as I hung up. I did it finally with a broom. The streak of lightning fled down the cellar stairs, maddening! Had he chosen to turn left he would have been outside and safe. But the cellar is huge and I suspect has holes in the walls, and there has been no sound since. . . .

Monday, August 2nd

I did get out into the garden yesterday afternoon and replenished the flowers in the house, but I was too tired to enjoy it. The mosquitoes were ferocious in the muggy heat. I could feel them biting through my shirt as I cut back the smothering grapevines and freed the perennials from weeds. In the end I was glad I had made the effort and cleared some space out there and in my mind. August is the dead end of summer, when everything goes to seed or becomes too lush, and there is a special August silence in the heavy air. The birds do not sing. The ocean sighs in the distance. The whole tempo slows down.

Lately I have been reading Alyse Gregory's journal sent to me by a friend in England. A large part of it is about her consuming love for her husband, Llewelyn Powys, and the anguish she suffered when he fell in love with a younger woman, Gamel Woolsey—a love she accepted and learned to live with until Llewelyn's death; she became his comforter and support through his despair when Gamel married Gerald Brenan and through his own long illness. The journal is chiefly the record of her own suffering, and I suppose it became her comforter, for she confided in no one else, apparently. It has had a strange effect on me. It has made me see once more how destructive passion is, how cruelly single-minded. For Llewelyn never seems to have been aware that his confiding in her caused continual pain and that to ask his wife to listen to his passionate involvement with another woman, to talk about her incessantly, to demand pity under these circumstances is very cruel. To take her understanding for granted when she is being horribly hurt seems quite intolerable, and here and there is a cry of anguish.

I was struck to the heart by the tragedy of being so wrapped up in one human being that nothing else exists or gives life. That was Alyse's state. She loved Llewelyn to the exclusion of everything and everyone else. "I must be self-sufficient. I live like a stunted tree in the shadow of a mountain, the warmth never reaches my branches." And another entry ends, "Llewelyn saw a stoat chasing a rabbit today and clapped his hands to frighten the stoat away. The rabbit was too frightened to run. I too remain stationary from fear."

All through my reading of this book I have felt immense relief that I am not attached in that way to anyone. For so much of my life I was, but now I am free of passion, I see that it is a great blessing not to be in its thrall. . . .

MONDAY, DECEMBER 13TH

Last Friday I flew to Cincinnati to help celebrate Heidi's seventy-fifth birthday at a dinner for eighty at the Losantiville Country Club and to do a book signing at the Crazy Ladies bookstore, a feminist cooperative. The contrast made for an invigorating two days that I shall be savoring as time goes on. But the Christmas frenzy is on, and I shall have to be brief here. It was beautiful to see Heidi and Harry in their magnificent apartment on the eleventh floor, spacious, filled with Harry's treasures, and animated by a secretive, elegant Himalayan cat called Mani and a Lhasa Apso, a ball-of-fluff-dog called Manu who is the most affectionate creature imaginable. I basked in all this beauty and luxury, had a nap, and then we all got dressed and drove off to the club. It was not quite the usual affair because Heidi had had the great adventure years ago of seeing India with Nehru's sister, Krishna, so the decorations and some of her own photographs spoke of India, as did the flower arrangements. The room was soon full of people, among whom I wandered in a daze, eating shrimp, drinking my Scotch, amused by the contrast it made with my life here where I almost never wear a long dress and where I am rarely among strangers. Soon the delightful grandchildren poured in, among them two little girls who had just been in a school performance of *Cinderella* and Chipper, my friend, looking extremely handsome and grown up in his first tuxedo. Altogether an occasion worthy of Heidi who, at seventy-five, still skippers her boat in Kennebunkport and still looks like a boy, partly because she is only five feet tall.

At three the next afternoon she drove me to a very different part of the city, a slum that is being rehabilitated, and there I found myself among "my people" at the Crazy Ladies—a subway crush of young and old but mostly young in blue jeans and sweaters, crowding around to get *Journal of a Solitude* signed (that is the one for the young) and of course *Anger*. Some had brought a great pile of my books from home. Many had things to say to me, but it was rather a rush as the line was long and the time short. At the end of two hours when I had not stopped making my mark, it looked as though the bookstore may have been saved (they are having a hard time), and everyone was happy. And on the way back to the Regency and Heidi, two women from the cooperative told me they thought they had sold $1,500 worth. Once more I felt lifted up on all the delightful caring of these people who read me.

It cannot be denied that it is these days a very good life for an old raccoon of seventy. . . .

WEDNESDAY, DECEMBER 22ND

Why is it, I wonder, that Christmas brings so much depression with it, so many people struggle against an undertow? It is partly because this moment of light shines out of the darkest and shortest days of the year, the lowest ebb of the cycle when wise animals dig themselves in for a long sleep, while we, driven creatures, spend immense energy on wrapping presents, sending off packages, baking cookies (this I used to do but have stopped doing myself, so other people's cookies are specially welcome). Partly it is that memories well up and not all are happy ones. We are dealing with a host of faces and times and sorrows and joys, and there is no time to sort them out.

Every year Christmas becomes a real creation for each of us, and as it is created we are re-creating the moment when Love is born again, Love that will know pain as well as joy.

As I was writing that last sentence Tim Warren, Judy's nephew, called—it is 8 A.M.—to tell me that Judy died last night. I have prayed that she might be allowed to slip away, and now she has. But it is always so sudden, so unexpected—death—and so final. When I went to see her last September and held her ice-cold hand in mine, at the very end of the half-hour when she had made no sign of recognition, she reached over and patted my hand and held it over her other one for a moment. I must remember that and that she is free at last of the failing body and mind and is wherever spirits dwell.

Surely she dwells in me and will as long as I live, with my mother and Jean Dominique and Anne Thorp and Eugénie Dubois. But Judy was the precious only love with whom I lived for years, the only one. There have been other great loves in my life, but only Judy gave me a home and made me know what home can be. She was the dear companion for fifteen years, years when I was struggling as a writer. We were poor then, for a time had no car even. But strangely enough I look back on those days as the happiest ones. And that is because there was a "we."

We met in Santa Fe and it is to that austere flaming landscape, sunset on the Sangre de Cristos, that my heart goes now and to a poem I wrote for Judy that ends:

> For after love comes birth:
> All we have felt and said
> Is now of air, of earth,
> And love is harvested. . . .

MONDAY, MAY 2ND

The last day of this seventieth year.

As I think over this year I wish I had a long empty time in which to think it over instead of a few minutes before I take Tamas out into the wet green world! In spite of the pressures of what is ahead—to clear my desk, sow the annuals, plant perennials, get back to the novel—I feel happy and at peace. My life at the moment is a little like a game of solitaire that is coming out. Things fall into place. The long hard work is bearing fruit, and even though I make resolves to see fewer people this summer than last, I know I shall be inundated as usual, be unable to say "no," but it does not matter, for I am coming into a period of inner calm. There will be months of seeing people and months of public appearances, but as surely as the dawn, there will be months of solitude and time to work. Who could ask for more? . . .

Permission Credits

Grateful acknowledgment is made to the following for permission to reprint copyrighted material: